FINANCIAL OPTIONS:

FROM THEORY TO PRACTICE

Edited by

Stephen Figlewski

William L. Silber

Marti G. Subrahmanyam

New York University

Salomon Brothers Center
for the Study of
Financial Institutions

Leonard N. Stern
School of Business
New York University

BUSINESS ONE IRWIN
Homewood, Illinois 60430

Project editor: Karen Nelson
Production manager: Diane Palmer
Jacket designer: Sam Concialdi
Printer: R. R. Donnelley & Sons Company

Library of Congress Cataloging-in-Publication Data

Financial options:from theory to practice/edited by Stephen
  Figlewski, William L. Silber, Marti G. Subrahmanyam.
      p.   cm.
    "Salomon Brothers Center for the Study of Financial Institutions,
  Leonard N. Stern School of Business, New York University."
    Includes index.
   ISBN 1-55623-872-X
    1. Options (Finance)—United States.   I. Figlewski, Stephen.
  II. Silber, William L.   III. Subrahmanyam, Marti G., date.
  IV. Salomon Brothers Center for the Study of Financial Institutions.
  HG6024.U6F56   1990
  332.64′5—dc20   90–3770

CONTENTS

PART 3—IMPLEMENTATION

PREFACE

In the last 20 years, we have seen a great proliferation in the number and variety of financial instruments known as "contingent claims" or "derivative securities." Prior to this, basic call and put options on individual stocks were traded over the counter, futures exchanges provided active markets in contracts based on agricultural and industrial commodities, and many kinds of securities like callable bonds contained features that we now think of as embedded options. But there was little effort to extend the scope of such markets toward other financial instruments, or to apply the limited amount of formal analysis done by academics to actual trading decisions. Options and futures were widely viewed as exotic, and very risky, instruments.

All of this began to change rapidly in 1973, with the opening of options trading at the Chicago Board Options Exchange and the advent of financial futures contracts based on foreign currencies at the International Monetary Market of the Chicago Mercantile Exchange. At the same time, in the academic world, Black and Scholes and Merton were publishing the fundamental papers on the option pricing model. Since then the pace of innovation has been extraordinary. In the markets, practitioners have had to deal with a bewildering array of new concepts, from volatilities and dynamic hedging to delta, gamma and other Greek letters, and occasionally even partial differential equations. Academics, for their part, have also had to scramble to keep up, as a cascade of new and increasingly complex option-type securities has required new and increasingly complex approaches to valuation and risk management.

In 1970, few business schools offered courses on derivative securities and little attention was paid to them on Wall Street except by those who were directly involved in the trade. In 1990, no one can be considered adequately prepared for a career in the financial markets without a basic understanding of these instruments.

THE RESEARCH PROJECT ON FINANCIAL FUTURES AND OPTIONS AT NEW YORK UNIVERSITY

In response to the widespread need for material on derivative securities to help practitioners in actual risk management situations, the Research Project on Financial Futures and Options was set up in 1984 under the auspices of the Salomon Center for the Study of Financial Institutions at the Leonard N. Stern School of Business of New York University. Stephen Figlewski has been the project director since its inception, and major funding for the project has been provided by grants from the American Council of Life Insurance.

One of the most important objectives of the research project has been to bridge the gap between the academic work on contingent claims and the potential application of that work by investors and other "real world" market participants. The initial focus was on the use of financial futures by institutional investors, and resulted in a book entitled *Hedging with Financial Futures: From Theory to Practice,* written by Figlewski in collaboration with John Merrick and Kose John. Thus the title of the present book, *Financial Options: From Theory to Practice,* represents continuity in form as well as substance. With input from a conference of academics and practitioners, the book is designed to span the interests of both communities. In addition to the books just mentioned, a number of other materials relating to financial futures and options have been produced under the Research Project, including computer software for option valuation, videotapes of presentations at the financial options conference, and research papers on more specialized futures and options applications and analysis. The interested reader may obtain a full list of available materials by contacting the Salomon Brothers Center at the NYU Stern School of Business.

OVERVIEW OF THE BOOK

We will now give an overview of the book, followed by a chapter outline to help orient the reader.

There are many books with the word options in the title. Most concentrate either on theory, presenting the mathematical models of modern option pricing and illustrating them with highly stylized examples, or on "practice," with detailed descriptions of trading strategies and institutional aspects of the markets. The former are typically used as textbooks in business school courses, while the latter are read by practitioners. But the nature of these markets has developed to the point that neither one-sided approach is adequate today. Students need to know more than the mathematics of option models; they also need to understand how those models are applied in analyzing, trading, and designing actual securities. Practitioners cannot be satisfied with payoff diagrams and contract specifications alone; they also need to understand how modern valuation methods apply to the markets and securities they are involved with.

Our overall goal in this book is to provide a link between option theory and practical application of that theory. We present the essential principles of option valuation in a rigorous but (hopefully) intuitive manner, and at the same time, we try to show how the theoretical concepts are applied to actual securities and markets. A key element in the presentation is the consistent use of the Binomial model to illustrate the properties of options. This approach offers a simple framework while also providing a general technique for solving actual option valuation problems.

Many options texts concentrate primarily on stock options. In the 1970s, equity options constituted the bulk of all exchange trading in options, so this focus was natural. But developments in the 1980s have greatly broadened the options markets and extended options trading to a wide variety of other financial instruments. Moreover, increasingly complex option features are now regularly incorporated into new securities issues, and there has also been a recognition that many features of such standard instruments as mortgages and callable bonds are actually best analyzed as options.

Thus, our focus has been made broader than traditional options books. In particular, after presenting the general principles of option trading and valuation, we offer chapters on specific types of financial options. These chapters are written by authors who are expert in both the theory and the practice of the particular market.

The book is divided into three parts: Theory, Applications, and Implementation.

Part I. Theory

The four chapters in this section provide the institutional and theoretical framework for understanding options and options markets. For those without any background in this area, the chapters should be read sequentially.

Chapter One defines the characteristics of options and then discusses the institutional structures that are peculiar to options markets, such as clearing arrangements and trading facilities. In addition, the chapter offers an overview of types of options, including a glimpse at how options theory can be applied to various securities.

The fundamentals of option pricing and trading are introduced in Chapter 2. A number of basic properties, stemming from principles of arbitrage, are shared by all types of options. Thus, the chapter develops relationships among option prices using put-call parity. The chapter also illustrates with payoff diagrams and practical discussion the most important trading strategies that follow from the fundamental price relationships, ranging from the protective put and the covered call to straddles, strangles and butterfly spreads.

Chapter 3 focuses on the explicit option valuation formulas that specify the fair value of an option prior to the expiration date. The celebrated Black-Scholes option pricing formula is sketched out along with the more intuitive Binomial model. Because the Binomial model is less complicated than the Black-Scholes formula, it will be used throughout the book to illustrate the properties of various options. The chapter provides precise numerical examples on how to implement the pricing models in valuing options on individual stocks, as well as offering insight on extensions of the models to options on other securities, e.g., the pricing of options on futures contracts. An appendix presents the continuous-time mathematics of modern option theory in more rigorous detail and shows how it is used to derive the Black-Scholes model.

The final chapter in Part I, Chapter 4, focuses on the distinction between European options, which can be exercised only on the expiration date, and American options, which can be exercised any time until expiration. Since it frequently does not pay to exercise American options prior to expiration, the two types of options often have the same value. The chapter focuses on the conditions when it pays to exercise early, hence when the prices of American and European options differ.

Part II. Applications

The seven chapters in Part II apply option pricing models to specific types of markets. Although the principles underlying various options are all the same, there are particular features of bonds, mortgages and foreign currencies, for example, that require special treatment. Moreover, creative application of options principles can produce guidelines for portfolio insurance purposes as well as providing insight into the option features of corporate securities more generally. The chapters make extensive use of the simple Binomial model but occasionally introduce other approaches to deal with specific complications.

Chapter 5 describes the valuation of options on stock indices, the most popular of all types of exchange-traded options during the 1980s. The chapter deals with a number of complications, including the fact that index options come in many varieties, ranging from broad-based indices such as the S&P 500 to narrow indices such as the Major Market Index. The fact that these index options are settled in cash rather than the underlying stocks receives special treatment. The chapter provides an overview of the portfolio strategies that can be implemented with index options, including an introduction to the basic principles of portfolio insurance.

Although Chapter 6 is called "Interest Rate Caps and Floors," it offers a general introduction to the valuation of interest rate options. In particular, the chapter describes two types of interest rate options, one written on the price of the underlying asset and the other on the interest rate itself. The chapter focuses on short term options, such as options on Eurodollar time deposits. Its main objective is to describe how these simple interest rate options can be used to establish a ceiling (cap) or set a floor to the cost of funds for a borrower or lender. Formal cap-floor valuation models are presented as well.

Foreign exchange options are described in Chapter 7, with special attention devoted to the wide variety of products offered in this area, including options on forward contracts, futures contracts, contingent options and multi-currency options. To simplify matters somewhat, the chapter begins with the basic hedging problem in foreign exchange, goes on to describe the structure of exchange traded options, and then turns to the modifications of the basic Black-Scholes model designed to accommodate foreign currencies.

Chapter 8 returns to the topic of interest rate options discussed in

Chapter 6, but takes a much broader view of the subject. In particular, the chapter describes the fundamental difficulties associated with applying the basic Black-Scholes model to value an option based on the price behavior of a fixed income security. A number of alternative models are considered, with most attention focused on valuing interest rate options by modeling the evolution of the term structure of interest rates within a kind of binomial framework. This permits a very general treatment of both explicit option contracts and also the embedded options present in securities like callable bonds. The use of bond options in hedging and immunization strategies is described along with an analysis of the duration and convexity of the underlying securities.

The main objective of Chapter 9 is conceptual: to describe how the fundamental insight offered by modern option pricing theory relates to the valuation of corporate securities. It turns out that basic securities, such as equities and zero coupon bonds, can be fruitfully viewed within the option pricing framework, and so can more complex securities, such as convertible bonds and warrants. Although it is fairly difficult to apply a formal options pricing model to value these securities in practice, the insight offered by the options theory perspective provides guidelines for understanding how these securities behave.

Mortgages are sufficiently different from other types of fixed income securities to warrant separate treatment in Chapter 10. Perhaps the main feature of mortgages that lends itself to option valuation is the right of the borrower to prepay the principal owed. The chapter describes how to integrate a prepayment model and options methodology to produce a pricing model for mortgages and mortgage-backed securities. An extensive glossary of mortgage-related terms is presented in the appendix.

Chapter 11 applies the principles of option theory to the creation of portfolio insurance for equity portfolios. The discussion begins with an explanation of when it might be necessary to replicate a put option via a trading strategy rather than simply purchasing the option outright. The advantages and disadvantages of such dynamic trading strategies are reviewed within the context of the 1987 stock market crash. The chapter concludes with a specific example of insuring a portfolio, including a discussion of deductibles, tracking error, volatility estimation, and execution costs.

Part III. Implementation

Those who actually trade options and those who must compute numerical estimates of option fair values are confronted by a number of common practical problems associated with implementing their craft. The three chapters in Part III are devoted to issues that transcend any particular options market, but extend beyond the purely theoretical framework of options pricing theory discussed in Part I. In particular, the chapters focus on the liquidity costs associated with executing trades, the techniques used to estimate volatility and the numerical methods that must be applied to solve many option valuation problems. Although the topics are of important practical significance, that does not imply that the chapters are appropriate for casual bedtime reading.

Chapter 12 is devoted to a description of how marketmakers quote bid and offer prices on options. Since the bid-asked spread is the most significant component of transactions costs, this topic is important to anyone actually trading options for hedging or speculative purposes. After a brief overview of how the exchange traded and over the counter options markets are organized, the chapter focuses on decision rules used by marketmakers in quoting option prices, including applications of put-call parity, butterfly spreads and formal option pricing models. The implications for investors, traders and speculators are presented in the last section.

The most difficult input in any options valuation formula is the volatility associated with the underlying asset. Chapter 13 describes two methods that are used to estimate volatility: (1) Historical data are combined via statistical techniques to provide an estimate based on past price behavior; (2) Actual options prices are used to derive the volatility implied by the options pricing formula. The chapter evaluates alternative procedures used in both approaches and discusses their advantages and disadvantages.

Chapter 14 confronts the fact that many option valuation problems can be solved only by numerical methods, that is by using a mathematical algorithm that computes an approximate solution for a specific set of parameters. This chapter introduces numerical methods and presents techniques that must be used to actually solve for the values of specific options, such as the American put option. The chapter requires more mathematical sophistication than the rest of the book. Appendix A to Chapter 3 on continuous time mathematics provides a useful introduction.

ACKNOWLEDGMENTS

A project of this size involves a great deal of time and effort from many people in addition to the authors. We would like to thank the American Council of Life Insurance for providing financial support for the overall project, and particularly Kenneth Wright, Nathaniel Cabanilla and Paul Reardon of the ACLI and Francis Schott of the Equitable Life Assurance Society, for their continued interest and support. Arnold Sametz, Director of the Salomon Center at N.Y.U. was especially instrumental in setting up the project.

Major thanks are due to Jim Cozby, for his careful and patient work in turning a collection of 14 separate manuscripts into a single document, and to Tavy Ronen and Nemmara Chidambaran for their able research assistance. Thanks also to Mary Jaffier, Robyn Vanterpool, Margie Guinyard, Ingrid Persaud, and Lyle Jaffier for their help throughout the project. Special thanks are due to Edie Shwalb, Linda Canina, Roni Michaely, Francesco Drudi, Hugh Thomas, Saturnino Mairal, and to countless Ph.D. and M.B.A. students at the Stern School for laboring through earlier drafts of the manuscript and uncovering (we hope) nearly all of the mistakes.

Stephen Figlewski
William L. Silber
Marti G. Subrahmanyam

PART 1

THEORY

CHAPTER 1

OPTIONS AND OPTIONS MARKETS

Stephen Figlewski
William L. Silber [*]

1.1 WHAT IS AN OPTION?

While options of one form or another have existed for centuries, in the last 15 years there has been a veritable explosion in the extent of options trading, in the variety of instruments that can be considered as options either explicitly or implicitly, and also in our understanding of the economics of options. In the next section we will describe this proliferation of options in more detail and give a number of examples to illustrate the range of financial instruments and contracts that can be treated as options. Subsequent chapters in the book will cover many of the most important kinds of options in detail. But first we must get acquainted with some definitions and options terminology.

There are two basic types of options, calls and puts. More complex option instruments can generally be treated as packages of these basic types.

---

[*]The authors are Professor of Finance and Professor of Finance and Economics, respectively, at the Leonard N. Stern School of Business, New York University.

A *call* option is the *right* to *buy* a specified quantity of some *underlying asset* by paying a specified *exercise price, on or before* an *expiration date.*

A *put* option is the *right* to *sell* a specified quantity of some *underlying asset* for a specified *exercise price, on or before* an *expiration date.*

The important terms in these definitions are italicized so that we can focus on them at greater length. Our discussion will lead to further definitions of the important features of these options.

Both calls and puts specify the terms of a financial transaction that can be made for a specific period of time in the future, i.e., until the option expires. The difference between them is that a *call* is the right to *buy* and a *put* is the right to *sell* the underlying asset.

The buyer of an option receives the *right but not the obligation* to make the specified transaction. For example, the holder of a call option has the power to choose whether to buy the underlying asset or not. If it is in the holder's interest to buy at the price fixed by the option contract, he or she may *exercise* the option and do so. But there is no obligation to buy the asset, if the option holder prefers not to; the option can be allowed to go unexercised without any penalty. It is the element of choice that is the defining characteristic of an option.

Note that the term "exercise" has a very precise meaning in this context. The holder of the option exercises it by informing the seller that he wishes to make the specified transaction. The seller must then perform the contractual obligation promised in the option contract.

Obviously, there are two parties to the option contract. Since the holder of the option has the right to choose whether the transaction will take place, his opposite number, known as the *option writer* or *grantor,* has given up this right. The writer commits to make the specified transaction only if the option holder wants to. In return, the writer normally receives a payment from the buyer, known as the option *premium,* at the outset. The buyer purchases the option from the writer, who then has a contractual obligation to enter into the transaction at a later time if the buyer chooses.

Exchange-traded option contracts are all of this form, with the option premium paid by the buyer to the writer at the time the option contract is purchased. But other optional arrangements are not uncommon, such as when a corporation awards stock options to its employees as a form of executive compensation, with no payment of a premium. Regardless of how, or whether, an option premium is paid, the essential point is that in giving the option holder the right to decide whether to exercise the option, the writer gives up something of economic value.

An option conveys the right to make a transaction in an *underlying asset*. For example, a call option on IBM stock, traded on the Chicago Board Options Exchange, gives the holder the right to buy 100 shares of IBM; a put option on Treasury bond futures traded at the Chicago Board of Trade gives the holder the right to sell a T-bond futures contract. In every case, the option specifies a transaction that is to be made in some other asset. The value of the option, and the holder's decision whether to exercise the option or not, will be contingent on what happens to the price of the underlying asset during the option's life. For that reason options, like futures contracts, are known as "contingent" claims or "derivative" securities. Their value is contingent on, or derives from, the value of their underlying asset.

The price at which the transaction will take place, if it takes place, is set by the terms of the option contract and is known as the *exercise price* or the *strike price*. Most options specify a single exercise price, although more complex arrangements are not uncommon. Many warrants, for example, have strike prices that change over time according to a schedule. The important thing is that the rules for determining the strike price and all other terms of the transaction are fixed at the outset by the option contract.

Finally, as we have seen, the option agreement specifies an *expiration date* that fixes the time period during which the holder can choose to make the transaction. There are two types of options that differ in when they allow the holder to exercise. *American* options can be exercised at any time the holder wishes up until the expiration date, while *European* options can only be exercised on the expiration date itself.

The terms American and European arose because of the way exercise terms were typically set in the past for options traded in those two parts of the world. This geographical distinction no longer has much validity. Today, most exchange-traded options in both the United States and Europe are "American," many over-the-counter options in both places are "European," and exceptions of all kinds abound.

A few options, such as the perpetual warrants issued by some corporations, have no expiration date at all. Again, the important thing is that the rules with respect to option expiration are specified.

1.2   INSTITUTIONAL ARRANGEMENTS IN OPTIONS MARKETS

The introduction of options trading on the Chicago Board Options Exchange (CBOE) in 1973, and the subsequent growth in exchange trading, marked a turning point in the history of the options market. Until then options were traded in the so-called over the counter market, where various securities firms acted as marketmaking dealers in particular stock options. Individuals wanting to trade options would contact their brokerage firms to buy from or sell to one of the option dealers. The Chicago Board Options Exchange brought greater visibility to options trading by providing an open forum where options could be bought and sold in an auction format similar to the way stocks were traded on the New York Stock Exchange and the way commodities were traded on the various futures exchanges. In addition, the CBOE introduced a number of other innovations that expanded the acceptance of options trading in the financial community. Among the most important innovations were the standardization of the terms of options contracts, the creation of centralized trading and price dissemination facilities, and the introduction of an options clearing corporation plus the associated regulatory structure. These innovations in options trading served to reduce the costs associated with trading options, thereby promoting an active secondary market where options could be easily bought and sold. To appreciate fully the importance of these institutional arrangements, let us first review the mechanisms associated with over the counter trading in options.

Over the Counter Options. Prior to 1973 all options contracts were traded in the over the counter (OTC) market. The over the counter market in options was organized much like the OTC market in common stock. Various securities firms would quote bids and offers on particular stock options, such as puts and calls on General Motors, General Electric and IBM. A stockbroker could call one of these "option marketmaking" firms and buy an option at the offer price or sell an option at the bid price for the account of one of the firm's customers.

Perhaps the most memorable feature of the pre-1973 OTC market was the bewildering array of strike prices and expiration dates associated with these options. In fact, there was an infinite variety of option terms on any given stock because a dealer would normally customize the option to accommodate the preferences of the buyer or seller.

This custom-tailoring of option terms is one of the reasons the OTC market in some types of options (such as on Treasury bonds and foreign exchange) continues to flourish alongside the exchange traded variety. On the other hand, the main problem with OTC options stems precisely from the fact that each option is different from every other option. This makes it difficult to transfer such options among third parties—even if that were permitted by the terms of the option contract. In point of fact, OTC options are not negotiable instruments. Thus, these contracts are illiquid and are almost always terminated either by exercise or by expiration. Moreover, ascertaining the price of a particular option is a time consuming and inaccurate procedure. In general, the only source of price information is the firm that originally bought or sold the option. Without the presence of an open auction format, price quotations suffer from lack of adequate competition.

A final problem associated with OTC options is default risk. As we saw in section 1.1, option buyers have rights and option sellers have obligations. The financial integrity of the securities firm that sells options is the only guarantee underlying the terms of the option. Buyers of OTC options must, therefore, evaluate the capital adequacy of option sellers to determine whether there is a reasonable chance of default. This credit risk exposure provides another stumbling block to OTC option trading.

The institutional innovations associated with exchange traded options were designed explicitly to overcome these drawbacks to the OTC options market. Perhaps the best way to proceed is to examine each of these innovations to see how they mitigated the barriers to OTC option trading.

Standardization of Option Terms. The first step in facilitating options trading on exchanges was to standardize option characteristics such as expiration dates and strike prices. For example, options on General Motors traded on the CBOE would expire four times a year, e.g., on a specific date in March, June, September and December. In addition, the exercise price of these options would be set in $5 increments surrounding the current price of the underlying stock. Thus, if GM stock were trading at $80, puts and calls with strike prices of $70, $75, $80, $85 and $90 could be listed for trading. In this way the proliferation of option expiration dates and strike prices is minimized. This serves to expand public order flow in listed options, thereby improving liquidity.

The specific rules for expiration dates and strike prices vary with the exchange on which the option is traded as well as with the price of the underlying security. For example, if a stock price is above $100, the strike prices on its options are set $10 apart. For options on futures contracts such as Treasury bonds (traded on the Chicago Board of Trade), the strike prices are set 2 points apart. Expiration dates also follow alternative rules. For example, there is a February, May, August, November cycle of expiration dates for some stocks rather than March, June, September and December. In addition, an option expiring at the end of the current month (whatever it is) is also sometimes listed for trading. Although the specific rules must be examined in each case, the overall principle is the same: fragmentation of strike prices and expiration dates is limited in order to promote market liquidity.

Centralized Trading Facilities. We have used the term liquidity rather loosely until now. In most contexts liquidity refers to the ability to transact quickly at prices that are close to the fair value of the asset. In this sense it is more properly defined as marketability, that is, the ability to uncover a ready buyer and/or seller quickly, without having to induce a purchase or sale by offering a huge discount or premium. Organized exchanges provide this service by disseminating bid and offer quotes from potential buyers and sellers over electronic quotation screens. In addition, marketmakers are attracted to an exchange because of the expected flow of public orders. These marketmakers quote bid prices at which people can sell and offer prices from which people can buy. Thus, when an exchange lists an option for trading it combines centralized order flow with standardized contract terms, both of which improve the marketability of the option and expand trading interest.

Clearing Arrangements. Our discussion has emphasized that buying and selling options conveys rights and obligations that last until either the option is exercised or expires. In particular, an option buyer has rights and an option seller has obligations. Option buyers should, therefore, monitor the credit worthiness of option sellers to make certain that the sellers have the financial integrity to meet their obligations. Concern with this credit risk exposure could seriously hamper the transfer of exchange traded options among buyers and sellers who do not normally do business with each other.

To solve this problem, all exchange traded options are settled through a clearing house, either the Options Clearing Corporation (OCC) for stock options or the clearing house for a particular futures exchange when dealing with options on futures contracts. The clearing house, which is composed of well capitalized brokerage firms, acts as the guarantor of each options transaction. Thus, once an option transaction has been completed on the floor of an exchange and a price for the option has been established, the buyer and seller of the option no longer look to each other to execute the contractual rights and obligations. Rather, the clearing corporation becomes the buyer to every seller and the seller to every buyer. This means, for example, that if a call buyer chooses to exercise the option contract to buy IBM at a strike of $100, the OCC must deliver IBM at that price. The OCC delivers IBM by assigning the obligation to someone who has sold these IBM calls. The OCC assigns this so-called "exercise notice" by choosing randomly among all outstanding writers of these options.

It is obvious that guaranteeing the performance of rights and obligations associated with an option contract is a serious matter. In particular, the OCC has risk exposure because the option seller, who has future obligations, may not be able or willing to perform. To protect itself the OCC imposes margin requirements on options writers. These margins are not downpayments as with stock but resemble margins on futures contracts which serve as a performance bond. The precise calculation of margin requirements is complicated because it varies with the risk exposure of the options writer's position. Even without the details, however, it is clear that margin requirements must be met when selling exchange traded options, and these margins serve to protect the integrity of the options clearing house.

An important benefit of the clearing corporation's activities is that exchange traded options can be *settled by offset*. Suppose a trader wrote an IBM call with a strike price of 100 and an expiration date in three months. If the price of IBM increased and the call writer wanted to terminate the obligation to deliver IBM he could simply go out and buy one 3 month IBM call with a strike price of 100. The trader's position in the clearing corporation would be long one call and short one call with the same strike and expiration date. These positions would cancel each other, leaving the trader without a position in IBM calls. A similar *settlement by offset* occurs if someone is long an option and subsequently sells an identical option. This arrangement makes buying and selling options an easily reversible process, once again expanding public interest in the marketplace. By way of contrast, as noted above, OTC options are not usually settled by offset because there is no centralized clearing facility or auction market to facilitate the process.

As an aside, it should be noted that the clearing house permits us to keep track of the total number of options contracts outstanding—known as the *open interest*. The open interest in a particular option, such as IBM calls, is nothing more than the total of all long positions, which is also equal to the total of all short positions.

1.3   OPTIONS TRADING

Perhaps the greatest testimony to the success of the innovations associated with exchange traded options is the dramatic growth in options trading as chronicled in Table 1-1. Trading volume on all U.S. exchanges grew by 320 percent between 1978 and 1988. Moreover, although the CBOE was the only exchange that listed options in 1973, all the major stock exchanges and futures exchanges sponsored options trading in 1988.

TABLE 1–1
Volume of options trading on major exchanges, 1973–1988.
(Figures are in thousands of contracts.)

Equity Options

	1973	*1978*	*1983*	*1987*	*1988*
CBOE					
Stock	1,119	34,277	71,696	73,315	49,393
Index	–	–	10,662	108,352	62,250
AMEX					
Stock	–	14,381	36,200	52,771	37,470
Index	–	–	2,693	18,193	7,549
PHLX					
Stock	–	3,270	16,608	18,088	13,093
Index	–	–	6	499	157
PSE					
Stock	–	3,290	11,156	18,952	13,069
Index	–	–	–	459	280
NYSE					
Stock	–	–	–	1,306	1,903
Index	–	–	–	2,193	724

Source: Market Statistics, CBOE.

TABLE 1–1, continued
Futures Options—12 month volume of trading on major exchanges for fiscal years ending September 30. (Figures are in thousands of contracts.)

Futures Options

	1982–1983	*1986–1987*	*1987–1988*
CSCE	8	383	1,464
CBT	1,143	22,684	26,493
CME & IMM	193	12,173	12,242
COMEX	288	3,218	3,368
NYFE	244	290	39
KCBT	–	30	36
MCE	–	13	20
MGE	–	1	2
NYCE	–	79	119
NYMEX	–	2,131	5,246

Source: CTFC Annual Reports

EXCHANGES

CBOE : Chicago Board Options Exchange

AMEX : American Stock Exchange

PHLX : Philadelphia Stock Exchange

PSE : Pacific Stock Exchange

NYSE : New York Stock Exchange

CSCE : Coffee, Sugar and Cocoa Exchange

CBT : Chicago Board of Trade

CME : Chicago Mercantile Exchange (IMM : International Monetary Market)

COMEX : Commodity Exchange

NYFE : New York Futures Exchange

KCBT : Kansas City Board of Trade

MCE : Mid-America Commodity Exchange

MGE : Minneapolis Grain Exchange

NYCE : New York Cotton Exchange

NYMEX : New York Mercantile Exchange

The composition of options listed for trading has also undergone considerable evolution. From 1973 through 1983 much of the growth in options trading stemmed from an increase in the number of stocks that the stock exchanges—primarily the CBOE and American Stock Exchange—found eligible for options trading. In 1983 two major changes occurred: (1) options on stock indexes were listed, led by the S&P 100 contract on the CBOE; and (2) options on futures contracts were introduced by the major futures exchanges.

It took less than two years for the S&P 100 contract to become the most widely traded options contract in the United States—accounting for more than half of all options traded by 1985. The success of the S&P 100 contract stems from the fact that obligations are settled in cash rather than stock—thereby avoiding the transactions costs of delivering the 100 different equities in the S&P100 index. In addition, as is pointed out in Chapters 2 and 5, portfolio diversification makes the cost of an option on an index much lower than the sum of the prices of each of the component options. Thus individuals could hedge against and/or speculate on movements in the market as a whole more cheaply with index options than with options on individual stocks.

The growth in options on futures contracts has also been substantial since 1983. The most popular option in this group is on Treasury bonds. The vast underlying market in Treasury securities accounts for much of the demand. In this case, however, exchange trading is supplemented by a large over the counter market in options on Treasuries. For many participants, the advantages of customized strikes and expiration dates in Treasury bond options outweighs the benefits of the exchange traded variety. Since trading volume is not available for OTC options it is not possible to determine which market dominates.

1.4   A FEW KINDS OF OPTIONS

In Table 1-2 we list some of the many kinds of options, securities with embedded option features, and financial arrangements that are not options but can be analyzed as if they were.

In 1973 when the Chicago Board Options Exchange first opened, and the academic papers by Black and Scholes introducing their option pricing model had just been published, puts and calls were thought of as exotic and

TABLE 1–2
A few kinds of options.

Basic calls and puts	Embedded options
Traded calls and puts on stocks	Callable securities
Stock index options	Convertible securities
Foreign currency options	Mortgage prepayment
Futures options	Portfolio insurance
Commodity options	
Warrants and rights	Financial arrangements as options
Primes and scores	Bankruptcy
Supershares	Senior/junior debt
Caps, floors, and collars	Insurance
Compound options	...and many others

specialized instruments. Stock options were traded in a rather illiquid over-the-counter dealer market. Other kinds of options existed, such as an option to buy a given piece of property that might be purchased by an investor in real estate, but there was little standardization, no secondary market trading, and no extensive effort to develop formal ways to analyze option valuation.

Since then options have proliferated. In addition to a tremendous increase in the volume of stock options activity, options contracts now exist for almost every other type of financial instrument. New kinds of securities with option features are being developed every day.

On the theoretical front, we have extended the basic option valuation paradigm in many ways: weakening and generalizing the assumptions used by Black and Scholes, finding efficient methods for computing option values, valuing new and different types of optional contracts, and using option theory to help us understand and value a wide variety of financial arrangements that had not previously been thought of as options. An example that will be covered in detail in a later chapter is the limited liability feature of corporate securities.

Most traded option contracts are straightforward calls and puts on different types of underlying assets. As described above, exchange-traded option contracts in the U.S. are standardized and traded under procedures governed by the exchanges and the Options Clearing Corporation. Over-the-counter options contracts traded by and through the major banks and other financial institutions tend to be less standardized: customized options can be created whose terms are limited only by the imaginations of the parties involved, at the cost of reduced liquidity and little or no secondary trading.

Since the most active exchange-traded options were those on stocks, option textbooks have tended to concentrate almost exclusively on stock options. Our focus in this book is purposefully much broader. Although in Chapters 2-4 we present the basics of option valuation mostly in the familiar terms of stock puts and calls, we then move on to examine the particular characteristics of the instruments, markets, and strategies for other kinds of financial options.

Stock index options, discussed in Chapter 5, resemble ordinary stock options, but they have some unique features. They are settled in cash, with no delivery of the underlying stock portfolio being possible at all. They make available a variety of interesting strategies for managing overall portfolio risk, but they also present a few valuation and hedging problems, due to cash settlement, the need to take into account the stream of dividends on a market index portfolio, and tracking error in positions involving non-index stock portfolios.

Possibly the largest volume of options trading is in options on foreign currencies that are traded over-the-counter by the large international banks. It is difficult to know exactly how large this market is because there is no central marketplace or clearing house. However, in March 1989, the Federal Reserve estimated that average daily foreign exchange transactions by 127 major U.S. banks alone was over $110 billion and that 4.3 percent of that was in options, a sixfold increase from 1986.[1] Currency options are discussed in Chapter 7.

Along with options trading based on financial instruments like stocks, bonds, and currencies, most futures exchanges have introduced options on futures contracts. For example, the most liquid Treasury bond options market is the market for T-bond *futures* options at the Chicago Board of Trade. Futures options are by no means restricted to financial futures; active markets exist for options on gold, oil, and soybean futures among many others. For a number of instruments, including stock indexes and currencies, there are active markets in futures, options on the underlying asset, and options on futures. This produces a great variety of arbitrage relationships among the different contracts that must all hold simultaneously.

---

[1]Federal Reserve Bank of New York, *Summary of Results of U.S. Foreign Exchange Market Survey Conducted in April 1989.* New York, September 13, 1989.

Unlike an ordinary option that leads to delivery of the underlying asset, exercise of a futures call (put) leaves the option holder with a long (short) position in the futures contract. This position is then marked to market as if it had been established at a futures price equal to the option's strike price. In other words, when a futures call is exercised, the call holder receives a *cash* payment from the writer equal to the difference between the current futures price and the option's strike price, and she is left with an open long futures position.

A second feature of American futures options is that they should normally be exercised before expiration. Futures options are discussed in several different chapters, including Chapter 4 (early exercise), Chapter 5 (stock index futures options), Chapter 8 (Treasury bond options), and Chapter 12 (marketmaking in oil futures options).

Commodity options have had a checkered past in the U.S. Because of incidents of fraud involving the sale of options on commodities traded in London, commodity options were banned during the 1970s by the Commodity Futures Trading Commission (CFTC). The prohibition was lifted in 1983 when the CFTC gave permission for pilot programs in one commodity option contract per exchange. The experiments were deemed successful and commodity options are now permitted. Options on commodities (in contrast to options on commodity futures) can be valued in the same way as options on stocks that do not pay dividends.

As discussed above, an exchange-traded stock option contract is an agreement between two private parties. Exercise of a stock option does not directly affect the corporation whose stock is involved. But corporations themselves issue two kinds of options, warrants and rights, for different purposes.

Warrants are call options that give holders the right to buy shares of the underlying stock from the company itself. Warrants are typically issued with rather long lifetimes, often five years or more, in contrast to the maturities of less than a year for traded stock options. Warrant exercise prices are frequently well above the current market price of the stock when they are issued. Often they are attached as a "sweetener" to make a new issue of bonds or other securities more attractive to buyers. A significant difference between a warrant and a call option is that when a warrant is exercised, new stock is issued and the capital structure of the firm changes. We discuss the implications of this in Chapter 9.

Rights are also call options issued by corporations, but they differ from warrants in several important ways. Rights are issued to existing stockholders when a firm decides to sell new stock. The purpose is to allow the current shareholders to maintain the same fractional ownership of the firm when the number of outstanding shares increases. Rights are generally issued with lifetimes measured in weeks rather than years, and with strike prices that are only slightly below the current price of the stock in the market.

Among the financial innovations spawned by widespread options trading during the 1980s are several types of options-related securities that are based on splitting up claims on the future value of an equity portfolio among a set of different instruments that then trade separately in the market. Two examples are Primes and Scores, and Supershares.

Primes and Scores are created by the establishment of an Americus Trust. Shares of the underlying stock, for example IBM, are deposited into the trust and for each share, the depositor receives one Prime and one Score. These can then be held or sold in the market, together or separately. The holder of the Prime receives the dividends that are paid by the shares in the trust (less a small fee that covers the cost of running the trust). After a few years, the trust matures, and the underlying shares are distributed to the holders of the Primes and Scores. This is done in such a way that the Score is essentially a call option and the Prime holder is in the position of someone who owns the stock and has written a "covered call" on it. These positions are discussed in more detail in Chapter 2.

Supershares are based on a similar idea of splitting up the future value of an underlying security, in this case either a diversified portfolio of stocks or a riskless portfolio of money market instruments. At the time this is being written, the creation of Supershares has been proposed by the firm of Leland, O'Brien and Rubinstein, but the Securities and Exchange Commission has not yet approved them for trading. The idea is discussed in Chapter 5.

As interest rate volatility has increased dramatically over the last 15 years, more and more financing is being done at floating rates. Borrowers hope that the rate they are obliged to pay will not float too high, and lenders worry that their future return on investment may fall far below today's rate. "Caps" and "floors" are option contracts that guarantee the maximum (cap) or minimum (floor) rate that can be reached. Many floating rate instruments, like variable rate mortgages, may have built-in caps and floors, but the instruments are also traded separately, mostly by major banks. Interest rate caps, floors, and related instruments are discussed in Chapter 6. Similar contracts for foreign exchange rates are covered in Chapter 7.

With the enormous variety of underlying instruments that have generated option trading, it should not be surprising that there are even options on options, or "compound" options. At this time, there are no explicit exchange-traded option on option contracts. There are, however, many options on securities that have *embedded* options, like callable bonds, or Treasury bond futures (that have several important delivery options). Chapter 9 shows how it can be useful to think about equity as an option on the value of the firm itself, which then makes a call on the stock into an option on an option.

Option theory is very important for understanding explicit option contracts, but it has also contributed to understanding and evaluation of many kinds of securities in which there is an element of choice that can be treated as an option. A callable bond is a good example. Nearly all corporate bonds are issued with call provisions that allow the firm to buy them back prior to maturity. This lets the firm retire bonds that had to be issued in times of high coupon rates, and refinance with less costly debt.

A callable bond can be valued as a package consisting of a straight, i.e., noncallable, bond plus a short position in a call option on the bond (that is retained by the company). Callability as an option is treated in Chapters 8 and 9.

Convertible securities are a similar case. The holder of a convertible bond, for example, has the option either to hold the bond and collect coupon interest, or to convert it into some number of shares of the issuing company's stock. In essence, this is the option to exchange one asset for another. To complicate matters, convertibles are often also callable. Chapter 9 describes how option principles can explain the behavior of these securities.

One of the most important options existing in what we might call "standard" securities is the option that a home buyer has to prepay a mortgage before maturity. Home mortgages are often 25 or 30 year instruments, but they are rarely outstanding for that length of time, simply because people move more frequently than that. More problematical for the lender than the uncertain maturity is the fact that when interest rates on new mortgages fall below the contract interest rate on an existing mortgage, the borrower has an incentive to prepay the loan and refinance at the lower rate. The effect of this prepayment option, and the uncertainty about how and when it will be exercised, has farreaching effects throughout the financial system. Several spectacular losses at major investment banks have been directly attributable to valuation problems with mortgage-related instruments. Chapter 10 explains how the mortgage prepayment option affects mortgages and mortgage-backed securities.

A different case in which options are closely tied up with an investment that is not an option itself is portfolio insurance. Portfolio insurance is a trading strategy that does not (normally) use options, but whose purpose is to make the value of an investment portfolio behave as if it contained some put options. The strategy involves using option theory to determine what portion of the portfolio should be invested in risky securities and what portion in riskless instruments at each point in time in order to replicate the desired payoff pattern. Chapter 11 describes the strategy in detail, as well as discussing the possible connection between portfolio insurance and the stock market crash on October 19, 1987.

Finally, as option valuation theory has developed, we have found more and more ways of applying its principles to other situations in which an element of choice is present, even though no option is directly involved. We will not cover many of the truly exotic applications of option theory to other kinds of problems in this book, but one important one will be explored in detail in Chapter 9. That is the insight that bankruptcy with limited liability can be treated as an option that is held by the stockholders of a firm, and effectively written by the bondholders.

Stockholders of a firm with debt outstanding have the following option when the maturity date for the bonds arrives: If the value of the firm's assets exceeds the required debt payment, the bonds will be paid off and the stockholders will get the remainder. But if the assets do not cover the required payment, the firm defaults. The bondholders receive less than was promised and the stockholders receive nothing (but they do not have to cover the shortfall out of their own resources). In effect, the shareholders have a call option on the firm's assets, with a strike price equal to the face value of the debt. The bondholders are short the call option.

This way of thinking about limited liability yields important insights about how management (which represents the shareholders) will behave when bankruptcy becomes a possibility. For example, under some circumstances, it may even make sense for the management to take on risky projects with negative net present values!

The same option principles that affect stockholders are also important in understanding debt claims with different priorities. Junior debt, in particular, changes from being "bond-like" to being "stock-like," with significant changes in the incentives of the junior debtholders, as the probability of default increases.

Lastly, an insurance contract may be usefully thought of as being a kind of put option. A fixed sum is paid at the outset, and the payoff depends on what happens to the value of the insured (i.e., underlying) asset. If the insured asset's value does not drop (i.e., there is no loss) there is no payoff (the option expires worthless). If there is a loss, the insurance company (option writer) makes a payment equal to the initial asset value less a deductible (equivalent to the put's strike price) minus the final value of the insured asset (the price of the underlying asset when the put is exercised). This is a very useful analogy for valuing explicit insurance contracts, and many types of related instruments such as loan guarantees. The analogy between put options and insurance is drawn in more detail in Chapter 11.

It is clear from this (nonexhaustive) list that we have a large amount of ground to cover in order to give even a brief overview of the subject of financial options. The next chapter begins the task with a discussion of the basic principles of option valuation.

CHAPTER 2

BASIC PRICE RELATIONSHIPS AND BASIC TRADING STRATEGIES

Stephen Figlewski[*]

In this chapter we will begin with the fundamentals of option valuation. There are a number of properties of option values that are so general that they must hold regardless of how the underlying asset price behaves. Some of these are obvious, such as that the value of an American option is never less than the amount you could realize by exercising it immediately. Other properties are not so intuitive, for example, that it should never pay to exercise an American call option early if the underlying asset is not going to pay any dividends or other cash distributions before the expiration date.

The principle we will use to demonstrate and prove these general properties is arbitrage, and its more powerful cousin, portfolio dominance. The term "arbitrage" is widely used, and often misused.

An *arbitrage* is a trade in which one buys something at one price and simultaneously sells essentially the same thing at a higher price, in order to make a riskless profit. The three important elements in this definition are first, that arbitrage involves buying and selling two things that are effectively the same (typically called "portfolios" since either or both might

---

[*]The author is Professor of Finance at the Leonard N. Stern School of Business, New York University.

involve transactions in more than one security); second, that the transactions are done at the same time; and third, that a riskless profit is produced.

An arbitrage amounts to a "free lunch"—an excess profit that involves no risk. *In theory* an arbitrage profit, like a free lunch, should not exist. If it did, clever investors should all take advantage of it, buying at a low price and immediately reselling at a higher price. In the process, they would drive the price of what they were buying up and the price of what they were selling down, until the arbitrage opportunity disappeared.

A price structure that permits an arbitrage profit can therefore not be an equilibrium in the market. Ruling out profitable arbitrage allows us to prove certain properties about how security prices must relate to each other in equilibrium. As we will see below, this leads to several important results about option prices. And as the next chapter will show, the arbitrage principle is the basis of the famous Black-Scholes option pricing model, and other modern theories of option valuation.

Throughout the chapter we will illustrate the valuation principles and basic option trading strategies using the set of option prices displayed in Table 2–1. These have been constructed using the Black-Scholes theoretical model (which we will cover in detail in the next chapter) so they will automatically satisfy all of the price relationships required for European options.

Table 2–1 shows prices for 1 and 3 month European calls and puts on an underlying asset whose current price S is 100. At this point, it may help intuition to think of the underlying asset as a share of stock, since this is

TABLE 2–1
Option prices[a]

	Calls		Puts	
Strike	1 Month[b]	3 Month[c]	1 Month[b]	3 Month[c]
95	6 7/16	9	13/16	2 1/8
100	3 3/16	6	2 9/16	4
105	1 1/4	3 5/8	5 5/8	6 3/4

[a]Prices are based on Black-Scholes theoretical values, with asset price $S = 100$, interest rate $r = 8\%$, volatility $\sigma = .25$, and no dividends.

[b]Prices are rounded to nearest 1/16 for 1 month contracts.

[c]Prices are rounded to nearest 1/8 for 3 month contracts.

consistent with most of the other options literature. The material presented here is quite general, however, and later chapters will show how it applies to options on all types of securities.

To keep things simple at first, we will assume there are no dividends to be paid in the next three months and that it is possible to borrow or lend money without risk at 8.00 percent (r). Finally, in order to apply the valuation model we have assumed the price volatility of the underlying stock is 25 percent per year, a typical value for a normal stock.

2.1 OPTION PAYOFFS

Let us first focus on the prices for 1 month call options. Three different strike prices are shown, 95, 100, and 105. The 95 strike call gives the holder the right to buy the underlying stock, which we will name XYZ, for 95 dollars per share one month from now. (If these were prices for ordinary exchange-traded stock options such as one might see in the newspaper, they would represent the price per share for a quantity of 100 shares.) Since the stock is currently selling for 100, the 95 strike calls are said to be 5 dollars *in-the-money*. An in-the-money option gives the holder the right to trade the underlying asset at a more favorable price than he currently could in the market. The price difference is known as the option's *intrinsic value,* 5 dollars in this case. An option that is in-the-money at expiration will be exercised.

The 105 strike call is *out-of-the-money*. It has no intrinsic value at present. The stock would have to go up at least 5 dollars by the option expiration date for it to be worth exercising this call. If the stock is still below the strike price at expiration, the holder will take advantage of the right to choose, and will not exercise the option. If he wanted to own the stock, it would still be cheaper to allow the option to expire unexercised and to buy the stock for less than 105 in the market.

An option whose exercise price is equal (or close to) the current market price for the underlying asset is *at-the-money*. At-the-money options are subject to the greatest uncertainty about whether they will ultimately be exercised or will expire worthless. They therefore embody the greatest value for the option of postponing the choice until later. For this reason, at-the-money options are generally the most actively traded and liquid in the options market.

At expiration, an option holder must decide whether to exercise or not.

At that time the option price will be equal to its intrinsic value. For a call, this will be the market price of the underlying asset (S) minus the exercise price (X) if $S - X$ is positive, or zero otherwise. This payoff pattern can be written succinctly as

$$\text{Call Payoff at Expiration} = \text{Max}\ (S - X, 0)\ . \qquad (2.1)$$

The call will be worth whichever is greater, the asset price minus the exercise price or zero.

It is often very useful to look at the payoff patterns of options positions graphically, as a function of the price of the underlying asset. The payoff on the 1 month at-the-money call at expiration is shown in Figure 2–1. It is zero for any price below 100, since in that case the option is worthless and will be allowed to expire unexercised. For prices above 100, the option value goes up dollar for dollar with the stock price. The payoff diagram rises at a 45 degree angle to the right of 100.

A put option specifies the price the holder will receive for selling the underlying asset, so a put is in-the-money when the current stock price is below the exercise price, and out-of-the-money when S is greater than X. So in Table 2–1, the 105 strike puts are in-the-money, with an intrinsic value of $(X - S) = 5$ dollars. The 100's are at-the-money and the 95's are out-of-the-money.

By the same reasoning as before, the payoff at expiration can be expressed mathematically as

$$\text{Put Payoff at Expiration} = \text{Max}\ (X - S, 0)\ . \qquad (2.2)$$

Figure 2–2 displays this payoff function graphically. It is a kind of mirror image of the call payoff diagram, reflected around the strike price of 100. Above 100 the put is worthless, since one would never exercise the put to sell the stock at 100 when its price in the market is higher. Below 100, the payoff rises dollar for dollar as the stock drops. Unlike the call, the put has a maximum value it can attain of X dollars, because the stock cannot go below zero.

2.2 PUT-CALL PARITY

One of the most important option price relationships that can be derived

FIGURE 2–1
Call option

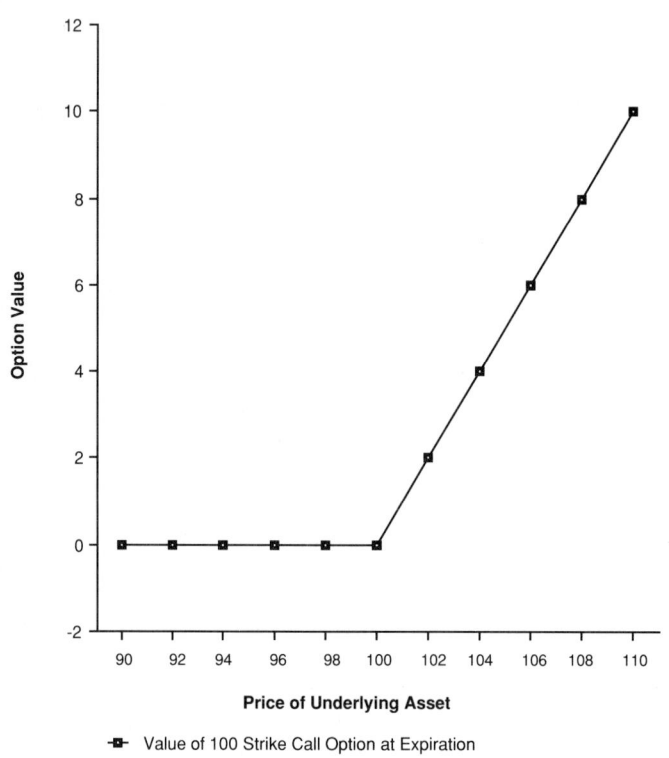

Value of 100 Strike Call Option at Expiration

directly from arbitrage is known as "put-call parity." If S is the price of the underlying asset, say XYZ stock, C is the price of a European call option on that stock, with an exercise price of X, and P is the price of a European put option with the same exercise price X and expiration date as the call, then

$$\text{Put-Call Parity:}\quad C - P = S - PV(X) \tag{2.3}$$

The call price minus the put price must equal the current stock price minus the present value of the strike price, discounted back from the option expiration date.

To prove put-call parity, let us consider two positions or "portfolios" corresponding to the left and right sides of the equals sign in equation (2.3).

FIGURE 2–2
Put option

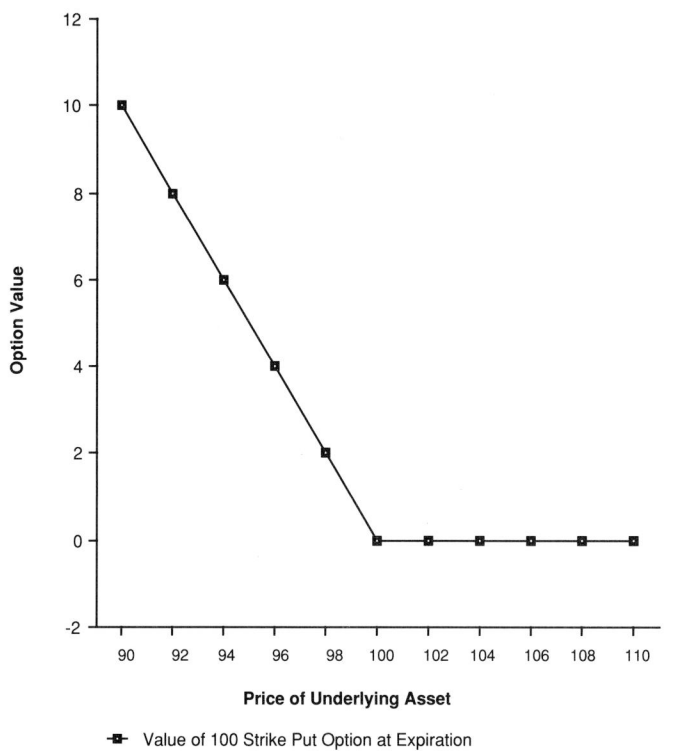

Price of Underlying Asset

☐ Value of 100 Strike Put Option at Expiration

Table 2–2 illustrates the portfolios.

Portfolio 1 consists of buying the call and writing the put option. The net cost is C dollars paid for the call, less P dollars received for writing the put.

Portfolio 2 consists of buying the stock and borrowing the present value of X dollars, i.e., borrowing an amount of money such that the total of principal and interest to be paid on the options' expiration date will be exactly X dollars. The net cost of Portfolio 2 at the beginning is $S - PV(X)$.

Now consider what these two positions will amount to as of option expiration. While we don't know what the stock price will be at that time, we do know that if it is above the strike price X, the call will be in-the-money and the put will be out-of-the-money. The reverse will be true if the stock price is below X. In analyzing options positions it is often very useful to set up a table like Table 2–2 detailing those two possibilities.

Table 2–2 shows that if the stock price at expiration is below X, we would not exercise the call, which will expire worthless. The put we have written will be exercised against us, and we will be obliged to buy the stock for X dollars. The total result will be that we end up owning the stock and paying out X.

If S is above X at expiration, the put expires worthless and we exercise the call. Again, we buy the stock and pay out X dollars. So as it turns out, regardless of whether the stock goes up or down, the result of holding Portfolio 1 is that at the options' maturity, we buy the stock and pay X dollars.

Portfolio 2 begins differently but winds up the same. In both cases, at option expiration we own the stock and repay X dollars. So even though we don't know what the stock price will be, we can say unambiguously that Portfolio 1 and Portfolio 2 will be worth the same amount.

Since the two portfolios will have the same value at expiration, if they didn't cost the same amount at the beginning, there would be an arbitrage. Investors would buy the cheaper portfolio, sell the more costly one, and keep the difference as a riskless profit. At expiration the proceeds from the portfolio they had bought would just offset what they owed on the one they were short. As long as the prices did not change, investors would continue

TABLE 2–2
Put-call parity

	Initial Cost	Value at Expiration	
		If $S_T \leq X$	If $S_T > X$
Portfolio 1			
Buy Call		Call expires	Exercise call
	$C - P$		
Write Put		Put exercised	Put expires
		In both cases: Pay X, buy stock	
Portfolio 2			
Buy Stock		Hold stock	Hold stock
	$S - PV(X)$		
Borrow present value of X		Repay X dollars	Repay X dollars

to do this trade in unlimited volume, so the situation can not be an equilibrium. The only stable possibility is that the two portfolios must cost the same, which proves that $C - P = S - PV(X)$, as equation (2.3) says.

Put-Call Parity and Synthetic Securities

The put-call parity relation shows how buying a call option and writing a put produces the same payoff pattern as buying the underlying asset and financing part of the purchase with borrowing. Options, in fact, offer a number of strategies for producing "synthetic" securities out of such combinations.

A good way to see what strategies exist is by rearranging the put-call parity equation. This section will illustrate several possibilities.

Equation (2.3) can be expressed as

$$\text{Long Call} + \text{Short Put} = \text{Long Underlying Asset} + \text{Borrowing} \quad (2.4)$$

In this equation, remember that the call and the put are matched as to strike price and expiration date. "Borrowing" means borrowing an amount equal to the present value of the options' strike price, so that the repayment at expiration date is X.

Equation (2.4) as it stands shows how to create a levered long position in the underlying asset, in other words, buying the stock on margin. The following four equations rearrange this to produce synthetic long positions in each of the four basic assets.

$$\text{Long Underlying Asset} = \text{Long Call} + \text{Short Put} + \text{Lending} \quad (2.5)$$

Buying a call, writing a put and investing the present value of the options' strike price in money market instruments produces a portfolio with exactly the same payoff as a long position in the underlying asset. The combined position should therefore cost the same in the market as the stock itself. ("Lending" here is just the negative of borrowing.)

$$\text{Long Call} = \text{Long Put} + \text{Long Underlying Asset} + \text{Borrowing} \quad (2.6)$$

This version of the equation will be analyzed in some detail below, in discussing the elements of value in a call option.

$$\text{Long Put} = \text{Long Call} + \frac{\text{Short Position in}}{\text{Underlying Asset}} + \text{Lending} \qquad (2.7)$$

Buying the stock, buying a put and writing a call creates a riskless hedged position. If prices in the market obey put-call parity, this position should earn the risk free rate of interest until the options' expiration date. This position is known as a *conversion*. An options market maker may write calls to satisfy a customer who wants to buy them, and then turn the trade into a riskless conversion by buying puts and the underlying asset. The comparable trade for puts, transforming the sale of a put into a riskless position by buying the call and shorting the underlying asset, is called a reverse conversion, or simply a "reversal."

$$\frac{\text{Riskless}}{\text{Lending}} = \text{Long Underlying Asset} + \text{Long Put} + \text{Short Call} \qquad (2.8)$$

The final position amounts to borrowing funds at the riskless interest rate (if the prices obey put-call parity).

It is easy to see how other short positions in the basic assets can be produced by reversing these equations.

2.3 ELEMENTS OF OPTION VALUE

One of the major achievements of modern finance theory is the option pricing model. It gives an easily implemented mathematical formula for the value of an option as a function of a small number of parameters, most of which are easily observable. We will put off developing the model in detail until later, but it is worth spending a few moments at this point to consider in general terms what gives value to an option.

Under the assumptions used in constructing Table 2–1, the exact fair value for a one month European call on XYZ stock with a strike price of 95 is 6 7/16, or $6.43 per share. What does this value derive from?

First, there is the option's intrinsic value. The 95 strike call gives the holder the right to buy XYZ stock for 5 dollars less than its current price in the market. Obviously, an American option that can be exercised at any time must always be worth at least its intrinsic value. Not quite so obvious, but true, is the fact that a European call must also be worth at least its intrinsic value, as long as no cash payouts will occur on the underlying asset before expiration date. A European put, on the other hand, may sell for less than its intrinsic value under certain conditions. We will elaborate on these points somewhat later. In any case, intrinsic value is an important component of option value. The deeper in-the-money an option is, the more it is worth.

Intrinsic value accounts for 5 dollars of the $6.43 value for the 95 strike one month call. The additional $1.43 is known as the *time value*. Prices of in-the-money options will include both intrinsic value and time value, while the prices of out-of-the-money options are entirely due to time value. An option's time value decays with the passage of time, so that at expiration only intrinsic value remains. An option that is out-of-the-money at expiration has neither intrinsic value nor time value and is therefore worthless.

Time value actually comes from two sources. One is the value of leverage. The 95 strike call is already fairly deep-in-the-money. If the stock price remains near 100 as expiration approaches, it will become increasingly likely that the option will eventually be exercised. The option feature, i.e., the right to decide later whether to exercise, becomes unimportant since it is virtually certain that the stock price at expiration will still be higher than 95.

However, even if we were sure to want to exercise the call, it would make sense to wait until the last minute to do so, since the longer we can delay paying out the exercise price, the longer we can earn interest on that money in other uses. So one component of a call option's time value is the interest that can be earned by investing the exercise price over the time from now until expiration. At the rate of 8 percent, this "leverage" value on a one month 95 strike call is $0.60. The leverage value will be greater the higher the interest rate is and the longer is the time to expiration.

The other component of time value is what we have referred to as the value of the option feature itself. The intrinsic value and leverage value together would give us the value of a forward contract, i.e., a binding commitment to buy XYZ for 95 in one month. The final component of the option price is the value of not having to buy the stock for 95 if the market price in a month should turn out to be lower than that. It stands to reason that this component of value depends on the probability that the stock price will end up below the strike price at expiration. This probability will depend on how far the call is in- or out-of-the-money, how much time remains for the price to change before expiration, and how much the stock's price usually moves over a given period of time (its price "volatility.")

In the case of our 95 strike call, the value of the option feature must be equal to

$$\$6.43 - \$5.00 - \$.60 = \$0.83.$$

That is,

$$
\begin{array}{ll}
\text{Call Value} = \text{Intrinsic value} & \left.\begin{array}{l} \\ \\ \end{array}\right\} \begin{array}{l} \text{Intrinsic} \\ \text{Value} \end{array} \\
\qquad\qquad\quad \text{Max } (0, S - X) & \\
\\
\qquad + \text{ Leverage value } [X - PV(X)] & \left.\begin{array}{l} \\ \\ \\ \end{array}\right\} \text{Time Value} \\
\\
\qquad + \text{ Value of the option feature} &
\end{array}
$$

Another way to think about the value of the option feature is that if the sum of the first two elements gives the value of buying XYZ for 95 in one month, the third component is the value of the right to undo that trade, selling the stock back at 95, if the market price is lower. That right to sell at 95 is simply a 95 strike put option.

If we substitute the put price for the "value of the option feature" in the last equation, we have

$$C = (S - X) + (X - PV(X)) + P$$

or $$C = S - PV(X) + P$$

which is just the put-call parity formula, equation (2.3) once again!

How does this work for a put option? The theoretical value of the one month 105 strike put is $5.59 per share, or $559 for a put contract on 100 shares. Like the 95 strike call we have been looking at, this option is also 5 dollars in-the-money when the stock price is 100. Like a call, a put's price should increase as its intrinsic value becomes greater.

The 105 strike put has time value in addition to its intrinsic value, equal to $(P - (X - S))$, or $0.59. Again, we can break this down into a portion that is due to the option feature and a portion that is due to the effect of delaying the payment of the exercise price until expiration. However, unlike the call, this latter effect works against the holder of the put.

Consider the situation faced by the holder of a very deep in-the-money put, say one with a strike of 120. It is virtually certain that this option will be in-the-money at expiration. But if it is a European put, the holder must wait until then before receiving the strike price of 120. What we have called the leverage value for a call is negative for a European put. The difference in value between receiving the strike price immediately and waiting until option expiration is $(PV(X) - X)$. The longer the delay and the higher the interest rate, the more it costs to wait.

The other component of time value for the put is the value of the option feature itself. Analogously to the argument we offered about this term above, one can think of the put as a commitment to sell the stock at expiration for 105 plus the right to undo the trade by buying the stock back at 105 if the market price at expiration is above that. The option feature for the put is then just a 105 strike call.

The breakdown of the elements of put value is therefore

$$P = \text{Max}\ (0\ ,\ X - S)\ \ +\ \ (PV(X) - X) + C.$$

$$(\text{Intrinsic Value})\ \ +\ \ (\text{Time Value})$$

So, unlike a call, time value for a put is made up of two components with different signs. In the case of the one month 105 strike put, the value of the option feature is $1.25 and the cost of waiting to receive the exercise price is $-0.66.

As the put goes deeper in-the-money, the value of the option feature (i.e., the call) goes to zero and the foregone interest term will dominate. Time value will become negative, so the European put before expiration can be worth less than its intrinsic value. The 120 strike one month put, for example, is 20 dollars in-the-money but its value is only $19.25.

An American put is not subject to this problem since it can be exercised at any time. American options can never be worth less than intrinsic value. This means that an American put will always be worth more than a European put because there is always some chance that one will want to exercise it early.

2.4 AMERICAN CALLS

A very important property of American call options can be derived from a similar portfolio argument to the one proving put-call parity. The property is that an American call on an asset that is not going to have any cash payout before option expiration will not be exercised early. For that reason, it must have the same value as a European call.

On the surface it seems as if an American option ought to be worth more than a European option. The American option allows you to do everything that you can with a European option, plus more. However, as we shall show, the right to exercise the American call early is of no value because it is never optimal to do it.

Consider the following two portfolios, shown in Table 2–3. Portfolio 1 is simply a long position in a European call option. Portfolio 2 is the same as the second portfolio in Table 2–2: buy the stock and borrow the present value of the call exercise price.

At expiration, if the stock price is less than or equal to the strike price, the call will expire worthless. If S_T is above X, the call is worth its intrinsic value, $S_T - X$.

The second portfolio is worth $S_T - X$ in both cases, since it is long the stock and requires that the loan of the present value of X be repaid. When S_T is above X, the two portfolios have the same value. But if S_T is below X, the value of Portfolio 2 is negative, while the call value is just 0, which is greater.

This is not exactly an arbitrage. One is not buying and selling the same thing, since the payoffs are not identical. But although the payoffs can differ, Portfolio 1 is at least as good as Portfolio 2 no matter what happens, and in some circumstances it is better. This means that Portfolio 1 *dominates* Portfolio 2.

TABLE 2–3
Call lower bound

	Initial Cost	Value at Expiration	
		If $S_T \leq X$	If $X < S_T$
Portfolio 1			
Buy Call	C	0	$S_T - X$
Portfolio 2			
Buy Stock	$S - PV(X)$	$S_T - X$	$S_T - X$
Borrow present value of X			

The principle of portfolio dominance is that if one portfolio dominates another, in equilibrium the dominant portfolio must cost at least as much in the market. Otherwise clever investors would buy it and sell the dominated portfolio for an immediate profit. The position would be completely hedged, and in some circumstances there would be a further cash payout.

Portfolio dominance in this case implies that

$$C \geq S - PV(X) \tag{2.9}$$

This gives us a useful lower bound for the value of a call.

But what does it have to do with American options? Whenever a call option is exercised, the value the holder realizes is the current stock price minus the exercise price, $S - X$. But equation (2.9) shows that a call option must be worth at least the stock price minus the *present value* of the exercise price, $S - PV(X)$, which will be greater than $S - X$ at any time prior to maturity. That means that regardless of whether the option is European or American, it pays to wait until the expiration date before exercising it.

If the holder wants to get out of her position in an American call prior to expiration, she should sell it in the market, where its price will be greater than what she could realize by exercising early. This observation is often summed up in the expression, "An American call is worth more alive than dead." However, it is important to remember that this only holds true when the underlying asset is not going to make any cash payouts before maturity.

2.5 THE CONVEXITY OF OPTION PRICES

The option prices in Table 2–1 exhibit the following pattern. In each column, it is always the case that the 100 strike option is worth less than the average of the prices for the 95 and 105 strike options. Another way of saying this is that if you formed a portfolio that was long one 95 strike option, long one 105 strike option, and short two 100 strike options, you would always have to pay more for the options you bought than you would receive for those you wrote. (This position that is long 1 call with a low strike price, long 1 call with a high strike, and short 2 calls with the strike in between is called a *butterfly* spread.)

For example, the butterfly spread using one month calls would cost $6\ 7/16 + 1\ 1/4 - 2 \times 3\ 3/16 = 1\ 5/16$. We will discuss butterfly spreads in more detail later, but at this point it is enough to know that if option prices did not obey this relationship between value and strike price, there would be an arbitrage.

Figure 2–3 plots the option value as a function of the strike price for one month calls under the assumptions about stock price, volatility, and so on that we use in Table 2–1. Figure 2–4 does the same for one month puts. The two curves exhibit the characteristic shape that they are bowed downward, or "convex" when viewed from below.

The convex shape translates into the property that if one takes any two strike prices, and a third that is a weighted average of the first two, then the value of the option with the middle strike is less than the same weighted average of the values of the outer options.

This can be expressed mathematically as follows:

Option Convexity: Take three strike prices X_1, X_2, and X_3, with $X_1 < X_2 < X_3$. X_2 is a weighted average of X_1 and X_3 with a weighting factor w equal to $w = (X_3 - X_2) / (X_3 - X_1)$.
That is,

$$X_2 = w\, X_1 + (1 - w)\, X_3.$$

Let C_1, C_2, and C_3 be the three call values corresponding to the three strike prices. Then

$$C_2 \le w\, C_1 + (1 - w)\, C_3. \qquad (2.10)$$

Proof: To prove this relationship holds, we set up two portfolios as before and look at their payoffs at expiration as a function of the stock price. Table 2–4 shows the example.

Portfolio 1 is just a long position in the X_2 strike call, while Portfolio 2 is the combination of $w\, X_1$ strike calls and $(1 - w)\, X_3$ calls. The object is to show that Portfolio 2 dominates Portfolio 1 so that it must cost more at the outset.

Because there are three strike prices, we must look at four possible outcomes at expiration, corresponding to 0, 1, 2, or all 3 options ending up in-the-money. Clearly, the two portfolios have the same value if $S_T \le X_1$ and all of the options expire out-of-the-money.

If S_T is between X_1 and X_2 only the X_1 strike call will be in-the-money. Portfolio 2 will have a positive value but Portfolio 1 will still be worthless.

FIGURE 2–3
Call value as a function of strike price

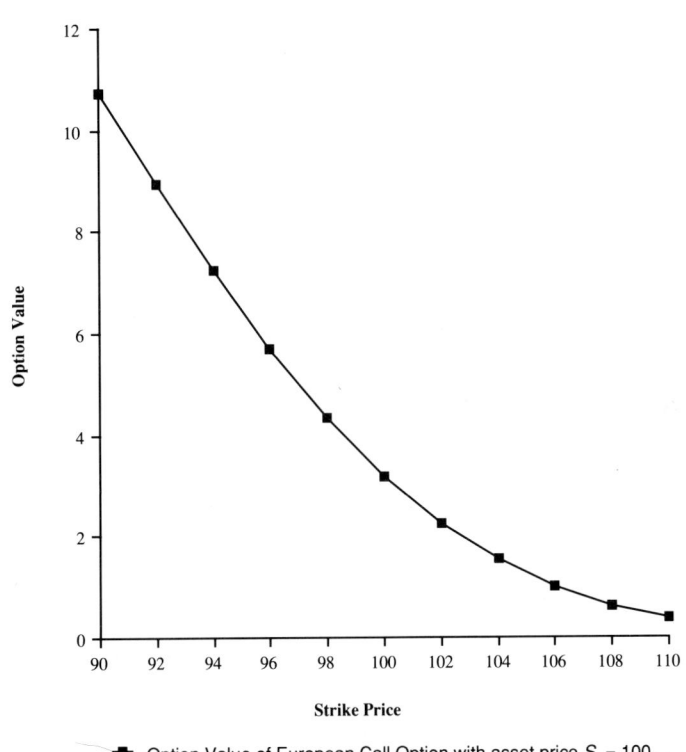

Option Value

Strike Price

Option Value of European Call Option with asset price S = 100, 1 month to expiration, interest rate r = 8%, volatility = .25, and no dividend payout.

If S_T is between X_2 and X_3, both positions are in-the-money, but it is not difficult to show that Portfolio 2's payoff is greater. Subtracting the payoff on Portfolio 1 from that on 2 gives

$$w(S_T - X_1) - (S_T - X_2) = (w - 1)(S_T - X_1) + (X_2 - X_1)$$

$$= \frac{X_1 - X_2}{X_3 - X_1} (S_T - X_1) + (X_2 - X_1)$$

$$= (X_2 - X_1)(1 - \frac{S_T - X_1}{X_3 - X_1})$$

FIGURE 2–4
Put value as a function of strike price

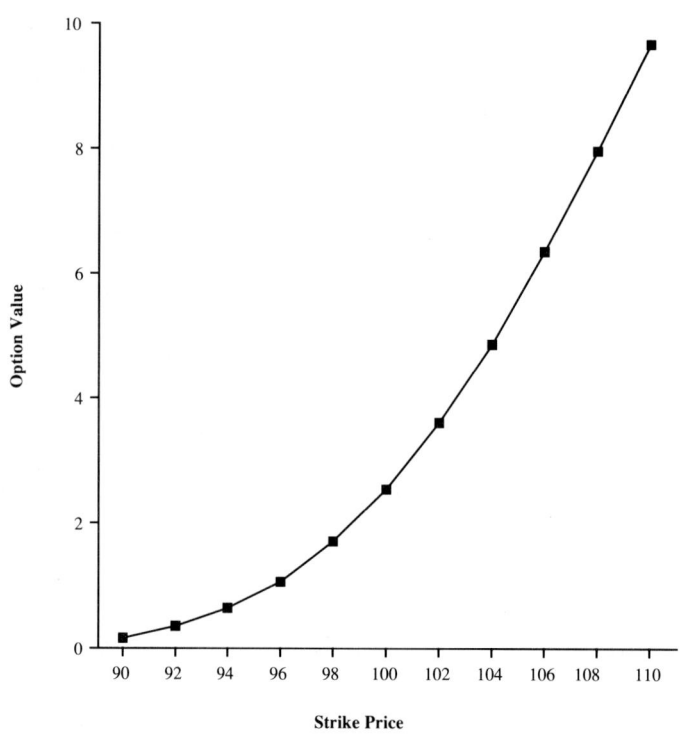

Option Value of European Put Option with asset price $S = 100$,
1 month to expiration, interest rate $r = 8\%$, volatility $= .25$, and
no dividend payout.

In this expression, the first term is clearly positive and so is the second, since S_T is less than X_3. This shows that Portfolio 2 is worth more than Portfolio 1 in this price range.

Finally, if all three options are in-the-money the two portfolios have equal value, because $w X_1 + (1 - w) X_3 = X_2$.

This shows that the payoff on Portfolio 2 is, in fact, always at least as great as on Portfolio 1 and in some cases greater. Since Portfolio 2 dominates 1, its initial cost must be higher in equilibrium, which proves the convexity relation, equation (2.10). A similar derivation proves convexity for puts.

End of Proof

TABLE 2-4

	Initial Cost	$S_T \le X_1$	$X_1 \le S_T < X_2$	$X_2 \le S_T < X_3$	$X_3 < S_T$
Portfolio 1					
Buy Call with X_2 Strike Price	C_2	0	0	$S_T - X_2$	$S_T - X_2$
Portfolio 2					
Buy w Calls with X_1 Strike Price	wC_1	0	$w(S_T - X_1)$	$w(S_T - X_1)$	$w(S_T - X_1)$
Buy $(1-w)$ Calls with X_3 Strike Price	$(1-w)C_3$	0	0	0	$(1-w)(S_T - X_3)$

2.6   AN OPTION ON A PORTFOLIO IS NEVER WORTH MORE THAN A PORTFOLIO OF OPTIONS

Another option property, related to convexity, is particularly important for options on indexes. It is that an option on the value of a portfolio of assets is never worth more than a portfolio of (comparable) individual options on those assets. It is nearly always worth less.

A tangible example of this would be options on the Standard and Poor's 100 index, the most actively traded stock index option contract. The option portfolio property says that a portfolio of at-the-money call options on the 100 stocks contained in the index (with each option represented in the portfolio with the same weight that its underlying stock has in the S&P 100 index) would be worth more than an at-the-money call on the index portfolio itself.

The following is a more formal statement of what we are calling the option portfolio property.

Option Portfolio Property: Suppose N assets with prices $S_1, S_2, \ldots, S_N$ are combined into a portfolio with weights $w_1, w_2, \ldots, w_N$. The value of the portfolio will be denoted as I, standing for "Index."

$$I = w_1 S_1 + w_2 S_2 + \ldots + w_N S_N$$

Each asset has a call option with strike price X_n whose value is C_n, and there is a call option on the portfolio with strike price X_I, where

$$X_I = w_1 X_1 + w_2 X_2 + \ldots + w_N X_N .$$

The strike price of the call on the index is a weighted average of the strikes on the individual calls. (For example, if $S_n = X_n$ for every stock, then $I = X_I$. That is, if all of the individual calls are exactly at-the-money, the call on the index is at-the-money also.)

Then,

$$C_I \le w_1 C_1 + w_2 C_2 + \ldots + w_N C_N \qquad (2.11)$$

The call on the portfolio with the weighted average strike price is worth no more than the weighted average of the individual call prices.

The same property holds for put options.

Proof: We will show how this can be proved for a portfolio of two assets. Extending the proof to more than two assets is straightforward, as is proving the same property holds for puts.

There are two assets with prices S_1 and S_2, and call options on these assets with strike prices of X_1 and X_2, valued at C_1 and C_2. The index portfolio $I = w_1 S_1 + w_2 S_2$ and the strike price on the index call option C_I is X_I.

As usual, we set up two portfolios and show that one dominates the other. Portfolio 1 is the portfolio of individual calls with weights w_1 and w_2 and Portfolio 2 is the call on the index. The two portfolio values are $w_1 C_1 + w_2 C_2$ and C_I, respectively.

It is somewhat cumbersome to set up a payoff table showing all possible outcomes as of expiration day, so we will simply describe the three cases of interest.

First, if at expiration $S_1 < X_1$ and $S_2 < X_2$, both individual options are out-of-the-money and Portfolio 1 is worth 0. Since

$$S_1 < X_1$$

and

$$S_2 < X_2,$$

then
$$w_1 S_1 + w_2 S_2 < w_1 X_1 + w_2 X_2$$

so
$$I < X_I$$

and the index call is also out-of-the-money. The two portfolios therefore have equal value if all of the individual options are out-of-the-money at expiration.

If both individual options are in-the-money at expiration, Portfolio 1 will be worth

$$
\begin{aligned}
\text{Portfolio 1 Payoff} &= w_1(S_1 - X_1) + w_2(S_2 - X_2)\\
&= (w_1 S_1 + w_2 S_2) - (w_1 X_1 + w_2 X_2)\\
&= I - X_I\\
&= \text{Portfolio 2 Payoff}
\end{aligned}
$$

and again the portfolio values are equal.

The third case is where one individual option is in-the-money and the other is out-of-the-money. Suppose C_1 is in-the-money. We have

$$S_1 > X_1$$

and
$$S_2 < X_2.$$

Portfolio 1's value is $w_1(S_1 - X_1)$. Portfolio 2 is worth $\text{Max}(I - X_I, 0)$. If the index option is out-of-the-money, it is clearly worth less than Portfolio 1, while if it is in-the-money, we have

$$
\begin{aligned}
\text{Portfolio 2 Payoff} &= I - X_I\\
&= w_1 S_1 + w_2 S_2 - w_1 X_1 - w_2 X_2\\
&= w_1(S_1 - X_1) + w_2(S_2 - X_2)\\
&< w_1(S_1 - X_1).
\end{aligned}
$$

The inequality in the last line comes from the fact that $S_2 < X_2$. Since the final expression is the payoff on Portfolio 1, it shows that for this case, Portfolio 2's payoff is lower than that on Portfolio 1.

This result would also hold if option 2 were in-the-money and option 1 out-of-the-money. Whenever at least one of the individual options is in-the-money and one is out-of-the-money, the portfolio of individual options has a greater payoff than the option on the portfolio of assets.

This proves that in equilibrium, the portfolio of individual options is never worth less than the comparable option on the asset portfolio, and the two can only be equal if it is certain that at expiration either all of the individual options will be in-the-money or all will be out-of-the-money. *End of Proof*

2.7 BASIC OPTION STRATEGIES

Options permit a great deal of flexibility in tailoring strategies to match an investor's price expectations and risk preferences. Many different payoff patterns can be produced from a basic set of building blocks that consists of an underlying asset, calls and puts, and borrowing or lending. Strategies can be bullish, bearish or neutral; they can be aggressive, defensive or virtually riskless; they can be designed to perform well in volatile markets or in calm markets; and there are many other possibilities.

In the following sections we will describe the most common option strategies and illustrate how they work using graphs of their payoffs. We will consider three different classes of strategies: those involving just one of the basic securities, those involving a combination of one option and the underlying asset, and those involving two or more options. The list is not meant to be exhaustive, but will give a good representation of the various ways options can be used.

The option payoff diagrams are based on positions constructed with the options shown in Table 2–1. We show the net profit or loss as a function of the price of the underlying asset at two points in time: today and at option expiration in 1 month. The former is computed using the Black-Scholes model to calculate option values for different current stock prices.

For each strategy, we show the initial cost per share to set it up, the maximum profit and loss possibilities, the breakeven price, the return if the stock price at expiration is the same as today, the market outlook for which the strategy is appropriate, and the degree of risk exposure. These results are expressed in symbols for the general case and also worked out for a specific example of the strategy based on the option prices in Table 2–1. In all cases, the profit analysis is done on a per share basis, while the payoff diagrams show results for trades with contracts of 100 shares.

One important factor we do not include in the return calculations is dividends. In evaluating any strategy that involves a long position in the underlying asset, all dividends and cash payouts expected before option expiration must be added to the return. The return on a trade involving a short position in the asset must be reduced by the value of any dividend payout, since the short seller will have to pay these.

Transactions Costs, Taxes, and Margins

The payoffs as shown do not include several important cost elements that have to be taken into account in actual options trading. One is commissions and "market impact" costs. In considering the payoff to an actual trading strategy, it is necessary to deduct the transactions costs that will be incurred getting into the position at the beginning and unwinding it at the end. These involve commissions on all of the securities that will be traded, plus market impact costs due to the fact that securities normally have to be purchased at the market's ask price and sold at the bid price, and a large transaction may also cause those prices to move unfavorably.

Commission levels are a function of the size of the transaction and can vary substantially among brokerage firms. Commissions for large trades are normally charged at a lower rate per contract and are negotiable. Market impact, on the other hand, tends to increase with the size of the trade. The quoted market bid and ask prices are only good for a limited number of contracts, and larger trades typically require a price concession. For example, the market quote for a liquid equity option might be given as 200 contracts offered at 2 with another 1000 available at 2 1/8.

Moreover, the effects of both commissions and market impact will depend on exactly how a position is set up. For example, writing a covered call against stock that is already owned will not involve a stock commission or market impact, so the only transactions costs will be those to trade the call. If the call expires worthless at maturity and the stock is not sold, there will also be no transactions costs to "unwinding" the trade. On the other hand, if the covered call is initiated with a purchase of stock at the outset and a sale at the end, costs will be significantly greater.

Taxes are another element that must be considered in evaluating an option strategy. Tax treatment for options is complex and also subject to frequent change. We will not cover taxation issues at all in this book, even though they are very important in practice, because of the enormous detail that would be required and the fact that tax information becomes obsolete too quickly. Before trading options the investor should consult with an expert to determine the tax treatment that will apply to the particular instrument and trading strategy he is considering.

One general observation, however, is that in the past a number of option strategies were popular solely because they reduced or postponed taxes by exploiting certain features of the U.S. tax code. Over the years, Congress and the Internal Revenue Service have largely eliminated these "loopholes." At this time, there remain few, if any, ways to avoid U.S. taxes easily by using options. A general principle now is that if a trade does not make sense on a before tax basis, it will not make sense after taxes either. In other countries, however, there remain option strategies that are made particularly attractive by their tax treatment.

Yet another important consideration in evaluating an option strategy is margin treatment. Options that are purchased must be paid for in full— there is no buying on margin permitted. Positions in which options are written may require a margin deposit that can be substantial, because of the need to guarantee that the writer can cover the future obligation if the option is exercised against her.

Margins are complex, to the point that it may be difficult to determine exactly how an involved position needs to be margined. Margin systems also change with some frequency, and different systems are in use in different markets. Like tax questions, we will not give a complete treatment of margin requirements in this book even though they can be quite important in practice.

Payoffs on Basic Securities

Riskless Lending: The simplest position of all is to invest in short term money market instruments. The interest that could be earned represents the opportunity cost of having funds tied up in any other strategy.

Initial Cost:	100
Profit:	$100 \times (e^{r \times T/365} - 1) = \$0.66$
Market Outlook:	Neutral
Risk Posture:	Riskless

Our examples assume a risk free interest rate of 8 percent. To be consistent with the way interest at an overnight rate of 8 percent cumulates, and also with the way the interest rate enters an option pricing model such as Black-Scholes, one should take account of daily compounding.

The interest earned on $100 over 30 days at 8 percent would be

$$100 \times ((1 + .08 / 365)^{30} - 1) = 0.65963$$

In the options literature, this is typically approximated using continuous compounding as

$$100 \times (e^{.08 \times 30/365} - 1) = 0.65970$$

where e represents the base of natural logarithms, approximately 2.71828.

Figure 2–5 shows the payoff diagram for a 1 month investment of $10,000 in the money market. The interest earned is obviously unaffected by the price of the stock at that time.

FIGURE 2–5
Riskless lending

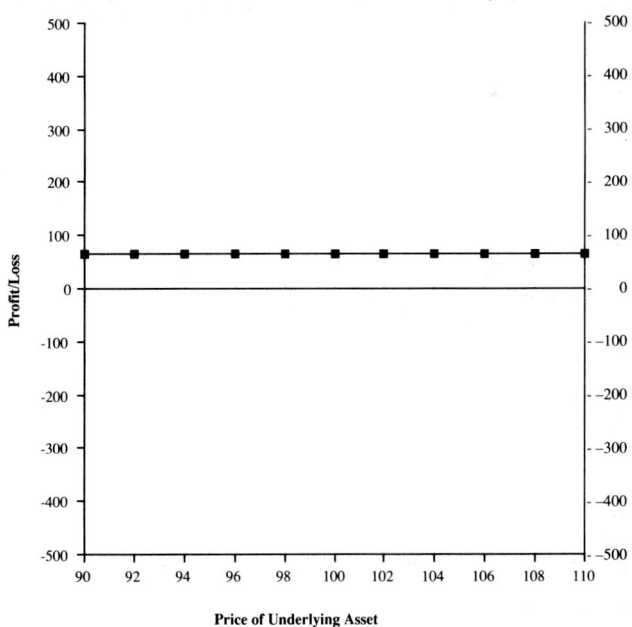

Long Stock: Figure 2–6 shows the profit on a long position in 100 shares of the stock, purchased today at a price of 100. Not surprisingly, the payoff increases dollar for dollar with the stock price and crosses the 0 line at a price of 100.

Initial Cost:	$S = 100$
Maximum Profit:	Unlimited if price rises
Maximum Loss:	$-S = -100$ if price falls to 0
Breakeven Price:	$S = 100$
Standstill Return:	0
Market Outlook:	Bullish
Risk Posture:	Aggressive

We have assumed there are no dividends during the month. If there were, the payoff line would be higher at each stock price by the amount of the dividend. Similarly, taking account of commissions and the market impact would lower the line by the amount of the transactions costs.

Buying the underlying asset is obviously a bullish strategy, since the return is higher when the stock price goes up. It is also an aggressive strategy, in the sense that it is exposed to substantial risk of loss. There is no limit to the profit that can be made if the price of the underlying asset goes in the hoped-for direction, but if it goes down, up to $100 per share can be lost. There is no profit or loss if the price simply stays the same.

Buying the stock outright is therefore an appropriate strategy for an investor who is confident that it will go up, and who is willing to take on significant risk of loss if he is wrong in order to pursue the maximum potential profit. The only more aggressive strategy is to take a leveraged long position, either by buying the stock on margin, or by using the money that would be invested in the stock to buy call options on a larger number of shares. Under current margin requirements, options make it easy to achieve a much more levered position than is possible by buying the stock alone.

Selling Short the Underlying Asset: The payoff for a short sale of the underlying asset shown in Figure 2–7 looks like the mirror image of that for a purchase. The trade breaks even at the initial price of 100, makes money below that, and loses dollar for dollar as the stock price goes up.

FIGURE 2–6
Long stock

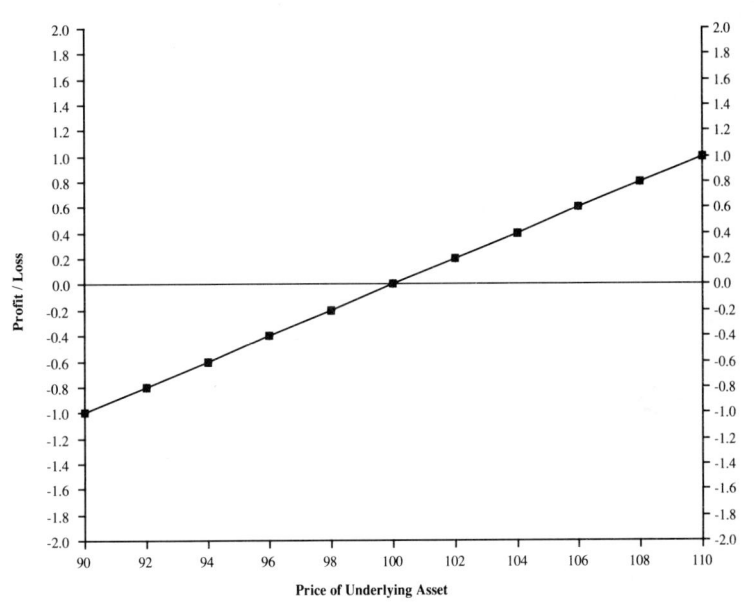

	Initial Cost:	Credit of $S = 100$
	Maximum Profit:	$S = 100$, if price falls to 0 (plus interest received on proceeds of short sale, if any)
	Maximum Loss:	Unlimited if price rises
	Breakeven Price:	$S = 100$ (plus interest received)
	Standstill Return:	0 (plus interest received)
	Market Outlook:	Bearish
	Risk Posture:	Aggressive

If there were dividends, the short seller would have to pay them to the lender of the shares that were sold. The profit line would be reduced by the amount of the dividends at every stock price.

FIGURE 2–7
Short stock

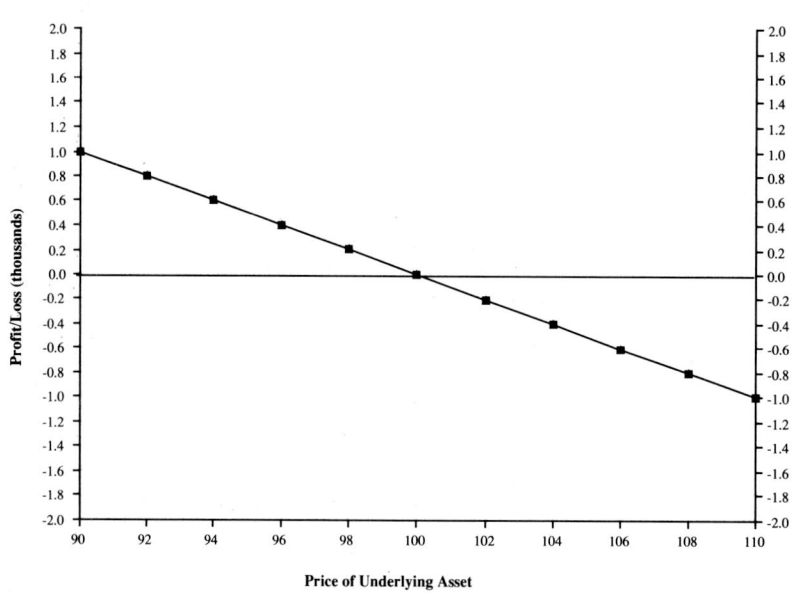

Price of Underlying Asset

When a stock is sold short, there are proceeds from the short sale. These are normally held in escrow by the short seller's brokerage firm as collateral. Investors are also obliged to post margin, currently equal to 50 percent of the value of the shares sold short. This often creates a significant asymmetry between buying an asset and selling it short. (Symmetric treatment would be for the investor to invest funds when he buys stock and to obtain funds that can be invested elsewhere when he sells short.) In practice, large traders can generally negotiate to have interest paid on the proceeds of a short sale at only a little below market rates (e.g., 85 percent of the broker loan rate). This goes a long way toward restoring symmetrical treatment. If interest is earned, it should be added to the profit line at every stock price.

Selling short is, of course, a bearish strategy. It only makes money if the price of the underlying asset goes down (or more precisely, if it does not rise by more than the interest received on the short sale proceeds). Like buying the asset, selling short is an aggressive strategy: exposed to risk of unlimited loss if the price rises, but profiting dollar for dollar if it should drop.

Buying a Call Option: Figure 2–8 shows the payoff pattern for the purchase of a 1 month call with a strike price of 100. Two profit lines are shown. One gives the difference between the call value at expiration (i.e., the intrinsic value) and the initial premium as a function of the stock price. The other shows how the value of the one month call would change if the stock price were to move to a new level immediately.

Initial Cost:	$C = 3\ 3/16$
Maximum Profit:	Unlimited if price rises
Maximum Loss:	$C = 3\ 3/16$, if the price at expiration is below X
Breakeven Price:	$X + C = 103\ 3/16$
Standstill Return:	Loss of the option's time value, $-(C - \text{Max}(0\ ,\ S - X)) = -3\ 3/16$
Market Outlook:	Bullish
Risk Posture:	Defensive

The figure shows the asymmetric payoff to a long call position. No matter how far the stock may fall below the strike price, the maximum loss is the initial cost C of the option, or 3 3/16 per share in this case. Potential profit is unlimited, if the stock goes up. But the price must rise above the strike price plus the initial option premium before the position breaks even. If the stock price simply stands still, the option loses its time value, which for this at-the-money option is the entire investment.

The strategy is bullish but defensive. It makes money if the price of the underlying asset rises, but the possible loss is limited if the price does not go up.

Before expiration, the value of the position changes smoothly as the stock price moves. It increases with the stock price at a rate that varies from almost zero, when the call is far out-of-the-money, to almost 1 for 1, when it is deep-in-the-money. The change in the option value caused by a 1 point increase in the stock price is known as the option's delta. We will discuss delta in more detail in the next chapter.

FIGURE 2–8
Long call

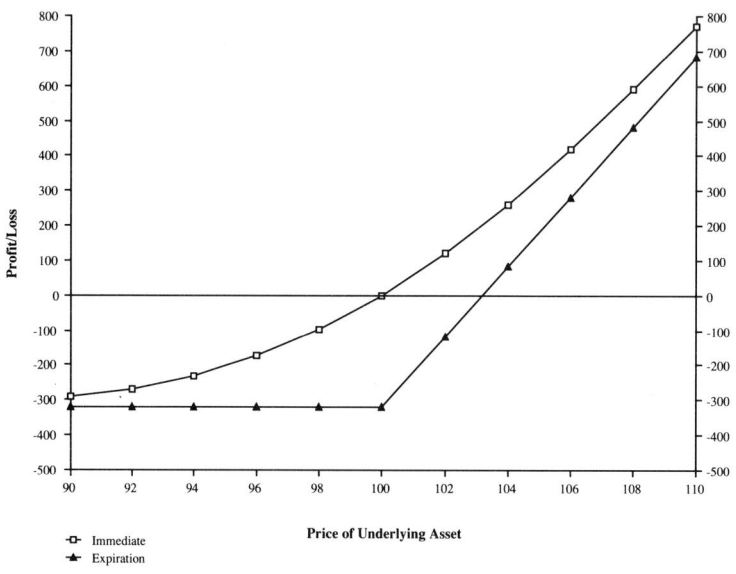

-□- Immediate
-▲- Expiration

Price of Underlying Asset

The position is also highly levered relative to an investment in the underlying asset itself. By paying the option premium of 3 3/16 the option buyer controls $100 worth of the stock. While buying call options is more defensive per share than buying the underlying stock, by investing a full $100 in calls one could use the leverage potential of the options to create a much more aggressive, and risky, position than would be possible with the stock alone.

Dividend payouts on the underlying asset tend to be unfavorable for call options. Exchange-traded options are not "payout protected," meaning the option holder does not receive the dividend and there is no adjustment to the strike price to offset the fact that the stock price will normally drop by approximately the amount of the dividend on ex-dividend day.

Buying a Put Option: The next figure shows the payoff pattern for the purchase of a 1 month 100 strike put.

FIGURE 2–9
Long put

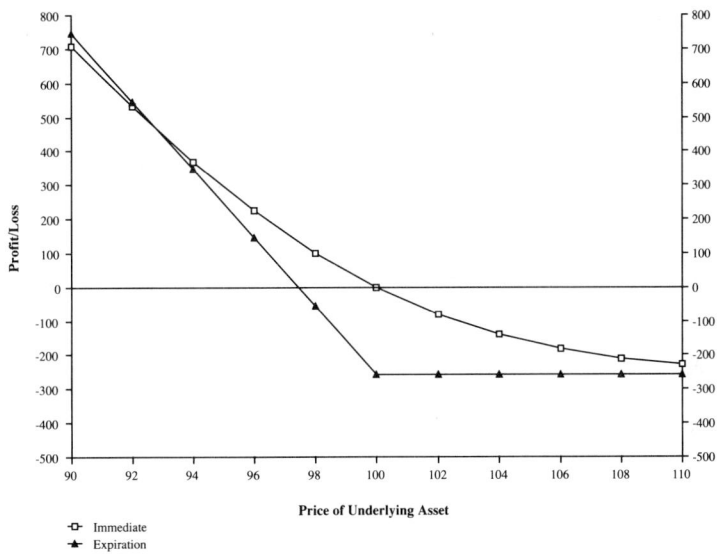

Price of Underlying Asset

-□- Immediate
-▲- Expiration

Initial Cost:	$P = 2\ 9/16$
Maximum Profit:	$X - P = 97\ 7/16$, if the underlying asset falls to 0
Maximum Loss:	$-P = -2\ 9/16$, if the price at expiration is above X
Breakeven Price:	$X - P = 97\ 7/16$
Standstill Return:	Loss of the option's time value, $-(P - \text{Max}(0\ ,\ X - S)) = -2\ 9/16$
Market Outlook:	Bearish
Risk Posture:	Defensive

Buying put options alone (as opposed to including a long put position as one component of an overall portfolio) is a bearish strategy. Similar to a short sale, it is a position that makes money only if the underlying stock goes down, and by an amount greater than the initial option time value. The time value in this case is the total premium of 2 9/16; if the underlying asset's price simply stands still until option expiration, the entire investment is lost.

However, buying puts is more defensive than selling the underlying asset short. No matter how wrong the investor might be, the most she can lose is the initial premium, but if there is a very large drop in price the potential profit on the put in dollars is only a few points less than that on the short sale, which is exposed to much greater possible loss. As a percent of the amount of capital at risk the potential profit on puts is much greater but, of course, the potential loss is 100 percent of the initial investment.

Because of the unfavorable treatment of margin on short sales, for most investors, buying puts is a much better way to assume an effective short position. With the advent of exchange-traded put options it became much easier for investors who expect falling stock prices to take positions that will be profitable. This is a good example of the way that introducing options extends the range of portfolio possibilities in the market.

Writing a Call Option: Figure 2–10 shows the payoff pattern for writing a 1 month 100 strike call "uncovered" or "naked," that is, without owning the underlying asset.

Initial Cost:	Credit of C = 3 3/16
Maximum Profit:	C = 3 3/16, if the price at expiration is below X
Maximum Loss:	Unlimited if the underlying asset price rises
Breakeven Price:	$X + C$ = 103 3/16
Standstill Return:	The option's initial time value, $(C - \text{Max}(0, S - X))$ = 3 3/16
Market Outlook:	Bearish to Neutral
Risk Posture:	Aggressive

Writing a naked call option entails the obligation to deliver the underlying asset to the option buyer, for the strike price of X = 100. If the investor owns the stock and can deliver it when the call is exercised, the position is known as a "covered" call. If she does not own the underlying

FIGURE 2–10
Short call

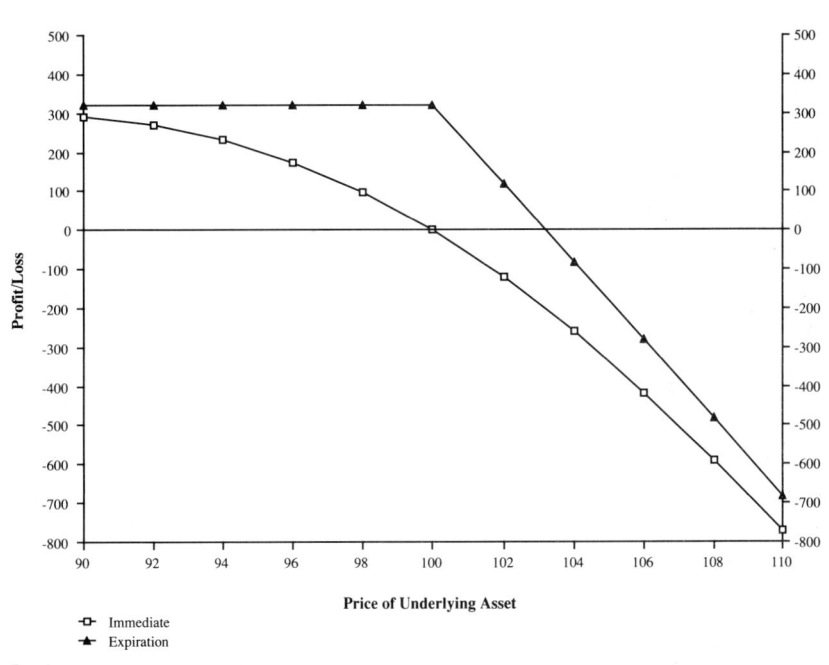

Price of Underlying Asset

-□- Immediate
-▲- Expiration

asset, it is a naked call. The potential loss on writing a naked call is un-limited, since the stock will have to be purchased at whatever the market price may be, and delivered to the option holder for the strike price.

Since the most that can be made from the trade is the initial call premium, it is an aggressive strategy. The compensation for the unfavor-able shape of the payoff pattern is the fact that it is a profitable trade if the asset price simply stands still. The position only loses if the asset price appreciates by more than the call's initial time premium.

Margin treatment for naked writing is quite unfavorable. Moreover, many institutional investors are prohibited from taking naked options positions, either by explicit regulation or because it involves risks that are felt to be inconsistent with their investment objectives.

Writing a Put Option: Figure 2–11 shows the payoff to writing a naked 1 month 100 strike put option.

FIGURE 2–11
Short put

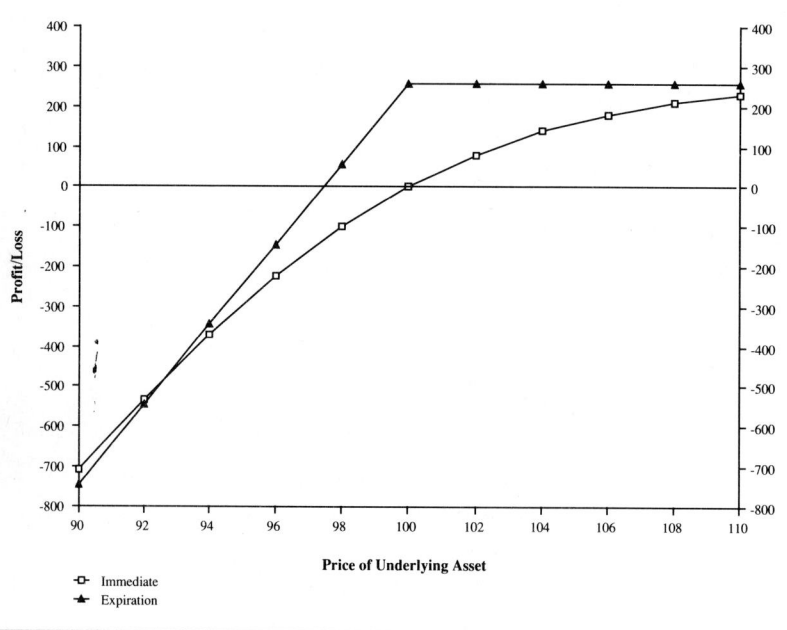

Initial Cost:	Credit of $P = 2\ 9/16$
Maximum Profit:	$P = 2\ 9/16$, if the price at expiration is above X
Maximum Loss:	$-(X - P) = -97\ 7/16$, if the underlying asset falls to 0
Breakeven Price:	$X - P = 97\ 7/16$
Standstill Return:	The option's initial time value, $(P - \text{Max}(0, X - P)) = 2\ 9/16$
Market Outlook:	Bullish to Neutral
Risk Posture:	Aggressive

Writing uncovered puts is widely regarded as being very risky. The position is exposed to the possibility of large losses and the potential profit is limited. The position is bullish, which is favorable since stocks and most other risky investments have a tendency to rise over the long run. However, it typically is observed that in a fixed time period, prices in the stock market, and other financial markets as well, can fall faster than they rise. This means that while there is a bias in the market toward profitability for the strategy of writing naked puts, the risk of large and very rapid losses is substantial.

2.8 COVERED STRATEGIES

The above strategies involved only a simple long or short position in one of the basic securities. However, many of the most common option strategies are designed to manage overall risk exposure by using the option in combination with the underlying asset. This section will describe four such "covered" option strategies.

The Protective Put: Buying a put option in combination with a long position in the underlying asset provides protection against major losses, for a fixed cost. The example examines the protective put strategy using the 1 month 100 strike contract.

Initial Cost:	$S + P = 102\ 9/16$
Maximum Profit:	Unlimited, if the stock price rises
Maximum Loss:	$X - (S + P) = -2\ 9/16$, if the underlying asset falls below X
Breakeven Price:	$S + P = 102\ 9/16$
Standstill Return:	Loss of the option's initial time value, $-(P - \mathrm{Max}(0, X - S)) = -2\ 9/16$
Market Outlook:	Bullish
Risk Posture:	Defensive

The protective put is one of the most common uses of options in a defensive investment strategy. In combination with an investment in the underlying asset, a put option acts very much like an insurance policy. For a fixed price, the initial option premium, the investor obtains the right to sell her holding in the risky asset for the option's exercise price at the expiration date. This guarantees a floor on the total value of her portfolio, no matter how far the underlying asset's price may fall in the market.

If the stock price falls, the maximum potential loss is equal to the initial put premium P plus the amount the stock has to fall before the put goes in the money $(S - X)$. After that point, all further price drops are covered (assuming puts have been bought against all of the underlying shares held, one-for-one.) If the puts are in-the-money when they are purchased, the most that can be lost is their time premium.

On the other hand, if the asset's price rises and the "insurance" proves to have been unnecessary, only the initial cost of the put is given up. In a large rally, the investor still makes most of the possible profit from price appreciation. It is this property of limiting risk on the downside while not limiting the possible profit on the upside that makes the protective put strategy so attractive to a defensive investor.

Whether the put ends up in- or out-of-the-money, however, the time value dissipates over its lifetime. This means that if the stock price stands still, there is always a loss. In order to break even, the stock price must rise by enough to cover the cost of the put. A protective put position is therefore only appropriate for an investor whose market outlook is bullish. But it is defensive, because it limits possible losses in exchange for giving up profit potential.

In looking at the payoff diagram for the protective put in Figure 2–12, it is apparent that the position is essentially the same as a long call option. This reflects put-call parity once again. Another rearrangement of that relationship shows that buying a put and buying the underlying stock is the same as buying a call and lending.

The insurance analogy is useful in thinking about the tradeoff between the strike price for the put and the degree of protection achieved. One can think of the put premium as the *price* of the insurance policy, that will be lost if the insurance turns out not to have been needed. The difference between the current asset price and the exercise price is like the *deductible* on the policy. It measures how far the asset's value has to fall before the insurance coverage begins.

Like other kinds of insurance, there is a tradeoff between the cost of insurance through puts and the degree of protectiveness of the policy. For example, buying put protection with a 1 month 100 strike put costs 2 9/16, and there is no deductible; losses are fully covered if the stock price falls below the initial price of 100.

In Table 2–1 we see that a less expensive policy with a 5 point deductible can be obtained by buying 95 strike puts for 13/16. This is a more bullish strategy. Less profit is given up if the market stays where it is or goes

FIGURE 2–12
Protective put

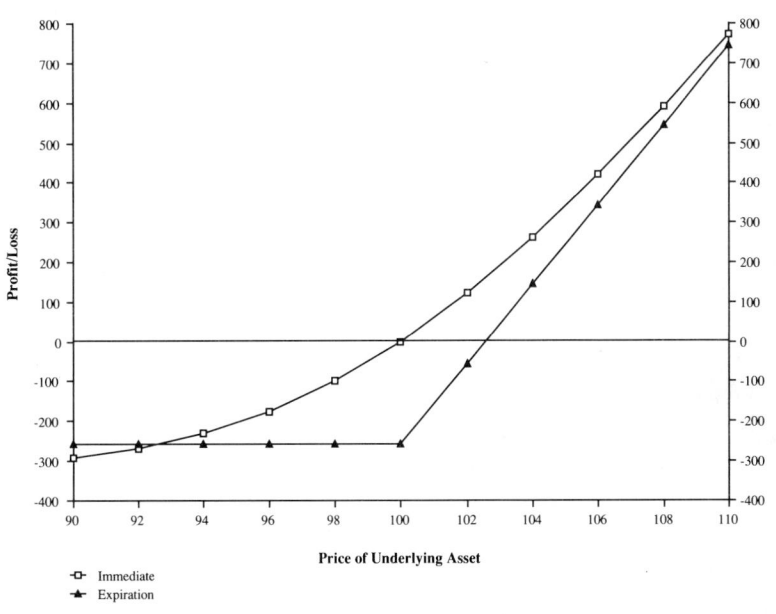

Price of Underlying Asset

-□- Immediate
-▲- Expiration

up, but the investor must bear the first 5 points of loss before insurance coverage begins. He is still protected against catastrophic loss, however.

Alternatively, he could buy very complete coverage with 105 strike puts at 5 5/8. This very protected position is not much different from selling the stock outright for 99 3/8, since that is what the position will be worth at any stock price below 105. Still, by giving up 5/8 of a point by buying deep-in-the-money puts instead of simply selling his stock today for 100, the investor is able to profit dollar for dollar if a sharp rise should take the price above 105. But if this were felt to be a high probability relative to the risk of a price drop, the investor would be better off buying puts with a lower exercise price and getting more participation on the upside.

An important issue that is deeper than it may appear at first glance is the question of how much a protective put strategy will cost over the long run. The simple answer, that the cost to insure for N months ought to be just N times the price of a 1 month put is clearly incorrect, since we can see that a three month 100 strike put costs only about 1 1/2 times as much as a 1 month put. Extending the maturity of in-the-money puts is even cheaper.

The problem is that the cost of a long run option strategy is "path dependent." This means that the total cost will depend on exactly what path the price of the underlying asset follows over the strategy's investment horizon. (Another problem is that in practice investors typically revise their strategies in response to what the price of the underlying asset does.)

For example, suppose that S rises to 105 in one month. At that price, rolling over the put protection for the next month by buying a new 1 month 100 strike put would now cost only about 13/16 since it would be 5 points out-of-the-money. At even higher stock prices the cost would become negligible. However, if S rises to 110, say, the protectiveness of a 100 strike put would be very limited. Many investors would raise their floor levels and buy a 105 or 110 strike option, rather than simply rolling over the contract at the same strike price. These would cost more, but in buying them they would lock in a portion of the gains that had been earned in the first month.

Although it does not deal correctly with the path dependency problem, a better estimate of what a long run fixed strike price put strategy would cost is the time value on a put whose maturity matches the strategy's time horizon. This thought is based on the general principle that in equilibrium all strategies that do the same thing should cost the same amount. This time value can be determined theoretically even if puts of that maturity do not exist.

The Covered Call: Buy the underlying asset and write a 1 month 100 strike call option against it.

Initial Cost:	$S - C = 96\ 13/16$
Maximum Profit:	$X - (S - C) = 3\ 3/16$, if the call finishes in-the-money
Maximum Loss:	$-(S - C) = -96\ 13/16$, if the asset price falls to 0
Breakeven Price:	$S - C = 96\ 13/16$
Standstill Return:	Gain of the option's initial time value, $(C - \text{Max}(0, S - X)) = 3\ 3/16$
Market Outlook:	Neutral to Mildly Bullish
Risk Posture:	Defensive

Writing covered calls is probably the single most common option strategy used by institutional investors. The payoff pattern is shown in Figure 2–13.

The call writer receives the option premium at the outset in return for standing ready to sell the asset for the exercise price at a later date. Writing the call limits the maximum profit that can be earned on the position, since the stock will be called away if its price ends up above the strike price. The maximum return is therefore what is often called the "If Called" return, since this is the return that will be earned if the call is exercised.

The If Called return is the difference between the strike price X and the initial investment $(S - C)$. Dividends, if any, should also be added. The If Called return is often expressed as an annualized percentage rate of return on the investment $(S - C)$.

Writing the call increases total return as long as the stock price does not rise higher than the exercise price plus the initial call premium. The

FIGURE 2–13
Covered call

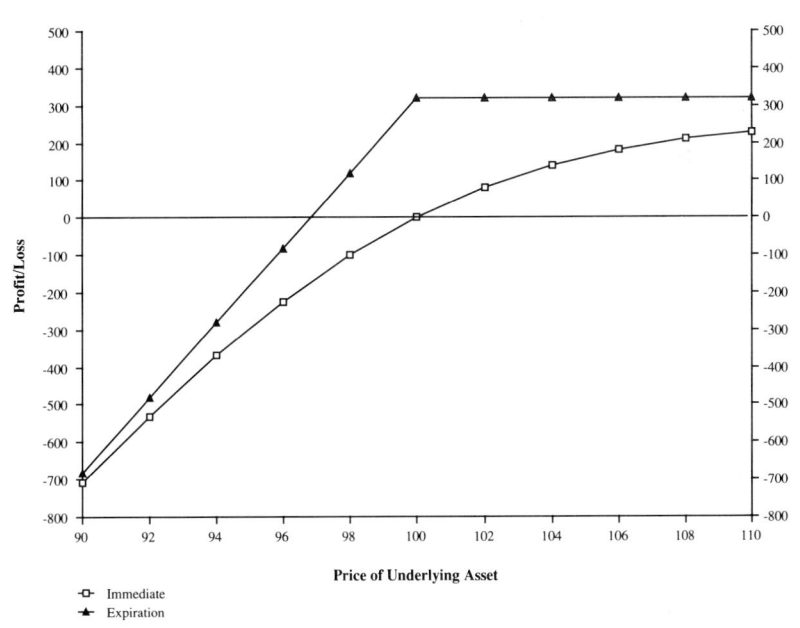

price $X + C$, 103 3/16 for this example, might be called the point of "Regret," because if the stock price goes higher than this, the return to a straight long stock position is greater than the return on the covered call, and the investor regrets writing the option.

The objective of writing the call is to generate extra income in a flat to down market, because the time value dissipates. The standstill return is positive, and equal to the option's initial time value. The call also provides a cushion if the stock price falls: the position breaks even when the stock has fallen by the amount of the premium received.

The position is neutral to mildly bullish because it makes money for any price above the breakeven price (which is below the current stock price), but if the stock price rises too far it passes the point of Regret and the investor would have been better off not selling the call. The position is exposed to the risk of substantial loss if the price of the underlying asset should drop sharply. Whether this payoff pattern makes the covered call position appear risky or not depends considerably on what it is being compared to.

In many cases, it is most natural to compare a covered call to a straight long position in the stock. Many covered call writers follow a strategy known as "overwriting," which is writing calls selectively against stocks they are already holding in investment portfolios. They view overwriting as an opportunity to earn an extra return on a security when they do not expect it to appreciate significantly in the immediate future. This expectation might arise either because they anticipate that the market as a whole is going to stagnate, or because they expect the particular asset to underperform the market.

Since the underlying asset is owned already, the investor is already exposed to the risk of loss if its price goes down. Writing a covered call that ultimately expires worthless just provides some extra return, so in this case it would seem that the covered call position reduces risk somewhat.

On the other hand, the position may be established as a "buy-write," in which the stock is purchased and the option sold at the same time. In this case, the appropriate comparison is not between the covered call position and the stock held alone. A buy-write is thought of as a single investment, and the risk of substantial loss if the stock price drops sharply would make it appear to be fairly risky.

This difference of perception between overwrites and buy-writes tends to be reflected in the strike prices that are chosen for the calls that are written. An investor doing an overwrite is generally looking for a little extra return on a security he expects to continue holding even though he does not anticipate that it will go up strongly in the short run. He will tend to write out-of-the-money calls, expecting that they will expire worthless.

Such an investor might think about the trade in the following way: Either the call will be exercised, in which case he is pleased to sell the stock at a price that is much better than he currently thinks likely, or else the call expires worthless and the trade just allows him to earn an extra return.

For other investors, having the security called away is regarded as a failure of the strategy, even though that event corresponds to its greatest possible return. (To prevent an unwanted exercise, the option, now in-the-money, should be bought back in the market prior to expiration.)

An investor doing a buy-write is more concerned about the immediate prospects for the stock and especially about the chance that it may go down. He will tend to favor calls that are already in-the-money that provide good downside protection (i.e., the breakeven price is well below the current stock price). In many cases, the primary objective of a buy-write is to earn a higher return, from the combination of option time value and stock dividends, than is available in the money market, while minimizing the risk of loss on the downside. It is expected that the call will be exercised—if it is not, it is because the stock has dropped and the buy-write position has earned a lower return than was hoped.

The "90/10" Strategy: The strategy consists of taking a fixed sum of capital and instead of investing it in an asset such as a portfolio of stocks, placing most of the funds in money market instruments and using the remainder to buy call options. The investment proportions should be set so that the interest earned is sufficient to preserve capital even if all of the options expire worthless, while the calls give market exposure if the price of the risky asset rises.

Initial Cost:	100, of which $100/(1+r) = 92.6$ in money market instruments and the rest in call options.
	NOTE: This is the cost of a 1 year 90/10 strategy.
Maximum Profit:	Unlimited, if the underlying asset price rises sharply

Maximum Loss:	0, if the purchased options expire out-of-the-money
Breakeven Price:	Any price below X
Standstill Return:	0
Market Outlook:	Bullish
Risk Posture:	Defensive

This strategy got its name in the early 1980s during a period of unusually high interest rates. At that time, it was possible to invest 90 percent of the capital of a fund in Treasury bills paying about 11 percent and guarantee that over an investment horizon of one year, the entire initial capital would remain intact. The remaining 10 percent of the funds were then available to be invested in call options. These were expected to provide significant extra income to the fund, if the stock market rose strongly.

The pattern of very limited risk on the downside plus participation in market advances on the upside is very attractive to many investors. The payoff to this strategy has the same shape as the protective put shown in Figure 2–12. As mentioned above, it is easily shown from put-call parity that buying a call and lending (a "90/10"-type strategy) amounts to the same thing as buying the underlying asset and buying a put (a protective put strategy).

Naturally, as interest rates have changed, the "90/10" portfolio proportions have had to be altered. The 90 component can be calculated easily as the present value of 100, discounted at the current money market interest rate. At 8 percent, it becomes a "92.6/7.4" strategy. Moreover, it is obviously not necessary that the standstill return be fixed at zero. As with a protective put, any floor portfolio value can be implemented (subject, of course to the limitation that no more than 100 percent of the funds can be invested in the money market, so that the floor return can not be above the riskless interest rate).

Notice that the payoffs described above refer to a 90/10 strategy that is kept in place for a year, meaning that the options must be rolled over as they expire. There is clearly an important tactical dimension to running such a strategy. For example, if the entire option component expires worthless in the first month, the strategy turns into a straight portfolio of money market instruments for the remainder of the horizon period.

Writing Cash Secured Puts: The investor writes naked 1 month 95 strike puts, but places enough cash in money market securities to cover payment of the exercise price if the puts are exercised against him.

Initial Cost:	$PV(X) - P = 94.37 - 13/16 = 93.56$
Maximum Profit:	$P + (X - PV(X)) = 13/16 + .63$ $= 1.44$, at any price above X
Maximum Loss:	$-(PV(X) - P) = -93.56$, if the asset price falls to 0
Breakeven Price:	$PV(X) - P = 93.56$
Standstill Return:	$P - \text{Max}(0, X - S) + (X - PV(X))$ $= 13/16 + .63 = 1.44$, the initial time value on the put plus the interest on the cash component
Market Outlook:	Mildly Bearish to Mildly Bullish
Risk Posture:	Defensive

While writing naked puts is often felt to be a very risky strategy, its effective risk can be substantially altered if the investor sets aside enough cash at the outset to cover paying out the strike price should the puts be exercised. The payoff pattern for the strategy then becomes the same as for a covered call. This can be seen by rearranging the put-call parity equation.

The strategy works as follows. The investor writes put options, normally out-of-the-money, and invests the present value of the exercise price at the risk free interest rate. At expiration, either the puts expire worthless and the premium received becomes extra income on a portfolio of money market securities, or else the puts are exercised and the investor ends up buying the underlying asset at a price well below its original market price. If the 1 month 95 strike puts in our example expire out-of-the-money, the position earns 1.44 on an initial investment of 93.56, or 1.54 percent over one month for an annualized return of 20.1 percent. On the other hand, if the asset price drops below 95 and the puts are exercised, the investor ends up buying it for an effective price of 93.56, which is about 6 1/2 percent cheaper than where it is selling today.

There are two sorts of risk in this position. One is that the asset price drops so far that even buying well below the current market price leads to a loss on the overall position. In that case, the investor would have been better off just investing in the money market without writing puts. The other "risk" is more a kind of opportunity loss: the asset price might rise sharply and the investor would have been better off simply to buy the asset at the current market price. Therefore, the strategy is most appropriate for an investor who expects a fairly stable market.

2.9 OPTION SPREADS

The strategies we have described so far involved just one call or put, or one option in combination with the underlying asset or money market instruments. These represent the most basic positions and the ones that are most frequently used by investors.

Combined positions involving more than one option allow more complex payoff structures. We will now discuss a few of the more common ones. Such positions include spreads, straddles, and others with more colorful names, like "strangles" and "butterflies." These are generally of greatest interest to options market makers and sophisticated investors.

Although these positions are complex, they are used by experienced option traders with enough frequency that market makers are generally quite willing to give a single price quote for the entire position. For example, a market maker might say "the June 95 / 105 call spread is 4 5/8 bid, offered at 5." When this is done, the prices at which the individual options in the position will be traded are somewhat arbitrary. They are set by the brokers involved so that they add up to the quoted price for the entire position and none of the individual options is recorded as trading at a price that is out of line with its current bid and offer on the trading floor. By convention, one "buys" a spread or other combined position if cash must be paid out initially; "selling" a spread brings cash in.

A spread involves buying an option and selling another of the same type (i.e., call or put) but with a different strike price or expiration date. In describing the positions we will use the letters L, H, and M to indicate "low," "high," and "middle" strike prices.

Bull Call Spread: Buy a call CL ($XL = 95$) and write another call CH with the same expiration date but a higher strike price ($XH = 105$).

$$\text{Initial Cost:} \qquad CL - CH = 6\ 7/16 - 1\ 1/4 = 5\ 3/16$$

Maximum Profit:	$(XH - XL) - (CL - CH) = 4\ 13/16$, for any price above XH
Maximum Loss:	$-(CL - CH) = -5\ 3/16$, if the asset price falls below XL
Breakeven Price:	$XL + CL - CH = 100\ 3/16$
Standstill Return:	$(CH - \text{Max}(0, S - XH)) - (CL - \text{Max}(0, S - XL)) = -3/16$, the time value on CH minus the time value on CL
Market Outlook:	Mildly Bullish
Risk Posture:	Defensive

Figure 2–14 shows the payoff pattern for a bullish call spread. Since the call that is bought has a lower strike price than the one that is sold, it will cost more $(CL > CH)$, and the position will always require a net investment of capital. It has both a limited potential for loss (equal to the initial investment, if both options finish out-of-the-money) and a limited possibility for profit. If both options end up in-the-money, the position will be worth the difference in their strike prices, so the maximum profit is $(XH - XL)$ less the initial investment $(CL - CH)$.

By expiration the time value of both options will go to zero. If the price of the underlying asset is the same then as today, the resulting standstill return can be either positive or negative, depending on which call had the higher initial time value. For the 95 – 105 spread, it is slightly negative, while it would be positive if the 100 strike call were sold in place of the 105.

The position is suitable for a mildly bullish market outlook. It makes money if the asset price rises, but if S goes up above XH, the investor would have been better off not writing the CH call.

A spread between options with differing strike prices is known as a "price" spread or a "vertical" spread. Option prices are normally reported in the newspaper in the same format as Table 2–1, with the rows corresponding to different exercise prices and columns corresponding to different expirations. A price spread is vertical because it is one between options in different rows of the same (vertical) column.

An alternative way to create a bull spread is to write a high strike price put PH and buy one with the same expiration and a lower strike price PL. For comparison, the payoff on a bull put spread is shown in Figure 2–15.

FIGURE 2–14
Bull spread (call)

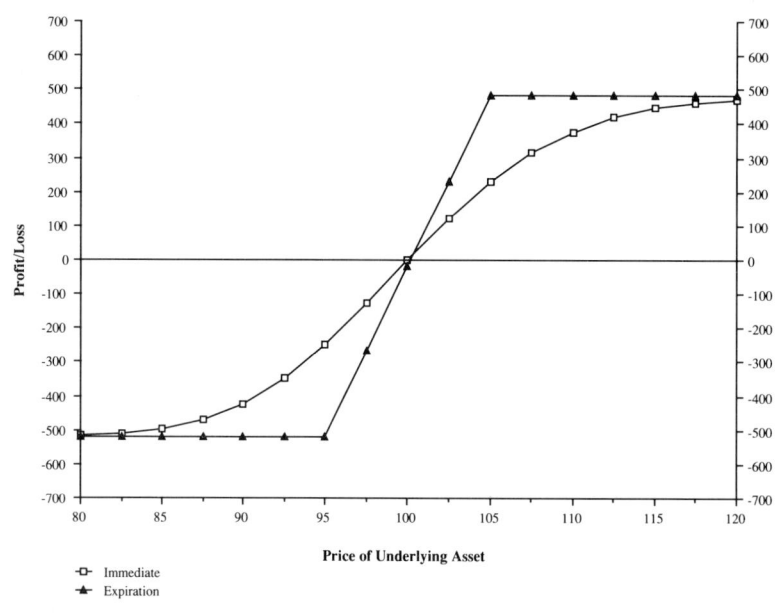

Price of Underlying Asset

-□- Immediate
-▲- Expiration

Naturally, since the values of the two positions at expiration are identical, in equilibrium, the two ways of creating a 95 / 105 bull spread should cost the same. If they did not, an investor should buy the cheap spread and write the expensive one (thereby creating a "Box spread"), and lock in an arbitrage profit.

Traders often think of a price spread as a way to buy an option cheaply, by writing another to offset a portion of its cost. Spread positions can also develop sequentially when an option position is traded actively. A trader may buy a call and find that the price of the underlying asset moves in the expected direction right away. With luck, he may then be able to write a call with a higher strike for the same price he paid for the first one. This turns the position into one in which he can make further profits, he can't lose money, and he will make some profit if the asset ends up at any price above the lower strike.

Bear Spreads: Spread positions that make money if the underlying asset price falls can be created easily from both calls and puts. The strategy

FIGURE 2–15
Bull spread (put)

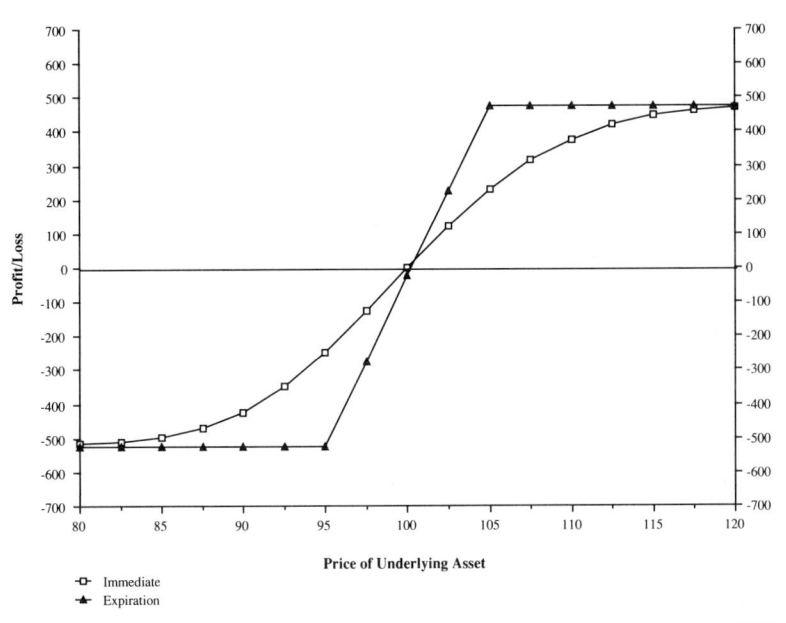

Price of Underlying Asset

-□- Immediate
-▲- Expiration

amounts to no more than selling a bull spread, i.e., writing the *CL* call and buying the *CH* call, or writing the *PL* put and buying the *PH* put. Figure 2–16 shows what the payoff pattern would look like.

Straddle: Buy a call and a put with the same strike price and expiration date. The payoff for a straddle using 1 month 100 strike options is shown in Figure 2–17.

Initial Cost:	$C + P = 5 \ 3/4$
Maximum Profit:	Unlimited, if the asset price rises sharply, and $X - (C + P) = 94 \ 1/4$, if the price falls to 0
Maximum Loss:	$-C - P = -5 \ 3/4$, if the asset price at expiration is exactly X and both options are worthless
Breakeven Price:	$X + C + P = 105 \ 3/4$, and $X - C - P = 94 \ 1/4$

FIGURE 2–16
Bear spread (call)

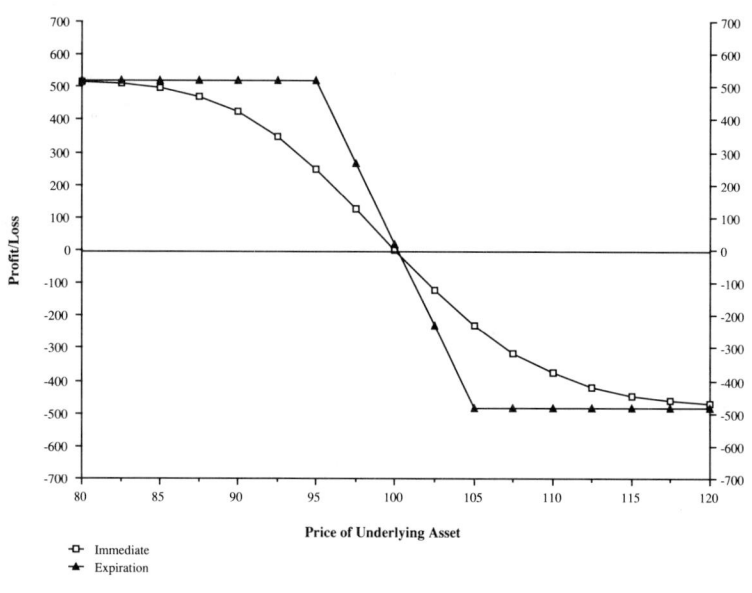

Price of Underlying Asset

-□- Immediate
-▲- Expiration

Standstill Return:	Max $(S - X, X - S) - (C + P)=$ −5 3/4
Market Outlook:	Neutral on price, high volatility
Risk Posture:	Speculative, but risk is limited

A straddle is a different type of option strategy from any we have looked at so far, because it is neither bullish nor bearish. The call makes money if the price of the underlying asset goes up strongly and the put makes money if it goes down strongly. Both options lose their time value by expiration date, so the standstill return is negative.

The position will lose money unless the stock price moves far enough from the strike price that one of the options is in-the-money by more than their combined initial cost. A straddle buyer is looking for a large price move in either direction. A straddle is therefore a strategy to profit from volatility in the price of the underlying asset.

This is a speculative position, but because it involves buying options, its risk is limited. One can not lose more than the sum of the two initial

FIGURE 2–17
Straddle

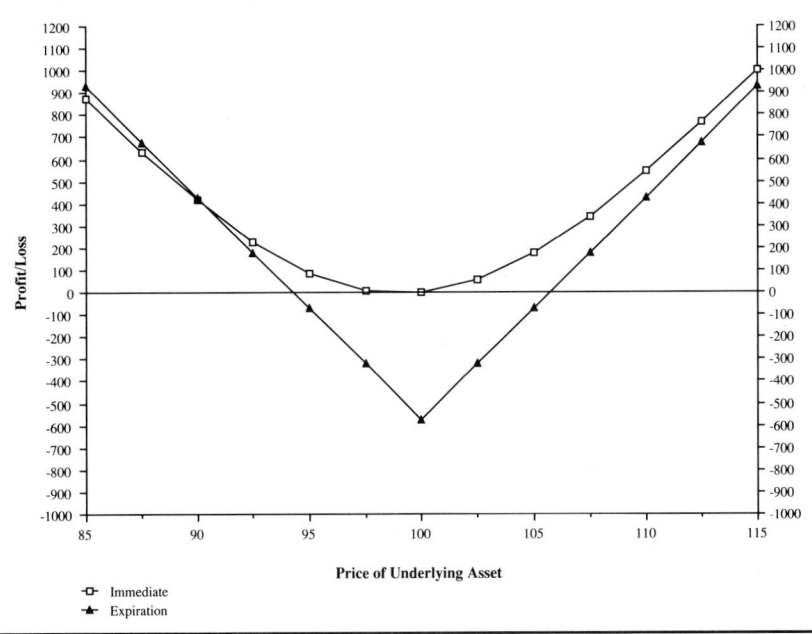

premiums, which can only happen if the asset price at expiration is exactly equal to the exercise price so neither option is in-the-money.

Selling a Straddle: The opposite position to buying a straddle is selling a straddle. The profit and loss figures are simply reversed from the previous case.

Initial Cost:	Credit of $C + P = 5\ 3/4$
Maximum Profit:	$C + P = 5\ 3/4$, if the asset price at expiration is X
Maximum Loss:	Unlimited, if the asset price rises sharply, and $C + P - X = -94\ 1/4$, if the price falls to 0
Breakeven Price:	$X + C + P = 105\ 3/4$, or $X - C - P = 94\ 1/4$
Standstill Return:	$(C + P) - \text{Max}\ (S - X, X - S) = 5\ 3/4$

Market Outlook: Price near *X*, low volatility

Risk Posture: Speculative

The payoff diagram for selling a straddle is simply the previous diagram, Figure 2–17, turned upside down. The position brings in a credit equal to the sum of the two option premiums at the outset. The maximum profit point at expiration occurs at the exercise price, where both options are worthless and the entire amount of both premiums can be retained. The position shows a profit for any asset price between the two breakeven points, but (virtually) unlimited potential loss outside that range.

Writing straddles makes sense for an investor who anticipates low volatility, so that the asset price is expected to remain in the profitable range. The investor must also be willing to take on a highly speculative position and bear the risk of large losses.

Strangle: A strangle is like a straddle, but the call's strike price, *XC*, is above the put's strike price, *XP*, and both options are out-of-the-money at the outset. Figure 2–18 shows the payoff diagram for a 1 month 95 – 105 strangle.

Initial Cost: $C + P = 2\ 1/16$

Maximum Profit: Unlimited, if the asset price rises sharply, and $XP - (C + P) = 92\ 15/16$, if the price falls to 0

Maximum Loss: $-C - P = -2\ 1/16$, if the asset price at expiration is between *XP* and *XC*

Breakeven Price: $XC + C + P = 107\ 1/16$, and $XP - C - P = 92\ 15/16$

Standstill Return: $\text{Max}\ (S - XC, XP - S, 0) - (C + P) = -2\ 1/16$

Market Outlook: Neutral on price, very high volatility

Risk Posture: Speculative, but risk is limited

A strangle is very like a straddle, but there is a middle range between

FIGURE 2–18
Strangle

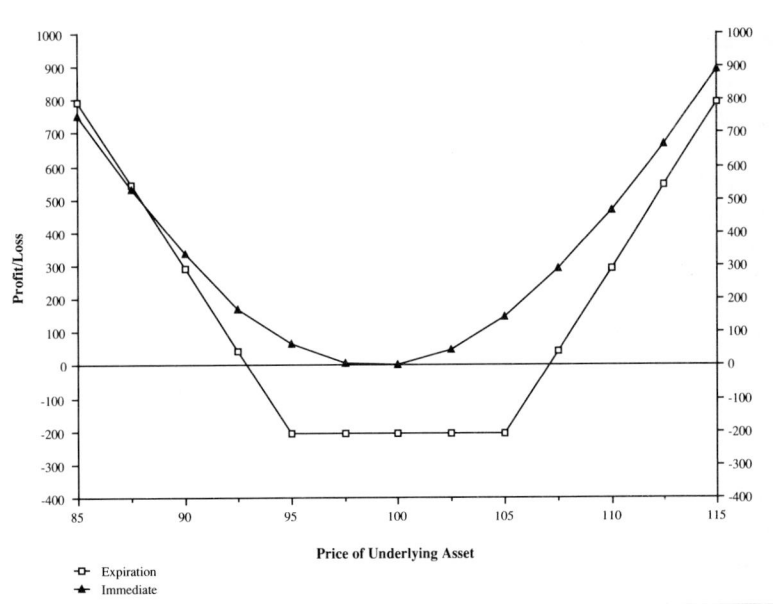

Price of Underlying Asset

-□- Expiration
-▲- Immediate

the two strike prices where both options can finish out-of-the-money. This is where the name of the strategy comes from: if the price of the underlying asset remains between *XP* and *XC* as time goes along, the investor strangles.

The breakeven prices for the 95 – 105 strangle are also farther apart than for the 100 strike straddle we just examined. The compensation for this less favorable range of profitability is that the strangle costs less than half as much as the straddle. An investor who expects volatility to be very high may find the strangle to be a good way to profit from it, because it is so highly leveraged. Yet, like the straddle, it has a strictly limited loss potential, since the most that can be lost is the sum of the two initial premiums.

Selling a Strangle: Similar to selling a straddle, the payoffs are easily determined by reversing the previous example. Interestingly, selling a strangle might seem slightly less risky than selling a straddle because the range of profitability is wider. Also, while it is lower than for the straddle, the strangle's maximum profit occurs over a broad range. The straddle's profit is concentrated at the common exercise price. Nevertheless, writing both strangles and straddles is highly speculative and carries the risk of substantial loss.

Butterfly Spread: A butterfly spread involves either three calls or three puts with different strike prices and the same expiration. The position is long one option with a low strike price, *CL*, long one with a high strike price, *CH* and short two options with the strike halfway between, *CM*. Figure 2–19 shows the payoff to a call butterfly using 1 month calls with strikes of 95, 100, and 105.

Initial Cost:	$CL + CH - 2 \times CM = 1\ 5/16$
Maximum Profit:	$(XM - XL) - (CL + CH - 2 \times CM) = 5 - 1\ 5/16 = 3\ 11/16$, if the asset price at expiration is *XM*
Maximum Loss:	$-(CL + CH - 2 \times CM) = -1\ 5/16$, if the asset price at expiration is below *XL* or above *XH*
Breakeven Price:	$XL + (CL + CH - 2 \times CM) = 96\ 5/16$, and
	$XH - (CL + CH - 2 \times CM) = 103\ 11/16$
Standstill Return:	Erosion of the time value on all three options,
	$(\text{Max}\ (0, S - CL) - CL) + 2 \times (CM - \text{Max}\ (0, S - CM) + (\text{Max}\ (0, S - CH) - CH) = (5 - 6\ 7/16) + (2 \times 3\ 3/16) + 1\ 1/4 = 3\ 11/16$
Market Outlook:	Price close to *XM*, low volatility
Risk Posture:	Low risk

FIGURE 2–19
Butterfly spread (call)

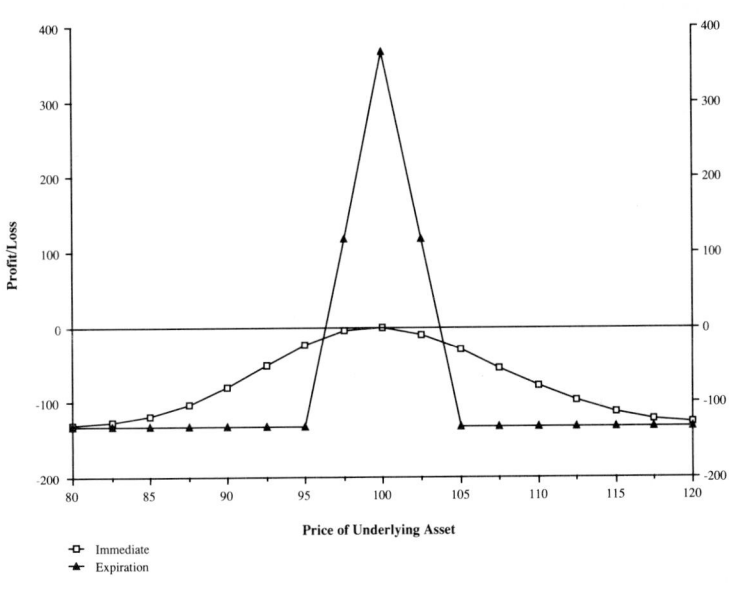

Price of Underlying Asset

-□- Immediate
-▲- Expiration

A butterfly spread appears to be a rather complicated position, since options with three different strikes are involved. It is also rather expensive to set up in terms of commissions. However, its payoff pattern has several virtues. Like selling a straddle, a butterfly spread focuses the position's return on a single price, the strike price of the middle call. But in contrast to the short straddle, risk is strictly limited since the most that can be lost is the relatively small net cost to set up the position initially. The result is that the investor is effectively able to bet that the stock price at expiration will be close to XM. If it is, the return will be several times the initial investment.

In this example, if the price stays at 100, the position makes a profit of 3 11/16 on an investment of 1 5/16, or 281 percent in one month. The possible loss in the position is only the 1 5/16 cost.

There is a concept in finance known as "complete markets" that is often a feature of theoretical models. A complete market exists when for each possible state of the world, it is possible to buy a security, known as a "state claim," that will pay off $1 if that state occurs, and nothing otherwise. A complete market allows an investor to tailor her investment portfolio exactly to match her needs and her expectations for every possible contingency.

Obviously, real financial markets are very far from being complete. However, the butterfly spread is something like a state claim. It pays off a positive amount only if the asset price is in the range between the lowest and the highest strike price, and it is worth 0 otherwise.[1]

Time Spread: A time spread or calendar spread is one involving two options with the same strike price but different expirations. We will use the letters N and F to indicate the "near" or "far" expirations. In the example, we buy the three month 100 strike call (CF) and write the one month call (CN).

Initial Cost:	$CF - CN = 2\ 13/16$
Maximum Profit:	CN minus the time decay on CF over time to near expiration = about 1 1/4, if asset price is X
Maximum Loss:	$-(CF - CN) = -2\ 13/16$, if the asset price at expiration goes to 0
Breakeven Price:	2 points (described below): = about 96 1/8 and 106
Standstill Return:	Time decay of CN minus time decay of CF
Market Outlook:	Price close to X, low volatility
Risk Posture:	Low

A time spread works quite differently from any of the others we have looked at. It does not depend only on a forecast of what the asset price will do. Instead, it is based upon the difference in the rate of time decay between options expiring at different dates. As we have seen above, an at-the-money

---

[1]Breeden and Litzenberger, in "State Contingent Claims Implicit in Option Prices," *The Journal of Business*, October 1978, analyze market completeness when there are enough strike prices that a complete set of butterfly spread positions can be formed to span the range of possible final stock prices. Hakansson, in "The Purchasing Power Fund: A New Kind of Financial Intermediary," *The Financial Analysts Journal*, November/December 1976, shows how a set of state claims could be created from a simple mutual fund stock portfolio.

FIGURE 2–20
Time spread

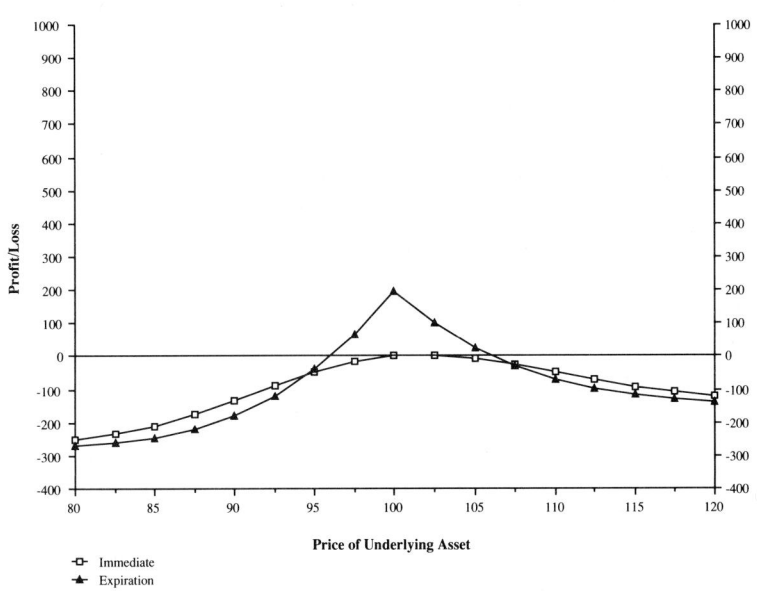

-□- Immediate
-▲- Expiration

option has the greatest time value and this value goes to zero at expiration if the option does not go into the money. Buying the far expiration call and writing the nearby call creates a position in which the option that is written decays faster than the one that is purchased. If the asset is exactly at the strike price at the expiration of the CN call, the disparity between time values is maximized. In our case, if the interest rate and volatility are unchanged in one month, the CF call that will now have two months to expiration will be worth 4 3/4 at a stock price of 100. Since the CN call will be worthless, the spread will have widened by 1 15/16.

The position should always require a net investment at the outset because the distant option has more time value. The most that can be lost on the position is just the net investment, if the options go so far out-of-the-money that they are both worthless by the time the near one expires.

If both are deep-in-the-money at that time, the maximum loss is smaller. The CN option will be worth its intrinsic value, having lost all of its time value. The *CF* option, on the other hand, can lose only the component of its time value due to the value of the option feature. The leverage value will remain, because there are still two months before it expires. For our example, the maximum loss on the downside is 2 13/16 but only about 1 1/2 on the upside.

No easy expression exists for the two breakeven stock prices. On the downside, the position breaks even when the loss in value of the *CF* option due to the combination of time decay and the stock price drop is just equal to the initial premium received for writing the *CN* call.

On the upside, the *CF* call gains intrinsic value as it goes farther in-the-money, but it loses time value due to the passage of time and also because the value of the option feature is reduced. Breakeven on the upside occurs at the point where this loss of time value on the distant option exactly offsets the nearby option's loss of its entire time value.

The position is similar to a butterfly spread in its risk posture and market outlook. Return is focused on a single stock price and risk of loss is limited.

In the same way that a price spread is sometimes called a vertical spread, a time spread is also known as a "horizontal" spread because it involves two options on the same *row* in the price table. Following the same naming convention, it is easy to see why a spread between options differing in both strike price and expiration date is a *"diagonal" spread.*

Box Spread: The last position we will discuss is the box spread, which involves four different options, with two strike prices and the same expiration. A box spread amounts to a "spread of spreads." One might think of it as buying a bull call spread and selling a bull put spread, or the reverse.

Initial Cost:	$(CL - CH) - (PL - PH)$
	$= 5\ 3/16 - (-4\ 13/16) = 10$
Maximum Profit:	0
Maximum Loss:	0
Breakeven Price:	Position breaks even at every stock price
Standstill Return:	0
Market Outlook:	Neutral
Risk Posture:	Riskless

The payoff on a box spread is just the difference between the high and low strike prices. If one has "bought" the spread by purchasing the in-the-money call and put (*CL* and *PH*) and selling the out-of-the-money options (*CH* and *PL*), the position requires an investment at the outset and pays off *XH* − *XL* at expiration. If all of the options are priced exactly in accordance with put-call parity, the initial cost should be slightly less than *XH* − *XL*, so that the riskless position earns the riskless interest rate over its lifetime. In this case, the options are slightly mispriced, so that the return on the spread is 0. Selling the spread brings in option premium at the beginning and there will be an outflow of *XH* − *XL* at expiration.

The box spread may seem like a very peculiar position, since it requires so many options to achieve a position that makes little or no profit. But it is a position that can arise for very good reasons in several ways. Most obvious is when option prices are somewhat out of line, as in this case. Since the position is riskless, even a small price discrepancy represents an arbitrage opportunity that may be worth taking advantage of. Here, for example, one has the chance essentially to borrow money for a month at zero interest by selling the box.

Box spreads can also come into being artificially, one might say, as components of a more complex option portfolio. Since the spread is riskless, it receives very favorable margin treatment. An investor holding a complex position may be able to reduce his overall margin requirement by treating options that can be combined in the right way as box spreads for margin calculations, regardless of how the positions were established initially.

Finally, in some cases options market makers may find it worthwhile to sell box spreads simply in order to bring needed funds into their trading accounts without increasing risk exposure. This is especially attractive if, as in this case, the effective interest cost for borrowing those funds is zero.

2.10 CONCLUSION

This chapter has covered a lot of ground, beginning with option price relationships that can be proved by arbitrage and portfolio dominance and ending with a quick presentation of the great variety of option trading strategies that are in use. Even so, we did not fully discuss either all of the dominance relations or all of the strategies.

In a sense, this chapter sums up what was known about the properties and uses of options before the development of theoretical valuation models. We are now prepared to go on to describe those models in the next chapter. But while mathematical option models will figure heavily throughout the rest of the book, we hope that the reader will take from this chapter an appreciation for the great variety of ways that options can be used to create payoff patterns that match an investor's expectations and willingness to bear risk. In particular, it is not necessary, or even desirable, to use a valuation model in all cases. Setting up a covered call or protective put position, for example, may be an excellent strategy under the proper circumstances, that does not require analysis by advanced mathematical methods.

References

Merton, Robert, (spring 1973). Theory of rational option pricing. *Bell Journal of Economics and Management Science, 4,* 141–183.

Gastineau, Gary, (1988). *The options manual.* New York: McGraw-Hill.

McMillan, Lawrence, (1986). *Options as a strategic investment.* New York: New York Institute of Finance.

Options Clearing Corporation, (1989). *Understanding the risks of traded options.*

CHAPTER 3

THEORETICAL VALUATION MODELS

Stephen Figlewski[*]

In the previous chapter, we saw that a great deal can be said about option valuation without specifying the expected return on the option or on its underlying asset. But the results that can be derived from considerations of portfolio dominance alone are not enough to pin down an option's fair value with precision. All we can obtain from this style of reasoning are boundaries, such as that the value of a call option on a non-dividend paying asset is no less than the asset's current price minus the present value of the option strike price. Ruling out dominant portfolios can not tell us *how much* greater than the boundary value the call price should be.

The problem of finding an explicit option valuation formula was first addressed in detail in the year 1900 by a French mathematician, Bachelier [1900]. Although Bachelier's work remained largely unknown for many years, we now see that it was path-breaking research for its time. He advanced a long way along the path that would develop into modern option pricing theory seventy years later.

The major stumbling block encountered by financial researchers trying to obtain an explicit option valuation model was that it seemed inherently to depend on two factors that could not be observed directly: the probability distribution for the price of the underlying asset at option

---

*The author is Professor of Finance at the Leonard N. Stern School of Business, New York University.

expiration and the appropriate risk-adjusted interest rate to use in discounting the option's expected payoff back to the present. It was only in 1972 that Fischer Black and Myron Scholes [1972,1973] were able to see through the problem and to find a solution, in the form of the celebrated Black-Scholes option pricing model.

In this chapter, we will first sketch out how Black and Scholes' use of the concept of an arbitrage portfolio made it possible to derive a model that did not depend explicitly on the expected price movement of the underlying asset. We will then introduce the Binomial model, an alternative approach that is consistent with Black-Scholes but is more intuitive. The Binomial model will be used throughout the book to illustrate the properties of different kinds of options.

After we have laid out the basics, we will describe how to implement the models, that is, what numbers to plug in, and how to use them in setting up a "delta-neutral" hedged position. We then discuss how to extend the basic formula to price options on assets paying dividends or other cash distributions, options on futures contracts, and options on foreign currencies.

3.1   THE GENERAL APPROACH

To see how considerations of arbitrage allow us to derive the fair value for a call option without having to know its expected payoff, let us take a very simple example.

Consider an asset currently priced at 100 that has a traded call option with strike price of 100. Assume the call's price is 10. Suppose that over the next day, the underlying asset's price will go either to 99 or to 101. If there is a formula that will give the fair value of the option as a function of the asset price, time to expiration, and other specifiable parameters, it will be able to tell us what the option is worth at asset prices of 99 and 101. Clearly the option will be more valuable when the asset price is higher, other things equal. *Suppose* such a formula exists and it says that the call is worth 9 1/2 if the asset's price goes to 99 and 10 1/2 if tomorrow's price is 101. These values are displayed in Table 3-1.

Looking only at the asset and the call option separately, it is not possible to determine the expected returns for either over the next day without knowing the relative probabilities the price will be 99 versus 101. But now consider a hedged position, in which one unit of the asset is

TABLE 3–1
The simplest case

		Next Day Value	
Position	Initial Cost	$S_1 = 99$	$S_1 = 101$
1. Buy 1 unit of asset	100	99	101
2. Buy 1 call option	10	9 1/2	10 1/2
3. Hedged position: Buy 1 unit of asset Sell 2 call options	100 -2×10	99 -19	101 -21
	80	80	80

purchased and two options are sold.

The initial cost of the position is $100 - 2 \times 10 = 80$. One day later, if the asset has dropped to 99, there is a 1 dollar loss on the one unit that is held. But the calls will also have dropped in price, so that buying them back would only cost $2 \times 9\ 1/2 = 19$ dollars. The profit and loss on the two components of the position cancel each other out, and the total value is unchanged at 80. Similarly, if the price rises to 101, the 1 dollar profit on the asset will be offset by the increase in the cost of the call options that were sold short, and the overall value of the hedged portfolio remains at 80.

It is clear that we do not need to know the probabilities that the price will go down to 99 or up to 101 here, because the value of the hedged position is the same in either case. The hedge eliminates risk over the next day. Since the position is riskless, it should be priced in the market to earn the same overnight rate of return as any other riskless asset. Otherwise there would be an arbitrage opportunity, in which funds could be raised at one rate and invested at a higher rate.

It is this principle, that an option can be combined with its underlying asset into a riskless hedge portfolio, that is the basis for all modern option valuation formulas. To prevent arbitrage, option prices in the market must be such that the hedge portfolio earns the riskless interest rate. Under a special set of assumptions, that we will describe shortly, Black and Scholes were able to derive a formula that gives the fair value for a call option so that the hedge portfolio does earn exactly the risk free interest rate. As you can see in this simplified example, it is not necessary to specify what the expected return on the underlying asset will be, or what the market's adjustment for risk is in valuing the option's payoff. By focusing on the hedged portfolio, a valuation for the option *relative to the price of the underlying asset* can be determined without knowing these parameters.

3.2   THE BINOMIAL MODEL

The concept behind the Black-Scholes model is easily grasped, but the mathematics involved in deriving it are rather daunting. Over the years, several "tricks" have been found that can greatly simplify the problem. One is the principle of "risk neutral" valuation. By placing the problem in the context of a riskless portfolio, the fair value for an option can be found without knowledge of investors' risk aversion. An option will be priced the same (given the price of its underlying asset!) regardless of how risk averse they are. In particular, a call will have the same value as if investors were all risk neutral, i.e., they were indifferent to risk and cared only about expected return. It turns out to be fairly easy to derive security valuation formulas for a risk neutral market environment, and the principle of risk neutral valuation says that these formulas also hold for options in a general risk averse market. The Appendix to this chapter illustrates the risk neutral valuation principle in detail and shows how it can be used to simplify the derivation of the Black-Scholes formula and many other option models.

Another approach to option valuation began as a modeling trick but has become a very important tool for explaining the principles of options and also for deriving numerical solutions to option problems in practice. That is the Binomial model, first mentioned by Sharpe in his *Investments* textbook[1] and then developed by Cox, Ross, and Rubinstein [1979]. We will now show how this model works.

The hedge portfolio argument we sketched out above worked because the asset's price could only go to two possible values, 99 and 101. What makes the mathematics of the Black-Scholes model difficult is that the asset price is allowed to move to any one of a large number of prices (in fact, an infinite number) in any finite period of time. This allows for realistic price behavior, similar to what we observe for real securities.

The Binomial model develops the two-price approach in a rigorous manner, apparently giving up realism in return for an intuitive structure and

---

[1]See William Sharpe, *Investments* (3rd edition), Englewood Cliffs, New Jersey: Prentice-Hall, 1985.

mathematical tractability. What makes the Binomial model so valuable, though, is that by taking its limiting case, as smaller and smaller price changes take place over shorter and shorter intervals, one arrives exactly at the Black-Scholes formula. Thus the Binomial model is a kind of special case of the Black-Scholes model, but it is easier to understand and to manipulate.

Let S represent the current price of the underlying asset. Over the next interval of time, assume the price can either move up to a value uS or down to dS. We can think of u as being "1 plus the rate of return if the asset goes up", and similarly for d, if the asset goes down. The possible price changes are shown on the left in Figure 3-1.

FIGURE 3–1
Possible asset prices over 1 period

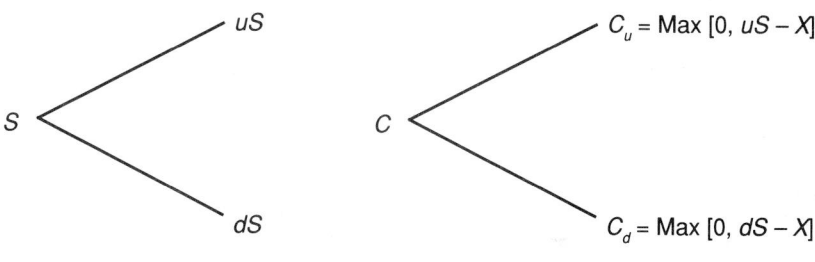

Suppose there is a 1 period call option on the asset, with an exercise price of X. When it expires next period, the call pays the greater of 0 or the asset price minus X. Today's call price, which we are trying to determine, is C. This is shown in the right-hand portion of Figure 3-1.

Finally, assume there is a riskless asset available that returns a total of R dollars next period for each $1 invested today. Gross interest R is 1 plus the interest rate, e.g., if the interest rate is 6 percent, $R = 1.06$. It is possible to lend or borrow freely at rate R.[2]

If the option's exercise price X is greater than uS, it will be out-of-the-

---

[2]Notice that to avoid arbitrage, we must have $u > R > d$. If, on the contrary, R were less than d, investing in the risky asset would always return more than the riskless asset. This could not be a market equilibrium because it would create an arbitrage in which investors would borrow unlimited amounts at rate R to invest in the "risky" asset. Similarly, if R were greater than u, the riskless asset would dominate the risky asset.

money regardless of whether the asset price is up or down. In that case, today's price C must be 0. X can be either greater or less than dS, but for ease of illustration, let us assume that $X > dS$. The other case can easily be worked out by the reader. So, if the asset goes up to uS, the call will be worth $uS - X$. If the asset goes down to dS, the call is worth 0.

Now, as before, we invoke the principle of arbitrage, which will permit us to derive the value of the option. If it is possible to construct a portfolio that consists only of some quantity of the underlying asset plus riskless borrowing or lending, and which has exactly the same payoffs next period as the option, that portfolio must cost exactly the same as the option, or else there is an arbitrage. Let us see how that could be done.

We are going to set up a position with h units of the risky asset and B dollars invested in the riskless asset that will replicate the option's payoff. We must have the payoff on the replicating portfolio equal to the option value in both the "up" state and the "down" state:

Portfolio Payoff		Option Value		
$h \times uS + RB$	$=$	$uS - X$	("up" state)	(3.1)
$h \times dS + RB$	$=$	0	("down" state)	(3.2)

This is a system of two equations in two unknowns, that is easily solved to yield

$$h = \frac{uS - X}{S\,(u - d)} \qquad (3.3)$$

$$B = \frac{-d\,(uS - X)}{R\,(u - d)} \qquad (3.4)$$

Since the portfolio of h units of the asset plus B dollars of riskless borrowing (borrowing, since B is negative) pays exactly the same as the one period call option, it must cost the same at the outset, so

$$C = h\,S + B$$

or,

$$C = \frac{(R - d)\,(uS - X)}{R\,(u - d)} \qquad (3.5)$$

This gives us an exact formula for the value of a one period call option.

h, the number of units of underlying asset in the replicating portfolio is known as the hedge ratio, or the "delta" of the option. Delta will be discussed in detail below.

Example: Suppose $u = 1.5$, $d = .5$, and $R = 1.10$. In this case, S can go to 150 or to 50 in the next period, and the riskless interest rate is 10 percent. If the option's strike price is 100, then

$$h = 50 / 100 = 0.5$$

$$B = -25 / 1.1 = -22.73$$

and $$C = .5 \times 100 - 22.73 = 27.27.$$

Now let us extend the analysis to a call with more than one period to expiration, with up and down moves u and d possible at each step. Figure 3-2 shows the "tree" diagram for the evolution of the stock price over two periods. At the end of the first period, there are two possible prices, uS and dS as before. If the first step is in the "up" direction, the possible prices at the end of the second period are uuS and duS. Similarly, if the first step is down to dS, then the possible period 2 prices become udS and ddS. Since duS is the same as udS, there are three possible prices that can occur in the second period.

In general, after T steps, there will be $T + 1$ possible outcomes, as shown in Figure 3-3. In terms of the figure, the ending prices will be arrayed from top to bottom, with the highest corresponding to $u^T S$, the next to $u^{T-1} dS$, and so on, down to $ud^{T-1} S$ and finally $d^T S$. That is, there will be $T + 1$ prices that differ according to whether they involve 0, 1, 2, and so on up to T, down moves over the T periods. Often the nodes are identified by step number and the number of prior up-moves. For example, the node $N(3,2)$ would be the node at step 3 at which there had already been 2 up-moves; the asset price would be $u^2d S$.

The bottom portion of Figure 3-2 shows the tree of call prices corresponding to the asset price tree above. But although there are more node points, the multiperiod binomial valuation problem is not really any more complicated than the single period problem we just solved. The only difference is that an equation similar to (3.5) must be solved repeatedly, once for each node.

FIGURE 3–2
Asset prices over 2 periods

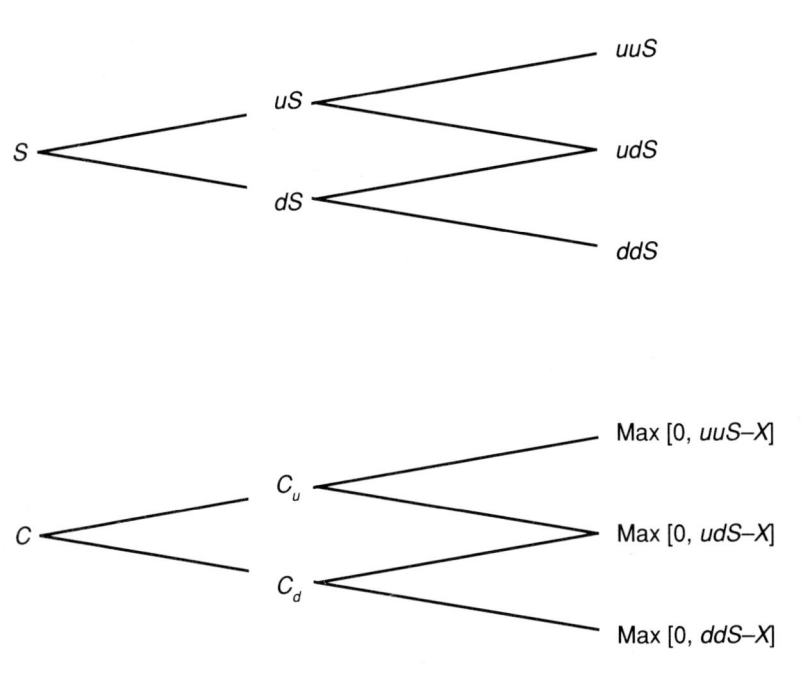

As before, we start from the right side of the tree where it is easy to determine the call values at expiration from the terminal asset prices. Given those values, equation (3.5) can be applied to value the calls one step earlier. The prices have been designated C_u and C_d.

Once we have filled in the option values at expiration, rolling the valuation back to the beginning period becomes straightforward. At each node we follow the same approach as before, forming a hedge portfolio from h units of the risky asset and B dollars of riskless borrowing or lending in order to replicate the same values next period as the call option, i.e., C_u if the asset price goes up to uS and C_d if it goes down to dS.

Using the prices from the example, the three terminal asset prices are

$$uuS = 1.5 \times 1.5 \times 100 = 225,$$

FIGURE 3–3
Asset price paths over *T* periods

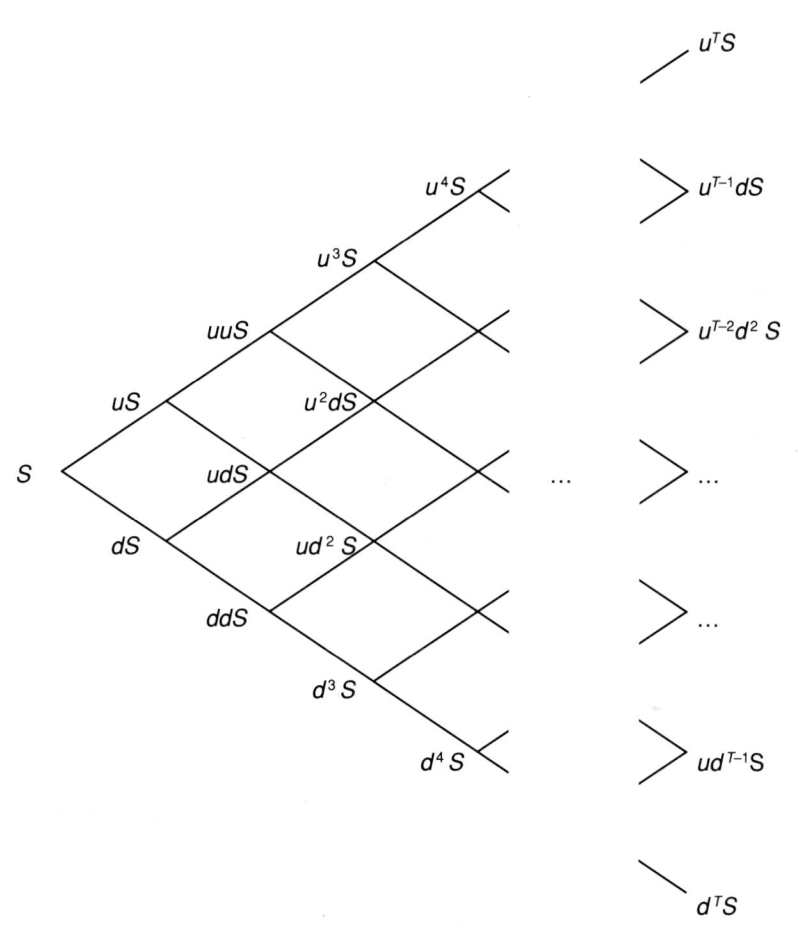

$udS = 75$, and

$ddS = 25$.

Applying (3.5) yields $C_u = 68.18$, $C_d = 0$. The option replication to derive the initial option value is

Portfolio Payoff		Option Value	
$h \times uS + RB$	$=$	C_u	("up" state)
$h \times dS + RB$	$=$	C_d	("down" state)

Solving for h and B gives

$$h = \frac{C_u - C_d}{S(u - d)} \qquad (3.6)$$

$$B = \frac{u C_d - d C_u}{R(u - d)} \qquad (3.7)$$

From (3.6) we have for our example

$$h = (68.18 - 0) / (100 \times (1.5 - .5))$$

$$= .6818 .$$

Equation (3.7) gives

$$B = (0 - .5 \times 68.18) / (1.1 \times (1.5 - .5))$$

$$= -30.99.$$

The value of the call option is then

$$C = \frac{C_u - C_d}{(u - d)} + \frac{u C_d - d C_u}{R(u - d)} \qquad (3.8)$$

Equation (3.8) is a general formula for rolling back the binomial tree one step. If C_u will be the next period option value for an up move and C_d for a down move, then equation (3.8) gives the only possible option value for the current time and asset price that does not allow an arbitrage profit.

This expression can be written in a more convenient fashion, if we define

$$p = (R - d)/(u - d).$$

Then we have

$$C = [p\, C_u + (1 - p)\, C_d] / R \qquad (3.9)$$

In solving a multiperiod valuation problem, (3.9) is used repeatedly.

With the values of u, d, and R assumed in the example, $p = .6$. It is easy to calculate the time 1 option values from (3.9):

$$C_u = (.6 \times (225\text{-}100) + .4 \times 0) / 1.1 = 68.18$$

$$C_d = (.6 \times 0 + .4 \times 0) / 1.1 = 0,$$

and the initial call value is

$$C = (.6 \times 68.18 + .4 \times 0) / 1.1 = 37.19.$$

As calculated from Equation (3.6) above, the call's delta is

$$h = \frac{68.18 - 0}{100 \times (1.5 - .5)}$$

$$= .6818.$$

We now have a complete procedure for valuing options in a Binomial framework. We start by constructing the tree of possible asset prices in each future period. Then, beginning with the final period, at expiration when the value of the option is easily established, we apply formula (3.9) to roll the valuation problem back one period, to determine the prices at all nodes in period $T-1$. Proceeding this way, one eventually gets to the beginning. The option value that results from this series of calculations is the only one that is consistent with there being no arbitrage opportunities at any future date.

One significant fact to note about the Binomial approach is that there is no difference in procedure whether one is valuing a European call option, a put, or any other derivative security. For example, in using the framework to value a put, the only difference with what we have just done would be that the terminal put values are given by Max[$0, X - S$] instead of Max[$0, S-X$] as for a call.

Once again, it can be seen that the option value does not depend on the expected price change for the asset (nothing has been said about the relative *probabilities* of u and d moves) nor does it depend on risk preferences. It *does* depend on the initial asset price S, the strike price X, the number of periods to expiration, T, the sizes of the up and down steps u and d, and the riskless interest rate R.

3.3   THE BLACK-SCHOLES MODEL

The Binomial Model can be developed much further than what we have done here, and subsequent chapters will do so. But at this point, we will move on to describe the option pricing formula established by Fischer Black and Myron Scholes, that has become one of the major theories of modern finance. The formula is derived and discussed in more technical detail in Appendix A.

The essence of the simple models we have looked at just now is that the possible price change for the asset over the next period is restricted to just two values, making it possible to replicate the change in the value of the option using the two fundamental securities (the risky asset and the riskless asset). At each step, the proportions in the hedge portfolio must be rebalanced, as a function of the price change that has just occurred.

Black and Scholes also limit the problem, but not in the same way. They do it by shortening the time interval between successive price changes for the underlying asset and assuming that the price moves continuously, though randomly, even in the limit. This leads to a process in which the price changes only by infinitesimal increments at each step, but with an infinite number of steps occurring during any finite time period. This is like looking at the limit for a binomial tree that becomes so dense that there are many steps in even an infinitesimal period.

The Black-Scholes (B-S) model is derived under a set of formal assumptions. There are several alternative paths to the formula, but the standard one is based upon the arbitrage principle we have illustrated above. In order to apply it we make assumptions about the market environment and assumptions about the mathematical properties of the price changes for the underlying asset.

Perfect Markets Assumptions

1. There is a risky asset, with current price S. It can be bought and sold freely, even in fractions of units. It can be sold short and the proceeds are available to the short seller, at least for investment in the riskless asset. The risky asset pays no dividends or other distributions before the option's expiration date.
2. It is possible to borrow and lend without risk at a fixed rate of interest. Interest accrues on a continuous basis at rate r. The gross interest rate R is now the compounded value

$$R = e^r$$

3. The option is European, with exercise price X and time to expiration T.
4. There are no outside factors affecting returns, such as taxes, transactions costs, or margin requirements.
5. The asset price evolves according to the equation

$$dS = \mu S \, dt + \sigma S \, dz \tag{3.10}$$

where, dS represents an infinitesimal change in the price,

dt represents an infinitesimal period of time,

μ ("mu") is the mean return on the asset per period, i.e., the proportional rate at which the price tends to drift upward over time,

σ ("sigma") represents the volatility of the asset's price,

dz is an infinitesimal random variable with mean $0 \, dt$ and variance $1 \, dt$.

Equation (3.10) embodies several important properties that are assumed about the price behavior of the underlying asset.

The price is continuous in time (e.g., the market is always open, and the price can not jump from one value to another without trading at all intervening prices).

The random component of the price change is embodied in the dz term. This is often called Brownian motion. A random variable that evolves according to an equation like (3.10), with a Brownian motion component, is known as a diffusion process or a Wiener process (after Norbert Wiener who did much to develop the mathematics of these processes).

Equation (3.10) denotes a continuous-time random process, in which randomness impinges upon the system at every instant, with each infinitesimal random increment being independent of every other one. Over a time interval of length T, the realizations of dz will cumulate to a value that is a normally distributed random variable with a mean of 0 and variance T (the standard deviation is $\sqrt{T}$). Such a process is essentially a random walk in continuous-time, which is consistent with the modern view of how most security prices move in an efficient market.

The instantaneous mean and variance of the price change are proportional to the current price S, so that the mean and variance of the (continuously compounded) rate of return per unit time are constant values, μ and σ^2, respectively. With the assumptions about dz, this means that the return on the asset over any period will be normally distributed, and the price S will be *lognormal*, i.e., its logarithm is normal. One characteristic of a lognormal distribution is that the size of the average price change is larger at higher price levels. Another is that the price cannot become negative, or even zero.

It is clear that a lognormal diffusion can only be an approximation to the behavior of actual security prices. For example, price changes are discontinuous when the market is closed overnight and on weekends. It is also generally found that the volatility of returns on real securities appears to change randomly over time. While these discrepancies can have important implications for marketmakers in options, and for the viability of particular trading strategies, they are ignored for the most part in deriving option valuation models, for the simple reason that treating them properly leads to enormous mathematical complexity.

Deriving the Black-Scholes Formula

Let C be the theoretical value of a European call option. The objective is to derive an equation that expresses C as a function of the strike price X, time to expiration T, and the characteristics that have been assumed for the market environment and for the price behavior of the underlying asset.

The first step is to look at a hedge portfolio containing one call option and some position in the underlying asset in the correct proportions so that whatever the price change on the asset is over the next instant, the profit and loss on the two components of the portfolio offset each other.

It is useful to compare this to the way in which the Binomial model was developed. In that case, we used the underlying asset and riskless borrowing to create a portfolio that replicated the payoff pattern of a call option. Here we turn the relationship among these securities around, combining positions in the asset and the call option into a riskless investment. The basic arbitrage relation at work is the same.

Let ∂C represent the amount that the value of the call option will change if the price of the underlying asset moves by a tiny amount ∂S. The ratio $\partial C/\partial S$ is the hedge ratio or the delta of the call for this set of parameters. We will use the symbol δ for delta.

Now think about the portfolio that is long one call option and short δ units of the underlying asset. If the asset price S moves by some amount y, the call value will change by δy. The value of the short position in δ units of the underlying asset will change by $-\delta y$, i.e., the same amount in the opposite direction. The position is therefore riskless overall for the next instant.

In the Binomial model, the amounts invested in the risky and the risk free assets were recalculated at every step. The same thing occurs in continuous-time models. Once the price moves, the delta changes too, and the position must be rebalanced by buying or selling some amount of the asset in order to achieve the new delta. That is why the price process must be continuous, to allow the continuous rebalancing that keeps the hedge portfolio riskless at *every* instant in time.

Under the assumptions set out above, it is possible to write the stochastic differential equation (similar to equation (3.10)) for the movement in the value of the call and of the hedge portfolio. And since this portfolio is instantaneously riskless, to prevent the possibility of arbitrage profits over the next interval dt it must return the riskless rate of interest, $r\ dt$. This relationship produces a "second order partial differential equation" that must be satisfied by the call value formula.

Such equations are seldom very easy to solve, but Black and Scholes were able to redefine the variables in the problem in such a way that it became like a well-known one from physics: the equation governing the diffusion of heat along a wire, whose solution was known.

The resulting Black-Scholes equation for the value of a call option can be written as follows.

$$C = S N [D] - X e^{-rT} N [D - \sigma \sqrt{T}] \qquad (3.11)$$

where,

S = the price of the underlying asset,

X = the exercise price,

T = time to option expiration,

r = the instantaneous riskless interest rate,

$$D = \frac{\ln (S / X) + (r + \sigma^2 / 2) T}{\sigma \sqrt{T}}$$

$ln[\cdot]$ = the natural logarithm,

σ = volatility of the underlying asset,

$N[\cdot]$ = the cumulative normal distribution function, i.e., the probability of observing a value less than the value in brackets when drawing randomly from a standardized normal distribution.

This formula gives the fair value for a call option as a function of only five variables: the price of the underlying asset, the strike price, the time to expiration, the riskless interest rate, and the asset's volatility. While the equation may appear somewhat complicated, it is quite easy to implement, even on a hand calculator. (Appendix B gives a formula for the cumulative normal distribution.)

Figure 3-4 plots the call value from this equation as a function of the price of the underlying asset.

Once again, it is worth reflecting on the variables that are not included in the model. The mean return on the asset, μ is not present, nor is any measure of market risk aversion. By focusing on the hedge portfolio, the model derives the fair price for the option *relative to the underlying asset*. The seemingly important variables (in particular, price expectations) that are not explicitly included in the formula enter nevertheless, because they are impounded in the price of the underlying asset.

FIGURE 3–4
Call option ($X = 100$, $T = 1$ month, $r = 6\%$, Volatility = 15%)

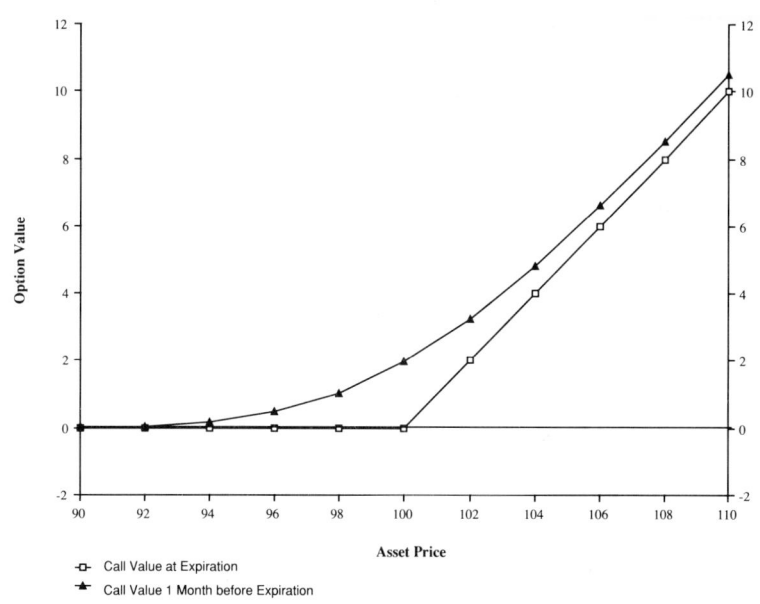

One thing that makes this model so valuable is that the Black-Scholes European call option model also applies to American calls. As we observed in the previous chapter, except for the effect of dividend payout, it is never optimal to exercise an American call early, so that American and European calls should be valued alike.

In addition to the fair call price, the Black-Scholes model also produces the all-important delta for the call.

$$\delta = N[D] \quad \text{(Call delta)} \qquad (3.12)$$

Delta measures the sensitivity of the option to changes in the asset price. Knowledge of the delta is essential for risk evaluation and for hedging an option position.

Combining equation (3.11) with the put-call parity relation, equation (2.3), leads easily to a comparable Black-Scholes formula for a European put.

$$P = X e^{-rT} N [-D + \sigma \sqrt{T}] - S N [-D]$$ (3.13)

The put value is plotted in Figure 3-5.
The put's delta is given by

$$\delta = -N [-D]$$ (Put delta) (3.14)

The put formula is a little less useful than the call formula because, unlike the American call, it is optimal to exercise American puts before expiration. Although it is widely used in practice for valuing both European and American puts, equation (3.13) does not take account of the economically valuable right to exercise early, and so it undervalues American puts.

FIGURE 3–5
Put option (X = 100, T = 1 month, r = 6%, Volatility = 15%)

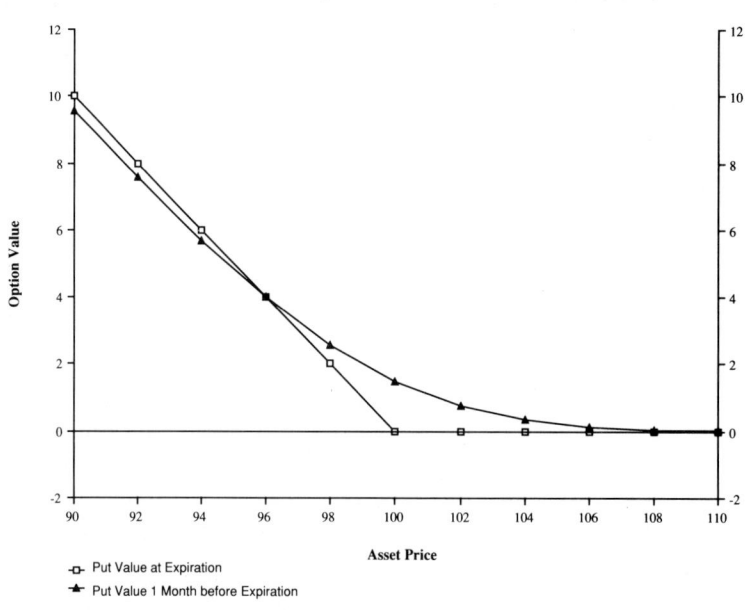

-□- Put Value at Expiration
-▲- Put Value 1 Month before Expiration

3.4   USING THE BLACK-SCHOLES MODEL

To illustrate how the model is implemented, we will now work through an example. Suppose we have the following parameter values for a three month at-the-money call option:

Initial Asset Price: $S = 100$

Exercise Price: $X = 100$

Time to Expiration: $T = 3$ months (91 days)

Interest Rate: $r = 6$ percent

Volatility: $\sigma = .15$

The initial asset price and the strike price need no explanation. The time to expiration must be converted into years, in order to be consistent with the way the other parameters are stated, so we use $T = 91/365$ in the formula.

The Interest Rate

The interest rate r in the model actually corresponds to a continuously compounded rate. That is, if $1 invested today becomes $1.06 in one year, we need the r that makes

$$e^{\,r} = 1.06$$

or, $\qquad\qquad r = \ln(1.06) = .0583$

As you can see, there are two adjustments that are made to obtain the value of r for the formula from a quoted interest rate. Most important, the rate must be entered as a decimal, i.e., .0583 not 5.83. Second, and of lesser importance quantitatively, if the rate is quoted on a "simple interest" basis, it should be converted to a continuously compounded rate.

On the other hand, if the rate used is an overnight rate expressed as an annual figure without compounding but quoted on the basis of a 365 day year, as is often done for money market instruments such as repurchase agreements, it should be entered into the formula without conversion. This is because the simple rate would actually be compounded if the overnight investment were rolled over for a year. For example, rolling over at an overnight rate of 6 percent for 365 days would yield $(1 + .06/365)^{365} - 1 =$ 6.18 percent in a year. Practically, this adjustment for continuous compounding does not have a very great impact on the computed option price, except for in-the-money calls with a long time to expiration.

Estimating Volatility from Past Prices

The volatility for purposes of the model is the standard deviation of the change in the natural logarithm of the underlying asset's price that is expected over the lifetime of the option, expressed as an annual rate. The volatility figure must be entered as a decimal. Chapter 13 will cover procedures for estimating volatility efficiently, so at this point we will only sketch out the simplest approach.

We begin with a series of prices from the recent past. There is no "correct" number of past prices to use, or even general agreement on whether it is better to use daily prices or those from longer intervals. Typically there are tradeoffs. Using more past prices increases statistical accuracy of the estimate, as long as the volatility does not change over time. But since actual volatilities do not seem to be constant, it is normally wise not to use data that are too old. Daily data allow more prices from the recent past to be used, but for some assets, such as small capitalization stocks, thin trading can induce artificial correlation in daily prices that affects the volatility calculation. In practice, volatility is estimated for most assets using 1 to 6 months of daily prices.

Assume we have daily prices from the last $K + 1$ trading days.

Step 1. Take the natural logarithms of the prices.

Step 2. Compute the changes in the logarithms. There will be K changes. We will denote them as y_t.

Step 3. Compute the mean $\bar{y}$ of the y_t.

Step 4. Compute the K deviations from the mean $(y_t - \bar{y})$. Square these deviations and sum them up.

$$Z = \sum_{t=1}^{K} (y_t - \bar{y})^2$$

Step 5. The estimate of the daily variance is $v^2 = Z / (K - 1)$. (Divide by $K - 1$ instead of K because one degree of freedom is used up in estimating the mean). Annualize the volatility by multiplying v^2 by the number of trading days in a year, about 260, to get σ^2.

Step 6. The volatility σ is the square root of σ^2.

Table 3–2 illustrates this calculation using closing values for the Standard and Poor's 500 index from February 1, 1988 through February 29, 1988. The annualized volatility during the month of February was .159. If this figure is used in valuing options with the Black-Scholes model, one is tacitly making the assumption that the S&P 500 index will continue to be as volatile from today until option expiration as it was during the month of February 1988.

Volatility is often described as the standard deviation of the annualized percent return on the underlying asset. For example, the volatility figure of .159 would commonly be called "a volatility of 15.9 percent." Computing volatility from percent returns rather than by the logarithmic formulation we have just described will be *approximately* correct, but not exact. For example, for the data displayed in Table 3-2, the standard deviation of the percentage rate of return comes out to be .1558.

Implied Volatility

The volatility estimate produced by analyzing past prices is known as "historical volatility." A different way to obtain a volatility estimate is by solving the valuation equation backwards, taking the price of the option in the market as given and finding the volatility that would make the theoretical value in equation (3.11) equal to the market price. This volatility figure is known as the "implied volatility" for the option, since if investors are using the Black-Scholes model to value options, the price that we observe in the market implies that it is the volatility estimate they are using.

Implied volatility is easy to compute given a valuation model appropriate for the option whose implied volatility one wishes to find. Chapter 13 describes efficient algorithms for estimating both implied and historical volatility.

The volatility that is relevant for establishing the value of an option is the volatility of its underlying asset from the present until option expiration. One problem with using implied volatility to estimate this value is that each

TABLE 3–2
Estimating volatility from historical prices

Date	S&P 500 Index	Log(S&P)	Change in Logs	Squared Deviations
01 Feb 88	255.04	5.541		
02 Feb 88	255.57	5.543	0.0021	0.000000
03 Feb 88	252.21	5.530	−0.0132	0.000250
04 Feb 88	252.21	5.530	0.000	0.000007
05 Feb 88	250.96	5.525	−0.0050	0.000057
08 Feb 88	249.10	5.518	−0.0074	0.000100
09 Feb 88	251.72	5.528	0.0105	0.000062
10 Feb 88	256.66	5.548	0.0194	0.000284
11 Feb 88	255.95	5.545	−0.0028	0.000029
12 Feb 88	257.63	5.552	0.0065	0.000016
16 Feb 88	259.83	5.560	0.0085	0.000035
17 Feb 88	259.21	5.558	−0.0024	0.000025
18 Feb 88	257.91	5.553	−0.0050	0.000058
19 Feb 88	261.61	5.567	0.0142	0.000136
22 Feb 88	265.64	5.582	0.0153	0.000162
23 Feb 88	265.02	5.580	−0.0023	0.000024
24 Feb 88	264.43	5.578	−0.0022	0.000023
25 Feb 88	261.58	5.567	−0.0108	0.000180
26 Feb 88	262.46	5.570	0.0034	0.000001
29 Feb 88	267.82	5.590	0.0202	0.000311
		Sum	0.048895	0.001759
		Mean	0.0026	

Daily Variance:	Sum/18	0.000098
Annual Variance:	Daily × 260	0.0254
Annual Standard Deviation:	$\sqrt{.0254}$	0.159

option produces its own figure, the volatility that makes the theoretical value equal to the current market price for that option. But a multiplicity of volatility figures is inherently contradictory.

A second problem with implied volatility is that since one picks the figure that makes the theoretical value match the market price, it is not of much use in trying to find options in the market that are *mispriced* relative to their underlying asset. A third problem, related to the second, is that the procedure inherently incorporates into the volatility estimate all sources of mispricing, including data errors, effects of the bid-ask spread and temporary imbalances in supply and demand.

On the other hand, a great advantage of implied volatility is that it is forward looking. Historical volatility estimates can not incorporate new information that is expected to change the underlying asset's volatility in the future. Such factors might include knowledge that a former source of uncertainty has been resolved: an election is held, an antitrust suit is settled, and so on; or that there is a new cause of volatility: a strike is called, the Federal Reserve adopts new operating procedures, etc. Since option investors incorporate their evaluation of what effect such factors will have on future volatility into current market prices, implied volatilities can reflect the information, while the historical estimate does not.

Briefly then, both ways of obtaining a volatility estimate are valid under the proper conditions. Typically the estimates will differ, sometimes by quite a lot. Which estimate to use depends largely on what purpose the investor has in using a valuation model. Most professional option traders pay attention to both, sometimes blending them together into a single composite figure. There is no single best approach, and in many ways estimating volatility continues to be as much an art as a science.

Black-Scholes Option Values

Finally, entering the parameter values shown above into the formula (3.11) yields the theoretical value for the 3 month call option as 3.74, i.e., $3.74 per unit of the underlying asset.

Or alternatively, since the asset's price is 100 one can think of this as 3.74 *percent* of the price of the underlying. The option pricing formula is "homogeneous of degree 1" in the asset price and strike price, meaning that multiplying both S and X by a constant factor c produces a theoretical option value c times as large. For example, a three month at-the-money call on an asset priced at 40, with volatility .15 and interest rate of 6 percent would be worth $(40 / 100) \times 3.74 = 1.496$.

In Table 3–3, we display the Black-Scholes prices and deltas for various parameter values. The reader can verify that these prices satisfy the relationships that were derived in the previous chapter from the principle of portfolio dominance. Call values increase for lower exercise prices, longer times to expiration, higher volatilities, and greater riskless interest rates.

A closer look at the numbers reveals another relationship that turns out to be generally true for calls. An increase in volatility or in time to expiration

TABLE 3–3
Sample option values (S = 100)

	X = 95		X = 100		X = 105	
	Value	Delta	Value	Delta	Value	Delta
Call Values						
σ = .15; r = .06						
T = 1 month	5.67	0.90	2.00	0.55	0.37	0.16
T = 3 months	7.13	0.82	3.74	0.59	1.61	0.34
T = 1 year	12.30	0.79	9.07	0.68	6.43	0.55
σ = .30; r = .06						
T = 1 month	6.80	0.75	3.73	0.54	1.76	0.32
T = 3 months	9.51	0.70	6.68	0.57	4.49	0.44
T = 1 year	17.23	0.70	14.63	0.63	12.34	0.57
σ = .15; r = .12						
T = 1 month	6.07	0.92	2.26	0.60	0.45	0.19
T = 3 months	8.18	0.86	4.55	0.66	2.09	0.40
T = 1 year	16.13	0.88	12.55	0.80	9.44	0.69
Put Values						
σ = .15; r = .06						
T = 1 month	0.20	−0.10	1.50	−0.45	4.85	−0.84
T = 3 months	0.75	−0.18	2.30	−0.41	5.09	−0.66
T = 1 year	1.92	−0.21	3.41	−0.32	5.49	−0.45

causes a larger percentage increase in an out-of-the-money than an in-the-money call. This is related to the fact that an out-of-the-money call is more highly leveraged. A large price move in the asset is magnified (in percentage terms) in the value of an out-of-the-money call. This has a marked impact on the risk borne by writers of options. Many options traders are very wary of writing out-of-the-money options out of a (justified) concern that huge losses can develop rapidly when a large market move occurs in the underlying asset. On the other hand, out-of-the-money calls lose value fastest as time elapses if the underlying asset does not move.

The last panel in Table 3-3 shows some representative put values. Naturally, these also satisfy the portfolio dominance relations of Chapter 2. Two interesting properties to notice here are first, that an at-the-money put is worth less than an at-the-money call, and second, that it is possible for a put close to expiration to be worth less than its intrinsic value. (If this happens, the value of the put is greater the *shorter* the time to expiration.)

This clearly could not happen for an American put, since one can realize the intrinsic value at any time simply by exercising the option.

These properties are both caused by the fact that the interest factor acts in opposite directions for calls and puts. A high rate of interest makes a call option more valuable because instead of buying the asset outright, one is able to control it with a small amount of capital while earning interest on the strike price that will not be paid out until option expiration.

A put's value, on the other hand, is negatively related to the interest rate. For a European put that is deep-in-the-money, the longer the holder has to wait before he can exercise, the longer he must go before he can begin to earn interest on the exercise price that he will receive. If the interest rate is very low, this effect is diminished. At an interest rate of zero, one would not exercise an American put early.

Delta, the Measure of Price Sensitivity

In the first section of Table 3–3, the delta of the three month at-the-money call is 0.59. If the price of the asset increases by 1 dollar to 101, the theoretical call value increases by about 59 cents. A hedged position would consist of a long position in the call and a short position in the underlying asset (or the reverse) with the proportions of 0.59 units of the asset against each call. Such a position would be hedged (or "delta neutral") for a small price movement in either direction. However, since delta changes when the asset price changes, the hedge only works for small changes, before the proportions need to be rebalanced.

Delta is integral to the *application* of option valuation theory in the financial markets. It provides a valuable measure of the option's exposure to the price fluctuations of the underlying asset. A call with a delta of .9 will be nine times as sensitive to price changes in the underlying asset as one with delta of .1. A put option has a negative delta, meaning its value goes down if the asset price rises.

It is clear from equations (3.12) and (3.14) that since delta is given by $N[D]$ or $-N[-D]$, it is a kind of probability. Thus it must lie between 0 and 1.0 for a call option, and between 0 and –1.0 for a put. A deep out-of-the-money option has a delta very close to zero—its value is only slightly affected by movements in the underlying asset, since the probability that the option will ultimately be exercised is low.

3.5 IMPLEMENTING THE BINOMIAL MODEL

Now we will show how the same example as in the previous section would be solved using the Binomial model. Table 3–4 displays the calculations. We have limited ourselves to 10 steps, in the interest of showing the entire tree for this example. Normally one would use a larger number of steps to value an option with three months to expiration.

The choice of the number of steps to use involves a tradeoff of accuracy versus speed and ease of computation. For a standard sort of problem, the degree of accuracy that can be achieved with even a small number of steps is quite good. The step size is about 9 days for this example and the theoretical call price ends up within 2 percent of the true option value. It is unlikely that in practice one would ever need a step size of less than one day, and a much coarser tree will typically be adequate.

To compute the asset price tree, we first need to convert the annual interest rate and volatility figures into "per step" values. Assuming, as before, that the 6.00 percent quoted interest rate corresponds to a continuously compounded rate of

$$r = \ln (1.06) = .0583,$$

the per step interest rate is

$$(r \times T / NS) = .0583 \times .0249 = .001452,$$

where T is the option maturity in years (91/365) and NS is the number of steps. This gives

$$R = 1.001452.$$

The per step volatility is

$$\sigma \times \sqrt{T / NS} = 0.15 \times \sqrt{.0249} = .0237 .$$

Next we compute the up and down state values u and d. We want the price volatility in the asset price tree to match that of the actual asset. But this leaves flexibility in setting up the tree, since we know that the expected return on the underlying asset does not directly affect the value of the option.

TABLE 3–4
Calculating a call value with a 10-step binomial procedure

Basic Parameters		Per Step Values			Binomial Parameters		
Asset Price:	100	1 Step	=	.0249 years	u	=	1.0255
Strike:	100	Interest:		.001452	d	=	0.9780
T to Expiration:	91 days	Volatility:		.0237	R	=	1.0015
Interest:	6.00%				p	=	0.4941
Volatility:	0.15						

Underlying Asset

Down						Step					
Steps	0	1	2	3	4	5	6	7	8	9	10
0	100.00	102.55	105.16	107.83	110.58	113.39	116.28	119.24	122.27	125.39	128.58
1		97.80	100.29	102.84	105.46	108.15	110.90	113.72	116.62	119.59	122.63
2			95.65	98.09	100.58	103.14	105.77	108.46	111.22	114.05	116.96
3				93.55	95.93	98.37	100.88	103.44	106.08	108.78	111.55
4					91.49	93.82	96.21	98.66	101.17	103.74	106.39
5						89.48	91.76	94.09	96.49	98.94	101.46
6							87.51	89.74	92.02	94.37	96.77
7								85.59	87.77	90.00	92.29
8									83.71	85.84	88.02
9										81.87	83.95
10											80.07

Call Value

Down						Step					
Steps	0	1	2	3	4	5	6	7	8	9	10
0	3.79	5.21	6.98	9.09	11.50	14.12	16.86	19.67	22.56	25.53	28.58
1		2.41	3.50	4.94	6.77	8.98	11.48	14.16	16.91	19.73	22.63
2			1.36	2.10	3.17	4.64	6.56	8.90	11.51	14.20	16.96
3				0.64	1.06	1.74	2.78	4.29	6.37	8.92	11.55
4					0.22	0.41	0.73	1.31	2.28	3.89	6.39
5						0.04	0.09	0.18	0.36	0.72	1.46
6							0.00	0.00	0.00	0.00	0.00
7								0.00	0.00	0.00	0.00
8									0.00	0.00	0.00
9										0.00	0.00
10											0.00

Model Values
Call Value = 3.79
Delta = 0.59

Still, the choice of u and d may well affect how accurate the Binomial algorithm is for a given step size. The following values work well in practice.

$$u = e^{r+\sigma}$$

$$d = e^{r-\sigma},$$

where both r and σ refer to their values per step. (Chapter 14 discusses alternative procedures for implementing the Binomial model.)

This is sufficient to fill out the asset price tree, beginning at $S_0 = 100$ and progressing to the right. In Table 3–4, each down step corresponds to going down one line as one goes from left to right in the tree. That is, uS in step 1 is 102.55 and dS is 97.80. At the final step, 128.58 corresponds to 10 consecutive up moves and 80.07 is 10 down moves.

Next the option price tree must be filled in, working backwards this time, from expiration at the right back to the initial value at step 0. The call values at expiration are easily determined, as $\text{Max}(0, S-X)$ for each possible asset price.

Filling in the option price tree is then accomplished by using equation (3.9), with

$$
\begin{aligned}
p &= (R - d) / (u - d) \\
&= (1.0015 - .9780) / (1.0255 - .9780) \\
&= .4941
\end{aligned}
$$

For example, to find the option value at step 9 assuming there have been 9 up moves and no down moves to that point, we take the two possible option prices that can be reached at step 10, 28.58 (if the next step is also up) and 22.63 (if it is down) and plug into equation (3.9):

$$
\begin{aligned}
C &= (.4941 \times 28.58 + .5059 \times 22.63) / 1.0015 \\
&= 25.53.
\end{aligned}
$$

This value is then entered at the top of the column at step 9.

Filling in the rest of the tree in the same manner leads eventually to a step 0 value for the call of 3.79. The delta, from equation (3.6) is

$$\begin{aligned}
\delta &= (C_u - C_d) / S \times (u - d) \\
&= (5.21 - 2.41) / 100 \times (1.0255 - .9780) \\
&= .59 \, .
\end{aligned}$$

These values can be compared to the exact figures of 3.74 and .59 that were derived above using the Black-Scholes model. The 10 step Binomial has overpriced the call by .05, a little over one percent of its correct value. The delta is correct to two decimal places.

3.6   HEDGING OPTIONS

Knowledge of an option's delta is essential in managing its risk. The obvious example is the hedge portfolio, in which the option is hedged by selling delta units of the asset. A position that is made riskless (for *small* price changes!) is called "delta neutral," because it has a delta of zero, and is neutral to both price increases and decreases.

It is also a straightforward matter to hedge one option with any other option on the same underlying asset by creating a delta neutral position. Since both options are affected by the same random price fluctuations, it is only necessary to hold them in the right proportions for the resulting changes in value to cancel out. If δ_1 is the delta for the first option and δ_2 is the delta for the second, selling (δ_1 / δ_2) units of option 2 for each unit of option 1 held long will create a delta neutral position.

For example, using the figures in Table 3–3, suppose we wanted to hedge a long position in the 3 month 105 strike call option when the volatility was .15 and the interest rate was 6 percent. The option's delta is .34, so we could sell .34 units of the underlying asset for each option. Or we could sell $(.34 / .16) = 2.13$ 1 month 105 strike calls, or sell $(.34 / .59)$ $= .58$ 3 month 100 strike calls. Another possibility would be to buy $(.34 / .66) = .52$ 3 month 105 strike puts. In all cases, we would end up with a delta neutral hedged position.

To illustrate this, suppose the asset price falls by one point and we have a delta neutral position that is long 100 of the 3 month 105 strike calls and short 58 of the 3 month 100 strike calls. The value of the long position should drop by about $100 \times -1 \times .34 = -34$. The short position in the 100 strike calls should make a profit of about $-58 \times -1 \times .59 = 34.2$. So if the prices in the market change by approximately the same amount as the changes in the theoretical values, the hedge should have very low risk.

Like all derivatives (delta is the derivative of the option value function with respect to a change in the price of the underlying), the delta of a combination, or portfolio, of several options is just the sum of the deltas of the individual option positions. This allows one to summarize the price sensitivity of even a very complex portfolio of options based on a given underlying asset in a single number, the delta. (Of course, when we are dealing with a portfolio involving a number of securities, delta is not limited to be less than 1.0).

For example, if an option position has a combined delta of 5000, for a small change in the price of the underlying, it will have the same profit or loss as 5000 units of the underlying asset. One of the major uses of option theory is option "replication," that is, setting up a position from just the underlying asset and borrowing or lending such that it replicates the payoff of a chosen option. Chapter 11 will describe how option replication is done in a portfolio insurance program, and its use by options market makers will be covered in Chapter 12.

Options Arbitrage

Since arbitrage between an option and its underlying asset plays such an important role both in the theory of option valuation and also in the practice of options trading, it is worth spending a few minutes to go over how an arbitrage trade to exploit a mispricing would actually be carried out.

Earlier, we computed the fair value for a 3 month call with strike price of 100, written on an asset whose price was currently 100. Volatility was assumed to be .15 and the riskless interest rate was 6 percent. According to the model, the option was worth $3.74 and its delta was 0.59.

Suppose this option were actually selling in the market for $4.25. At that price it is overvalued by $0.51. In the theoretical world of perfect markets that was assumed in deriving the model, this mispricing can be turned into a riskless profit through arbitrage. How does one do it?

Since the market price is too high, we want to write the option and hedge the position by buying the underlying asset. We buy 59 units of the asset and sell calls on 100 units to produce a delta neutral position. The total cost to set up the hedge portfolio is $5,475.

The Hedge Portfolio:

Buy 59 units of the underlying asset at 100	5900
Sell calls on 100 units of the asset at 4.25	$\underline{-425}$
Total cost	5475

Notice that since the market has priced the option above the value we have computed, the volatility implied in the market price is higher than our estimate of 0.15 (which we are assuming to be the true volatility). At a price of \$4.25, the implied volatility for this option is .176. At any value higher than 0.15, the option will be priced too high in the market. It is important in hedging and valuing the option that the true volatility always be used in the calculations, and not the implied volatility. (Of course, determining the true volatility is easier said than done.)

This hedge portfolio is riskless over the next short interval of time. Constantly rebalancing the proportions of calls and the underlying asset according to the formula until the options expire, will lock in a return equal to the riskless rate of interest on the capital invested in the position, plus an excess return of \$0.51 per call, or \$51 on the position.

Now suppose that over the first day, the asset price rises to 102. Plugging the new price into the valuation formula, with time to expiration one day less, we find that the call is now theoretically worth \$5.00 and the delta has become 0.69.

If the market is now pricing the options using the true volatility of 0.15 (perhaps because of the trading of arbitrageurs), the portfolio will be worth $-100 \times 5.00 + 59 \times 102 = \$5518$.

Since the options are now correctly priced, there is no further excess profit to be made, so the arbitrage position should be unwound. The total profit will be \$43, of which less than \$1 is accounted for by overnight interest, and the remainder is due to the repricing of the call options to their fair value.

The \$43 profit is less than the theoretical profit of \$51. The discrepancy is due to the fact that we did not rebalance the hedge. As the price of the underlying asset rises from 100 to 102, the delta changes from .59 to .69. To remain completely delta neutral, the position needs to be rebalanced continuously as the delta is changing. If that is not done, the hedge does not keep up completely as the price rises, so the realized profit is less than the theoretical value.

Typically, however, it may take longer than one day for a mispricing to disappear. Suppose that after the price rises to 102 the calls are still priced in the market on the basis of a 0.176 volatility. In that case, they will be selling for about 5 1/2. In order to realize the theoretical excess return from this mispricing, it will be necessary to maintain the arbitrage position.

The proportions of calls and the underlying asset must be rebalanced to adjust for the new delta of .69. This must be done by buying 10 units more of the underlying asset. (If instead, a portion of the short call option position were covered to achieve the correct portfolio proportions, one would be buying overpriced options in the trade and dissipating some of the theoretical profit.)

While many options arbitrage positions can be unwound quickly because prices come into line, it is perfectly possible for a difference in opinion about volatility to persist for long periods. In that case, the hedge might have to be maintained until option expiration. This is sufficiently cumbersome in practice, and the transactions costs associated with frequent rebalancing can grow so large that it becomes not worthwhile to enter into the trade for only a moderate expected return. This is compounded by risk stemming from the fact that future volatility can not be predicted perfectly. Thus fairly wide deviations from Black-Scholes model option values can develop in some markets without inducing massive arbitrage trading to push prices back into line.

Price jumps, that are assumed away in developing the model, but are a part of most real world financial markets, also cause trouble for the options arbitrageur. We saw this when we considered the returns on a hedged position when the asset price went from 100 to 102 and there was no rebalancing in between. The hedge underperformed. The general principle is that in a hedged position in which options are written, a price jump causes the hedge to underperform, while a hedge that contains a long option position will be enhanced by a price jump. This makes sense in terms of the model, because a price jump can be thought of as high volatility. When the market is more volatile than expected an option's value is higher than expected. You make extra returns if you own the option and you lose if you are short the option. In the jargon of the options markets, owning options makes you "long volatility" while writing them makes you "short volatility."

3.7   GAMMA, THETA, AND THE OTHER DERIVATIVES

Delta is a very important characteristic to know about an option, but other parameters can also be very important to understanding how the option value will behave as market conditions change, and to evaluating and managing total risk exposure in an options position. Table 3–5 displays these parameters for a variety of options.

Lambda

Delta gives the dollar change in the option value caused by a one dollar change in the price of the underlying asset. In many cases it is not the dollar changes but *percentage* changes that are most relevant. The "leverage ratio" or "elasticity" is a scaled delta that gives the percent change in the option value due to a one percent rise in the underlying asset price. This is often called lambda, and it is equal to delta times the asset price divided by the option price:

$$\text{Lambda} = \lambda = \delta\, S/C$$

Gamma

We have already seen that delta is not constant, but changes as the underlying asset price changes. Delta also changes gradually over time even if there is no price movement on the asset. The change in the delta for a given change in the asset price is known as gamma. Variations in delta require that a hedged position be rebalanced if it is to remain delta neutral after the asset price has changed. How much adjustment is necessary will depend on how much the delta changes, that is, on gamma.

The effect of gamma can be seen graphically in Figures 3–4 and 3–5, in the curvature of the option value function. A sharp curve means that the slope is changing rapidly over that range of prices, so gamma will be high. Gamma is a measure of "convexity," referring to the upward bow shape of both the call and the put value function. Note that "convexity" here refers to how the option value changes with changes in the asset price, while in the previous chapter, we proved that the option value was a convex function of the strike price. These two meanings of convexity for an option are related but not exactly the same.

TABLE 3–5
Option sensitivity to changes in input parameters. (Asset Price = 100)

Strike Price	Maturity	r	Volatility	Model Value	Delta	Lambda (Elasticity)	Gamma	Theta (per day)	Kappa (per .01)	Rho (Interest Sensitivity) (per 1.0%)	Beta (relative to asset)
Calls											
95	1 mo.	6%	.15	5.67	.90	15.9	.039	−.025	.049	.068	16.0
100	1 mo.	6%	.15	2.00	.55	27.5	.090	−.037	.115	.043	27.7
105	1 mo.	6%	.15	0.37	.16	43.2	.056	−.020	.072	.013	44.1
95	3 mo.	6%	.15	7.12	.82	11.5	.035	−.023	.131	.176	11.5
100	3 mo.	6%	.15	3.74	.59	15.8	.052	−.025	.194	.130	15.8
105	3 mo.	6%	.15	1.59	.34	21.4	.049	−.020	.181	.079	21.1
100	1 mo.	6%	.30	3.73	.54	14.5	.045	−.064	.116	.040	14.5
100	3 mo.	6%	.30	6.68	.57	8.5	.026	−.041	.196	.118	8.5
100	1 mo.	12%	.15	2.26	.60	26.5	.089	−.045	.113	.043	26.4
Puts											
95	1 mo.	6%	.15	0.20	−.10	−50.0	.039	−.010	.049	−.008	−47.9
100	1 mo.	6%	.15	1.50	−.45	−30.0	.090	−.021	.115	−.037	−29.7
105	1 mo.	6%	.15	4.85	−.84	−17.3	.056	−.003	.072	−.071	−17.2
100	3 mo.	6%	.15	2.30	−.41	−17.8	.052	−.009	.194	−.101	−17.8
100	1 mo.	6%	.30	3.24	−.46	−14.2	.045	−.049	.116	−.039	−14.2
100	1 mo.	12%	.15	1.30	−.40	−30.8	.089	−.015	.113	−.032	−31.1

Delta is almost zero for deep-out-of-the-money calls, and it changes little at first when the asset price moves, so gamma is small. Gamma is greatest for options that are at-the-money, but then goes toward zero again as the deep-in-the-money call's delta goes to 1.0. Both calls and puts have positive gamma because deltas for both increase (algebraically) if the asset price rises.

Gamma indicates how much rebalancing will be needed in a delta neutral position. A hedge involving an option with a large gamma becomes unbalanced rapidly when the asset price moves. To understand this from a different angle, gamma is a measure of how much risk exposure a hedged position will develop when the price jumps and the hedge is not, or cannot be, adjusted.

Theta

Theta refers to the rate of time decay for an option. It is the derivative of the option value with respect to time. As we have said, an option is a "wasting asset." If the price of the underlying asset is constant, an option loses value day by day. Theta measures the rate at which the value decays. A common way of expressing this decay is simply as the loss in value over the next day if the underlying asset remains at the same price.

Theta measures the cost of holding an option long, and the reward for writing it. Options with the greatest time value will also have the largest rate of decay of that value. Theta tends to be greatest in dollar terms for at-the-money options, but as a percent of value, theta is larger for out-of-the-money options.

As we saw earlier, a deep-in-the-money European put can be worth less than its intrinsic value, due to the opportunity loss from not being able to exercise it immediately and begin earning interest on the exercise price that would be received. Over time, the put must rise to its intrinsic value. So in this case only, theta will be positive.

Notice that theta is the derivative of option value with respect to time, expressed as a daily rate. That makes it the negative of the derivative with respect to T, time to maturity, in equation (3.11) or (3.13). T becomes smaller as time elapses.

Kappa, the Measure of Volatility Sensitivity

Since volatility is such an important determinant of option value, many options are quite sensitive to a change in volatility. In the financial community, volatility sensitivity is often known as "vega." This term is conveniently short, but it is unfortunately not a letter in the Greek or any other alphabet. (Vega is either the name of a bright star in the constellation Lyra, or alternatively, a model of Chevrolet.) Instead, we will adopt a frequently used alternative term for the change in option value caused by a change in volatility, the Greek letter "kappa," written κ.

For example, an increase in σ from .15 to .16 raises the value of the 3 month 100 strike call option from 3.74 to 3.91. Kappa is uniformly positive for calls and puts. (Of course, in a spread position where one option is written and another is held long, the sensitivity to a change in volatility for the portfolio will be the difference between the two kappas, which may have either sign.)

A derivative is normally expressed as the change in the function for a unit change in the parameter of interest. But since volatility for most financial assets tends to be in the range of about .10 to .40, a change of 1.0 in volatility is not really meaningful. It is more useful to express kappa in terms of the change in option value for a .01 change in σ.

Rho, the Measure of Interest Sensitivity

The final parameter in the option formula is the riskless interest rate. The derivative of the option value with respect to the interest rate is known as rho. As we have discussed already, the time value for a call option comes partly from the interest that can be earned by investing the strike price from the present until the expiration date. The higher the interest rate, the greater the call's time value, other things equal; hence rho is positive for a call. The opposite is true for a put, since the put holder loses interest while waiting until option maturity to receive the strike price. For both calls and puts, the longer the time to expiration, the larger is the effect of the interest rate on option value. The effect is also greater for options that are in-the-money; since the exercise price is more likely to be paid, the discounting of it becomes relatively more important. Table 3–5 illustrates these patterns in rho for the options displayed.

Beta

Beta for a stock refers to the percentage change in stock price associated with a one percent move in a market index. Since stock option values change with the stock price, an option will have a beta also. It is a function of the stock's beta, the option's delta, and the stock and option prices (in order to convert dollar price changes into percents.)

$$\text{Beta of Option} = (\text{Beta of Asset}) \times \delta \times (S / C) \qquad (3.15)$$

The option beta has the same sign as the delta, so a put's beta is negative. Since the option is levered, its beta is always greater in magnitude than that of the underlying asset. It also varies with the stock price, rising in absolute value as the option goes out-of-the-money and approaching the beta of the underlying asset (or minus the asset's beta for a put) for a deep in-the-money option. Note that the symbol C in (3.15) refers to the price of the particular option under consideration, whether it is a call, a put, or something else.

3.8 VARIATIONS ON THE THEME: OPTIONS ON OTHER TYPES OF ASSETS

The Black-Scholes model is valid for European calls and puts on assets that obey the assumptions set out above. Many assets satisfy most of the requirements, but they pay dividends, coupon interest, or some other kind of cash distribution. In this section we will describe several variants of the model to handle such securities.

Assets with Cash Payouts

The problem in valuing a call option on an asset that has a cash payout prior to the expiration date, is that the holder of the asset receives the payout but the holder of a call does not. When the security goes "ex-dividend" it will normally drop in price by approximately the amount of the distribution. Sometimes an option is "payout protected," meaning that the strike price is reduced by the value of any distribution that occurs during its lifetime. But this is rare. Normally the option holder has no compensation for the ex-dividend price drop. In that case, expected payouts will naturally affect the fair value of the option.

Consider an asset that is expected to pay out one cash distribution of Q dollars on a given date between now and option maturity. On that date the asset price will drop by Q. But at every other time, the price evolves according to the lognormal diffusion shown in equation (3.10). It can be shown that as far as option value is concerned, it is as if the asset began at a lower price initially and made no payout over the period.

That is, a European call on the asset currently priced at S and paying out Q dollars in the future has the same value as if the asset were priced today at $S - PV(Q)$ and made no subsequent distribution. The call value is given by

$$C = S* N[D*] - X e^{-rT} N[D* - \sigma \sqrt{T}] \qquad (3.16)$$

where the variables are as defined in equation (3.11) above, except that $S*$ $= S - PV(Q)$ replaces S everywhere in the formula. A similar substitution into equation (3.13) gives the value of a put on an asset with one future cash payout.

The same reasoning can easily be extended to assets with multiple payouts. Simply define

$$S* = S - PV (\text{all future payouts})$$

and apply (3.16).

Notice that this approach allows us to deal with a European option on an asset with distributions, but not with American options. When a call is deep-in-the-money and close to maturity, the impending payment of a large dividend will cause the holder of an American option to exercise early, in order to realize the intrinsic value before the price drops. The right to do this imparts additional value, beyond what is shown in (3.16), to an American call on an asset that makes cash payments over the option's lifetime. Valuing options with early exercise features is the subject of Chapter 4, and we will defer further discussion of this point until then.

The Continuous Payout Model

For some kinds of assets, the distributions are so numerous that (3.16) becomes unwieldy. An example is a broad-based stock market index port-folio, in which nearly every day one component stock or another will pay a dividend. Foreign currencies also make effective distributions daily, in the form of interest accruals.

Merton [1973] has derived a variant of the Black-Scholes formula for an asset that pays dividends *continuously*. The payout is assumed to be a constant proportion of the current asset price, so that the payout over an instant dt is equal to $q\,S\,dt$. The model is then

$$C = S\,e^{-qT}\,N\,[\,D_q\,] \; - \; X\,e^{-rT}\,N\,[\,D_q - \sigma\,\sqrt{T}\;] \qquad (3.17)$$

where q is the instantaneous proportional payout rate,

$$D_q = \frac{\ln\,(S\,/\,X)\; +\; (r - q + \sigma^2\,/\,2)\,T}{\sigma\,\sqrt{T}} \qquad (3.18)$$

and the other parameters are as defined for (3.11).

The discerning reader will notice that (3.17) is actually the same as (3.16) with $S^* = S\,e^{-qT}$. The one difference is that unlike the model with cash distributions of a fixed size, a continuous payout affects the option's delta.

$$\delta \; = \; e^{-qT}\,N\,[\,D_q\,] \qquad (3.19)$$

As alluded to above, one application of the continuous payout model is in valuing foreign currency options. If the underlying asset is a given quantity of a foreign currency, the interest accruing on it is an effective cash distribution that is proportional to the asset value. For currency options, q becomes the foreign riskless interest rate, while r is the domestic rate. And again, the foreign interest rate will enter in the delta. Currency options are covered in detail in Chapter 7.

Options on Futures Contracts

There is a variant of the basic formula, developed by Black [1976], that applies to options on futures and forward contracts.

$$C = F e^{-rT} N[D_f] - X e^{-rT} N[D_f - \sigma\sqrt{T}] \qquad (3.20)$$

where F refers to the futures price and

$$D_f = \frac{\ln(F/X) + \sigma^2 T/2}{\sigma\sqrt{T}} \qquad (3.21)$$

The delta is given by

$$\delta = e^{-rT} N[D_f] \qquad (3.22)$$

This formula is clearly related to the earlier ones, particularly the continuous dividend model in (3.17)–(3.19). Futures options will be discussed more fully in Chapter 4.

The Option to Exchange One Asset for Another

One final useful formula covers the option to exchange one asset for another. In a sense, a normal call option can be thought of as an option to exchange one asset (an amount of cash equal to the call's strike price) for another (the underlying asset). This kind of option becomes special, however, when both assets involved are risky. Then the option value will depend on the random price movements on both assets. One example of such an option would be a convertible bond, which can be thought of as being the same as a normal bond plus an option to exchange the normal bond for shares of the issuing company's stock.

Margrabe [1978] derived the value of an option to exchange asset 2 for asset 1, when the Black-Scholes assumptions hold for both of them. That is, at the option's maturity date if the price of asset 2 is less than asset 1, the holder will exercise the option, delivering asset 2 to the writer and receiving asset 1 in return. If asset 2 is selling for more than asset 1 on that date, the option will be allowed to expire worthless. The exchange option's value is given by

$$C = S_1 N[D_x] - S_2 N[D_x - \sigma_x\sqrt{T}], \qquad (3.23)$$

where, S_1 = the price of asset 1

σ_1 = asset 1 volatility

S_2 = the price of asset 2

σ_2 = asset 2 volatility

ρ_{12} = correlation between asset 1 and asset 2 returns

$\sigma_x = \sqrt{\sigma_1^2 + \sigma_2^2 - 2\rho_{12}\sigma_1\sigma_2}$

$$D_x = \frac{\ln(S_1/S_2) + \sigma_x^2 T/2}{\sigma_x\sqrt{T}} \tag{3.24}$$

The delta of the exchange option in terms of units of asset 1 per option is

$$\delta = N[D_x]. \tag{3.25}$$

Finally, one should recognize that an exchange option is both a put and a call at the same time. That is, it is equivalent to think of it as an option to *call* asset 1 in exchange for asset 2, or as an option to *put* asset 2 and receive asset 1. Therefore there are not separate formulas for calls and puts in this case.

Table 3-6 summarizes the various formulas we have presented.

TABLE 3–6
European option valuation formulas

Black-Scholes

Call $= S\,N[D] - X\,e^{-rT}\,N[D - \sigma\sqrt{T}]$	Delta $= N[D]$
Put $= X\,e^{-rT}\,N[-D + \sigma\sqrt{T}] - S\,N[-D]$	Delta $= -N[-D]$

where S = price of underlying asset

X = exercise price

T = time to option expiration

r = riskless interest rate

$D = \dfrac{\ln(S/X) + (r + \sigma^2/2)T}{\sigma\sqrt{T}}$

σ = volatility

$N[\cdot]$ = cumulative normal distribution

Continued on next page

TABLE 3-6
European option valuation formulas—continued

Option on Asset with Discrete Cash Payout

Call $= S^* N[D^*] - X e^{-rT} N[D^* - \sigma \sqrt{T}]$ Delta $= N[D^*]$

Put $= X e^{-rT} N[-D^* + \sigma \sqrt{T}] - S^* N[-D^*]$ Delta $= -N[-D^*]$

where S^* = price of underlying asset minus present value of all cash paid out prior to expiration

     D^* = same as D above with S^* replacing S

All other variables defined as above

Option on Asset with Continuous Payout

Call $= S e^{-qT} N[D_q] - X e^{-rT} N[D_q - \sigma \sqrt{T}]$ Delta $= e^{-qT} N[D_q]$

Put $= X e^{-rT} N[-D_q + \sigma \sqrt{T}] - S e^{-qT} N[-D_q]$ Delta $= -e^{-qT} N[-D_q]$

where q = rate of continuous payout, i.e., payout $= S(e^q - 1)$ per period

$$D_q = \frac{\ln (S/X) + (r - q + \sigma^2/2)T}{\sigma \sqrt{T}}$$

Futures Option

Call $= F e^{-rT} N[D_f] - X e^{-rT} N[D_f - \sigma \sqrt{T}]$ Delta $= e^{-rT} N[D_f]$

Put $= X e^{-rT} N[-D_f + \sigma \sqrt{T}] - F e^{-rT} N[-D_f]$ Delta $= -e^{-rT} N[-D_f]$

where F = Futures price

$$D_f = \frac{\ln (F/X) + \sigma^2 T/2}{\sigma \sqrt{T}}$$

Exchange Option *(option to exchange Asset 2 and receive Asset 1)*

Option Value $= S_1 N[D_x] - S_2 N[D_x - \sigma_x \sqrt{T}]$

Delta $= N[D_x]$ units of Asset 1

where S_1 = Asset 1 price, σ_1 = Asset 1 volatility

     S_2 = Asset 2 price, σ_2 = Asset 2 volatility

     $\sigma_x = \sqrt{\sigma_1^2 + \sigma_2^2 - 2\rho \sigma_1 \sigma_2}$

     ρ = correlation coefficient between returns on Assets 1 and 2

$$D_x = \frac{\ln (S_1/S_2) + \sigma_x^2 T/2}{\sigma_x \sqrt{T}}$$

APPENDIX A TO CHAPTER 3

CONTINUOUS-TIME MATHEMATICS AND THE BLACK-SCHOLES MODEL

The Black-Scholes model and much of modern contingent claims valuation theory is derived under the assumption that the price of the underlying asset evolves according to a lognormal diffusion process like equation (3.10). This Appendix will describe the mathematics of such processes and show how the Black-Scholes model is derived.

The first section describes continuous-time stochastic processes and relates them to the more familiar discrete-time processes. The following section presents Itô's Lemma, the primary tool used in analyzing option price dynamics. In Section 3A.3 we develop the Fundamental Partial Differential Equation of contingent claims pricing. And finally, in Section 3A.4, we use the Risk Neutral Valuation Principle to derive the Black-Scholes option equation.

3A.1 Diffusion Processes

Diffusion processes belong to the general class of Markov processes. A Markov process is a random function on two (kinds of) variables, X and t, where X represents the "state" and t the "index". For our purpose, t refers to time and is a nonnegative real number, while $X(t)$ is the state of the system under consideration at time t and may well be a vector of variables. It could be the exchange rate between two currencies, the price of a particular stock, a vector of rates of return on different securities in an investment portfolio, etc.

A defining characteristic of a Markov process is that the random increments to X are independent over time. In other words, the probability of going from state X_0 at time t_0 to another state X_1 at a later time t_1 is independent of what state the system has been in at any time before t_0. When $X(t)$ refers to the market price in a financial market, the Markov property implies ("weak form") market efficiency. Once the current price is known, there is no further information about future price movements that can be gained from consideration of prices in earlier periods.

The Binomial model of asset prices we have been examining is a good example of a Markov process operating in discrete time. That is, the time variable t takes on only integer values and the state of the system is only defined at those points. By contrast, a diffusion process is continuous in time, with randomness impinging upon the system constantly.

Diffusions are one of two fundamental classes of continuous time Markov processes, the other being Poisson processes. In a diffusion, small changes in state occur continually. During a short interval of time only local movements can take place, but there is some change no matter how infinitesimal the time interval. The prototype physical analog to a diffusion is the Brownian motion of a tiny particle suspended in a fluid. Under constant bombardment by molecules of the fluid, its position continually changes by small random amounts. A graph of the path of such a particle would show that it followed a continuous, though erratic, trajectory.

Poisson or "jump" processes, on the other hand, are characterized by discontinuous changes of state (jumps) that occur only at random intervals. At a given instant there is either no change or a jump. Such a process could be used to describe the way the prime rate of interest moves over time, or any similar system of administered prices, such as fixed exchange rates. The Markov property is reflected in the fact that the probability of a jump occurring within the next time interval of a given length is independent of how long it has been since the previous jump. While some work has been done on option valuation for Poisson processes,[*] primary interest has focused on the diffusion model. A major reason for this is that jumps in the price of the underlying asset make riskless arbitrage impossible (except for isolated special cases), so the standard procedure for deriving an option model does not work.

Let us see how a diffusion process arises as the limiting case of a discrete time stochastic process when the time interval between observations goes to zero. Consider a discrete time model of a variable X that has in each period an expected change μ and a random increment $\xi(t)$ that has variance σ^2. We can write the equation describing X as

$$X(t + 1) = X(t) + \mu + \sigma \xi(t + 1)$$

---

[*] See, for example, J. Cox and S. Ross (January/March 1976), "The Valuation of Options for Alternative Stochastic Processes," *Journal of Financial Economics*, pp. 145–166.

with $E[\xi] = 0$

$\text{Var}[\xi] = 1$

$\xi(t)$ and $\xi(s)$ independent for $t \neq s$,

or,

$$X(t + 1) - X(t) = \Delta X(t) = \mu + \sigma \xi(t + 1). \qquad (3\text{A}.1)$$

The random increment ξ may be drawn from any probability distribution with a finite variance. The binomial would be one possibility.

Now let us change the focus a little, and consider a process like (3A.1) in which the same kind of price changes are taking place but at shorter intervals, so that the change over one period is actually the cumulative result of n small changes occurring regularly at subintervals of length $h = 1/n$ throughout the period. Let the change over the ith subperiod be given by

$$X(t + ih) - X(t + (i - 1)h) = \mu h + \sigma \varepsilon(i)\sqrt{h} \qquad (3\text{A}.2)$$

where $E[\varepsilon] = 0$

$\text{Var}[\varepsilon] = 1$

$\varepsilon(i)$ and $\varepsilon(j)$ are independent for $i \neq j$.

The mean change over one subinterval is μh and the variance is $\sigma^2 h$.

The change in X over the whole period is the sum of the changes in every subinterval.

$$X(t + 1) - X(t) = \sum_{i=1}^{n} \{X(t + ih) - X(t + (i-1)h)\} \qquad (3\text{A}.3)$$

$$= \sum_{i} (\mu h + \sigma \varepsilon(i)\sqrt{h})$$

$$= \mu + \sigma\sqrt{h} \sum_{i} \varepsilon(i).$$

The one period mean and variance of this new process are

$$E[X(t + 1) - X(t)] = E[\mu + \sigma\sqrt{h} \sum_{i} \varepsilon(i))] \qquad (3\text{A}.4)$$

$$= \mu + \sigma\sqrt{h} \sum_{i} E[\varepsilon(i)]$$

$$= \mu$$

$$\text{Var}[\, X(t+1) - X(t)\,] \tag{3A.5}$$

$$= (\sigma\sqrt{h}\,)^2 \,\text{Var}[\, \sum_i \varepsilon\,(i)\,]$$

$$= \sigma^2 h \,\{\, \sum_i \text{Var}[\varepsilon\,(i)] \;+\; \sum_i \sum_{j \neq i} \text{Cov}[\varepsilon\,(i),\, \varepsilon\,(j)]\}$$

$$= \sigma^2 h \,(\, n + 0\,)$$

$$= \sigma^2$$

Thus the mean and variance per unit time of the new process remain the same as for the old even though the new one has random disturbances occurring much more frequently. The one difference is that in the new process, the change in X over one period is a sum of n identically and independently distributed random variables with finite variance. By the Central Limit Theorem, as n goes to infinity, $X(t+1) - X(t)$ will be normally distributed regardless of the actual distribution of the ε's.

Now imagine the result as the number of subintervals goes to infinity. In the limit, we will have a process whose mean and variance per unit time will still be μ and σ^2 respectively, but for which the stochastic element will be in the form of infinitesimal time independent random shocks occurring at every instant of time: a Markov process in continuous time.

This limiting process is known as a stochastic differential equation, and is written formally as

$$dX = \mu\, dt + \sigma\, dz. \tag{3A.6}$$

where $dz = z\sqrt{dt}$ and z is a time independent standard normal random variable with mean 0 and variance 1.

Notice that dX is made up of a deterministic part $\mu\, dt$ and a stochastic part $\sigma\, dz$. The basic diffusion process denoted by dz is called a Wiener process.

The constants μ and σ are known as the instantaneous mean and standard deviation. More general processes in which the instantaneous mean and variance are allowed to depend on the current state and time are known as Itô processes and can be written as in (3A.7).

$$dX = \mu\,(X, t)\, dt + \sigma\,(X, t)\, dz. \tag{3A.7}$$

A major problem that arises in dealing with discrete time models is that while a period model such as equation (3A.1) can be reasonably tractable by itself, it is normally very difficult to use it to analyze functions of X, and it becomes worse when X is a vector of random variables. One feature that makes diffusion processes particularly useful in financial modeling is that any smooth function of Itô process variables also follows an Itô process.

3A.2 Itô's Lemma

Itô's Lemma, also known as the Fundamental Theorem of the Stochastic Calculus, is the basic tool for manipulating diffusion processes. It provides the way to determine the stochastic differential equation for a function of diffusion process variables.

If X follows an Itô process and $Y = F(X, t)$, where $F(.)$ is a twice differentiable function, then

Itô's Lemma: $$dY = \frac{\partial F}{\partial X} dX + \frac{\partial F}{\partial t} dt + \frac{1}{2} \frac{\partial^2 F}{\partial X^2} (dX)^2 \qquad (3A.8)$$

where dX is the stochastic differential of X as in (3A.7) and calculation of the term $(dX)^2$ is governed by the multiplication rules

$$(dt)^2 = 0$$

$$(dt)(dz) = 0$$

$$(dz)^2 = 1 \, dt .$$

If X is a vector of Itô process variables, Itô's Lemma becomes

$$dY = \sum_i \frac{\partial F}{\partial X_i} dX_i + \frac{\partial F}{\partial t} dt + \frac{1}{2} \sum_i \sum_j \frac{\partial^2 F}{\partial X_i \partial X_j} dX_i \, dX_j \qquad (3A.9)$$

with the addition to the multiplication rules stated above:

$$(dz_i)(dz_j) = \rho_{ij} \, dt$$

where ρ_{ij} is the instantaneous correlation coefficient between dz_i and dz_j.

Derivation of Itô's Lemma

It is instructive to see how Itô's Lemma and its associated multiplication rules arise from the peculiar nature of stochastic differential equations. Consider solving for $dY = Y(t + dt) - Y(t)$ by expanding in Taylor's series.

$$Y(t + dt) = F(X + dX, t + dt)$$

$$= F(X, t) + \frac{\partial F}{\partial X} \, dX + \frac{\partial F}{\partial t} \, dt + \frac{1}{2} \frac{\partial^2 F}{\partial X^2} \, (dX)^2$$

$$+ \frac{1}{2} \frac{\partial^2 F}{\partial t^2} \, (dt)^2 + \frac{\partial^2 F}{\partial X \, \partial t} \, (dX)\,(dt) + R_3$$

where R_3 is a term involving higher powers of dX and dt. For ease of exposition, let us assume dX has a constant μ and σ, as in (3A.6).

The term dt, of course, refers to an infinitesimal change in the time index. Any terms involving a finite quantity multiplied by a power of dt greater than 1, such as $(dt)^2$ or $(dt)^{3/2}$ are of a smaller order of magnitude than dt so that they are effectively zero. In the above Taylor expansion, R_3 and the two previous terms are therefore negligible. Dropping them and moving $F(X, t)$ to the left hand side gives dY on the left and we have Ito's Lemma, equation (3A.8).

The next question is how to evaluate $(dX)^2$. Squaring the expression for dX gives

$$(dX)^2 = \mu^2 \, (dt)^2 + 2\mu\sigma \, (dt)(dz) + \sigma^2 \, (dz)^2$$

$$= \mu^2 \, (dt)^2 + 2\mu\sigma\xi (dt)^{3/2} + \sigma^2 \, \xi^2 \, dt.$$

By the above reasoning, the first two terms are zero, giving us the first two multiplication rules. The last term is more interesting. It is of order dt, so it will not be negligible, and since it involves ξ^2, the square of a standard normal variable, it is apparently stochastic. But, consider its expected value and variance.

$$E\ [(dX)^2] =\ E\ [0 + 0 + \sigma^2\ \xi^2\ dt]$$

$$=\ \sigma^2\ dt\ E\ [\xi^2]$$

$$=\ \sigma^2\ dt$$

$$\text{Var}[(dX)^2]\ =\ \text{Var}[\ \sigma^2\ \xi^2\ dt]$$

$$=\ \sigma^4\ (dt)^2\ \text{Var}[\xi^2]$$

This shows that the variance of $(dX)^2$ is of the order $(dt)^2$ which is again effectively zero. Thus $(dX)^2$ is actually nonstochastic and equal to $\sigma^2\ dt$ with probability 1. This gives us the third multiplication rule.

It is the continuous nature of diffusion processes that makes the great simplification in Itô's Lemma possible. In discrete time we would not be able to ignore the higher order terms in the Taylor expansion nor the higher moments of the stochastic part of dX.

Using Itô's Lemma

Itô's Lemma is an extremely powerful tool for manipulating models involving diffusion processes, since it allows one to write out the stochastic differential equation for any well behaved function of Itô process variables very simply.

As an example, consider $Y = e^X$, where X follows the diffusion process given in equation (3A.6). This function is the one most frequently used to model security returns in financial markets. By Itô's Lemma,

$$dY\ =\ e^X\ dX + (e^X /\ 2)(dX)^2$$

$$=\ e^X\ (\mu\ dt\ +\ \sigma\ dz\ +\ 1/2\ \sigma^2\ (dz)^2\ )$$

$$=\ Y\ ((\mu + \sigma^2 /\ 2)\ dt\ +\ \sigma\ dz\ )$$

or,

$$dY\ /\ Y\ =\ (\mu\ +\ \sigma^2 /\ 2)\ dt\ +\ \sigma\ dz. \qquad (3A.10)$$

By this equation, the continuously compounded rate of change of Y (i.e., the rate of return, if Y is an asset price) follows a diffusion process with mean $\mu_s = (\mu + \sigma^2/2)$ and variance σ^2 per unit time.

Stochastic differential equations are similar to ordinary differential equations but they have some important differences. For example, they are continuous (meaning you can trace out the path of X without lifting the pen from the paper) but they are not differentiable. (The fact that the dz term is of the order $\sqrt{dt}$ makes the sample path too choppy.) This latter property makes it necessary to define a special kind of stochastic integral in order to describe the time path of X. This will allow us to calculate the probability distribution of X at a time t_2, given where it is at an earlier time t_1.

The Itô integral satisfies the relation

$$\int_0^t dz = \xi\sqrt{t} \tag{3A.11}$$

where ξ is a normally distributed random variable with mean zero and variance 1.

Stochastic integration of diffusion processes can be accomplished by applying Itô's Lemma and (3A.11). For the process of (3A.6), we have

$$X(t) = X(0) + \int_0^t \mu\, dt + \int_0^t \sigma\, dz$$

$$X(t) = X(0) + \mu t + \sigma\xi\sqrt{t} \tag{3A.12}$$

$X(t)$ will be normally distributed with mean $X(0) + \mu t$ and variance $\sigma^2 t$.

3A.3 Deriving the Fundamental Partial Differential Equation

We now have the mathematical tools to derive option pricing equations. There are several approaches to this. We will first describe how Black and Scholes obtained their solution by solving a partial differential equation. We will then, in the next section, carry out a simpler derivation based on the Risk Neutral Valuation Principle. This method has the advantage that it can be applied in a comparable fashion to other option problems without the necessity of dealing with partial differential equations.

The price of the underlying asset is assumed to follow the diffusion process

$$dS / S = \mu_s \, dt + \sigma \, dz. \qquad (3A.13)$$

The similarity to (3A.10) is apparent.

Black and Scholes used (3A.13) and Itô's Lemma to write the stochastic differential equation for the call value.

$$dC = \frac{\partial C}{\partial S} \, dS + \frac{\partial C}{\partial t} \, dt + \frac{1}{2} \, S^2 \sigma^2 \frac{\partial^2 C}{\partial S^2} \, dt \qquad (3A.14)$$

The delta of the call is given by the partial derivative of the call function with respect to the stock price, so a hedged portfolio will be long one call and short $\partial C / \partial S$ shares of stock. Its value is

$$V = C - \frac{\partial C}{\partial S} \, S$$

The change in value of the hedge portfolio is given by

$$dV = dC - \frac{\partial C}{\partial S} \, dS$$

and, substituting from (3A.14) the two terms involving the random change in the stock price, dS, cancel out, leaving

$$dV = \left(\frac{\partial C}{\partial t} + \frac{1}{2} \, S^2 \sigma^2 \frac{\partial^2 C}{\partial S^2} \right) dt \qquad (3A.15)$$

With the terms involving dz cancelling out, the hedge portfolio is riskless over the next instant, and since every riskless investment should earn the same risk free rate of interest r per unit time, we must also have

$$dV = r \, V \, dt$$

Combining this with (3A.15) leads to the partial differential equation shown in (3A.16). This is sometimes called the Fundamental Partial Differential Equation of Contingent Claims Pricing.

Fundamental P.D.E. of Contingent Claims Pricing

$$rC - rS \ \frac{\partial C}{\partial S} - \frac{\partial C}{\partial t} - \frac{1}{2} \ \sigma^2 S^2 \ \frac{\partial^2 C}{\partial S^2} \ = 0 \qquad (3A.16)$$

The solution to (3A.16) is a function $C(S, t)$ that gives the value for the option for each date t and stock price S. In order to solve it, we need three boundary conditions. We must specify what happens to the option value at option expiration, what happens before that time when S becomes arbitrarily low, and what happens when S becomes arbitrarily high.

For a European call option, the boundary conditions are:

1. The call value at expiration is Max(0, $S_T - X$).
2. At $S_t = 0$, the call value is 0.
3. As S_t goes to infinity, $\partial C / \partial S$ goes to 1.

Solving (3A.16) subject to these three boundary conditions yields the Black-Scholes equation.

The great importance of the Fundamental Partial Differential Equation is that it must hold for *all* contingent claims. Looking back at equation (3A.14), we see that nothing that went into its derivation restricted it to apply only to a call option: it could relate to any contingent security whose value depended on the underlying asset and time. This would include European and American calls and puts, futures and forward contracts, and any other kind of derivative security. What makes the equation for a call different from one for a put is the set of boundary conditions associated with it.

One of the major uses for the Fundamental P.D.E. is in deriving approximate solutions for option valuation problems. Chapter 14 describes several such techniques, based on approximating (3A.16) by a second order difference equation.

3A.4 Deriving the Black-Scholes Equation under Risk Neutrality

Equation (3A.16) does not depend on the expected return on the stock μ_S, or any parameters involving investors' risk aversion or possible risk premia on risky assets. The solution will therefore be the same regardless of risk preferences. So if a solution can be obtained for a particular degree of risk aversion, it will hold in every case. The most convenient assumption is that investors are risk neutral, and the principle that the option value obtained under risk neutrality holds in general has come to be known as the Risk Neutral Valuation principle.

Since $dS / S = d(\ln(S))$, equation (3A.13) implies that the logarithm of S_T is normally distributed with

$$E[\ln(S_T)] = (\ln(S_0) + \mu_S T)$$

$$\mathrm{Var}[\ln(S_T)] = \sigma^2 T.$$

S_T is therefore lognormal with

$$E[S_T] = S_0 \exp(\mu_S T + \sigma^2 T / 2),$$

where $\exp(x)$ denotes the exponential function, e^x. The extra term $\sigma^2 T / 2$ enters because of the nonlinearity in the log and exponential functions.

In a risk neutral world, the expected return on every asset must be the same, and equal to the risk free rate. The expected return on the stock is therefore r per unit time, so

$$E[S_T / S_0] = \exp(rT),$$

and by substitution,

$$\mu_S = r - \sigma^2 / 2.$$

Proceeding to the call option, its value in a risk neutral world is its expected payoff at expiration, discounted at the risk free interest rate, or

$$C = e^{-rT} E[\mathrm{Max}(0, S_T - X)]$$

$$C = e^{-rT} \int_X^\infty (S_T - X)\, \ell(S_T)\, dS_T \qquad (3\mathrm{A}.17)$$

where $\ell(S_T)$ is the lognormal probability density function.[*]

---

[*]The lognormal density function for a variable x is given by

$$\ell(x) = \frac{1}{x}\, \frac{1}{\sigma\sqrt{2\pi}}\, \exp\left(\frac{-(\ln(x) - E[\ln(x)])^2}{2\sigma^2}\right)$$

We are going to solve this integral equation in two parts, beginning with the term involving the strike price X. First let us simplify the notation by defining

$$L = \ln(S_T), \quad \bar{L} = E[\ln(S_T)], \quad \text{and } v = \sigma\sqrt{T}.$$

L is the log of the stochastic terminal stock price, and $\bar{L}$ and v are the expected value and standard deviation of L, respectively.

The second term can then be written,

$$e^{-rT} X \int_X^\infty \ell(S_T) \, dS_T$$

$$= e^{-rT} X \int_X^\infty \frac{1}{S_T} \frac{1}{v\sqrt{2\pi}} \exp\left(-\frac{1}{2v^2}(L - \bar{L})^2\right) dS_T \tag{3A.18}$$

Now define a new variable $Y = (L - \bar{L})/v$. Y is now a standardized normal variable.

We have $dY = dS_T/(S_T v)$ and $Y = (\ln(X) - \bar{L})/v$ when $S_T = X$.

Now writing (3A.18) in terms of Y, we have

$$e^{-rT} X \int_{\frac{\ln(X) - \bar{L}}{v}}^\infty \frac{1}{\sqrt{2\pi}} \exp\left(-\frac{Y^2}{2}\right) dY$$

The integrand is now in the form of a standardized normal density function in which we are integrating over the upper tail of the distribution, so it can be written

$$e^{-rT} X \left(1 - N\left[\frac{\ln(X) - \bar{L}}{v}\right]\right)$$

and finally, since $1 - N[z] = N[-z]$, substituting back for $\bar{L}$ and v, we have the second term in the Black-Scholes equation,

$$e^{-rT} X N \left[\frac{\bar{L} - \ln(X)}{v}\right]$$

$$= e^{-rT} X N \left[\frac{\ln(S_0/X) + (r - \sigma^2/2)T}{\sigma\sqrt{T}}\right]$$

Now let us work on the first term of (3A.17). First we rewrite the expression, using the fact that $z = \exp(\ln(z))$, and then we expand the lognormal density function.

$$e^{-rT} \int_X^\infty S_T \ \ell(S_T) \ dS_T$$

$$= S_0 \exp(-\ln(S_0)) \ e^{-rT} \int_X^\infty \exp(\ln(S_T)) \ \ell(S_T) \ dS_T \qquad (3A.19)$$

$$= S_0 \int_X^\infty \frac{1}{S_T} \ \frac{1}{v\sqrt{2\pi}} \ \exp(\ln(S_T) - \ln(S_0) - rT) \exp\left(\frac{-(L-\bar{L})^2}{2v^2}\right) dS_T$$

Using the definitions for L, $\bar{L}$, and v, the exponent in the first exponential expression of (3A.19) is equal to

$$L - \left(\bar{L} + \frac{v^2}{2}\right)$$

Completing the square gives us the sum of the two exponents as

$$-\frac{1}{2v^2}\left(L - \left(\bar{L} + v^2\right)\right)^2$$

The integral can now be written as

$$S_0 \int_X^\infty \frac{1}{S_T} \ \frac{1}{v\sqrt{2\pi}} \ \exp\left(-\frac{(L - [\bar{L} + v^2])^2}{2v^2}\right) dS_T \qquad (3A.20)$$

Once again, we want to turn this expression into a standard normal density function, which we do by defining

$$w = \frac{L - (\bar{L} + v^2)}{v}.$$

We have

$$dw = \frac{d\,S_T}{v\,S_T}$$

Substituting into (3A.20) makes the integral now

$$S_0 \int_{\frac{\ln(x) - (\bar{L} + v^2)}{v}}^{\infty} \frac{1}{\sqrt{2\pi}} \exp\left(-\frac{w^2}{2}\right) dw \qquad (3A.21)$$

As we wanted, (3A.21) is the integral over the upper tail of a standard normal density function. Substituting out the variables gives

$$S_0 \left(1 - N\left[\frac{\ln(X) - (\bar{L} + v^2)}{v}\right]\right)$$

$$= S_0 N\left[\frac{\ln(S_0/X) + (r + \sigma^2/2) T}{\sigma \sqrt{T}}\right]$$

Finally, combining the two expressions we have developed from equation (3A.17) results in the Black-Scholes equation.

$$C = S_0 N[D] - X e^{-rT} N[D - \sigma \sqrt{T}] \qquad (3A.22)$$

where

$$D = \frac{\ln(S_0/X) + (r + \sigma^2/2) T}{\sigma \sqrt{T}}$$

One might justifiably feel that this "simplified" derivation of the Black-Scholes equation is pretty challenging. That is the nature of option problems: deriving closed form solutions is challenging at best, and in most realistic cases impossible. However, for minor variations on the basic model, such as an option on a stock with a continuous dividend payout, it is not hard to see how the above derivation should be modified to arrive at the correct solution. More importantly, the principle of Risk Neutral Valuation is extremely useful in deriving approximate solutions to option problems using numerical methods. Later chapters will illustrate this, and Chapter 14 will examine several approaches in detail.

APPENDIX B TO CHAPTER 3

Formula to Evaluate the Cumulative Normal Distribution

The cumulative normal function has to be approximated. There are several formulas that work. This one is very accurate.

We want $N[z]$, for some number z. That is, the probability of getting a value less than or equal to z. The probability of a number *greater* than z is $(1 - N[z])$, which is also equal to $N[-z]$.

First, define

$$w = +1 \text{ if } z \text{ is positive or zero}$$
$$w = -1 \text{ if } z \text{ is negative.}$$

$$y = \frac{1}{1 + 0.231649 * w * z}$$

where * denotes multiplication.

Also, to prevent computer overflow, it is good to limit the size of z. For example, if $z < -6$, set $z = -6$, and if $z > 6$, set $z = 6$.

Next define the following constants:

$$C1 = 2.506628$$
$$C2 = 0.3193815$$
$$C3 = -0.3565638$$
$$C4 = 1.7814779$$
$$C5 = -1.821256$$
$$C6 = 1.3302744$$

Then,

$$N[z] = .5 + w * (.5 - (e^{-z*z/2}/C1) * (y * (C2 + y *$$

$$(C3 + y * (C4 + y * (C5 + y * C6))))))$$

References

Classic Articles

Bachelier, L. (1900). Théorie de la Speculation. Reprinted in Cootner (ed.), (1967), *The random character of stock market prices.* Cambridge, Massachusetts: M.I.T. Press, 17–78.

Black, F. (January-March 1976). The pricing of commodity contracts. *Journal of Financial Economics, 3*, 167–79.

Black, F., and Scholes, M. (May 1972). The valuation of option contracts and a test of market efficiency. *Journal of Finance, 27*, 399–418.

Black, F., and Scholes, M. (May-June 1973). The pricing of options and corporate liabilities. *Journal of Political Economy, 81*, 637–59.

Cox, J., Ross, S., and Rubinstein, M. (September 1979). Option pricing: A simplified approach. *Journal of Financial Economics, 7*, 229–63.

Margrabe, W. (March 1978). The value of an option to exchange one asset for another. *Journal of Finance, 33*, 177–86.

Merton, R. (spring 1973). Theory of rational option pricing. *Bell Journal of Economics and Management Science, 4*, 141–83.

Smith, C. (January-March 1976). Option pricing: A review. *Journal of Financial Economics, 3*, 3–51.

Textbooks

Cox, J., and Rubinstein, M. (1985). *Options markets.* Englewood Cliffs, New Jersey: Prentice-Hall.

Hull, J. (1989). *Options, futures, and other derivative securities.* Englewood Cliffs, New Jersey: Prentice-Hall.

Ritchken, P. (1987). *Options theory, strategy, and applications.* Glenview, Illinois: Scott, Foresman and Co.

CHAPTER 4

THE EARLY EXERCISE FEATURE OF AMERICAN OPTIONS

Marti G. Subrahmanyam [*]

4.1 AMERICAN VERSUS EUROPEAN OPTIONS

A European-style (or European) option can be exercised only on its expiration date. In contrast, an American-style (or American) option can be exercised at any time before its expiration date, at the option of the buyer. This basic difference has implications for the payoffs from the two types of options, and hence, their valuation and hedging. The simplest way to illustrate the differences between the two types of options is by reference to the boundary conditions derived in Chapter 2.

In the case of American call options, arbitrage considerations imply that, at all times, the price must be at least as large as the difference between the stock price and the exercise price, or zero, whichever is larger:

$$C \geq \text{Max} [S - X, O] \tag{4.1}$$

The reason is that, otherwise, the buyer of the call option could realize an

*Research Professor of Finance and Economics, Leonard N. Stern School of Business, New York University.

arbitrage profit by exercising it immediately. In contrast, for a European call option, there is no similar arbitrage-based restriction prior to the expiration date based on *immediate* exercise: the restriction is based on the weaker condition of stochastic dominance, as discussed in Chapter 2. Of course, in both cases, the value of the call option on the expiration date equals its immediate exercise value. However, on any other date, due to the additional privilege of premature exercise available to the holder of an American call option, it must be worth at least as much as, and sometimes more than, a comparable European call option.

Similar considerations apply in the case of American versus European put options. For put options, arbitrage considerations imply that American options must be worth at least as much as the difference between the exercise price and the stock price or zero, whichever is larger:

$$P \ \geq \ \text{Max} \ [\ X - S, O \ ] \hspace{3cm} (4.2)$$

Again, there is no comparable arbitrage condition for European put options based on immediate exercise. However, the value of an American put option must be at least as large as that of a European put option on the same terms, due to the additional privilege of early exercise available to the holder of an American option.

American call options

Under what conditions does it pay to exercise an American option early? Consider the case of an American call option some time prior to its expiration date. Assume that the underlying asset, say a stock, does not pay any dividends during the period between the current date and the expiration date. The immediate exercise value of the option is given by the right-hand side of equation (4.1) above. Since there can be a benefit from early exercise only if the option is in-the-money, i.e., if $S > X$, let us explore this case. On any date prior to the expiration date, the holder of the option has three choices. She can exercise the option, do nothing, i.e., wait until the expiration date of the option, or, sell the option.

If she exercises the option immediately, she receives the stock which sells for a price, S, by paying the exercise price X. If she waits until the expiration date, she will receive the stock which may be selling at a different price, by paying the same amount X, but later on. However, if the price of the stock declines below X in the meantime, she has the choice of not exercising the option. The third alternative of selling the option would yield the holder the market value of the option. As such, this choice is not directly related to the exercise decision.

The price of the American call option, C, has to be compared with the exercise value, $S - X$, the difference between the price of the underlying asset, S, and the exercise price, X, to determine the benefits of premature exercise. However, since the exercise decision can be postponed until the expiration date, this condition can be further tightened using the principle of portfolio dominance discussed in Chapter 2 [see equation (2.9)]. Using this principle, we can specify that the value of the American call option, C, has to be at least as large as the difference between the price of the underlying asset, S, and the present value of the exercise price, X. In other words,

$$C \geq S - PV \text{ of } X \tag{4.3a}$$

or

$$C = S - PV \text{ of } X + IV(C) \tag{4.3b}$$

where $IV(C)$ is the additional amount a buyer is willing to pay for the *insurance value* of the call option, i.e., the protection it offers on the downside while maintaining the upside potential. Rewriting equation (4.3b) by adding and subtracting X leads to:

$$C = S - X + X - PV \text{ of } X + IV(C) \tag{4.4a}$$

or

$$\underbrace{C - (S - X)}_{\substack{\text{Loss due to} \\ \text{Early} \\ \text{Exercise}}} = \underbrace{(X - PV \text{ of } X)}_{\substack{\text{Time Value} \\ \text{of Money on} \\ \text{the Exercise} \\ \text{Price}}} + \underbrace{IV(C)}_{\substack{\text{Insurance} \\ \text{Value of the} \\ \text{Option}}} \tag{4.4b}$$

Note that both the terms on the right hand side of equation (4.4b), the time value of money on the exercise price and the insurance value of the option, are positive. Hence, the left hand side of the equation is also positive, i.e. the American call option is worth more than its immediate exercise value. This amount is lost if the option is exercised prematurely.

There are, therefore, two considerations that influence the decision to exercise the American call option early. One is the time value of money or the interest foregone by paying the exercise price prematurely, rather than waiting until the expiration date. The other is due to the fact that if the option is exercised early, the holder receives the stock immediately and loses the insurance value of the option. If the stock price increases between the premature exercise date and the expiration date of the option, she is no worse off on this account than if she waited until the expiration date to exercise the option. However, if the price decreases during this period to a level below X, she is worse off, since she is fully exposed to the decline. In contrast, if she had held on to the option, she need not exercise it on the expiration date if the price falls sufficiently. Hence, the maximum loss she would suffer is the price she paid for the call option.

Thus, by exercising the American call option prematurely, the holder of the option loses on two counts: the time value of money on the exercise price and the removal of the "insurance" protection obtained by holding the call option rather than the stock. Therefore, it does not pay to exercise an American call option early, if the underlying asset does not pay dividends. In other words, an American call option on an asset that does not pay dividends is treated the same way as a European call option—both of them are exercised at maturity if they happen to be in the money. This, in turn, implies that the value of an American call option will be the same as the value of a European call option on a non-dividend paying stock, since the additional flexibility offered by the former compared to the latter is never used and, hence, is of no value.

American put options
Similar considerations apply in the case of American put options. However, in this case, unlike the case of American call options, early exercise *may* be optimal. To see this, consider the case of an American put option on a stock that does not pay dividends. Suppose that the holder of the option also owns the underlying stock.[1] The decision regarding whether to exercise the option early or wait until the expiration date is dependent on the payoffs at the two points in time.[2] From the boundary conditions for an American put option, the payoff from exercising the option on the prior date is $(X - S)$, i.e., the difference between the striking price X, and the then prevailing stock

---

[1] This assumption does not affect the early exercise decision but makes the analysis more intuitive.
[2] The put option holder has a third choice—she can sell the option. As in the case of the call option, this alternative is not related to the exercise decision.

price, S, provided this difference is positive. [If this difference is negative, early exercise is irrational.] If the option is exercised on the expiration date, the payoff is the difference between the striking price and the stock price on the later date. Hence, between the current date and the expiration date, we can use the tighter boundary condition [analogous to equation (4.3a)] for the value of the put option, P:

$$P \geq PV \text{ of } X - S \qquad (4.5a)$$

As in the case of American call options, we can write equation (4.5a) as

$$P = PV \text{ of } X - S + IV(P) \qquad (4.5b)$$

where $IV(P)$ is the value of the insurance protection offered by the put option, i.e., a benefit if the price of the underlying asset moves down, with a cap on the loss if it moves up. Rewriting equation (4.5b) by adding and subtracting X yields:

$$P = X - S + PV \text{ of } X - X + IV(P) \qquad (4.6a)$$

or

$$\underbrace{P - (X - S)}_{\substack{Gain/Loss \\ due\ to \\ Early \\ Exercise}} = \underbrace{(PV \text{ of } X - X)}_{\substack{Time\ Value \\ of\ Money\ on \\ the\ Exercise \\ Price}} + \underbrace{IV(P)}_{\substack{Insurance \\ Value\ of\ the \\ Option}} \qquad (4.6b)$$

In this case also, the insurance value is always positive. However, the time value of money has the opposite sign, i.e., it is always negative except on the expiration date. Hence, the sign of the right hand side, and therefore of the left hand side of the equation, is ambiguous in the case of put options.

There are, again, two considerations influencing the decision whether to exercise the American put option prematurely. The first is the receipt of the exercise price, X, earlier rather than later which means that the option holder *earns* the time value of money on this amount. This is in contrast to the case of the American call option where the holder of the option *pays* the time value of money on the exercise price by exercising the option prematurely.

The other aspect of the decision is that if the put option is exercised prematurely, the holder of the put option receives the difference between the exercise price, X, and the prevailing market price, S. Since she already owns the stock, this amounts to saying that she sells the stock for the exercise price, X, rather than the prevailing market price, S. If she exercises the put option early and the stock price declines subsequently, the drop in the stock price is exactly offset by the increase in the payoff from the put. Thus, the holder of the option is unaffected by the early exercise decision. Hence, she is no worse off by exercising the option prematurely rather than on the expiration date. However, if the stock price increases later on, so that the put option finishes out-of-the-money, the put holder is worse off by exercising the option early, since she does not participate in the upward move in the stock price. In other words, she forgoes the benefit from the increase in the stock price that she would have obtained had she waited and decided not to exercise the put option. Hence, in this case, she is better off keeping the option alive rather than exercising it prematurely.

In the case of an American put option, therefore, there are two conflicting effects to consider in the decision regarding whether to exercise the option prematurely: the time value of money on the exercise price which is received if the option is exercised early; and, the flexibility or insurance protection which is lost by exercising the option early. Hence, in some cases, an American put option may be exercised prematurely if the first effect dominates the second. This may happen if the interest rate is relatively high and if the volatility is relatively low, meaning that the price of the underlying stock will not fluctuate much and hence, the flexibility provided by the option is not very valuable.

4.2   EARLY EXERCISE OF AMERICAN OPTIONS ON STOCKS

American Call Options

It was argued above that it is never optimal to exercise an American call option early if there are no payments such as dividends on the underlying asset. This conclusion has to be modified for American call options on dividend-paying stocks. As we shall see below, the case of a dividend-paying stock is the most obvious example of a general problem where the underlying asset loses value between the current date and the expiration date in a predictable manner.

We shall explain this with reference to a simple example. Consider an American call option on a dividend-paying stock. Suppose there is a single dividend payment between the current date and the expiration date of the call option. Suppose also that the ex-dividend date of the stock is just a few days prior to the expiration date of the option, and that the amount of the dividend payment is known with certainty. In addition to the two considerations discussed previously—the loss of the time value of money on the exercise price and the downward protection offered by owning a call option rather than the underlying stock—there is a third aspect introduced by the payment of dividends that affects the exercise decision. On the ex-dividend date, the price of the underlying stock falls since buyers on this day and after do not qualify for the current dividend.[3]

Suppose the American call option is "protected" against the payment of dividends, i.e., the exercise price of the option is marked down by the amount of the dividend. In this case, the arguments of the previous section continue to hold. The loss of the time value of money on the exercise price as well as the loss of protection on the downside dictate against early exercise of the American call option. Furthermore, since the exercise price of the option is adjusted following the payment of the dividend, the holder of the option does not lose any value from postponing exercise even though the share price declines, since she is protected against this eventuality by a downward adjustment in the exercise price.

Now, consider the case where the American call option is not protected against the dividend payment, which is the usual arrangement in options markets. In this case, no adjustment is made to the exercise price following the dividend payment. Since this reduces the benefit to the option holder if she decides to postpone exercise, there are now three factors to be reckoned with.

This can be illustrated by a modification of equations (4.3b) and (4.4b) to account for the dividend payment, D, on the underlying stock, against which the option is not protected:

$$C = S - PV \text{ of } X + IV(C) - PV \text{ of } D \qquad (4.7a)$$

or

---

[3]On average, the drop in the price of the stock around the ex-dividend day is somewhat less than the amount of the dividend. This has been documented in numerous empirical studies. See Michaely (1989) for a recent example.

$$C - (S - X) \quad = \quad (X - PV \text{ of } X) \quad + \quad IV(C) \quad - \quad PV \text{ of } D \quad (4.7b)$$

| Gain / Loss due to Early Exercise | Time Value of Money on the Exercise Price | Insurance Value of the Option | PV of Dividend Payment |

Note that the adjustment is for the *present value* of the dividend to be paid on the underlying asset later on. As before, the first two terms on the right hand side of the equation are positive, while the third term is negative. On the one hand, the loss of the time value of money on the exercise price and the loss of protection on the downside subsequent to exercise, bias the exercise decision in favor of postponement. On the other hand, the gain of the dividend which is received by the option holder only if the option is exercised prior to the ex-dividend date induces the option holder to exercise early. The combination of these factors *may* cause the option to be exercised early.

Before the ex-dividend day, looking forward, the likelihood of early exercise of an American call option is influenced by several factors, which also determine the value of a European call option:

1. The stock price as a proportion of the exercise price, S / X.
2. The riskless rate of interest, r.
3. The volatility of the underlying stock, σ.
4. The time remaining to the expiration date of the option, t, and
5. The amount of the dividend, D.

We shall now discuss each of these effects sequentially. The level of the stock price, S, in relation to the exercise price, X, is important because it determines the benefit from exercise. If this ratio, S / X, is small, i.e., if the option is only slightly in-the-money, it may not be worthwhile to exercise the option. Hence, the greater the ratio, other things remaining the same, the greater the chances of early exercise. The riskless rate of interest, r, determines the opportunity cost of paying the exercise price earlier rather than later. The greater the riskless rate, the smaller the net benefit from early exercise and hence, the smaller the likelihood of doing so. The volatility of the stock, σ, determines the fluctuations in the stock price and hence the value of the downside protection obtained by not exercising the option early. The greater the volatility, the larger the value of this protection and hence the smaller the chances of early exercise.

The time to expiration of the option, t, has two effects. In combination with the riskless rate, it determines the opportunity cost of early exercise in terms of the time value of money foregone. Also, since the square of the volatility parameter, σ^2, is specified per unit of time, the time to expiration is also an input in determining the amplitude of fluctuations in the stock price and hence the value of the downward protection offered by the option. For both effects, the larger the period of time left to the expiration date of the option, the smaller the benefit from exercising early, and hence, the less likely the early exercise of the option. The last effect to be considered is the size of the dividend payment, D. Since the motivation for early exercise of American call options stems from this variable, it is reasonable to expect that the larger this amount is, the greater will be the benefit from early exercise and hence, the likelihood of doing so. The direction of the impact of each of the parameters on the probability of exercise is summarized in Table 4–1:

TABLE 4–1
Effects of parameters influencing the probability of early exercise of American call options on dividend paying stocks

Parameter		Probability of Early Exercise
S	↑	↑
X	↑	↓
r	↑	↓
σ	↑	↓
t	↑	↓
D	↑	↑

One point regarding the early exercise of an American call option on dividend paying stocks deserves emphasis. Since it is the payment of the dividend (or rather, the qualification for the dividend payment) that triggers early exercise, it is never worthwhile to exercise the option except immediately prior to the ex-dividend date. On any other date, the same reasons for not exercising the option prematurely would apply as the case where no dividend payments are made. Hence, early exercise *may* take place for an

American call option on a dividend paying stock, but then only just prior to the ex-dividend date. Note that this reasoning applies to call options on *any* underlying asset that makes cash payments prior to the expiration date of the option, provided the option is not protected against this payout.

American Put Options

The same type of analysis can be extended to the case of American put options on stocks. Since the price of the underlying stock falls, on average, on the ex-dividend date, the payoff to a put option that is not payout-protected increases as a result of the dividend payment. Hence, with dividend payments, it may pay to wait for the ex-dividend date rather than exercise the put option prematurely. In general, other things remaining the same, the greater the dividend payments, the smaller the chance of premature exercise before the dividend payment. Equations (4.5b) and (4.6b) can be modified for the case of American put options, when there is a dividend payment on the underlying asset:

$$P = PV \text{ of } X - S + IV(P) + PV \text{ of } D \tag{4.8a}$$

$$\underbrace{P - (X - S)}_{\substack{Gain \,/\, Loss \\ due \text{ to } Early \\ Exercise}} = \underbrace{(PV \text{ of } X - X)}_{\substack{Negative \text{ of} \\ Time \text{ Value} \\ of \text{ Money on} \\ the \text{ Exercise} \\ Price}} + \underbrace{IV(P)}_{\substack{Insurance \\ Value \text{ of the} \\ Option}} + \underbrace{PV \text{ of } D}_{\substack{PV \text{ of} \\ Dividend \\ Payment}} \tag{4.8b}$$

In the case of put options, the first term on the right hand side is negative, while the second and third terms are positive. Hence the early exercise decision depends on the net effect of the three factors.

The sensitivity analysis of the probability of early exercise of an American put option is summarized in Table 4–2. As in the case of American call options, the probability of premature exercise depends on:

1. The stock price as a proportion of the exercise price S / X.
2. The riskless rate of interest, r.
3. The volatility of the underlying stock, σ.
4. The time remaining to expiration of the option, t, and
5. The amount of the dividend, D.

TABLE 4–2
**Effects of parameters influencing the probability of early
exercise of American put options on dividend paying stocks**

Parameter	Probability of Early Exercise
S ⬆	⬇
X ⬆	⬆
r ⬆	⬆
σ ⬆	⬇
t ⬆	?
D ⬆	⬇

Unlike the case of American call options, the greater the stock price, S, the smaller the chance of early exercise for American put options. Similarly, the higher the striking price, X, the larger the probability of early exercise. Hence, the probability of early exercise is inversely related to the ratio of S/X, and directly related to the depth in-the-money of the put option, X/S. Since the time value of money earned on the striking price is the variable that may trigger early exercise, the greater the riskless interest rate, r, the greater the time value of money, and hence, the higher the probability of early exercise. Since the volatility of the option, σ, is the main factor determining the benefit of protection from the option and hence, keeping the option alive, the greater the volatility, the smaller the probability of premature exercise.

As in the case of American call options, the time to expiration, t, has two effects, one due to the risk free rate, r, and the other through the volatility parameter, σ. Unlike the case of American call options, the two effects act in opposite directions for put options. The time value of money effect increases the chance of early exercise, while the volatility effect reduces it. Thus, the net effect is difficult to predict, in general, since it depends on the precise magnitudes involved. The last factor, the amount of the dividend, D, acts to reduce the chances of early exercise before the ex-dividend day, as argued earlier.

TABLE 4–3
Summary of early exercise decision for options on dividend paying stock

	Call Options	Put Options
Stock pays no dividends	• Never exercised early • $C_A = C_E$	• May be exercised early • Can occur any day • $P_A \geq P_E$
Stock pays dividends	• May be exercised early • Early exercise only just before stock goes ex-dividend • Dividends induce early exercise • $C_A \geq C_E$	• May be exercised early • Can occur any day • Dividends delay early exercise • $P_A \geq P_E$

A summary of the conclusions regarding early exercise of American options is presented in Table 4–3, where subscripts A and E refer to American and European options respectively. When the underlying asset pays no dividends, it is never rational to exercise an American call option early; however, it may pay to exercise an American put option at any time. This implies that, in the absence of dividends, American and European call options are equally valuable, while American put options are more valuable than their European counterparts. When dividends are paid on the underlying asset, early exercise may occur for both American puts and calls. Again, American puts may be exercised at any time, whereas American calls may be exercised only just prior to ex-dividend dates. It follows that American put and call options are worth at least as much as their European equivalents, for the case of a dividend-paying asset.

4.3   THE EARLY EXERCISE OF AMERICAN OPTIONS: SOME BINOMIAL EXAMPLES

We shall now discuss some numerical examples which make the intuitive arguments regarding early exercise discussed in the previous section more precise. These examples are all in the context of the binomial process for the underlying asset that was discussed in detail in Chapter 3. We shall analyze the early exercise decision for both American put and call options on stocks. We shall also discuss the early exercise decision for options on underlying assets other than stocks, the most important examples being futures contracts and foreign currencies. As we shall see, there is an analog of dividend payments in these cases that may trigger premature exercise for American options. We begin with an example involving American put options, for which, as we argued earlier, early exercise is more likely to occur for stocks that do not pay dividends.

American Put Option on a Stock

Suppose the underlying stock (which does not pay dividends during the period under discussion) follows a binomial process as described in Figure 4–1.

FIGURE 4–1
Binomial tree for S, the stock price

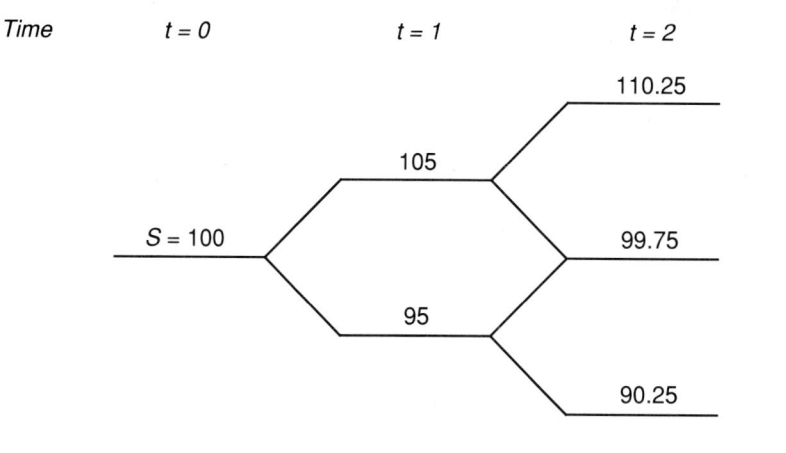

The stock price, S, is $100 at time 0 and may either go up to $100 \times 1.05 = \$105$, or go down to $100 \times 0.95 = \$95$ at time 1. In the next period, the price may go from $105 to either $105 \times 1.05 = \$110.25$ or $105 \times 0.95 = \$99.75$; and from $95 to either $95 \times 1.05 = \$99.75$ or $95 \times 0.95 = \$90.25$. The riskless rate of interest is 0.5% per period. Hence, in terms of the notation in Chapter 3, $u = 1.05$, $d = 0.95$ and $R = 1.005$.

Consider an American put option at an exercise price, X, of $100. (This option is at-the-money at time 0.) The payoffs from the put option, if exercised, at the various nodes in the binomial tree, are given by Max $[X - S, 0]$, and are represented in Figure 4–2. For example, the put option pays Max $[100 - 90.25, 0]$ or $9.75 in the lowest branch at time 2. In the upper branch at time 1, when the stock price is $105, the option is out-of-the-money, since Max $[100 - 105, 0] = 0$.

FIGURE 4–2
Binomial tree for Max[X – S, 0], the exercise value of the put option on the stock

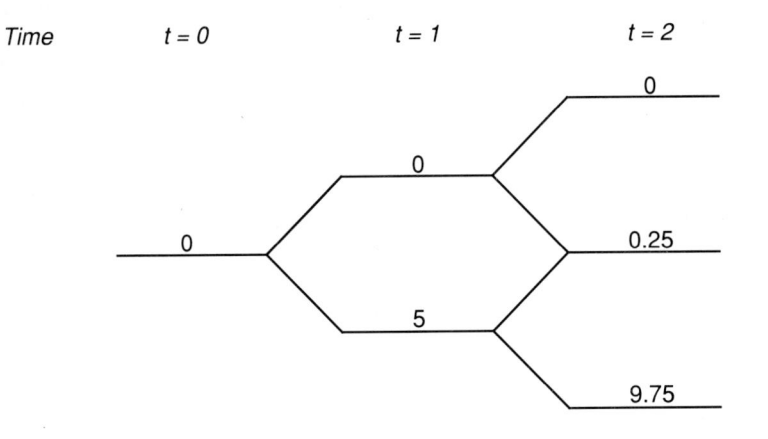

As noted in Chapter 3, these early exercise values are not necessarily the fair values of the put option except at time 2, when the option expires and, therefore, has to be exercised, if it is in-the-money. The fair value of the option on other dates can be computed from the value of a riskless hedge consisting of long positions in the put option and the underlying stock, which must earn the riskless rate of interest. This implies that the option can be valued by computing the expected value of the future cash flows using the "risk-neutral" probability, p, and discounting this cash flow at the riskless rate of interest. From equation (3.9) in Chapter 3, the "risk-neutral" probability, p, can be computed from:

$$p = \frac{R - d}{u - d} = \frac{1.005 - 0.95}{1.05 - 0.95} = 0.55 \qquad (4.9)$$

Hence, the values of the put option, if left unexercised at time 1 are shown in Figure 4–3. At the upper node at time 1, when $S = \$105$, (see panel A of Figure 4–3), the value of the put is given by:

$$P = \frac{1}{1.005} [0.55 \times 0 + 0.45 \times 0.25] = \$0.1119 \qquad (4.10)$$

At the lower node at time 1, (see panel B of Figure 4–3), the value of the put option when $S = \$95$ is :

$$P = \frac{1}{1.005} [0.55 \times 0.25 + 0.45 \times 9.75] = \$4.5025 \qquad (4.11)$$

Comparing the above values to the payoffs from the put by exercising it at time 1, it is clear that if $S = \$105$, the put is better left unexercised. Its fair value, $0.1119, is greater than the payoff if exercised, which is less than 0, since it is out-of-the-money (compare Figure 4–2 with panel A of Figure 4–3). On the other hand, if $S = \$95$ at time 1, it is rational to exercise the put option, since the immediate payoff, $5, exceeds its value if left unexercised, $4.5025 (compare Figure 4–2 with panel B of Figure 4–3).

The value of the put option at time 0 is based on a rational exercise strategy conditional on prices at time 1—exercise if the stock price falls to $95 and do not if the price goes up to $105. Hence, the value of the put at time 0 (see panel C of Figure 4–3) is given by:

$$P = \frac{1}{1.005} [0.55 \times 0.1119 + 0.45 \times 5] = \$2.3001 \qquad (4.12)$$

Since this value is greater than the payoff if the put is exercised at time 0, it does not pay to exercise the option then. The value of the put for the various outcomes of the stock price over the two periods is given in

FIGURE 4–3
Binomial tree for *P*, the value of the put option at different nodes

Panel A: Time t = 1; S = 105

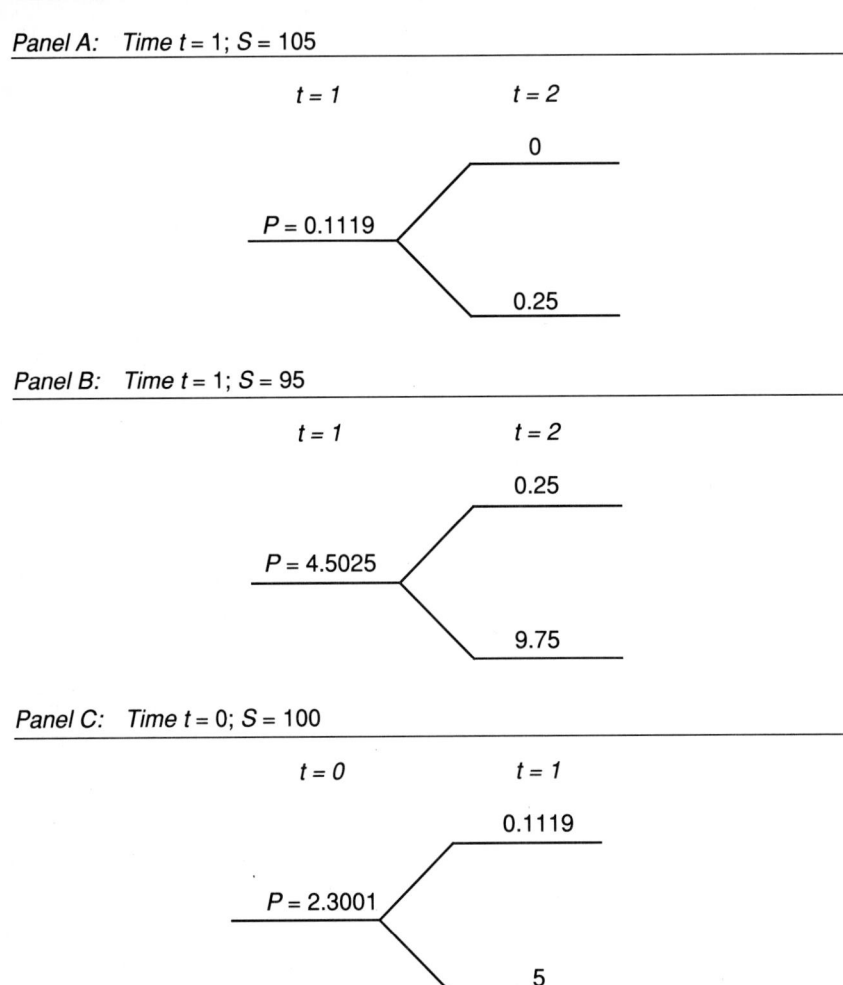

Figure 4–4. The value of the put, when it is optimal to exercise the option immediately, is marked.

The same type of analysis can be extended to cover more stages or periods by proceeding backwards from the expiration date. At each node, one should check to see if it is worthwhile to exercise the option prema-

FIGURE 4–4
Binomial tree for *P*, the value of the put option, and the optimal
exercise strategy

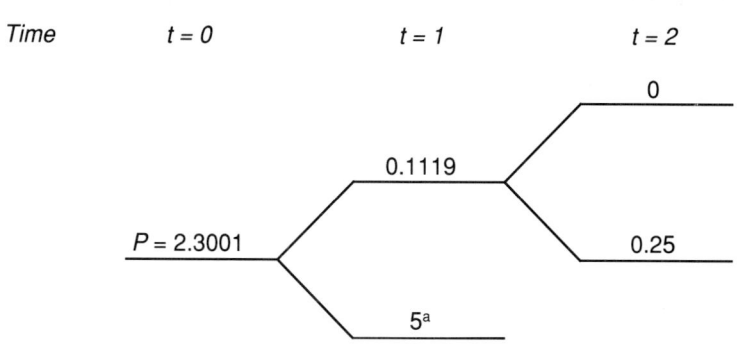

| Time | t = 0 | t = 1 | t = 2 |

ªIndicates optimal early exercise of the put

turely. This is done by comparing the fair value of the option with the immediate exercise value. The higher of the two values is used in computing the fair value one period earlier.

American Call Option on a Dividend-Paying Stock

Consider a stock that pays a dividend of $2 at time 1 and whose price follows a binomial process as in Figure 4–5. The process is similar to the previous case except that the (known) dividend of $2 reduces the stock price at time 1. Specifically, the stock price, *S*, is $100 at time 0 and may either go up to $105 ($u = 1.05$) or down to $95 ($d = 0.95$) at time 1. This is on a cum-dividend basis, indicated by *CD* in Figure 4–5. An instant later, still at time 1, the stock goes ex-dividend and pays a dividend per share (known in advance) of $2. In the upper branch, from a level of $105, cum-dividend (*CD*), the stock price drops by $2 to $103, ex-dividend (*XD*).[4] In the lower branch, from a level of $95, cum-dividend (*CD*), the prices fall by $2 to $93, ex-dividend (*XD*). Between time 1 and 2, the stock prices again move up

---

[4]This assumption is made in the interest of simplicity. As mentioned earlier, the drop in the price of a stock when it goes ex-dividend is usually less than the amount of the dividend. On average, the drop in the stock price on the ex-dividend day is about 80–85% of the dividend payment. The example can be easily modified to take into account a smaller drop in the stock price than the amount of the dividend.

FIGURE 4–5
Binomial tree for S, the stock price

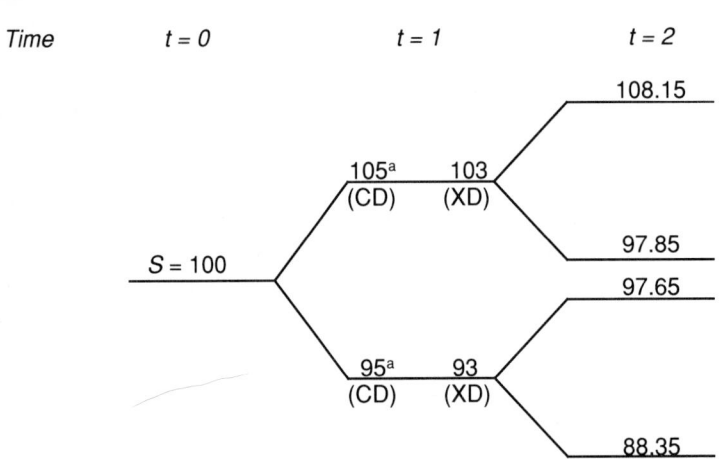

ᵃDividend per share is $2, paid in period 1

CD = Cum-dividend

XD = Ex-dividend

by a factor of 1.05 or down by 0.95 as in the previous stage. As in the previous example, suppose that the riskless rate is 0.5% per period.

Consider an American call option on the stock that is not protected against the payment of dividends. Suppose that the exercise price of the option, X, is $100 and the option expires at time 2. Hence, the option is at-the-money at time 0. The payoff to the holder of the call option, Max [$S - X, 0$], based on immediate exercise at different points in time for the various outcomes, is represented in Figure 4–6. Again, as in the case of the American put option, the exercise values are not the fair values of the option, except on the expiration date, time 2, when the option is exercised, if it is in-the-money. For example, the payoff from the call option in the top branch at time 2 is Max [$108.15 - 100, 0$] = $8.15. Similarly, the payoff in the bottom branch at time 2 is Max [$88.35 - 100, 0$] = 0, since the option is out-of-the-money. Note that in the upper branch at time 1, a payoff of $5 is obtained by exercising the call option just prior to the time the stock goes ex-dividend. However, after the stock goes ex-dividend, the payoff from exercise is only $3. In the other states, the call option is not worth exercising and its payoff is 0.

FIGURE 4–6
Binomial tree for Max[S – X, 0], the exercise value of the call option on the stock

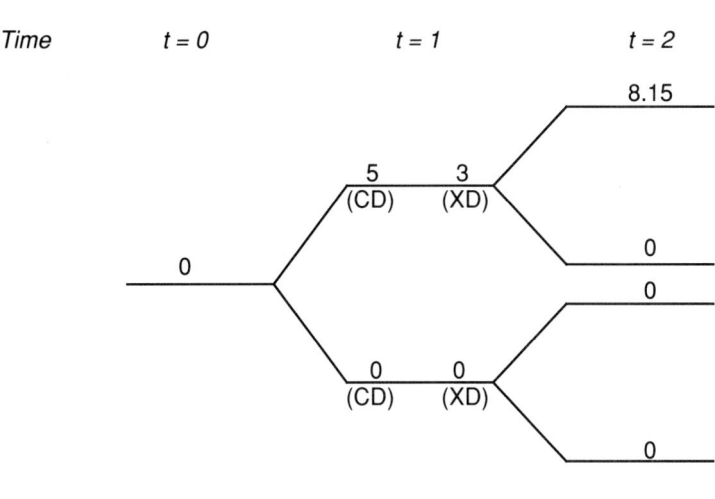

Time   t = 0   t = 1   t = 2

                                                                          8.15

                                     5   3
                                    (CD)   (XD)

                                                                          0
                    0   0

                                     0   0
                                    (CD)   (XD)

                                                                          0

CD = Cum-dividend
XD = Ex-dividend

The value of the call option can be computed by forming a riskless hedge consisting of a long position in the underlying stock and a short position in the call option. This riskless hedge must earn the riskless rate of interest. This is equivalent to valuing the call option by computing the expected value using the "risk-neutral" probabilities, p, and discounting this cash flow at the riskless rate of interest. In this case, p can be computed as before:

$$p = \frac{R - d}{u - d} = \frac{1.005 - 0.95}{1.05 - 0.95} = 0.55 \qquad (4.13)$$

Consider the upper branch of the tree at time 1 as shown in panel A of Figure 4–7. The value of the call option if left unexercised at time 1, after the stock goes ex-dividend, i.e., when $S = \$103$ (XD), can be computed as follows:

$$C = \frac{1}{1.005} [0.55 \times 8.15 + 0.45 \times 0] = \$4.4602 \qquad (4.14)$$

FIGURE 4–7
Binomial tree for *C*, the value of the call option at different nodes

Panel A: Time t = 1; S = 103 (XD)

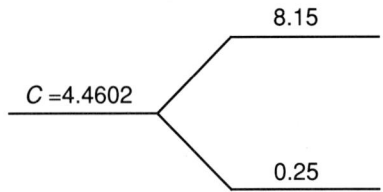

Time	t = 1	t = 2
		8.15
	C =4.4602	
		0.25

Panel B: Time t = 1; S = 93 (XD)

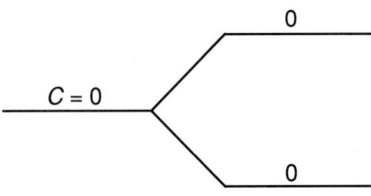

Time	t = 1	t = 2
		0
	C = 0	
		0

Panel C: Time t = 1; S = 105 (CD)

Time		t = 1
C = 5		C = 4.4602
(CD)		(XD)

Panel D: Time t = 1; S = 95 (CD)

Time		t = 1
C = 0		C = 0
(CD)		(XD)

FIGURE 4–7—continued

Panel E: Time t = 0

Time	*t = 0*	*t = 1* (CD)

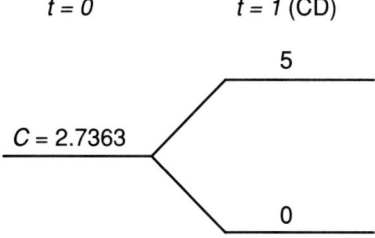

Similarly, in the lower branch, (see panel *B* of Figure 4–6), when S = $93 (*XD*),

$$C = \frac{1}{1.005} [0.55 \times 0 + 0.45 \times 0] = \$0 \qquad (4.15)$$

In the upper branch, at time 1, the fair value of the option, $4.4602, is less than its immediate exercise value an instant earlier, $5, when the stock is still trading cum-dividend, (compare panel *C* of Figure 4–7 with Figure 4–6). Hence, it is optimal to exercise the option. In the lower branch at time 1, the option is better left unexercised since it is out-of-the-money (see the lower branch of Figure 4–6). However, the value of the option at this node is zero, since there is no prospect of a payoff at time 2. Hence, the option may be abandoned at this point.

The value of the call option at time 0 is based on following a rational exercise strategy at time 1, i.e., exercising the option if the stock price increases and abandoning it if the price declines (see panel *E* of Figure 4–7). In other words, the value at time 0 is given by:

$$C = \frac{1}{1.005} [0.55 \times 5 + 0.45 \times 0] = \$2.7363 \qquad (4.16)$$

Since the fair value of the option at time 0 is greater than the immediate exercise value, 0, it does not pay to exercise the option at that time. The value of the call option and the optimal exercise strategy in the various states is given in Figure 4–8. In the diagram, the node where premature exercise is optimal is marked.

FIGURE 4–8
Binomial tree showing C, the value of the call option, and the optimal exercise strategy

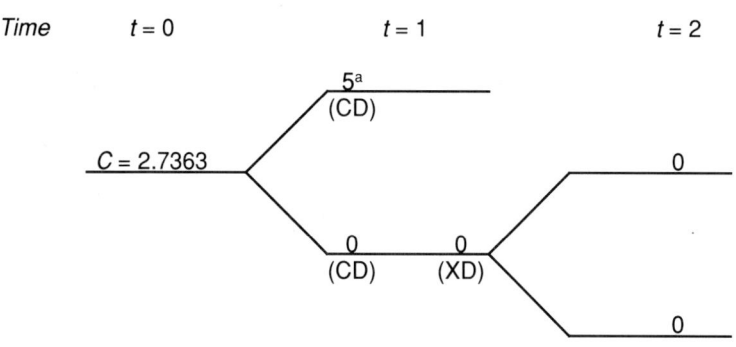

ᵃIndicates optimal early exercise of the call

As in the case of American put options, the same type of analysis can be extended to cover more stages in a backward iterative computation starting with the expiration date. However, there is one difference. In the case of American call options, the only reason to exercise the option prematurely is a reduction in the value of the underlying asset against which the option is not protected. In other words, it is optimal to exercise an American call option prematurely only if the reduction in the value of the underlying asset (or the cash flow foregone) is large enough to offset the benefits from postponing exercise—the time value of money on the exercise price and the insurance protection on the down side. Hence, it is sufficient to check whether this is so just prior to each ex-dividend date. In contrast, premature rational exercise of the American put option may take place *at any time,* and hence each stage has to be checked for early exercise.

The reason why it may pay to exercise an American call option (that is not payout-protected) prematurely, is the prospect of depreciation in the value of the underlying asset. In addition to the case of American call options on dividend-paying stocks, there are other cases of American call options on depreciating assets, where there is an opportunity cost of not exercising the option early. Two important examples of such options are options on futures contracts and options on foreign currency. In these cases, there is an opportunity cost of not exercising the option which is very similar to the dividend payment analyzed in the case of American options on stocks. In the case of options on futures, it is the decay in the futures price over time in relation to the underlying spot price due to the declining cost of carry. In the case of foreign exchange options, there is a potential depreciation (or appreciation) of the foreign currency, based on the interest rate differential between the foreign currency and the domestic currency. We now provide binomial examples of options on futures contracts and on foreign exchange.

American Call Option on a Futures Contract
Consider a spot asset (e.g., a commodity such as gold) whose price follows a binomial process as in Figure 4–9.

FIGURE 4–9
Binomial tree for *S*, the price of the spot asset

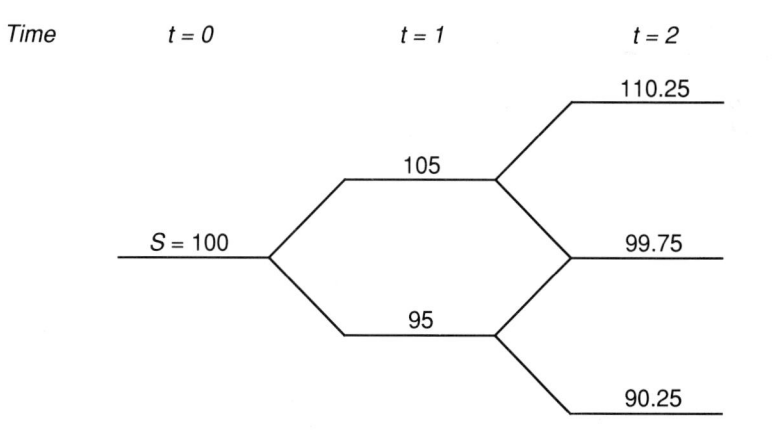

Time	$t = 0$	$t = 1$	$t = 2$
			110.25
		105	
	$S = 100$		99.75
		95	
			90.25

The process is similar to that in Figure 4–1 for a stock that does not pay a dividend. Specifically, the spot price, *S*, is $100 at time 0 and may either go up to $105 ($u = 1.05$) or down to $95 ($d = 0.95$) at time 1. At time 1, the stock can again go up or down by 1.05 and 0.95 respectively. In the upper branch, the price could move from $105 to either $110.25 or $99.75. In the lower branch, the price could move from $95 to either $99.75 or $90.25. Again, suppose that the riskless rate is 0.5% per period.

Since there is no uncertainty in the riskless interest rate, a futures contract on this spot asset is priced just like a similar forward contract. Also, since there are no cash payments on the spot asset, the cost-of-carry model for forward and futures pricing implies that the fair price of the futures contract is the compounded value of the spot price at the riskless rate of interest. Specifically, the futures price, F, on any date, is given by:

$$F = S (1 + r)^t \qquad (4.17)$$

where t is the number of periods left until the maturity of the futures contract. The binomial process for the futures price is given in Figure 4–10.

FIGURE 4–10
Binomial tree for F, the price of the futures contract

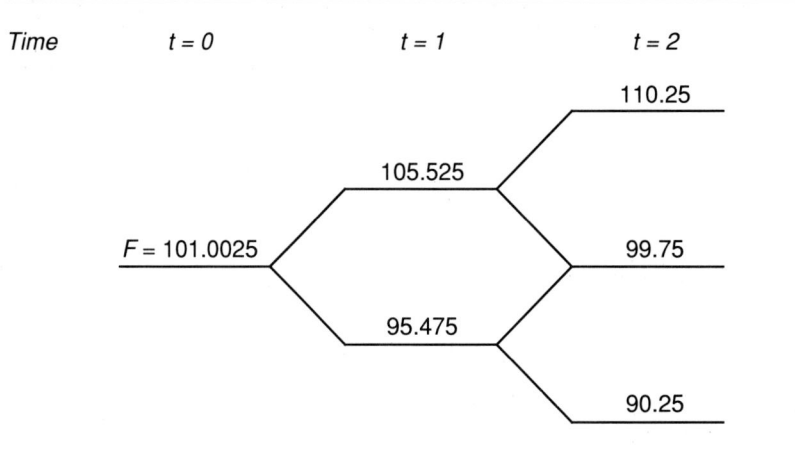

Time	$t = 0$	$t = 1$	$t = 2$

110.25

105.525

$F = 101.0025$ 99.75

95.475

90.25

At time 0, when the spot price is $100 and the futures contract has two periods to expiration, the futures price is given by:

$$F = 100 (1.005)^2 = \$101.0025 \qquad (4.18)$$

Similarly at each of the two nodes at time 1, the futures price is given by the same formula but compounded at the riskless rate of interest for one period:

$$F = 105\ (\ 1.005)^1 = \$105.525 \tag{4.19a}$$

$$F = 95\ (\ 1.005)^1 = \$\ 95.475 \tag{4.19b}$$

respectively. At time 2, the futures contract expires and the futures price is, by definition, equal to the spot price. (Compare the prices at time 2 in Figures 4–9 and 4–10, respectively.)

Consider an American call option on the futures contract. Suppose that the exercise price of the option, X, is \$98 and that the option expires at time 2. Hence, the option is in-the-money at time 0. The payoff to the holder of the call option, Max $[F - X, 0]$, based on immediate exercise at different points in time for the various outcomes, is represented in Figure 4–11.

FIGURE 4–11
Binomial tree for Max[$F - X$, 0], payoff from exercising the call option on the futures contract

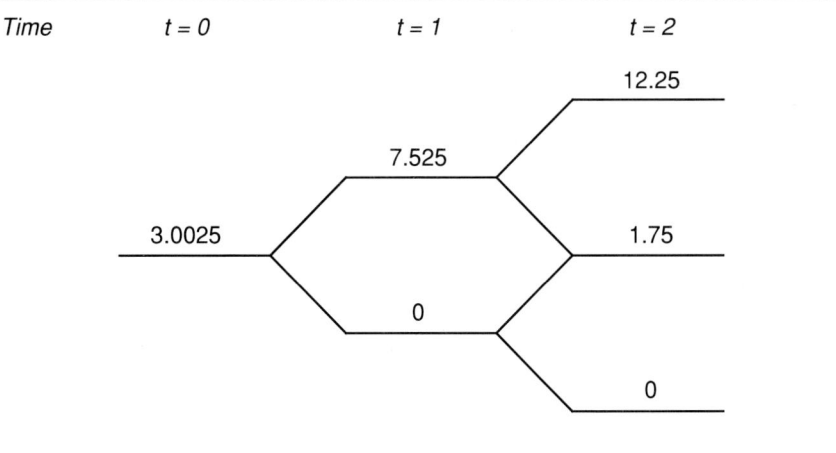

Time	$t = 0$	$t = 1$	$t = 2$

12.25

7.525

3.0025   1.75

0

0

As in the previous cases, the exercise values are not the fair values of the option, except on the expiration date, time 2, when the option is exercised, if it is in-the-money. For example, the payoff from the call option in the top branch at time 2 is Max [110.25 − 98, 0] = \$12.25. Similarly, the payoff in the bottom branch at time 2 is Max [90.25 − 98,0] = 0, since the option is out-of-the-money. In one of the states, the call option is not worth exercising and its payoff is 0.

The value of the call option can be computed by forming a riskless hedge consisting of a long position in the underlying futures contract and a short position in the call option. This riskless hedge must earn the riskless rate of interest. This is equivalent to valuing the call option by computing the expected value using the "risk-neutral" probability, p, and discounting this cash flow at the riskless rate of interest. However, since there is no cash outlay in taking a long position in a futures contract, the probability p can be computed by replacing R in the previous formula by 1.[5] Thus, in this case, p can be computed as:

---

[5]Consider a hedge portfolio consisting of a long position in one call option on the futures contract and short position of Δ futures contracts. Suppose the futures price follows a binomial process: from a current price of F, it can either increase to uF or decrease to dF. Since the portfolio is riskless, it must have the same payoff in both states:

$$-\Delta (uF - F) + C_u = -\Delta (dF - F) + C_d$$

where C_u and C_d are the cash flows on the call option in the up and down states respectively. Note that the short position in the futures contract results in a cash flow that is equal to the difference between the current and future prices of the contract. This yields a hedge ratio of:

$$\Delta = \frac{C_u - C_d}{uF - dF}$$

Substituting the expression for the hedge ratio Δ in the left (or right) hand side of the previous equation yields, after simplification, a cash flow in both states of:

$$\frac{(1 - d)C_u + (u - 1)C_d}{(u - d)}$$

In an arbitrage-free market, the present value of this cash flow must be equal to the initial investment in the hedge portfolio. Since there is no cash flow on the futures contract when the hedge is set up, the only cash flow at that time is the price paid for the call option. Hence, the current value of the call option is the present value of the above cash flow or:

$$C = \frac{1}{R} \times \frac{(1 - d)C_u + (u - 1)C_d}{(u - d)}$$

$$= \frac{1}{R} \left[pC_u + (1 - p)C_d \right]$$

where the risk-neutral probability p is equal to $(1 - d) / (u - d)$.

$$p = \frac{1-d}{u-d} = \frac{1-0.945274}{1.044776 - 0.945274} = 0.55 \qquad (4.20)$$

In the upper branch of the tree at time 1 as shown in panel *A* of Figure 4–12, the value of the call option if left unexercised at time 1 can be computed as follows:

FIGURE 4–12
Binomial tree for *C*, the value of the call option on the futures contract at different nodes

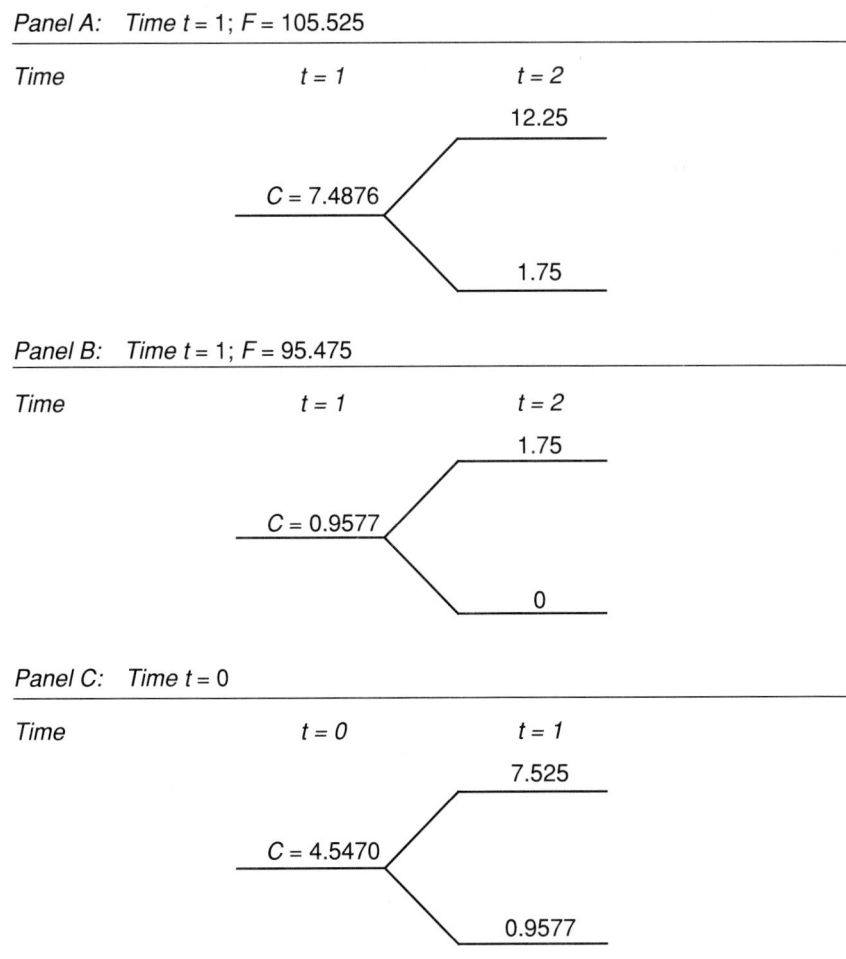

Panel A: Time *t* = 1; *F* = 105.525

Time	*t* = 1	*t* = 2
		12.25
	C = 7.4876	
		1.75

Panel B: Time *t* = 1; *F* = 95.475

Time	*t* = 1	*t* = 2
		1.75
	C = 0.9577	
		0

Panel C: Time *t* = 0

Time	*t* = 0	*t* = 1
		7.525
	C = 4.5470	
		0.9577

$$C = \frac{1}{1.005} [0.55 \times 12.25 + 0.45 \times 1.75] = \$7.4876 \quad (4.21)$$

Similarly, in the lower branch, (see panel B of Figure 4–12), when F = $95.475, the value of the option is:

$$C = \frac{1}{1.005} [0.55 \times 1.75 + 0.45 \times 0] = \$0.9577 \quad (4.22)$$

In the upper branch, at time 1, the fair value of the option, $7.4876, is less than its immediate exercise value,$7.525 (compare panel A of Figure 4–12 with the upper branch at time 1 in Figure 4–11). Hence, it is optimal to exercise the option. In the lower branch at time 1, the option is out-of-the money and hence better left unexercised (see the lower branch at time 1 in Figure 4–11). However, since there is no prospect of a payoff at time 2, the option can be abandoned, once this node is reached, and hence its value is 0. Intuitively, it pays to exercise the call option of the futures contract in the upper branch at time 1 because the potential decline in the futures price exceeds the insurance value of the option and the time value of money on the exercise price taken together.

The value of the call option at time 0 is based on following a rational exercise strategy at time 1, i.e., exercising the option if the futures price increases and abandoning it if the price declines (see panel C of Figure 4–12). In other words, the value at time 0 is given by:

$$C = \frac{1}{1.005} [0.55 \times 7.525 + 0.45 \times 0.9577] = \$4.5470 \quad (4.23)$$

Since the fair value of the option at time 0 is greater than the immediate exercise value, 0, it does not pay to exercise the option at that time. The value of the call option and the optimal exercise strategy in the various states are shown in Figure 4–13. The diagram indicates the node where premature exercise is optimal.

The same type of analysis can be extended to cover more stages in a backward iterative computation starting with the expiration date. As in the case of American put options on stocks, premature exercise may be rational and may take place at any time. Hence each stage has to be checked for early exercise. A similar calculation could be made for the case of an American put option on the futures contract. In this case, the probability of early

FIGURE 4–13
Binomial tree showing *C*, the value of the call option on the futures contract and the optimal exercise strategy

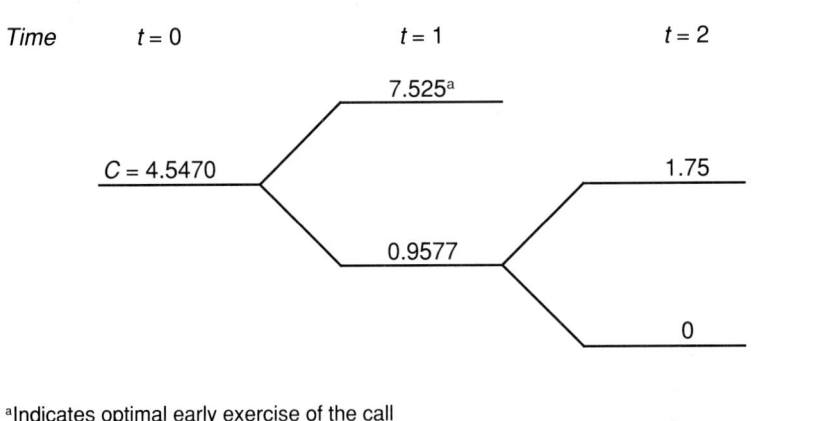

Time	$t = 0$	$t = 1$	$t = 2$

7.525[a]

$C = 4.5470$

1.75

0.9577

0

[a]Indicates optimal early exercise of the call

exercise is smaller than that for an American put option on the underlying spot asset.

American Call Option on Foreign Exchange

Consider an American call option on the pound sterling bought by a dollar investor. This call option is similar to an American put option on the dollar from the viewpoint of an investor in pounds sterling.[6]   Suppose the movement of the $/£ spot exchange rate, *S*, from time 0 to time 2 can be described by a binomial process as shown in Figure 4–14. The foreign exchange rate can either move up or down by 2% ($u = 1.02$ and $d = 0.98$). The exchange rate could move from 180 ¢/£ ($1.80/£) at time 0 to either 183.60 or 176.40 at time 1. The same proportional up and down movements can occur between time 1 and time 2. In this example, the domestic riskless rate of interest (i.e., in dollars) is 0.5% per period and the foreign riskless rate of interest (i.e., in pounds sterling) is 1.0% per period.

Consider an American call option on the pound sterling at an exercise price, *X*, of 180 ¢/£ ($1.80/£) – the option is at-the-money at time 0. The payoffs from exercising the option on different dates for the various outcomes of the $/£ foreign exchange rate are given in Figure 4–15. The

---

[6]See Chapter 7 for a discussion of this and other issues relating to foreign exchange options.

FIGURE 4–14
Binomial tree for S, the $ / £ spot foreign exchange rate in ¢ / £

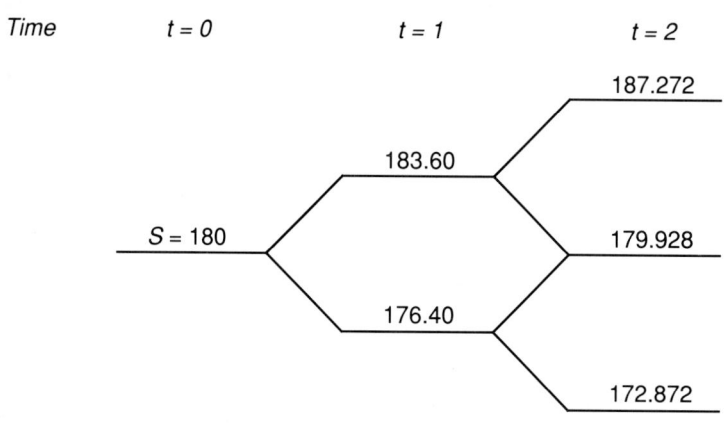

Time	t = 0	t = 1	t = 2

187.272

183.60

S = 180   179.928

176.40

172.872

FIGURE 4–15
Binomial tree for Max[S − X, 0], the payoff from exercising the call option on the $ / £ foreign exchange rate in ¢ / £

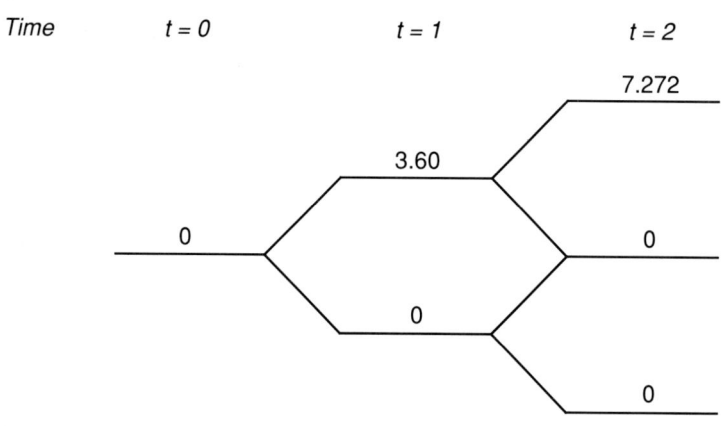

Time	t = 0	t = 1	t = 2

7.272

3.60

0   0

0

0

payoff is $S - X$ if the option is in-the-money. Otherwise, the option is not worth exercising and the payoff is 0. For example, in the upper branch at time 2, the call option is in-the-money and the payoff is 7.272. In the lower branch on the same date, the option is out-of-the-money and the payoff is 0.

The call option can be valued by the technique of forming a riskless hedge in dollars, the domestic currency. The hedge consists of a long position in the riskless asset denominated in pounds sterling (lending) and a short position in the riskless asset denominated in dollars (borrowing).[7] $R*$ and R are, respectively, one plus the foreign and domestic riskless rates of interest. As in the previous cases, this is equivalent to valuing the call option by computing the expectation using the "risk-neutral" probabilities, p, and discounting this cash flow at the riskless rate of interest. However in this case, p can be computed as follows:

$$p = \frac{(R/R*) - d}{u - d} = \frac{(1.005/1.01) - 0.98}{1.02 - 0.98} = 0.37624 \quad (4.24)$$

Consider the upper branch of the tree at time 1 as shown in panel A of Figure 4–16. The value of the call option if left unexercised at time 1, when the exchange rate goes to 183.60 ¢/£ can be computed as follows:

$$C = \frac{1}{1.005} [0.37624 \times 7.272 + 0.62376 \times 0] = 2.7224 \ ¢ \quad (4.25)$$

Similarly, in the lower branch, (see panel B of Figure 4–16), when the exchange rate declines to 176.40, the option value is :

$$C = \frac{1}{1.005} [0.37624 \times 0 + 0.62376 \times 0] = 0 \ ¢ \quad (4.26)$$

In the upper branch, at time 1, the fair value of the option, 2.7224 ¢, is less than its immediate exercise value, 3.60 ¢, (compare panel A of Figure 4–16 with the upper branch at time 1 in Figure 4–15). Hence, it is optimal to exercise the option in that node. In the lower branch at time 1, it is not worth exercising the option, since it is out-of-the money (see Figure 4–15). However, the option has no value either, since there is no chance of a payoff in the next period.

The call option value at time 0 is based on pursuing a rational exercise strategy at time 1, i.e., exercising the option if the stock price increases and abandoning it if the price declines (see panel C of Figure 4–16). The value

---

[7]The proof of this equation for p is similar to that shown in footnote 5. Note that the opportunity cost of investing in one unit of the foreign currency is $R/R*$.

FIGURE 4–16
Binomial tree for *C*, the value of the call option on the $ / £ spot foreign exchange rate at different nodes in ¢/£

Panel A: Time t = 1; S = 183.60

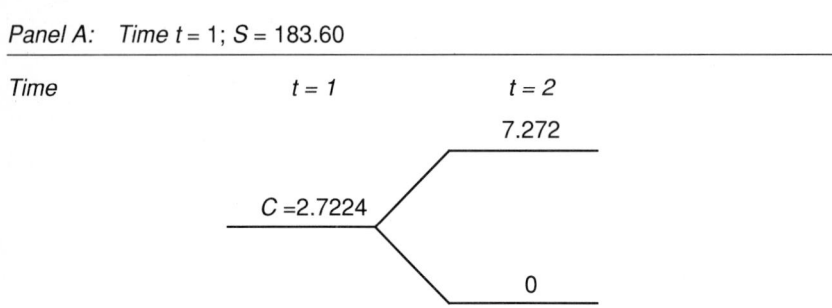

Panel B: Time t = 1; S = 176.40

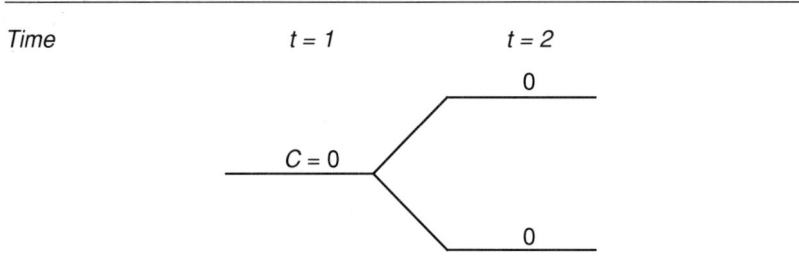

Panel C: Time t = 0

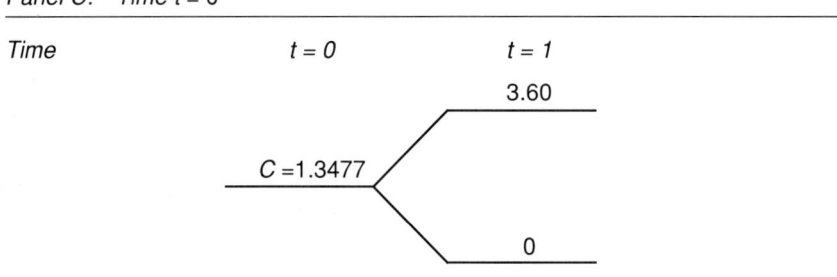

at time 0 is given by:

$$C = \frac{1}{1.005} \; [0.37624 \times 3.60 + 0.62376 \times 0] = 1.3477 \; ¢ \qquad (4.27)$$

The value of the option at time 0 is greater than its immediate exercise value, 0. Hence, it does not pay to exercise the option at that time. The value of the call option and the optimal exercise strategy in the various states is given in Figure 4–17. In the diagram, the node where premature exercise is optimal is indicated.

FIGURE 4–17
Binomial tree showing *C*, the value of the call option on the $ / £
spot foreign exchange rate and the optimal exercise strategy in ¢/£

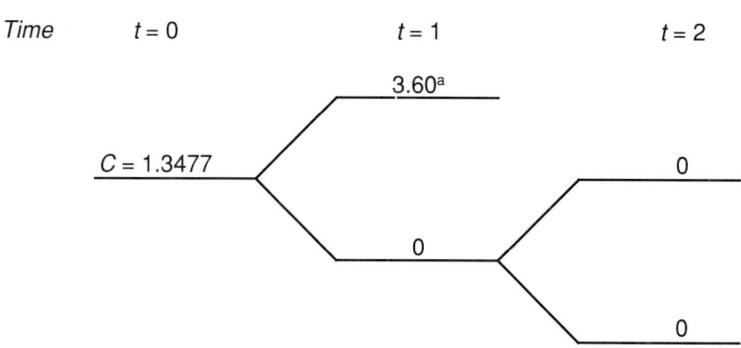

[a]Indicates optimal early exercise of the call

As in the previous cases, the above procedure can be extended to the case of multiple stages, by starting at the expiration date and working backwards. At each node, the value of the option should be compared with its immediate exercise value and the greater of the two should be used in the computation for the prior stage. As in the case of options on futures contracts, early exercise may occur at any time and hence the exercise decision must be considered for every node. An important difference between foreign exchange options and options on stocks is that a call option on the foreign currency, say the pound sterling, denominated in the domestic currency, say dollars, is like a put option on the domestic currency denominated in the foreign currency. Hence, early exercise is possible for both put and call options, depending on the difference between the domestic and foreign interest rates.[8]

---

[8]For further details, see Chapter 7, this volume.

4.4. BINOMIAL APPROXIMATIONS OF AMERICAN OPTION VALUES AND HEDGE RATIOS

In the case of European options, one can usually derive closed-form expressions for both values and hedge ratios.[9] An important example of a European option valuation and hedging model is the Black-Scholes formula derived and discussed in Chapter 3. In contrast to European options, there is, in general, no closed-form expression for American option values and hedge ratios. Typically, one has to resort to numerical methods to compute values and hedge ratios in the case of American options.

There are two main numerical approaches used in the valuation of American options. One approach is to set up the partial differential equation that must be satisfied by all claims contingent on the underlying asset.[10] The alternative approach is to use the binomial approach described in the previous section, but allowing for many stages. In the first approach, American option values can be obtained by solving the partial differential equation subject to certain boundary conditions. The special condition that defines American options is that they can be exercised at any time. Since the partial differential equation does not have a closed-form solution in the case of American options, one has to resort to numerical methods. The standard numerical solution of partial differential equations involves approximating the partial differential equation by difference equations which are then solved by finite difference methods.[11] This approach assumes small discrete changes in the price of the underlying asset and the time to expiration of the option, the two state variables that determine the price of any contingent claim. The smaller the changes considered in the two state variables, the better the approximation the numerical solution will be to the continuous case. The difference equations are then solved numerically subject to the boundary conditions to determine the value of the option. The delta, gamma, and theta are calculated in the course of the computation. Kappa (vega) and rho must be approximated by changing these parameters

---

[9]In the case of option valuation, a closed-form expression is a mathematical relationship where the parameters such as volatility can be plugged into the right-hand side of an equation to yield the option value on the left-hand side.

[10]See Appendix A to Chapter 3 for details of the partial differential equation approach to the valuation of options.

[11]See Chapter 14 for a detailed discussion of finite difference methods of solving the partial differential equation for the value of an option.

slightly and solving the problem again to determine the effect on option value.

The alternative approach using a multi-stage binomial process is also a numerical approximation. In this case also, a better approximation to the continuous time case is obtained as the number of stages increases, with the price change in each stage getting smaller.[12] Again, the hedge ratio can be calculated directly from the price tree, while the other derivatives are obtained by valuing the option again with a slightly different parameter value to determine the change in the option price for a small change in the parameter.

Tables 4–4a and 4–4b provide the option values and hedge ratios for three-month European call options on a stock using the binomial approach for different values of the parameters. In these calculations, the stock price is $100, the time to expiration is 1/4 year, the riskless interest rate is 8% and there are no dividends paid on the underlying stock. As can be seen from Table 4–4a, the call option value converges rapidly to the correct analytical (i.e., Black-Scholes) value. For example, for σ = 20%, S = $100, X = $100, and t = 1/4 year, and r = 8%, the value of a call option is $4.9670 or within 0.98%, with 20 stages, and $4.9969 or within 0.39% with 50 stages, of the correct analytical value of $5.0163. The behavior of the hedge ratio is similar. For the same parameters, the hedge ratio is 0.5994 and 0.5990 for 20 and 50 stages respectively, or within 0.12% and 0.05% of the hedge ratio in the correct analytical model of 0.5987.

We turn next to some examples of the value of the early exercise premium for typical parameter values.[13] Tables 4–5a and 4–5b provide a comparison of European and American put option values and hedge ratios respectively for the same parameters as the previous tables. In Table 4–6a, at a strike price of $110 and volatility of 15%, it pays to exercise the American put option immediately and hence its value is $110 – $100 = $10. The values of the European puts for the various expiration dates are lower, since European options cannot be exercised prematurely. Indeed, as a result, European put option values decline with maturity, due to the higher

---

[12]The calculations of the up and down movements in each stage, u and d, as a function of the volatility parameter, σ, are described in Chapter 3.

[13]For the purpose of our discussion here, we do not consider the case of the American and European call options on stocks that do not pay dividends. In this case, the values and the hedge ratios of the two types of options are the same, since it is never rational to exercise the American option early in this case.

TABLE 4–4a
Binomial approximations of the prices of call options

Volatility (%)	Strike price ($)	Number of stages in the binomial tree			
		20	50	100	inf.
15	110	.6278	.6450	.6433	.6438
	100	4.0185	4.0411	4.0489	4.0558
	90	11.9124	11.9159	11.9179	11.9199
20	110	1.3289	1.3594	1.3538'	1.3542
	100	4.9670	4.9969	5.0070	5.0163
	90	12.2633	12.2567	12.2544	12.2534
25	110	2.2012	2.1875	2.1777	2.1784
	100	5.9252	5.9623	5.9748	5.9866
	90	12.7445	12.7385	12.7547	12.7542
30	110	3.1160	3.0730	3.0656	3.0662
	100	6.8877	6.9320	6.9470	6.9615
	90	13.4124	13.3861	13.3778	13.3696

Parameter Values:
  S = 100
  r = 8%
  t = 1/4 (3 months)
No dividends

TABLE 4–4b
Binomial approximations of the hedge ratios of call options

Volatility (%)	Strike price ($)	Number of stages in the binomial tree			
		20	50	100	inf.
15	110	.1767	.1720	.1694	.1669
	100	.6196	.6195	.6195	.6195
	90	.9517	.9549	.9556	.9563
20	110	.2515	.2464	.2434	.2410
	100	.5994	.5990	.5989	.5987
	90	.8952	.9005	.9022	.9038
25	110	.3065	.2996	.2969	.2946
	100	.5894	.5886	.5883	.5880
	90	.8505	.8548	.8551	.8567
30	110	.3472	.3394	.3369	.3347
	100	.5844	.5833	.5829	.5825
	90	.8106	.8153	.8170	.8188

Parameter Values:
  S = 100
  r = 8%
  t = 1/4 (3 months)
No dividends

TABLE 4–5a
Binomial approximations of the prices of European vs.
American put options

Volatility (%)	Strike price ($)	European Put			American Put		
		Time to Expiration (Years)					
		1/12	1/4	1/2	1/12	1/4	1/2
15	110	9.3017	8.4650	7.7743	10.0000	10.0000	10.0000
	100	1.4055	2.0686	2.4661	1.4651	2.2672	2.8811
	90	.0060	.1357	.3818	.0061	.1426	.4209
20	110	9.4313	9.1755	9.0846	10.0000	10.1266	10.5163
	100	1.9728	3.0267	3.7711	2.0299	3.2205	4.1857
	90	.0533	.4722	1.0411	.0540	.4896	1.1172
25	110	9.6683	9.9994	10.4458	10.0478	10.6830	11.5486
	100	2.5419	3.9946	5.1025	2.5972	4.1843	5.5150
	90	.1772	.9725	1.8845	.1792	1.0021	1.9990
30	110	9.9928	10.8873	11.8296	10.2682	11.4365	12.7648
	100	3.1119	4.9668	6.4461	3.1658	5.1536	6.8569
	90	.3746	1.5955	2.8950	.3784	1.6367	3.0321

Parameter Values:
  S = 100
  r = 8%
No dividends
100 stages in the binomial tree

TABLE 4–5b
Binomial approximations of the hedge ratios of European vs.
American put options

Volatility (%)	Strike price ($)	European Put			American Put		
		Time to Expiration (Years)					
		1/12	1/4	1/2	1/12	1/4	1/2
15	110	−.9784	−.8306	−.6777	−1.0000	−1.0000	−.9655
	100	−.4303	−.3805	−.3335	−.4549	−.4310	−.4124
	90	−.0047	−.0444	−.0782	−.0047	−.0470	−.0879
20	110	−.9326	−.7566	−.6233	−1.0000	−.8890	−.7837
	100	−.4426	−.4011	−.3616	−.4597	−.4365	−.4174
	90	−.0250	−.0978	−.1376	−.0254	−.1023	−.1504
25	110	−.8834	−.7031	−.5867	−.9414	−.7814	−.6855
	100	−.4487	−.4117	−.3761	−.4618	−.4386	−.4188
	90	−.0575	−.1449	−.1819	−.0582	−.1505	−.1960
30	110	−.8338	−.6631	−.5594	−.8727	−.7159	−.6286
	100	−.4519	−.4171	−.3836	−.4623	−.4387	−.4180
	90	−.0918	−.1830	−.2156	−.0929	−.1890	−.2293

Parameter Values:
  S = 100
  r = 8%
No dividends
100 stages in the binomial tree

present value cost. Note also that as the volatility parameter increases, it may no longer be optimal to exercise the American put option immediately, and they are worth more than their immediate exercise value. However, in all cases, the American put is worth more than its European counterpart. From the table, it is clear that the early exercise premium decreases with the volatility, but increases with the depth in-the-money of the option as discussed in section 4.2. The sensitivity with respect to the time to expiration is ambiguous since the time value of money and the volatility effects act in opposite directions. However, for realistic values of volatility and the riskless rate of interest, the volatility effect dominates. For example, when the volatility is 30%, the strike price is $90 and the time to expiration is 1/12 year, there is hardly any difference between the American and European put values $0.3784 versus $0.3746. However, when the volatility is 15%, the strike price is $110 and the time to expiration is 1/2 year, the American put is worth $10.0000 against $7.7743 for the European put.

The hedge ratios of American versus European put options reflect the same pattern. In the case of put options, the hedge ratio essentially reflects the extent to which the option behaves like a short position in the underlying asset. Since there is always a likelihood of premature exercise for American put options, their hedge ratios are always more negative than their European counterparts. The hedge ratio for American puts is -1, for a volatility of 15%, when it is rational to exercise immediately, whereas it is not as negative for the European put. Also, the difference between the hedge ratios is greater as the time to expiration and the depth-in-the-money increase and the volatility decreases.

We turn next to the impact of dividends on option values and hedge ratios. Tables 4–6a and 4–6b provide the estimates of the value and hedge ratio for American versus European call options for various parameters when a dividend of $2 is paid on the underlying asset in the middle of the period until maturity. The American call option is worth more than its European counterpart whenever there is some probability of premature exercise. For example, in Table 4–6a when the volatility is 15%, the strike price is $90, and the time to expiration is 1/12 year, there is a substantial probability of premature exercise since the volatility is low, the depth in the money is high and the time to expiration is short. Hence, as argued in section 4.2, there is a large early exercise premium reflected in the difference between the value of the American and European options, $10.2995 versus $8.6286. However, a large part of this difference is simply due to the present value of the dividend payment, which the holder of the American option can

TABLE 4–6a
Binomial Approximations of the Prices of European vs.
American Call Options

Volatility (%)	Strike price ($)	European Call			American Call		
		Time to Expiration (Years)					
		1/12	1/4	1/2	1/12	1/4	1/2
15	110	.0083	.3720	1.5214	.0084	.3740	1.5214
	100	1.1240	2.9369	5.1523	1.4906	3.0977	5.1525
	90	8.6286	10.0563	12.1298	10.2995	10.9515	12.2200
20	110	.0663	.9341	2.6963	.0675	.9387	2.6963
	100	1.6719	3.8983	6.5149	2.0009	4.0213	6.5150
	90	8.7328	10.5023	12.8956	10.3060	11.1899	12.9455
25	110	.2105	1.6526	3.9902	.2150	1.6598	3.9902
	100	2.2309	4.8877	7.8760	2.5217	4.9899	7.8760
	90	8.9277	11.1019	13.8597	10.3448	11.6199	13.8889
30	110	.4480	2.4483	5.3212	.4565	2.4570	5.3212
	100	2.7849	5.8711	9.2350	3.0412	5.9557	9.2350
	90	9.2014	11.7839	14.8816	10.4462	12.1846	14.9020

Parameter Values:
  S = 100
  r = 8%
Dividend of $2 at time 1/2 t
100 stages in the binomial tree

TABLE 4–6b
Binomial Approximations of the Hedge Ratios of European vs.
American Call Options

Volatility (%)	Strike price ($)	European Call			American Call		
		Time to Expiration (Years)					
		1/12	1/4	1/2	1/12	1/4	1/2
15	110	.0065	.1108	.2589	.0067	.1121	.2589
	100	.3877	5157	.5965	.5361	.5595	.5966
	90	.9835	.9238	.8910	.9997	.9725	.9017
20	110	.0321	.1856	.3245	.0333	.1877	.3245
	100	.4202	.4794	.5849	.5255	.5483	.5849
	90	.9460	.8634	.8303	.9943	.9168	.8367
25	110	.0714	.2448	.3707	.0744	.2472	3707
	100	.4414	.5256	.5809	.5202	.5453	.5809
	90	.9035	.8156	7864	.9755	.8613	.7901
30	110	.1149	.2899	.4044	.1192	.2922	.4044
	100	.4563	.5307	.5805	.5179	.5450	.5805
	90	.8640	7804	.7571	.9447	.8169	.7595

Parameter Values:
  S = 100
  r = 8%
Dividend of $2 at time 1/2 t
100 stages in the binomial tree

obtain by early exercise, but the holder of the European option cannot. This is also reflected in the relatively small difference in the respective hedge ratios: 0.9997 versus 0.9835 in Table 4–6b. In contrast when the volatility is 30%, the strike price is $110, and the time to expiration is 1/2 year, there is a low probability of premature exercise since the volatility is high, and the depth-in-the-money is low. Here, the American and European call options have the same value $5.3212. This similarity gets reflected in the hedge ratios which are identical at 0.4044.

As argued earlier, the payment of dividends on the underlying asset decreases the probability of early exercise before the ex-dividend date in the case of American put options. Hence, the differences in term of both values and hedge ratios between American and European options are smaller with dividends (after adjusting the European values for the present value of the dividends) than without. The impact of dividends on the difference between the hedge ratios of the two types of options is similar.

The Early Exercise Boundary

As is clear from the above discussion and the analysis in section 4.2, the probability of early exercise increases with the depth-in-the-money and decreases with volatility for both American put and call options. In addition, for American call options, the likelihood of early exercise diminishes as the time to expiration of the option increases. However, in the case of American put options, the effect of changing the time to expiration is ambiguous. These relationships can be presented on a graph of the depth-in-the-money versus the time to expiration, for different levels of the volatility parameter. The graph shows the critical value of the depth-in-the-money at which early exercise become optimal. In the case of calls, the critical value of the depth-in-the-money represents the price of the underlying asset above which it would be optimal to exercise the option at a given time to expiration. In the case of puts, the critical value represents the price of the underlying asset below which it would be optimal to exercise the option.

Figures 4–18a, 4–18b and 4–18c are examples of optimal exercise boundaries for options on spot and futures contracts, derived by using the finite difference methods discussed previously. The X-axis in these figures represents the time to expiration of the option in days and the Y-axis is the ratio of the price of the underlying asset to the exercise price. The Y-axis is a measure of the depth-in-the-money for call options and its inverse in the

FIGURE 4–18a
Put options on a non-dividend paying spot asset

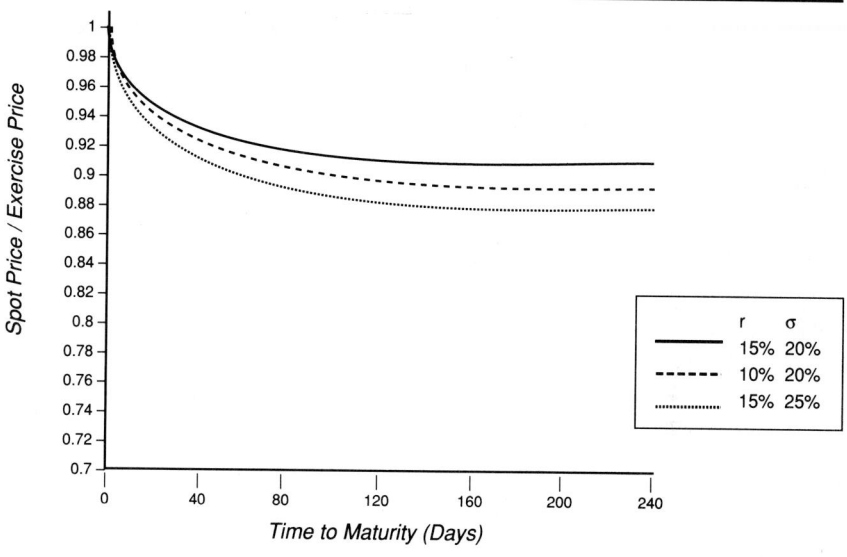

FIGURE 4–18b
Call options on a futures contract

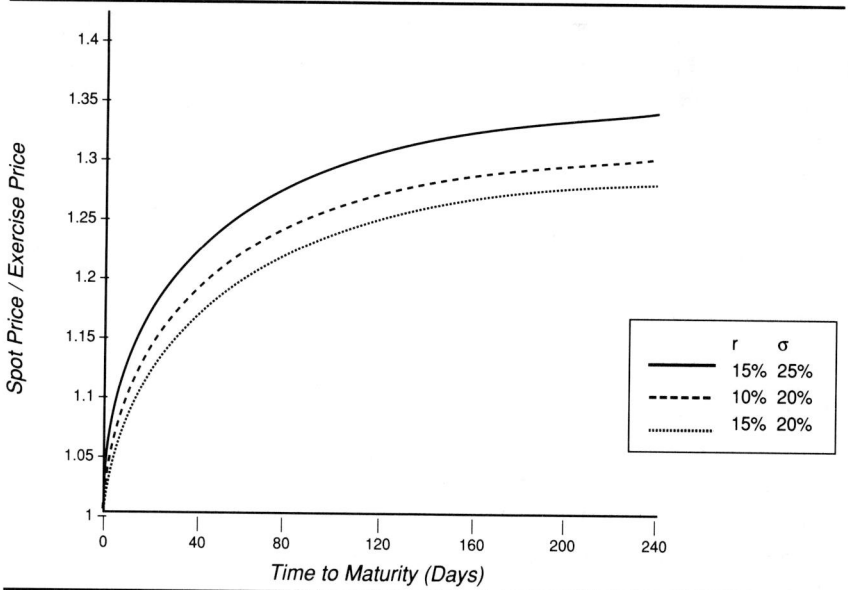

FIGURE 4–18c
Put options on a futures contract

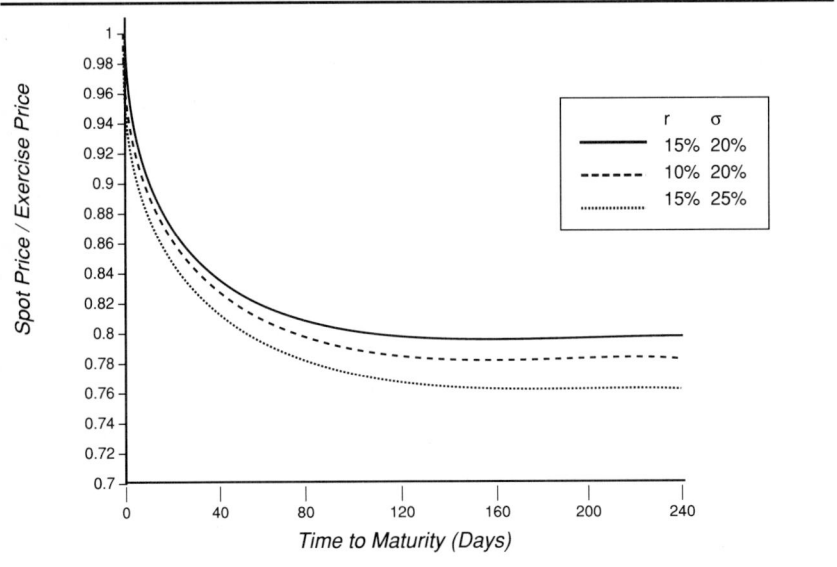

case of put options.[14]   From Figure 4–18a, it is clear that for put options on a spot asset that does not pay dividends, early exercise is optimal for a larger and larger range of spot prices as the time to expiration gets shorter.[15]   At a volatility of 25%, (the lowest graph in Figure 4–18a), early exercise is optimal when the spot price is 87% or lower of the exercise price when the time to expiration is 180 days. However, when the time to expiration is only 30 days, it is optimal to exercise the option even if the spot price is 91% or lower of the exercise price. As volatility falls to 20%, early exercise is optimal over a wider range of spot prices, as seen from the middle graph in Figure 4–18a.

For call options, the early exercise boundary is interpreted somewhat differently. For example, in Figure 4–18b for call options on a futures contract, when the volatility parameter is 25% (the top graph in the figure),

---

[14]The graphs have been "smoothed" to eliminate to effects of the discreteness of changes in the time to maturity and the price of the underlying asset. See Brenner, Courtadon and Subrahmanyam (1985) for details.

[15]If the spot asset pays a dividend, there would be a discontinuity in the boundary on the ex-dividend date. Early exercise is optimal at a higher asset price after it has gone ex-dividend.

it is optimal to exercise the option when there are 180 days to expiration, if the price of the underlying asset is 132% of the exercise price or above it. This critical value falls with the time to expiration and becomes 117% or higher of the exercise price when there are 30 days to expiration.

The early exercise boundaries for the other types of options would be similar to the above cases. For example, in the case of call options on stocks that pay dividends, there is only one point in time when it may be rational to exercise the option and that it just prior to the ex-dividend day. Hence, exercise boundaries would consist of points associated with the ex-dividend day with no critical price defined on other days. This is in contrast to the exercise boundary for put options, with or without dividends, which is smooth, with the critical value falling with the time to expiration. In the case of put options on a futures contract, the boundary is smooth as shown in Figure 4–18c.

4.5   ANALYTIC VALUATION OF AMERICAN OPTIONS

From the discussion in the previous section, it is clear that, in general, the value of the early exercise feature, and hence, of American options, can be computed only by the use of numerical methods. The question arises as to whether it is possible to develop an analytic approach to the valuation of American options by imposing some additional restrictions on the problem. This approach, pioneered by Roll (1977) and Whaley (1981) for the American call option and Johnson (1983) and Geske and Johnson (1984) for the American put option has two merits over the numerical methods. First, it provides a framework for the comparative statics analysis of the values and hedge ratios of American options. Using such a framework, one can develop a feel for how the solutions may change as the restrictions are gradually eased. Second, it is possible that such an approach may offer a more efficient computational technique for the solution of the valuation problem than other numerical methods.

Let us now turn to the type of restriction on the problem that may facilitate an analytic solution to the valuation and hedging of American options. Since the need for a numerical solution to the valuation problem arises from the (infinitely) large number of dates and underlying asset prices at which early exercise may occur, one approach would be to restrict one or the other of these two variables. (Indeed, the numerical methods using the binomial and finite difference approaches may be viewed as restricting the dates and underlying asset prices to discrete values.)

The most obvious example of this is the case of American call options on stocks that pay a dividend. In this case, early exercise may be optimal, but then only just prior to the ex-dividend day. In the case where there is just one dividend payment between the current date and the maturity date of the option, it should be simple, in principle, to check whether this is so. This is the approach taken by Roll (1977) and corrected by Whaley (1981) for American call options. This analytic approach is further generalized by Johnson (1983) and Geske and Johnson (1984) to the case of American put options, or indeed any contingent claim with an early exercise privilege, by placing restrictions on the number of dates when exercise can occur and obtaining a direct solution to the valuation problem.

The Geske and Johnson formulation of the analytic solution to the American option problem is in the context of a geometric Brownian motion in the price of the underlying asset. However, their general technique can be applied to any stochastic process for the price of the underlying asset for which the hedging argument applies. We shall explain their approach without making any specific assumption regarding the stochastic process followed by the price of the underlying asset.

Consider an American put option that can be exercised at any time before time $t = 2$ at an exercise price X.[16] Let us approximate the value of this option by the value of another put option that can be exercised only at one point in time before the expiration date. For convenience, let us assume that the option can be exercised only at time $t = 1$, which falls mid-way between the initial date $t = 0$ and the expiration date $t = 2$, in addition to the expiration date $t = 2$. Suppose the prices of the underlying asset at time $t = 1$ and $t = 2$ are given by S_1 and S_2 respectively. The exercise decision at time $t = 1$ and hence the value at time $t = 0$ of the American put option can be determined by comparing the exercise value at time $t = 1$ with the value at $t = 1$ of a put option expiring at time $t = 2$. The payoff from the put option at $t = 1$ is the higher of the two and can be written as:

$$\text{Payoff at time } (t = 1) \quad = \quad \text{Max } [X - S_1, P_1(S_2, X)] \qquad (4.28)$$

---

[16]Exercise can occur at any instant before the expiration date, $t = 2$.

where $P_1(S_2, X)$ is the price at time $t = 1$ of a European put option expiring at time $t = 2$, expressed as a function of its underlying asset price, S_2 and the exercise price X.

The above equation can be rewritten as

$$\text{Payoff at time } (t = 1) \quad = \quad \text{Max } \{ \text{ Max } [X - S_1, 0], P_1(S_2, X)\} \quad (4.29)$$

since $P_1(S_2, X) \geq 0$, or as ,

$$\text{Payoff at time } (t = 1) \quad = \quad \text{Max } [X - S_1, 0] + \\ \text{Max } [\{P_1(S_2, X) - \text{Max } [X - S_1, 0]\}, 0] \quad (4.30)$$

Equation (4.30) represents the payoffs at time $t = 1$ for a put option expiring at time $t = 2$, that can be exercised prematurely at time $t = 1$. The first term in the equation is the payoff of a European put option expiring at time $t = 1$. The second term is the payoff at time $t = 1$ from a compound option at an exercise price equal to Max $[X - S_1, 0]$. A compound option is a European option on a European option. In this case, the compound option is a call option expiring at time $t = 1$ on a put option, $P_1(S_2, X)$, expiring at time $t = 2$. Thus, the payoff at time $t = 1$ of an American put option exercisable either at time $t = 1$ or $t = 2$ can be represented as the value of a European put option expiring at time $t = 1$ plus the payoff from a compound call option at a stochastic exercise price equal to the payoff from a European put option expiring at time $t = 1$. In turn, the same relationship holds for the value of the American put option in terms of the value of the other two options.

The value of a European put option expiring at time 1 can be determined using the methods outlined in Chapter 3. In particular, if the underlying asset price follows a geometric Brownian motion, the value is given by the standard Black-Scholes model for European call options and the put-call parity condition. The value of the compound option deserves further comment. In this case, the compound option is a European call option on a European put option. What determines whether the compound option will be "in-the-money" at time $t = 1$? As with any call option, the compound option is "in-the-money" when the underlying asset price exceeds the exercise price. In this case, the underlying asset price is the value of a European put option expiring at time 2, while the (stochastic) exercise price is the payoff from a European put option expiring at time 1.

This compound option is in-the-money when the underlying asset price is below a critical level, say S^*. This level has to be low enough such that the value of the European put option expiring at $t = 2$ is *above* the payoff of a European put option expiring at $t = 1$. Only in this case would it be worthwhile to keep the option "alive." The value of the compound option can be computed by integrating (i.e., summing) the difference between the stock price and the exercise price over all possible stock prices below the critical stock price.

This approach can be extended to the case of an American put option that can be exercised at one of three or more points in time. In general, at each point in time, the option will be exercised if it has not already been exercised and if the payoff from exercising it exceeds the value if not exercised. This suggests a critical stock price level, below which it is optimal to exercise the option. At the first point in time, there is no probability that the option has already been exercised. Hence, we just integrate or sum the difference between the stock price and the exercise price over all stock prices below the critical level. At the next point in time, the integration is similar, but cases where the put has already been exercised have to be excluded. This is done by integrating over prices where the stock price at the first point in time is above the first critical level but the stock price at the second point in time is below the second critical level. The next point in time involves cases where the option was not exercised on the two previous dates, i.e., where the stock price was above the critical prices on the first two dates but is below the critical price on the third date. The approach can be extended to more exercise dates using the same approach.

In general, the equation derived by Geske and Johnson for the case of a geometric Brownian motion in the price of the underlying asset involves expressions in terms of bivariate, trivariate and, in general, multivariate standard normal variates. These follow from the compound option extensions of the Black-Scholes model as proposed by Geske (1979). Since it is very expensive in terms of computer time to go beyond multivariate normal distributions involving four variables, numerical interpolation methods are used to go from the two-, three-, four-date values to the n-date values.[17] Specifically, the Richardson approximation is used to approximate the value of an n-date option, as n tends to infinity, using the one-, two-, three-, and,

---

[17]See Geske and Johnson (1984) for details.

possibly, the four-date values. This approach is computationally efficient, in addition to providing an analytical formulation.

Recently, Kim (1989) has extended the approach of Geske and Johnson (1984) to obtain the continuous limit of the American put option valuation formula, when the price of the underlying asset follows a geometric Brownian motion. In other words, he lets the number of intermediate exercise dates in the Geske and Johnson method become very large. He formulates the valuation problem as a free-boundary problem and obtains an explicit analytic solution by characterizing the critical stock price, above or below which exercise is rational. Apart from providing better intuition for the importance of the early exercise feature of American options and, in particular, put options, this approach provides a more accurate and efficient computational technique for their valuation and hedging.

Another approach to the problem of valuation of American options is to obtain an approximate analytic solution. An example of this approach is the quadratic approximation method used by Macmillan (1986), Barone-Adesi and Whaley (1987), and Omburg (1987). The basic idea behind this approach is that since the fundamental partial differential equation of Black and Scholes (1973) (see equation 3A.16 in Chapter 3) applies to both European and American options, it also applies to the early exercise premium of American options.

The approximation is based on writing the partial differential equation for the early exercise premium and setting its value to be zero, for very short term options or for very long term options, when the exercise price is allowed to increase over time at the riskless rate. By using this approximation, the Black and Scholes partial differential equation becomes quadratic in the differential operation with respect to the price of the underlying asset. This leads to an approximate analytic solution to the original problem of valuation of the early exercise premium. After imposing the appropriate boundary conditions for the type of option (e.g., put or call option) and the nature of the underlying asset (e.g., dividend-paying stock, futures contract, foreign exchange), the value of the option with the early exercise feature can be obtained from the approximate analytic solution.[18]

---

[18]See Macmillan (1986) and Barone-Adesi and Whaley (1987) for details.

4.6 CONCLUSION

The distinguishing feature of an American option is the privilege the holder has to exercise the option prematurely. This feature makes American options more valuable than their European counterparts. In this chapter, we discussed the rationale for early exercise and provided examples of various types of American options using the binomial model. We also analyzed the variables that influence the early exercise decision and hence the value of American options. The principal variables are the depth-in-the-money of the option, the riskless rate of interest, the time to maturity, the volatility parameter and the timing and magnitude of dividend payments on the underlying asset. The chapter provided an intuitive understanding of how these variables influence the likelihood of early exercise and hence the value and hedge ratio of American options.

The chapter also provided the basic background necessary to study the numerical methods used to determine the value and hedge ratio of American options, explained in more detail in Chapter 14. More advanced issues such as analytic methods for valuing American options were discussed at an introductory level. Since American options are common in many markets such as those for foreign exchange, bonds and other interest rate dependent instruments, corporate securities and mortgage-backed securities, interested readers will find applications of the ideas discussed in the other chapters in the book.

References

Barone-Adesi, G., and Whaley, R. (June 1987). Efficient analytic approximation of American option values. *Journal of Finance, 42,* 301–20.

Black, F., and Scholes, M. (May/June 1973). The pricing of options and corporate liabilities. *Journal of Political Economy, 81,* 637–54.

Boyle, P. (May 1977). Options: A Monte Carlo approach. *Journal of Financial Economics, 4,* 323–38.

Brennan, M. J., and Schwartz, E. (May 1977). The valuation of American put options. *Journal of Finance, 32,* 449–62.

Brennan, M. J., and Schwartz, E. (September 1978). Finite difference methods and jump processes arising in the pricing of contingent claims: A synthesis. *Journal of Financial and Quantitative Analysis, 13,* 461–74.

Brenner, M., Courtadon, G., and Subrahmanyam, M. (December 1985). Options on the spot and options on futures. *Journal of Finance, 40,* 1303–17.

Courtadon, G. (December 1982). A more accurate finite difference approximation for the valuation of options. *Journal of Financial and Quantitative Analysis, 17,* 689–703.

Geske, R. (March 1979). The valuation of compound options. *Journal of Financial Economics, 7,* 63–81.

Geske, R., and Johnson, H. E. (December 1984). The American put option valued analytically. *Journal of Finance, 39,* 1511–24.

Geske, R., and Shastri, K. (June 1985). The early exercise of American puts. *Journal of Banking and Finance, 9,* 207–19.

Johnson, H. E. (March 1983). An analytic approximation for the American put price. *Journal of Financial and Quantitative Analysis, 18,* 141–48.

Kalay, A., and Subrahmanyam, M. (January 1984). The ex-dividend day behavior of option prices. *Journal of Business, 57,* 113–28.

Kim, I. J. (December 1990). The analytic valuation of American options. *Review of Financial Studies, 3,* 547–72.

MacMillan, L. (1986). An analytic approximation for the American put price. *Advances in Futures and Options Research, 1,* 119–39.

Michaely, R. (1989). Ex-dividend day stock price behavior: The case of the 1986 Tax Reform Act. New York University: Solomon Bros. Center working paper.

Omberg, E. (1987). The valuation of American put options with exponential exercise policies. *Advances in Futures and Options Research, 2,* 117–42.

Parkinson, M. (January 1977). Option pricing: The American put. *Journal of Business, 50,* 21–36.

Roll, R. (November 1977). An analytic valuation formula for unprotected American call options on stocks with known dividends. *Journal of Financial Economics, 5,* 251–58.

Whaley, R. (June 1981). On the valuation of American call options on stocks with known dividends. *Journal of Financial Economics, 9,* 207–12.

PART 2

APPLICATIONS

CHAPTER 5

STOCK INDEX OPTIONS

Menachem Brenner*

5.1 INTRODUCTION: INDEX OPTIONS

Options on stock-market portfolios were first offered by insurance companies. In 1977 when the Harleysville Insurance Company provided 'portfolio insurance' for investors in certain mutual funds, the company was actually selling put options on the fund portfolios. At the same time, life insurance companies in the U.K. and Canada were offering equity-linked life insurance policies with minimum value guarantees. They were, in effect, offering a fixed payment combined with a call option on an equity portfolio.[1] The benefits of options on a market portfolio have been discussed by several scholars[2] long before the introduction of exchange

*Professor of Finance, New York University and Hebrew University. The author would like to thank Steve Figlewski, Bill Silber, Marti Subrahmanyam, Mark Rubinstein, Fischer Black, Howard Baker, Joe Stefanelli, David Krell, Gary Katz, Ethan Etzioni, and Richard Bookstaber for their helpful comments and suggestions.

[1]These plans are also equivalent to an equity portfolio with an attached put option. For a detailed discussion of these plans see Brennan and Schwartz (1976).

[2]For example, Hakansson (1976), Leland (1980). Also, in 1977 Mark Rubinstein prepared a statement at the request of the Philadelphia Stock Exchange (PHLX), that provides an economic justification for index options. (See Cox and Rubinstein (1985), pp. 446-468).

traded index options, which did not occur until options on stock market indices were introduced in 1983.

In March 1983 options on Standard & Poor's (S&P) 100 index[3] (ticker symbol: OEX) began trading at the Chicago Board Options Exchange (CBOE) and within its first year of trading the option became the most actively traded option on the CBOE.

In the past few years other index options, including index futures options, were introduced. Table 5–1 summarizes the features of the different contracts. These options are based on market indices that include as few as 20 stocks and as many as 1700 stocks. Currently, the OEX option accounts for about 80 percent of the daily volume traded in all stock index options (see Table 5–2) and its open interest, i.e., the number of contracts outstanding, is more than 50 percent of total open interest in index options (on February 15, 1989, OEX open interest was 1,050,387 contracts while the open interest for all index options combined was 1,860,710).

Though the indices differ in number of stocks included in the index and in the weighting and averaging method, the correlations among their weekly as well as daily returns are generally above 0.9 (see Table 5–3). For example, the S&P500 index has a correlation of .98 with the Dow Jones index. While options on the different indices could be used as substitutes for one another in hedging and arbitrage strategies, their distinguishing features, summarized in Table 5–1, should be taken into account in choosing the options that suit the investor best. For example, an institutional investor who wants a two year insurance policy that provides protection against losses in his stock market portfolio may be interested in buying two-year European-style Institutional Index (XII) options. An individual who anticipates a large drop in the Dow-Jones Industrial Average (DJIA) in the near future would buy short term put options on the Major Market Index (XMI), an index of 20 blue-chip stocks that has a correlation, in daily returns, of .99 with the DJIA (see Table 5–3).

In the next section the OEX and XMI options are used to illustrate the effect of the options' features on the valuation of index options. The third section deals with options on stock index futures. The fourth section describes various hedging strategies and other uses of index options. The fifth section provides a summary of options features and of forthcoming index products. Finally an up-to-date report on the global trend in index options is provided.

---

[3]Originally the index was called the CBOE 100.

TABLE 5–1
Features of index options

Index	Ticker	Ex-change [a]	Type	Expiration [b]	Size [c] ($)	Open Interest [d]	Futures
Options on Cash Indexes							
S&P100	OEX	CBOE	American	4 near mos.	28,090	1,050,387	no
Major Market Index	XMI	AMEX	European	3 near mos.	45,322	192,647	yes
S&P500	SPX	CBOE	European	2 near + 4 in quarterly cycle + long (to 2 years)	29,424	501,205	yes
NYSE Composite Index	NYA	NYSE	American	3 near mos.	16,531	24,164	yes
Institutional Index	XII	AMEX	European	3 near + 2 in quarterly cycle + long (to 2 years)	29,350	80,354	no
Value Line Index	VLE	PHLX	European	3 near + 2 in quarterly cycle	26,079	2,286	yes
National OTC Index	XOC	PHLX	American	2 near + 2 in quarterly cycle	27,864	269	no
Financial News Composite Index	FNC	PSE	European	2 near + 2 in quarterly cycle	21,040	9,398	no
Options on Index Futures							
S&P500	SPX	CME	American	2 near + 2 in quarterly cycle	147,115	42,889	
NYSE Composite Index	NYA	NYFE	American	2 near + 2 in quarterly cycle	83,075	2,304	

[a] *Exchanges*

    CBOE = Chicago Board Options Exchange   PSE = Pacific Coast Stock Exchange
    AMEX = American Stock Exchange   CME = Chicago Mercantile Exchange
    NYSE = New York Stock Exchange   NYFE = New York Futures Exchange
    PHLX = Philadelphia Stock Exchange

[b] *Expiration* indicates the number of available maturities. For example, XII has options that expire in February, March and April + options that expire in June and in September + options that expire in two years.

[c] *Size* means the dollar value of a contract. The size of all index option contracts is $100 × index (tick size is 1/16). The size of an index futures option is 1 futures contract, which is itself worth $500 × futures price (tick size is .05).

[d] Open interest and size as quoted on February 15, 1989.

TABLE 5–2
Comparative participation in broad-based index options—1988 volume of trading

Exchange	Contract	Total	Average Daily	% Market Share	% Customer Volume [a]	% Firm Volume [b]
AMEX	XMI	6,464,051	25,550	9.13	27.16	5.22
	XII	1,042,677	4,121	1.47	12.52	11.05
	Total	7,506,728	29,671	10.60	25.13	6.02
CBOE	OEX	57,433,506	227,010	81.14	25.47	5.32
	SPX	4,399,557	17,389	6.22	29.67	11.67
	NSX	417,337	1,650	0.59	17.54	26.14
	Total	62,250,400	246,049	87.95	25.71	5.91
NYSE	NYA	724,889	2,865	1.02	23.21	3.15
PSE	FNC	280,393	1,108	0.40	6.14	2.53
PHLX	VLE	22,681	146	0.03	18.67	20.22
OCC	Total	70,785,091	279,839	100.00	25.58	5.90

[a]Volume of trades for customer accounts as reported by their brokers.
[b]Volume of trades done for the firm account.

Source: American Stock Exchange Statistics

5.2   THE VALUATION OF STOCK INDEX OPTIONS

Though stock index options have been very successful, the valuation of these options is not a simple matter.[4] To value an option we need to know the features of the underlying asset and the specifications of the option contract (see Table 5–1).[5] The following features are important for

---

[4]For a detailed discussion of valuation issues see Brenner, Courtadon, and Subrahmanyam (1985, 1987).

[5]We have not included options on narrow-based indices like the Computer Technology Index (XCI) or the Oil Index (XOI) because their volume of trading and open interest are very small. From the start these options drew very little interest because they fall in between stock options and options on the market as a whole. Institutions that typically hold diversified portfolios and individuals who invest either in funds or in small portfolios, across sectors, cannot efficiently use options of a specific sector. Also, a market maker in these options would not provide a liquid market since he does not have a liquid hedging vehicle like a stock or a futures contract.

TABLE 5–3a
Daily index return correlations (January 2, 1988–August 1, 1988) [a]

	DJIA	NYA	OEX	SPX	XII
NYA	.984				
OEX	.981	.987			
SPX	.985	.998	.991		
XII	.982	.989	.996	.993	
XMI	.989	.976	.986	.980	.986

TABLE 5–3b
Weekly index return correlations (1986–1988)

	DJIA	NYA	OEX	SPX	XII
NYA	.978				
OEX	.978	.977			
SPX	.982	.997	.986		
XII	.974	.975	.991	.985	
XMI	.981	.952	.972	.962	.972

Table 5–3c
Monthly index return correlations (1979–1988)

	XMI	NYA	OEX
NYA	.911		
OEX	.921	.919	
SPX	.941	.977	.938

[a]Index ticker symbols are defined in Table 5–1.

valuation. First, the composition of the underlying asset: Is it a small index, say 20 stocks, like XMI, or a large one, 1,600 stocks, like the NYSE index? An index of fewer stocks is more manageable as a hedge vehicle than a very large index, but it is less representative of the market as a whole. How is the value of an index option affected if there is a futures contract on the same index? Is the futures contract a good substitute for the spot? This question is related to the second feature, early exercise. The effect of a futures contract on option valuation is different for American style options and European style options. The third feature, that is related to early exercise and is an important factor in pricing index options, is 'cash settlement.' [6] Finally, time to maturity is an important feature in option strategies and valuation. Most options are short term, 3 to 6 months, but some have maturities of up to 2 years, for example, options on XII and options on the S&P500 index.

We will start the discussion on valuation with the OEX, an index of 100 blue-chip stocks listed on the NYSE. All but one of the stocks have equity options trading on the CBOE. This index is capitalization weighted (meaning, the component stocks are weighted in the index in proportion to their total market value) and it is computed continuously during trading hours. The ten largest stocks in the index, including IBM, Exxon, and GE, account for about 40 percent of the overall value of the index. In 1988 the correlation of daily returns of the OEX index with the Dow Jones Index was .98, and with the S&P500 index, it was .99 (see Table 5–3).

An option contract on OEX represents a value of $100 \times$ Index and the minimum price change in the option (tick size) is $1/16 = \$6.25$. At any point in time there are four nearby monthly expirations. The options are American style, i.e., they could be exercised early.[7] When the option is exercised it is settled by the payment of cash, not by delivery of the underlying portfolio of stocks, as is the case with stock options. For example, suppose an investor exercises a call with a strike price of 270 and the OEX settles on that day at 290, his account will be credited with $(290 - 270) \times \$100 = \$2000$ while the account of an option writer is debited by the same amount.

Given the above specifications how do we price such an option? The common approach has been to assume that the stock index follows a geometric Wiener process, which leads to the Black-Scholes (BS) model discussed in Chapter 3. The same assumption is made with regard to prices of individual stocks but it seems that such a process, in which the price changes continuously without jumps, fits a stock index better than it fits most stocks.[8]

In applying the BS model to index options we must also take into account the dividend payments on the stocks in the index. For broad-based

---

[6]The 'cash settlement' procedure is explained in the next page.

[7]On the expiration day all options that are owned by customers and are at least $.10 in-the-money and all options owned by exchange members that are at least $.01 in-the-money are automatically exercised.

[8]Technically, it is inconsistent to assume that stock prices and the index of these prices both can follow a geometric Wiener process because the sum of lognormal variables does not have a lognormal distribution. Practically, however, it is a more reasonable assumption for the index than for many individual stocks.

indices, like the S&P500 index or the New York Stock Exchange (NYSE) index, the dividend stream spreads over the entire year (see Figure 5–1). It has been shown that, in pricing of options on such indices, a constant dividend yield is a very good approximation of the actual dividend stream.[9] The formula for a European call option with a constant dividend yield was derived by Merton (1973) and is given in Chapter 3, equation (3.17)

$$C = Se^{-qT} N [D] - Xe^{-rT} N [D - \sigma\sqrt{T}\,] \qquad (5.1)$$

where S is the value of the index and q is the dividend yield on the index. The other variables X, T, r, σ, and D are defined in Chapter 3.

This formula is most appropriate for European style options on broad-based indices like SPX. For other European style options that contain a relatively small number of stocks, XMI for example, we may use the modified BS formula given by equation (3.6) where $S^* = S - PV$ (dividends). S^* is the index value adjusted for the present value of all dividend payments on the stocks in the index.

Valuation of American Index Options
Although the OEX includes only 100 stocks we consider it to be a broad-based index and use a constant dividend yield in the valuation process. However, OEX and most other index options are American style options. The early exercise privilege can make these options more valuable than similar European style options. The difference in values will depend on the probability of premature exercise.[10] In the case of American index options where there is a stream of dividend payments, the valuation model does not have a closed form solution and it has to be solved numerically.

How important is early exercise, leaving aside the cash settlement issue that will be discussed later? In the following example we show the theoretical values of an American index option compared with a European index option using the same underlying index. We use equation (5.l) to value the European options and a finite difference approximation technique to solve numerically for the values of the American options.[11] We make the following assumptions:

---

[9]See Brenner, Courtadon and Subrahmanyam (1987).

[10]Chapter 4 discusses early exercise in detail.

[11]These techniques are described by Schwartz (1977) and Courtadon (1982). A general discussion of numerical methods in option pricing is given in Chapter 14.

FIGURE 5–1
NYSE Composite Index—dividend distribution (1989)

Amount[a]

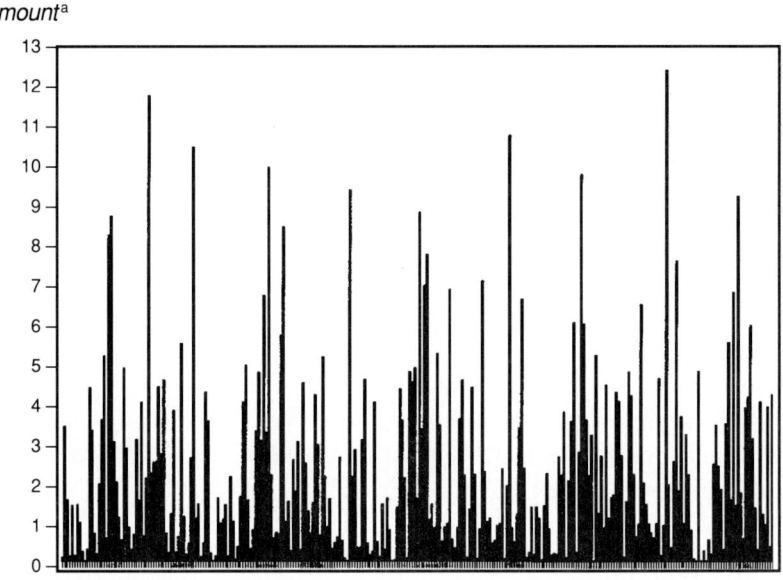

[a]Scale: The dividends are in index units.
Source: NYSE Statistics

Initial Index Value	S	= 300
Exercise price	X	= 300
Time to expiration	T	= 90 days
Interest rate	r	= 8 percent
Dividend yield	q	= 4 percent
Volatility	σ	= .20

In Table 5–4 we provide the values of a European (E) call and a European put as well as an American (A) call and an American put when the options are at-the-money, in-the-money and out-of-the-money. We also show how the difference between American values and European values changes with time to expiration.

An in-the-money American call with $S = 330$ and $X = 300$ and 30 days to maturity has a value of $31.21, almost identical to the European call that is worth $31.20. The same is true for the other calls whose values are given

TABLE 5–4
Theoretical prices of European and American index options

	Index Call				Index Put			
	90 Days		30 Days		90 Days		30 Days	
Days to Maturity								
Index Value	European Style	American Style	European Style	American Style	European Style	American Style	European Style	American Style
270	2.49	2.51	.24	.26	29.28	30.73	29.16	30.00
300	13.22	13.24	7.33	7.35	10.31	10.51	6.35	6.39
330	34.91	34.93	31.20	31.21	2.29	2.31	.32	.32

$X = 300$
$r = .08$
$\sigma = .20$
$q = .04$

in the table. The difference between European and American call options is small, mainly due to the assumption of a constant dividend yield. Option values in Table 5–4 assume the index goes ex-dividend continuously by an infinitesimal amount at each instant. The incentive to exercise, at any instant, depends largely on the size of the forthcoming dividend payments relative to the rate of interest, as well as on other parameters. Given the above parameters, including the dividend yield, the probability of exercising early an index call is extremely small. This is different from the case of dividend paying stocks where the payments are infrequent but relatively large and may cause a sharp drop in the price of the stock on the ex-dividend day. In that case early exercise may be valuable and the difference between American options and European options could be substantial.[12]

Although for index calls there is only a small difference between American and European values, for index puts the difference is not negligible. When $S = 270$ and $X = 300$ the 90 day American put is worth 5 percent more than the European one ($30.73 vs. $29.28). The continuous dividend payments do not overcome the effect of the rate of interest that

[12]This is true, though to a lesser extent, for options on indices with a small number of stocks, like XMI, and industry indices, where only a few dividend payments may be left before the options expire.

makes early exercise of calls irrational and makes early exercise of puts rational.

We may summarize the above discussion with the following statement: The values of American style index calls are almost identical to European style calls for a wide range of parameter values. The values of American style index puts may exceed their European counterparts by significant amounts especially for in-the-money options.

The Cash Settlement Feature of Index Options

The valuation of index options, as discussed above, assumed implicitly that upon exercise there is delivery of the underlying index (i.e., the stocks in the index, in proportion to their market value). However, unlike stock options, all index options are settled in cash. For example, the holder of a February 260 OEX call notifies his broker that he would like to exercise his call. The broker informs the Options Clearing Corporation (OCC) which will assign the exercise notice to one of its member firms which in turn assigns it to one of its clients with an open short position in February 260 calls. If the index closed, say, at 280 the option holder would be paid by the writer in cash $(280 - 260) \times \$100 = \$2000$. While the option holder knows at the end of the trading day that his income is $2000, the writer of the option will only discover the next morning (usually before the opening) that she has been assigned and that her account was debited for $2000.

Cash settlement adds an 'exercise risk' to index options writers. To clearly identify this risk let's look at a position that is considered riskless, a conversion. Assume, for example, that the holder of an IBM conversion is short a February 120 call, long a February 120 put and long 100 shares of IBM. As shown in Chapter 2 this is a riskless position. In case of early exercise of the call option, the 100 shares of IBM are delivered and the holder faces no risk from movements in the price of IBM stock at the opening of trading the next day.

Assume now that he holds an OEX conversion instead: short a February 260 call, long a February 260 put and long the appropriate amount of the OEX index portfolio. In the event of early exercise this conversion is not riskless. On February 7, 1989, the OEX closed at 286.35. Assume that the February 260 call was exercised. On the morning of February 8 the conversion holder was notified that he was exercised and that he was debited for $(286.35 - 260) \times 100 = \$2635$. When trading opened at 9:30 on February 8 he was long a put, with a closing price of 1/16 on February 7, and long the OEX index portfolio. His riskless position had become a risky one. If the OEX had opened, for example, at 284 he would have experienced a loss[13] of $(286.35-284) \times 100 = \$235$. This additional source of risk, due to early exercise and cash settlement, cannot be eliminated by hedging. Because, unlike the IBM case where the stock is delivered out of the portfolio, the OEX conversion holder pays cash and still holds the stocks which must be liquidated. Thus, in equilibrium, the options should command a risk premium that will depend on the probability of early exercise, risk aversion and the other option parameters. The derivation of a model to price this risk is beyond the scope of this chapter.[14]

It should be noted that cash settlement at expiration, unlike prior to expiration, does not come as a surprise to the option writer and therefore does not cause problems. The hedged option writer who holds the index portfolio and does not want to assume a risky position in the index can sell the stocks on the close of trading at expiration. He can do so by submitting Market On Close (MOC) orders on the stocks he is holding. There is no price risk because he will be selling his stocks at the prices that make up the closing index value, which is the value that is also used to settle all in-the-money options.

The Index as a Traded Asset: Problems and Solutions
Another important assumption in pricing options is that the underlying asset is traded continuously and that transactions costs are negligible. This assumption is more problematic for broad-based indices than for most stocks with exchange traded options. Replicating the S&P500 index exactly requires executing trades in 500 stocks in three markets, NYSE, AMEX, OTC. Such a trade is time-consuming and involves non-trivial transactions costs, mainly due to the less liquid stocks. The alternative approach to trading in all stocks is to choose a sample that consists of the more liquid stocks and is highly correlated with the index.

Let us go through a specific example, this time ignoring the cash settlement issue. On the close on November 21, 1988 the December 150

---

[13]With 10 days to expiration the value of the 260 put remains 1/16.

[14]A theoretical model, in a market with stock index futures, is derived in Brenner, Courtadon and Subrahmanyam (1987). The actual cash-settlement risk premium can be estimated in several ways. Using a small sample of in-the-money calls, the estimates of this risk premium were as large as 3.5 percent of the option's value.

calls and puts on the NYSE composite index (NYA) were selling at the same price (2 7/16). The index was at 150.09. An arbitrageur who thought that the put was too expensive relative to the call[15] could have sold the put and bought the call for "even money." She then would have a synthetic long position in NYA.[16] If she had wanted to hedge, she should have sold short all NYA stocks (about 1650) in a matter of minutes, which is an impossible task.[17] Instead she could have chosen a small sample of highly liquid stocks that are highly correlated with NYA, for example, the 20 stocks included in the Major Market Index (XMI). The index has a correlation of .95 and a beta of 1 with NYA and the stocks are among the most liquid ones on the NYSE.[18] Since on November 21 XMI was 2.7 times NYA ($405.38 = 2.7 \times 150.09$) she could have bought 27 synthetic NYA's for every 10 XMI that she was selling short. With the income obtained from the short sale she could have bought bonds that mature on December 16 (the expiration day for December options). Since the synthetic long position combined with being short XMI was obtained at no cost, she should have ended up with the interest income on the bonds she had bought irrespective of the level of the market at expiration.

Now let's see what happened on December 16. NYA closed at 155.16 and XMI closed at 423.13. The 27 calls were exercised and they generated $27 \times (S - X) \times 100 = 27 \times (155.16 - 150) \times 100 = \$13,932$. Assuming 8.5 percent continuously compounded annual interest on the bonds that she bought for 16 days, her interest income was $\exp(rT) - 1 = (\exp(.085 \times .0438) - 1) \times \$405,380 = \$1,510$. Total income was $\$13,932 + \$1,510 = \$15,442$. If she did not want to keep the short positions she needed to buy back the stocks in XMI. On the close, Friday December 16, XMI closed at 423.13. Buying back the stocks she sold short would have cost her $\$423,130 - \$405,380 = \$17,750$. Despite the favorable start-up conditions she ended up losing $\$17,750 - \$15,442 = \$2,308$. This is an example of 'tracking error' and it is due to the fact that even with a very high correlation

---

[15]Put-call parity does not hold for American options. An at-the-money put may cost as much as an at-the-money call and more..

[16]'Synthetic' positions are discussed in Chapter 2.

[17]While it may be possible to buy stocks in a reasonable time frame, it is next to impossible to sell short so many stocks in a short time span. Problems like the need to borrow the stocks and the 'uptick' rule are just two of many problems in executing this trade.

[18]In general, the ratio of two indices reflects the difference in the base index values and in their betas. E.g., a 2.7 ratio could be a result of a 1.8 base ratio and a beta ratio of 1.5 ($2.7 = 1.8 \times 1.5$).

we may have occasional shifts in one index and not in the other one, resulting[19] in an unexpected gain or loss on a position that is considered riskless.

Another alternative to hedge index options is to use a stock index futures contract. Many traders do use such futures contracts. It has been estimated that 30 percent of the volume of the S&P500 futures contract trading on the Chicago Mercantile Exchange (CME) is being used to hedge OEX options and options on the S&P500 index (SPX). The advantages of using a futures contract are speed of execution, low transactions costs and the ability to short the futures contract with no restrictions.[20] However, here too we may encounter some serious problems. The futures contract can serve as a perfect hedge only for European index options that are cash settled at the same time that the futures contract on the same index is settled. This is strictly true only for XMI options and futures. If the futures contract does not settle when the options do, or if there is no futures contract on the same index as the options and other futures are being used, we are faced with two potential problems: one, the futures contract may deviate from its fair value (a 'basis' problem) and two, the index underlying the futures contract may deviate from the index underlying the option contract (the 'tracking' error problem).[21]

Traders in OEX use two futures contracts to hedge their positions;[22] the S&P500 and the recently introduced, CBOE 250. Hedging OEX options with futures contracts may be the cheapest way to hedge these options but it does not solve the cash settlement problem. Here too the option writer faces 'exercise risk.' Upon exercise of the option, the writer who has used a futures contract for hedging will be left with his unhedged futures position.

---

[19]This may also happen due to the fact that an index with many stocks will always have some stocks that have not traded but their prices are included in the index computation. A 20 stock index, like XMI, on the other hand reflects almost always current prices.

[20]The only problem is the marking-to-market procedure that requires the management of cash flows in the trader's account. The effect of interest rate uncertainty on hedge performance is assumed to be negligible and is not discussed here.

[21]SPX options in the quarterly cycle are in the same category as XMI options but for their off quarterly expirations (e.g., January, February) there is no futures contract.

[22]It should be noted that in hedging with a futures contract we use $N(D)e^{-rT}$ as the hedge ratio and not $N(D)$ that is used if we hedge with the cash index. The reason is that a futures contract has a premium over cash that decays continuously towards the cash level and it is paid out continuously because of the marking-to-market procedure. This is a standard adjustment, known as "tailing" the futures hedge.

5.3   OPTIONS ON STOCK INDEX FUTURES

In addition to cash settled options on stock indexes, there are also options on index futures. Currently there are two stock index futures contracts that offer options. The S&P500, the most liquid index futures contract, offers options with 3, 6, and 9 month maturities. Both the futures and the options trade on the Chicago Mercantile Exchange (CME). The other exchange that offers options on its futures contracts is the New York Futures Exchange (NYFE).

The main distinguishing feature of these options is the method of delivery. When a futures option is exercised, the positions of both the buyer and the writer are transformed into futures positions.[23] A long call becomes a long position in the futures contract and the call writer gets the matching short futures position. These are then marked to market, based on the difference between the option's strike price and the current futures price.

The value of an option on a futures contract was derived by Black (1976) and is given in Chapter 3, equation (3.20). Black's formula assumes that the option is a European style option.[24] The existing futures options, however, are American style and could, in principle, be exercised early. In the case of the American call on the stock index futures contract, the valuation problem is similar to the valuation of options on an index. Since the futures price converges smoothly toward the spot price at maturity depending on the force of interest, the call option on the futures contract is similar to one on a stock paying a continuous dividend. This arises from the fact that, if the spot price remains constant over a period of time, the futures price decreases relative to the price of its underlying asset as the maturity date approaches. Note that this effect is independent of dividend payments on the index and would arise even if there were no dividend payments. In this case, too, the valuation problem does not have a closed form solution and has to be solved numerically.[25]

Figure 5–2 shows the values of American options on stock index futures compared with values obtained from Black's model (equation 3.20)

---

[23]Options on futures are available monthly while the index futures are on a quarterly cycle. Options in the off quarterly cycle settle with the near quarter futures contract. For example, the January options, when exercised, settle with the March futures contract.

[24]The hedge ratio is given by $PV[N(D)]$. As we discussed before if one hedges with a futures contract, he needs less futures contracts than in hedging with the actual index.

[25]See Brenner, Courtadon and Subrahmanyam (1985), Ramaswamy and Sundaresan (1985) and Whaley (1986).

for European futures options. While for spot call options the minimum values for American and European options coincide, as shown by Merton (1973), for calls on futures, C_F, the minimum value of the American call is always larger than the minimum value of the European call.

Since an in-the-money European call can only be exercised at maturity, the value of $F - X$ is only its present value, $(F - X)e^{-rT}$. The American call, however, carries the right to obtain $F - X$ immediately and $F - X$ is always larger than $PV(F - X)$. Thus, C_F for American futures options must always be larger than for European futures options due to arbitrage possibilities. Buying American calls and selling European calls for credit (i.e., at a higher price) would provide a profit on a no-investment no-risk position.

The valuation of puts on futures contracts is similar to the valuation of calls except that the boundary conditions are different. The minimum values, for in-the-money puts, are $(X - F)e^{-rT}$ for European puts and $X - F$ for American puts. Again, the valuation problem does not have a closed form solution and must be solved numerically.

Options on the Index and Options on Futures: A Comparison

Two stock market indices, SPX and NYA, have options on the index and options on the futures contract on the same index. What should be the relationship between an index option and an index futures option? While the option on SPX is European and the option on the SPX futures contract is American, the option on NYA and the option on the NYSE futures contract are both American.

The value of an index call is given by (5.1) as described before. The value of a European option written on the futures contract is given by Black (1976) (equation 3.20). Assuming that the futures contract is priced correctly vis-à-vis the index, we have

$$F = Se^{(r-q)T} \tag{5.2}$$

If we substitute this expression for F in Black's model we will find that the value of the European option on the futures contract should be the same as one on the cash index.[26] Since we have shown before, that American options on futures, like the SPX futures options, should be priced higher than

---

[26] In case the futures contract is not priced correctly according to (5.2) we may find the futures options to be priced differently than the index option, but this will provide opportunities for arbitrage. A detailed discussion is beyond the scope of this chapter.

FIGURE 5–2
American and European call values

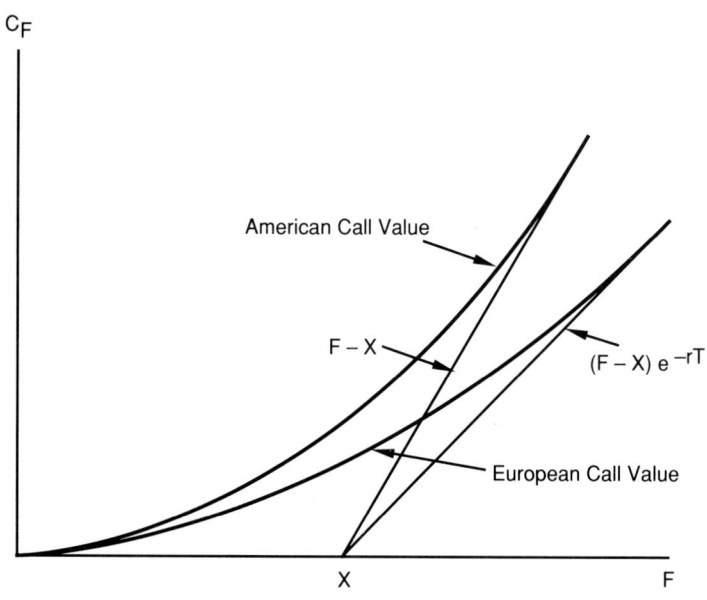

European futures options, it implies that SPX futures options should be priced higher than SPX index options. For example, on February 14, 1989, the at-the-money February and March 290 calls on the S&P500 closed at 3 1/4 and 7 respectively. The February and March 290 calls on futures closed at 4.05 and 7.15 respectively.[27]

The comparison of NYA index options with the futures options is more complicated. In general, the values of these two American options should be different. Again assuming that the futures contract is priced correctly, the main reason for the potential difference in values is the spread between the riskless rate of interest and the dividend yield. The larger is this spread (i.e., the higher r is relative to q) the more valuable will be the futures call option relative to the index call option. The reverse is true for the put

---

[27]This is used as an example. It should be noted that there is a problem of simultaneity especially with closing prices, since the futures options close a few minutes after the cash options.

options. Take for example, the extreme case that there are no dividends paid on the index. We know already that it will not be rational to exercise such an American index call and it will be priced the same as the European call. The futures call, however, may be exercised early and therefore will be priced higher than the index call.

To see by how much these values can differ we provide in Tables 5–5A and 5–5B the values of calls and puts for index options and for futures options. For example, the index is at 80, the exercise price is 100, volatility is 20 percent, the yield on a six-month T-bill is 8 percent and the dividend yield is 4 percent. An American put that matures in six months will be valued at $20, and exercised immediately, if the underlying is the index itself. It should cost only $18.5, slightly above the exercise value $X - F$, if the underlying is a futures contract on the index, assuming the futures is priced correctly with respect to the index. The difference between call options is much smaller. Using the parameter values in the example above, except with the index at 120 rather than at 80, the value of the futures call is only $0.6 more than the value of the index call ($22.6 vs. $22.0).

The difference between a call on an index and a call on the futures contract seems to be insignificant for short maturity and/or out-of-the-money options. However, at longer maturities, the option on the index could be lower than the option on the futures contract by .5 to 1.5 percent of the index. The difference increases the deeper in-the-money the options are. It is important to note, however, that for lower dividend yields the difference in values increases. On the other hand, for a sufficiently high dividend payment, given the rate of interest, the values of the two options could be about the same.

The difference in values is naturally related to the difference in the probability of early exercise. Regarding call options, a large dividend payment on the index will increase the probability of early exercise for the futures options. As far as put options are concerned, a larger dividend payout will increase the probability of early exercise of the futures put option. However, the effect of an increase in dividends on the probability of early exercise of the index put option is ambiguous. A large dividend may delay exercise but will also increase the probability of reaching low stock prices that trigger exercise.

Options on the index and options on index futures are two competing instruments that fund managers should weigh as alternatives in their trading strategies. Choosing the option that best suits the investor depends not only

TABLE 5–5a
Values of index call options and index futures call options[a]

Days to Maturity	30 Days		90 Days		180 Days		270 Days	
I / X	Index Option	Futures Option	Index Option	Futures Option	Index Option	Futures Option	Index Option	Futures Option
.80	.000	.000	.000	.000	.004	.004	.010	.010
.90	.001	.001	.008	.008	.021	.022	.034	.034
1.00	.024	.025	.044	.044	.065	.065	.081	.082
1.10	.104	.104	.116	.117	.134	.136	.149	.153
1.20	.203	.204	.209	.212	.220	.226	.232	.240

r = Interest Rate = .08

σ = Standard Deviation = .20

q = Dividend Yield = .04

I / X = how far the option is in-the-money or out-of-the-money. For example, if the Strike Price (X) = 100, the Index (I) = 120, and the Days to Maturity (T) = 90 days, the futures call value is 21.2 while the index call value is 20.9.

TABLE 5–5b
Values of index put options and index futures put options[a]

Days to Maturity	30 Days		90 Days		180 Days		270 Days	
I / X	Index Option	Futures Option	Index Option	Futures Option	Index Option	Futures Option	Index Option	Futures Option
.80	.200	.197	.200	.192	.200	.185	.200	.181
.90	.100	.097	.102	.098	.107	.102	.112	.105
1.00	.021	.021	.035	.035	.047	.046	.056	.053
1.10	.001	.001	.008	.008	.017	.017	.025	.024
1.20	.000	.000	.001	.001	.005	.005	.010	.010

r = Interest Rate = .08

σ = Standard Deviation = .20

q = Dividend Yield = .04

I / X = how far the option is in-the-money or out-of-the-money. For example, if the Strike Price (X) = 100, the Index (I) = 80, and the Days to Maturity (T) = 90 days, the futures put value is 19.2 while the index put value is 20.

[a]The values in the tables are the ratio of the option price to the strike price.

on the type of option (American vs. European, cash or futures) but also on institutional factors. The various options trade on different exchanges and futures options are subject to different regulations than index options.[28] For example, margin requirements are quite different for the two types of options. The margin system on index options is in principle the same as on stock options while the margin system in futures options tends to be similar to futures margining.[29] Arbitrageurs also should be aware of the risk involved in writing an index option against an identical futures option. Being long the futures option does not provide complete protection when the cash option is exercised, especially because there is always a delay in assigning the exercise notice.

An institutional investor who uses index options should take into account the various factors of liquidity, margin requirements, price limits, type of option and other transactions costs. Take, for example, a fund manager who wants to protect his portfolio against a market decline in the coming six months. Assuming he does not want to substitute his portfolio for a call and a bond and does not want to engage in dynamic hedging, he will look for a six month index put. Which one? OEX options are the most liquid, are based on 100 blue-chip stocks, and are of the American type with 4 nearby monthly expirations. SPX options are less liquid, are based on an index of 500 stocks, are European style and have up to two-year maturities. The fund manager may prefer the SPX options for several reasons. First, he can match his horizon rather closely with existing options and does not need to buy a new put when an existing put expires. Second, the broader 500 stock index provides a better match for most institutional stock funds. Third, the European option is cheaper than the American. There is no point in paying for the early exercise feature when there is no need for it. Finally, since the fund manager is not engaging in daily trading the liquidity issue is of little concern to him. Another alternative he may consider are the S&P500 futures options. These options have lower transactions costs, but are more expensive than the S&P500 cash option, due to their early exercise feature and thus may be less desirable for the purpose specified above.

---

[28]Index options are regulated by the SEC while futures options, such as index futures, are regulated by the CFTC.

[29]'Delta' margining is common practice for exchange members. In this system all options are translated into futures equivalents using the hedge ratio, delta, from the BS model.

5.4 STRATEGIES WITH INDEX OPTIONS AND OTHER USES

Options on stock market indices have created new opportunities for all investors. Institutional investors, securities firms, individuals and other market players are likely users of these options.

Index options can be used in portfolio strategies in ways similar to the use of stock options in single stock strategies.[30] While it is possible to use individual stock options to change the risk-return characteristics of any portfolio, index options may be preferred for broader strategies that involve a portfolio as a whole. They provide a risk-return profile that matches closely most diversified portfolios and they are 'cheaper' than a portfolio of stock options.[31]

The Protective Put

The purpose of this strategy is to protect a portfolio of stocks from declining in value below a given level. This portfolio insurance strategy is becoming even more popular since the October 1987 Crash.[32] In this strategy the portfolio manager uses index puts. As in any insurance there is a tradeoff between the cost of the insurance and the level of protection. For example, assume a diversified portfolio, with a beta of 1, that for simplicity is currently valued at $29,202,000 while the current S&P500 index is 292.02 (February 10, 1989). The manager is considering several options to protect his gain in the recent market runup. He would like to profit from stock market increases and is willing to pay some premium to protect most of his gains. One strategy is to buy index puts. Which index should he use? What maturity should he use? What strike price?

To shorten the discussion here we will assume that he would like to buy protection (insurance) for four months, until the expiration of the June '89 contract. Since the only liquid index option with June maturity is the SPX contract, he examines these options. SPX also has the advantage of being a European option and therefore should cost less than a comparable

---

[30]Since many portfolio strategies are essentially identical to the single stock strategies we will emphasize the special aspects of index strategies. See Chapter 2 for a detailed discussion of stock option strategies.

[31]See Chapter 2 for a proof that an option on a portfolio is worth less than a portfolio of options.

[32]Before the Crash, portfolio insurance strategies were mainly dynamic strategies using index futures. Chapter 11 discusses these strategies in detail.

American option.[33] On February 10, 1989 the put prices for S&P500 puts were as follows:

Strike Price:	250	260	270	280	290	300
Put Price:	1	$1\frac{3}{16}$	$2\frac{13}{16}$	$4\frac{7}{8}$	$7\frac{3}{4}$	$11\frac{1}{4}$

The closing value of the S&P500 was 292.02. The number of puts needed to guarantee a floor for the value of the portfolio is given by

$$\frac{\text{value of portfolio}}{\text{S\&P500} \times 100} \times \text{beta} = \frac{29,202,000}{29,202} \times 1.0 = 1,000$$

The combined value for the portfolio with 1,000 puts is given in Table 5–6.

The portfolio manager may choose not to protect the portfolio, in which case he may see it decline by the same rate as the S&P500 index. However, by giving up some of the potential increase he may protect the portfolio from declining below a floor that is given by, the strike price minus the price of the put. For example, by buying 1000 puts with a 280 strike price he obtains a floor of $27,512,500 but he gives up $487,500 of the potential increase in the value of the portfolio in the next four months.[34] Higher strike prices provide a higher floor at greater cost.

In many cases the portfolio manager is looking for longer-term protection. The existence of long-dated options enables portfolio holders to buy protection for up to two years. In case the portfolio beta is different from 1, let's say 1.5, then the number of puts needed to guarantee a floor is 1.5 times the number of puts needed for an index portfolio. Also, each desired floor is obtained by puts with higher strike prices that are determined by the size of beta. For example, a minus 15 percent floor could be approximately achieved by one and a half 10 percent out-of-the-money puts.

Another strategy that is similar to the protective put is the so called *90/ 10 strategy,* a combination of 90 percent T-bills and 10 percent index calls.[35]

---

[33]He can also examine the highly liquid OEX option. It is an American option and would require rolling over at some point before its expiration in June. OEX options carry risk when rolled over and are more expensive because they can be exercised early.

[34]The computation is: (strike price − put price) × 100 = 'floor' value of 1 index contract. I.e., (280 − 4.875) × 100 = 27,512.5. Multiplying this by 1,000 contracts gives the floor for the entire portfolio.

[35]Initially the idea was to buy enough T-bills to guarantee that the interest income would restore the initial value of the portfolio even if all of the options expired worthless. See also the discussion in Chapter 2.

TABLE 5–6
Value of portfolio protected with puts with different strikes
(in $ '000)

Percentage Change in S&P500	−20	−10	−5	0	+5	+10
S&P500	233.62	262.82	277.42	292.02	306.62	321.22
Value of Portfolio (no puts)	23,362	26,282	27,742	29,202	30,662	32,122
Value of Portfolio (with puts)						
X = 260	25,819	26,100	27,561	29,021	30,481	31,941
X = 270	26,719	26,719	27,461	28,921	30,381	31,841
X = 280	27,513	27,513	27,513	28,715	30,175	31,635
X = 290	28,225	28,225	28,225	28,427	29,887	31,347
X = 300	28,875	28,875	28,875	28,875	29,537	30,997

In principle, the strategy requires selling the equity portfolio and using the funds to purchase bonds and call options for the desired period at a ratio that replicates the combination of the portfolio plus the put. The extent to which these strategies mimic one another depends on how well put-call parity holds, which in turn depends on the type of options (American, European), liquidity, transactions costs and other parameters. For example, a portfolio combined with an American deep-in-the-money put could not be closely replicated by a T-bill combined with an out-of-the-money call option.

Covered Call Writing
A recent survey of mutual funds, conducted and published by the CBOE (1987), identifies 435 funds that are allowed to use options. The most popular strategy among these funds is covered call writing, used by about 86 percent of the funds vs. 74 percent buying puts, the second most popular strategy. Covered writing is used by holders of large portfolios who believe that the market is going to be rather 'stable' in the near future. Thus, writing index calls may enhance portfolio returns.

The risk-return profile of such a position depends on the exercise level of the option. In the following example the portfolio manager can choose among three alternative profiles. Assume he manages a $29,202,000 S&P500 index fund (on February 10, 1989 the S&P500 index was at 292.02). The fund manager believes that in the next 4 months the index will trade in the range of 280 to 300. The premiums for the June 290, 295, and 300 SPX calls were 15 1/2, 12 1/4, and 9 1/4 respectively. If he wants to write calls against the entire portfolio he should sell 1,000 index calls. He arrives at this number by dividing the value of the fund by the value of the contract (index level of 292.02 × contract size of $100).

The fund manager faces the risk-return profile shown in Table 5–7.

Writing-in-the-money calls reduces the dispersion of the outcomes more than writing at-the-money or out-of-the-money options. In fact, writing a very deep-in-the-money call amounts to 'freezing' the fund at its current value (there is no dispersion).[36]

'Synthetic' Portfolios

First, recall that a long position in a portfolio of equities could be obtained by buying an index call, writing an index put and buying T-bills that match the expiration of the options. Thus, this strategy could be used as a substitute to buying a large diversified portfolio. For example, on February 10, 1989 the SPX June 290 call and put prices were 15 1/2 and 7 3/4 respectively. The S&P500 index closed at 292.02. Buying the 290 call at 15 1/2 and selling the 290 put at 7 3/4 would require a net outlay of $775 for the combination. To make it comparable with an investment in an index fund, we buy 4 month T-bills in a face amount equal to the strike value of the options which is $29,000. If the S&P500 increases by 5% to 306.62 the put will expire worthless and the call will provide $1,662. Combined with the maturing T-bills at $29,000 we have the same payoff as the S&P500. The same is true for a 5% decrease in value where the short put makes us lose the same percentage as the index did. This 'synthetic' position could be executed faster than buying a large portfolio of stocks. It also provides diversification for small investors who, until now, were forced to buy mutual fund shares in order to diversify.

Moreover, a portfolio manager who already has a long equities

---

[36]A similar strategy could be enacted by selling futures contracts, using a hedge ratio derived from an option pricing model. He would then dynamically operate the strategy by selling futures when the market moves up and buying some of them back when the market moves down. This strategy, however, provides an unknown payoff distribution and requires active management.

TABLE 5–7
Value of portfolio covered with written calls with different strikes (in $ '000)

Percentage change in S&P500	−10	−5	0	+5	+10
S&P500	262.82	277.42	292.02	306.62	321.22
Value of Portfolio	26,282	27,742	29,202	30,662	32,122
Value of Covered Portfolio					
X = 290	27,832	29,292	30,550	30,550	30,550
X = 295	27,507	28,967	30,427	30,725	30,725
X = 300	27,207	28,667	30,127	30,925	30,925

position and wants to 'get out' for a period of time (he predicts a market downturn) could simply sell a synthetic (i.e. sell a call and buy a put). When he later reverses his options position, or it matures, he becomes long again. In doing this he may save transactions costs and achieve relatively fast execution.

Second, using the above principle it is possible to initiate a short market portfolio position by writing an index-call and buying an index put with the same strike and expiration. Due to short-sales restrictions and other transactions costs it is much more difficult to sell short a market portfolio dealing only in the spot market.

Tactical Asset Allocation

Index options can be used in a variety of strategies that are currently the domain of index futures and other financial assets. Two such examples are Tactical Asset Allocation (TAA) and the creation of fixed income instruments linked to the S&P500 Index.

The objective of TAA is to enhance investment returns by varying the allocation of funds among broad asset classes, typically between a stock market index, long term bonds and cash equivalents[37] in order to exploit inefficiencies in relative prices of securities in these classes. The allocation

---

[37]See Sharpe (1987) for a discussion on asset allocation strategies.

is changed when there is a change in the perceived risk or expected return of any of the assets.

For example, a fund manager may believe that the normal long-run relationship of bond yields to dividend yields is about two to one. A significant drop in the dividend yield coupled with an increase in the bond yield, as happened in the summer of 1987, would trigger a shift from the equity market to the bond market. This could be done using stock index futures and bond futures, leaving the mix of cash bonds and common stocks in the investment portfolio intact. An opposite move in the relative yields, back to the assumed 'normal' ratio would call for a reversal of the futures positions. Alternatively, one could use index options and bond options in various combinations. One way would be to sell in-the-money index calls and buy in-the-money bond calls.

A different approach to asset allocation could be to use only an equity portfolio combined with index options to create a 'synthetic' stock-bond combination. As discussed in Chapter 3 we can create the equivalent of a bond position by buying stocks and selling call options at the delta neutral hedge ratio. Thus, if we would like to create a 50/50 mix of stocks and bonds, we could invest in an index fund and sell at-the-money index calls against it. The hedge ratio of at-the-money calls is approximately .5. Therefore, being long x units of the index combined with being short at-the-money calls on $2x$ units of the index is comparable to being long x bonds.

An important feature of an asset allocation strategy using stock index options is that a change in the level of the market automatically alters the portfolio's exposure in the different asset classes. The appropriate option position can therefore rebalance the portfolio in the desired direction without the need for any transaction. For example, if we had started with a 50/50 allocation by writing index calls and an increase in the index increases the hedge ratio of the call options to .6 each, every call option turns 60 percent of the index unit into a riskless asset, in effect changing the mix to a 60/40 allocation. A very large increase will turn our position into a 100 percent bond position. A very large drop in the market will turn the position into a 100 percent equity position.

The 50/50 initial position could also be created by a combination of an equity portfolio with a long position in at-the-money index puts. In this case an increase in the stock market index shifts the assets' actual exposure more into stocks and a decrease in the market more into bonds.

An asset allocation strategy, sometimes called "a fence", combines the index fund with an out-of-the-money long put and an out-of-the-money short call.[38] The long puts and short calls turn some of the equity into a bond. Thus, the asset mix consists of a small proportion of bond equivalents. As the market moves either up or down, the asset mix moves more into bond equivalents and away from equity.[39] More complicated asset allocation schemes use futures and options in the bond and stock markets combined with an initial bond/stock mix. For example, if the stock market is expected to rise and the bond market to decline we may change our exposure by buying an index call bull-spread and selling a bond call bull-spread.

Fixed Income Instruments Linked to the Stock Market

In 1987, several banks began to offer CD's linked to the S&P500 index. They pay less interest than conventional CD's but contain an option to participate in the increase of the S&P500 index if it rises beyond a given strike price. Specifically, the Chase Market Index Investment (CMII) would pay the larger of an annual interest rate of 4% or 30 percent of the increase in the S&P500, if the funds were invested for 6 months.

The following figures illustrate the payoff on this instrument:[40]

S&P500 index at opening	285.57
S&P500 index at maturity	342.68
Increase during 6 months	57.11 or 20%
30% of the increase is	6%

On an annual basis the return is 12.36 percent. This return is obtained due to the call option on the S&P500 that was attached to the CD. The cost of the option is the difference between the CD rate at Chase and the 4% guaranteed rate.

Chase offered these CMII's at different minimum rates and with 3, 6, 9 and 12 month maturities. From the investor's point of view this instrument was competing with SPX and other index options. They were not perfect substitutes since strike prices and maturities were seldom matching. The bank, on the other hand, can use exchange traded index options to hedge its

---

[38]Using the bond market terminology, this strategy is similar to a "collar," created by a 'cap' and 'floor.'

[39]The beta of this position, the percentage change in the position's return with a one percent change in the market's return, changes from a beta close to 1 to a beta close to 0 as the market moves away from its current level.

[40]The example is taken from a Chase Manhattan Bank brochure advertising the CMII.

position. Most banks that offered these products were using index futures for hedging, but the events of October 1987 have affected their approach and made them use index options rather than futures. As a writer of options, the bank had a "negative gamma," so that even when it was hedged, it could lose if there was a big change in stock prices, in a short time interval.[41] Hedging with futures may make the position 'delta neutral' but it does not affect the gamma of the position. However, hedging the written options by buying comparable index options, which have positive gamma, can make the position 'gamma neutral' as well as delta neutral and reduce the risk from both small and large price changes. The success of this hedging strategy depends on how well the bank can match the terms of the CMII with the available index options.[42]

The Market Factor Hedge

Index options could also be used by investors and dealers in strategies that involve individual stocks. It is claimed that at least 40 percent of the volatility in individual stocks is due to market volatility and for some stocks it is much higher. For these stocks index options could be an efficient instrument to hedge the so called 'systematic risk.' For stocks that have no listed options, and for stocks that have illiquid options, index options are the only hedging tool. Moreover, many investors who own non-indexed portfolios may still want to buy what might be called 'disaster insurance,' i.e., insurance for events like October 1987. Index options are an efficient tool for this purpose.

5.5   NEW INDEX PRODUCTS

In designing an index option contract or an option-like instrument the exchanges try to assess who the potential users might be and specify the features that will appeal to these users. For example, the American Stock Exchange has recently changed the exercise terms of their XMI contract and made it a European style option. The main reason given for this change is

---

[41]The term "gamma" is defined and explained in Chapter 3.

[42]It should be emphasized that index options may have a limited appeal to banks for at least two reasons: one, there are position limits on exchange traded options and two, the cost of transacting a large order could be very high due to a wider bid-ask spread demanded for large orders.

that index options are mostly used for covered call writing and as protective puts. For these uses there is no need for the early exercise privilege and it adds uncertainty. As discussed in part 5.2, the features of the contract determine the valuation model that should be used.

Options on an International Index

The most recent innovation in the area of options on indices is an option on an *internationally* diversified stock market index. The AMEX and the Coffee, Sugar, Cocoa Exchange (CSCE) have developed an International Market Index (IMI) and in the Spring of 1989 began trading futures and options on the index. The index is capitalization weighted based on 50 "blue chip" securities which trade in form of American Depositary Receipts (ADRs) in the U.S. Since the stocks of these companies trade as ordinary shares in overseas markets, American and foreign investors who hold portfolios of foreign securities could use these futures and options to hedge their positions. The so-called ADR option is European-style, settled by cash and has 3 to 6 month maturities. Another international index being considered for options and futures trading is Morgan Stanley's EAFE (Europe, Australia, Far East) index. The trading in these instruments, subject to SEC and CFTC approval will take place at the CBOE and the CME.

An Exchange Traded Index

Another instrument that is not an option but may be important for option uses and valuation is the Equity Index participation (EIP).[43] The EIP is a security which gives the holder the equivalent of a position in the portfolio of an entire index. In effect, EIPs mimic the spot index portfolio and give investors an easy way to invest in the market indices themselves. Thus, EIPs could be used to hedge option positions. These EIPs have, in some sense, set the stage for the most recent new product proposal; the supershares.

SuperTrusts and SuperShares

The idea of a 'superfund' that sells 'supershares' was introduced many years ago by Professor Nils Hakansson (1976). As originally proposed, a

---

[43]The EIP was trading at the AMEX and a very similar product, Cash Index Participation (CIP), was trading on the PHLX. Following a court ruling, that these instruments are not a security, the exchanges stopped trading them. The exchanges have asked the full court to review the ruling.

'supershare' gives its owner a claim, at expiration, to a certain proportion of the fund's assets if the value of these assets is in a given range, otherwise he gets zero. In other words, an investor could choose a specific range of potential payoffs and buy claims for just that part. For example, if the Dow Jones Industrial Average (DJIA) were the index portfolio of a 'superfund,' then a "2000 - supershare" would be a claim that paid off only if the DJIA ended up in the range 1990 to 2010; it would be worthless otherwise.[44] One of the reasons that such securities are not traded is the lack of liquidity in instruments that may appeal to a small group of investors.[45]

The most recent innovation, the SuperTrust and its Super Shares, is an attempt to introduce an instrument that is based on the original superfund idea. A registration statement,[46] by Leland O'Brien Rubinstein (LOR) Associates, has been filed with the Securities and Exchange Commission. The SuperTrust will offer two basic securities with a maturity of three years: Index Trust SuperUnits backed by a common stock portfolio designed to track the S&P500, and Money Market Trust SuperUnits backed by a portfolio of short-term, high-quality money market instruments. Though there are several differences, the Index Trust as such is similar to the EIPs proposed by the AMEX and the PHLX. The Index Trust, however, provides an important extension, the SuperShares. An investor may split each of the Index Trust SuperUnits into two separate securities: an Appreciation SuperShare and an IndexIncome SuperShare.[47] Appreciation SuperShares have the right at expiration to all capital appreciation of the Index Trust beyond a given price. These shares have the same features as a call option on the Index Trust with the given strike price and a three year maturity. The Income SuperShares have the right to all the remaining value of the Index SuperUnit including dividends and other distributions.

For example, assume that the strike price is $100, the Index SuperUnit finishes at $120 and the dividends are $4 a year. The holder of the Appre-

---

[44]Currently one can achieve only a 'triangular' payoff scheme by buying a 'butterfly spread' in the range of available strike prices, for example using XMI options with 390, 400 and 410 strike prices. See Chapter 2.

[45]The lack of success of options on industry indices is an indication of what may happen to other narrow-based instruments.

[46]A detailed description of these instruments is given in the prospectuses filed with the SEC. A short description is given in the following paragraphs.

[47]These SuperShares are the equivalents of the "Primes" and "Scores" offered by Americus Trust for individual stocks and traded on the AMEX.

ciation SuperShare receives $120 – $100 = $20 at termination. The holder of the Index Income share gets $100 at expiration plus a $4 dividend every year during the three years. If the Index Super Unit had finished at 100 or less the Appreciation share would have been worthless.

The Money Market Trust may be split into Protection SuperShares and Money Market Income SuperShares. Protection SuperShares are like put options. They will appreciate in value as equities decline and lose all their value if equities increase or stay the same. The Money Market Income SuperShare would get interest income for three years and at the end of the period it would get back some or all of the principal depending on the performance of the stock market. If the market did well Money Market Income SuperShares will get more than the rate of interest. If the Index SuperUnit declined in value then these money market SuperShares will lose part of their value because it goes to the Protection SuperShares. The Protection SuperShare provides a long-term put option with a gain limited to a maximum that is reached if the market drops 30 percent. This SuperShare is intended to provide static portfolio insurance that avoids the problems associated with dynamic hedging.

5.6   CONCLUSIONS

A recent survey, commissioned by the American Stock Exchange,[48] provides a perspective of options investors a year after the October 1987 crash. Option investors express intentions to increase future use of stock options and stock index options. In particular, 86 percent of those who have positions in stock index options expect their use of index options to increase or remain the same.

A survey conducted by the CBOE[49] finds that the number of funds permitted to use stock index options increased to 40 percent in 1987 from 8 percent in 1985.

Another recent survey on the use of financial futures and options by life insurance companies was conducted by Stephen Figlewski (1989). One of his conclusions is that the lack of activity in many companies is due to

---

[48]Conducted by Yankelovich Claney Shulman of Westport, Connecticut, and published November 1988 by the AMEX OPTIONS division.

[49]Published by the CBOE in *Options for Mutual Funds,* December 1987.

lack of understanding of the instruments and their potential uses, and that this could change in the future as the firms gain experience. In this context it is interesting to note that among the larger firms only 13 percent are using index options *but* 53 percent have stated that they are likely to use them in the future.

The introduction and use of index options is now a global trend and many countries are joining the ranks. The most recent additions are the Swiss Market Index (SMI) options, trading since December 1988, and the French OMF50 trading since October 1988 on the OMF.[50] An option on the Nikkei Stock Average is trading on the Osaka Securities Exchange (OSE) since June 1989.[51]

Most countries nowadays that plan the introduction of options start with index options rather than stock options.[52] There are two major reasons for this. First, users of index options will mainly come from actual and potential holders of portfolios, the large and active participants in the market. Second, in most stock markets there is a serious concern about possible manipulation of prices of individual stocks and their effect on option trading. It is less likely that a portfolio of stocks, contained in an index, will be manipulated.

The success of a financial product depends on its specifications. The important issues are: First, should index options be accompanied by a tradable underlying asset? Most exchanges are planning a futures contract on the index and some are considering a tradable spot index. Second, should the option be a European style option or an American style option? In less liquid markets it may be advisable to make the option American so that investors who want to liquidate are not dependent on an illiquid market. Third, since cash-settlement seems to be the only reasonable way to settle index options, how do we reduce exercise risk faced by the writer of the options? Fourth, should we introduce long-dated options that are important in some strategies but have so far been rather illiquid or should we concentrate on short-term options?

Finally, there is another trend, mainly in the U.S., towards new

---

[50]The OMF50 option is trading electronically on the Options Market France (OMF). There is also the CAC40 option, an option on a futures contract trading on the MATIF.

[51]Several financial institutions offer over-the-counter options on the Nikkei index, the S&P500 and other stock market indices.

[52]Other countries in an advanced state of planning are Germany and Israel.

instruments that have option features and are stock index related. The most recent example in this category are the Super Shares suggested by LOR. Another example is options on the volatility of a market index suggested by Brenner and Galai (1989).[53]

References

Black, F. (January/March 1976). The pricing of commodity contracts. *Journal of Financial Economics, 3,* 167–79.

Black, F., and Scholes, M. (May/June 1973). The pricing of options and corporate liabilities. *Journal of Political Economy, 81,* 637–59.

Brennan, M., and Schwartz, E. (June 1976). The pricing of equity-linked life insurance policies with an asset value guarantee. *Journal of Financial Economics, 3,* 195–213.

Brenner, M., Courtadon, G., and Subrahmanyam, M. (December 1985). Options on the spot and options on futures. *Journal of Finance, 40,* 1303–17.

Brenner, M., Courtadon, G., and Subrahmanyam, M. (March 1987). The valuation of index options. New York University, Salomon Brothers Center for the Study of Financial Institutions working paper No. 414.

Brenner, M., Courtadon, G., and Subrahmanyam, M. (September 1989). Options on stocks and options on futures. *Journal of Banking and Finance,* pp. 773–82.

Brenner, M., and Galai, D. (July/August 1989). New financial instrument to hedge changes in volatility. *Financial Analysts Journal,* pp. 61–5.

Chicago Board Options Exchange. (December 1987). *Options for mutual funds.*

Courtadon, G. (December 1982). A more accurate finite difference approximation for the valuation of options. *Journal of Financial and Quantitative Analysis, 17,* 697–703.

Cox, J., and Rubinstein, M. (1985). *Options markets.* Englewood Cliffs, NJ: Prentice-Hall.

Figlewski, S. (Spring 1988). Arbitrage based pricing of stock index options. *Review of Futures Markets,* pp. 250–70.

Figlewski, S. (March 1989). The use of financial futures and options by life insurance companies. *Best's Review,* pp. 94–7.

Hakansson, N. (November/December 1976). The purchasing power fund: A new kind of financial intermediary. *Financial Analysts Journal, 32,* 49–59.

Leland, H. (May 1980). Who should buy portfolio insurance? *Journal of Finance, 35,* 581–94.

---

[53]These options are discussed in Brenner and Galai (1989).

Merton, C. (Autumn 1973). Theory of rational option pricing. *Bell Journal of Economics and Management Science, 4,* 141–83.

Ramaswamy, K., and Sundaresan, M. (December 1985). The valuation of options on futures contracts. *Journal of Finance, 40,* 1319–40.

Schwartz, E. (March 1977). The valuation of warrants: Implementing a new approach. *Journal of Financial Economics, 4,* 79–93.

Sharpe, W. (September/October 1987). Integrated asset allocation. *Financial Analysts Journal, 44,* 25–32.

Whaley, B. (March 1986). Valuation of American futures options: Theory and empirical evidence. *Journal of Finance, 41,* 127–50.

CHAPTER 6

INTEREST RATE CAPS AND FLOORS

*Richard C. Stapleton**
*Marti G. Subrahmanyam***

6.1 INTRODUCTION

The increase in the volatility of interest rates in the major currencies coupled with the deregulation of international financial markets in recent years has heightened the interest of various market participants in hedging their exposure to fluctuations in interest rates. A corporate treasurer who is concerned about the possibility of rising interest rates and its impact on the interest payments on his floating-rate debt obligations, may seek to reduce his risk by either switching to fixed-rate denominated debt or buying a "cap" on the (floating) interest rate. As we shall see in this chapter, a cap is a financial arrangement that limits the exposure of a floating-rate borrower to

*Wolfson Professor of Finance, Lancaster University.
**Research Professor of Finance and Economics, Leonard N. Stern School of Business, New York University.

220

upward movements in interest rates. Similarly, a bond portfolio manager seeking to limit the down-side exposure of a floating-rate denominated portfolio to falling interest rates may wish to either switch to fixed-rate denominated securities or obtain a "floor" on interest rates. A floor permits an investor in floating rate debt (i.e., a lender) to obtain some protection against falling interest rates.

In the past decade, there has been a variety of interest rate-related derivative securities introduced in the world financial markets. These range from forward and futures contracts to various types of option contracts on fixed income instruments or interest rates. Some of these products are listed on organized exchanges and others are traded over-the-counter. In general, the exchange-traded contracts tend to be standardized, with relatively short expiration dates, whereas over-the-counter products are custom-made to suit the preferences of the buyer or seller and have a range of possible expiration dates. In the recent past, there has been a tremendous growth of over-the-counter interest rate products such as interest rate swaps (arrangements to exchange fixed-rate debt for floating-rate debt), caps and floors, which may all be used to manage interest rate exposure.

The purpose of this chapter is to provide an analysis of interest rate caps and floors, which are portfolios of interest rate call and put options. Section 6.2 provides an introduction to simple interest rate options, descriptions of the common contracts and the definitions of the costs and payoffs from the contracts. Section 6.3 explores the alternative hedging choices in a typical situation and the costs and benefits of these choices. Section 6.4 provides a description of interest rate cap and floor contracts and their relationship to simple interest rate options. This section focuses on the standard market conventions used in defining the cost of, and cash flows from, caps and floors. The next section, Section 6.5, deals with relationships between the prices of caps and floors, with different characteristics based on arbitrage considerations. In particular, the section discusses the derivation of arbitrage-based parity relationships. Section 6.6 values simple interest rate options and then caps and floors, using a simple binomial model.[1] This approach is extended to the closed-form solution of the valuation of caps and floors for a continuous distribution of possible future interest rates in Section 6.7. Two alternative distributions of interest

---

[1] See Chapter 3 for a description of the simple binomial model and its application to the valuation of options.

rates, the normal and the lognormal, are analyzed and cap-floor valuation models based on these alternative assumptions are developed. Section 6.8 explores the hedging implications of these models. Section 6.9 examines extensions of the basic valuation and hedging framework to related products such as swaptions and captions and presents a summary and the conclusions.

6.2   SIMPLE INTEREST RATE OPTIONS

This section defines simple, i.e., single period options, and explains the market conventions that determine the costs and payoffs from such options. Apart from providing an understanding of what interest rate options are, this section will serve as a building block for the analysis of the costs and payoffs of caps and floors and the valuation and hedging of these instruments. As explained later on in this chapter, a cap or a floor can be thought of as a series of interest rate options. Hence, an understanding of simple interest rate options is crucial to any analysis of interest rate caps and floors. Interest rate options are of two types based on how the underlying asset is defined. The "underlying asset" could be an *interest rate* itself, such as the six-month interbank deposit rate for dollars (6 month $LIBOR), or the U.S. prime interest rate. Alternatively, the "underlying asset" could be the *price* of a fixed income instrument such as the price of a 182 day U.S. Treasury bill or the price of a futures contract on Euro-dollar certificates of deposit. These two types of simple interest rate options are illustrated below by examples.

Example 1

A 6 Month Call Option on 6 Month $LIBOR at a Strike Level of 8% and a Face Value of $10 Million, Costing $30,000 today

Option Type:	European-style Call Option
Expiration Date:	6 Months (183 days)
Underlying Interest Rate:	6 Month $LIBOR
Strike Level:	8%
Face Value:	$10 Million
Cost of the Option:	$30,000 (or 30 basis points of face value)
Current 6 month $LIBOR Interest Rate:	8%

The option in this example is a *call option* written on an *interest rate.* This option gives the buyer the right to receive the difference between the 6 Month $LIBOR interest rate prevailing in six months time and the 8% *strike level,* if the former happens to be greater, on a face value of $10 million. The buyer of such an option thus receives a higher payoff as interest rates rise. The option is *European-style,* i.e., it can be exercised only on the *expiration date,* which happens to be six months hence. The precise number of days to the expiration date is determined by the actual day count, which, in this case, happens to be 183 days. The *strike level* is defined in terms of the interest rate the option is written on, in this case, the 6 month $LIBOR. The *face value* determines the size of the contract and hence the cost and the payoffs. The *cost of the option* is specified either as a dollar amount today or expressed as a percentage of the face value. The *current level* of 6 month $LIBOR happens also to be 8%.

If the 6 month $LIBOR interest rate happens to be less than or equal to 8%, six months hence, it does not pay to exercise the call option, since the payoff from the option is negative or zero. Another way of thinking about the choice is that it does not pay to borrow at an interest rate of 8%, when the market interest rate is lower. On the other hand, if the interest rate is higher than 8%, there is a positive payoff from exercising the option. The payoff function is as follows:

6 month $LIBOR Interest Rate	Call Option Payoff
$\leq 8\%$	0
$> 8\%$	$(i - 8\%) \times 182/360 \times \$10$ Million

The payoff is determined by the difference between the actual interest rate in six months, i, expressed as an annual rate in percent, and 8%, the strike level. According to the conventions in the $LIBOR market, this difference is multiplied by the actual number of days in the subsequent six month period as a proportion of 360 days in the year, and the face value of the option. Note that this payoff is received on the maturity date of the underlying interest rate, i.e., $183 + 182 = 365$ days from today. The three dates that are relevant to the definition of the contract are shown in Figure 6–1. The current time, 0 days, is when the options contract is written. The contract expires 183 days hence, with the payoff on the underlying face being received 365 days from today.

FIGURE 6–1

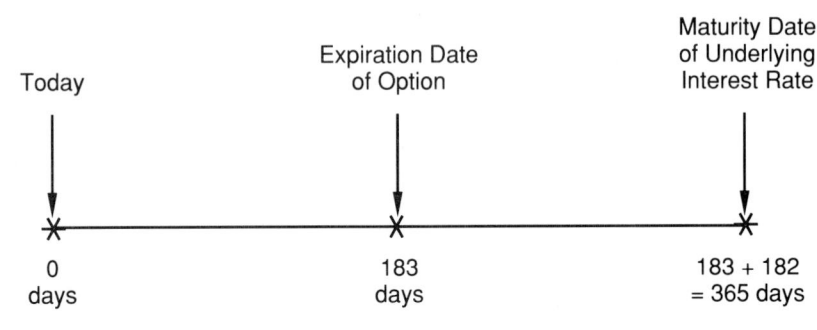

For example, if the actual interest rate in 183 days' time happens to be 9%, the payoff from the option is computed as follows:

6 month $LIBOR
Interest Rate   *Call Option Payoff*
9% $(9\% - 8\%) \times 182/360 \times \$10$ Million
$= \$50,555$

The payoff of $50,555 is received 365 days from today. Alternatively, the present value of this amount, discounted for six months interest is received 183 days from today. The payoff diagram from this option is presented in Figure 6–2. The shape is the same as that for any call option. However, since the x-axis represents the interest rate and the y-axis the payoff in dollars, the slope is not equal to one, unlike in the case of the options on the price of an underlying asset, as discussed in Chapter 2.

A question that is frequently asked in the context of analyzing options is: At what level of the underlying asset does the option break even? In our example, this question could be paraphrased as follows: At what level of the 6 month $LIBOR in 6 months time would the *total* borrowing cost be the same with and without the call option? Let this interest rate be $i\%$. In the absence of the option, the cash flow on the repayment of the loan of $10 million on the maturity date (365 days from today) based on $LIBOR conventions would be:

$$\$10 \text{ Million} \times [1 + (i\% \times 182/360)]$$

FIGURE 6–2
Payoff diagram for interest rate call

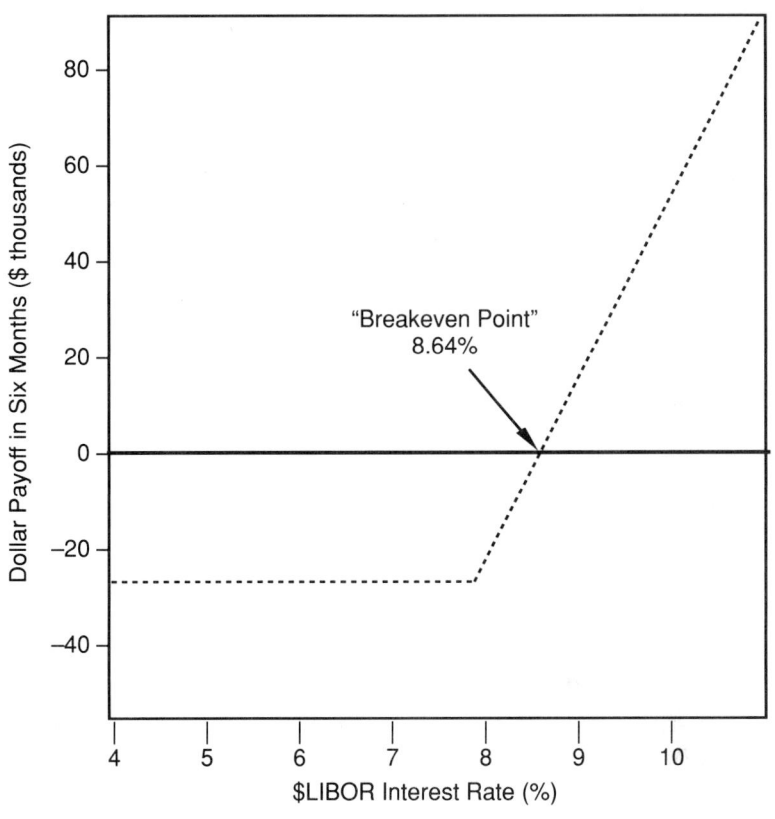

With the call option, the interest rate on the loan itself would be "capped" at 8%. Hence, the *total* payment on the loan on the maturity date would be:

$$\$10 \text{ Million} \times [1 + (8\% \times 182/360)]$$

In addition, the option itself costs \$30,000 today. To determine the cost on the maturity date, this amount has to be compounded forward. The interest rate for the first six months is known today—8%. However, the interest rate for the second six month period is not known today. Hence, the compounded value of the cost of the option is:

$$\$30,000 \times [1 + (8\% \times 183/360)][1 + (i\% \times 182/360)]$$

where the first and second terms in square brackets are the compound factors for the first and second six month periods respectively.

The "breakeven point" is the interest rate i at which the total cost of the loan is the same with and without the option. In other words:

$$\$10 \text{ Million} \times [1 + (i\% \times 182/360)]$$

$$= \$10 \text{ Million} \times [1 + (8\% \times 182/360)]$$

or

$$+ \$30,000 \times [1 + (8\% \times 183/360)][1 + (i\% \times 182/360)] \quad (6.1)$$

$$[\$10 \text{ Million} - \$31,220)][1 + (i\% \times 182/360)]$$

$$= \$10 \text{ Million} \times [1 + (8\% \times 182/360)] \quad (6.2)$$

or

$$i = 8.64\% .$$

Note that the breakeven calculations could have been made in terms of cash flows at the expiration date of the option 183 days from today. The result would be the same. The "breakeven" interest rate of 8.64% is the interest rate on the expiration date above which the option starts to pay. In other words, if the 6 month $LIBOR interest rate six months from today turns out to be greater than 8.64%, the buyer of the interest rate call option would be better off with the option than without it. At an interest rate below 8.64%, the buyer would have been better off without the option. We shall discuss the implications of this breakeven number for the hedging decision in the next section, but before we do so, let us consider another example of a simple interest rate option, this time based on the price of the Eurodollar CD futures contract.

Example 2
A 3 Month Put Option on the June Eurodollar CD Futures Contract at a Strike Price of 92, Costing 0.80 today

Option Type:	American-style Put Option
Expiration Date:	June (91 days from today)
Underlying Asset:	June Euro $ CD Futures
Strike Price:	92
Face Value:	$1 Million
Cost of the Option:	0.80
Current 3 month	
$LIBOR Interest Rate:	8%

Here, the option is a *put option* written on the *price* of the Eurodollar CD futures contract. As interest rates rise, the price of the Eurodollar futures contract declines. Since this is a put option, it pays off in this eventuality. Hence, a put option on the Eurodollar futures contract has payoffs similar to those on a call option on an interest rate. This option is American-style and hence can be exercised at any time before the expiration date. However, in this example, we shall assume implicitly that it does not pay to exercise the option before the expiration date.[2] The option has 91 days to expiration. The strike level, 92, is defined in terms of the price of the Eurodollar futures contract, which itself is defined as 100 minus the 3-month $LIBOR interest rate expressed in points of a 100. The current futures price happens to be 92 which is consistent with a 3 month $LIBOR interest rate of 8%. The cost of the option, defined in points of 100, is 0.80. The face value of this standardized contract is $1 Million. [This contract is traded on the International Monetary Market (IMM) of the Chicago Mercantile Exchange (CME), the London International Financial Futures Exchange (LIFFE) and the Singapore International Monetary Exchange (SIMEX).]

If the Eurodollar futures price on the expiration date is greater than or equal to 92, it does not pay to exercise the put option, since the payoff from the option is negative or zero. Of course, if the Eurodollar futures price is lower than 92 (i.e., interest rates rise above 8%), it pays to exercise the put option. Notice that the exercise decision for the put option on Eurodollar futures is similar to that for a call option on the 3 month $LIBOR. The former is not worth exercising if the Eurodollar futures price is more than or equal to 92, which corresponds to the latter not being worth exercising if 3 month $LIBOR is less than or equal to 8%. The payoff function for the put option on Eurodollar futures is as follows:

---

[2]See Chapter 4 for an analysis of the early-exercise feature of American-style options.

June 3-month Eurodollar
Deposit Futures Price   *Put Option Payoff*

≥ 92	0
< 92	$(92 - F) \times 1/100 \times 90/360 \times \$1$ Million

The payoff is determined by the difference between the actual futures price in June, F, and the strike price of 92. This difference is multiplied by $1/100$, to adjust for the fact that the quotation is in points of a 100, as well as the face value of $1 Million. Also, an adjustment is made for the fact that the interest rate is for a 3-month period, which, *by convention,* is taken to be 90 days in a year of 360 days. For example, if the actual futures price is 91 (which corresponds to a 3 month interest rate of 9%), the payoff from exercising the put option is as follows:

June 3-month Eurodollar
Deposit Futures Price   *Put Option Payoff*

$$91 \qquad (92 - 91) \times 1/100 \times 90/360 \times \$1 \text{ Million}$$
$$= \$2,500$$

The payoff diagram for this option is presented in Figure 6–3. The shape of the payoff function is similar to that of any put option. The payoff from the put option declines as the futures price increases until it reaches a lower bound—the price paid for the put option. In the range where the payoff from the option declines, it does so one-for-one with the futures price, as in the case of a put option on a stock. Note that the futures price moves inversely with the 3-month interest rate as discussed earlier.

As in the previous example, we could work out the breakeven point for the option. Suppose this breakeven level for the futures price is F. The payoff from a (long) position in the put option on the futures contract on the expiration date (in 91 days time) is:

$$(92 - F) \times 1/100 \times 90/360 \times \$1 \text{ Million}$$

The cost of the option today is:

$$0.80 \times 1/100 \times 90/360 \times \$1 \text{ Million} = \$2,000 \qquad (6.3)$$

Hence, the future value of this payment in three months or 91 days time is:

$$2{,}000 \times [1 + (91/360 \times 8\%)] = \$2{,}040.44 \qquad (6.4)$$

Note that the current interest rate is 8% and the time value of money calculations are based on the \$LIBOR conventions. The breakeven point can be determined by equating the cost of the option and the payoff:

$$(92 - F) \times 1/100 \times 90/360 \times \$1 \text{ Million} = \$2040.44$$

or $\qquad\qquad\qquad\qquad\qquad\qquad F = 91.184 \qquad (6.5)$

as shown in Figure 6–3.

FIGURE 6–3
Payoff diagram for Eurodollar futures put

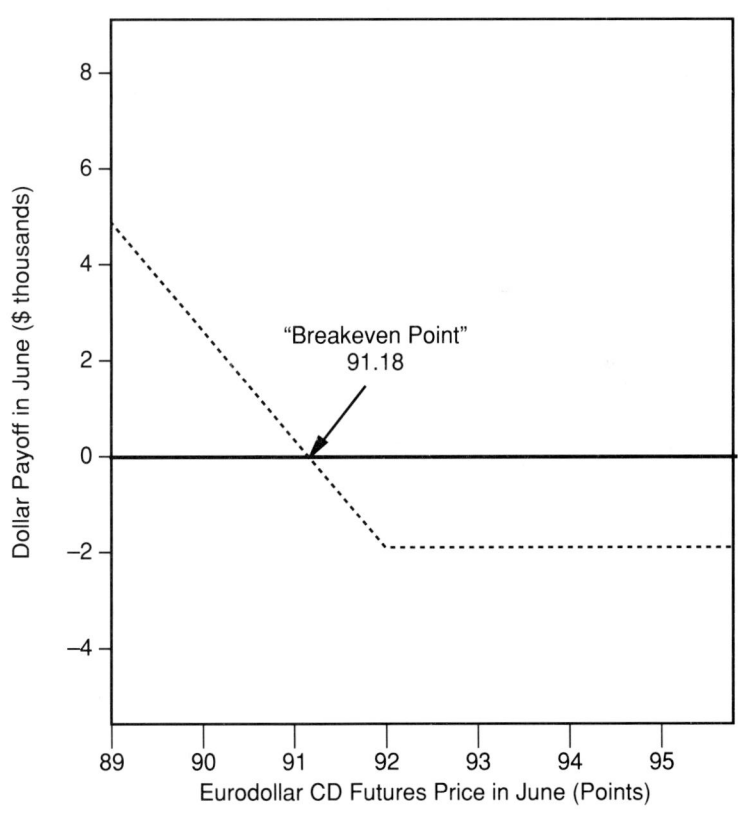

6.3   HEDGING WITH SIMPLE INTEREST RATE OPTIONS

The use of options to hedge interest rate risk is best illustrated by considering an example with one cash flow that is subject to interest rate fluctuations. In this case, the risk reduction problem can be handled with simple interest rate options of the type discussed in Section 6.2.

Example 3

A $50 Million Borrowing Requirement in 6 Months time (September) for 6 months

	Strike Level	Cost of the Call Option
Current Interest Rate: 8%		
6 Month Interest		
Rate Call Options:	8%	$150,000
	9%	$50,000

The various alternatives available to change the risk-reward (or risk-cost of loan) relationship are as follows:

1. Stay unhedged, wait for 6 months and borrow at whatever the 6 month $LIBOR interest rate happens to be at that time.
2. Enter into a forward rate agreement (FRA) and "lock-in" the interest rate today.
3. Buy a 6 month call option on the 6 month $LIBOR interest rate.
4. Buy a 6 month put option on the September Eurodollar CD futures contract.
5. Write a 6 month put option on the 6 month $LIBOR interest rate.
6. Write a 6 month call option on the September Eurodollar CD futures contract.

These alternative strategies deserve further discussion. The first strategy is the most risky one in the sense that the borrower is fully exposed to the uncertainty of the 6 month interest rate in September. This is illustrated in Figure 6–4 where the effective interest rates for the unhedged alternative vary linearly with the actual interest rate. The second alternative represents the other extreme in terms of risk. By entering into a forward contract, the borrower undertakes to pay the same interest rate independent of the actual interest rate in September—the relationship between the effective interest rate and the actual interest rate is a horizontal line.[3] A similar, although not exactly equivalent, position can be achieved by selling the September Eurodollar CD futures contract. If interest rates rise, the price of the futures contract will fall, offsetting the effect of the higher interest rate. If interest rates fall, the futures contract falls in price, nullifying the benefit of the lower interest rate. The reason why the futures position differs from the forward position is that the futures contract is marked-to-market each trading day, creating intermediate cash flows, both positive and negative, before the contract expires. Also, in our example, the interest rate to be hedged is 6 month $LIBOR, in contrast to the futures contract which is based on 3 month $LIBOR. These two interest rates are not necessarily the same although they are highly correlated.

As discussed in Section 6.2, a call option on the interest rate is essentially the same as a put option on the price of the futures contract. Hence, alternatives 3 and 4 have the same payoffs. Similarly, a put option on the interest rate is analogous to a call option on the price of a futures contract. Therefore, alternatives 5 and 6 have the same payoffs. Referring to Figure 6–4, notice that alternatives 3 and 4 limit the risk, in the sense that there is a level above which higher market interest rates have no effect on the effective interest rate paid by the hedger. In that sense, risk is limited by either of these alternatives but at a cost—the price of the option bought. In contrast, alternatives 5 and 6 generate a cash inflow but do not limit the maximum dollar payoff. Note that the effective interest rate is lower but increases at the same rate as the unhedged alternative 1. In other words, the effective interest rate lines are parallel to one another after a point. In that sense, alternatives 5 and 6 cannot be thought of as hedging choices, since they do not limit the upside risk.

We now turn to another aspect of the hedging choice—the cost of the hedge versus the risk reduction achieved. This is best illustrated using the data from the example. Buying an interest rate call option at a lower strike level is more expensive, but places a lower ceiling on the effective interest rate to be paid. In contrast, buying an interest rate call at a higher strike level is cheaper, but offers less protection against an upward movement in interest rates: the maximum effective interest rate is higher than in the case

---

[3]Strictly speaking, this contract does not completely eliminate risk, if the credit standing of the borrower changes. The borrower receives or pays the difference between the forward rate and the actual interest rate in September.

FIGURE 6–4
Effective rates for alternative hedging strategies

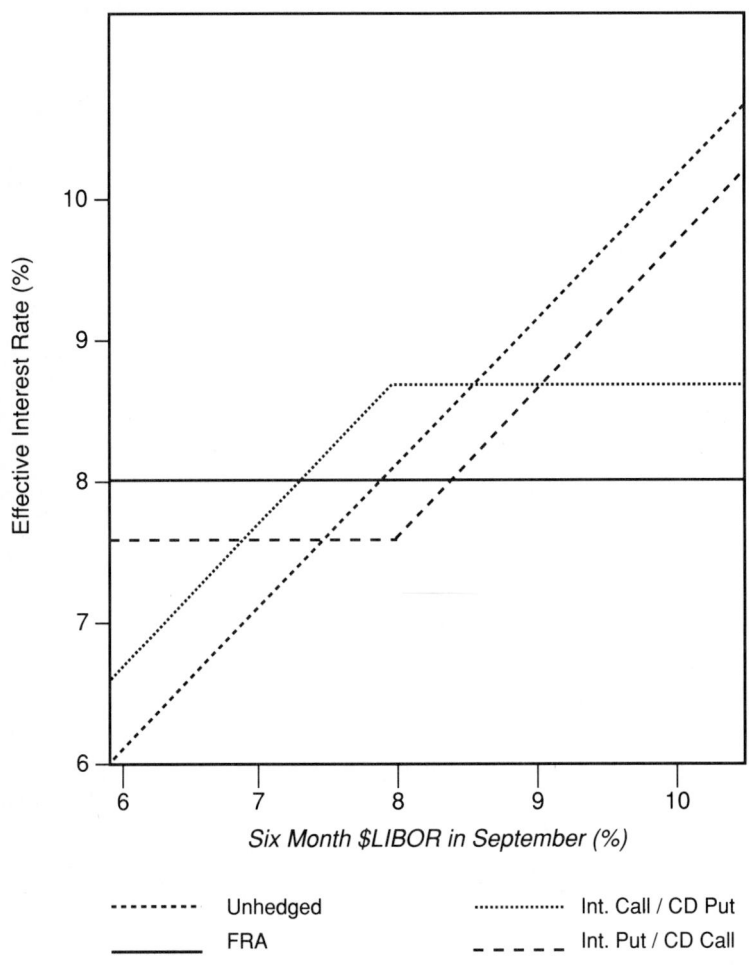

of the call option at a lower strike level. This issue is closely related to the notion of the *deductible* versus the *premium* paid in buying an insurance policy. The greater the deductible, the lower the level of protection achieved and the lower is the premium charged.

This trade-off can be easily illustrated by the data from the example. At a strike level of 8%, the call option costs $150,000 today or

$$150,000 \times \left[1 + 8\% \times \frac{183}{360} \right] = \$156,100 \text{ in 6 months time} \quad (6.6)$$

By buying such an option, the borrower "caps" his interest payment in 12 months time at a maximum of 8% in 6 months time. This means that the cash flows the borrower faces if interest rates exceed 8% are as follows:

FIGURE 6–5
Cash flow diagram for a hedged loan with an 8% cap

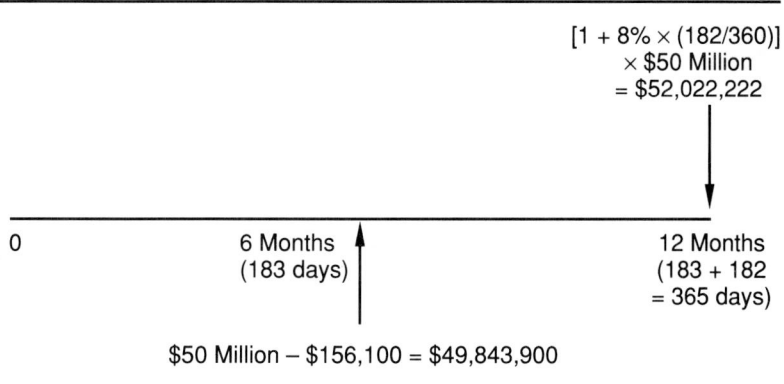

The cash inflow in 6 months time is the amount of the borrowing, $50 million, less the future value of the amount paid for the option, $156,100. The cash outflow in 12 months time is the amount due at a "capped" $LIBOR interest rate of 8% or $52,022,222. The *maximum* effective interest rate is calculated using the $LIBOR conventions as the interest rate, i, that equates

$$49,843,900 \left[1 + i\% \times \frac{182}{360} \right] = 52,022,222 \quad (6.7)$$

or

$$i = \frac{52,022,222 - 49,843,900}{49,843,900} \times \frac{360}{182} = 8.64\%$$

Here, the "premium" is 0.64% and the "deductible" is 8% for a maximum effective interest rate of 8.64%. Of course, if $LIBOR falls below 8%, the interest rate call option will not be exercised, but the effective interest rate will also be lower.

What if the borrower buys an interest rate call option at a strike level of 9%? The cost of the option today is $50,000 or:

$$50,000 \times \left[1 + 8\% \times \frac{183}{360}\right] = \$52,033 \tag{6.8}$$

in 6 months time. Using the same arguments as before, the cash flows paid and received by the borrower, if the interest rate in 6 months time exceeds 9%, are as follows:

FIGURE 6–6
Cash flow diagram for a hedged loan with a 9% cap

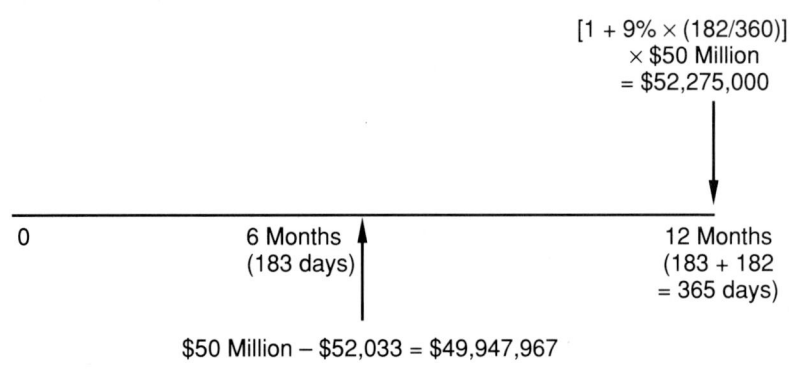

The maximum effective interest rate, i, is given by:

$$49,947,967 \left[1 + i\% \times \frac{182}{360}\right] = 52,275,000 \tag{6.9}$$

or

$$i = \frac{52,275,000 - 49,947,967}{49,947,967} \times \frac{360}{182} = 9.22\%$$

The "premium" for the 9% strike level is 0.22% and the "deductible" is 9%. Figure 6–7 shows the relationship between the actual interest rate and the effective interest rate for the two strike levels compared with the unhedged position where the effective and actual interest rates coincide.

6.4   CAPS AND FLOORS: CONTRACT CONVENTIONS AND CASH FLOWS

An interest rate cap is a series of interest rate European call options. It is thus a portfolio of call options on interest rates in successive periods. An interest rate floor is a series of interest rate European put options or a portfolio of put options on interest rates in successive periods. In addition to these basic definitions, there are several features of interest rate caps and floors that need to be defined in practice. Some of these are relevant even for a simple interest rate option, but others arise due to the portfolio nature of caps and floors.

The main features of caps and floors can be illustrated by using an example of each.

Example 4

A 5 Year Cap on 6 Month $LIBOR at 8% with a Face Value of $100 Million

Option Type:	Interest Rate Cap
Term:	5 years
Underlying Interest Rate:	6 Month $LIBOR
Reset (Determination) Dates:	January 13, July 13
Strike Level:	8%
Trade Date:	January 13
Settlement Date:	January 15
Underlying Amount:	$100 Million
Up-Front Fee:	3% or $3 Million

The option in the example is an interest rate *cap* or a series of European interest rate call options. The *trade date*, the date when the contract terms are set, in the example is January 13. The *settlement date*, the date when the contract takes effect, is typically two days later, or January 15 in this example. The *underlying interest rate* is the 6 month $LIBOR interest rate

FIGURE 6–7
Effective rates for alternative hedging strategies

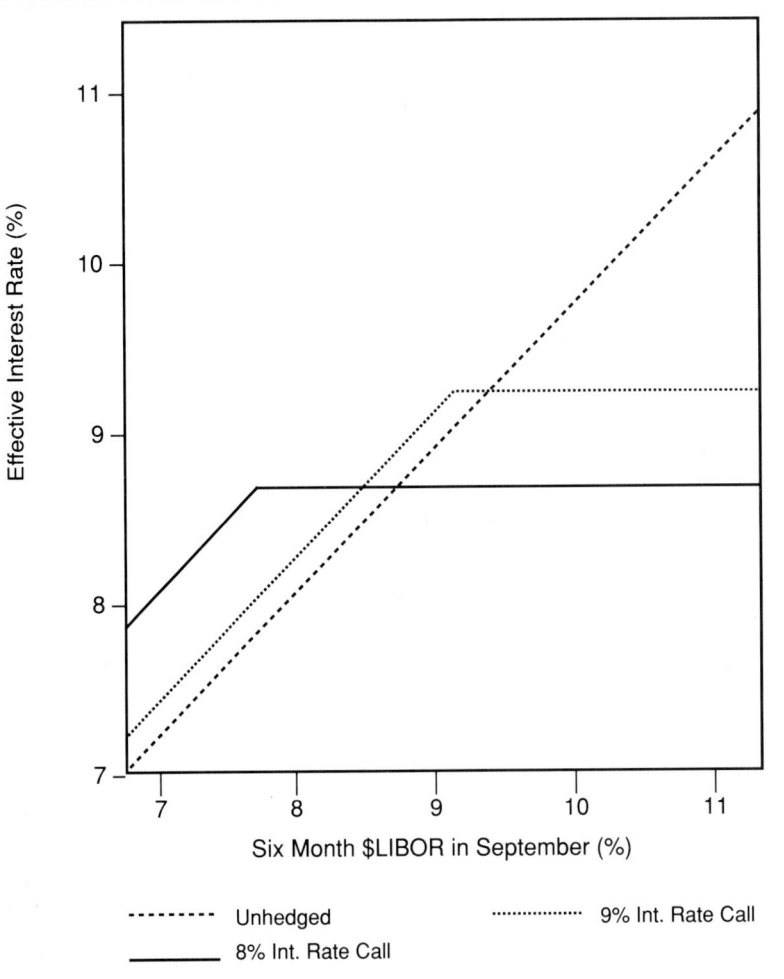

and is the basis for determination of the payoffs to the buyer of the cap based on the difference with respect to the *strike level* of 8% based on $LIBOR conventions. Alternatives for the underlying interest rate and the strike level are the prime interest rate, the Treasury bill rate, the certificate of deposit (CD) rate or the commercial paper (CP) rate. The *underlying amount* could be fixed or changing in a predetermined manner over time.

In this case, it is fixed at $100 Million. The *up-front fee* could be specified as a dollar amount, $3 Million in this case, or as a percentage of the face value, 3%. Alternatively, the fee can be set as a stream of periodic payments. Since the *term* of the cap is 5 years, there are ten 6-month periods involved. However, since the underlying interest rate for the first period is the interest rate today and, therefore, is known, there is no option involved. Thus, there are nine options in the cap, with the payoffs being determined on the reset dates—January 13 and July 13, with the first option expiring on July 13 and the last one on January 13 five years hence.

For illustrative purposes, the payoffs from the cap can be thought of as a stream of cash flows to be balanced against the up-front fee amortized over the term of the cap. Specifically, the up-front fee of $3 Million amortized over 9 half-yearly periods at a semiannual interest rate of 4% (which is assumed to be the semiannual interest rate for a 5 year maturity) represents a stream of cash flows as in Figure 6–8:

FIGURE 6–8
Amortization of the up-front fee of a cap

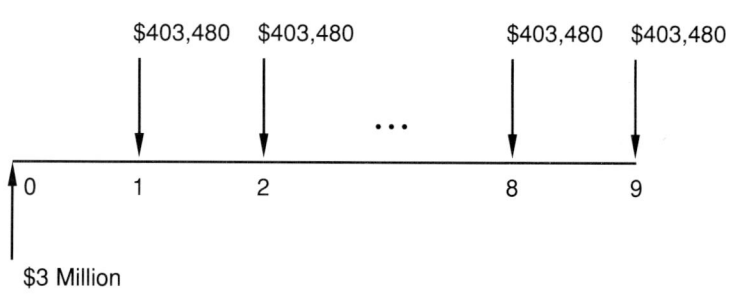

In Figure 6–8, the time scale is given in semiannual periods. The stream of (amortized) outflows can be compared with the payoffs from the sequence of options to determine the effective cost of funds of the cap *and* a floating interest rate loan. However, unlike a simple interest rate option, where we specified only one actual interest rate, we need to consider, for the multi-period scenario of the cap, a whole sequence of actual interest rates. For example, suppose the actual $LIBOR interest rate starts out at 8% at time 0, and then rises to 9% at time 1, and remains at that level for the next

5 years. The cash flows for the loan and the payoffs from the cap can be computed as shown in Table 6–1. The first column refers to the semiannual period. The second column specifies the realization of the 6 month $LIBOR interest rate on each reset date. The remaining columns show the cash flows from the loan, the cap payoff, the cap cost and the net cost of the capped loan in each period. For example, the loan cash flow in period 2 is equal to $100 million $\times$ 9% $\times$ 182.5 / 360 = $4.5625 million. The cap payoff is equal to $100 million $\times$ (9% – 8%) $\times$ 182.5 / 360 = $0.5069 million.

The effective interest rate of the capped loan is the internal rate of return of the stream of cash flows for each semiannual period. This is 4.43% per semiannual period, or 8.73% on an annual basis based on $LIBOR conventions. The effective interest rate on the capped loan for alternative scenarios may be compared with the interest rate on a fixed-rate loan. This is similar to the analysis in Section 6.3 where a forward rate agreement (FRA) and a call option on interest rates were compared. As before, the breakeven point could be determined. Since a cap is a portfolio of options, the future payoffs from the cap depend on the interest rate that prevails on each reset date, rather than on a single expiration date, as in the case of a single option. Thus, the payoffs from the cap depend on the whole sequence of future interest rates.

TABLE 6–1
Net cost of capped loan[a]—($ in millions)

Semi-annual Period	$LIBOR	Loan Cash Flow	Cap Payoff	Cap Cost (Amortized)	Net Cash Flow on Capped Loan
0		+100.00			+100.00
1	8%	−4.0556	0	−0.4035	−4.4591
2	9%	−4.5625	+0.5069	−0.4035	−4.4591
3	9%	−4.5625	+0.5069	−0.4035	−4.4591
4	9%	−4.5625	+0.5069	−0.4035	−4.4591
5	9%	−4.5625	+0.5069	−0.4035	−4.4591
6	9%	−4.5625	+0.5069	−0.4035	−4.4591
7	9%	−4.5625	+0.5069	−0.4035	−4.4591
8	9%	−4.5625	+0.5069	−0.4035	−4.4591
9	9%	−4.5625	+0.5069	−0.4035	−4.4591
10	9%	-104.5625	+0.5069		-104.0556

[a]For ease of calculation, it is assumed that the number of days in each semiannual period is exactly half the number of days in the year, 182 1/2 days. The extra day in a leap year is also ignored.

There are several alternative scenarios for the path of future interest rates. Consider the scenario where the interest rate remains at the same level for the 5 year term of the loan. In this case, it is clear that the cost of the cap on an annual basis is roughly 73 basis points per year (8.73% – 8%). Clearly, this amount has to be recouped, so that at the break-even fixed interest rate of 8.73%, the borrower is indifferent between the capped loan and the fixed rate loan.[4] This breakeven point can be illustrated by a payoff diagram as in Figure 6–9, where the effective interest rates on a floating rate loan, with and without a cap, are plotted as a function of the 6 month $LIBOR. Note that, as in Section 6.3, we could compare the risk-reward tradeoffs at different levels of protection by comparing the effective interest rates for caps at different strike levels.

We now turn to an analysis of floors on interest rates. Since the floor is a series of put options on interest rates, it pays off when interest rates decline. Just as a cap is useful in reducing the risk of upward movements in interest rates from the perspective of a borrower, a floor puts a limit on the down-side risk of a lender. Consider the following example of a floor.

Example 5
A 3 Year Floor on 6 Month $LIBOR at 8% with a Face Value of $10 Million

Option Type:	Interest Rate Floor
Term:	3 years
Underlying Interest Rate:	6 month $LIBOR
Reset(Determination) Date:	March 13, September 13
Strike Level:	8%
Trade Date:	March 13
Settlement Date:	March 15
Underlying Amount:	$10 Million
Up Front Fee:	1.5% or $150,000

As in the case of the cap, the up front fee of the floor can be amortized over the term of the agreement as in Figure 6–10. The time scale is again in semiannual periods and the semiannual interest rate is currently 4%. Again, the stream of (amortized) outflows for the options can be compared

---

[4]The breakeven point can be computed in a similar manner for other scenarios of future interest rates. Note that it is not necessary for the interest rates to be the same at each reset date.

FIGURE 6–9
Effective interest rate on floating rate loan plus cap

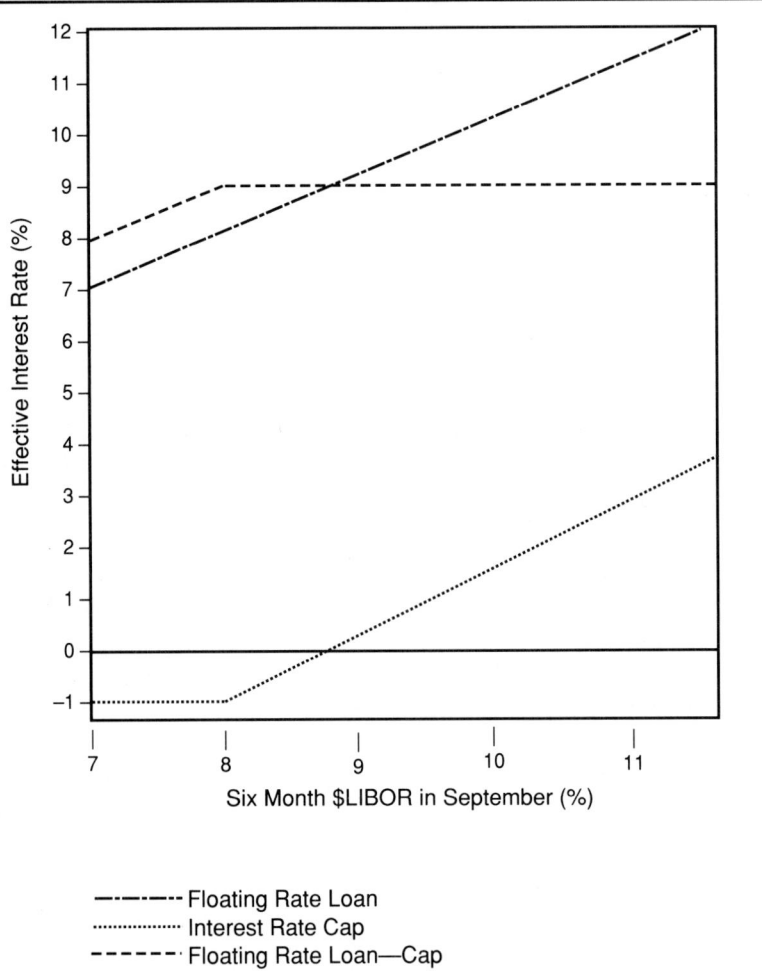

Floating Rate Loan

Interest Rate Cap

Floating Rate Loan—Cap

with the stream of option payoffs to determine the effective yield on floating interest rate lending *plus* the floor. We define the scenario of future interest rates as a current 6 month $LIBOR interest rate of 8% falling to 7% at time 1 and staying at that level over the term of the floor. The cash flows for the floating rate lending and the payoffs from the floor are given in Table 6–2.

FIGURE 6–10
Amortization of the up-front fee of a floor

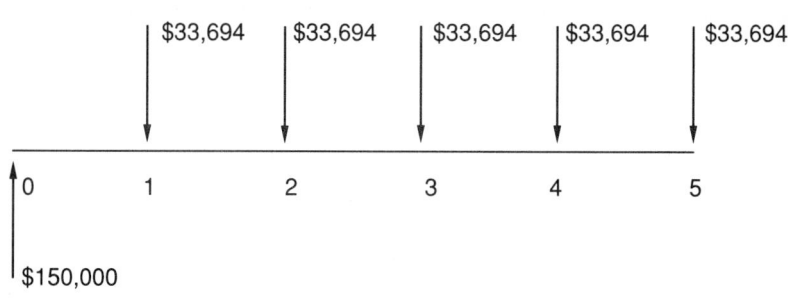

In Table 6–2, the first column indicates the semiannual period. The second column gives the interest rate on each reset date. The other columns indicate respectively the cash flows from the lending, the floor payoff, the floor cost and the net return from the lending in each period. The calculations are similar to those in Example 4 for a cap.

The effective return on the floating rate lending with the floor is 3.77% for each semiannual period or 7.44% on an annual basis using the $LIBOR conventions. The effective return on the floating rate lending with the floor, for alternative sequences of interest rates over the term of the loan, may be compared with the return on fixed rate lending. This is analogous to the comparison of the return on a forward rate agreement and a put option on interest rates. Note, however, that as in the case of floating rate borrowing with a cap, the breakeven interest rate depends on the whole sequence of interest rates. For the case where the interest rate drops to 7% and remains at the same level for the term of the lending, the cost of the floor is roughly 56 basis points (the strike level of 8% minus the return on the loan of 7.44%) per year over the term of the floor. For the investor to be indifferent between the floating rate loan with a floor and a fixed rate loan, the breakeven fixed rate is 7.44%. As in the case of caps, the risk-reward tradeoff may be analyzed by considering floors at various strike levels. These may be viewed as insurance policies with alternative "premiums" and "deductibles."

TABLE 6–2
Net return on floating rate lending with a floor[a] ($ in millions)

Semiannual Period	$LIBOR	Floating Rate Lending Cash Floor	Floor Payoff	Floor Cost (Amortized)	Net Cash Flow on Floating Rate Lending with Floor
0		-10.0000			-10.0000
1	8%	+0.4056	0	-0.0337	+0.3719
2	7%	+0.3549	+0.0507	-0.0337	+0.3719
3	7%	+0.3549	+0.0507	-0.0337	+0.3719
4	7%	+0.3549	+0.0507	-0.0337	+0.3719
5	7%	+0.3549	+0.0507	-0.0337	+0.3719
6	7%	+10.3549	+0.0507		10.4056

[a]For ease of calculation, it is assumed that the number of days in each semiannual period is exactly half the number of days in the year, 182 1/2 days. The extra day in the leap year is also ignored.

6.5   BASIC PARITY RELATIONSHIPS BETWEEN CAPS-FLOORS-FORWARDS-SWAPS

Put-Call Parity

The most important parity relationship between options based on arbitrage considerations is the relationship known as put-call parity. (See Chapter 2 for a detailed discussion.) For a European-style call and a European-style put option struck at the same exercise price, this says:

$$C(X) - P(X) = S - Xe^{-rT} \qquad (6.10)$$

where

$C(X)$ is the price of the European-style call option at an exercise price of X

$P(X)$ is the price of the European-style put option at an exercise price of X

S is the price of the underlying asset on which the options are written

X is the exercise price of the put and the call option

T is the expiration date of the options

r is the continuously compounded interest rate on an annualized basis for maturity T.

The put-call parity relationship in equation (6.10) derives from a more fundamental parity between the payoff at time T on the put, call, and forward contracts. The payoff from a long position in a European-style call and a short position in a European-style put at a strike price X is the same as the payoff on a long position in a forward contract to buy the asset at a price X. Using a subscript T for the payoffs at time T, this can be shown in Table 6–3 where the two portfolios are compared.

Note that in Table 6–3, the total payoff at time T from the positions in the call and the put taken together is equal to the payoff from the forward contract. This is true whether the price of the underlying asset turns out to be greater than, equal to, or less than the exercise price X. In other words, we can write, using subscript T for the payoffs at time T:

$$C_T(X) - P_T(X) = S_T - X \tag{6.11}$$

The left hand side of (6.11) is the payoff from a long call and a short put position. The right hand side is the payoff from a long position in a forward contract to buy the underlying asset at a price X. It is also worth

TABLE 6–3
Put-call parity: Payoffs at expiration

	$S_T > X$	$S_T = X$	$S_T < X$
Portfolio 1:			
Payoff from the long position in the call	$S_T - X$	0	0
Payoff from the short position in the put	0	0	$-(X - S_T)$
Total Payoff	$S_T - X$	0	$S_T - X$
Portfolio 2:			
Payoff from the long position in the forward contract	$S_T - X$	0	$S_T - X$

noting that, if the put and the call contracts are struck at an exercise price of $X = F$, where F is the current forward price of the asset for delivery at time T, we have a payoff:

$$C_T(F) - P_T(F) = S_T - F \qquad (6.12)$$

The payoff on the right hand side of equation (6.12) is the terminal payoff on a forward contract struck at the current forward price since $S_T = F_T$. By the definition of a forward contract, this has a zero value, since a forward contract struck today has a zero outlay. It follows that the *current value* of the payoff at T from the call equals that from the put, which means that the current value of the call equals the current value of the put:

$$C(F) - P(F) = 0 \qquad (6.13)$$

or

$$C(F) = P(F) \qquad (6.14)$$

Put-call parity can refer to any of the relationships (6.10), (6.11), (6.12) or (6.14). In our discussion of interest rate options and caps and floors we will concentrate initially on the future payoff relationships (6.11) and (6.12).

Parity Relationship 1
Consider one option in the series of call options in an interest rate cap. This is a European-style call option on an interest rate with strike price x and expiration date T. Consider the corresponding option in the series of put options in an interest rate floor. This is a European-style put option on an interest rate with strike price x and maturity T. Then, using equation (6.11), and noting that $S_T = F_T$, we can write:
   The payoff from a long position in the call option and a short position in the put option on the interest rate is equivalent to a forward agreement to borrow at the rate of interest, x.

Example 6
A One-year Call and Put Option versus a One-year FRA on 3 Month $LIBOR.

Consider the payoff from a forward rate agreement (FRA) to borrow $1 million at 10% for 3 months (say, 91 days) one year from now. This contract pays off:

$$(i - 10\%) \times \frac{91}{360} \times \$1,000,000$$

15 months from today, where i is the 3 month $LIBOR interest rate in 12 months time. If i turns out to be 11%, the contract pays:

$$(11\% - 10\%) \times \frac{91}{360} \times \$1,000,000 = \$2,527.78 \qquad (6.15)$$

On the other hand, if i turns out to be 9%, the contract pays:

$$(9\% - 10\%) \times \frac{91}{360} \times \$1,000,000 = -\$2,527.78 \qquad (6.16)$$

A call option at a strike level of 10% on 3 month $LIBOR has a payoff:

$$(i - 10\%) \times \frac{91}{360} \times \$1,000,000, \qquad \text{if } \$LIBOR > 10\%$$

$$0 \qquad \text{if } \$LIBOR \leq 10\%$$

For example, if $LIBOR is 11%, the payoff is $2,527.78. If i is 9%, however, the payoff is $0.

A put option at 10% on 3 month $LIBOR has a payoff:

$$0 \qquad \text{if } \$LIBOR \geq 10\%$$

$$(10\% - i) \times \frac{91}{360} \times \$1,000,000, \qquad \text{if } \$LIBOR < 10\%$$

If $LIBOR a year hence happens to be 9%, the payoff is $2,527.78. The payoffs on the various contracts are shown in Figure 6–11.

Put-call parity refers to the relationship between a call minus a put on the one hand and a forward on the other. In Figure 6–11, if we take the negative of the put payoff and add it to the call payoff, we have the same

FIGURE 6–11
Call, put and forward payoffs

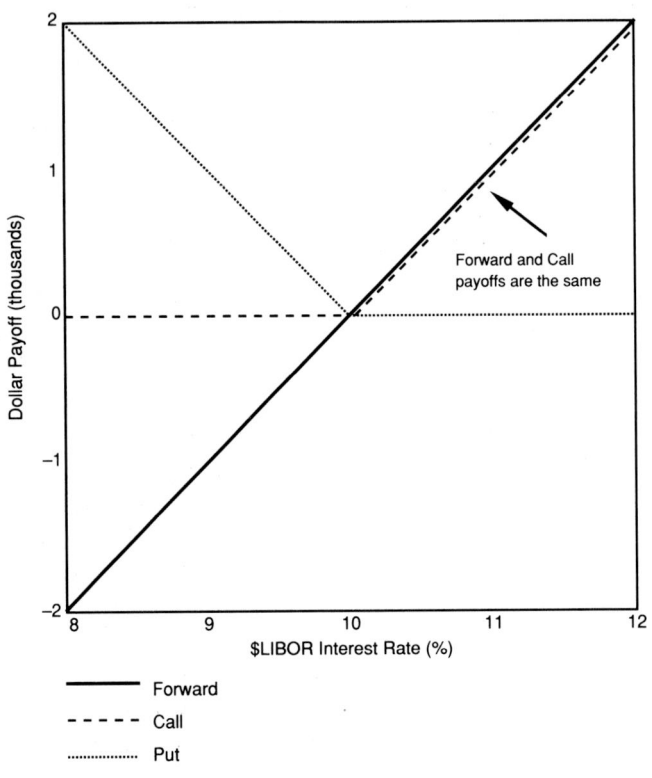

payoff as the forward . For example, if $LIBOR is 9%, the call pays $0 and short position in the put pays –$2,527.78. The net position is –$2,527.78 which is the same as the payoff from the forward. At 11%, the call pays $2,527.78 and the put pays $0. The net position is +$2,527.78, which is identical to the payoff from the forward.

The put-call parity payoff diagram in Figure 6–11 illustrates the relationship in equation (6.11), for the case of interest rate options. The payoff on a call minus a put at 10% is the same as that on a forward contract to borrow at 10%. It follows also that if the forward interest rate (that is the rate at which a zero value forward contract can be struck) is, say 9.8%, then a call at 9.8% has the same *value* as a put at 9.8%. This illustrates the relationship in equation (6.12).

Cap-Floor Parity

Since a cap is a portfolio of call options and a floor is a portfolio of put options, we can extend the notion of put-call parity to caps and floors. We will consider caps and floors based on the same interest rate index and struck at the same strike level. We will relate caps and floors, which can be thought of as series of call and put options, respectively, on interest rates, to *interest rate swaps,* which are series of forward agreements on interest rates. An example would be useful to clarify the nature of the relationship.

Consider a borrower who initially has a five year floating rate loan linked to six month $LIBOR, with the interest rate being reset every six months. Such an arrangement would mean that the interest rate payable over each six-month segment of the five year period is determined by the six-month $LIBOR interest rate prevailing at the beginning of the period. Suppose this borrower decides to switch from a floating interest rate loan to a fixed interest rate loan over the same five-year term. He can do so by entering into a *fixed-for-floating interest rate swap* at a given *fixed interest rate*. If the swap is at the market-determined *swap rate*, no payments are made initially to enter into the arrangement. This is similar to the situation of a borrower facing a floating interest rate on six month borrowing in the future, who enters into a FRA to exchange the floating interest rate for a fixed interest rate. The only essential difference is that there is a whole *series* of these FRAs in the case of a swap. There is, therefore, a clear analogy between one-period interest rate call and put options, and FRAs on the one hand and caps, floors and swaps on the other. We shall now compare the incremental cash flows from a fixed-for-floating interest rate swap with those from caps and floors struck at the same interest rate as the swap rate.

Parity Relationship 2

A cap minus a floor (at a strike rate, x) is equivalent to a forward agreement to borrow at $x\%$ on each reset date of the cap/floor. This follows immediately from put-call parity. Each call in the cap can be matched by a corresponding put in the floor. Each pair of a long call and a short put pays the same as a forward agreement to borrow on the specified date at $x\%$. Hence, the cap minus the floor is a series of such forward agreements. Such an agreement is similar to the fixed side of a swap agreement. Hence, we can state:

The payoff from a long position in a cap and a short position in a floor equals that on the fixed side of a swap, where the strike level of the cap and floor are set equal to the swap rate.

Inequality 1

A cap is a portfolio of interest rate call options, a floor is a portfolio of interest rate put options and a swap is a portfolio of forward rate agreements. However, a cap should be contrasted with another interest rate option, the option to enter into a fixed-for-floating interest rate swap. Similarly, a floor is quite different, in general, from an option to enter into a floating-for-fixed interest rate swap. Such *options on swaps*, sometimes known as *swaptions*, have only one exercise date, unlike caps and floors which have several. We shall now explore the differences between caps and floors on the one hand and swaptions on the other, in some detail.

A cap on a given interest rate index is worth at least as much as a (call) option to enter a fixed-for-floating interest rate swap agreement on the same index at the same strike rate, and like maturity and face amount. Similarly, a floor is worth at least as much as a (put) option to enter into floating-for-fixed interest rate swap agreement at the same strike rate, like maturity and face amount.

We can write

$$\text{CAP}\ (x, T, u, p, A)\ \geq \text{SWAPTION}_F\ (x, T, u, p, A)$$

$$\text{FLOOR}\ (x, T, u, p, A)\ \geq \text{SWAPTION}_f\ (x, T, u, p, A) \qquad (6.17)$$

where

   CAP(x, T, u, p, A) is the value of a T year cap at a strike level of $x\%$, defined on a given underlying interest rate index u, with a reset period of p years, on a face value of A.

   FLOOR(x, T, u, p, A) is the value of a T year floor at a strike level of $x\%$ defined on a given underlying interest rate index u, with a reset period of p years, on a face amount of A.

   SWAPTION$_F$ (x, T, u, p, A) is the value of a European-style option on a fixed-for-floating interest rate swap at a strike level of $x\%$, defined on a given underlying interest rate index, with an expiration date of p years, over a total period T, on a face amount of A.

   SWAPTION$_f$ (x, T, u, p, A) is the value of a European-style option on a floating-for-fixed interest rate swap at a strike level of $x\%$, defined on a given underlying interest rate index u, with an expiration date of p years, over a total period T, on a face amount of A.

We shall discuss the case of the cap versus the option to enter into a fixed-for-floating interest rate swap and note that the case of the floor versus the option to enter into a floating-for-fixed interest rate swap is similar. The reason why an option to enter a swap agreement is worth less than a cap is that the cap gives the borrower the option *at each reset date* to either borrow at the rate x or at the market rate of interest existing at the time. A European-style option on a swap requires a decision to borrow at a fixed rate x for the maturity of the agreement. A similar American-style option on a swap would give the buyer flexibility as to when to exercise the option, but still there is only one option involved. Thus, if the option on the swap is in-the-money and the swap is entered into at time p, the borrower may win or lose in subsequent periods according to whether the market rate of interest turns out to be greater or less than x. Thus, a cap or a floor may be thought of as a *portfolio of options*. In contrast, an option on a swap is similar to an *option on a portfolio*. A portfolio of options offers more choices than a similar option on a portfolio, and hence the former can never be worth less than the latter.

Example 7
A One-year Cap on 3 Month $LIBOR with a 3 Month Reset versus a 3 Month Option on a One-year Fixed-for-floating Swap

In Figure 6–12, we assume that the interest rate follows a simple binomial process. Specifically, in 3 months time, 3 month $LIBOR could be either 11% or 9%. In 6 months time, it could then move to 12% or 10% from 11%, and to 10% or 8% from 9%. In Figure 6–12, the first number is the three-month $LIBOR on that date. We also assume in this example that the term structure is always flat, i.e., the $LIBOR interest rates for 3 months, 6 months, and 9 months maturity are identical.

We now compare the payoff from a 3 month option on a swap with a cap on 3 month $LIBOR. Both the option and the cap have a strike rate of 10%. The cap has three exercise dates (month 3, 6, 9). In contrast, the option on the swap is exercisable only at month 3. However, if the option on the swap is exercised at month 3, it means that money must be borrowed at the swap rate of 10% for 3 months at month 3, 6, and 9. Hence, the swaption will be in-the-money (and exercised) if the 3 month $LIBOR rate goes to

FIGURE 6–12
Payoffs from a cap vs. an option on a swap

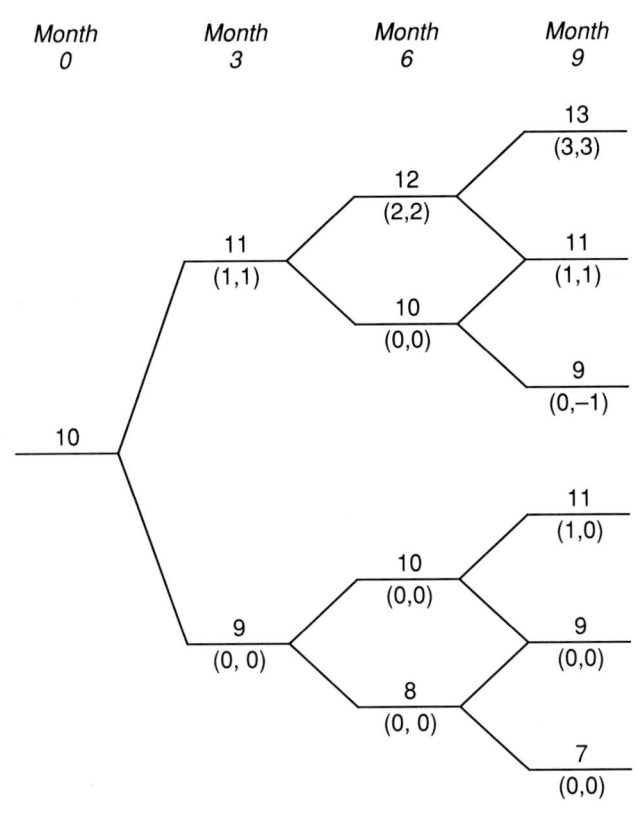

| Month 0 | Month 3 | Month 6 | Month 9 |

11% at month 3 and will not be exercised if it goes to 9% at month 3.

The profits (in terms of percentage points rather than dollar cashflows, for simplicity) are shown in brackets in Figure 6–12. The actual cash payoff can be found by multiplying the number in percentage points by 91/360 times the discount factor. However, in this context, it is sufficient to discuss the payoff simply in terms of $i - x$, the difference between the market interest rate and the strike rate. The first number in brackets is the payoff on the cap. This is simply Max($i - x$, 0).

If interest rates reach 11%, the cap pays 1%. If they go to 12%, it pays 2% and so on. Since the cap holder has the option in each 3 month period to receive the difference between the market rate and 10%, he either makes a positive gain or zero. The second number in brackets is the gain or loss from the option on the swap. If the rate goes to 9% at month 3, the option expires out of the money. At all subsequent times and states, the payoff on the option is zero. Even if the interest rate finishes up at 11%, the option on the swap has expired and pays 0%. On the other hand, if the interest rate goes to 11% at month 3, the option on the swap is exercised. This means that there may be losses to the option holder if the interest rate declines subsequently.

The first difference between the cap and the option on the swap is the payoff in the 11% state at month 9, following the 10% state at month 6. The cap pays off 1% regardless of how the 11% state is reached. However, the option on the swap only pays off if the rate first goes to 11% at month 3 (followed by the state at month 6 and then the 11% state at month 9). The second difference arises in the 9% state at month 9 following the 10% state at month 6. This produces a loss of 1% on the swap option if the interest rate at month 3 was 11% and the option was exercised at month 3. Hence, it is possible to *lose* money on an option on a swap relative to not exercising it, if interest rates decline subsequently. If the option is in the money at month 3 and exercised, but the swap becomes unprofitable at a later date, a negative cash flow is incurred relative to not exercising the option. In the case of the 3 month $LIBOR cap, no negative cash flows arise since there is an option for each date. The cap is worth more than the option on the swap in this case. In general, it must be worth at least as much, because unlike the option on a swap where the decision to enter the swap has to be made once and for all, the cap offers an extra option to get out of the floating rate loan agreement or get back in at a later date. In most cases, caps and floors of long maturity will be considerably more valuable than options to get into or out of a swap contract.

A similar argument applies for the comparison between the values of caps and floors with different reset dates. A 6 month cap (that is, a cap with 6 month reset dates) is, in general, not as valuable as a 3 month cap. [This also holds for 6 month versus 3 month floors.] The holder of the 3 month cap has the opportunity to exercise the option every 3 months and receive the difference between the market rate of interest and the strike rate x at each point in time. The holder of the 6 month cap is locked into a rate for 6 months at a time. This must be less beneficial because it could be that the 3 month $LIBOR rate falls after 3 months in one of the 6 month periods. Essentially, the 6 month cap is a portfolio of options, each of which gives the right to enter a 6 month fixed rate agreement. By the argument of the previous section, this cannot be worth more than a portfolio of options to borrow at 3 month $LIBOR.

We shall first discuss the somewhat simpler case of a call (or put) option on 6 month money compared to a 3 month call (or put option) and a 6 month call (or put option), respectively, on 3 month money. We shall then extend this example to the case of caps and floors.

Inequality 2
A series of calls on a given interest rate index (say 3 month $LIBOR) over a given term is worth at least as much as a single call on an interest rate index defined over the whole term (say 6 month $LIBOR), at the same strike rate.

For example, a *t* month call option on 3 month $LIBOR and a *t* + 3 month call option on 3 month $LIBOR (i.e., one expiring in *t* months and the other in *t* + 3 months) is worth more than a single *t* month call option on 6 month $LIBOR. Here, we assume that the term structure is flat (that is, the 3 month $LIBOR rate is equal to the 6 month rate). Note also that a similar statement can be made about put options. We shall now illustrate this with an example involving a 3 month call option on 6 month $LIBOR versus a 3 month plus a 6 month call option on 3 month $LIBOR.

Example 8
A 3 Month Call on 6 Month $LIBOR vs. a 3 Month Plus a 6 Month Call on 3 Month $LIBOR

In Figure 6–13, we show the payoffs on options at strike rate *x* of 10.5%, using a binomial interest rate process similar to the one used earlier. We assume a flat term structure as in the previous example. As before, the top figure at each node in the binomial tree refers to the interest rate. The first figure in brackets is the payoff on the 3 month call plus the 6 month call on 3 month money. The second figure is the payoff on the 6 month call on 6 month money. We compare a 3 month *and* a 6 month option on 3 month $LIBOR with a 3 month option on 6 month $LIBOR. The portfolio of the two options on 3 month $LIBOR pays

$$\max(i - 10.5\%, 0)$$

FIGURE 6–13
Payoffs from a 3 month call option on 6 month $LIBOR vs.
payoffs on a 3 month and a 6 month call options on 3 month
$LIBOR

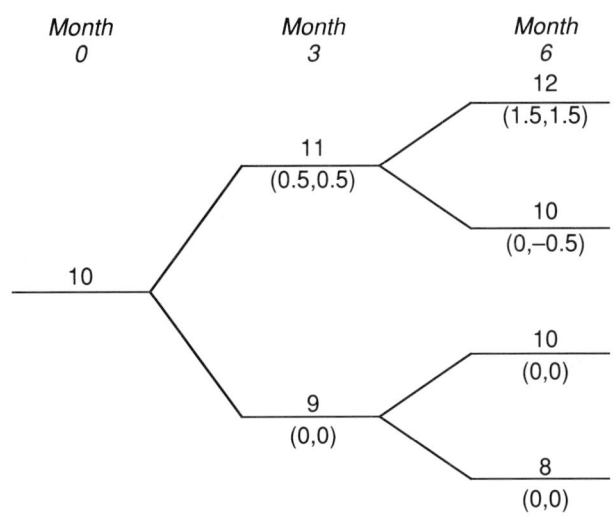

on *each* date, i.e., 3 months and 6 months hence. In contrast, however, the option on 6 month $LIBOR *loses* 0.5% if the option is exercised at month 3, when the interest rate is 11%, but the subsequent rate at month 6 is only 10%. The option on longer period money is similar to an option on a swap, and in this example, it will be worth less than the series of options on shorter period money.

We can extend the above example to the more complicated case of the 3 month versus the 6 month cap reset dates. This is really just a series of comparisons of two options on 3 month money compared to a single option on 6 month money. Again, if the term structure is flat, the holder of the 3 month cap must have at least as much value as the holder of a 6 month cap at the same strike price.

Inequality 3
A cap on a given interest rate index with a given reset period is worth at least
as much as a cap with a longer reset period on an interest rate index defined

over a correspondingly longer period, the strike rate, the term and face amounts of the caps being identical.

Using the same notation as before,

$$\text{CAP}(x, T, u, p, A) \geq \text{CAP}(x, T, u', p', A) \tag{6.18}$$

where $p' > p$ and u' is the interest rate index corresponding to the reset period p'.

For example, a 5 year cap on 3 month \$LIBOR with a 3 month reset period is worth at least as much as a similar cap on 6 month \$LIBOR with a 6 month reset period. Here again, we assume a flat term structure of interest rates. Again, a similar statement can be made for floors on interest rates.

Example 9
A Cap on 6 Month \$LIBOR vs. a Cap on 3 Month \$LIBOR

In Figure 6–14, we show the gains and losses (compared to borrowing at 3 month \$LIBOR at each point) from a cap on the 6 month \$LIBOR (a 6 month cap) at 10% and a cap on the 3 month \$LIBOR (a 3 month cap) at a strike rate of 10%. We assume that the options are exercised if the interest rate exceeds the strike rate of 10%. The top figure at each node of the binomial tree is the interest rate for the date (both the 3 month and 6 month rates, since the term structure is assumed to be flat). The first number in brackets is the profit on the 3 month cap. The second number is the profit on the 6 month cap. The gains/losses are compared to borrowing at the 3 month \$LIBOR rate.

In the 9% states, two sets of numbers are given in brackets when there are two alternative paths for reaching the states. These represent the payoffs at 9% if 9% is reached via 10% (the first bracket) and via 8% (the second bracket). The 6 month cap is worth less than the 3 month cap if the 9% state is realized via 10%. For example, the 6 month cap loses 1% if an interest rate of 9% occurs at month 3. This is because the first element in the cap is exercised at months 0, 6 and 12. If the subsequent interest rate is 9%, a 1% loss is made at the subsequent date.

Some care has to be taken in comparing a 6 month and a 3 month cap, because of the term structure of interest rates. The inequalities 2 and 3 are not strict inequalities since they assume a flat term structure. It is possible, for example, if the current 6 month \$LIBOR is higher than the 3 month

FIGURE 6–14
A cap on 6 month $LIBOR vs. a cap on 3 month $LIBOR

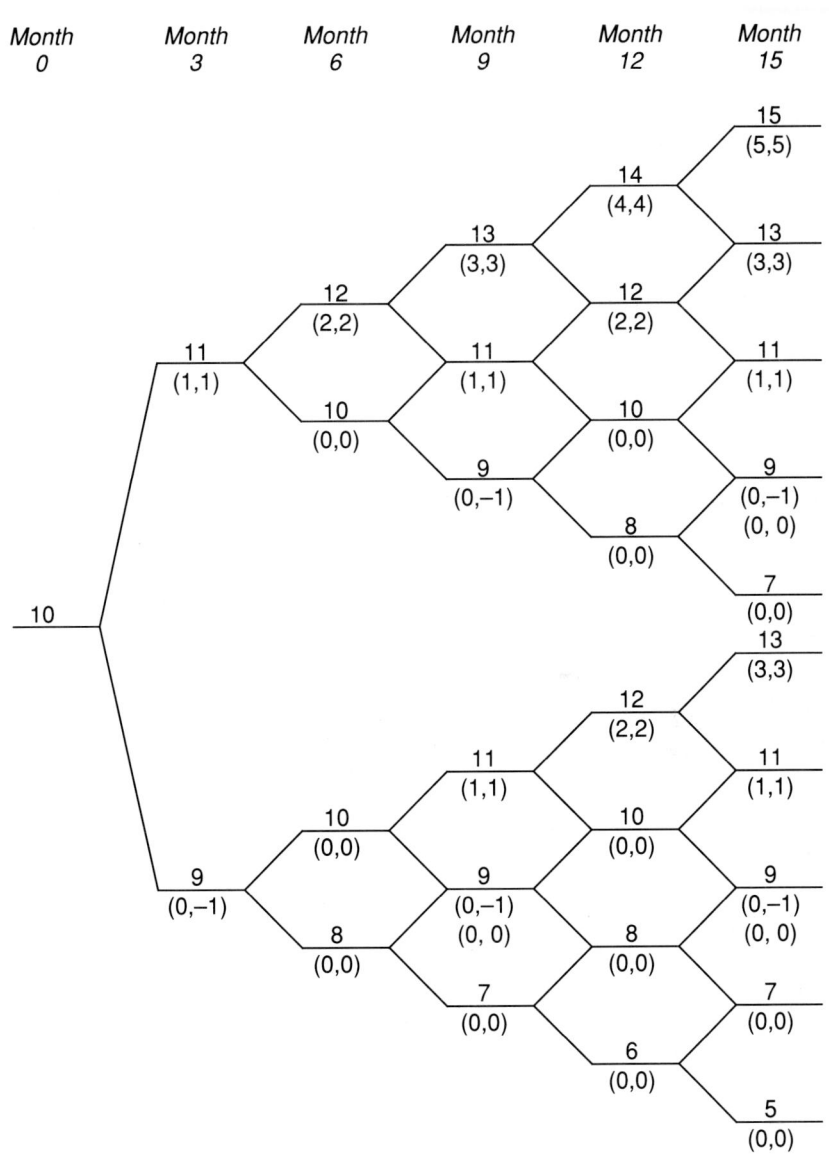

$LIBOR, that the 6 month cap *could* be worth more than the 3 month cap. However, this would not normally be the case. We shall state inequalities 2 and 3 then as "weak inequalities" that we would normally expect to hold in the market. The parity and inequality relationships discussed in this section are just examples of relationships that apply for any options. For instance, the put-call parity condition for interest rate options is an example of the put-call parity relationship that holds for puts and calls on any underlying asset. Similarly, the inequalities that apply to caps and floors are examples of a general inequality that applies to options on portfolios versus portfolios of options. In general, as shown in Chapter 2, an option on a portfolio at an appropriate strike price is worth less than a portfolio of options. In our case, an option on a swap is an option on a portfolio of loans whereas a cap is a portfolio of options on loans. Also, a 6 month cap is a portfolio of options on portfolios of (two 3 month loans) compared with a 3 month cap which is a portfolio of options on 3 month loans.

6.6   VALUATION OF CAPS AND FLOORS USING A BINOMIAL MODEL

In order to illustrate the general principles involved in valuing caps and floors we will assume a "risk neutral" model. In this model, investors evaluate alternative gambles in the interest rate market by computing the expected value of the payoffs from the gamble. There are two major implications of this assumption. First, the term structure of interest rates conforms to the "pure expectations hypothesis." This means that the forward price of a bill is equal to its expected price and the forward interest rate is roughly equal to the expected spot interest rate. The second implication is that options can be valued quite simply by weighing the option payoffs by the probability of the payoff occurring. At this point we should note that this assumption of risk neutrality is not *required* for the valuation of caps and floors. It is made at the moment only for expositional purposes. When we value caps and floors in the subsequent section using a modification of the Black and Scholes model, no such assumption will be required. Any risk aversion that may exist in the market is built into the forward price of the bills, or the forward rate of interest. It is automatically taken care of in the option pricing formulae which use the forward rate as an input. In the context of the binomial model used in Chapter 3, the effect of risk aversion is incorporated in the "risk-neutral" probabilities.[5] Option values can then be evaluated assuming "risk neutrality" with respect to those probabilities.

Example 10
A 6 Month Call and a 6 Month Put Option on 6 Month $LIBOR

We will first consider a single period example. We will assume that the 6 month $LIBOR interest rate today is 10% and that there is a 50% chance ($q = 0.5$) of the rate rising to 11% in 6 months time and a 50% chance ($1 - q = 0.5$) of it falling to 9%. The expected 'spot' interest rate is 10%. Suppose that we wish to value an at-the-money interest rate call option ($x = 10\%$) and an at-the-money interest rate put option ($x = 10\%$). Figure 6–15 shows the payoff on the two options. We assume that the options have a maturity of 183 days and that they are options on 182 day loans. We also assume that face amount of the options is $1 million.

The first point to note from Figure 6–15 is that the call option payoff in the 11% state (when discounted at 11%) is less than the put option payoff in the 9% state (when discounted at 9%). The reason for this is that the option contract pays off the discounted value of the payoff based on the 6 month interest rate in 183 days time. The discount rate obviously varies from state to state, and so does the discounted value.

The present value (at time 0) of the call, given risk-neutrality is:

$$\text{Call price } = (\text{Discount factor}) \times \sum_{\text{states}} [(\text{probability}) \times (\text{payoff})]$$

or

$$C(10\%) \; = \; \frac{1}{1 + 0.1 \times 183/360} \times [0.5 \times \$4{,}789.22 + 0.5 \times 0]$$

$$= \$2{,}278.77 \tag{6.19}$$

The discount factor incorporates the *current* rate for 6 month (183 day) money.

---

[5]As explained in Chapter 3, even under risk aversion, option prices can be compared by computing the discounted value of the expectations of the payoffs with respect to the "risk-neutral" probabilities. Similarly, the forward price of a payoff one period hence is also the expected value of the payoff using the "risk-neutral" probabilities but without discounting, since there is no net investment required to enter into a forward contract.

FIGURE 6–15
Value of options on 6 month $LIBOR

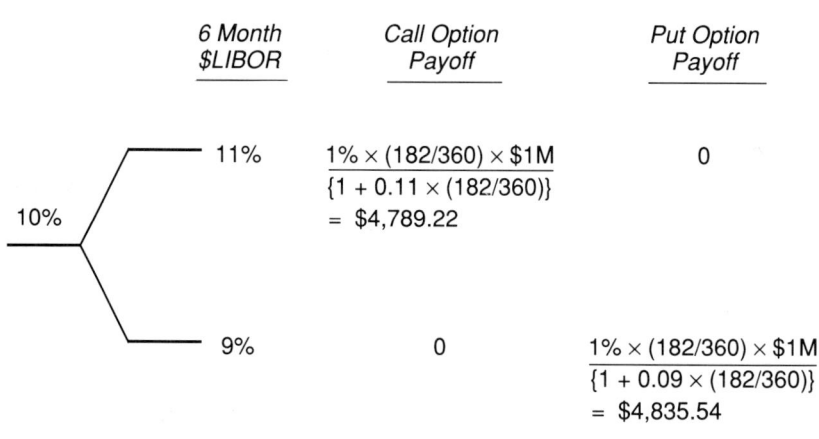

	6 Month $LIBOR	Call Option Payoff	Put Option Payoff
	11%	1% × (182/360) × $1M ——————————————— {1 + 0.11 × (182/360)} = $4,789.22	0
10%			
	9%	0	1% × (182/360) × $1M ——————————————— {1 + 0.09 × (182/360)} = $4,835.54

By a similar calculation, the put option is worth

$$P(10\%) = \frac{1}{1 + 0.1 \times 183/360} \times [0.5 \times \$4{,}835.54 + 0.5 \times 0]$$

$$= \$2{,}300.81 \tag{6.20}$$

The noteworthy feature of these calculations is that put-call parity does *not* hold when the options are struck at the current interest rate of 10%. This is not a violation of the put-call parity equation (13) however, because 10% is *not* the forward rate of interest. Assuming risk neutrality, the forward price of a 6 month bill in 6 month time (or, more accurately, an 182 day bill in 183 days time) with a forward value of $1 is

$$F = \left\{ 0.5 \times \left[\frac{1}{1 + 0.11 \times 182/360} \right] \right\} + \left\{ 0.5 \times \left[\frac{1}{1 + 0.09 \times 182/360} \right] \right\}$$

$$= 0.951899 \tag{6.21}$$

The forward 6 month $LIBOR rate for delivery in 183 days time that yields this forward price is f in

$$0.951899 = \frac{1}{1 + f \times 182/360}$$

or

$$f = 9.9953\%$$

(6.22)

It is easy to check that calls and puts struck at this forward rate have equal value. Both the put and the call at a strike rate of 9.9953% are worth $2,289.50.

Valuation of Longer Term Interest Rate Options

In the example above, the interest rate used to discount the option payoff back from T, the exercise date, to the present was 10%, the existing $LIBOR 6 month rate. Strictly speaking, the discounting should be done period by period over each time interval over which the interest rate changes. In other words, in the case of longer term options, we have to acknowledge that the discount rate is itself stochastic. The option payoff has to be discounted period by period at the interest rate that exists at each future period of time. In the examples below, we assume that the interest rate to be used for discounting is the $LIBOR rate on which the option is written. This assumption, to be relaxed in later models, is equivalent to using a one factor model for interest rates—i.e., assuming that all the relevant interest rates are influenced by the same stochastic factor.[6]

In the previous examples, we have seen the effect of the exact day count on the value of $LIBOR options. In the following examples, for simplicity, we shall assume that the options are written on 1 year interest rates, thus avoiding the day count problem. Also, the interest rate options will be written on a face amount of $1.

Example 11
2 Year Call and Put Options on the One Year Interest Rate
    In Figure 6–16 we trace the value of two 2 year options on 1 year

---

[6]See Chapter 8 for a discussions of one-factor versus alternative models of term structure movements.

FIGURE 6–16
Value of 2 year options on 1 year $LIBOR

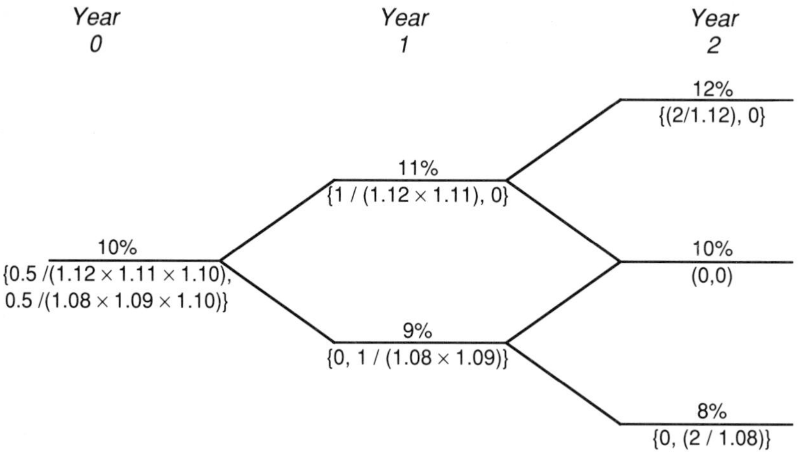

money. The top number at each node is the interest rate. The brackets include the call option price as the first number, and the put option price as the second one. All branch probabilities are 0.5. All numbers are in %. The call at 10% pays 2%/(1.12) at year 2 if the interest rate is 12%, and the put at 10% pays 2%/(1.08) at year 2 if the interest rate is 8%. There is no payoff in the other two states, in each case. This payoff is then discounted back to year 1 at 11% for the call, since 11% is the 1 year interest rate at year 1 which will occur prior to the state when the call option is in the money. Similarly, the interest rate state of 9% occurs at year 1 just before the state when the put option is in the money, and the payoff is discounted at 9%.

Both options are then discounted back at 10% to time 0. The option prices are

$$C(10\%) = \frac{2 \times 0.5 \times 0.5}{1.12 \times 1.11 \times 1.10} = 0.3656 \qquad (6.23)$$

$$P(10\%) = \frac{2 \times 0.5 \times 0.5}{1.08 \times 1.09 \times 1.10} = 0.3861 \qquad (6.24)$$

In this example, the difference between the put and call prices is greater than in the previous single period example.

$$\frac{0.3861 - 0.3656}{0.3656} = 5.6\% \qquad (6.25)$$

In general, the longer the interest rate option maturity (and the more that the option is out of the money) the greater will be the impact of the discounting effect. The reason is that the differences between the various paths of the future interest rate over time become larger. Further, the more out-of-the money the option, the more is its value influenced by extremely high or extremely low interest rates.

Again, however, as we shall see later, this effect is accounted for by the forward price (or interest rate). An option written at the forward rate of interest will have the same price whether it is a call or a put.

Valuation of Caps and Floors

A cap is a portfolio of calls on interest rates and a floor is a portfolio of puts. We can, therefore, now value a cap by simply adding the values of the interest rate options, each of which has been valued as in the previous example.

Example 12
A 2 Year Cap and a Floor on the One Year Interest Rate

In Figure 6–17, we trace the value of an at-the-money ($x = 10\%$) cap and floor. The second option in the cap is the same as that in Figure 6–16 above. It pays $2\%/(1.12)$ in the 12% state at year 2. The corresponding put pays $2\%/(1.08)$ in the 8% state at year 2.

The figure on top at each node is the one year interest rate observed. The figures in brackets are the prices of the cap and the floor, respectively. As before, all branch probabilities are 0.5 and all numbers are in percentages. The first option in the cap pays $1\%/(1.11)$ at year 1 if the 11% state occurs. The corresponding put pays $1\%/(1.09)$ if the 9% state occurs. The corresponding second options in the cap and floor respectively pay the same amounts as in Figure 6–16. The cap and floor values are shown as the sums of the two call and put options, respectively, in brackets in Figure 6–17. At year 0, the prices are:

FIGURE 6–17
Value of 2 year cap/floor on 1 year $LIBOR

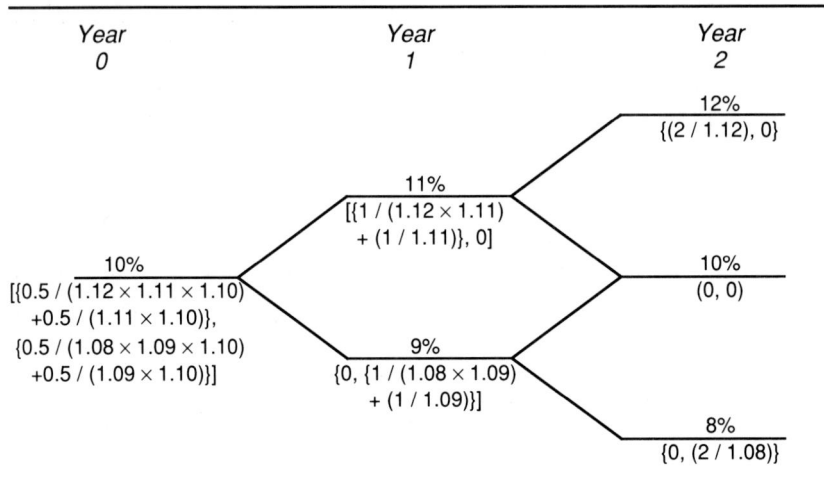

$$CAP(10\%) = \left\{ \frac{0.5}{1.12 \times 1.11 \times 1.10} \right\} + \left\{ \frac{0.5}{1.11 \times 1.10} \right\} = 0.7751 \quad (6.26)$$

$$\begin{array}{c} FLOOR \\ (10\%) \end{array} = \left\{ \frac{0.5}{1.08 \times 1.09 \times 1.10} \right\} + \left\{ \frac{0.5}{1.09 \times 1.10} \right\} = 0.8031 \quad (6.27)$$

The percentage difference between the prices of an at-the-money cap and a floor is rather less than for the longest call and put options in the cap, since the cap and floor prices represent the sums of both short-term and long-term options. As a result, the difference between the prices of the cap and the floor is smaller than in the single option case in equation (6.25). In this case, the difference is

$$\frac{0.8031 - 0.7751}{0.7751} = 3.6\% \quad (6.28)$$

compared to 5.6% in the single option case.

6.7   VALUATION OF CAPS AND FLOORS USING THE BLACK AND SCHOLES MODEL

The Black and Scholes (BS) model for pricing an option applies to options on assets whose prices are instantaneously normally distributed or lognormally distributed over a longer period. Derivation of the model also assumes (in the usual derivation) that the risk free interest rate is non-stochastic. (See Chapter 3 for details.) Some difficulty arises in directly applying BS to the case of the interest rate options in caps and floors since the options are written on an interest rate (not the price of an asset) and because interest rates are stochastic (otherwise interest rate options would not be relevant). However, these problems can be circumvented in the following ways:

1. An interest rate option can be re-stated as an option on the price of a zero coupon bond or bill of a particular maturity.

2. It can be shown that the required adjustment in the option price to take into account stochastic discounting (i.e., discounting at the period by period interest rate as in the examples above in section 6.2) is achieved by applying the Black (1976) model. The Black model prices an option on a futures contract. The option is valued and then discounted at the current spot risk free rate for the interval between the current date and the expiration date of the option. In the case of interest rate options where the discount rate is stochastic, the Black model can be applied with the forward price substituted for the futures price. In effect, the forward price of the bill captures the effect of stochastic discounting.[7]

We will explore the two adjustments to the basic BS model as applied to interest rate options in some detail. We first consider the difference that arises from the fact that the options are on an interest rate rather than the price of a bill.

The Relationship Between Interest Rate and Bill Options

We will now show the equivalence between the payoffs on a *call* option on an *m*-period interest rate and an expiration date of *T* years and those on a *put*

---

[7]This argument for using the BS model in the presence of stochastic interest rates has been derived by Heath, Jarrow and Morton (1987). The method is applied to options on interest rates and bonds by Jamshidian (1989). See also Satchell, Stapleton and Subrahmanyam (1989) for a general approach to the problem.

option on the price of an *m*-period discount instrument such as a bill, with the same expiration date. Recall the discussion about the similarity between these two options following Example 2. We will derive the precise number of put options on the price of a bill that are equal to one call option on the interest rate. Also, we will demonstrate how to relate the strike price from the interest rate call option, expressed as an annual interest rate in percentage to the strike price of the put option on the bill, expressed in dollars.

Example 13
A Call Option on 3 Month $LIBOR vs. a Put Option on the Price of a 3 Month Bill

Consider a call option on 3 month $LIBOR with a maturity of *T* years. Let the strike price of the option be *x*%. We define the 3 month (91 day) period of the $LIBOR contract as *m* years, where $m = 91/365$. Given an actual interest rate, *i*%, the call option on a face amount of $1 pays an amount at expiration equal to:

$$\frac{[\{i \times (91 / 360)\} - \{x \times (91 / 360)\}]}{[1 + \{i \times (91 / 360)\}]}$$

at time *T*, if it is in-the-money. Otherwise, it pays nothing. (See Example 1 for details.)

Now, consider α puts on 3 month discount bills, with a strike price of $1 / [1 + x \times (91/360)]$ and a maturity of *T* years. The payoff on these α puts is:

$$\alpha \left[\frac{1}{\{1 + x \times (91/360)\}} - \frac{1}{\{1 + i \times (91/360)\}} \right].$$

Now, suppose that we choose α so that:

$$\frac{[\{i \times (91/360)\} - \{x \times (91/360)\}]}{[1 + \{i \times (91/360)\}]}$$

$$= \alpha \left[\frac{1}{\{1 + x \times (91/360)\}} - \frac{1}{\{1 + i \times (91/360)\}} \right] \tag{6.29}$$

We have

$$\alpha = \{1 + x \times (91 / 360)\} = \{1 + x \times (91 / 365) \times (365 / 360)\} \quad (6.30)$$

or, in general

$$\alpha = \{1 + (365 / 360) \times x \times m\} \quad (6.31a)$$

where m is the period of the \$LIBOR contract as a fraction of a 365 day year. Then, the right-hand side of (6.29) becomes

$$1 - \frac{[1 + \{x \times (91/360)\}]}{[1 + \{i \times (91/360)\}]} = \frac{[\{i \times (91/360)\} - \{x \times (91/360)\}]}{[1 + \{i \times (91/360)\}]} \quad (6.32)$$

or the same as the payoff from the interest rate option. It follows from the example that 1 call option on \$LIBOR at a strike rate of x% is equivalent to α put options of a bill with a strike of X where, in the example,

$$X = \frac{1}{[1 + \{x \times (91 / 360)\}]} \quad (6.33)$$

is the strike price of the bill option and

$$\alpha = \{1 + x \times (91 / 360)\} = \frac{1}{X} \quad (6.34)$$

In general,

$$\alpha = \{1 + (365 / 360) \times x \times m\} = \frac{1}{X} \quad (6.31b)$$

By a similar argument, it can be shown that 1 *put* option on \$LIBOR at x% is equivalent to $\alpha = 1/X$ *call* options on a bill where X is the strike price of the bill options.

In summary:

One call (put)option on m period \$LIBOR at a strike rate of x% is equivalent to $\alpha = [1 + x \times m \times (365/360)]$ put (call) options on the price of a 91 day bill at a strike price of X = 1 / [1 + x \times m \times (365/360)].

If the strike rate, x, is 10%, and m is 91/365 years, for example,

$$\alpha = \{1 + 0.10 \times (91 / 365) \times (365 / 360)\} = 1.0253 \quad (6.35a)$$

and

$$X = 0.9753 \tag{6.35b}$$

In other words, a call option on the 3-month interest rate on a face amount of $1 at a strike rate of 10%, is equivalent to 1.0253 put options on the price of a 3-month T-bill with a face amount of $1 at a strike price of 0.9753, the expiration dates of the options being identical. We can, therefore, proceed to value and hedge call (put) options on $LIBOR rates by valuing and hedging α puts (calls) on the price of 91 day bills.

Valuation of Caps and Floors when the Bill Prices are Lognormally Distributed

A fairly straightforward application of the BS model to caps and floors is available when the prices of bills are lognormally distributed. [See Chapter 3 for a discussion of the BS model.] A cap (floor) is a portfolio of n interest rate options with maturities $T_1, T_2, \ldots, T_n$, where n is the number of reset dates. The value of the cap (floor) is the sum of the values of the n interest rate options. Each of the n interest rate calls (puts) is equivalent to α puts (calls) on the price of an m period bill where

$$\alpha = \{1 + x \times m \times (365 / 360)\} \tag{6.36}$$

and x is the strike rate of the cap (floor). For example, if $m = 91/365$, as in the above example

$$\alpha = \{1 + x \times (91 / 365) \times (365 / 360)\}$$
$$= \{1 + x \times (91 / 360)\} \tag{6.37}$$

The price of a put option with maturity T_i on the price of a bill is denoted by $P(T_i, X)$, and the price of a call option is defined as $C(T_i, X)$, where X is the strike price of the options on the bill. The cap with n interest rate call options is then valued as

$$\mathrm{CAP}(x) = \sum_{i=1}^{i=n} \alpha P(T_i, X), \tag{6.38}$$

where

$$X = \frac{1}{\{1 + x \times m \times (365 \,/\, 360)\}}$$

The floor is similarly valued as

$$FLOOR(x) \;=\; \sum_{i=1}^{i=n} \alpha\, C(T_i, X), \qquad\qquad (6.39)$$

where

$$X = \frac{1}{\{1 + x \times m \times (365 \,/\, 360)\}}$$

Suppose the price at time 0 of a bill with maturity $T_i + m$ is denoted by $B_{0,\,T_i + m}$, and the price of the bill at T_i, $B_{T_i,\,T_i + m}$ is lognormally distributed with volatility $m\,\sigma_{T_i}$. The volatility $m\sigma_{T_i}$ is the volatility of the price of an m-period bill, given that the price volatility of the bill on an annualized basis is σ_{T_i}.

$$C(T_i, X) = B_{0,\,T_i + m}\, N(d_1) - B_{0,\,T_i}\, X N(d_2) \qquad\qquad (6.40)$$

where

$$d_1 = \frac{\ln\,(F_{T_i,\,T_i + m}\,/\,X) + \dfrac{m^2}{2}\,\sigma_{T_i}^2\, T_i}{m\,\sigma_{T_i}\,\sqrt{T_i}}$$

and

$$d_2 = d_1 - m\,\sigma_{T_i}\sqrt{T_i}$$

$F_{T_i,\,T_i + m} = \dfrac{B_{0,\,T_i + m}}{B_{0,\,T_i}}$ is the T_i period forward price of the $T_i + m$ period bill with a face value of \$1

B_{0, T_i} is the current price of a T_i period bill with a face value of \$1

$m \, \sigma_{T_i} = \sqrt{\text{var} \left(\ln B_{T_i, T_i + m} \right)}$ is the price volatility of the $T_i + m$ maturity bill.

The value of the call option on the $T_i + m$ period bill shown in equation (6.40) is exactly the same as the BS model applied to the case of a call option on a bill. To see this, recall that from Chapter 3, the BS model for a call option can be written as (after changing the notation for the underlying asset to the bill price B)

$$C(T_i, X) = B_{0, T_i + m} \, N(d_1) - B_{0, T_i} \, X N(d_2) \qquad (6.41)$$

where

$$d_1 = \frac{\ln (B_{0, T_i + m} / X) + (r + \frac{m^2}{2} \sigma_{T_i}^2) T_i}{m \, \sigma_{T_i} \sqrt{T_i}}$$

and

$$d_2 = d_1 - m \, \sigma_{T_i} \sqrt{T_i}$$

where d_1 can be simplified using $B_{0, T_i} = e^{-rT_i}$ to

$$d_1 = \frac{\ln (B_{0, T_i + m} / X) - \ln(e^{-rT_i}) + \frac{m^2}{2} \sigma_{T_i}^2 T_i}{m \, \sigma_{T_i} \sqrt{T_i}}$$

$$= \frac{\ln (B_{0, T_i + m} / X) - \ln(B_{0, T_i}) + \frac{m^2}{2} \sigma_{T_i}^2 T_i}{m \, \sigma_{T_i} \sqrt{T_i}}$$

$$= \frac{\ln (B_{0, T_i + m} / B_{0, T_i} X) + \frac{m^2}{2} \sigma_{T_i}^2 T_i}{m \, \sigma_{T_i} \sqrt{T_i}}$$

$$= \frac{\ln (F_{T_i, T_i + m} / X) + \dfrac{m^2}{2} \sigma_{T_i}^2 T_i}{m \, \sigma_{T_i} \sqrt{T_i}} \tag{6.42}$$

or the same as in equation (6.40).

From the put-call parity relationship in equation (6.10) we have

$$P(T_i, X) = C (T_i, X) + X B_{0, T_i} - B_{0, T_i + m} \tag{6.43}$$

where $B_{0, T_i} = e^{-rT_i}$ is the price of a T_i period bill at time 0.

Hence,

$$P(T_i, X) = B_{0, T_i} X [1 - N(d_2)] - B_{0, T_i + m} [1 - N(d_1)] \tag{6.44}$$

The cap can now be valued by substituting equation (6.44) in equation (6.38). The floor can be valued by substituting equation (6.40) in equation (6.39).

Example 14
A 3 Year Cap on 6 Month $LIBOR.

Assume that the current 6 month (182 day) $LIBOR rate is 8% and the cap has an exercise price of 8%. The cap consists of 5 options which are exercisable at the end of 6 months (183 days), 12 months (365 days), 18 months (548 days) 24 months (730 days) and 30 months (913 days). The first option in the cap is on 182 day $LIBOR, the second is on 183 day $LIBOR, the third is on 182 day $LIBOR, the fourth is on 183 day $LIBOR and the fifth option is on 182 day $LIBOR.

In terms of our notation the periods over which each 6-month rate is applicable and the expiration dates of the options are as follows:

$$
\begin{array}{ll}
T_1 = 183/365 & m_1 = 182/365 \\
T_2 = 365/365 & m_2 = 183/365 \\
T_3 = 548/365 & m_3 = 182/365 \\
T_4 = 730/365 & m_4 = 183/365 \\
T_5 = 913/365 & m_5 = 182/365
\end{array}
$$

Note the periods, m_i, where the subscript indicates the option being referred to, are not exactly equal to 0.5, since each six-month period has either 182 or 183 days, in this example. In general, the period is based upon the precise day count. Using an equation similar to equation (6.32) the strike price on the equivalent put options on bills is, for the first option in the cap, for example,

$$X_1 = \frac{1}{\{1 + 0.08 \times (182 / 360)\}} = 0.9611$$

The input data required for the cap-floor valuation model is summarized in Table 6–4. In column 1 the expiration dates are shown in days from the initiation of the cap. The first five dates show the maturity of the five options in the cap, i.e., $T_i \times 365$. For example, the last number is $(T_5 + m_5) \times 365$, which is the maturity of the last option in the cap. The second column shows the assumed value of a zero coupon bond with a maturity equal to the number of days in the first column. In the third column, we show the current value of a zero coupon bond with a maturity $T_i + m_i$. The fourth column shows the strike price for each option (on the bill price) in the cap. The fifth column records the continuously compounded interest rate implied by the zero bond prices in the second column. In the sixth column, we show the forward price of the zero coupon bond on which the option is written. This is simply $B_{0, T_i + m}$ in the third column divided by $B_{0, T}$ in the second column. In the final column, we show the volatility assumed for the Black and Scholes model calculation. This is the $m \, \sigma_{T_i}$ volatility in equation (6.40). In this example we assume that the annualized volatility is 1% for each of the

TABLE 6–4
Input data for cap-floor valuation model

Option Maturity Days	Bill Price B_{0, T_i}	Bill Price $B_{0, T_i + m}$	Exercise Price X_i	Continuously Compounded Interest Rate	Forward Price $F_{T, T_i + m}$	Volatility
183	0.9609	0.9250	0.9611	0.0795	0.9626	0.0100
365	0.9250	0.8890	0.9609	0.0780	0.9611	0.0100
548	0.8890	0.8548	0.9611	0.0784	0.9615	0.0100
730	0.8548	0.8129	0.9609	0.0784	0.9615	0.0100
913	0.8219	0.7903	0.9611	0.0784	0.9615	0.0100
1035	0.7903					

6 month bills on which the options in the cap are written (the volatility is approximately 1% for each option, the precise number is $0.02 \times m_i$). As we saw in equation (6.38), the value of a cap is equal to the sum of a series of a certain number of puts on the value of a bill with appropriate maturity. In Table 6–5 we show that Black-Scholes values of each option on the bill price. For example, a 183 days put option on a 182 bill (with face value $1) has a Black-Scholes value of 0.00196133 or 19.6133 basis points. In the lower half of the table, this value is adjusted for the α factor. α is the number of put options on bills that is equivalent to one call option on the interest rate. In this case, α_1 for the first option in the cap is, from (6.31b),

$$\alpha_1 = \frac{1}{X_1} = \frac{1}{0.9611} = 1.0405$$

Using this factor, we find the value of the first option in the cap, in basis points is:

TABLE 6–5
Values of a cap-floor (all values in basis points)

	Value of an Option on the Bill Price		
Option Maturity Days	Option	Put	Call
183	1	19.6133	33.6639
365	2	34.6903	36.4439
548	3	39.8620	43.5135
730	4	43.8998	49.1652
913	5	48.0490	51.4250

	Value of an Option on the Interest Rate	
Option	Call	Put
1	20.4065	35.0254
2	36.1010	37.9259
3	41.4742	45.2734
4	45.6850	51.1646
5	49.9923	53.5049
	Cap	Floor
	193.6591	222.8942

$$19.6133 \times 1.0405 = 20.4065 \text{ basis points.}$$

The same procedure is followed for all the other options in the cap. Adding the values of the five options in the cap, the value of the cap is:

$$\text{CAP}(8\%) = 193.6591 \text{ basis points.}$$

Also shown in Table 6–5 is the value of a floor at 8%. The floor is valued as the sum of a certain number of call options on bills. The floor at 8% is worth rather more than the cap since if it is slightly in the money. Also, in the Black-Scholes model, even at-the-money calls on bills are worth more than puts at the same strike price, due to the lognormality assumption. Hence, at-the-money floors are worth more than at-the-money caps. The value of the floor in this example is 222.8942 basis points.

Modification of the Cap and Floor Valuation Model for Alternative Assumptions Regarding the Distribution of Bill Prices

The BS model prices for the options on bills which have been used to value the cap and the floor rely on the assumption that the prices of discount bills are lognormally distributed. This, in turn, implies that interest rates (that is, the continuously compounded interest rates) are normally distributed. This assumption may be appropriate for interest rates in some circumstances. However, it has two features that are objectionable from both a theoretical and empirical perspective. First, since the distribution of the interest rate itself is normal, it allows for the possibility of negative interest rates, which is obviously unrealistic. Second, given the same volatility parameter, the volatility of interest rates is independent of the level, i.e., the same changes in interest rates are possible at both high and low interest rates, which may not be empirically reasonable. An alternative assumption that may be more reasonable in many cases is that interest rates are themselves lognormally distributed.

It is somewhat difficult to incorporate lognormal interest rates into the model in a direct manner for interest rate options, and, hence, for interest rate caps and floors. However a simple modification can be made which captures the essence of the effect of lognormal interest rates. We can assume that the "bankers discount rate," which is defined as one minus the bill price with a face value of \$1, $(1 - B_{T, T+m})$, is lognormal. Since a call on $B_{T, T+m}$ at a strike price X is equivalent to a put on $(1 - B_{T, T+m})$ at a strike price of $(1 - X)$, we can use a modified BS model to value the options with $(1 - B_{T, T+m})$ being assumed to be lognormal. In applying the Black-Scholes model in this case we use an application of the Black model for options on forwards. In this method, we use as an input the forward price of the asset and determine the value of the option on the forward. Since the option on the forward has the same value as the option on the spot, when both are European style, this gives us the values we need under stochastic interest rates. However, since we are valuing an option on $1 - B_{T, T+m}$, we use $1 - F_{T, T+m}$ as the forward price of the asset, and $1 - X$ as the strike price.

Example 15

A 6 Month Option on a 12 Month Bill using the Lognormal Model

This is the bill option that is required to value the first option in the cap in Example 14. We will use the same input data as in that example, i.e., the forward price of the 12 month bill is 0.9626 (from Table 6–4). The strike price of the option is 0.9611, the continuously compounded rate of interest is 7.95% and the volatility of the price of the 12 month bill is 1%.

In Table 6–6 we show the input and output for the lognormal interest rate model. Instead of the price of the asset, we use

$$1 - F_{0.5, 1} = 1 - 0.9626$$
$$= 0.0374$$

TABLE 6–6
Lognormal interest rate option pricing model

Value of Options on the Bill Price			
			Basis Points
Bill forward price	0.0374	Call price	34.1423
Strike price	0.0389	Put price	20.0916
Interest Rate Volatility	25.66%		
Interest Rate	7.95%		
Days to expiration	183.000		

In place of the strike price, we put in

$$1 - X = 1 - 0.9611$$
$$= 0.0389$$

In place of the volatility of the bill (1% in Example 14) we use the volatility of $1 - B_{T, T+m}$. To make the example roughly consistent with Example 14, we input a volatility of 25.66% since

$$0.2566 = 0.009973 \times \frac{0.9626}{0.0374}$$

where $0.009973 = 0.02 \times (182 / 365)$ is the precise volatility used in the first option in Example 14. In other words, 25.66% is the same volatility as before expressed as a percentage of $1 - F_{0.5, 1}$ rather than as a percentage of $F_{0.5, 1}$.

The value of the call on a bill price (i.e., a put on interest rates) is the BS value (with a zero interest rate, since we use the Black model for an option on a forward) discounted at the interest rate of 7.95%. This gives a value of 34.1423 basis points, slightly more than in Example 14 where the corresponding price was 33.6639 basis points. The put on the bill price has a value of 20.0916 basis points, which is also larger than the corresponding price (19.6133 basis points) in Example 14. The differences between the values of the options in the two cases are a direct consequence of the differences in their assumptions regarding the stochastic process generating interest rates. In the lognormal interest rate model, puts on bills (i.e., calls on interest rates) are worth more and calls on bills (i.e., puts on interest rates) are worth less than in the normal interest rate model. This is because the lognormal version permits more interest rate variation on the up-side and less on the down-side.

There are alternative stochastic processes for the short-term interest rate that essentially fall between the two extremes of lognormal and normal distributions. In continuous time, the interest rate process may be modeled as

$$di = i^* \, dt + i^\beta \, \sigma \, dz \tag{6.45a}$$

or
$$di = i^* \, idt + i^\beta \, \sigma \, dz \tag{6.45b}$$

where

dz is a Wiener or instantaneously normally distributed random variable,

di is the instantaneous change in the interest rate,

i is the current interest rate,

$i*$ is the mean insterest rate, and

σ is the instantaneous standard deviation of dz, which is a constant.

This implies that

$$\hat{\sigma}\ (i)\ =\ i^{\beta}\ \sigma$$

where

$\hat{\sigma}\ (i)$ is the instantaneous standard deviation of the interest rate when the interest rate is i.

Note that the coefficient β can take different values ranging from 0 to 1. If $\beta = 0$ in equation(6.45a), we get the normally distributed interest rate model because the change in interest rates is independent of the level i. If $\beta = 1$ in equation (6.45b), we get the lognormally distributed interest model, where the changes in interest rates depend on the interest rate level, i. A commonly used assumption is the so-called "square root process" for interest rates which falls between the two extremes by setting $\beta = 1/2$ in equation (6.45a). This avoids the possibility that interest rates could become negative by allowing the variation in interest rates to decline as interest rates fall.

Another device that is commonly used is an adjustment of the stochastic process to account for mean reversion. Mean reversion refers to a tendency of interest rates to be "pulled back" to some long-run level, say $i*$. This effect could be appended to the previous process as follows:

$$di = \gamma\,(i - i^*)dt + i^*\ dt + i^{\beta}\ \sigma\,dz \tag{6.46}$$

Mean-reversion causes the volatility of longer term bill prices to taper off with maturity and become less than the simple BS model would imply. The mean-reversion parameter, γ, is an index of the strength of this effect. The greater the value of γ, the stronger the "pull" back to the long-run level and, hence, the lower the volatility of interest rates in the long run.

A further problem with the use of the BS model is the existence of 'fat tails' in the distribution of interest rates. 'Fat tails' imply that there are departures from the normal distribution at the extreme ends on both the high and low side. These departures may be caused by "jumps" in interest rates, i.e., due to the fact that interest rates do not change smoothly. An alternative cause may be that the volatility parameter itself is not a constant. This problem is a common one in valuing options on many other types of underlying assets such as foreign exchange, commodities, etc. This means that market prices might be higher than model prices for "out of the money" caps and floors. Again, a modification of the BS formula can be used to value the individual options in the cap (floor) by changing the volatility parameter.

6.8   HEDGING CAPS AND FLOORS

The use of the BS model to value options when interest rates are stochastic relies on a forward hedging argument. The writer of an option can hedge the forward price of the option with appropriate transactions in the forward market. It is important to note that when interest rates are stochastic, the hedge ratio from the BS model should be specified in terms of the *forward* price rather than the *spot* price of the asset. Spot hedging is inefficient because spot prices of bills reflect the stochastic discounting differently from the option. In contrast, the forward contract incorporates the stochastic discounting in a manner similar to the option.

From equation (6.40) for the call option on a discount bill, we have the forward price of the call option

$$C^f(T_i, X) = \frac{C(T_i, X)}{B_{0,T_i}} + F_{T_i, T_i+m} N(d_1) - XN(d_2) \qquad (6.47)$$

where the forward price of the option is simply its compounded value over the time period from 0 to T_i. Hence, the appropriate hedge ratio for forward hedging is

$$\frac{\partial C^f(T_i, X)}{\partial F_{T_i, T_i+m}} = N(d_1) \qquad (6.48)$$

By a similar argument, for the put we have

$$\frac{\partial P^f\,(T_i,\,X)}{\partial F_{T_i,\,T_i+m}} = -[1 - N(d_1)] \tag{6.49}$$

These hedge ratios indicate the number of T_i period *forward* positions in period T_i+m bills required to hedge the option that has been written. These hedge positions then need to be aggregated over the different put (call) options in the cap (floor) to compute the hedge ratio for the cap (floor). This hedge can then be stated as positions in the underlying spot bills. This approach can be illustrated using the previous example where we valued interest rate caps and floors.

Example 16
A 3 Year Cap on 6 Month $LIBOR

Suppose that the Black-Scholes model implying normally distributed interest rates is used to value the cap in Example 14. We now illustrate the forward hedging strategy which is consistent with that model. In Table 6–7 we show in the first column the hedge ratio appropriate for hedging one put on the value of a bill. The hedge ratio, -0.4134, for example, is from equation (6.40):

$$-[1 - N(d_1)] = -0.4134$$

where $$d_1 = 0.5866$$

In the second column, we adjust the hedge ratio to account for the fact that one call option on the interest rate is α puts on the value of a bill. This yields,

TABLE 6–7
Hedge ratios for hedging a cap with forwards

Option Maturity Days	Put on Value	Call on Rates	Hedge Position in Bills					
			6 Month	12 Month	18 Month	24 Month	30 Month	36 Month
183	−0.4134	−0.4301	0.4140	−0.4301				
365	−0.4902	−0.5101		0.4903	−0.5101			
548	−0.4836	−0.5032			0.4838	−0.5032		
730	−0.4792	−0.4986				0.4795	−0.4986	
913	−0.4861	−0.5057					0.4863	−0.5057
			0.4140	0.0601	−0.0263	−0.0237	−0.0124	−0.5057

for example, for the first option in the cap, a hedge ratio of:

$$\alpha_1 \left[-[1 - N(d_1)]\right\} = 1.0405 \times (-0.4134)$$
$$= -0.4301$$

The forward hedging strategy for the first option in the cap requires a short position in 0.4301, 6 month forward contracts on the 12 month bill. For the second option in the cap, the strategy requires a short position in 0.5101, 12 month forward contracts on the 18 month bill; and so on for the later options in the cap. As mentioned before, these forward positions can themselves be "manufactured" by appropriate spot positions in bills of different maturity. For example, a 6 month forward position in a 12 month bill is created by buying one 12 month bill and selling $F_{0.5,1}$, 6 month bills where

$$F_{0.5,1} = \frac{B_{0,1}}{B_{0,0.5}} = 0.9626 \tag{6.50}$$

To see this, note that the time 0 cost of this portfolio is

$$-B_{0,1} \qquad + \qquad \frac{B_{0,1}}{B_{0,0.5}} \qquad \times \quad B_{0,0.5} \quad = \quad 0$$

$$\uparrow \qquad\qquad\qquad \uparrow$$

cost of one   sale proceeds
12 month bill   of $(B_{0,1} / B_{0,0.5})=F_{0,0.5}$
6 month bills

The cash flow in month 6 is $-(B_{0,1}/B_{0,0.5})$, i.e., the forward price of a 12 month bill, and the month 12 cash flow is $1. Thus, this strategy allows us to "manufacture" a 6 month forward on a bill maturing in month 12.

Since the hedging of the first option is the cap requires -0.4301 forwards in the (current) 12 month bill, this is achieved by a short position in 0.4301, 12 month bills and a long position in

$$0.4301 \times 0.9626 = 0.4140$$

6 month bills. These positions are shown in the third and fourth columns of Table 6–7. The same procedure is followed for the other options in the cap.

The hedging of the cap is the sum of the hedge positions for the individual options in the cap. These are shown in the bottom line of Table 6–7. Note that the hedge for the whole cap consists of a positive position in 0.4140 6 month bills and a negative position in the 36 month bill. The positions in the intermediate maturity bills are quite small. This indicates that a reasonably good hedge in practice could be achieved by minor adjustments to positions in only the 6 month bill and the 36 month bill.

Hedging Caps and Floors: Some Practical Considerations

The forward hedging strategy gives the perfect 'delta' hedge for the cap (floor). However, two problems remain. First, the instruments may not be available or may be too expensive to deal in. The delta hedge may therefore be impractical. Second, even a perfect delta hedge may be ineffective because of (a) jumps in the interest rate process or (b) changes in volatility of interest rates. The second set of problems is common to all option hedging and will not be discussed here. The first problem is particularly acute in the case of interest rate options and requires comment.

In the case of stock options, the hedging instruments (i.e., the underlying stocks) are readily available and traded in liquid markets. To create a delta hedge in an interest rate option we need to deal in zero coupon bonds of varying maturities up to at least 5 years. In most currencies, the only liquid interest rate related contracts are fairly short-term futures contracts on bills and bonds. In practice, a hedge position has to be created in futures contracts on short-term interest rates or in interest rate swaps. It is often possible to use the concept of duration to locate a reasonable hedge in terms of the futures contract. In other cases it is possible to hedge with swaps or forward rate agreements (FRAs). Furthermore, the hedging for various interest rates products such as swaps, caps, and floors is done together in one book.

6.9   EXTENSIONS AND CONCLUSIONS

In this chapter we have outlined the essential principles underlying the valuation and hedging of options on short-term interest rates. In particular, we have examined the market conventions and product specifications that are common in both exchange-traded and over-the-counter products that depend on short-term money market rates. Much of the analysis has centered around caps and floors on interest rates. It should be noted, however, that these are but two examples, although quite important in today's markets. There is an array of possible variations around these basic products. Two examples will serve to illustrate the possibilities of extension of the framework used in this chapter.

The first example deals with "captions," which are options to buy or sell a cap in the future. Essentially, these are options on options and can be analyzed using the compound options methodology outlined in Chapter 4. The second extension is to the case of "swaptions" or options on swaps. An example of a swaption would be the right to switch from the fixed side to the floating side of a swap sometime in the future before a certain expiration date. These may be either American-style or European-style. In principle, these are similar to options on bonds since the price of the fixed side of the swap fluctuates just like that of a bond, whereas the floating side has very little interest rate risk. Swaptions may, therefore, be valued and hedged using the approaches outlined in the bond options chapter (Chapter 8) with appropriate adjustments.

References

Black, F. (January/March 1976). The pricing of commodity contracts. *Journal of Financial Economics, 3*, 167–79.

Black, F., and Scholes, M. (May/June 1973). The pricing of options and corporate liabilities. *Journal of Political Economy, 81*, 637–59.

Briys, E., Crouhy, M., and Schöbel, R. (June 1988). The pricing of interest rate cap and collar agreements. Centre - HEC working paper.

Cox, J., Ingersoll, J., Jr., and Ross, S. (March 1985). A theory of the term structure of interest rates. *Econometrica, 53*, 385–407.

Heath, D., Jarrow, R., and Morton, A. (1988). Bond pricing and the term structure of interest rates. Cornell University working paper.

Jamshidian, F. (March 1989). An exact bond option formula. *Journal of Finance, 44*, 205–09.

Satchell, S., Stapleton, R., and Subrahmanyam, M. (August 1989). Futures, forwards, options and the equivalent martingale measure. New York University working paper.

CHAPTER 7

FOREIGN EXCHANGE OPTIONS

Richard C. Stapleton
*Constantine Thanassoulas**

7.1 INTRODUCTION

The last few years has seen a dramatic growth in the purchase and trading of Foreign Exchange (FOREX) Options. In this chapter we describe the contracts offered in the traded FOREX options markets and on the over the counter (OTC) markets. The emphasis is on the nature of the various contracts and their pay-offs. In section 7.2 we discuss the use of options for hedging foreign currency risk. Section 7.3 describes the contracts available on the major traded FOREX options markets in Philadelphia and Chicago. In this section we distinguish options on cash from options on futures. In the case of FOREX options it is important to realize that the American feature of options on cash can be of significant value.

The valuation of simple FOREX options is looked at in section 7.4 in the context of the Black and Scholes (B-S) model. The B-S model can be adapted to value European style FOREX options by making an adjustment for the interest differential between the foreign currency and the domestic currency.

*The authors are Wolfson Professor of Finance, University of Lancaster (U.K.), and Head of Risk Management, Barclays Bank, respectively.

One of the features of the OTC FOREX options market is the great variety of complicated products that are offered. Section 7.5 describes the nature of the most commonly encountered contracts including the Range Forward, Conditional Forward and the Participating Forward Contracts. We also discuss more exotic offerings, such as Contingent FOREX options, Compound options and Multi-Currency options. We describe these various option contracts by plotting their pay-off diagrams.

Finally, in section 7.6 we discuss the problem of hedging FOREX options from the point of view of the option writer.

7.2 THE USE OF FOREX OPTIONS TO HEDGE CURRENCY RISK

An Example: A U.S. manufacturing company is due to receive a payment of 30 million Deutschemarks (DM) in 6 months time. The current exchange rate is DM 1 = $0.50. The company is considering the use of various hedging instruments (forwards, futures, options) to reduce the risk of the US $ it will receive, when it exchanges the DM for dollars.

The company has a number of possible strategies. The most important ones are:

1. Do not hedge. Convert DM at the spot exchange rate in six months time.
2. Hedge 100 percent using a forward sale at the 6 month forward rate
3. Hedge less than 100 percent using a forward sale as above.
4. Buy 'at-the-money' DM puts at a strike price of $0.51.
5. Buy 'out-of-the-money' DM puts at a strike price of $0.49.

The market prices are summarized in Figure 7–1 and the results of following the various strategies are plotted in Figure 7–2. The current price of the DM is $0.50 and the 6 month forward rate is $0.51. (This indicates that the DM is a 'premium' currency). The first two strategies shown in Figure 7–2 are straightforward. Either wait until the DM 30 million are received in 6 months time and then convert at the going exchange rate (i.e., the No Hedge strategy 1) or sell forward and agree to receive $15.3 million ($30 \times 0.51$) for certain in 6 months time (strategy 2). Note that a similar result to strategy 2 can be obtained by using the futures market. However, we will not explicitly consider the purchase or sale of futures in this chapter.

The problem of selling the DM 30 million forward is the 'regret'

FIGURE 7–1
Hedging example data

DM – $ quotes

Spot DM $0.500
6 month forward DM 0.510
Put option on DM at strike = $0.510 ....0.010
Put option on DM at strike = $0.490 ....0.005

Contract Size

Futures .... DM 125,000
Options (cash) .... DM 62,500

Number of contracts to hedge DM 30 million

Futures (30,000,000 / 125,000) = 240 contracts
Options (30,000,000 / 62,500)   = 480 contracts

FIGURE 7–2
Hedging strategies

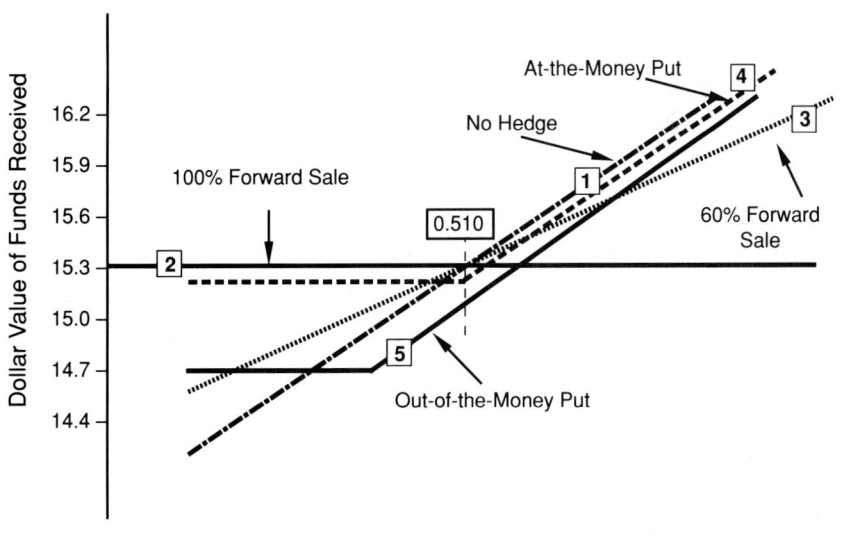

factor. If the DM rises above $0.51 the company gains no benefit, since it is obliged to convert at the agreed rate of $0.51. This can be important if its competitors have not sold forward and are able to gain from the strength of the DM. One way of overcoming this 'regret' factor is a '60:40' strategy. Sell 60 percent of the DM 30 million forward and take a chance with the exchange rate by not hedging the remaining 40%. This partial hedge is illustrated in Figure 7–2. Note that the slope of relationship 3 is just 60 percent of that in the 'no hedging' case (1). With strategy 3 some gains are made (compared to the forward sale at $0.51) if the exchange rate rises, but losses are incurred if the exchange rate falls.

The advantage of options is that they place a floor under the dollar proceeds. In the case of strategy 4, which involves the purchase (see Figure 7–1) of 480 put option contracts at a strike price equal to the forward rate ($0.51), the minimum proceeds are $15 million. This is because we have assumed an option premium of $0.01. At any price less than or equal to $0.51 the firm can sell its DM for $0.51. However it pays the premium of $0.01, so that the net proceeds per DM are $0.51 - $0.01 = $0.50. The put option at $0.51 can be regarded as an insurance contract. A premium of $0.01 is paid. This is the insurance premium. The firm is then guaranteed a FOREX sale of at least the forward price, $0.51. They have insured against a fall in the DM below its forward price.

An alternative insurance contract is the 'out-of-the-money' put option. Here the firm in effect agrees to cover the first part of any fall in the price below $0.51 itself in return for a lower premium. For example, in Figure 7–2 strategy 5, it is assumed that the firm can buy an option to sell DM at $0.49 for $0.005. Net proceeds are $0.485 or $14.55 million if the FOREX is at or below $0.49 per DM. The smaller premium of $0.005 is seen by comparing the payoffs on strategies 5, 4, and 1. This out-of-the-money option represents insurance with a 'deductible' of 2 cents.

7.3   EXCHANGE TRADED FOREX OPTIONS

As with options on any other underlying security it is possible to write or buy puts or calls on FOREX. These puts and calls may be either exercisable at the maturity date (European) or at any time up to the maturity date (American). Also, the options may be written on the foreign currency itself or on foreign currency futures. Finally, the FOREX options may be tradeable on a secondary market or may be sold 'over the counter' by a bank. Over the counter (OTC) options are custom made and, as we shall see, come in many different varieties. The FOREX option market differs from other option markets in the proportion of business that is done in the OTC market. Perhaps because the underlying security is so homogeneous and liquid it is relatively easy to structure custom made deals where both parties can negotiate exactly what the contract entails.

As shown in Figure 7–3, Traded options on FOREX are available on the Philadelphia Stock Exchange (PHLX) and the Chicago Mercantile Exchange (CME). These are the two principal marketplaces for traded FOREX options. However, FOREX options are also traded, in much

FIGURE 7–3
Exchange traded option contracts

Traded Options

PHLX   American options on Cash .... DM SFr C$ STG FFr ¥ Ecu
CME   American options on Futures ... DM SFr C$ STG FFr ¥ Ecu
Other   (LIFFE, Amsterdam, Montreal, Singapore)

Principal Exchange Traded Option Contracts

Currency (Symbol)	Contract Size	Exchange[a]	Average Monthly Volume[b]
Deutschemark (DM)	125,000	CME	200,000
Deutschemark (DM)	62,500	PHLX	262,000
Pound Sterling (STG)	12,500	PHLX	160,000
Pound Sterling (STG)	12,500	LSE	600
Swiss Franc (SFr)	62,500	PHLX	60,000
Japanese Yen (¥)	6,250,000	PHLX	240,000
Canadian Dollar (C$)	50,000	PHLX	22,500
Australian Dollar (A$)	100,000	PHLX	50,000
European Currency Unit (ECU)	62,500	PHLX	3,400
Netherlands Guilder (NLG)	10,000	EOE	50

[a] PHLX = Philadelphia Stock Exchange

   CME = Chicago Mercantile Exchange

   EOE = European Options Exchange (Amsterdam)

   LSE = London Stock Exchange

[b]All volume figures refer to the first half of 1988.

smaller volumes, in London, Singapore, Amsterdam and Montreal. Since, its inception in 1982, volume on the PHLX has steadily increased to a daily average of around 40,000 contracts, representing approximately $600 million in terms of the underlying currencies on which the options are written. The CME had a similar volume of trade in options on FOREX futures.

One feature of the traded options markets is that it is only possible to buy options on a small number of currencies. Also, although option prices are quoted on 8 currencies on PHLX, there is significant volume only in 4 (Deutsche Mark [DM], Yen [¥], Pound Sterling [£] and Swiss Franc [SFr]). Although it is interesting to note that options are quoted for the European Currency Unit, a basket of currencies, trading in ECU options is negligible. The other important feature to note is that the only FOREX options traded are US dollar denominated. No traded market exists for Deutsche Mark/Swiss Franc options for example. This is an important limitation of the traded options markets and may explain the relative importance of the OTC market. The OTC market has grown during 1986-1988 at a phenomenal rate. Although 'official' figures on volume do not exist, our estimates put the average daily volume in excess of $20 billion.

Options versus Futures on FOREX
A long forward position is equivalent to a long call plus a short put at the same strike price. A futures contract is similar to a tradeable forward. Although there are slight differences, we will use the terms 'forward' and 'futures' interchangeably.[1] On the other hand, the distinction between an option contract and a forward/futures contract is a fundamental one. In the context of FOREX it is particularly important. In Figure 7–4 we illustrate the difference. A forward contract to buy DM for $ together with a forward contract to buy $ for £ is simply a contract to buy DM for £. However, the same is not true if we combine a DM/$ call and a $/£ call. In fact, the combined cost of the two $ denominated calls will be more than the DM/£ call. There are situations where the $ calls pay off and the DM/£ call does not. For example, if the $ falls to 1DM = $.60 and to £ 1 = $2.50, the option to buy DM at $.50 yields a profit of $.10. However, the option to buy $.50 at £ 0.25 expires out-of-the-money. Similarly, because the DM = £ 0.24, a call to purchase 1 DM for £ 0.25 is also worthless. The two $ options are worth $.10 whereas the DM/£ option is worthless.

---

[1] For an analysis of the differences, see Cox, Ingersoll and Ross (1981).

FIGURE 7–4
Cross-currency options and forwards

Forward Contracts

Forward DM / \$	+ Forward \$ / £	= Forward DM / £
Buy 1 DM at \$0.50 per DM	+ Buy \$0.50 at £0.50 per \$	= Buy 1 DM at £0.25

Option Contracts

Option DM / \$	+ Option \$ / £	≠ Option DM / £
Call 1 DM at \$0.50	+ Call \$0.50 at £0.25	> Call 1 DM at £0.25

The distinction between options and forward contracts is important. It means that the existence of \$ denominated traded options on PHLX and CME does not mean that the market for FOREX options is complete. There is room for banks to offer OTC options on nondollar FOREX rates, and these cannot be duplicated by combinations of \$ traded options.

Options on Cash versus Options on Futures

Traded options volume on FOREX expanded rapidly between 1982 and 1987 on the Philadelphia Stock Exchange. PHLX options are options on cash, i.e., when the contract is exercised the holder of the option either purchases or sells foreign currency. Options on cash may seem to be a straightforward type of contract. However, because of interest differentials between currencies, the pricing of these options is somewhat complicated. American call options may sell at a premium to European calls for example. Partly for this reason, a thriving market has developed in options on Futures on FOREX. Traded options on Futures, traded on the Chicago Mercantile Exchange, have recently exceeded volumes on the PHLX.

In order to illustrate the difference between options on cash on FOREX and options on Futures on FOREX, we will first show why American options on Cash are in general worth more than European options on cash.

In Figure 7–5 we assume that the exchange rate follows a Binomial process. The DM could rise over 3 months to \$0.53 or fall to \$0.48. Over the second 3 month period it could rise further to \$0.56, fall back (or rise from \$0.48) to \$0.51 or fall further to \$0.46. The Binomial process has been

FIGURE 7–5
DM/$ exchange rate process

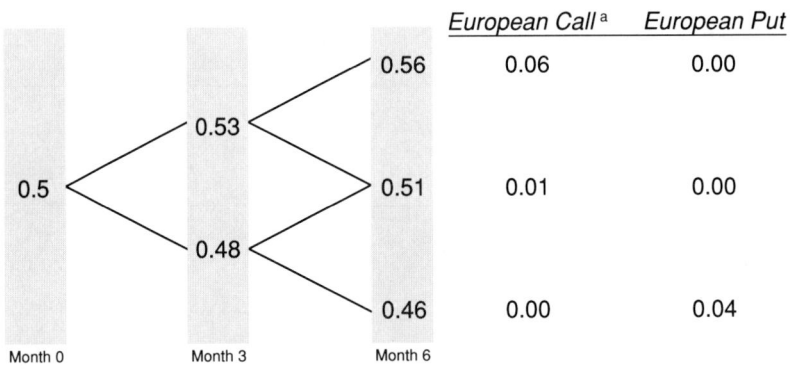

	European Call [a]	European Put
0.56	0.06	0.00
0.51	0.01	0.00
0.46	0.00	0.04

Month 0   Month 3   Month 6

Volatility = 5% per quarter
Interest rate: DM = 1.5% for 3 months, 3.0% for 6 months
    $ = 2.5% for 3 months, 5.0% for 6 months

[a]At-the-money options

centered around the 6 month forward rate of $0.51. In this example we assume also a 3 month forward exchange rate of $0.505. The first stage of the Binomial process is centered around the 3 month forward rate.[2]

Figure 7–5 shows the pay-off on an at-the-money European Call option and an at-the-money European Put option. Notice that the Call option pays off more heavily than the Put option. This is because the Binomial process for the DM exchange rate is upward biased. It is centered on $0.51 and the options are written at $0.50. This upward bias causes the Call to be worth more than the Put.

In Figure 7–6 we illustrate the process for the month 6 futures price of a DM. The assumption made is that the interest differential between $ and DM is nonstochastic. It is at the present moment 1 percent for 3 month money and it will be 1 percent also for 3 month money in 3 month's time. Thus the premium of the month 6 futures price over the spot price at the end of 3 months is 1 percent. For simplicity we assume that the premium is a

---

[2]It follows from Interest Rate Parity that the interest rate differential between the $ and DM is 1 percent over 3 months and 2 percent over 6 months, i.e., 4 percent at an annual rate.

FIGURE 7–6
DM/$ futures price process

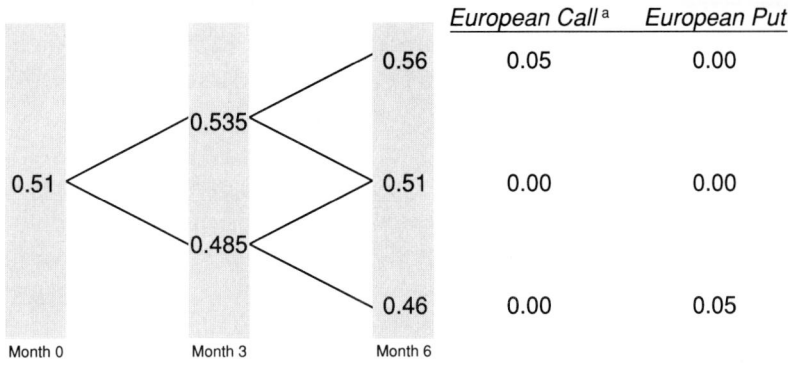

	European Call [a]	European Put
0.56	0.05	0.00
0.51	0.00	0.00
0.46	0.00	0.05

[a]At-the-money options

fixed amount (0.005) rather than a fixed percentage above the spot price. Compared with Figure 7–5 we see that the premium narrows over time from $0.01 at month 0 to zero at month 6. By definition the month 6 futures price at month 6 is the spot price of the currency.

If we now define an at-the-money option on the DM futures to be an option struck at 0.51, the current 6 month futures price, we see that the payoffs on at-the-money European put options on futures and European call options on futures are symmetrical. It follows that the options will be equally priced.[3]

The difference between the European options on cash (Figure 7–5) and on futures (Figure 7–6) is purely a matter of definition. An at-the-money option on the futures is an option with an exercise price of $0.51 rather than $0.50 as in the case of an option on the cash currency. In fact, the payoff on a European option with a given exercise price is the same for options on cash or futures. This is because the month 6 futures price is the same as the month 6 exchange rate.

[3]This follows from put-call-forward parity. A call minus a put at the forward price has zero value.

American Options on Cash

American options on futures are less likely to be exercised early than options on cash. The example in Figure 7–6 illustrates this. In the example, the current 6 months futures/forward price is $0.51. The current 3 months futures/forward price is $0.505. The Binomial process for the futures price in Figure 7–6 has been centered on the current 3 and 6 month futures prices. The volatility is the same as in Figure 7–5.

An American option will be exercised if the exercise pay off exceeds the value that the option will have if it is not exercised. Assuming the exchange rate follows the process shown in Figure 7–5, one sees that in the case of the American option on cash there is an incentive to exercise the American Put at the end of the 3 months. For example, an American put with an exercise price of $0.51 pays $0.51 – $0.48 = $0.03, if exercised at the end of 3 months in the 'down' state. This has to be compared to the value of an option which pays ($0.51 – $0.51 = 0), in the 'up' state or ($0.51 – $0.46 = $0.05), in the 'down' state at the end of 6 months. If the uncertain prospect of $0.05 at the end of 6 months is worth less than a certain $0.03 at the end of the 3 months, the American Put will be exercised early in the 'down' state.

Now consider an American option on the futures, assuming the futures price tree is as shown in Figure 7–6. An American Put at $0.51 pays $0.51 – $0.485 = $0.025 at the end of the 3 months in the 'down' state. If the American option on the futures is not exercised at month 3 it pays ($0.51 – $0.51 = $0) in the 'up' state or ($0.51 – $0.46 = $0.05) in the 'down' state at month 6. (Assuming for simplicity that no exercise is allowed between month 3 and 6). It may still be optimal to exercise early and gain $0.025 at month 3. However, the incentive is reduced considerably when we compare this option to the American Put option on cash.

7.4   THE VALUATION OF EUROPEAN FOREX OPTIONS.

We have seen above that the payoff on a European option on a currency depends upon the interest differential between the two currencies involved. For example, a call option to buy £ for $ will be more likely to pay off, and hence be more valuable, if the £ interest rate is less than the $ interest rate. In this case the forward rate for £ exceeds the spot rate. A call option at a given strike price on £ is worth more in this case than it would be if there were no interest rate differential. The converse is true for put options.

The Black-Scholes model for the valuation of stock options can be adapted to capture this interest rate differential effect. The B-S model values options on nondividend paying stocks. We have for example:

$$C = C\,(S, X, T, \sigma, r)$$

where: C = the call value,
            S = the spot price,
            X = the exercise price of the option,
            T = the time to maturity,
            r = the interest rate (quoted on a continuous basis)
and σ = the volatility of the stock.

The precise formula for the call option value is:

$$C = SN[D] - X\,e^{-rT}\,N[D - \sigma\sqrt{T}\,] \qquad (7.1)$$

where

$$D = \frac{\ln(S\,/\,X) + (r + \sigma^2\,/\,2)\,T}{\sigma\sqrt{T}}$$

and $N[\cdot]$ = the Normal Cumulative Probability function.

In order to value FOREX options, the B-S formula (7.1) has to be adjusted for the interest rates in the two currencies involved. Garman and Kohlhagen (1983), Grabbe (1983), and Bodurtha and Courtadon (1987) derive the following relationship for a **call option** on FOREX:

$$C = e^{-r_f T}\,S\,N[D] - X\,e^{-r_d T}\,N[D - \sigma\sqrt{T}\,] \qquad (7.2)$$

where: C = the call value
            S = the spot price of the foreign currency
            X = the exercise price of the option
            T = time to maturity in years
            r_d = the 'domestic' interest rate
            r_f = the 'foreign' interest rate
            σ = volatility

and
$$D = \frac{\ln (S / X) + (r_d - r_f + \sigma^2 / 2) T}{\sigma \sqrt{T}}$$

The delta of the currency option is given by

$$\textbf{call delta} = e^{-r_f T} N [D].$$

The valuation formula for a FOREX **put option** is given by

$$P = Xe^{-r_d T} N [-(D - \sigma \sqrt{T})] - Se^{-r_f T} N [-D]$$

$$\textbf{put delta} = -e^{-r_f T} N [-D],$$

which can be derived from (7.2) by applying put-call parity.

The normal practice is to program the value of equation (7.2) with the additional variable r_f. We will illustrate with the following examples:

Example 1:
A 182 day call option on £ denominated in $, with a strike price of $1.60 per £. We assume:

$$S = \$1.60$$
$$r_d = 0.10$$
$$r_f = 0.10$$
$$\sigma = 0.12$$

In this example $T = 182/365$.

Substituting in equation (7.2) we obtain: $C = \$0.0514$.

Comment: In this case the equation for the call has a zero differential $(r_d - r_f = 0.0)$. This special case is interesting because the put option value for an at-the-money option is also $0.0514.

Example 2:
A 182 day call option on £ denominated in $, with a strike price of $1.60. We now assume:

$$S = \$1.60$$
$$r_d = 0.10$$
$$r_f = 0.11$$
$$\sigma = 0.12$$

Example 2 is the same at-the-money option as in example 1. However, the foreign (£) interest rate is now 11 percent per annum. Sterling is a discount currency, which has a forward rate less than $1.60. The option is worth, according to (7.2): $C = \$0.0476$.

Comment: In this case $r_d - r_f = -0.01$ and this expected decline in Sterling is reflected in the call value. In the case of an at-the-money put we find: $P = \$0.0552$.

The Relationship between Black-Scholes and the FOREX Option Pricing Formula

The FOREX option pricing formula was presented in equation (7.2) above as a 'black box.' We can get an intuitive feel for the formula if we consider the relationship to the simpler B-S formula (7.1).

If we place $r_f = 0.0$ in equation (7.2) we find that it reduces to the B-S formula (7.1) with $r_d = r$. An option on a foreign currency can be thought of as an option on an asset that pays a dividend. In the case where $r_f = 0.0$, the dividend is zero and we can use the 'regular' B-S formula, which values options on nondividend paying assets. If $r_f > 0.0$, as we would invariably expect, we have to adjust the B-S formula to account for the fact that the underlying asset on which the option is written pays a positive dividend. In the case of a nondividend paying stock with price S, the B-S approach calculates the forward price:

$$F = S\,e^{rT} \tag{7.3}$$

For a currency, the forward price F depends on the interest rate differential. In fact, if r_d and r_f are the continuously compounded interest rates in the domestic and foreign currency:

$$F = S\,e^{(r_d T - r_f T)} \tag{7.4}$$

Equation (7.4) results from applying the interest rate parity theorem in the case of continuously compounded interest rates.

In order to have the correct forward price in the B-S model we must input an adjusted spot price of the currency, S', such that

$$S' e^{r_d T} = F = S e^{(r_d T - r_f T)} \qquad (7.5)$$

re-arranging (7.5):

$$S' = S e^{-r_f T} \qquad (7.6)$$

It follows that the correct FOREX option price can be obtained by substituting $S e^{-r_f T}$ for S in the regular B-S equation (7.1). Therefore, substituting S' for S in (7.1):

$$C = S' N [D] - X e^{-r_d T} N [D - \sigma \sqrt{T}]$$

where

$$D = \frac{\ln (S' / X) + (r_d + \sigma^2 / 2) T}{\sigma \sqrt{T}}$$

which is the same as (7.2).

To calculate the FOREX option values using the B-S formula, we have:

Example 1:
Instead of $S = \$1.60$, we input $S' = \$1.60 \, e^{-0.1 T} = \$1.5220$, which gives a B-S call value of $C = \$0.0514$.

Example 2:
Instead of $S = 1.60$, we input $S' = \$1.60 \, e^{-0.11 T} = \$1.5146$, which gives a B-S call value of $C = \$0.0475$.

Essentially, all that is involved in valuing European options on FOREX is a shift in the spot price input to the Black-Scholes calculation. The shift involves discounting the spot price by the foreign interest rate.

Are the Black and Scholes Assumptions Correct for FOREX Options?

We have seen how to adjust the B-S model for the forward premium or discount of a foreign currency. We now ask whether the other assumptions involved in the B-S valuation model apply in the case of FOREX. The most important assumption of the B-S model is the distributional assumption regarding price of the underlying asset: lognormality and nonstochastic variance.

In the case of FOREX prices there is well documented evidence, that the volatility is stochastic and that prices depart significantly from the B-S assumption of lognormality. Studies by So (1987) and Taylor (1986) looked at daily exchange rates, spot and futures, for the major currencies over the period 1974–1981. They, like previous work by McFarland, Pettit and Sung (1982), Rogalski (1978), and Calderon-Russel (1982) found that the historical distribution of FOREX rates showed significant kurtosis, i.e., 'fat tails.' This was relatively more important for the minor currencies.

Compared to a lognormal distribution, which the Garman and Kohlhagen (1983) extension of the Black and Scholes (1973) model to FOREX options assumes, exchange rates have 'fat tails.' This means that the probability of an extreme outcome occurring is higher than the B-S model assumes. In turn this means that the B-S model tends to undervalue out-of-the-money options on FOREX. The degree of the undervaluation depends upon the extent of kurtosis for the particular currency. The evidence suggests that the inaccuracy of the B-S model is relatively small for the major currencies such as DM, £ and ¥.

7.5   OVER THE COUNTER FOREX OPTIONS

OTC options are contracts negotiated on a custom made basis with a bank. The main participants in this market are the large international banks who write the options and corporate clients and banks who buy the options. By definition these options may be of any type. However, most contracts are based on the cash currency rather than the futures. Also, the majority of contracts tend to be American rather than European.

The principal OTC options are summarized in Figure 7–7. These are:

A.   Straight Option Contracts

These are the same as the Exchange Traded options except that the currencies involved, and the exercise prices and maturity dates are more varied. Thus it is possible to buy an option to buy DM for £, for example, as well as currencies priced in US $. Also long dated options (2 - 5 years)

FIGURE 7–7
Types of over the counter FOREX options

A. Straight Option Contracts (varying strike rates, maturities)
B. Zero Cost Options
   • Range forward (cylinder options)
   • Conditional forward (forward reversing options)
   • Participating forwards (shared option forward agreement)
C. Contingent FOREX Options
D. Compound Options (options on options)
E. Multicurrency Options

may be bought or sold in this market. As in the Traded Options Market, the premium on a straight option contract is paid up front, when the contract is negotiated. However, in custom made contracts arrangements can be made to pay option premia in instalments.

B. Reduced or Zero 'Cost' Combinations

One of the important innovations in the OTC market has been the marketing of option contracts that have a zero apparent cost. What this means is that a contract is written which involves no cash payment at the time the deal is made. Since forward contracts involve no such cash payment, these option contracts are often referred to as forwards of various types. However, this terminology is somewhat confusing. In each case, the contracts are combinations (i.e., portfolios of straight options). The combinations are arranged so that the net cost (of buying one option and selling others) is zero.

Before describing the three most common forms of zero cost options we should consider some of the reasons why these contracts are so popular. First, there may be a desire on behalf of a corporate client to delay the impact of the option cost on the published accounts, and on the firm's cash flow. Option contracts represent insurance against changes in the FOREX rate and it is natural to want to match the timing of the insurance payment and the benefits (if any) of the insurance. However there may also be more substantial tax benefits to paying option premia out of the proceeds of the contract.

B.1 The Range Forward (or Cylinder Option) Contract

This contract allows the holder to ensure that his future exchange rate is between a maximum x_1, and a minimum x_2. For example, if a firm in the United States wishes to purchase £ in 6 months' time and the current forward rate is \$1.60 it might be able to do the following deal. If the exchange rate in 6 months' time is greater than, say, \$1.61, the firm has the right to purchase £ at \$1.61. If the market rate is below, say, \$1.595, the firm must purchase at \$1.595. In between \$1.61 and \$1.595 it must purchase at the market rate.

The Range Forward contract is a generalization of a simple forward contract, except that over a given range, in this case \$1.595 to \$1.61, the holder of the contract is prepared to take some risk on the future market price of £. His exchange rate is shown in Figure 7–8A. Below \$1.595 he has to pay \$1.595 and his loss, compared to the market is shown in Figure 7–8B. Above \$1.61 he gains as in a conventional forward contract.

The flexibility of the Range Forward contract arises from the fact that the range is defined by two points. A high rate x_1, and a low rate x_2. The customer can pick one of the rates, say x_1, and the Bank can pick the other rate (x_2). In effect, the customer chooses a rate (x_1) which is the guaranteed maximum on the exchange rate. The Bank then says that it will sell the contract for a zero price if the customer agrees to purchase FOREX at an exchange rate no less than x_2. The lower x_1 is, the higher x_2 must be to compensate.

The Range Forward Contract can be replicated by a portfolio of puts and calls on FOREX. In the example above, the gains and losses are the same as on the portfolio

$$C\,(1.61, 6) - P\,(1.595, 6)$$

where the notation $C\,(X, T)$, $P\,(X, T)$ refers to payoffs on calls and puts with exercise price X and maturity T (months). The holder of the portfolio gains when the price exceeds \$1.61 and loses when it is less than \$1.595. Since the call and put contracts can be valued separately, the Bank can effectively choose an exercise price on the put (\$1.595) which compensates it for giving away a call option (at \$1.61).

FIGURE 7–8A
The range forward contract

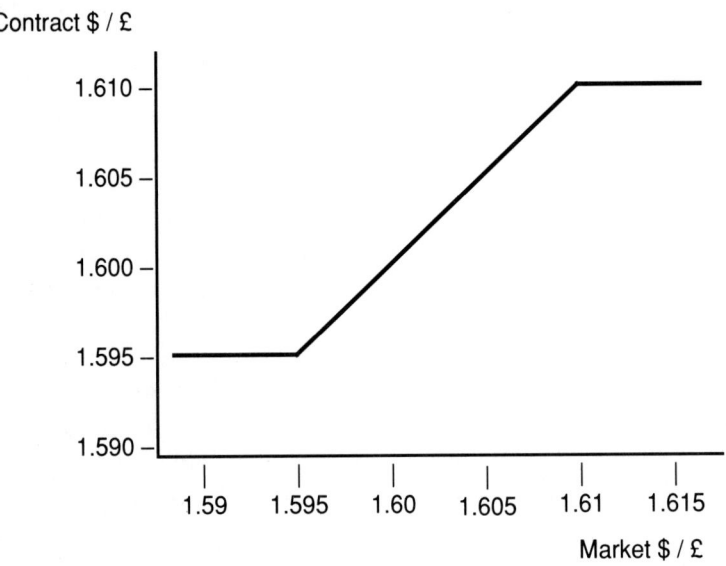

FIGURE 7–8B

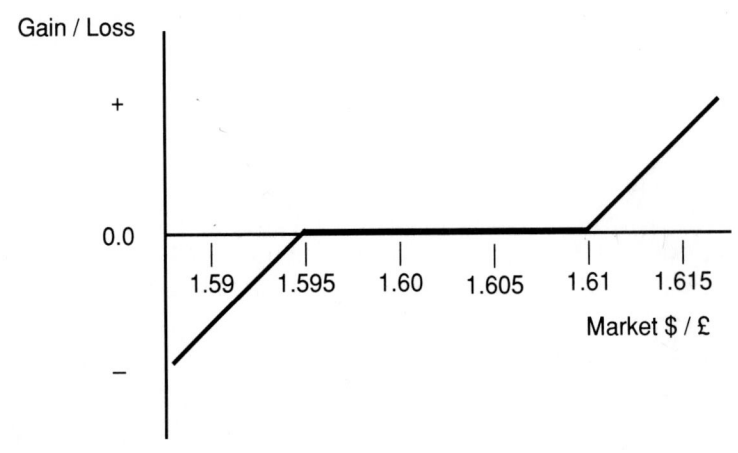

B.2 The Conditional Forward (Forward Reversing Option) Contract

The Conditional Forward is the same as a straight FOREX option except that the option premium is paid in the future and is only paid if the FOREX price is below a specified level. The customer again specifies a price x_1 for £ above which she is not prepared to go, for example $1.61. The Bank then quotes a premium which is to be paid if and only if the FOREX price plus the premium is less than $1.61.

The effect of this contract is shown in Figure 7–9A. Here we assume that the (conditional) premium to be paid is $0.01. Hence, if the FOREX price is $1.58, the customer pays $1.59. If it is $1.60 she pays $1.61 but this is her maximum price. The gains and losses from this contract compared to purchasing FOREX at the market price are shown in Figure 7–9B. They show a similar pattern to the gains and losses on a straightforward call option. Here there are losses as well as gains in the future and the expectation of the losses in effect pays for the prospect of the gains.

The Conditional Forward Contract can be replicated by a portfolio of puts and calls on FOREX. In the example above, the gains and losses are the same as on the portfolio:

$$C\ (1.61,6)\ -\ [P\ (1.61,6) - P\ (1.60,6)].$$

The call at $1.61 provides the gains that occur when the market price exceeds $1.61. The put spread in the square bracket is the 'cost' of the call option. Below $1.60 the spread loses $0.01. Between $1.60 and $1.61 it loses an amount equal to the difference between the FOREX rate and $1.60. Another way of viewing the contract is

$$F\ (1.61,6)\ +\ \ P\ (1.60,6)$$

where $F\ (X,\ T)$ is payoff on a T period forward contract with forward price X. Here the customer can be viewed as purchasing a put which is paid for by agreeing to a disadvantageous forward agreement.

B.3 The Participating Forward (Shared Option Forward) Contract

In this contract the purchaser is fully protected against a rise in the exchange rate, but below a given exchange rate ($1.605 in Figure 7–10A) he agrees

FIGURE 7–9A
The conditional forward contract

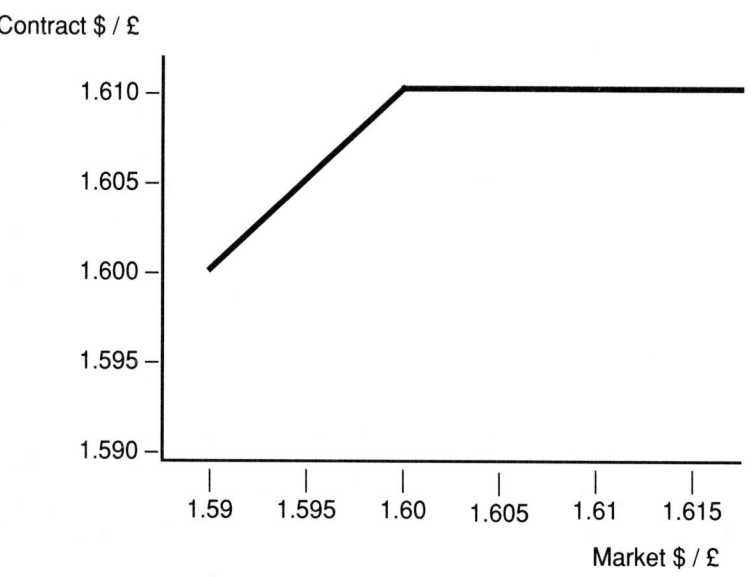

FIGURE 7–9B

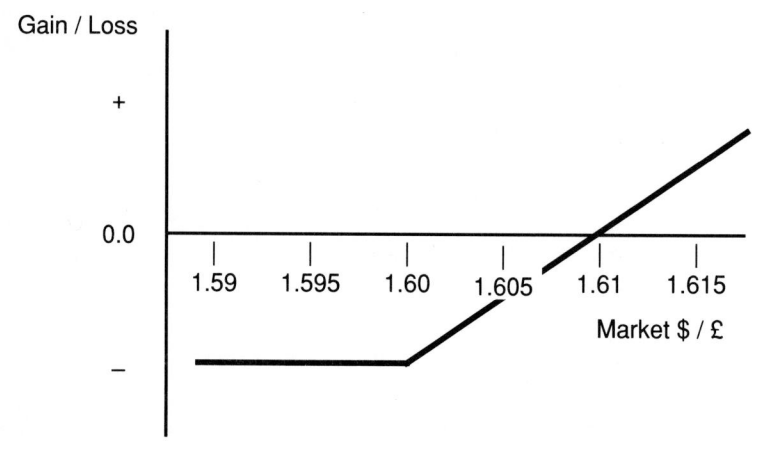

FIGURE 7–10A
The participating forward contract

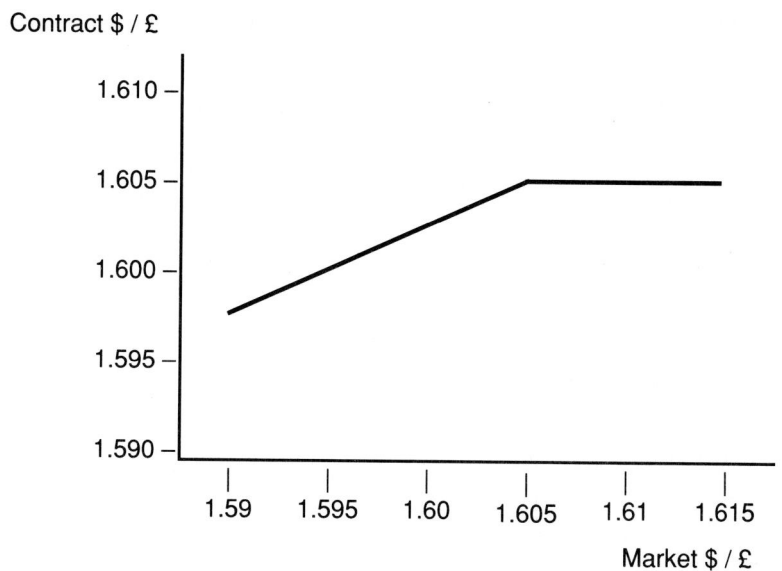

Contract $ / £

FIGURE 7–10B

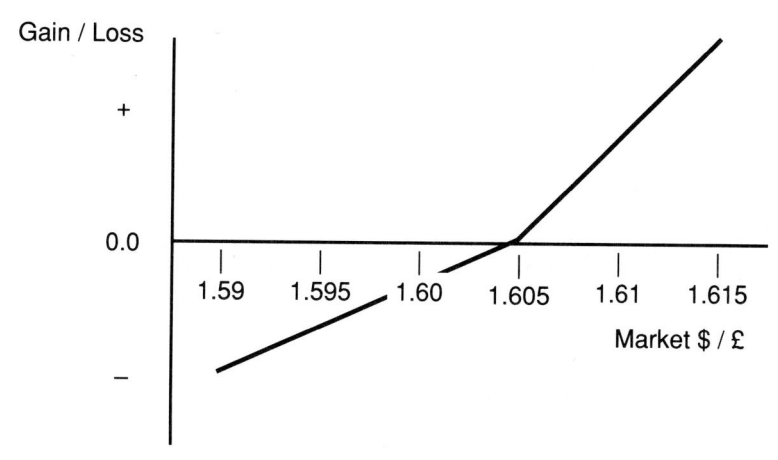

Gain / Loss

to pay a proportion of any decrease in the FOREX price. The proportion is 0.5 in the example shown in Figure 7–10A. At $1.59 for example, he pays $1.5975. This is $1.59 + 0.5 × ($1.605-$1.59). This contract is similar to an outright forward contract,except that the costs on the downside are reduced by an amount equal to the writer's participation rate.

The Participating Forward Contract is just one of an infinite variety of zero 'cost' contracts that can be made which give the purchaser partial cover against exchange rate movements. The contract with the gains and losses shown in the Figure 7–10B can be replicated by a portfolio of puts and calls

$$C\ (1.605,\ 6)\ -\ 1/2\ P\ (1.605,6)$$

This time a 6 month call option on £ at 1.605 is obtained in exchange for writing 50 percent of a put at $1.605. The results of entering these three contracts are compared with a simple forward and a simple option contract in Figure 7–11.

FIGURE 7–11
Effective exchange rate

Exchange Rate[a]	1.57	1.58	1.59	1.60	1.61	1.62	1.63
Contract							
Forward[b]	1.60	1.60	1.60	1.60	1.60	1.60	1.60
Range Forward[c]	1.595	1.595	1.595	1.60	1.61	1.61	1.61
Conditional Forward[d]	1.58	1.59	1.60	1.61	1.61	1.61	1.61
Participating Forward[e]	1.5875	1.5925	1.5975	1.6025	1.605	1.605	1.605
At-the-money Call Option[f] (Premium 0.005)	1.575	1.585	1.595	1.605	1.605	1.605	1.605

[a]The future spot exchange rate is shown in the first row. The other numbers are the effective exchange rates achieved by purchasing the contract.

[b]The forward rate is assumed to be $1.60.

[c]For the range forward, x_2 = $1.595 and x_1 = $1.61 define the range.

[d]For the conditional forward, x_1 = $1.61 and the conditional premium is $0.01.

[e]For the participating forward, x_1 = $1.605, and the participation rate is 50%.

[f]The at-the-money option is struck at the forward rate ($1.60) and has a premium (paid in the future) of $0.005.

The three contracts that are the most popular products in the OTC FOREX options market have been described above. The zero 'cost' of the contract which mimics the standard forward contract is achieved by forming a portfolio of puts and calls which has zero value at the bank's offer prices. In the illustrations above we envisage the customer as a potential purchaser of FOREX. For a seller, the contracts can be reversed by replacing calls with puts and vice-versa. Also these three contracts are just the most common of the contracts that are used. Banks will sometimes sell more complex combinations of puts and calls. As an example, consider the portfolio

$$C(1.61,6) - P(1.595,6) + 0.5\ C(159.5,6)$$
$$- C(1.60,6)\quad + 0.5\ C(1.605,6) - 0.5\ P(1.61,6)$$
$$+ P(1.605,6) - 0.5\ P(1.60,6)$$

This portfolio of options has the payoff shown in Figure 7–12. The payoff is similar to that of the Range Forward and illustrates the flexibility that is afforded by combinations of options. It uses the principal involved in the Participating Forward to smooth the exchange rate between the lower floor of $1.595 and the ceiling of $ 1.61. The value of a combination option can be found by adding up the values of the component options in the combination.

The nature of the contracts outlined above has been analyzed by Courtadon (1987). Their valuation and hedging properties are discussed in Boyle and Turnbull (1987). However, since the contracts are merely portfolios of puts and calls, all the problems associated with valuation and hedging are those that apply to straightforward options.

C.   Contingent FOREX Options

If a firm is tendering for a contract in a foreign country it may wish to prepare for the possibility of it winning the contract and then needing to buy or sell FOREX. In the OTC market a small number of banks will quote for options or forwards which are contingent on particular circumstances arising, such as a contract being awarded. These are often called Tender To Contract deals.

In the case of a contingent FOREX option, the payoff depends on two

FIGURE 7–12A
Generalized participating forward

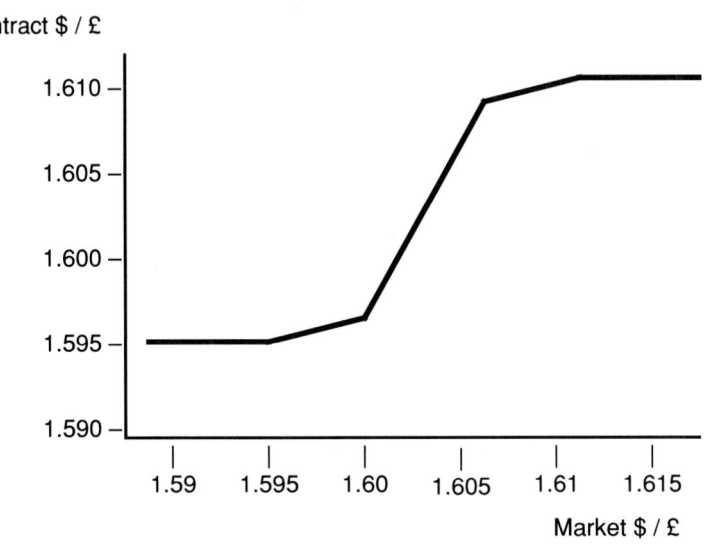

FIGURE 7–12B

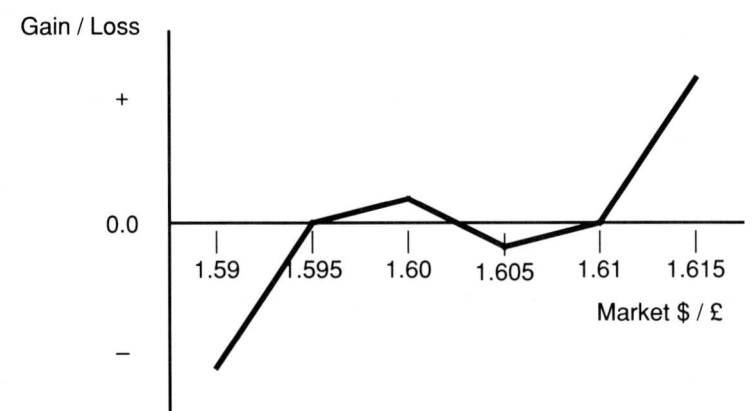

FIGURE 7–13
Payoff on a contingent FOREX option

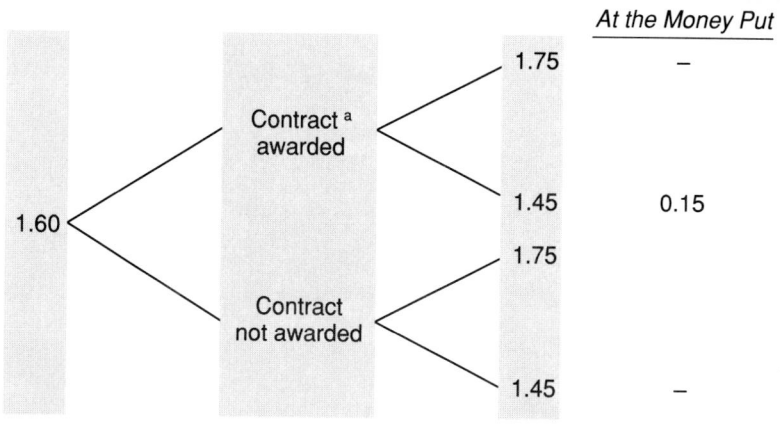

^aContract is to sell goods in £

events: whether or not the specific contract is awarded to the firm, and whether the FOREX price rises or falls. The payoff on such an option is illustrated in Figure 7–13. In this example, the firm will receive £ if the contract is awarded. The current $/£ rate is 1.60, and it wishes to protect itself against a fall in the $ value of its receipts. However, it wants the protection only if it wins the contract.

The payoff on a contingent put option is illustrated in Figure 7–13. The option is written at $1.60, but it pays off only if the FOREX rate falls and the contract which the firm is bidding for is awarded. The value of the option is clearly less than that of a straightforward put option. The difference will depend on the probability of the contract being awarded.

Contingent FOREX options are problematic for the bank that is writing them, from both a valuation and a hedging point of view. Often the firm buying the option has more knowledge about the contract situation than the Bank. It is difficult in these circumstances to agree upon a price for the option. It is also extremely difficult for the bank to hedge an instrument that depends for its value on two sources of uncertainty, one of which is usually nonhedgeable by its very nature because it is unique to the firm tendering for the contract.

D. Compound Options on FOREX

A compound option is an option to purchase or sell another option at a pre-specified premium. Compound options are not common in general, although some are written in the interest rate options market. Some banks do offer compound options on FOREX and this is one area where some development might take place in the future as both traders and bank customers become more sophisticated. Compound options are also known as "Split Fee" options since the purchaser agrees to pay an option premium (or fee) up front, and if the FOREX rate moves in favour of the option, a further premium in the future (the back fee) to obtain the FOREX.

In order to illustrate the pay-off on a compound option and the way it differs from that of a straightforward option we assume in Figure 7–14A a very simple valuation formula for the option (1) on which the compound

FIGURE 7–14A
Binomial tree for exchange rate and $1.60 strike call option

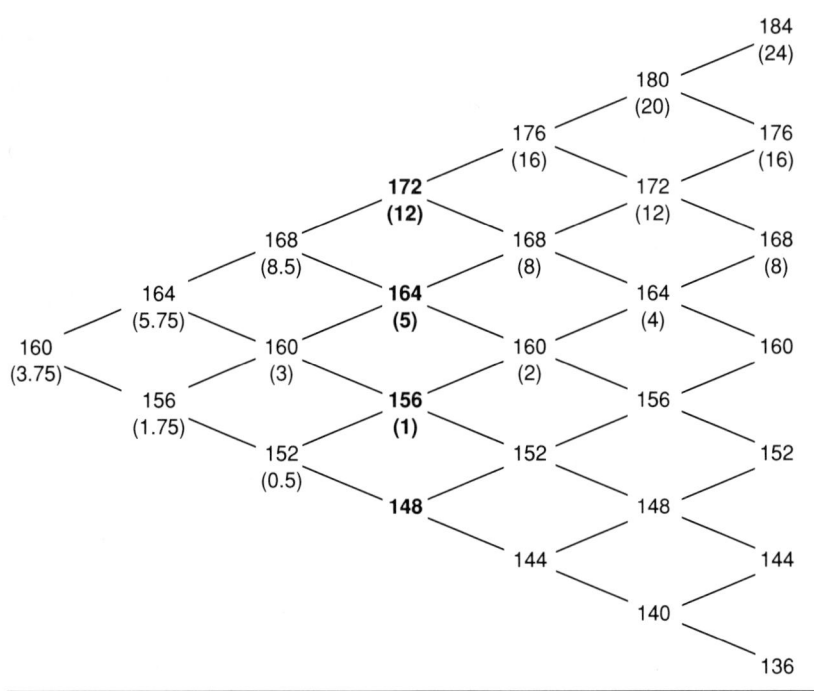

option (2) is written. In Figure 7–14A the \$/£ rate is assumed to follow an additive process where each increment (over one month) is ±4 cents. The chance of a positive increment over any month is 50 percent. The current 6 month forward rate is \$1.60, so the £ is neither a premium nor a discount currency. In parentheses we show the value of a call option with exercise price \$1.60 on a period by period basis using a simplified option pricing model. In this model, the period t option price is:

$$\text{Option price } (t-1) = .5 \text{ Option price } (t, +)$$
$$+ .5 \text{ Option price } (t, -)$$

where Option price $(t, +)$ is the option price in the next period if the FOREX rate rises and Option price $(t, -)$ is the next period price if the rate falls. The option pricing model is a crude one, since it assumes both a very simple stochastic process for the FOREX rate and no time discounting of the option price. However, it serves to illustrate the essential nature of the compound option.

In Figure 7–14A, the at-the-money call option on the FOREX rate, option (1), sells at the nondiscounted, expected value of its future pay-off. In Figure 7–14B we show the payoff on a compound option (2) which is a call option to buy option (1) in 3 months' time for a premium of 4 cents. Its value, again using the nondiscounted, expected values, is 1.375 cents at month 0.

In this example the fees paid consist of a Front fee of 1.375 cents paid for option (2) and a Back fee of 4 cents which has to be paid in 3 months time to obtain option (1).

There are two points to notice about the scale of these fees:-
1. The sum (Front fee + Back fee) exceeds the value of the straight-forward 6 month option

$$\text{Front fee (1.375)} + \text{Back Fee (4)} >$$
$$\text{premium on an at-the-money option (3.75)}$$

2. The Sum (Front Fee + expected value of Back Fee) is less than the value of a straightforward 6 month option

$$\text{Front fee (1.375)} + \text{expected Back Fee (2)} <$$
$$\text{premium on an at-the-money option (3.75)}$$

The customer who purchases a compound option has to pay a further fee in 3 months' time to obtain the FOREX. If Sterling rises over the first 3 months his compound option goes into the money and he pays a further fee of 4 cents. In this event he pays a total of 5.375 cents to obtain the FOREX at $1.60. This is more than he would have paid if he had purchased a straightforward 6 month option for 3.75 cents. However, looking at Figure 7–14B, we see that there is only a 50 percent chance of the compound option (2) being exercised at month 3. The expected value of the future fee is $0.5 \times 4 = 2$ cents. The expected cost of purchasing the FOREX for $1.60 is thus only

$$1.375 + 2 = 3.375 \text{ cents.}$$

Compound options represent a cheaper form of options-based insur-

FIGURE 7–14B
Binomial tree for compound call option on a $1.60 strike call option

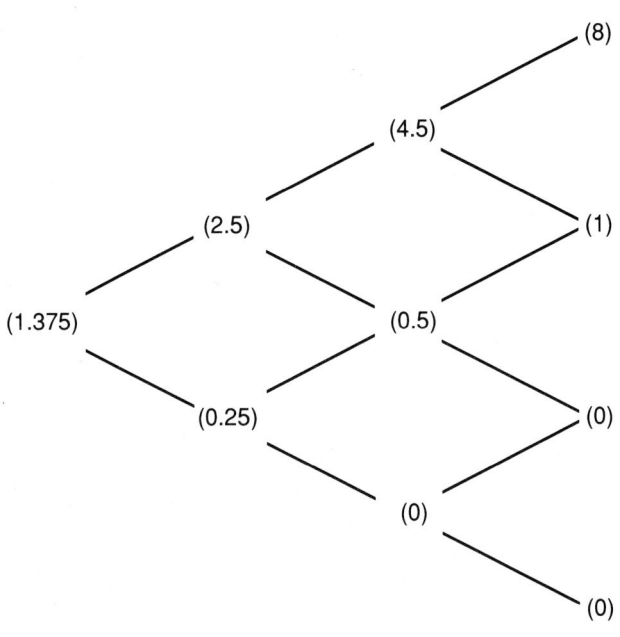

ance. In the long run, the costs of the insurance equal the sum of the expected fees. However, the insurance is cheaper only because the events insured against are different and less comprehensive than those involved in a regular option. The compound option purchase strategy pays off if the FOREX rate rises over the first 3 months and then continues to rise. However, the purchaser may be caught out if the £ falls over the first 3 months and subsequently rises. For example, if the rate falls to $1.56 after 3 months and the compound option expires worthless, but it then rises to $1.68, the purchaser of the compound option is unprotected. It is this event which is covered by the regular option and not covered by the compound option.

Compound options add a new dimension to the range of FOREX option products available on the OTC market. They represent partial insurance. However, unlike out-of-the-money options or the Participating Forward Contract, the payoff on the options depends on the path of the FOREX rate over time. Basically the gamble involved is a more complicated one whose outcome depends on both the FOREX rate at the end of the period of the underlying option and the FOREX rate at some intermediate point. Normally, compound options are European options on European options. However, European options on American underlying options and other combinations may be negotiated.

The valuation of compound FOREX options is more complex than for straightforward options. The general problem of compound option valuation has been solved by Geske (1977). In practice, FOREX compound options can be valued using the method illustrated in Figure 7–14. To solve the problem we have to generate a grid of option values for the underlying option (1) as in Figure 7–14A. At month 3 we can use a regular FOREX option pricing model to find the contingent option prices for a given grid size. The compound option (2) can then be valued given its exercise price as in Figure 7–14B. However, this relatively straightforward procedure is complicated when volatility is itself stochastic. To some extent, the compound option is an option on volatility, and as such it has a value in addition to its value as a partial insurance on the FOREX itself. Uncertain volatility also affects the hedging of compound options. In the absence of uncertain volatility the compound option can be hedged using the underlying FOREX or the futures. However, if volatility is stochastic, full protection for the writer requires that compound options are hedged using regular options.

E.   Multicurrency Options

A multicurrency option gives the right to exchange one currency ($) for one of a number of foreign currencies at pre-set rates of exchange. For example, if the FOREX rates at a given moment are

$$\$1 \ = \ 2\,DM$$

$$£1 \ = \ \$2$$

a customer could purchase an option to buy either 4DM or £1 for $2.00. Here the exercise price of the option is $2.00 but a further option exists which allows the purchaser to buy either DM or £ for the $2.00. The pay-off from such an option is illustrated in Figure 7–15.

We assume in Figure 7–15 that the DM will go from $0.50 to $0.55 or $0.45 with a 50 percent probability. £ will go from $2.00 to $2.30 or $1.70 also with a 50 percent probability. However, the movements of the DM and £ rates are related because of their common dependence upon the $. In Figure 7–15 we assume that there is an 80 percent chance of the £ rising to $2.30 if the DM has risen to DM = $0.55. If the DM falls to DM = $0.45 there is an 80 percent chance of the £ falling to $1.70. This simple process for the joint behavior of the DM and £ FOREX rates is sufficient to illustrate the multicurrency option contract.

The option payoff depends upon the two currency movements. If the DM and £ rise in value, £ is purchased since it is worth $2.30 as against $2.20 for the 4DM. In the example, the variance of £ is greater than that of the DM. If the DM rises but £ falls the option holder receives DM and makes a profit of $0.20. The expected payoff on the option is

$$.4 \times \$0.30 \ + .1 \times \$0.20 \ + .1 \times \$0.30 \ = \ \$0.17$$

This is an indicator of the option's likely value.

The value of the multicurrency option depends upon the correlation between the two currency exchange rates, i.e., the extent to which the DM and £ rates move together. The maximum value of the option will occur when the two FOREX rates are inversely related (i.e., if the DM goes down to $1.80, the probability is high that £ will rise to $2.30). In this case the option is almost guaranteed a valuable outcome. However, the more likely

FIGURE 7–15
Multicurrency option

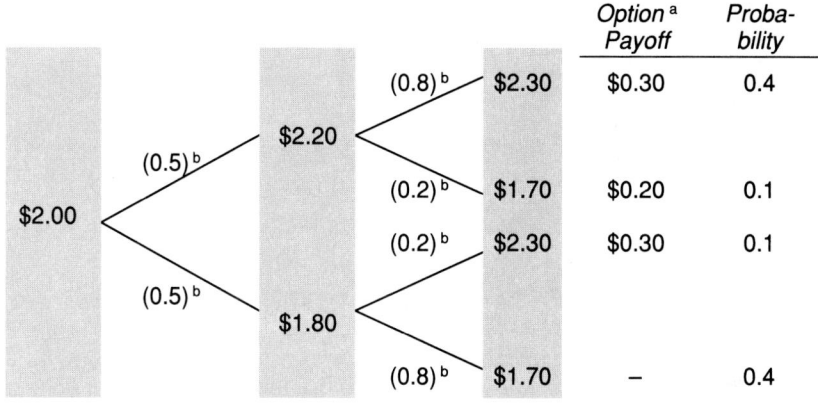

	Option [a] Payoff	Proba- bility
$2.30	$0.30	0.4
$1.70	$0.20	0.1
$2.30	$0.30	0.1
$1.70	–	0.4

[a]Call option to buy 4 DM or £1 for $2
[b]Probability

case is where the two FOREX rates are positively related as in the example in Figure 7–15.

7.6   HEDGING PROCEDURES FOR FOREIGN CURRENCY OPTIONS

FOREX option values are affected by a number of variables, namely: the spot exchange rate, volatility, exercise rate, deposit rates and time left to maturity. Once an option is written, the only variable that will remain fixed till maturity is the exercise rate. Changes in the values of the remaining variables during the life of the option will produce corresponding changes in option prices. In a 'static' world the effect of each variable on option prices can be quantified. E.g., a rising spot rate will, *ceteris paribus,* increase call option prices and reduce put option prices, while a reduction in volatility will decrease both call and put prices. In a 'dynamic' world, however, events can occur simultaneously, hence a rising spot rate may produce a decline in call prices, if, say, volatility is reduced by an amount enough to offset the spot rate effect.

Hedging the risk associated with the movements of all the above variables can be an impossible task. Although, the most obvious way to hedge the risk on a written option is to purchase (ignoring default risk) an identical option, in practice this may not be possible, or the cost of purchasing the option may be prohibitive. In fact, the most common form of hedging is the so called 'delta hedge.' The delta of an option measures its sensitivity to changes in the spot price of the underlying asset. (Assuming that all other variables remain constant).

In theory, if there were no transaction costs, it would be possible to continuously adjust the Delta hedge so that the risk from spot price movements is completely eliminated. However, continuous hedging is not feasible in practice. Even 'frequent' adjustments can be quite costly and perhaps unattainable in a fast moving spot market.

Hence, the problem of finding an optimal hedging strategy has become one of the main areas of research among the market practitioners. Most of the strategies employed involve a mixture of Delta hedging together with 'fine tuning' of the composition of the options portfolio. E.g., particular emphasis may be placed on the average strike (exercise) rate of the portfolio and options may be bought or sold at various strike rates to maintain a 'target' strike rate and/or reduce the overall sensitivity of the portfolio to spot price movements. More complex strategies may involve, in addition to the above, adjustments to the maturity 'ladder' by buying or selling options of different maturities.

7.7   CONCLUSIONS

Options on foreign exchange are written and traded in many different forms and combinations. In this chapter we have distinguished options on cash and futures and described many of the complex combinations found in the market place. We have also discussed how the Black-Scholes valuation model can be modified to the case of European FOREX options.

References

Black, F., and Scholes, M. (May/June 1973). The pricing of options and corporate liabilities. *Journal of Political Economy.*

Bodurtha, J., and Courtadon, G. (1987). The pricing of foreign exchange options. New York University, Solomon Bros. Center for the Study of Financial Institutions monograph No. 1987–4/5.

Bodurtha, J., and Courtadon, G. (March 1986). Efficiency tests of the foreign currency market. *Journal of Finance.*

Boyle, P., and Turnbull. S. (November 1987). Pricing and hedging capped options. AGSM working paper.

Calderon-Russel, B. (Fall 1982). The behaviour of FOREX rates. *Journal of International Business Studies.*

Courtadon, G. (1987). Recent trends in the valuation of foreign currency options. Mimeograph.

Cox, J. C., Ingersoll, J., and Ross, S. (December 1981). The relationship between forward prices and future prices. *Journal of Financial Economics, 9,* 321–46.

Garman, M., and Kohlhagen, S. (December 1983). Foreign currency option values. *Journal of International Money and Finance.*

Geske, R. (November 1977). The valuation of corporate liabilities as compound options. *Journal of Financial and Quantitative Analysis.*

Grabbe, J. (December 1983). The pricing of call and put options on foreign exchange. *Journal of International Money and Finance.*

McFarland, J., Petit, R., and Sung, S. (June 1982). The distribution of foreign exchange price changes: Trading day effects and risk measurement. *Journal of Finance.*

Rogalski, V. (Fall 1978). Empirical properties of FOREX rates. *Journal of International Business Studies.*

So, J. (March 1978). The distribution of foreign exchange price changes: Trading day effects and risk measurement: A comment. *Journal of Finance.*

Taylor, S. (1986). *Modelling financial time series.* New York: Wiley.

CHAPTER 8

OPTIONS ON INTEREST SENSITIVE SECURITIES

Thomas S. Y. Ho
Allen A. Abrahamson *

8.1 INTRODUCTION

Changing interest rates have a pervasive impact on the market value of all securities. Security valuation is based on discounting a security's promised or forecasted cash flows at appropriate interest rates. Uncertainty with respect to the levels of future discount rates therefore makes the correctness of market valuations less certain.

Risk means unanticipated or uncertain changes in security prices or yields. In the case of interest rate risk, this definition may apply to a particular rate, such as the 30 year Treasury bond yield, or the 30 day Treasury bill rate. More generally, however, interest rate risk entails overall shifts in the level and shape of the entire yield curve. In extreme cases, the magnitude of particular rate movements can be stunning. In a few days around "Black Monday," October 19, 1987, the rate on long term Treasury

*Thomas Ho is Professor of Finance, Leonard N. Stern School of Business, New York University and President, GAT Corporation. Dr. Abrahamson is Director of Research at GAT Corporation

bonds dropped 150 basis points in two days. The shape of the yield curve is likewise far from stable. In the late 1970s, the curve shifted rapidly from a normal to an inverted shape and back as the "short rate" (e.g., the one year Treasury bill rate) more than doubled from 7 percent, and subsequently dropped back again, while the thirty year bond rate rose from 8 percent to exceed 10 percent.

These are examples of unusually large rate changes, but interest rate risk is substantial on average. The standard deviation of the percentage change of the long rate has been approximately 12 percent per annum. This means, for example, that a spot rate of 10 percent would have a standard deviation of 120 basis points over a one year period, and the price of a long term coupon bond whose duration was 10 years would have about 12 percent volatility. By way of comparison, the Standard and Poor's stock index typically has volatility of around 15 percent.

Fixed income portfolio management matches the return and interest rate risk exposure of an investment with the preferences and objectives of the investor. Many investors, such as pension fund managers, are quite averse to interest rate risk. Managers then reduce the exposure to losses and shortfalls from adverse rate movements by hedging or immunization. On the other hand, risk takers and speculators often take positions with significant exposure to rate movements, hoping to profit by correctly forecasting or guessing the direction of changes in interest rates. Options on fixed income securities provide unique flexibility for adjusting the volatility exposure and return of a portfolio. Intelligent use of options can align a portfolio's investment risk and return profile with the preferences and objectives of the investor.

Three broad categories define the types of fixed income options. The first category is *exchange traded options*. Organized exchanges, notably the Chicago Board of Trade and the Chicago Mercantile Exchange, offer trading of standardized put and call options on interest rate sensitive instruments. Options on the futures contracts for 20 year Treasury bonds, 10 year Treasury notes, and on short term Eurodollar futures are among the most actively traded instruments in our securities market, which attests to their importance. All active exchange traded fixed income options are for futures contracts, rather than underlying cash instruments. This serves to enhance liquidity and promote standardization. Standardization allows these options to be traded in a central location. Trade data, transaction prices, and volume information is readily available to the public market.

Exchange traded options offer liquidity and conceptual simplicity, and are used in a great variety of hedging and speculative strategies.

The second category of options includes *over-the-counter options*. Broker dealer firms and banks make markets for specialized or "custom" options on fixed income securities, portfolios, or loans. In principle, these options can have any features for which there is a market. The interest rate "caps and floors" market, described in Chapter 6, is an important OTC market. Many commercial loans are now written with interest rates that float in parity with some key rate such as the LIBOR rate, T-bill rate, or prime rate. Cap or floor agreements attached to a loan specify that the rate charged will not exceed, or fall below, the cap or floor levels, respectively. This market is large and growing, since many banks and other primary lenders often look to major broker dealers or larger institutions to underwrite the options, which the banks then effectively "re-sell" to their commercial loan clients.

The third category encompasses *embedded options* in the payment terms for bonds and other interest rate sensitive instruments. "Embedded" means the options cannot be traded in isolation, but are a part of the underlying security and must be bought and sold along with it. Embedded option valuation is thus an integral part of analysis of such securities. In many ways, these options are the most complex, least understood, and most interesting of the three categories. Methods suitable for the analysis of simple options on interest rates or simple bonds are generally not valid for embedded options.

The oldest and the most familiar type of embedded option is the call feature of a bond. A call feature typically gives the issuer the right to buy the bonds back from the holders at a specified price, regardless of the market price of the bond at the time of call. That means that the holder of a callable bond is effectively "long" the bond and "short" the call option.

Even a simple European-type bond call feature is inherently complex. One reason is that its value depends not just on the price of the underlying bond, but potentially on the entire structure of interest rates. Figure 8–1 illustrates relative valuation of a 15 year bond that can be called at par in 10 years. It can be seen that the value of the European call at its "expiration date" is related to the values of two noncallable bonds, of 15 year and 10 year maturities, as well as to the value of a European put option on a 5 year bond with a 10 year expiration.

Figure 8–1 shows three positions with identical payoffs. The first is

FIGURE 8–1
Call, put, and straight bond equivalences: Years in which cash flows are received

	Interest rates in year 10	
Position	High	Low
1. 15 Year Bond Callable at Par in Year 10	Years 1 – 15	Years 1 – 10 (Bond Called)
2. 15 Year Bond Noncallable *and* Write Call to Buy 5 Year Bond in Year 10	Years 1 – 15 (Call Expires)	Years 1 – 10 (Call Exercised)
3. 10 Year Bond Noncallable *and* Write Put to Sell 5 Year Bond in Year 10	Years 1 – 15 (Put Exercised)	Years 1 – 10 (Put Expires)

simply to buy the 15 year bond callable in year 10 at par. On the call date, the bond will have 5 more years to maturity. If its coupon is greater than the current market yield on 5 year instruments, the issuer will call it and its stream of cash flows will end at that point. If the 5 year rate is above the bond's coupon rate, it will not be called and the cash flows will continue for another 5 years.

The second position essentially separates the call feature from the bond and considers a 15 year "straight" (i.e., noncallable) bond plus writing a call option. The call is written on a 5 year bond with the same coupon as the 15 year bond, and has maturity of 10 years and strike of 100. It is very easy to see that this is exactly the option that the issuer of the callable bond in the first position has, and it will be exercised under the same conditions at year 10, leading to the same stream of cash flows for the two positions.

The third position shows that the same cash flows can be obtained by buying a 10 year straight bond and selling a put on a 5 year instrument.

Figure 8–1 demonstrates how the current shape and evolution of the whole yield curve which affects the bond price directly, will have an indirect influence on option prices.

It is apparent that what sometimes is termed an "interest rate" option is actually an option on future cash flows. In Figure 8–1, exercise affects the bond holder's cash flows from the 11th to 15th years of the bond's life. Both put and call values must therefore be related to the present value of those cash flows, since their receipt by the bondholder is conditional on the option's exercise.

It is essential that modern fixed income practitioners understand interest rate options. This is especially true for managers who wish to apply active hedging and investment strategies. Even portfolio managers who do not trade in the exchange options markets or the OTC market need to understand the basic concepts. Risk and return characteristics of buy and hold portfolios are sensitive to the options that are embedded in the bonds in the portfolio. By the same token, assets and liabilities of financial institutions usually have options of various kinds embedded on both sides of their balance sheets. These options can impact asset/liability matching, earnings, and net worth.

The connection between option valuation and the behavior of the entire term structure makes bond options inherently more complicated than equity options. A model for fixed income options requires a model of interest rate movements. Unfortunately, there is no single, widely accepted theory. The next section discusses several different approaches from which bond option models have been derived. Section 8.3 describes the Arbitrage-free Rate movements (AR) term structure model of Ho and Lee that we will use in the rest of the chapter to analyze bond option behavior.

The following section discusses duration and option risk, and introduces the "performance profile," which will used to examine bond option behavior under different interest rate scenarios. Finally, in Section 8.5 we are able to apply the tools developed in the earlier sections to illustrate the characteristics of fixed income options. Section 8.6 offers a brief summary of the results.

8.2 INTEREST RATE OPTION MODELS

This section describes a number of approaches to modeling interest rate movements that produce alternative bond option models. There are two general types of theories: those based simply on specifying the behavior of a single interest rate or bond price over time, and equilibrium models that model the entire term structure of rates.

The Black-Scholes model is essentially a model of the first type, but is not a very good model for bond options. It assumes that the riskless interest rate is constant (while bond yields are obviously variable), and that uncertainty about the price of the underlying asset grows uniformly as the time to option maturity increases (while a bond's price must go to par as it nears maturity). A number of bond option models adjust the basic Black-Scholes approach for these features. Three will be discussed: Merton's stochastic interest rate model, the Brownian Bridge model, and the model of Shaefer and Schwartz. All of them are subject to certain shortcomings.

Equilibrium models deal with the entire term structure, and produce theoretical values for all securities based on interest rates, including options. The model we will adopt for further analysis is of this type. The Ho-Lee AR model will be introduced in this section and described in detail in the next section.

All modern options models are developed from an assumption about the stochastic process that defines the way in which the underlying asset's value (or return) changes over time. A particular stochastic process governs a probability distribution for the value of the underlying asset at all points in the future, from which option values can be taken.

If the option is European, the analysis next makes use of the "boundary condition" that relates the call option value to the price of the underlying asset at expiration. When the price of the underlying asset at expiration is S, a call option's value will then be Max$[(S - X) , 0]$. From the probability distribution of S at maturity, the expected value of the option's terminal payoff follows directly. Discounting this expected value to the present provides the value of the option.

The Black Scholes model (1973) described in detail in Chapter 3 is developed under the assumption that returns obey one of the simplest of all continuous stochastic processes: "Brownian motion," or "Wiener diffusion." The Wiener process can be defined by a differential equation describing the dynamics of stock price changes over each instant in time. This differential equation and the boundary conditions gives the well known Black-Scholes closed form solution to the option pricing problem.

Equivalently, the process can be described not by its behavior at each instant but by the probability distribution of security value at expiration. The Wiener process implies that the continuously compounded rate of return R obtained by holding an asset for a given interval of time is normally distributed with a variance that is proportional to the holding period. This basic assumption can be expressed as:

$$S(t) = S(0) \exp(Rt), \quad \text{or}$$

$$\log[\, S(t) \,/\, S(0) \,] = Rt.$$

Since R has a normal distribution with variance proportional to t, prices have a lognormal distribution. The Black-Scholes solution could be obtained by taking the expected value of the option payoff at the terminal boundary using the appropriate lognormal distribution of value of the underlying stock at expiration.

Because there is generally correspondence between stochastic processes and implied probability distributions, there are two equivalent approaches to option valuation. The choice of methodology is, generally, motivated by considerations of simplicity and the relative lucidity of the alternatives. Chapter 14 describes option valuation methods based on the differential equation expression of stochastic processes; here, we concentrate more on binomial approximations of probability distributions.

In either case, once some fundamental principles of model construction are accepted and verified, it is possible to price options on assets with very complex assumed distributions of returns.

It is critically important to recognize that an option model will be appropriate for valuation only if the assumed stochastic process is an adequate description of the returns generated from holding the underlying instrument. Future bond returns are not unconstrained as they are assumed to be in the basic Black-Scholes model. In modelling stock returns, one stock is conceptually very much like another. The returns process of IBM can be viewed as the same as that of, say, General Motors, up to differences only in the values of such parameters as volatility and dividend rate. In principle, nothing constrains the domain of possible future prices, other than that they must be nonnegative. In other words, the nature of equity returns does not require volatility to be different at different points in time.

In contrast to the simple dynamics of equity prices, a stochastic description of fixed income prices is complicated by several factors. The domain of reasonable bond prices is constrained on both upside and downside. Like stocks, bond prices cannot fall below zero. On the upside, a bond has a maximum price, if interest rates cannot be negative. The upper bound for the price of a series of future cash flows is their sum, i.e., their present value at a discount rate of zero. Further, the price of a bond will converge to its face value at maturity, regardless of discount rates or volatility.

With bonds, it is important to distinguish yield to maturity from the rate of return. An important definition that formalizes the latter concept of yield is the "holding period return," or HPR. The holding period return of an asset is the measure of the value of all cash flows received over a period of time plus the change in market value of the asset during the period, as a percent of the beginning market value. In this chapter, bond "return" should be understood as holding period return over the next interval of time unless otherwise specified.

The Time Dependent Nature of Fixed Income Asset Volatility

The principal complication in modelling fixed income returns is that they cannot have a constant variance over the life of the bond.

Figure 8–2 shows two possible paths a coupon bond price could take until maturity. For a time after issue, the value of the bond can rise or fall substantially, because the price will reflect the present value of the remaining coupons. From T_0 to T_M, the distribution of bond prices is increasingly dispersed. More elapsed time increases the chance of large changes in yield. After T_M until maturity, the chance of diffusion to a broader domain of prices is increasingly offset by the "pull to par" of the bond.

As bond life shortens, two effects work to restrict price movement. Even if yield is very high, discounting the future payments will have relatively little effect, because there are fewer discounting periods until maturity. Also, with fewer payments remaining, the upper bound on possible price (i.e., the sum of future payments) is relatively lower. Therefore, as maturity is approached, the maximum attainable price is smaller, and the probable minimum price is greater. At maturity, of course, both of these effects converge as the bond price goes to the face value.

The effect of the changing variance of bond returns over time has been investigated by a number of researchers. Three alternative specifications will be discussed.

Merton's Model. Merton's model of the risk structure of interest rates (1975) was the first to describe use of time dependent variance to price bond options. He showed it is theoretically possible to value a debt option,

FIGURE 8–2
Two paths for price over a bond's life showing "pull to par"

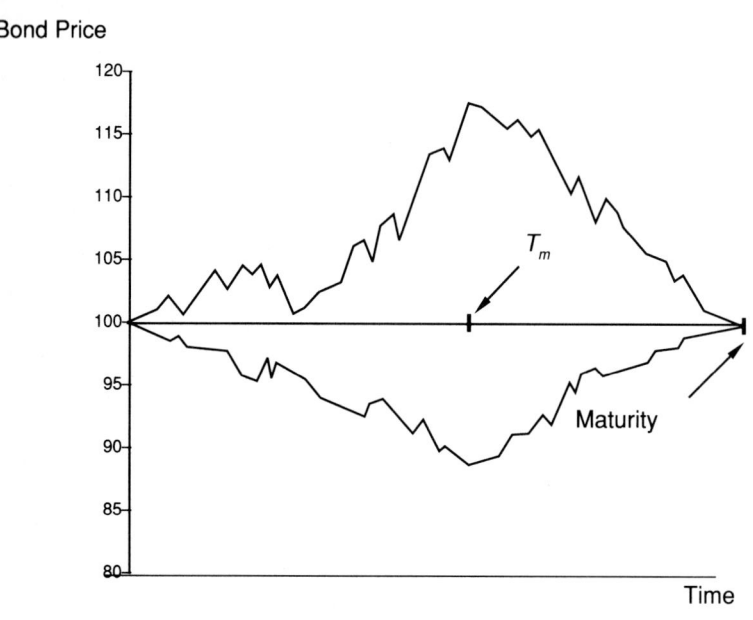

Bond Price

Time

assuming the underlying bond returns follow a Wiener process, by generalizing the solution obtained by Black and Scholes to the case where
variance is a function of time to maturity. Merton applied continuous
arbitrage arguments similar to those discussed in Chapter 3 to derive an
expression for the value of a debt option.

The resulting equations will not be reported here. Their theoretical
importance overshadows the practical application. The solution of option
value requires specification of the bond return variance, and contains an
expression that involves the average expected return variance over the time
interval until expiration, along with the covariance between return and a
short term rate. With few guidelines for estimating this average variance in
practice, the model would be difficult to implement.

Merton's model was an immediate extension of his often cited
compendium work on generalized option pricing (1973). Together with the
Black-Scholes model, which appeared at the same time, his analysis forms
the cornerstone of modern option theory.

The Brownian Bridge Model. This model specifies bond price change as a stochastic process with variance that first increases and then decreases over time. Ball and Torous (1983) suggested that bond prices can be modelled by a "Brownian Bridge" process. This process, sometimes termed "tied-down Brownian motion," defines random motion when both the beginning and ending points are fixed ex ante. This circumstance quite well describes the certainty of the current and maturity values for a bond.

This ingenious idea models the price of a discount bond as it converges to its face value at maturity in such a way that the variance of the rate of return is constant over time. Ball and Torous then make use of Merton's formula for an option when the risk free interest rate is stochastic to determine a formula for the value of a European option on a discount bond.

For technical reasons, the instantaneous variance and expected return parameters of the Bridge process cannot describe exactly all of the characteristics of bond return. A significant weakness of the approach is that the constant variance of return implies that the variability of yield to maturity increases without bound as the bond approaches maturity. However, the Brownian Bridge is still an important normative characterization of bond return behavior under the constraints inherent in bond price behavior. In part, this work led to the model discussed next.

The Schaefer and Schwartz Duration Model. This third approach models bond returns by a Wiener process augmented by an explicit model of the instantaneous variance of bond return.

Schaefer and Schwartz (1987) developed a model that relates the instantaneous return variance to bond duration. They assume that the standard deviation of return on a bond is proportional to the bond's duration, which is a simple and realistic explanation of bond price changes over time.

As will be discussed below, there is a well defined link between bond return and duration. For simple riskless bonds, an explicit formulation of duration is possible, and the instantaneous variance of the bond return process can be identified. However, implementation of the Schaefer and Schwartz model for general use, is again quite involved.

Each of these three models was motivated by the goal of pricing options on bonds. A taxonomy would place all three in the family defined by the solution methods of Black-Scholes and Merton, and a common root is the recognition of changing bond return variance. The primary differences among them are in the specification of precisely how it changes.

An alternative approach has given rise to fixed income option models that have begun to dominate securities applications. These techniques relate values of the debt option to movements in the term structure of interest rates.

Equilibrium Term Structure Models and Option Valuation

Figure 8–1 illustrated that the value of a debt option should depend on the present value of the cash flows being optioned. It logically follows that option value must be a function of the term structure of rates corresponding to the present value factors used to value those cash flows.

The above models of bond price behavior all specified the HPR of a specific bond or type of bond. Modelling the term structure of interest rates avoids the need for explicit explanations of the complex structure of holding period returns. Once a term structure model is specified, then any bond price, its HPR behavior over time, and the prices of options on that bond, can all be examined as consequences of that common underlying structure.

A term structure model must perform two tasks for option valuation purposes. First, the model must provide a stochastic process and/or probability distribution that identifies the possible future term structures. The evolution of the term structure into the future implied by the stochastic process must be economically rational and consistent with observed behavior. Second, the model should be consistent with the actual term structure observed at any point in time.

A number of different theories of equilibrium term structure have been proposed in finance and economics. Details of these theories will not be treated here. Interested readers are encouraged to study the papers by Cox, Ingersoll and Ross (1985), Vasicek (1977), Brennan and Schwartz (1982), and Courtadon (1982), and their references, to gain insight into this important area of theory. A number of descriptive comments are warranted here.

An important underpinning of equilibrium term structure models is that they provide *arbitrage free* rate movements. An easy and valid "reality check" on a model is to answer the question: "If the market actually functions according to the model, can trading strategies be developed that yield arbitrage returns?" If no such strategies can be found, then the model is arbitrage free. If the model is proven to be arbitrage free, the question need not be asked.

Formally, an arbitrage free term structure implies that no security or combination of securities can provide consistently higher expected holding period returns than any other with the same degree of risk. The arbitrage free condition is necessary for maximum validity and practical acceptance of an option model. Correct relative pricing of options on different cash flows relies on the condition. Accordingly, arbitrage free rate movements play an important role in the model development below.

All equilibrium term structure models are derived by assigning stochastic processes to one or more "factors" or "state variables," which in this case are term interest rates. The models of Vasicek and Courtadon are single factor models, where the state variable is the "short rate" of interest. Equilibrium levels of all other rates are derived from it. Brennan and Schwartz present a two factor model. There the dynamics of the term structure are related to the rate on a perpetuity, or "consol rate," in addition to the short rate. Cox, Ingersoll and Ross provide a general equilibrium structure. While they explicitly study a one factor model, it can be generalized to higher factor dimensions as well.

Practical difficulties restrict the use of equilibrium term structure models for pricing debt options. First, the models require estimation or specification of the stochastic process for one or more term interest rates. Second, they require the estimation of a parameter that is determined by investor utility functions. This parameter relates to risk aversion, and is termed the *market price of risk*. Application of equilibrium models for option valuation is thus quite dependent on computational methodology, and requires considerable skill and analytical insight. The final practical barrier to implementation is that the solution methodology for option valuation usually involves the numerical solution of differential equations. This is not a significant hardship for those endowed with powerful computers and advanced mathematical aptitude, but the requirement stands in contrast to the simple application of the Black-Scholes model, or solutions based on direct modelling of the probability distribution of future term rates.

While equilibrium models of the term structure possess the necessary property of arbitrage free rate movements, another potential concern exists within the context of options pricing. Since the conditions of equilibrium are specified within the model, it can easily happen that the term structure actually observed in the bond market is not an "equilibrium" of the model. Some would argue that a model's consistency with the existing term structure is as important a "reality check" as is the condition of arbitrage freedom. In practice, for debt option pricing, we view consistency with the observed term structure as a necessity.

The alternative to specification of equilibrium parameters is simply to accept the current observed term structure as consistent with an unobserved and unspecified equilibrium. From this platform, feasible arbitrage free movements of term rates can be modeled. The first such approach was the model of Ho and Lee (1986), termed the *arbitrage free rate movements,* or "AR" model. Rather than modeling the behavior of one or more interest rates in order to derive the future term structure, the AR model begins with the existing term structure and models how it might evolve over time. This approach has immediate advantages for option pricing without some of the problems that attend *a priori* equilibrium specifications.

The main advantage of the AR development is that it utilizes the full information of the term structure to price options. By tautology, the market's price of risk and general time preferences must be reflected in the array of current term rates. Moreover, the shape of the yield curve directly determines cash flow present values and thereby affects prices of options on those flows.

Most importantly, utilization of term structure information automatically determines option prices that are consistent with underlying asset values, and all other fixed income security prices as well. The arbitrage free property of feasible rate movements insures that "straight" bond prices derived from the model today will be identical to market prices determined by the current term structure. The practical importance in valuation of embedded options is the direct attribution, or separation, of value and return into the option features and straight cash flow features of any bond. By construction, the value of an embedded option feature is the price difference between the bond with the option feature and the identical bond without the option.

The AR model possesses a straightforward binomial representation. Option pricing in a binomial model is relatively simple, and provides ready insight into the properties and behavior of debt options. The next section describes the AR model in more detail.

8.3   DEVELOPING AN OPTION PRICING FRAMEWORK FROM THE AR MODEL

It is most correct to say that the AR model develops a binomial lattice for the prices of zero coupon bonds of all maturities. This is because arbitrage free rate movements really mean that the prices of bonds in future states preclude arbitrage. The structure imposed on rates by the AR model is a consequence of price determination in the model.

For clarity, it will be assumed that the bonds and options on them are riskless in the sense that all cash flows will be paid when promised. This is not a necessary condition, of course. The basic development can be directly extended to treatment of bonds with credit risk.

In binomial modeling, possible prices for a discount bond at the end of a period are represented by two values: the "upstate" and the "downstate." These are defined by two functions, h and h^*, respectively, that serve the same role in fixing the possible evolution of the entire discount function as the constants u and d have for the asset price in the standard Binomial model. Figure 8–3 shows a four period binomial lattice. At $t = 0$, the prices of the four discount bonds are determined by the spot term structure, which is a "flat" yield curve of 8 percent in the example. At each node, the first number on a line gives the maturity of a discount bond and the second number is its price (in the upper panel) or yield (in the lower panel).

From these initial conditions, prices at the subsequent nodes of the lattice are constructed so that the prices are arbitrage free. In the binomial model of Figure 8–3, it is assumed that the risk neutral probability of an upmove is the same as a downmove, i.e.,

$$p = (1 - p) = .5.$$

For an initial term structure, a set of forward prices (and forward rates) can be derived. Forward prices can be explained by reference to Figure 8–3. With an investment horizon of two years, an investor could buy a two year zero coupon bond for 85.734, and be assured of 100 at maturity. Alternatively, a one period bond could be purchased at time 0 for 92.593. After one year, 100 could be reinvested for the next year. If the market price of 1 year bonds in one year were 92.593, the return from the "rollover," buying 1.08 units face value of (then) one year bonds would be exactly that of the two year investment.

The price of a one year zero coupon bond in one year that would equate the returns of the two strategies is termed the *forward discount function*, $F(1)$. In this example, the forward price of a one period discount bond $F(1)$ has the same value as $B(1)$, the current spot price of a one period bond. In general this is not true; here, it reflects the flat yield curve. In every case, however, the forward discount function is completely specified by the

FIGURE 8–3
An arbitrage free binomial term structure[a]

Spot Discount Factors

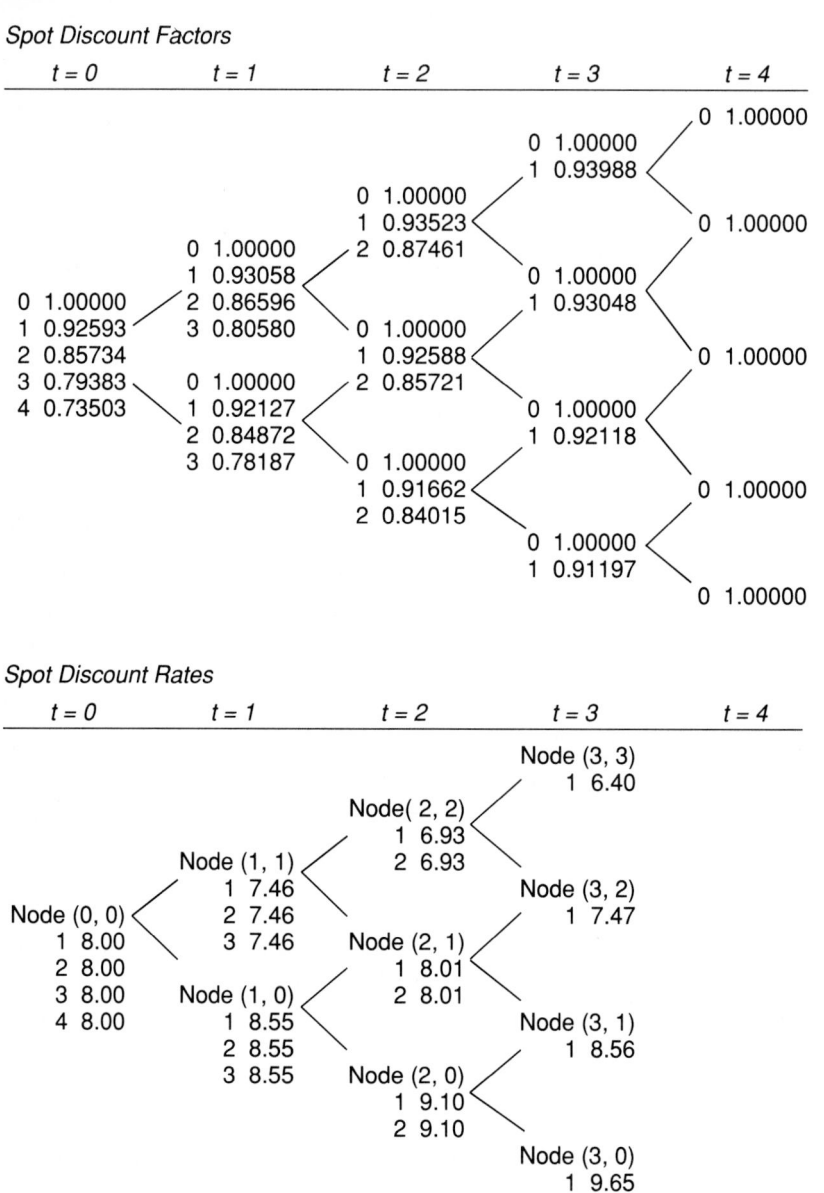

t = 0	t = 1	t = 2	t = 3	t = 4

Spot Discount Rates

t = 0	t = 1	t = 2	t = 3	t = 4

[a]Each entry in the lattice shows the number of years to maturity for a zero coupon bond, followed by the discount factor or yield to maturity that applies to it.

initial discount function. The forward discount of a T period bond, determined for time n, is given by:

$$F_i^n(T) = B_i^n(T+1) / B_i^n(1) \tag{8.1}$$

(In this notation, $F_i^n(T)$ is the forward price for a bond maturing at T, as of time n, if there have been i up moves in the discount function prior to that point, and similarly for $B_i^n(T)$.)

At any node (n, i) on a lattice, the upstate price beyond that node, for a bond with maturity T, is expressed in terms of the forward prices:

$$B_{i+1}^{n+1}(T) = F_i^n(T) h(T). \tag{8.2}$$

In the downstate, the definition is:

$$B_i^{n+1}(T) = F_i^n(T) h^*(T). \tag{8.3}$$

Arbitrage free bond price equilibrium requires the expected HPR to be equal for all bonds. Equivalently, the AR condition can be expressed in terms of the ratio of prices. At any node, the next expected price divided by the price at that node must be the same for all maturities. That this is true everywhere in Figure 8–3 can be easily verified. For example, consider a two period bond at $t = 0$. This ratio is

$$\frac{(.5)(.93058) + (.5)(.92127)}{.85734} = \frac{.925925}{.85734}$$

$$= 1.08,$$

or 1 plus the 1 period spot rate. The same applies to all four bonds at $t = 0$.

Because the AR condition requires equal returns for any T-period bond and the one period bond, the expected value condition is:

$$\frac{\dfrac{p \, B_i^n(T+1) \, h(T)}{B_i^n(1)} + \dfrac{(1-p) \, B_i^n(T+1) \, h^*(T)}{B_i^n(1)}}{B_i^n(T+1)} = \frac{1}{B_i^n(1)} \tag{8.4}$$

The left side of equation (8.4) shows the ratio of the expected price of a zero coupon bond (under the risk neutral probabilities) one period in the future, divided by the initial price. This ratio is equated to the certain maturity value of 1 for a one period bond, divided by that bond's initial price.

After clearing terms common to both sides:

$$p \, h(T) + (1 - p) \, h*(T) = 1 \qquad \text{for all } T.$$

One additional constraint on the binomial lattice allows specification of the AR prices at every node of the lattice. This constraint is termed the "Path Independence Condition." Path independence means that the discount function at node (2,1), for example, should be the same whether that node is reached with a downmove to (1,0) followed by an upmove, or by moving first to (1,1) followed by a downmove.

The AR condition and the Path Independence condition combine to express $h(T)$ uniquely in terms of p, $h(1)$, and $h*(1)$. If δ is defined as $h*(1) / h(1)$, it can be shown, (refer to Ho and Lee for details), that

$$h(T) = 1 / [\, p + (1 - p) \, \delta^T \,], \quad \text{and} \qquad (8.5a)$$

$$h*(T) = \delta^T \, h(T) \qquad (8.5b)$$

This result can be applied recursively to specify the AR term structure at each node. That is, at time n and state i:

$$B_i^n(T) = \left[\frac{B(T + n)}{B(n)} \right] \left[\frac{h(T + n - 1) \, h(T + n - 2) \, \dots \, h(T)}{h(\,n - 1) h(n - 2) \, \dots \, h(0)} \right] \delta^{T(n - i)} \quad (8.6)$$

With this AR specification, both discount bonds and coupon paying bonds will be priced correctly, relative to the spot curve and to each other. Any bond's cash flow stream can be considered to be a sum of discount bonds. Any two bonds' prices will likewise be consistent and arbitrage free. By extension, options on the cash flow streams of any bonds will then be valued in the same relative pricing framework.

Estimation of the Spot Discount Function

Because the AR model relies heavily on the spot term rates, implementation of the AR model begins with estimation of the spot curve. In principle, a spot curve is observable because of the equivalence between the discount function and the price of discount, or zero coupon, bonds. In practice, however, the observable prices of most of the bonds that represent the spot discount function are for coupon bonds. Such observations represent sums of the spot discount factors of many different maturities. Further, the bond market is not complete; that is, within the population of traded bonds, there is not necessarily a bond maturity or coupon payment for all points in time. Conversely, there may be many different bonds with cash flows occurring at a particular point in time. For example, a majority of U.S. Treasury bonds pay their coupons on either the 15th of February and August, or May and November. Estimation of the spot curve with these practical limitations therefore requires a merging of an econometric regression technique, to resolve the "multiple" cash flow issue, with an interpolation technique, to resolve the incompleteness problem.

A number of alternative methods have been advanced for estimation of the spot discount function. Probably the most widely known procedure is that of McCulloch (1975), which is termed *cubic spline estimation*. The interested reader is referred to that paper, or the paper by Litzenberger and Rolfo (1984) for description and examples of application.

Estimation of AR Binomial Parameters Using Bellwethers

The lattice in Figure 8–3 was constructed with artificial values for p, $h(T)$ and $h^*(T)$. In practice, these parameters must be estimated in order to implement the AR model for option valuation. Because the AR approach is built upon a foundation of current market information, these parameters are estimated from the current bond price environment. This process is termed "fitting" or "tuning up" of the model.

The AR model will provide consistent relative prices for any noncallable security, *irrespective* of the values of the three parameters. To provide relative prices for observable callable securities in the market, the next step in implementing the AR model is estimation of the parameter values that are most consistent with the observed prices of callable bonds.

As in the case of estimation of the spot curve, this procedure is conceptually very simple. Essentially, the estimation searches for the values that minimize the difference between the prices of the bellwether bonds and the AR model prices. In practice, this requires a criterion of "goodness of fit," and a systematic and robust procedure to search among the pairs of possible values for the best fit. Current practice employs nonlinear estimation algorithms to find the values of p and δ that best explain the prices of the bellwether bonds.

The population of callable bonds used to estimate p and δ is termed a "Bellwether Portfolio." In principle, the bellwether should be chosen to most closely replicate the type of security on which options are to be evaluated. For example, for custom options to be written on bonds, a bellwether with similar options would ensure derived values that are correct relative to similar other offerings in the market.

Best fit estimates of p and δ, relative to the bellwether portfolio, combine with the estimated spot curve to fully identify the AR model. When this is accomplished, the model can be used to value any security, option, or embedded option. A simplified procedure can be used if an estimate of volatility of the short term interest rate is available, and equal probabilities of up and down moves on the lattice are acceptable. The delta parameter is functionally related to the variance of the short rate. Specifically, if σ is given exogenously (in basis points per year) and S is the number of lattice nodes per year, then for $p = .5$, δ is given by

$$\delta = \exp[-2\,\sigma/S^{3/2}] \tag{8.7}$$

Valuing Callable Bonds Using the AR Model

A fixed income security is priced by "backwardation," or rolling back, of the successive cash flows of the bond, beginning at maturity and discounting back to the present.

Figure 8–4 illustrates the valuation procedure applied to an 8 percent annual coupon bond of 4 year maturity. At every node (n, i), the value is the sum of two terms. The first term is the expectation, or weighted average, of the bond values at nodes $(n+1, i)$ and $(n+1, i+1)$, discounted at the one period rate at that node, $B_i^n(1)$. This is then added to the cash flow at node

FIGURE 8–4
Valuation of a noncallable 4 year note[a]

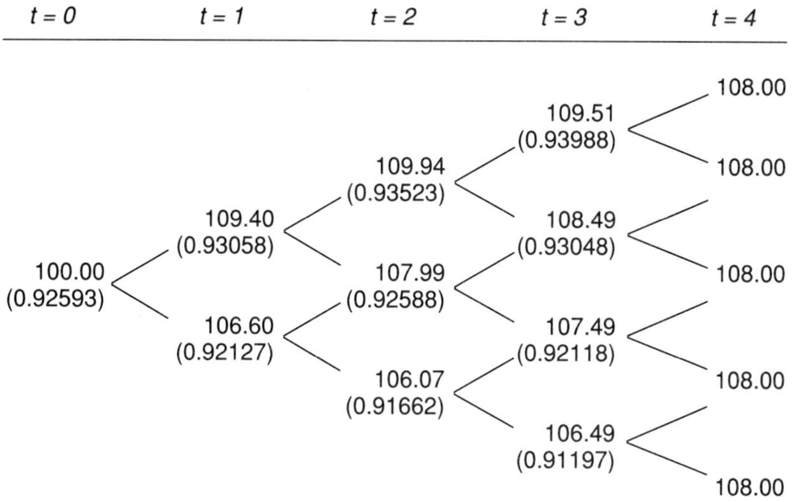

$t = 0$	$t = 1$	$t = 2$	$t = 3$	$t = 4$

[a]Discount factors in parentheses

(n, i). Each node in Figure 8–4 also shows the one period discount factor that would prevail under the AR specification. For example, at node $(1, 1)$, Figure 8–4 shows that the one period discount factor would be .93058, and the price of the bond (with 3 years left to maturity) would be $101.40 + 8.00 = 109.40$, because the value at the node includes the coupon payment of 8.00. As required, the price of the bond at time 0 is par.

Backwardation uses only the one period rate at each node. The complete term structure, shown in the upper panel of Figure 8–3, is not required. The price at each node could be obtained by discounting the bond's remaining cash flows using the complete discount function at that node. Because of the AR construction, there is no need to take on this additional work. The price thus obtained will always be equal to the answer given by backwardation. It is precisely this fact that facilitates use of the binomial lattice to price callable securities.

Figure 8–5 values a 4 year note callable at 101 on or after the first year. In time 3, the value at node $(3, 3)$ is replaced with the lesser of the rollback price and the call price plus the coupon payment, 109.00. This value is then employed in the subsequent rollback to node $(2, 2)$. Node $(2, 2)$ will also

FIGURE 8–5
Valuation of 4 year note callable at 101 plus interest[a]

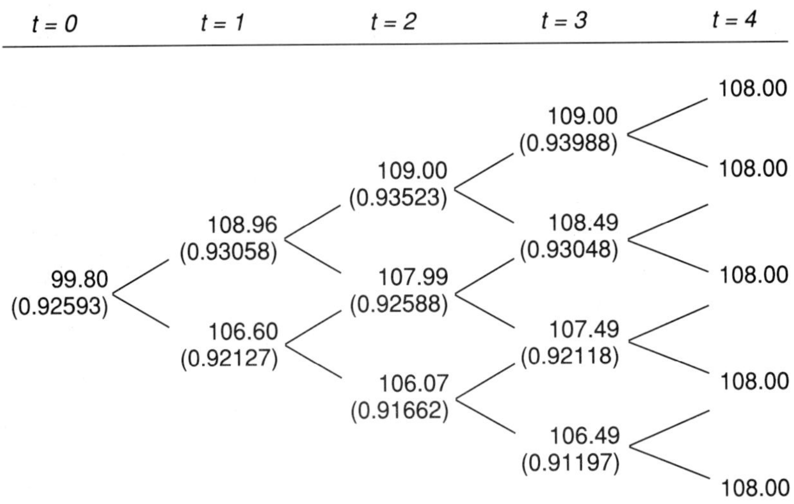

$t = 0$	$t = 1$	$t = 2$	$t = 3$	$t = 4$

				108.00
			109.00	
			(0.93988)	108.00
		109.00		
		(0.93523)	108.49	
	108.96		(0.93048)	
	(0.93058)			108.00
99.80		107.99		
(0.92593)		(0.92588)	107.49	
	106.60		(0.92118)	
	(0.92127)			108.00
		106.07		
		(0.91662)	106.49	
			(0.91197)	
				108.00

[a]Discount factors in parentheses

have a value greater than 109.00, so this value, too, is replaced by the call price plus the interest payment. After the rollback is completed, the price of the callable note is shown to be 99.80.

It is important to note that in Figure 8–4, the noncallable bond's value at node (1, 1) is 109.40. Yet, Figure 8–5 indicates the callable bond would not be called at that node. In general, the price that would prevail at a particular node for a noncallable bond with the same maturity and coupon does not provide an inference about the optimal time to call. The "called" states for a bond are given only by the lattice of that bond. The time of call is also the earliest node of substitution along an up diagonal of the lattice. In the case of Figure 8–5, the bond would be called at state (2, 2); it should never reach node (3, 3).

Several general statements regarding the pricing of callable bonds relative to similar bonds without call features can be made, and the AR model could be used to verify these principles.

- For callable bonds currently selling above par, the price of the callable bond will be less than the price of a similar straight bond that matures on the first call date.

- For callable bonds currently selling below par, the price of the callable bond will be less than the price of a similar bond that matures at the same time as the callable issue.

Other Binomial Models

The AR model is not the only binomial representation of rate movements that is possible. The paper by Dyer and Jacob (1988) provides an interesting informal discussion of some alternatives. In every case, the condition of arbitrage freedom constrains the way the models can be developed and solved. One of the advantages of the AR model is that it incorporates a systematic and insightful method for making arbitrage freedom endogenous to the construction.

Bond Option Prices in the AR Model versus Black-Scholes

The models that have been presented can be compared in terms of ease of application. The Black-Scholes model can be implemented on a hand held calculator. Binomial models require a modest amount of computer programming, and simplified versions can be written for Lotus 1-2-3. Equilibrium specifications require sophisticated econometric estimation and software for solution of differential equations.

Direct comparison of alternatives is impossible. No set of inputs can simultaneously satisfy all of the assumptions for all models, as some would conflict with others. Any test against actual data is subject to a type of selection bias. All of the models require parameter estimation, or "tuning up" to actual data via different parameters. This itself would destroy comparability.

For a practitioner, the most important comparison would probably be between the Black-Scholes model and the results obtained from binomial lattice pricing. Accordingly, Black-Scholes call option results for both zero coupon bonds and a par coupon bond will be compared to those obtained with a commercially available implementation of the AR model.

Table 8–1 shows the results of the two models, for the parameters shown. The initial spot curve is flat at 10 percent. For the zero coupon bond every call exercise price is equal to the 10 percent compound value of the current price. These calls are thus the term structure equivalent of "at-the-money" options. For the calls on the par bond, the strike price is always 100.

TABLE 8–1
Comparative pricing of interest rate options—Black-Scholes Model and AR Model

10 Year Zero Coupon Bond: *Current price* = 37.69
                             Volatility = 9.58 % p.a.

Expiration	Strike Price	AR Model Price	Black-Scholes Price
3 month	38.63	0.64	0.73
6 month	39.59	0.85	1.00
9 month	40.54	1.04	1.26
1 year	41.55	1.17	1.48
2 year	45.80	1.36	2.09
5 year	61.40	1.40	3.29
9 year	90.71	0.36	4.41

10 Year 10% Coupon Bond: *Current price* = 100.00
                           Volatility = 9.58 % p.a.
                                      = (102 BP)

Expiration	Strike Price	AR Model Price	Black-Scholes Price
3 month	100.00	1.10	1.88
6 month	100.00	1.47	2.58
9 month	100.00	1.72	3.09
1 year	100.00	1.94	3.48
2 year	100.00	2.19	4.46
5 year	100.00	1.83	5.30
9 year	100.00	0.35	4.87

In computing Black-Scholes values , we have fixed the "riskless" interest rate at 10 percent, and assumed a constant volatility of 9.58 percent per annum. The bond price is entered for S in the formula.

The Black-Scholes prices increase monotonically with the time until expiration for both bonds, since the model assumes that the bond prices can drift without bound. In contrast, the AR prices are not monotonic. This is a direct reflection of the "pull to par" on both bonds, as evidenced by the significant reduction in value of the options with 9 year term.

The two models produce significantly different results even for very short term options. This can be partially attributed to different amounts of "drift" in the two stochastic processes, even though they possess the same variance. Drift refers to a nonzero mean rate of change of the underlying variable. Because of the nonlinear relationship between price and yield, in the Black-Scholes model the prices drift, but the rates do not. In the AR model that was used in the comparison, expected price does not drift significantly; moreover, price changes of the bonds are automatically associated with changes in the rates of discount of the cash flows that produce the present value of the final payoffs unlike the B-S model, which treats the bond price as variable but the riskless rate as a fixed constant.

Bond Futures Options: The AR versus the Black Model

The clear implication of Table 8–1 is that the Black-Scholes model is not appropriate for use with debt options. However, this is not at all the case for analysis of traded options on Treasury Bond and Note futures contracts.

Black (1976) published a model for use with futures options that is very close to the original Black-Scholes option model. The futures model, referred to informally as "Black '76" in reference to the year of publication, is identical to the original, with one substitution. Everywhere in the original formulation, the current price (in this case, the trading price of the futures contract) is replaced by the current price discounted continuously at the riskless rate from the expiration of the option. The model can then be given as:

$$c = e^{-rT} [FN(d_1) - XN(d_2)]$$
$$d_1 = [\ln(F/X) + .5\,\sigma^2\,T]/\sigma\sqrt{T} \qquad (8.8)$$
$$d_2 = d_1 - \sigma\sqrt{T}$$

where
T = time to call expiration
F = futures price, and
X = strike price

Table 8–2 compares the results of AR pricing with prices calculated from the Black '76 model. June 1989 Treasury bond futures contracts prices are shown as of November 15, 1988. Both models give results that are quite close to the closing market prices. This is because the constant variance assumption is quite accurate when the underlying asset is a futures contract. Here, the underlying security is a price for a standardized, hypothetical bond of 20 year maturity (10 year in the case of notes) with an 8 percent coupon rate. The futures price could be considered to be an index on the 20 year bond yield. Therefore, changes in the underlying price do not imply changes in the riskless (i.e., short term) rate, nor do changes imply any specific movement of the term structure.

Valuation of debt options is a vital input into portfolio analysis and management. Thus far, this chapter has dealt with the construction and use of debt option models. The next section relates debt options to the tasks of fixed income portfolio management.

TABLE 8–2
Comparative pricing of interest rate options—Black '76 Futures Option Model and AR Model

June 1989 futures price = *88.13*
Standard Deviation = *11.15% p.a.*
Riskless Rate = *8.35% continuous*

| | *Prices* | | |
Option	*Observed*	*AR Model*	*Black '76*
88 put	2.81	2.82	2.86
88 call	2.97	2.93	2.98
90 put	3.91	3.92	3.87
90 call	2.06	2.09	2.08
92 put	5.19	5.21	5.15
92 call	1.41	1.44	1.39

8.4 ANALYZING BOND OPTION PRICE BEHAVIOR: DURATION AND THE PERFORMANCE PROFILE

A binomial term structure model directly relates option values to the yield curve. At the outset of this chapter, interest rate risk was defined as an unexpected shift of the yield curve. With this commonality, interest rate risk exposure of all fixed income securities can be systematically investigated in an integrative framework. To study effects of options on portfolios, it is then sufficient to consider the effects of yield curve shifts on value and performance.

The fundamental measure of the effect of yield curve shifts on assets is the simple and very powerful standard of *Effective Duration*.

Definitions of Duration

Duration measures the price sensitivity of a bond with respect to shifts of the yield curve. Duration does not rely upon any individual interest rate forecast or subjective views of the market. It is derived independently of the expected yield curve shape, interest rate volatility, or the distribution of the future interest rates. Duration is completely determined by cash flow characteristics, and uses the same market factors used in bond pricing.

Bond texts and reference works have, in the past, generally developed and discussed Macaulay duration. This measure is often described as a weighted average time to cash flow payment. Effective Duration is a closely related, but more powerful and appropriate measure. It is very simple to define, yet powerful enough to have broad applications.

A measure of bond price exposure should reflect a "typical" future movement of the yield curve. Unfortunately, the yield curve's historical movements offer no readily discernable pattern. In cases such as this, generally the simplest reasonable assumption is no worse than any other, and may provide insights that more complexity would obscure. Effective duration assumes instantaneous yield curve shifts are parallel, either up or down. In fact, over small intervals of time, it can be observed that the parallel shift assumption is typically a reasonable approximation. Further, effective duration is closely associated with the assumptions of the AR model, since yield curve changes therein are approximately parallel shifts over short intervals of time.

Effective duration of a bond, or other interest rate sensitive security, is the ratio of the proportional drop in bond price to a small parallel upward shift of the yield curve. A simple numerical example can illustrate this point. Say a particular bond has a price of $125 and is known to have an effective duration of 10 years. Then, if the yield curve shifted 1 basis point upwards, the price of that bond would fall by 0.1 percent, or $.0001 \times 10 \times \$125 = \$0.125$. Note that the basis point is expressed as a decimal fraction, and the price is expressed as a whole number percent of face value. This is conceptually very closely related to the "price value of one basis point" currently used by portfolio managers and traders.

Duration is nominally expressed in units of time, usually years. With Macaulay duration, this time dimension is relevant for many applications, such as determining optimal asset holding periods. For effective duration, the interpretation of the time dimension is less clear, but also less important. Without loss of meaning, one can simply take duration as a pure number that measures sensitivity to interest rate changes, much like an equity beta coefficient measures a stock's sensitivity to broad market movements.

Here is a more formal definition. Let the yield curve make a parallel, infinitesimally small shift (dr). Since the shift is parallel, dr is the same for all maturities. Thus the new yield curve at every maturity T is given by $r1(T) = r(T) + dr$. Let the new bond price be $B1 = B + dB$. Then, the change in bond price is:

$$dB = B1 - B \qquad (8.9a)$$

and

$$dB / B = B1 / B - 1 = \text{instantaneous HPR} \qquad (8.9b)$$

Effective duration D is then defined by:

$$dB / B = -D \, dr. \qquad (8.10)$$

Table 8–3 shows the values of effective duration, along with some calculated zero coupon bond prices before and after shifts of the yield curve. Yields are perturbed by "large" changes of ± 50 basis points, and by smaller changes of 1/3 as much, i.e. ± 17 basis points. The price changes shown can be obtained using the effective duration. Consider, for example, the 5 year bond in Table 8-3. The base price is 66.07. The change in price for a 17 basis point increase in yield is given, using duration, as:

$$dB\ (+17BP) = -[66.07 \times 4.789 \times .0017] = -.54.$$

This is correct up to a small rounding error.

TABLE 8–3
Effective duration for zero coupon bonds

Maturity	Effective Duration	Prices for Basis Point Shifts				
		−50	−17	0	+17	+50
1 Year	0.953	92.74	92.47	92.32	92.18	91.89
5 Year	4.789	67.67	66.60	66.07	65.54	64.51
10 Year	9.574	44.38	42.99	42.31	41.64	40.33
20 Year	19.142	18.15	17.58	17.03	16.50	14.99
30 Year	28.876	9.60	8.72	8.31	7.92	7.20

For zero coupon bonds, effective duration numbers are always slightly less than the maturity. Macaulay duration always equals the maturity for zeros, while effective duration is equal to Macaulay duration divided by $(1 + r)$. The negative sign on the definition above indicates the inverse relationship of bond price and yield. Since present value always moves inversely to change in yield, duration numbers are typically reported without the sign. The only exceptions to this are "short" positions, and, more importantly, put options. Puts are reported with negative duration numbers, indicating that they have a positive relationship between price and yield change.

Effective Duration of Debt Options

Effective duration can be determined for debt options as well as bonds. Table 8–4 illustrates effective duration and option elasticity for some options on the 10 year security in Table 8–3, obtained with an AR model.

The duration of an option is related to elasticity, discussed in Chapter 3. Option durations equal the duration of the underlying security times the elasticity of the option. With C and B denoting option price and underlying security price, respectively, and dC and dB denoting small changes, then elasticity is defined by:

$$dC \, / \, C \; = \; \text{option elasticity} \times dB \, / \, B.$$

Dividing both sides of this expression by dr and applying equation (8.10), it follows immediately that effective duration D is

$$D \text{ (option)} = \text{elasticity} \times D \text{ (underlying)}. \qquad (8.11)$$

Elasticity is large for an out-of-the-money option; therefore, so is the duration. For options in-the-money, the elasticity approaches unity, and the duration of the option approaches the duration of the underlying bond. These relationships can be seen in Table 8–4.

Effective duration has the same interpretation for any interest rate sensitive security, so the duration measures in Table 8–4 directly assess the interest rate exposure of options. For example, Tables 8–3 and 8–4 together show that an at-the-money call option on a 10 year zero coupon bond has a duration of 107.42, compared with the underlying bond's duration of 9.547. This means that the call price is $(107.42 \, / \, 9.547) = 11.25$ times more sensitive to interest rate changes than the underlying asset. These observations are equally applicable to put options, except movements are of

TABLE 8–4
Duration and elasticity for interest rate options

10 year zero coupon bond, 9% yield, with price of 42.31 (See Table 8–3)

	Strike = 40		Strike = 42		Strike = 44	
	Put	Call	Put	Call	Put	Call
Price	0.32	4.08	0.88	2.59	1.97	1.45
Duration	−205.86	82.43	−169.46	107.42	−138.98	139.06
Elasticity	−21.50	8.61	−17.70	11.22	−4.52	14.52

opposite direction. A put option price rises along with rising interest rates. Therefore, the put option has negative elasticity and, as noted above, duration is also negative.

Effective duration is the basis of fixed income hedging applications, because it is similar to the hedge ratio or delta for an equity option. However, duration is not as straightforward as the hedge ratio. The latter statistic defines a dollar change in option price with respect to a 1 dollar stock price change. Duration of a bond and a bond option gives proportional price change with respect to interest rate changes. Simple ratios of durations do not directly provide hedge proportions . The additional complexity of using debt options to hedge bonds is simplified by development of performance profiles, which will be described in the next section.

Performance Profiles

A Performance Profile is a graphic representation of the risk exposure, showing how asset value changes with respect to an instantaneous parallel shift of the yield curve.

Figure 8–6 shows the performance profiles for zero coupon bonds with maturities of 10 years and 2 years. They graphically represent the data in Table 8–5. These prices are the most simple performance profiles, being the present values of the $100 face value, discounted at 9 percent. Throughout this section, a flat yield curve of 9% will be assumed.

TABLE 8–5
Prices of 2 year and 10 year zero coupon bonds under various yields

Yield	2 Year	10 Year
7.0%	87.50	49.31
8.0%	85.83	44.79
9.0%	84.20	40.69
9.5%	82.61	36.99
10.0%	81.06	33.65
Duration	1.91	9.56

FIGURE 8–6
Performance profiles for 2 year and 10 year zero coupon bonds

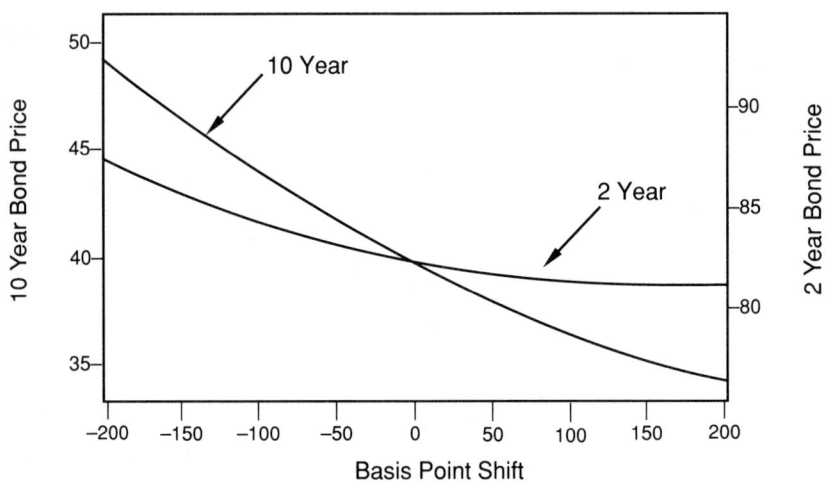

Performance profiles of zero coupon bonds are negatively sloped, nearly straight, lines. The slope of the profile at each point is related to duration at that level of yield. Equation (8.10), shows that the slope of the performance profile equals effective duration multiplied by the price of the bond. The slope of the performance profile will show the interest rate exposure expressed in dollars, much as the delta of an equity option does.

If a straightedge is placed tangent to a performance profile, a characteristic increase in slope into the region of lower interest rates can be observed. Also, the entire curve will lie above the straightedge. This phenomenon is termed *convexity*.

Convexity measures the rate of change of the slope of the performance profile. Positive convexity means that as the yield moves in the direction that increases the price, an asset gains value at an increasing rate. Convexity is therefore a very desirable property in fixed income assets. As rates fall, the bond gains value at an increasing rate. Conversely, as rates increase, the bond loses value at a decreasing rate. It will be shown below that the treatment of convexity along with duration can markedly increase the performance of bond hedges.

8.5   THE PRICE BEHAVIOR OF BOND OPTIONS

Analyzing Interest Rate Options Using Performance Profiles

Performance profiles of straight bonds do not provide much insight, since there is little that is subtle or complex about zero coupon bond prices. For debt options, however, performance profiles are much more valuable.

The price of a debt option incorporates a tradeoff between two fundamental sources of price risk. First, the option price reflects the price risk of the underlying asset and the relative chances of favorable and unfavorable price change due to shifts in market yields. Secondly, option value accounts for the loss of value that the option itself faces until its expiration. Because options have a shorter life than their underlying assets, an option will experience "time decay" even when the value of the underlying asset is constant.

For short term debt options, the dominant pricing factor is underlying asset risk. Over a short time horizon the volatility of the underlying asset will be relatively constant. In that case, a short term debt option will behave much like an equity option. As time to expiration increases, however, performance profiles show that debt options lose more and more of the character of equity options.

Figure 8–7 shows performance profiles for simple call options on a 10 year zero coupon bond with a present yield of 9 percent. The strike price for each option is the bond price as of option expiration at which the bond will have a 9 percent yield. The performance profile for the 1 year call is quite like the profiles for equity options. It falls to zero asymptotically as interest rates rise and the underlying asset price moves out of the money, and rises rapidly for yields that put the underlying bond price in the money. On the other hand, the performance profile for the longest term option, with nine years to expiration, is quite flat and almost linear, similar in shape to the performance profile of the underlying asset itself. The intermediate option, with 5 years to expiration, is less convex than the 1 year, but decidedly more "option like" in appearance than the 9 year. Interestingly, the value of the 5 year and 1 year calls are almost the same at-the-money. This could never be true of two equity calls with such different maturities, which illustrates that the intuition of pricing equity options, like the models themselves, is often out of place in debt option analysis.

FIGURE 8–7
Performance profiles for 1 year, 5 year, and 9 year call options

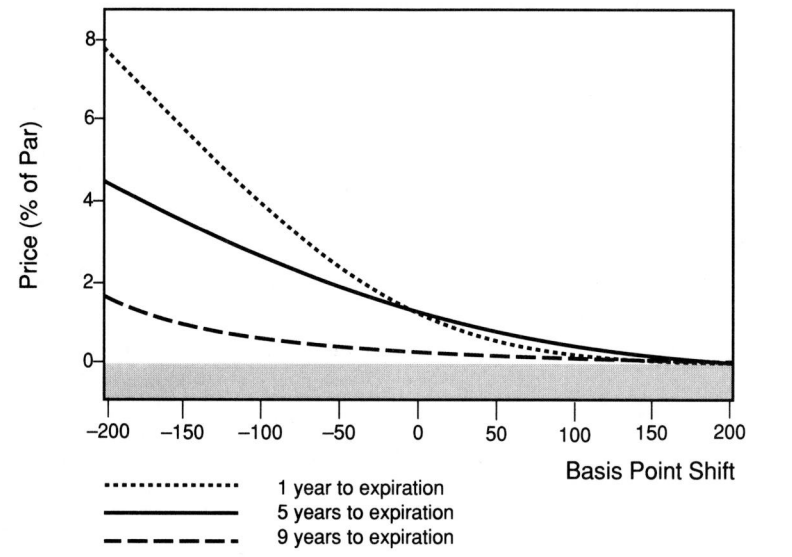

········· 1 year to expiration
———— 5 years to expiration
— — — 9 years to expiration

FIGURE 8–8
Performance profiles for 1 year, 5 year, and 9 year put options

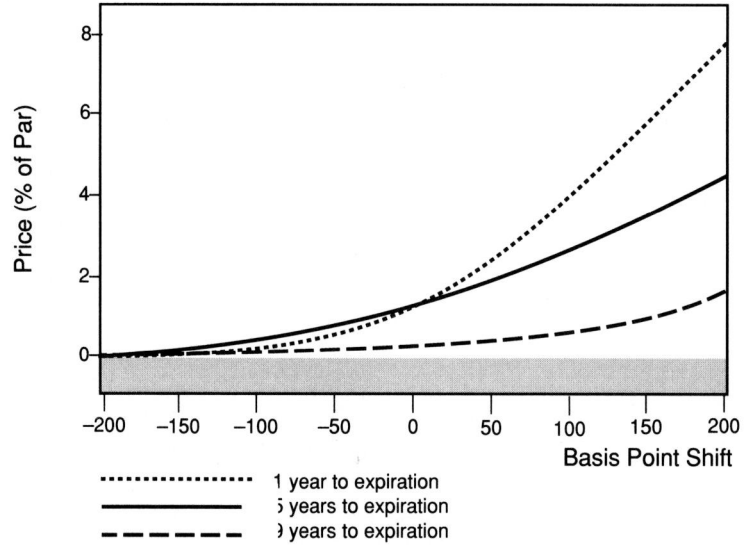

········· 1 year to expiration
———— 5 years to expiration
— — — 9 years to expiration

Figure 8–8 shows the performance profiles of puts corresponding to the calls above. As is the case in equity options, put prices are not precise mirror images of corresponding calls. In the case of debt options, a simple explanation of this is that the convexity of an underlying bond is not symmetric around the strike price, so the profiles of the put and call cannot be symmetric, either.

For European equity options, the passage of time reduces the value of a call option for a fixed stock price, whether the stock price is in-, out-of, or at-the-money. Debt options do not have an unambiguous time decay effect. This is shown in Figure 8–9.

To understand this effect, consider an extreme case when a call is so much in-the-money that the possibility of the option expiring with no value is negligibly low. This would be represented by options towards the left of Figure 8–9. With the passage of time the price of a zero coupon bond will almost certainly appreciate. This effect dominates the time decay effect. On the other hand, if the option is deeply out-of-the-money, any final value

FIGURE 8–9
Typical time decay behavior of a 5 year call on a 10 year zero coupon bond

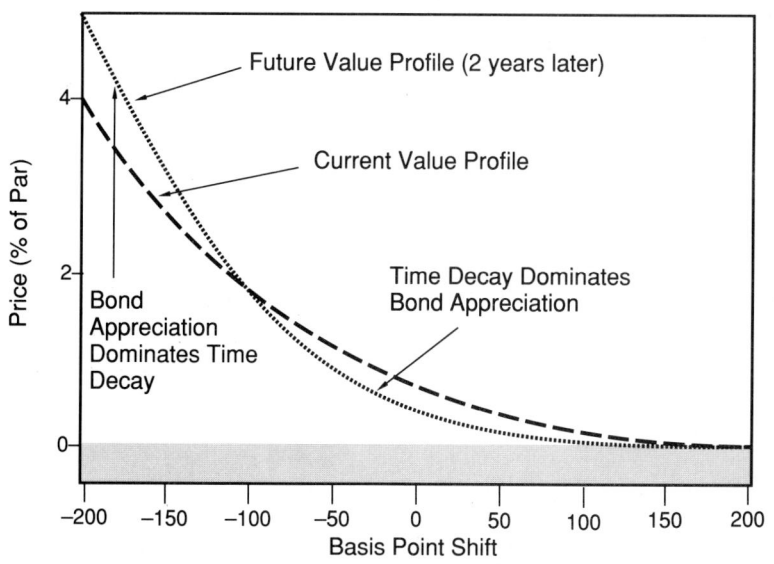

depends on a relatively small chance of a favorable bond price change. Then, as in the equity case, the less time that remains for a favorable yield shift, the lower the option price will be. Time decay can then dominate the price appreciation effect of the bond.

The time decay is even more complicated in the case of coupon bonds. If yield remains constant over time, the bond will either increase or decrease in price, depending on whether it is selling at a discount or premium. Analysis of options on coupon bearing bonds requires application of a pricing model.

Complete Specification of Bond Price Change

Effective duration was defined in equation (8.10) as the link between relative bond price change and yield change. For debt options, additional factors must be included to provide a complete representation of price change. These factors can be included as explicit factors in the pricing of underlying bonds as well. These additional factors are: convexity, G; time effect, "theta"; and volatility effect, "vega."

The extended specification of relative price change is then:

$$dB \, / \, B = -D \, dr + G \, (dr)^2 \; + \text{theta } dt + \text{vega } d\sigma \qquad (8.12)$$

Fixed income portfolio immunization is a strategy to remove interest rate sensitivity of a portfolio. If values of D, G, theta and vega are known for a portfolio, and some calls and puts with different strike prices and expiration dates, the options can be directly used in immunization. Elementary immunization typically concentrates only on matching duration, by forming a hedge for which the first term in (8.12) is equal to zero. However, the portfolio will then face price risk because of the effects of convexity, time effect on the options, and changing volatility. Of these additional factors, convexity has the greatest impact for options. Because of this, hedges using options are far better when convexity minimization is included along with duration as an objective of the hedge.

Table 8–6 illustrates the magnitude of the four factors described in equation (8.12). The data are generated by a straightforward application of that equation. In the AR model, closed forms are not available for these factors, as they are in the case of equity options using the Black-Scholes model. Therefore, all elements must be approximated by differences.

To estimate the duration, each option price $C0$ is first calculated.

Then, the yield curve is shifted a small amount, such as 5 basis points, both up and down. These new yields give two new T bond futures prices, which in turn provides two more observations on the call price, $C(up)$ and $C(dn)$. Considering only the duration term of equation (8.12), *ceteris paribus*, then duration is approximated by:

$$D(up) = - \{C(up) - C0\} / (C0 \times .0005) \qquad (8.13a)$$

and

$$D(dn) = - \{C0 - C(dn)\} / (C0 \times .0005). \qquad (8.13b)$$

A good estimate of effective duration is obtained by the average of these two numbers.

TABLE 8–6
Price risk components for T bond futures puts and calls

Price data for October 11, 1988.
Futures prices :   December = 89.97
March= 89.38

| Strike | | December | | March | |
		Call	Put	Call	Put
88	Price	2.55	0.58	3.19	1.83
	D	271.13	−403.98	181.45	−178.97
	G	357.50	2155.34	183.08	74.63
	theta	2.02	8.82	1.09	1.96
	vega	3.93	16.68	6.65	11.56
90	Price	1.25	1.30	2.14	2.75
	D	378.93	−358.08	209.58	−167.76
	G	1590.90	1587.15	256.04	282.37
	theta	4.60	4.49	1.64	1.26
	vega	9.69	9.45	10.24	7.97
92	Price	0.55	2.56	1.38	3.91
	D	475.24	−261.52	240.70	−146.73
	G	1657.84	338.75	400.70	152.75
	theta	9.02	1.88	2.35	0.78
	vega	18.44	3.96	14.74	5.17

Two duration approximations are used because convexity is the rate of change of duration. Therefore, the estimate of convexity follows immediately:

$$G = \{D(up) - D(dn)\} / (C0 \times .0005) \qquad \text{(8.14a)}$$

$$= \{C(up) + C(dn) - 2\,C0\} / (C0 \times .0005 \times .0005) \quad \text{(8.14b)}$$

Because of the large magnitude of the convexity number, current "street" convention is to report the convexity figure divided by 100. This is done in Table 8–6.

A similar perturbation of time to expiration, and then sigma, in turn, provides the other two factors.

A number of general characteristics can be observed in the data of Table 8–6.

- Price behavior is similar in character to equity options. Call prices increase as the options are more in-the-money, and the time decay is evident between the prices of the March and December expirations.
- The effective duration of the calls increases for out-of-the-money calls. This effect is the same for puts, where out-of-the-money means lower strike prices. The durations of puts are negative numbers. As time to expiration increases, the duration of both puts and calls falls in absolute value. Convexity also increases for out-of-the-money options. Unlike duration, the convexity of both calls and puts is positive. This reflects the fact that both types of options provide their holders with unlimited upside return and protection from downside risk.
- Convexity is positive for a *holder* of a call option, so the presence of an embedded call will diminish the convexity of a bond, since the bondholder is short the embedded call. As bond prices increase because of falling yields, callable bonds will not increase in price above their call (i.e., strike) prices. This situation must be taken into account in hedging callable bonds with noncallable issues or futures. On the other hand, a puttable bond increases convexity, because a bondholder is then long a put with positive convexity.
- The time effect, theta, shows that near term options tend to lose value fastest, particularly the out-of-the-money options.

- The volatility effect, vega, increases for puts and calls out-of-the-money. In the money, the effect of volatility on short term contracts is smaller, because the price behavior of the underlying bond is more homogeneous in the smaller time interval. At the money, vega tends to be quite similar for puts and calls. It was demonstrated earlier that futures options can be priced by the constant variance Black '76 model.

   This implies the vega of the underlying futures contract must be quite close to zero; there is little "directional" difference reflected between puts and calls. While not necessarily an optimal strategy, it is clear that buying a put and selling a call will tend to hedge away volatility risk.

Examples of Options Strategies

As a practical matter, hedging and immunization can be concentrated on duration and convexity if options are used as the hedge vehicles. Option positions used in hedges always need periodic monitoring and possibly adjustment. Therefore, any improvement in hedge effectiveness that would accrue to immunization in all four factors would be difficult to evaluate *ex ante*.

   Table 8–7 shows the results of immunization by matching both duration and convexity. This is accomplished by solving a system of equations with two unknowns (8.15a) and (8.15b). One equation equates duration; the other, convexity. These equations match the product of the duration and price of the bond portfolio with weighted products for a put and call:

$$-P_b \times D_b = n_c \times P_c \times D_c + n_p \times P_p \times D_p \qquad (8.15a)$$

$$-P_b \times G_b = n_c \times P_c \times G_c + n_p \times P_p \times G_p \qquad (8.15b)$$

   A hedge of $10,000,000 face value of a 30 year Treasury bond on October 31, 1988 is illustrated. Duration/convexity immunization, through solution of equations (8.15a and 8.15b), requires (rounded) transactions of $n_p = 114$ put contracts long against $n_c = 118$ call contracts short.

   The initial option transaction had a net inflow of $101,531, with margin on the short transaction being covered by the long bond position.

TABLE 8–7
**Duration and convexity hedge using Treasury bond futures put
and call**

Securities:	T Bond 9 1/8s 5/18	TB Futures 90 Call	TB Futures 90 Put
Price 10/31/88	104.09375	2.671875	1.875000
Duration	10.14	203.32	−210.49
Convexity	1.83	213.15	231.13
Price 11/30/88	100.25000	1.046875	2.859375

Transactions/Values:	Initial	Final
T Bond 9 1/8s May, 2018	(10,409,375)	10,025,000
Accrued Interest	(419,056)	37,811
Short 118 March 90 Call	315,281	(123,531)
Long 114 March 90 Put	(213,750)	325,969
Portfolio Value with Hedge	(10,726,900)	10,265,249
Coupon paid 11/15/88		456,250
7% interest on coupon		1,314
		10,722,813

Portfolio Value Under Parallel Yield Shifts:

	Basis Point Change				
	−200	−100	0	100	200
Bond Alone	168.44	116.39	104.44	94.45	86.05
With Hedge	107.92	107.20	107.13	107.24	107.26

When the hedge was sold out on November 30, the transaction inflow was $202,438. Also, a coupon payment of $456,250 was received on November 15. The sum of these three cash flows offset the decline experienced in bond value due to changing interest rates. Considering accrued interest, and interest of 7% per annum on the interim coupon payment, the net result of the hedge was a cost of about $4,000. Considering the magnitude of the transactions, and the fact that the bond changed about 4 percent (almost $400,000) in value, this "zero duration/convexity" hedge shows practice almost closely approximating theory.

Next, the use of options to alter the performance profiles of a bond can be illustrated. The same bond is combined with a short call, and then a long put in two different cases.

Case I: Hold $10 million position in the long bond.

Case II: Hold the same bond as in Case I, and write 100 contracts of the 88 strike price March futures calls shown in Table 8–6.

Case III: Hold the same positions as in Case II, and additionally buy 100 put contracts with 92 strike March futures puts, as shown in Table 8–6.

Table 8–8 shows the *ex ante* holding period returns (not annualized) for the term October 31, 1988 to January 31, 1989, for five different rate scenarios.

In Case I, one can observe the convexity of the long bond: for the lower rate scenarios, the magnitude of the return is greater than the loss in the higher rate scenarios.

In Case II, the addition of the option premiums captured from the writing of the calls increases the return in the "no change" scenario, but at the expense of lower returns when the bond increases in value. Note further that the writing of the calls provides almost no downside protection for the bond position.

In Case III, the addition of the put options to the position provides

TABLE 8–8
Holding period returns for different rate scenarios

	Basis Point Change				
	–200	*–100*	*0*	*100*	*200*
Case I	25.91	12.99	2.22	–6.82	–14.46
Case II	9.10	6.83	3.16	–5.79	–13.52
Case III	7.35	5.11	1.88	–0.66	–1.41

substantial downside protection. Also, the range of results over the five scenarios is less than in either of the other cases. The net effect of this position is to lower significantly the effective duration. Note, however, that the convexity of the position remains positive.

One may be tempted to draw a conclusion that one of these positions is superior to the other two. In fact, no such "global" assertion can be made: as a consequence of the option model, the expected value of each position, analyzed over all possible scenarios, will be equivalent. However, in terms of an individual's risk preferences, one position may be superior to another. Of the cases above, Case III is clearly the best choice for an investor who wishes to face as little interest rate risk as possible, even at the expense of foregoing the chance of large gains. Similarly, Case II would be the best choice for one who envisions little change in interest rates in the near future.

8.6   SUMMARY AND CONCLUSION

This chapter has described the attributes of options on interest rate sensitive securities. Options on, or embedded in, fixed income securities, have proliferated in recent years. The most common form of debt options are the call features embedded in bonds. In addition, there are now options traded on organized exchanges, and active over the counter markets for products with interest rate option features. Further, many bonds issued today have complex embedded options in the form of puts, performance covenants, or equity participations. It is impossible to fully understand the fixed income market without an understanding of the dynamics of these options.

Equity option models described elsewhere in this book are generally not appropriate for the pricing of debt options. This is principally due to the constraints on the price behavior of bonds, especially the fact that a bond has a known price at its maturity, barring default of the issuer.

The complex stochastic process governing bond price and return can best be handled by incorporating the term structure of interest rates, as an alternative to explicit consideration of the behavior of bond prices. Modern valuation models for debt options accordingly use equilibrium models of the term structure of interest rates as an underpinning.

Any fixed income asset is viewed as the sum of its cash flows discounted at rates that correspond to the term until payment of each cash flow. Every bond price is thereby related to all others, and an efficient market would require that no combination of bonds would yield superior returns to any other without an increase in risk. This is termed an "arbitrage free" market, and serves as the constraint on the modelling of term structure movements and equilibrium.

A model of interest rate option prices, like any finance model, is beneficial only if it makes a positive contribution to assessment of risk and analysis of performance. Assessment of risk of fixed income securities is embodied in the concepts of effective duration and convexity. Debt options provide the opportunity to alter the interest rate sensitivity of fixed income portfolios in a way that matches the preferences of the investor.

A principal tool for the assessment of performance of fixed income assets or portfolios is a "performance profile." This is a graphical or tabular representation of the price behavior of the assets under alternative scenarios of interest rate change. By construction of performance profiles, the price behavior of options can be studied. By the addition of the profiles of component securities, the behavior of portfolios or securities with embedded options can be developed, so that the manager can find the composition that best suits his or her preferences and goals.

References

Ball, C.A., and Torous, W. (1983). Bond price dynamics and options. *Journal of Financial and Quantitative Analysis, 18*, no. 4, 517–30.

Black, F. (1976). The pricing of commodity contracts. *Journal of Financial Economics, 3*, 167–79.

Black, F., and Scholes, M. (May/June 1973). The pricing of options and corporate liabilities. *Journal of Political Economy, 81*, 637–54.

Brennan, M.J., and Schwartz, E.S. (September 1982). An equilibrium model of bond pricing and a test of market efficiency. *Journal of Financial and Quantitative Analysis, 17*,303–29.

Courtadon, G. (September 1982). The pricing of options on default free bonds. *Journal of Financial and Quantitative Analysis, 17*, 75–100.

Cox, J.C., Ingersoll, J.E., and Ross, S.A. (March 1985). A theory of the term structure of interest rates, *Econometrica, 53*, 385–407.

Dyer, L.T., and Jacob, D.P. (1988). *A practitioner's guide to fixed income option models.* New York: Morgan Stanley Research.

Global Advanced Technology Corporation. (1988). *Integrative bond system.* New York: GAT Corporation.

Ho, T.S.Y., and Lee, S.B. (December 1986). Term structure movements and pricing interest rate contingent claims. *Journal of Finance, 41,* 1011–29.

Litzenberger, R.H., and Rolfo, J. (March 1984). An international study of tax effects on government bonds. *Journal of Finance,* 1–22.

McCulloch, J.H. (June 1975). The tax adjusted yield curves. *Journal of Finance, 30,* 811–30.

Merton, R.C. (March 1975). On the pricing of corporate debt: The risk structure of interest rates. *Journal of Finance, 29,* 449–70.

Merton, R.C. (1973). Rational theory of option pricing. *Bell Journal of Economics and Management Science, 4,* 141–83.

Schaefer, S.M., and Schwartz, E.S. (1987). Time dependent variance and the pricing of bond options. *Journal of Finance, 42,* no. 5, 1113–28.

Vasicek, O.A. (November 1977). An equilibrium characterization of the term structure. *Journal of Financial Economics, 5,* 177–88.

CHAPTER 9

OPTION FEATURES OF CORPORATE SECURITIES

Sang Yong Park[*]
Marti G. Subrahmanyam[**]

9.1 INTRODUCTION

An important aspect of modern option pricing theory is its relevance to the analysis of corporate securities. This insight was first pointed out by Fischer Black and Myron Scholes in their celebrated article published in 1973. It has since been elaborated upon, and the options framework has been applied to individual corporate securities by several authors over the past fifteen years. In this chapter, we provide a framework for valuing corporate securities based on their option features, and analyze the major types of corporate securities in some detail. In each case, we define the option features involved and provide a simple approach to their valuation in the context of the binomial option pricing model discussed in Chapter 2.[1] Our focus is on developing the basic intuition behind the models rather than providing the mathematical details.

[*]Graduate School of Business Administration, Yonsei University.
[**]Leonard N. Stern School of Business, New York University. The authors acknowledge with thanks the helpful comments of R. Ambarisha and E. Stiles.
[1]The appendix discusses the extension of these results to the continuous time model.

In general, a corporate security has three possible sources of value: (1) the terminal value of the security on its maturity date; (2) the interim cash flows, such as coupon or dividend payments; and (3) the value of the security in the event of recapitalization of the firm. For corporate bonds, for example, the promised terminal value is usually the face value of the bond and the interim cash flows are the coupon payments to the bondholders. The third source of value arises from a recapitalization of the firm, which may be triggered off by the actual realization of some uncertain state variable, such as interest rates. For example, in the case of a callable bond, the bondholder does not necessarily receive the face value of the bond on the terminal date. If interest rates decline sufficiently, the bond may be "called" by the issuer and the investor may receive the call price (which is typically higher than the face value) even before maturity. In this chapter, we look at all three sources of value in an options context.

We first examine basic corporate securities whose value arises from just the first source, the terminal value of the security. Basic securities, such as stocks that do not pay a dividend, and zero-coupon bonds, are used to show a correspondence between options and corporate securities. We then look at coupon bonds and dividend-paying stocks which derive their value from both the terminal and the intermediate cash flows. Next, we analyze securities whose value is partly derived from the third source, the cash flow when the firm is recapitalized. Examples of such securities include callable bonds and convertible bonds. Finally, we discuss the valuation of warrants and more recent innovations in designing corporate securities with option-like features.

9.2   BASIC SECURITIES: STOCKS AND ZERO-COUPON BONDS

Consider a firm which has only two securities outstanding: zero-coupon bonds maturing at time T and common stock. The total current market value of the firm, V, is the sum of the market values of the two securities:

$$V = S + B \qquad (9.1)$$

where S is the current market value of the stock on which no dividends are paid before the maturity date of the bonds, T, and B is the current market value of the zero-coupon bonds with a face value F payable at date T. Also, assume that the total market value of the assets of the firm on the maturity date of the bonds, V_T, will be distributed either as a payoff to the bondholders, B_T, or as a payoff to stockholders, S_T. The contractual payoff of these securities can, therefore, be stated as:

$$B_T = \min [V_T, F] \tag{9.2}$$

$$S_T = \max [V_T - F, 0] \tag{9.3}$$

The terminal payoffs on the two basic securities are expressed in equations (9.2) and (9.3) and are illustrated in Figure 9–1. Inspection of the equations and the figure shows that the payoffs on both securities are *contingent* upon the realized value of the assets of the firm, V_T, on the maturity date of the bonds. In fact, looking back at the figures in Chapter 2, Figure 9–1A looks like the payoff diagram for a long call position. Similarly, Figure 9–1B is like the payoff diagram for a covered-write (i.e., being long the underlying asset and short the call option) or short put position. More specifically, the payoff on the bonds on the maturity date, T, is the *minimum* of the terminal value of the firm's assets, V_T, and the face value of the bonds, F. The payoff on the stock, on the other hand, is the *maximum* of $V_T - F$ and zero. The payoff function of the stock is, therefore, directly analogous to that of a European call option on common stock, whose payoff on the expiration date is the maximum of either the excess of the stock price over the striking price, or zero. This correspondence between the common stock of a levered firm and a call option on stock results from the fact that stocks represent *residual claims* with *limited liability*. In other words, if the value of the firm at date T, V_T, falls short of the promised payment to the bondholders, F, the stockholders can simply walk away from the firm. Since the payoff pattern for the common stock at maturity in this case is the same as for a European call option on a stock on the expiration date, C_T, it follows that the value of the common stock is equal to that of a European call option written on the firm value, V, with an exercise price equal to the face value of the bond, F. The expiration date of the option is the same as the maturity date of the bonds. Thus, if C denotes the current value of a European call, we obtain:

$$S_T = C_T \tag{9.4a}$$

FIGURE 9–1A
Possible values of stock

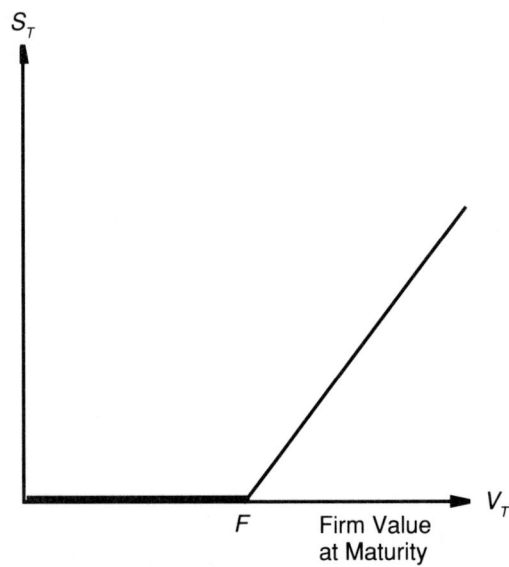

Stock Value
at Maturity

S_T

F Firm Value
at Maturity

V_T

FIGURE 9–1B
Possible values of bonds

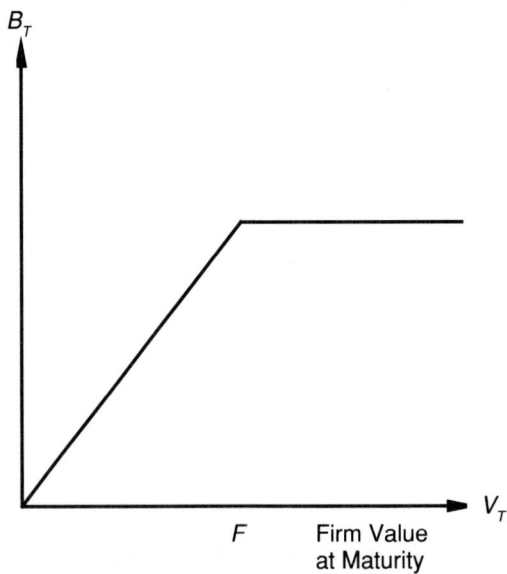

Bond Value at
Maturity

B_T

F Firm Value
at Maturity

V_T

and
$$S = C\ (V, F, T),$$ (9.4b)

where the value of the call option is a function of the value of the underlying asset, V, the face value of the bonds or the exercise price, F, and the time to expiration, T.

There is also a correspondence between options and corporate bonds. As mentioned earlier, the payoff diagram for a corporate bond with default risk looks like that of a covered-write or short put position. This follows from the fact that the value of the firm's bonds is, by definition, the difference between the value of the firm's assets and the value of the common stock. This difference, in turn, can be valued as an option. To see this more clearly, we can rewrite the payoff function of the bonds in equation (9.2) as:

$$B_T = F - \max\ [F - V_T, O]$$

$$= F - P_T$$ (9.5)

where P_T is the payoff of a European put option on the firm value with an exercise price equal to F, and an expiration date equal to the maturity date of the bonds, T. The current value of bonds today is, then, equal to:

$$B = PV(F) - P(V, F, T)$$ (9.6)

where $PV(F)$ is the present value of the face amount, F, discounted at the riskless rate, and P is the value of a European put option on firm value, V, at a striking price F and time to expiration T. The only difference between equations (9.5) and (9.6) is that the payoffs on the expiration date, T, are replaced by their respective current market values.

A risky zero-coupon bond can thus be viewed as a portfolio of a long position in a default risk-free bond and a short position in a European put option. The put option represents the *limited liability* claim owned by the stockholder and written by the bondholder. Under the limited liability arrangement, the stockholder can "walk away" from the firm in case its value falls short of the promised payment to the bondholder on the maturity date. The greater the risk of default on the debt, the higher is the value of the put option. A high grade bond such as a AAA-rated bond has a relatively small probability of default and a correspondingly small value of the put option. A "junk" bond, on the other hand, may have a high probability of default and hence, a high value of the put option. The put option value is the reduction in the current value of the future promised payments due to the likelihood of default, relative to the value of a riskless Treasury bond of similar maturity. This reduction is small for AAA-rated bonds and relatively large for junk bonds and can be thought of as the value of the stockholders' limited liability arrangement. In other words, if a bond is guaranteed, rendering it free of default risk and thus yielding what a riskless bond would in an arbitrage-free market, then the *fair value* of the guarantee (fee) is equal to the value of the put option.

Another way of looking at this relationship is as follows. We have seen in Chapter 2 that from put-call parity, an underlying asset can be replicated by a long position in a European call option on the underlying asset, a short position in a European put option on the same asset at the same striking price, and risk-free lending equal to the present value of the striking price. The identical put-call parity relationship also holds among corporate securities, with the underlying asset being the value of the firm. To see this, we can combine equations (9.1), (9.4b) and (9.6) to obtain:

$$V = S + B$$

$$= C(V, F, T) + PV(F) - P(V, F, T) \tag{9.7a}$$

or, $$S = C(V, F, T) = V - PV(F) + P(V, F, T) \tag{9.7b}$$

Equation (9.7a) is a demonstration of put-call parity in the case of corporate securities, with the underlying asset being the value of the firm. Equation (9.7b) shows that the common stock can be interpreted either as a call option on the value of the firm's assets, as discussed earlier, or as a long position in the firm's assets with riskless borrowing and a long position in the limited liability put option.

Note that when corporate securities are described as options, the underlying asset is the *total market value of the assets of the firm* or the value of the firm, for short. Thus, we can only value each corporate security as an option relative to a *known* value of the firm. By the accounting identity of assets and claims on the firm, the total market value of all the assets of a firm is equal to the total market value of all its liabilities. It is often difficult to observe the market value of the firm's assets directly. However, the value of the firm can be inferred indirectly from the market values of the component securities of the firm, or from similar assets that are publicly traded.

Numerical Example 1: We shall now show how to value the basic corporate securities, debt and equity, using, as we shall throughout the chapter, the binomial option pricing model discussed in Chapter 3.[2] Suppose the *current* market value of the firm, V, is 100. The rate of return on the assets of the firm, over one period, is either $u - 1 = 20\%$ with probability q or $d - 1 = -20\%$ with probability $1 - q$. In other words, the assets will be worth either 120 (the "up state") or 80 (the "down state") at the end of the period. As we shall see, these probabilities are not directly relevant to the valuation of corporate securities. The risk-free interest rate is given as $r = 10\%$, or $(1 + r) = 1.1$. Finally, the *face value*, i.e., the promised payoff at the end of one period, of the (risky) discount bond issued by the firm is 100. The movements of the firm value and the bond value can then be represented by binomial processes as shown in Figure 9–2.

In a manner analogous to the case of an option on a stock in Chapter 3 for the binomial process, we now form a portfolio consisting of the assets of the firm and a riskless borrowing or lending position in such a way that the payoff from the portfolio is identical to that of the bond *regardless* of the firm value at maturity. In other words, we form a portfolio that *replicates* the payoffs from the risky bond. Specifically, a long position in the bond can be created by a long position in the assets of the firm and a long position in the riskless asset. Denoting by h and m the proportions of the firm and the riskless money market position in the replicating portfolio, we obtain:

$$B_u = hV_u + m(1 + r) = 120h + 1.1m = 100 \qquad (9.8a)$$

$$B_d = hV_d + m(1 + r) = 80h + 1.1m = 80 \qquad (9.8b)$$

Solving the two equations simultaneously, we find $h = 0.5$ and $m = 36.36$. Thus, a portfolio consisting of a long position in half of the assets of the firm and a lending position of 36.36 will replicate the discount bond. (It is easy to check that this is true by substituting h and m in equations (9.8a) and (9.8b)). For arbitrage to be precluded, the current value of the bond must then be equal to the current value of the replicating portfolio.[3] That is:

---

[2]We will leave the units of the value unspecified to avoid tedious notation.

[3]These arguments are discussed in Chapter 3. The intuition is that two securities with identical payoffs in every state should sell for the same price. Otherwise, it would pay to buy the cheaper security and sell the more expensive one for a sure profit.

FIGURE 9–2
Possible firm and bond value changes over one period

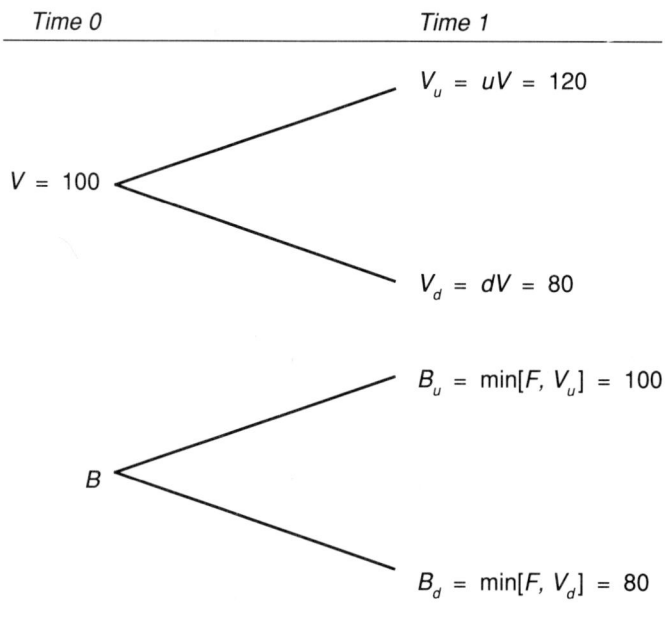

| Time 0 | Time 1 |

$V_u = uV = 120$

$V = 100$

$V_d = dV = 80$

$B_u = \min[F, V_u] = 100$

B

$B_d = \min[F, V_d] = 80$

V = value of the firm at time 0
B = value of the bond at time 0
V_u = value of the firm in the up-state at time 1
V_d = value of the firm in the down-state at time 1
B_u = value of the bond in the up-state at time 1
B_d = value of the bond in the down-state at time 1

$$B = hV + m$$

$$= 0.5\,(100) + 36.36$$

$$= 86.36 \tag{9.9}$$

The value of the equity can be obtained in a similar manner by forming a replicating portfolio consisting of a fraction of the assets of the firm and riskless borrowing. Alternatively, however, once the value of the bond is obtained, we can find the value of stock directly by subtracting the bond value from the firm value. Therefore, in our example:

$$S = V - B$$
$$= 100 - 86.36$$
$$= 13.64 \tag{9.10}$$

The interested reader may confirm this result by computing the stock value from a strategy that replicates the payoff from the stock.

We have seen in Chapter 3 that a solution for h and m gives rise to a simple valuation formula: discount the expected payoff on options at the riskless interest rate with the expectation taken over "risk-neutral" probabilities, $p = [(1 + r) - d]/(u - d)$ and $1 - p = [u - (1 + r)]/(u - d)$. In our example, $p = (1.1 - 0.8)/(1.2 - 0.8) = 0.75$. Therefore,

$$B = [(0.75 \times 100) + (0.25 \times 80)] / 1.1 = 86.36 \tag{9.11}$$

In the examples in the rest of the chapter, we shall bypass the process of forming replicating portfolios and go directly to the simple discounting method using the expected value with the "risk-neutral" probabilities.

The price of the risky bond can be interpreted in different ways. The first interpretation is to compare the value of the risky bond with a riskless bond with the same face value. Such a riskless bond would have a value of $100 / 1.1 = 90.91$, since the appropriate discount rate to use would be the riskless rate of 10%. In other words, the risky bond is worth $90.91 - 86.36 = 4.55$ less than the riskless bond with same face value. This difference is the value of the put option as indicated in equation (9.6). Another way of interpreting the price of the risky bond is to transform it into a *promised* yield. In this case, since the bond has one year to maturity, the promised yield of the risky bond is:

$$(100/86.36) - 1 = 15.79\%$$

or 5.79% above the riskless interest of 10%.

What are the determinants of the difference in value (or yield) between a risky bond and a riskless bond with an identical face value? In general, in the absence of coupon payments the value of a risky bond is a function of V, F, $u - d$, r and T. The specific valuation method developed above, which is valid for any option contingent on the value of the firm's assets, V, can be used to determine the sensitivity of the value of the risky bond with respect to each of the parameters in the binomial model. The ratio V / F is an index of the depth in-the-money of the option; $u - d$ is a measure of the volatility of the firm value; r is the risk-free interest rate; and, T is the time to expiration. In the present context of risky debt, we can interpret the depth in-the-money as a measure of the degree of leverage or *financial risk*. The greater the leverage, or financial risk, the smaller the ratio V / F, and the smaller the value of the bonds in relation to their face value. The volatility parameter, $u - d$, measures the *business risk* of the firm. The larger the volatility parameter, the smaller the value of the risky bond, although the precise magnitude of the impact also depends on the depth in-the-money of the limited liability put option. When the put option is deep in-the-money, as is the case for very low quality junk bonds, or deep out-of-the-money, as is true for AAA-rated bonds, changes in volatility have little or no effect on the value of the put option at low levels of volatility. This is because there is little or no chance that the depth in-the-money of the option will change dramatically over the life of the option, if the volatility is small. However, at higher levels of volatility, the value of the limited liability option invariably increases with volatility, irrespective of the depth in-the-money of the option. Hence, the value of bonds, at various points on the quality spectrum, declines with increases in volatility. This effect is greatest, relatively speaking, when the put option is close to being at the money.

The binomial example may be generalized to give a more realistic model of valuing risky bonds. This extension is similar in spirit to the Black-Scholes model and represents a similar generalization of the basic binomial example. The Appendix provides details of this extension to the continuous-time setting.

We now turn to an example of a recent issue of zero coupon junk bonds to illustrate the calculation of the risk premium in relation to default-free bonds.

Zero-Coupon Junk Bond	*Example*
Issuer	Damon Clinical Labs Acquisition Corporation Inc.
Issue Size	$96.5 Million Senior Subordinated Discount Notes.
Issue Date	May 23, 1989.
Maturity Date	May 15, 1999.

Coupon	0% prior to May 15, 1992; "at a rate to be determined thereafter, until maturity."
Price	64.74
Call Feature	Callable on or after May 15, 1992.
Sinking Fund Feature	25% of issue including accrued interest on May 15, 1996.
Security	Subordinate.
Rating	B2 (Moody's).

This issue is below investment grade and is generally classified as a "junk" note. To keep our discussion simple, we shall ignore the call and sinking fund features. We shall also assume that the note will definitely be called at par on the first call date. In other words, we shall treat the note as a 3 year zero coupon note with a payoff at maturity of 100.

We can quantify the risk of the note in relation to a default-free Treasury note of similar maturity in one of two ways:

a) Yield of the note in relation to the yield of the Treasury note. Using the semiannual discounting conventions of U.S. bonds, the yield of the note can be computed from:

$$64.74 = \frac{100}{[1 + y\% / 2]^6}$$

or $y = 15.03\%$. This yield may be compared with the yield on 3 year Treasury zero coupon notes which were about 8.30% at the time of the issue. Thus, the risk premium of the note was 6.73%.

b) Price of the note compared with a Treasury note with similar promised payments. The price of a 3 year zero coupon note with a promised payment of 100 in 3 years would be equal to:

$$\frac{100}{[1 + 8.30\% / 2]^6} = \$78.35$$

This should be compared with the issue price of the junk note of $64.74, a difference of $13.61.

So far, in order to demonstrate the correspondence between corporate securities and options, we have assumed that the firm issues only basic securities, stocks that do not pay dividends and zero-coupon bonds. Our analysis shows that these securities are like simple, European-style options. We now turn to other types of corporate securities which are more complex options and may be American-style rather than European-style. Although the valuation of more complex corporate securities is rather involved, the basic insight that any corporate security can be represented as a combination of options is the fundamental principle we shall rely upon.

9.3   COUPON BONDS

Coupon bonds will, in general, have cash flows in more than one period. If a firm has coupon bonds outstanding with more than one period left until maturity, we can view the common stock as a "compound option," or an "option on an option." To see this, suppose the bond is valued before the second to last coupon date. On the maturity date, the last coupon and the face value of the bond are to be paid. By paying the last coupon plus the face value on the maturity date, the stockholders exercise their option to buy the firm from the bondholders for the face value of the bonds. Let us call this "option 1." Right before the second to last coupon date, i.e., one period before the terminal date, the stockholders have an option to buy option 1 by making the second to last coupon payment. (If they fail to make this coupon payment, the bondholders will take over the firm). Calling this "option 2," we can see that the stockholders have an option to buy option 1, until just before the second to last coupon payment is made. The current value of the stock is then equal to the value of the option 2. Option 2 is exercised by the payment of the second to last coupon and option 1 is exercised by payment of the last coupon and the face value of the bonds.

We shall now analyze this "compound option" in some detail. In our analysis, we assume that any cash payout to securities is made by the liquidation of assets. (Alternative assumptions regarding how the cash payments are financed will produce somewhat different values for the "compound option," although the qualitative aspects of the following analysis will be preserved.) If new financing is precluded, any default on the promised coupon will force the firm to go bankrupt and thus, the stock value will go to zero. Under these assumptions, a coupon bond can still be represented as a *European-style compound* option because a stockholder's choice at each coupon date with respect to default is a trivial one: the stockholders will always make the coupon payment if the firm value exceeds the promised coupon payment. In other words, the values of the stock and the coupon bond will depend only on the relationship between the value of the firm and the promised coupon payment, and not on other factors such as the issue of additional equity and/or bonds.

Before we value the coupon bonds, we shall describe the two-period binomial process of the firm value, which will be used throughout the rest of this chapter. As before, the rate of return on the assets of the firm is $u - 1$, with probability q, or $d - 1$, with probability $1 - q$. (Note that, as in the single period example, the probability, q, does not play a role in valuation, but is relevant for describing the risk of the assets of the firm, as we shall see later on.) However, this assumption holds for each period. If any cash payout, coupon c and/or dividend D, is made at time 1, then the *ex-payout* firm value will change by either $u - 1$ or $d - 1$ over the second period. The firm value can, therefore, be represented by the binomial process as shown in Figures 9–3 and 9–4. The firm value with and without * denotes the cum-payout firm value and the ex-payout firm value, respectively.[4] Dividends and coupon are paid at time 1. In Figure 9–4, the reduction in the value of the firm from the cum-payout date to the ex-payout date, for example from V_u^* to V_u, is indicated by an arrow pointing down.

In all examples in the rest of the chapter, we assume, unless otherwise specified, the following parameter values: $V = 150$, $u = 1.2$, $d = 0.8$, and $(1 + r) = 1.05$ in each period, which we assume to be half a year. The value of the firm in the absence of any cash payout at time 1 will then move according to the binomial process shown in the bottom panel of Figure 9–3. When there are cash payments such as dividends and coupon payment at time 1, the process has to be modified as shown in Figure 9–4. Note that once we specify the distribution of the firm value, as in Figure 9–3, without regard to the firm's debt policy and dividend policy, we are implicitly assuming that those policies do not affect the total value of the *assets of the firm*. In other words, we are assuming that the Modigliani-Miller propo-

---

[4]The more general analysis that allows for the possibility of paying coupons from any one of the many sources (operating cash flows, sale of assets or new financing), is considerably more complex than the discussion here. However, the essential principles are similar to those used here.

FIGURE 9–3
Possible firm values over two periods without payments at time 1

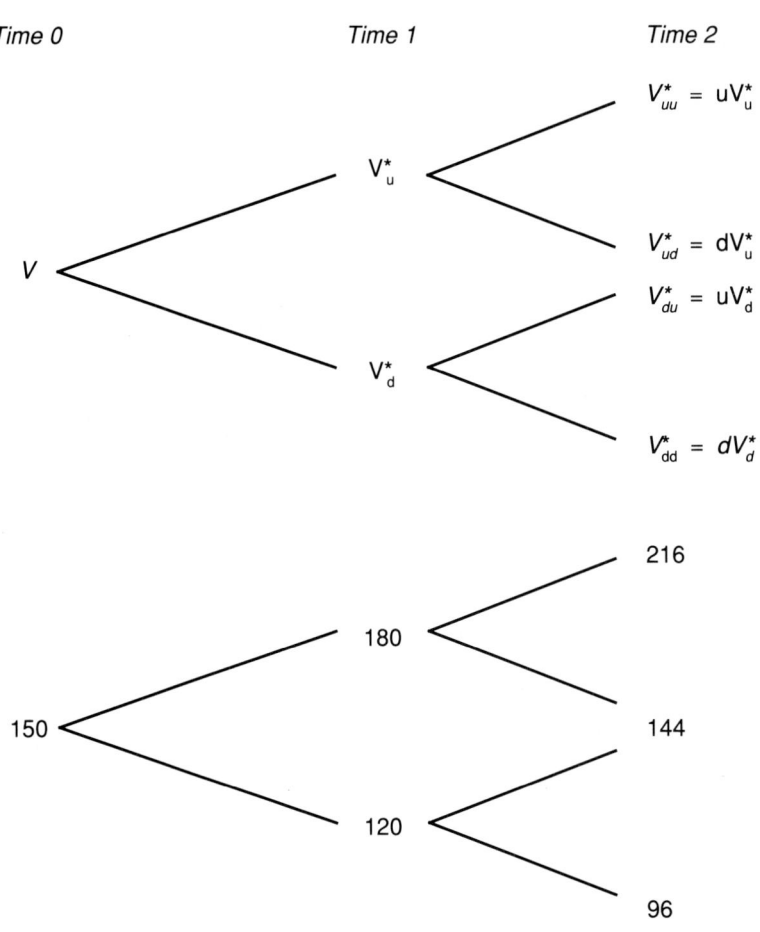

V = value of the firm at time 0
V_u^* = value of the firm in the up-state at time 1
V_d^* = value of the firm in the down-state at time 1
V_{uu}^*, V_{ud}^*, V_{dd}^*, V_{du}^* = value of the firm in the respective states at time 2

FIGURE 9–4
Possible firm values over two periods with payments at time 1

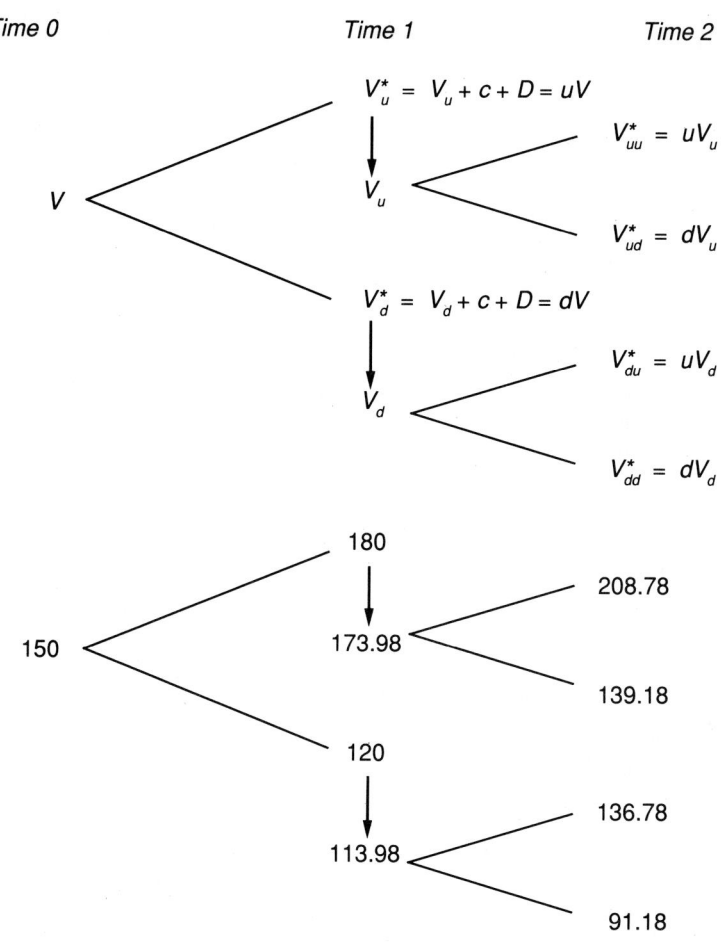

V = value of the firm at time 0
V_u = ex-payment value of the firm in the up-state at time 1
V_u^* = cum-payment value of the firm in the up-state at time 1
V_d = ex-payment value of the firm in the down-state at time 1
V_d^* = cum-payment value of the firm in the down-state at time 1
$V_{uu}^*, V_{ud}^*, V_{dd}^*, V_{du}^*$ = cum-payment value of the firm in the respective states at time 2
c = coupon on the bond
D = dividend on the stock

sition holds—the firm value is independent of its financing policies.[5] This proposition holds, given the investment decisions of the firm, in a perfectly competitive capital market where there are no frictions, such as taxes and transaction costs, impeding trading.

For a given probability distribution of the firm value, the movement of the coupon bonds can be represented by the binomial process as shown in Figure 9–5. In Figure 9–5, the value of the bonds with an "*" denotes the cum-coupon value. Also, note that for simplicity of exposition, we have assumed there is no probability of default on coupon payments at time 1, i.e., the lower firm value, V_d^*, exceeds the coupon payment, c. This is quite reasonable in many cases, since coupon payments are a much smaller proportion of the value of a firm's assets than the face value of the bonds it issues.

Now, as described in Chapter 3 for multiperiod valuation, we use the recursive technique to move backward one period from the maturity date and compute the ex-coupon bond value at time 1. That is:

$$B^*_u = [p\, B_{uu}^* + (1-p)\, B_{ud}^*] / (1+r) \qquad (9.12)$$

$$B^*_d = [p\, B_{du}^* + (1-p)\, B_{dd}^*] / (1+r) \qquad (9.13)$$

where, as before, p represents the "risk-neutral" probability of an increase in firm value at time 1. Finally, the current value of the bonds can be computed from:

$$B = [p\, B_u^* + (1-p)\, B_d^*] / (1+r) \qquad (9.14)$$

Numerical Example 2: Suppose the firm pays no dividends on the stock at time 1, which is six months away from time 0. For a given coupon, we can then compute the current value of the bond using equations (9.12), (9.13) and (9.14). Here, however, we shall fix the value of the risky bond equal to the face value of 100 and compute the coupon that will result in par pricing (i.e., equal to 100). This is in order to permit us to use the "straight" (i.e., without other option features) coupon bond priced at par as a benchmark for easy comparison with more complex bonds to be valued later on in the chapter. Although the calculation of the coupon for a fixed bond price

---

[5]The proposition that, in the absence of taxes, the value of a firm in a competitive market is independent of its financing policies, was first rigorously demonstrated by Modigliani and Miller in 1958. This proposition has subsequently been clarified and extended by several authors.

FIGURE 9–5
Possible values of coupon bonds over two periods

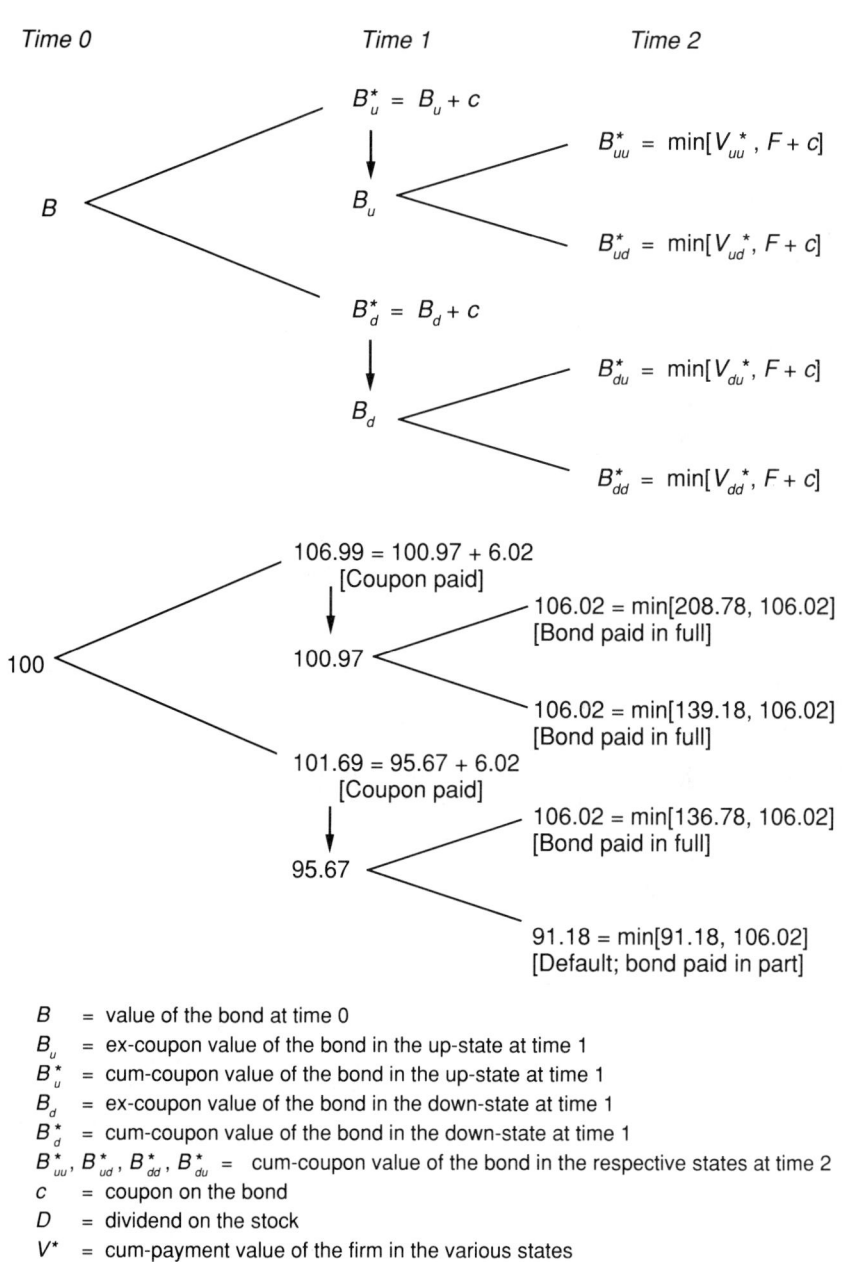

B = value of the bond at time 0
B_u = ex-coupon value of the bond in the up-state at time 1
B_u^* = cum-coupon value of the bond in the up-state at time 1
B_d = ex-coupon value of the bond in the down-state at time 1
B_d^* = cum-coupon value of the bond in the down-state at time 1
$B_{uu}^*, B_{ud}^*, B_{dd}^*, B_{du}^*$ = cum-coupon value of the bond in the respective states at time 2
c = coupon on the bond
D = dividend on the stock
V^* = cum-payment value of the firm in the various states

is cumbersome, the procedure is similar to that in the previous example. In Numerical Example 1, we computed the current price of a risky bond given its future payoffs. In order to determine the coupon that would lead to par pricing, we have to reverse this procedure and determine the coupon that would yield a price of 100, using the "risk-neutral" probabilities.

For the given parameter values, the semiannual coupon for the bond to be priced at par is 6.02 (i.e., the promised semiannual coupon yield is 6.02%, compared to a risk-free interest rate of 5% per half-year.) The firm values in the various states are shown in Figure 9–4. All the corresponding values for the risky bond, obtained by using equations (9.12), (9.13), and (9.14) iteratively working backwards from time 2, are shown in the lower panel of Figure 9–5. Note that the firm will default partly on the promised payment in one of the four states at time 2, when the realized firm value is $V_{dd}^* = 91.18$ at maturity. For this default possibility, the firm pays a default risk premium of $6.02\% - 5\% = 1.02\%$.

In general, the value of the corporate bond depends on the level of the riskless interest rate and the default risk. The default risk, in turn, depends on the firm's investment policy, dividend policy, and debt policy. The firm's manager, acting on behalf of the stockholders, may then change the firm's financial policies after the bonds are issued to make them riskier, and thus, less valuable. This is because, if changes in financial policies do not affect the total value of the firm's assets, as assumed here, a decrease in the bond value will be accompanied by an increase in the stock value. Such a possibility of transferring wealth from the bondholders to the issuing firm's stockholders constitutes an important difference between traded options and corporate securities viewed as options. In the case of traded options such as options on stocks, the option buyer and the option writer are essentially trading a "side-bet" on the future stock price. This bet does not have any direct effect on the firm that issued the stock. In contrast, in the case of corporate securities viewed as options, their issue and exercise may involve transfer of wealth between the stockholders and the other claimhold-ers such as the bondholders. It should be emphasized, however, that this possibility was known and should have been rationally taken into account by bondholders in the price they paid when they initially bought the bond. The following extensions of the example show the consequences of *unanticipated* changes in financial policies on the value of the component securities.

Dividend Policy: Suppose the firm that just issued a coupon bond paying a semiannual coupon of 6.02% at par, i.e., at its face value of 100, declares a total cash dividend payment of 10 to its stockholders at time 1. Since the dividend will reduce the firm value at time 1, the firm value will be lower at maturity (date 2). Although this amount of dividend will not result in a default in other states, the firm value in the default state, V^*_{dd}, will be reduced from 91.18 (see Figure 9–5) to $\{(120 - 6.02 - 10) \times 0.8\}$ or 83.18. A calculation similar to the previous one then shows that the current bond value will immediately decline from 100 to 98.98, a fall of 1.02 in value, for which the bondholders are not compensated. Alternatively, with a dividend of 10 at time 1, the semiannual coupon rate for par pricing would have had to be 6.64%. Thus, the bondholders would lose in terms of the promised semi-annual coupon yield by 6.64% – 6.02%, or 0.62%, if they experienced an unanticipated dividend payment of 10 to the stockholders at time 1.

Debt Policy: Suppose the firm that just issued a bond with a semi-annual coupon of 6.02% , at par, issues 50% more bonds *pari passu*, i.e., on equal terms, including seniority, with the outstanding bond. (This is normally not permitted, since, as we shall see below, the previous bond-holders would suffer a loss in the value of their holdings.) The face value of the total debt is now 150, with the promised coupon $6.02 \times 1.5 = 9.03$. Let us assume that the proceeds from the new issue of debt are used to repurchase the equity. Under this assumption, the investment policy of the firm remains unchanged. The *total* value of debt is now 133.65. Since the old debt comprises two thirds of the total debt, its value would become 89.10, a decrease of 10 .90. The semiannual coupon rate for par pricing of the old debt in the presence of new debt would have to be 16.32%. Thus, the bondholders would lose in terms of the promised semiannual coupon yield by 16.32% – 6.02% or 10.30%, if the new debt with an equal priority is issued unexpectedly. Notice that the new bondholders neither gain nor lose because they pay a fair price for the promised payments and do not suffer a reduction in the value of their bonds. The total value of the new bonds is 133.65 – 89.10 or 44.55.

Investment Policy: Suppose the firm that just issued a 6.02% coupon bond, at par, decides to substitute more risky assets for existing, less risky assets. More specifically, under the new, riskier investment policy, the rate of return on the firm is either $u – 1 = 25\%$ or $d – 1 = -25\%$ in each period, as opposed to 20% or –20% under the old, safer investment policy. Assume that the probability of an upward movement, q, in the value of the assets of the firm is 0.75 under both the old and new investment policies. The expected return on the firm is 12.5% and its standard deviation is 21.65% under the new investment policy; while it was 10% and 17.32%, respectively, under the old investment policy.[6] In other words, the new investment policy then results in a higher return and higher (business) risk without changing the total value of the firm today.[7] Under the new investment policy, the bond value becomes 98.10 , a decrease of 1.90. This decrease in the bond value is a direct result of an increase in default risk, which, in turn, is induced by an increase in the business risk or volatility of the value of the firm's assets. The semiannual coupon for par pricing under the new investment policy is 7.20%. Thus, if the bondholders had not anticipated this eventuality, the bondholders lose in terms of the promised semiannual coupon yield by 7.20% − 6.02% = 1.18%.

A recent example of this "risk-shifting" problem is the crisis in the U.S. Savings and Loan Associations. It has been argued that the crisis developed, at least in part, due to the reckless investment strategies pursued by failing thrift institutions. It has been alleged that they enticed investors with high interest rates on their deposits and invested the proceeds in high risk projects. If the projects did well, the shareholders in the thrifts stood to gain substantially. If they failed, the Federal Savings and Loan Insurance Corporation, that guaranteed the deposits, was left holding the bag. One policy recommendation that has been made to prevent further disasters in the industry is for regulatory authorities to automatically suspend dividend payments to the shareholders long before a thrift goes bankrupt. Similar practical illustrations can be given for the other corporate policies that transfer wealth between the claimholders.

In all these examples, a loss to the bondholders will be reflected as a

---

[6]   Expected return $= q (u-1) + (1-q)(d-1)$

$$= \begin{cases} 0.75 \times (+20\%) + 0.25 \times (-20\%) = 10\% \\ 0.75 \times (+25\%) + 0.25 \times (-25\%) = 12.5\% \end{cases}$$

Standard deviation of return $= [\{q (1-q)\}^{1/2} (u-d)]$

$$= \begin{cases} [0.75 \times 0.25]^{1/2} \times (1.20 - 0.80) = 17.32\% \\ [0.75 \times 0.25]^{1/2} \times (1.25 - 0.75) = 21.65\% \end{cases}$$

[7]The value of the firm would also change, in most cases. However, if the "beta" or systematic risk does not change, the firm value would be unaffected. We use the latter assumption in order to keep the computations simple and illustrate the main effect of an increase in volatility, without a corresponding change in firm value.

gain to the stockholders. As stated before, rational bondholders, who anticipate the potential wealth loss, will impose covenants in the bond indenture agreement, restricting the unexpected changes in financial policies that might provide a windfall gain to the stockholders, at the expense of the bondholders. These examples illustrate the rationale behind the restrictive covenants usually contained in the bond indenture agreement. In addition, these examples show that the option pricing model enables us to analyze the impact of changes in firm's financial policies on corporate securities.

We shall now discuss the application of the above approach to the computation of the risk premium for a recent issue of coupon bearing junk bonds.

Coupon Junk Note	*Example*
Issuer	Kay Jewelers Inc.
Issue Size	$100 Million.
Issue Date	July 27, 1989.
Maturity Date	August 1, 1999
Coupon	12.875%
Price	96.5
Call Feature	Callable after August 1, 1994 according to a declining call schedule from 104.828 to 100.
Put Feature	Puttable at par plus accrued interest upon a change in control.
Sinking Fund Feature	On August 1, 1997 and 1998, 25% each.
Security	Unsecured, but *pari passu* with other senior subordinated notes.
Rating	B2 (Moody's).

This issue of coupon bearing notes is below investment grade. As before, we shall ignore the call and sinking fund features and focus on the default risk. We shall also assume that the notes are not called before maturity. The risk of the notes can be quantified in relation to Treasury notes of similar maturity in two ways:

a) Yield of the coupon note in relation to Treasury notes of similar maturity. The yield of the junk bond is given by:

$$96.50 = \frac{12.875/2}{[1 + y\%/2]} + \frac{12.875/2}{[1 + y\%/2]^2} + \ldots + \frac{100 + 12.875/2}{[1 + y\%/2]^{20}}$$

or, $y = 13.52\%$. On the issue date, 10 year Treasury notes were yielding 7.85%. Thus, the risk premium was 5.67%.

b) Price of the coupon note in relation to a Treasury note with the same promised payments. The price of a 10 year Treasury note with an annual coupon of 12.875% would be:

$$\frac{12.875/2}{[1+7.85\%/2]} + \frac{12.875/2}{[1+7.85\%/2]^2} + \ldots + \frac{100 + 12.875/2}{[1 + 7.85\%/2]^{20}}$$

or 134.37, which should be compared with the issue price of the junk bond, 96.50: a difference of 37.87.

One aspect of the above issue that is fairly common today, with the growing importance of takeover threats, through the vehicle of leveraged buyouts or otherwise, is the put feature incorporated into the terms of the issue. In the event of a takeover threat, especially a highly leveraged one, the default risk on the currently outstanding bonds of a firm typically increases substantially, and the market price falls. Since such an eventuality is usually associated with a change in control, a put feature, that is triggered off when this occurs, will protect the interests of the bondholders.

9.4   CALLABLE BONDS

Many corporate bonds have a call provision that allows the firm to repurchase (i.e., call) the bond during a specified period (call period) for a pre-specified price (the call price) plus the accrued coupon since the last coupon date. The call period may start immediately after the issue (immediate call) or, more often than not, after a certain period (call protection period) has elapsed (rolling call). In some cases, such as floating rate notes (FRN's), however, the debt is callable only on coupon dates (stepped call). The call price may be equal to the face value of the bond, or above it. The call price over and above the face value, i.e., the *call premium*, may be fixed over the life of the bond or, more typically, declining over the life of the bond to reach the face value by maturity (a declining call schedule). When the firm decides to call the bond, i.e., exercise its call, it has to notify the bondholders of an impending call before the actual call date. The amount of notice required is generally around 30–45 days for a FRN and 45–90 days for a fixed rate bond.

The firm calls its bond either to refinance the debt at a lower interest cost or to obtain operating flexibility by removing restrictive covenants that may impede mergers, acquisitions, or other major investment projects. A call for refinancing will be exercised either when the general level of interest rates has declined or when the firm's prospects have improved, so that the default risk premium on a new issue can be less than that on the outstanding issues. In this chapter, we abstract from interest rate risk and focus only on firm value uncertainty which affects the default risk of the bonds.[8] In other words, we assume that there is no uncertainty in default-free interest rates such as the yields on U.S. Treasury securities. Therefore, a lower interest cost due to a lower default risk premium is the relevant rationale here for refinancing through a call. Incidentally, most FRN's are subject to little interest rate risk, since, typically, their rates are reset every three or six months. However, they usually have call provisions that permit the firm to take advantage of an unanticipated improvement in its credit quality. Thus, for FRN's, a lower default risk premium is the primary source of benefits from refinancing through a call. Our analysis applies to the case of FRN's, or to an environment where interest rates are quite stable, in relation to the default risk premia. Hence, the main motivation for the firm to call its debt is a decline in its default risk. The firm can, then, refinance its existing debt at a lower promised yield than before by calling it and issuing new debt in its place.

During the call period, the equity of the firm can be viewed as an *American-style* call option on the firm. This contrasts with the equity of the firm that issued discount or coupon bonds without a call provision. Since, as discussed in Chapter 4, the right to exercise an option before the expiration date may have value, the equity of the firm with a callable bond should not be less valuable than that of a firm with an otherwise comparable non-callable bond. By the same token, the callable bond should not be more valuable than an otherwise comparable non-callable bond. This follows

---

[8]The effect of interest rate risk on the value of callable bonds is discussed in Chapter 8 , dealing with the valuation of bond options. The interaction between default risk and interest rate risk, which is important in some practical problems, makes the analysis much more complex.

from the Modigliani-Miller proposition, under which the value of the firm, i.e., the sum of the debt and equity values, is a constant.

How should we value a callable bond? In order to answer this question, note first that the equilibrium value of a callable bond is defined as that value which does not offer an opportunity of arbitrage profit to investors, given that the firm pursues an optimal policy with respect to calling the bonds. Given this sensible definition of the equilibrium value of a callable bond, we then have to determine *when* it is optimal for the firm to call the bonds.

When does it then pay to call the bonds? From our previous discussion, we first note that, given the total value of the firm's assets, the value of the firm's equity is maximized by pursuing a call strategy that minimizes the value of the callable bonds. The firm should, therefore, not allow the callable bonds to rise in value above the price at which it is currently callable, K (excluding accrued interest). Hence, under an optimal call strategy, the ex-coupon value of a callable bond will never exceed the call price: $B \leq K$. On the other hand, it will not be optimal to call the bonds when the ex-coupon value is less than the call price, since this would result in a windfall gain to the bondholders at the expense of the stockholders. Therefore, the optimal call strategy dictates that the firm should call the bond when its ex-coupon value reaches the call price: i.e., call when $B = K$.

An alternative way of determining the optimal call strategy is as follows. First, we can express the value of the callable bond as the difference between the value of an otherwise comparable non-callable bond, B_{NC}, and the value of a call option, C. That is,

$$B = B_{NC} - C, \tag{9.15}$$

Equation (9.15) can be rewritten as:

$$C = (B_{NC} - K) + (K - B) \tag{9.16}$$

Equation (9.16) can be interpreted in an interesting manner. Note from the equation that the firm can minimize the value of the callable bond by maximizing the value of the call option. In order to keep the capital structure of the firm, i.e., the mix of debt and equity, constant, assume that, after the call, the firm will issue an otherwise comparable non-callable bond. The payoff to the firm is the exercise value of such a call option, i.e., max $[B_{NC} - K, 0]$. However, even if this exercise value, $B_{NC} - K$, is positive, the firm may not exercise the call. As with any American option, a positive exercise value will not, in general, trigger early exercise. This is because the firm may lose the "premium" of the call option over the exercise value, $K - B$, if the bond is called when the premium is positive. What is the optimal exercise policy, or when is the call value at a maximum? The firm should wait until the interest cost is sufficiently low so that the premium over the exercise value reaches zero. This occurs when the market price of the callable bond reaches the call price.[9]

We now turn to the valuation of a callable bond. It should be clear from our discussion, so far, that the value of a callable bond depends on the optimal call strategy which investors *believe* the firm will pursue. The valuation should then incorporate a call policy constraint dictated by an optimal call strategy, i.e., $B \leq K$. Under this constraint, before maturity, the value of a callable bond without accrued interest is min $[B, K]$; i.e., the value of a bond when not called, or the call price, whichever is lower. The top panel of Figure 9–6 describes the possible values of a callable bond when the bond can be called at the call price K at time 1.

The value of the bond at time 1 is the lower of the price when called, and when not called, after accrued interest has been taken into account. If the bond is not called, the bond "lives" for one more period, with the payoffs at time 2 being dependent on the value of the firm's assets, as in the case of the straight (i.e., non-callable) bond.

Numerical Example 3: Suppose the firm pays no dividends on the stock at time 1. In order to allow comparison with a non-callable bond, let us assume that the semi-annual coupon yield is as assumed in Numerical Example 2, 6.02%, and the face value is 100. Assume that the call price on an ex-coupon basis is 100 (i.e., 106.02 on a cum-coupon basis). As shown in the lower panel of Figure 9–6, if the firm value increases at time 1 the cum-coupon bond value, when not called, is 106.99, which exceeds the call price plus the accrued coupon of 106.02. Thus, the firm will call the bond at time 1 in this state and its value becomes 106.02. (Note that in a model with more stages and smaller changes per stage, the call is optimal when the bond value, when not called, *just* exceeds the call price.) On the other hand, if the firm value decreases at time 1, the cum-coupon bond value, 101.69, when not called, is less than the call price plus the accrued interest, 106.02.

---

[9]We shall discuss later observed departures from this exercise criterion.

FIGURE 9–6
Possible values of a callable bond over two periods

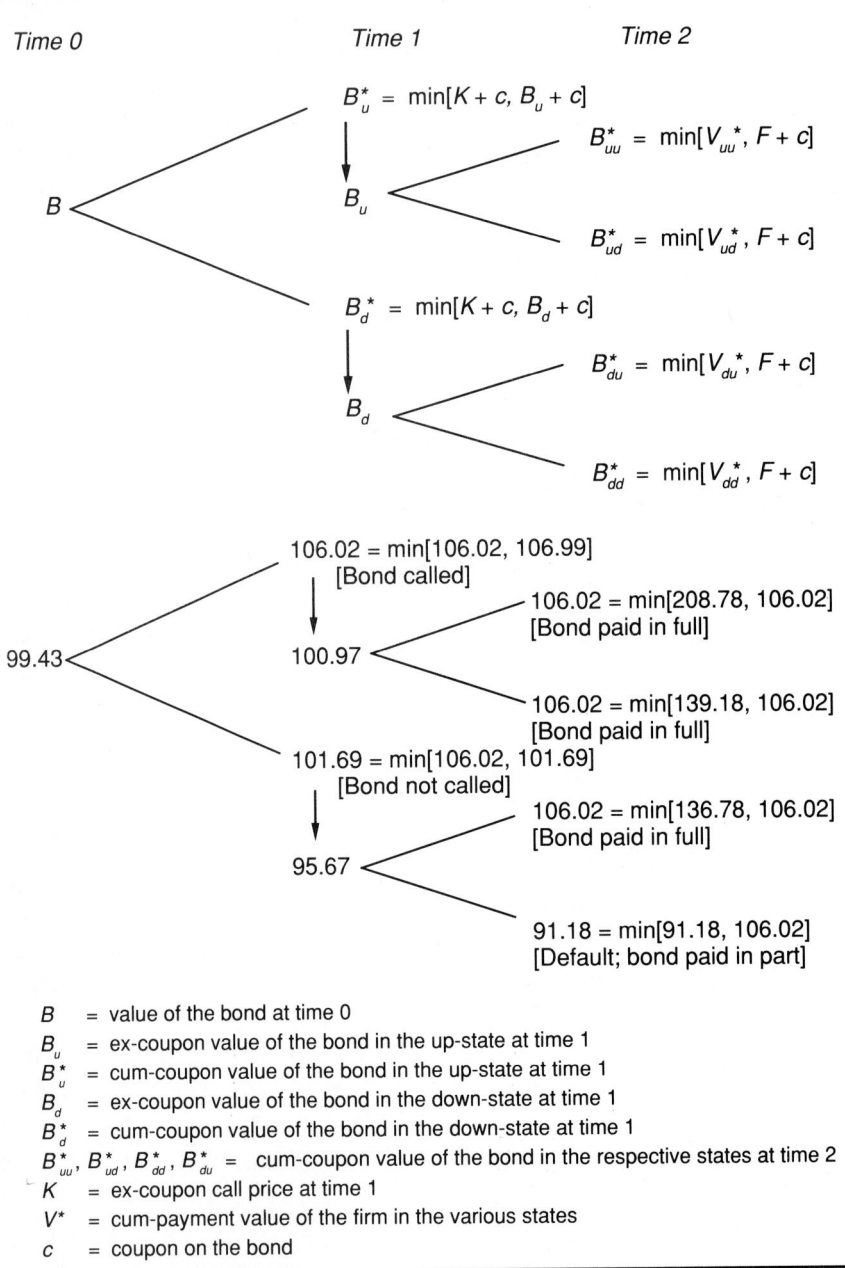

Time 0	*Time 1*	*Time 2*

$B_u^* = \min[K + c, B_u + c]$

$B_{uu}^* = \min[V_{uu}^*, F + c]$

B_u

$B_{ud}^* = \min[V_{ud}^*, F + c]$

B

$B_d^* = \min[K + c, B_d + c]$

$B_{du}^* = \min[V_{du}^*, F + c]$

B_d

$B_{dd}^* = \min[V_{dd}^*, F + c]$

$106.02 = \min[106.02, 106.99]$
[Bond called]

$106.02 = \min[208.78, 106.02]$
[Bond paid in full]

100.97

$106.02 = \min[139.18, 106.02]$
[Bond paid in full]

99.43

$101.69 = \min[106.02, 101.69]$
[Bond not called]

$106.02 = \min[136.78, 106.02]$
[Bond paid in full]

95.67

$91.18 = \min[91.18, 106.02]$
[Default; bond paid in part]

B	= value of the bond at time 0
B_u	= ex-coupon value of the bond in the up-state at time 1
B_u^*	= cum-coupon value of the bond in the up-state at time 1
B_d	= ex-coupon value of the bond in the down-state at time 1
B_d^*	= cum-coupon value of the bond in the down-state at time 1
$B_{uu}^*, B_{ud}^*, B_{dd}^*, B_{du}^*$	= cum-coupon value of the bond in the respective states at time 2
K	= ex-coupon call price at time 1
V^*	= cum-payment value of the firm in the various states
c	= coupon on the bond

Thus, the firm will not call the bond in this state. The current bond value is shown to be equal to 99.43. The call option then has a value of $100 - 99.43 = 0.57$. Alternatively, the semi-annual coupon yield for par pricing of the callable bond can be computed to be 6.56%. Therefore, the additional coupon to be promised to investors to compensate them for the call option owned by equity holders is $6.56 - 6.02 = 0.54$ or an incremental yield of 0.54%. It is easy to demonstrate that if the promised yield differs from 6.56% when the non-callable bond yields 6.02%, there is an arbitrage opportunity. We leave this as an exercise to the reader.

We shall now discuss a recent issue of callable bonds to illustrate the application of some of these concepts.

Callable Bond	*Example*
Issuer	Texas Instruments Inc.
Issue Size	$150 Million.
Issue Date	July 16, 1989.
Maturity Date	July 15, 1999.
Coupon	9%.
Price	99.40
Call Feature	Callable on or after July 15, 1996 at par plus accrued interest.
Sinking Fund Feature	None.
Security	Unsecured.
Rating	A1 (Moody's)

This note can be thought of as a non-callable note on similar terms *minus* a 7-year call option on a three year note (maturing in 1999). The *direct* valuation of such an option requires the application of the principles of bond option valuation discussed in Chapter 8. However, we can get an *indirect* valuation of the call option by a comparison with a non-callable note of similar maturity and risk.

On July 14, 1989, 10-year Treasury notes were yielding 8.02%. Assuming a yield spread of 60 basis points of A1 notes over Treasury notes of 10 year maturity, a non-callable note by an issuer with a similar rating would have yielded approximately 8.62%. In other words, the price of a *non-callable* note with a similar coupon would be:

$$\frac{9/2}{[1 + 8.62\% \ / \ 2]} + \frac{9/2}{[1 + 8.62\% \ / \ 2]^2} + \ldots + \frac{100 + 9/2}{[1 + 8.62\% \ / \ 2]^{20}}$$

$$= \ 102.51$$

By writing a call option *and* buying a non-callable note with a similar coupon and maturity from the issuer, the investor has reduced his investment to 99.40. The implicit price of the call option is, therefore, 102.51 − 99.40, or 3.11. Alternatively, we could compare the yield to maturity on the callable note with the yield to maturity on an otherwise similar non-callable note. The yield to maturity on the callable note is given by:

$$99.40 = \frac{9/2}{[1 + \ y\%/2]} + \frac{9/2}{[1 + \ y\%/2]^2} + \ldots + \frac{100 + 9/2}{[1 + \ y\%/2]^{20}}$$

or, $y = 9.09\%$, compared with the yield on the comparable non-callable note of 8.62%.

We now turn to a discussion of the empirical evidence on the exercise of the call option by firms issuing callable (but non-convertible) bonds. As mentioned earlier, the decision to call such bonds may be motivated by either a decline in the general level of default-free interest rates, or an improvement in the credit standing of the firm. (Our analysis in this chapter has focused on the latter argument. In the chapter on bond options, Chapter 8, the other motivation is discussed). In a study of 133 calls of non-convertible callable bonds by Vu (1986) over the period October 1962 to April 1978, it was found that:

a) most firms in the sample called their non-convertible bonds when the market value was below the call price. The average discount of the market price of the bond to the call price just before the announcement date was found to be 4.7%.

b) several firms in the sample did not call their bonds even when the market prices of the bonds exceeded the call price. The delay in many cases was as long as 12 months.

c) When bonds were called for refunding purposes (i.e., reissued at a lower promised yield), there was a decline in the average coupon from 6.14% to 5.76%, a drop of about 38 basis points.

We may conclude from this evidence that there may be other factors that influence the decision of a firm to call its bonds besides those relating to interest rate risk and default risk. A fruitful area of current research in this area is the role of asymmetric information between the firm and the bondholders regarding the future prospects of the firm.

9.5   CONVERTIBLE BONDS

A convertible bond offers investors the right to convert the bond into the stock of the issuing firm during the conversion period at the specified conversion terms. The *conversion* ratio states the number of shares of common stock into which a bond can be converted. Alternatively, bond-holders can convert their bonds into shares of common stock at the specified *conversion price*, which is defined as the face value of the bond divided by the conversion ratio.

The conversion terms expressed either way can, however, be restated in a manner that is easier to interpret for our purpose. Suppose there is a single issue of convertible bonds and all bondholders behave identically in exercising their conversion options.[10] We can then express the conversion terms more simply in terms of the dilution factor, "*a*." Noting that con-version requires the firm to issue new shares of stock, we define the *dilution factor* as the fraction of the post-conversion equity value that accrues to the bondholders. For example, if there are 40 shares of common stock outstanding and the entire convertible bond can be exchanged for 60 shares of common stock, then, upon conversion, the bondholders will hold 60 / (40 + 60) = 60% of the post-conversion equity value. In this case, the dilution factor, a, would be 60%. If there are no securities outstanding other than stocks and convertible bonds, then the post-conversion equity value will be equal to the firm value.   In this case, the conversion value of the convertible bond is simply aV, where V is the value of the firm's assets.

A convertible bond can be viewed as a package of an otherwise comparable non-convertible bond plus warrants which are essentially call options written on the issuing firm's common stock.[11] Conceptually, a convertible bond would then be equivalent to a non-convertible bond with warrants attached, where the warrants are not detachable from the non-

---

[10]The effect of relaxing this assumption is discussed in Section 9.7 below.

[11]Warrants are discussed in Section 9.7 below. Also, there are other types of convertible securities, such as debt with warrants attached and convertible preferred stock, which can be valued using the same principles. It should be noted that there are differences, in details, between a convertible bond and a package of debt with warrants attached, e.g., the scrip used for the exercise of the option, tax treatment, and so forth.

convertible bond and the bond has to be used as the scrip (in lieu of cash) in exercising the warrants.

How should we value a convertible bond? As was done for a callable bond, we first define the equilibrium value of a convertible bond. However, in this case, the option is to be exercised by the bondholders rather than by the stockholders. The equilibrium value of the bond is the value that does not offer an arbitrage opportunity to the bondholders, given that the bondholders pursue an optimal strategy with respect to conversion. Given this definition, we then need to determine when it is optimal to exercise the conversion option. Later on, the optimal conversion strategy will be incorporated in the valuation problem as the boundary condition the equilibrium bond value must satisfy.

We first discuss the optimal conversion policy and the constraint on value imposed by it on the maturity date. At maturity, the convertible bond-holder receives the higher of two values: either the value of the shares the bonds could be converted into, or the face value of the bond plus the terminal coupon. The firm value at maturity, V_T, is above, below, or equal to the promised payment, $F + c$, where F is the face value of the bond, and c is the coupon payment. If it is less than the promised payment, the firm will default and the bondholders will receive the firm value. If it is equal to the promised payment, the firm will not default, but the bondholders will still receive the firm value. If, on the other hand, the firm value exceeds the promised payment, the bondholders will receive either the conversion value, aV_T, or the promised payment, $F + c$, whichever is larger. Hence, the value of the convertible bond is max $[aV_T, \min (V_T, F + c)]$, where V_T is the firm value at maturity.[12]

We now turn to the optimal conversion policy and the convertible bond value constraint on the maturity date. Note first that the bondholders will always find it optimal to convert the bond if its value, when not converted, falls below the conversion value. Therefore, the cum-coupon value of a convertible bond can never fall below the conversion value. On the other hand, it will never be optimal to convert if the bond value, when not converted, exceeds the conversion value. Therefore, the convertible bond will be optimally converted when its value is equal to the conversion value. Under the above optimal conversion strategy, the value of the convertible bond will be max $[aV, B + c]$, i.e., the conversion value or the

---

[12]This terminal value can be equivalently expressed as $\min[V_T, \max (aV_T, F + c)]$.

cum-coupon value of the convertible bond, whichever is higher. Note that the above constraint to be satisfied by the value of the convertible bond presumes that conversion does not carry an accrued coupon. This presumption reflects not only the substitution, upon conversion, of dividends for coupons for long term bonds, but also the institutional fact that for most convertible bonds, the bondholders do not receive the accrued interest upon conversion.[13]

Before we value a convertible bond by incorporating the constraint on value, max $[aV, B + c]$, we shall examine more closely the optimal conversion strategy that led to the above constraint. For the purpose of simple exposition, let us assume, for the time being, that the bond will mature one period hence. The ex-coupon value of the bond is then just the present value of the payoff on the bond on the maturity date. Therefore, the current cum-coupon bond value when not converted can be expressed as:

$$c + B = c + PV\{\max[aV_T, \min(V_T, F + c)]\} \qquad (9.17)$$

where $PV\{\cdot\}$ indicates the present value of $\{\cdot\}$.

Suppose further, again for expositional simplicity, that the current value of the firm, V, is sufficiently high that the firm will not default at maturity. Making use of the fact that the present value of the firm value at maturity, $PV(V_T)$, is equal to the current ex-payout value of the firm, $V - c - D$, where D is the amount of the dividend paid, we can rewrite the equation (9.17) as:

$$
\begin{aligned}
c + B &= c + PV\{\max[aV_T, \min(V_T, F + c)]\} \\
&= c + PV\{\max[aV_T, F + c]\} \\
&= c + PV\{aV_T + \max[0, F + c - aV_T]\} \qquad (9.18) \\
&= c + a(V - c - D) + PV\{\max[0, F + c - aV_T]\} \\
&= aV + [(1 - a)c - aD] + PV\{\max[0, F + c - aV_T]\}
\end{aligned}
$$

In other words, the cum-coupon bond price is equal to the current coupon plus the present value of the terminal cash flow on the bond. The latter can be defined as the higher of the payoffs with and without conversion. Redefining the conversion value as an increment over the value without conversion, the cum-coupon bond price can be written as the sum

---

[13]This is true also for involuntary conversions, as in the case of callable convertible bonds to be discussed in Section 9.6 below.

of the three terms in the last line of equation (9.18), (a) proportion of the value of the firm, (b) a term that indicates that the bondholder receives the current coupon but gives up the dividend by not converting early, and (c) the value of the option not to convert on the expiration date. Where there is more than one period left until maturity, it can be shown that the second term on the right hand side of the above equation is replaced by its present value.[14] Thus, we obtain:

$$c + B = aV + PV[(1 - a)c - aD] + PV\{\max [0, F + c - aV_T]\} \quad (9.19)$$

In equation (9.19), we have decomposed the value of a convertible bond into three parts:

a. the conversion value, aV;
b. the present value of a quantity called the "yield advantage" of the bond relative to the stock, $PV[(1 - a)c - aD]$, i.e., the benefit of receiving coupon payments on the bonds, rather than dividend payments on the stock; and
c. the value of a European option to "put" the conversion value at maturity and receive the promised payment, $PV\{\max[0, F + c - aV_T]\}$.

Since the value of a put option is *never* negative, it follows that a convertible bond will never be converted if the yield advantage is positive.[15] For example, if dividends are not paid on the stocks, a convertible bond should not be prematurely converted for the same reason that an American call option on non-dividend paying stocks should not be exercised early as discussed in Chapter 4. This is because, by converting a bond, the bond-holders not only forgo coupons but also give up a valuable option not to convert at maturity.

On the other hand, if the dividends to be paid are large enough to make the yield advantage negative, it *may* pay to prematurely exercise a conversion option. The necessary, but not sufficient, condition for early exercise is then $(1 - a)c - aD < 0$ or $c < a(c + D)$. Under the assumption that the total cash payout by the firm does not change following a conversion, the condition states that early exercise of the conversion option *may* be

---

[14]We assume here that the interim coupon and dividend are known with certainty. Also, c and D can be interpreted as multiple coupons and dividends by indexing them by the date of payment in the future.
[15]If there is a positive probability of default at maturity, the value of the put option will be less than stated in equation (9.19). Nevertheless, the put will have some non-zero value, in general.

FIGURE 9–7
Possible values of convertible bonds over two periods (without dividends)

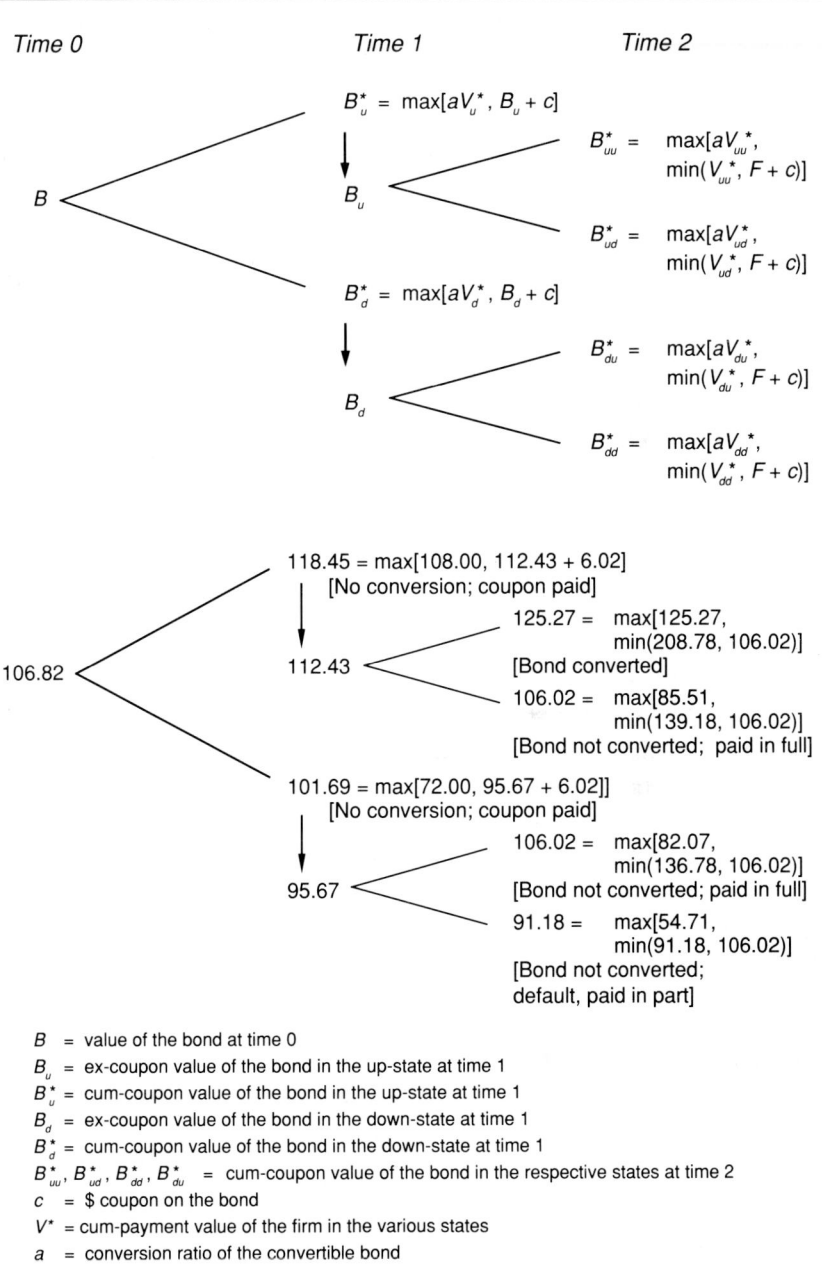

Time 0	*Time 1*	*Time 2*

$B_u^* = \max[aV_u^*, B_u + c]$

$B_{uu}^* = \max[aV_{uu}^*, \min(V_{uu}^*, F + c)]$

$B_{ud}^* = \max[aV_{ud}^*, \min(V_{ud}^*, F + c)]$

$B_d^* = \max[aV_d^*, B_d + c]$

$B_{du}^* = \max[aV_{du}^*, \min(V_{du}^*, F + c)]$

$B_{dd}^* = \max[aV_{dd}^*, \min(V_{dd}^*, F + c)]$

$118.45 = \max[108.00, 112.43 + 6.02]$
[No conversion; coupon paid]

$125.27 = \max[125.27, \min(208.78, 106.02)]$
[Bond converted]

$106.02 = \max[85.51, \min(139.18, 106.02)]$
[Bond not converted; paid in full]

$101.69 = \max[72.00, 95.67 + 6.02]]$
[No conversion; coupon paid]

$106.02 = \max[82.07, \min(136.78, 106.02)]$
[Bond not converted; paid in full]

$91.18 = \max[54.71, \min(91.18, 106.02)]$
[Bond not converted; default, paid in part]

B = value of the bond at time 0
B_u = ex-coupon value of the bond in the up-state at time 1
B_u^* = cum-coupon value of the bond in the up-state at time 1
B_d = ex-coupon value of the bond in the down-state at time 1
B_d^* = cum-coupon value of the bond in the down-state at time 1
$B_{uu}^*, B_{ud}^*, B_{dd}^*, B_{du}^*$ = cum-coupon value of the bond in the respective states at time 2
c = $ coupon on the bond
V^* = cum-payment value of the firm in the various states
a = conversion ratio of the convertible bond

beneficial to the bondholders. This happens if the amount of coupon payments they will forgo after conversion, c, is less than the fraction of total payout, $a(c + D)$, they will receive as dividends after conversion.

The necessary condition for early exercise may be alternatively stated in terms of the yields. To see this, denote by i and k, the current yield on the bond and the dividend yield on the stock, respectively. The necessary condition can then be rewritten as $iB < a(iB + kS)$. When early conversion occurs, the bond price equals its conversion value, $B = aV$, hence $S = (1 - a)V$.

Substituting these expressions into the condition, we find an equivalent condition in terms of the yields: $i < k$. Thus, $(1 - a) c - aD$ can be interpreted as the yield advantage of bonds. In sum, an early conversion will occur only when the present value of the bond's yield advantage is sufficiently negative to offset the loss of the value of the put option to receive the face value plus the terminal coupon on the bond rather than the conversion value.

The top panel of Figure 9–7 illustrates the possible values of a convertible bond. Here, it is assumed that the bond can be converted into a fraction of the post-conversion equity value (i.e., the firm value in the absence of other securities) at time 1 or at time 2 (maturity). As in the case of the callable bond in the previous section, the valuation problem and the optimal conversion strategies are solved for simultaneously.

Numerical Example 4: Suppose a firm that pays no dividends on its stock issues a bond with a 6.02% semi-annual coupon and a face value of 100. Suppose this bond can be converted into 60% of firm value either at time 1 or at time 2 (maturity). The current bond value is then 106.82, as shown in the lower panel of Figure 9–7. Thus, the value of conversion option is $106.82 - 100 = 6.82$ (the difference between a convertible bond and a non-convertible bond with an identical semi-annual coupon). Notice that the bondholders will convert the bond if the most favorable outcome for firm value, $V_{uu}*$, is realized at maturity. However, the bond will not be converted at time 1, even if the firm value increases over the first period. Thus, this is an example showing that a convertible bond will not be converted before maturity, since no dividends are paid on the stock until maturity.

Previously, we showed that if the yield advantage is positive, it is never optimal to prematurely exercise the conversion option. In our example, since for the given coupon and other parameter values, the dividend is less than 4.01 [$D < (1 - a) c / a = (1 - 0.6) \times 6.02 / 0.6 = 4.01$], the convertible bond will not be converted at time 1. Thus, the minimum dividend, at time 1, above which a conversion *may* be triggered, is 4.01. On the other hand, the minimum dividend over and above which a conversion *is* triggered can be calculated using the equation (9.19), which takes into account both the "yield advantage" and the value of the put option—to receive the promised payments rather than the conversion value—forgone by early conversion. For example, if the firm value increases to 180 at time 1, the firm value in the next period, time 2, will become either $1.2 \times (180 - 6.02 - D)$ or $0.8 \times (180 - 6.02 - D)$. Thus, solving after substituting in equation (9.19) yields:

$$[(1 - 0.6) \times 6.02 - 0.6D] +$$
$$[0.625(0) + 0.375\{106.02 - 0.6(0.8)(180 - 6.02\text{-}D)\}] / 1.05$$
$$= 2.408 - 0.6D + 8.039 + 0.171D$$
$$= 10.447 - 0.429D$$

which should be set to be equal to 0.

In other words, the minimum dividend to trigger early conversion is 24.38.[16] Here, because the value of put option, 12.22, is fairly large due to the short maturity of the bond, the minimum dividend at which conversion is triggered is also very large relative to the semiannual coupon. For convertible bonds with a longer maturity, however, even a slightly negative yield advantage *may* trigger a conversion, since the present value of the difference between the dividend and the coupon payments over a long period of time may be considerable.

In Figure 9–8, we consider the case of a 25 dividend at time 1. The firm value declines at time 1 by 31.02, (the sum of the 25 dividend and the coupon payment of 6.02). In this case, it pays for the convertible bondholder to convert the bond in the up-state at time 1, just before the stock goes ex-dividend, in order to receive the 25 dividend.

---

[16]Readers may confirm from Figure 9–8 that a dividend of 25 will trigger conversion at time 1, if the firm value is V_u^* and $B = 98.05$.

FIGURE 9–8
**Possible values of the firm and convertible bonds over two
periods (with dividends)**

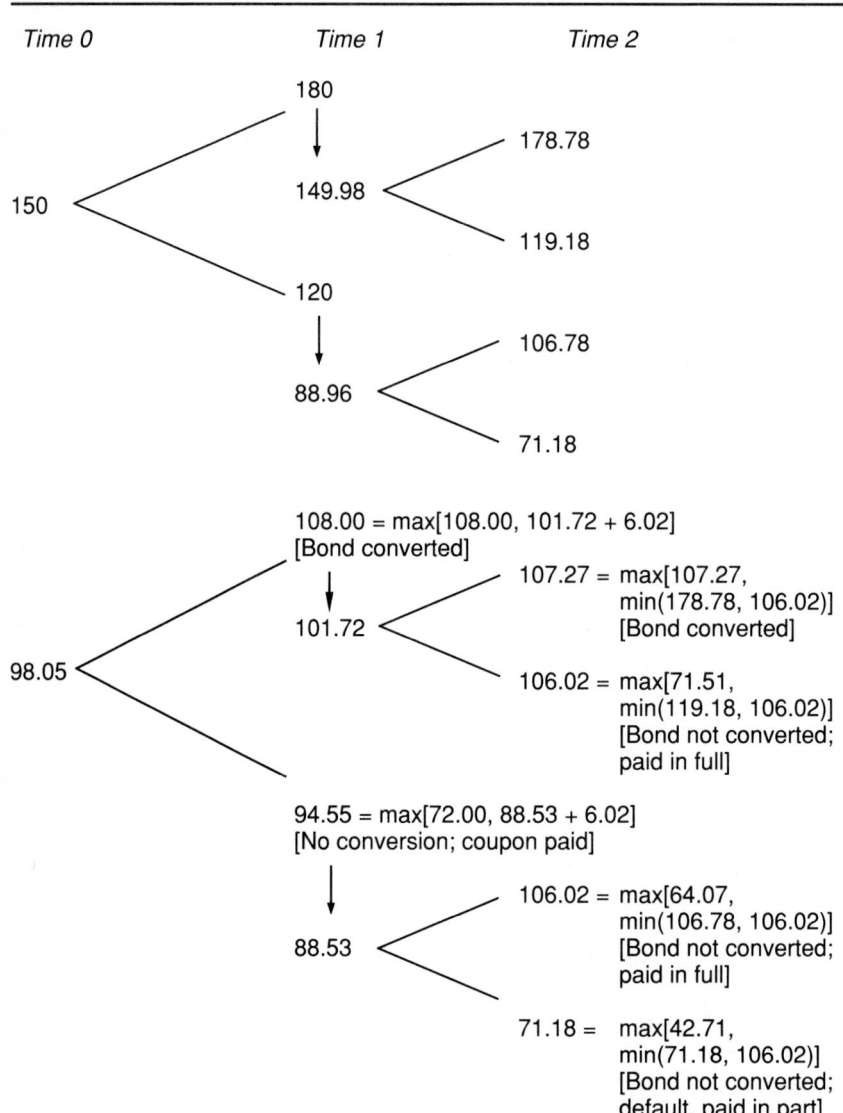

Time 0	Time 1	Time 2

180
↓
149.98
178.78
119.18
150
120
↓
88.96
106.78
71.18

108.00 = max[108.00, 101.72 + 6.02]
[Bond converted]
↓
101.72
107.27 = max[107.27,
min(178.78, 106.02)]
[Bond converted]
106.02 = max[71.51,
min(119.18, 106.02)]
[Bond not converted;
paid in full]
98.05
94.55 = max[72.00, 88.53 + 6.02]
[No conversion; coupon paid]
↓
88.53
106.02 = max[64.07,
min(106.78, 106.02)]
[Bond not converted;
paid in full]
71.18 =   max[42.71,
min(71.18, 106.02)]
[Bond not converted;
default, paid in part]

9.6   CALLABLE-CONVERTIBLE BONDS

Callable-convertible bonds offer the firm the right to call the bond, and the bondholders the right to convert the bond into shares of common stock. The equilibrium value of such a bond is the value at which there is no arbitrage opportunity to investors, given that the firm follows the optimal call policy and the bondholders follow the optimal conversion policy. As before, we shall first determine the optimal strategies with respect to call and conversion. The value constraints implied by these optimal exercise policies are then incorporated into the analysis in valuing the callable convertible bond.

Let us denote by B^* the cum-coupon value of the callable convertible bond when neither called nor converted. Similarly, denote by K^* the call price plus the accrued coupon. Since the callable bond is (trivially) called at maturity, if the firm value exceeds the promised payment, the value of the callable convertible at maturity is the same as that of an otherwise comparable, non-callable convertible bond.

Now, we turn to the optimal exercise strategies before maturity.[17] Note first that the optimal strategies will depend on (a) the relative magnitude of the conversion value, aV, (b) the call price plus the accrued coupon, K^*, and (c) the cum-coupon value of the bond when kept "alive," i.e., neither called nor converted, B^*. Since, as we shall see shortly, there is a potential interaction between the conversion and call decisions, it is necessary to determine the optimal strategies on dates before maturity by examining all possible cases regarding the relative magnitudes of aV, B^*, and K^*.

Case 1: $aV > B^*$: Convert voluntarily

If the conversion value exceeds the value of the bond when "alive," then the bondholders will voluntarily convert the bond into shares of common stock. Once the bond is converted, the firm's call option is extinguished as well. This is similar to the previous case of (non-callable) convertible bonds.

Case 2: $aV < B^*$: Do not convert voluntarily

If the conversion value is less than the value of the bond when alive, the bondholders will not convert the bond voluntarily, but may be forced to do

---

[17]We ignore exercise strategies relating to the transfer of control rights between the old shareholders and the convertible bond holders, for example, in takeover contests.

so if the bond is called by the issuer before the maturity date. Given this condition, when will the firm call the bond? There are two cases in which the firm will call the bond: (a) to force conversion and (b) to refinance on more favorable terms.

Case 2.1: $K^* < aV < B^*$: Call to force conversion

In this case, the conversion value is more than the call price, but less than the bond value when "alive." Since the firm acts in the interests of its *current* shareholders, it has an incentive to minimize the bond value. This can be done by calling the bond. Upon being called, the bondholders will convert the bond because the conversion value exceeds the call price. Thus, the optimal call policy for forcing conversion can be stated as follows: the firm should call as soon as the conversion value reaches the call price, K^*. This optimal call strategy is sensible because, through a call, the firm can "kill" the bondholder's conversion option early, i.e., it can revoke the bondholders' opportunity to participate in the upward movement in the stock prices, without losing their downside protection. In other words, the firm can remove a class of "superior" (potential) shareholders enjoying upside potential and downside protection, thus protecting the interests of the present shareholders.

Case 2.2: $aV < K^* < B^*$: Call to refinance

In this case, the firm will not call the bond in order to force conversion because the call price exceeds the conversion value. Upon being called, the bondholders will surrender the bond and receive the call price. This case is, however, a pathological one, if the only uncertainty is in the value of the firm's assets, and not in the level of the default-free interest rates of similar maturity. This is because, given that the call price is no less than the face value, the bond value is not likely to be more than the call price, when the conversion value is less than the call price. This case is, however, likely to happen in the presence of interest rate uncertainty for a firm whose value is positively related to the level of interest rates. Hence, when the general level of default-free interest rates declines, the value of the firm falls. Although there is no incentive to call the bond to force conversion, there may be an incentive to call the bond because interest rates are low, and the bond price is at or above its call price. This is similar to the rationale for calling a non-convertible, callable bond.

Case 2.3: $aV < B^* < K$: Do nothing

In this case, neither the bondholders nor the firm have an incentive to exercise their options.

The value constraint implied by the optimal conversion and call strategies before maturity can be written as $\max[aV, \min(K^*, B^*)]$. In the two-period binomial case, the movement of the callable convertible bond value can be represented by the binomial process in the top panel of Figure 9–9.

Numerical Example 5: Suppose the 6.02% semi-annual coupon bond, with a face value of 100 is callable at par plus the accrued coupon, and convertible into 60% of the firm value, with both options exercisable either at time 1 or at time 2 (maturity). If the firm pays no dividends at time 1, then, as shown in the lower panel of Figure 9–9, the bond will not be voluntarily converted at time 1, because its conversion value, 108, is less than the bond value "alive," 118.45. The bond value alive, 118.45, at time 1, exceeds the call price plus the coupon, 106.02. Thus, the firm would find it worthwhile to call the bond. Since the conversion value, 108, exceeds the call price plus the coupon, 106.02, the bondholders would always convert the bond upon a call notice by the firm, although this is less desirable from the bondholders' point of view than keeping the conversion option "alive." The current value of the bond is shown to be 100.60. The semiannual coupon for par pricing in this example is 4.76%.

By a similar calculation, if the firm pays a dividend of 25 at time 1, the bond value "alive" at time 1 becomes 107.74 if the firm value goes up over the first period (see Figure 9–8). Since it is less than the conversion value, 108, the bondholders will voluntarily convert the bond at time 1 to capture some of the dividend. If the firm value falls over the first period, neither a conversion nor a call occurs. Readers may confirm that the current bond value in this case is 98.05, which is the same as the value of the non-callable convertible bond in footnote 16 and Figure 9–8 when the firm pays a dividend of 25 at time 1.

FIGURE 9–9
Possible values of a callable, convertible bond over two periods

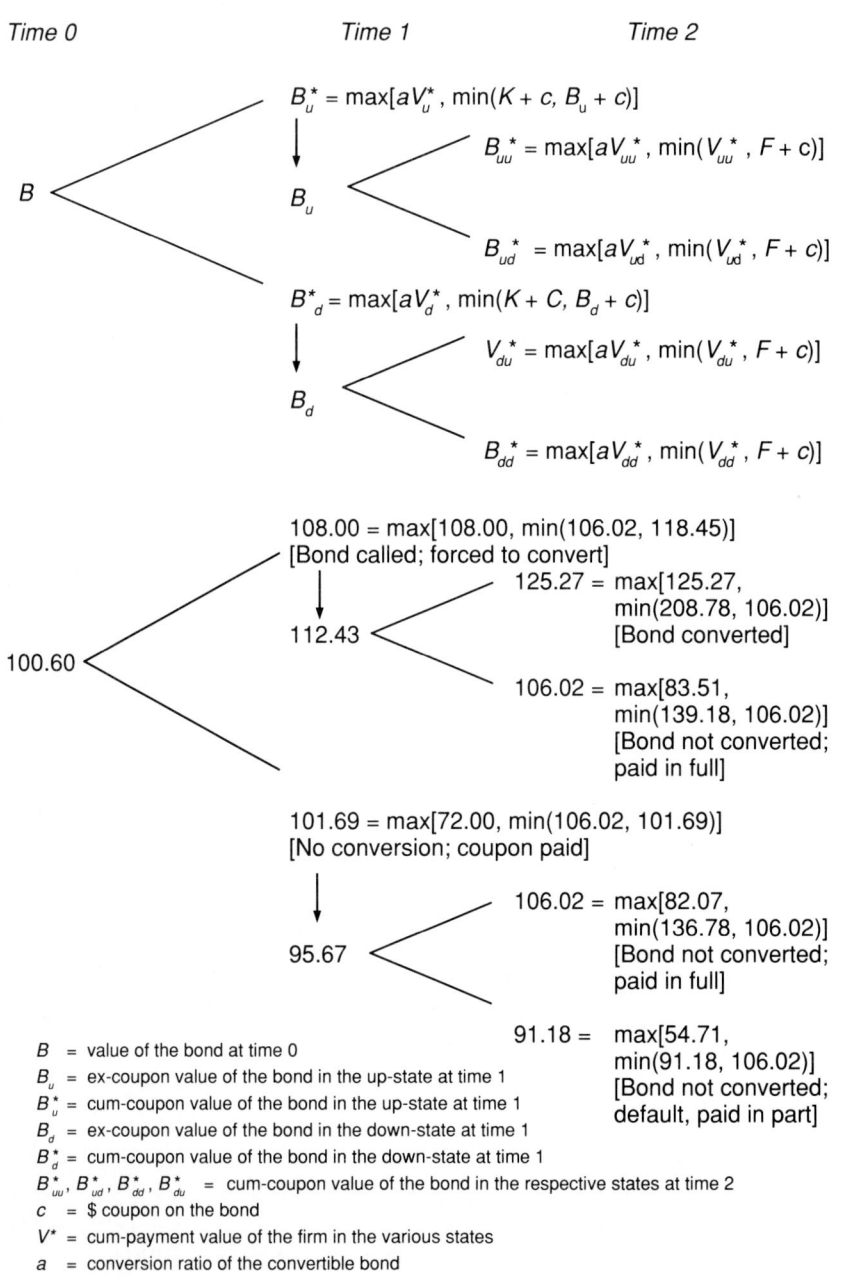

Time 0	Time 1	Time 2

$B_u^* = \max[aV_u^*, \min(K + c, B_u + c)]$

$B_{uu}^* = \max[aV_{uu}^*, \min(V_{uu}^*, F + c)]$

B_u

$B_{ud}^* = \max[aV_{ud}^*, \min(V_{ud}^*, F + c)]$

$B_d^* = \max[aV_d^*, \min(K + C, B_d + c)]$

$V_{du}^* = \max[aV_{du}^*, \min(V_{du}^*, F + c)]$

B_d

$B_{dd}^* = \max[aV_{dd}^*, \min(V_{dd}^*, F + c)]$

108.00 = max[108.00, min(106.02, 118.45)]
[Bond called; forced to convert]

125.27 = max[125.27, min(208.78, 106.02)]
[Bond converted]

112.43

106.02 = max[83.51, min(139.18, 106.02)]
[Bond not converted; paid in full]

100.60

101.69 = max[72.00, min(106.02, 101.69)]
[No conversion; coupon paid]

106.02 = max[82.07, min(136.78, 106.02)]
[Bond not converted; paid in full]

95.67

91.18 = max[54.71, min(91.18, 106.02)]
[Bond not converted; default, paid in part]

B = value of the bond at time 0
B_u = ex-coupon value of the bond in the up-state at time 1
B_u^* = cum-coupon value of the bond in the up-state at time 1
B_d = ex-coupon value of the bond in the down-state at time 1
B_d^* = cum-coupon value of the bond in the down-state at time 1
$B_{uu}^*, B_{ud}^*, B_{dd}^*, B_{du}^*$ = cum-coupon value of the bond in the respective states at time 2
c = $ coupon on the bond
V^* = cum-payment value of the firm in the various states
a = conversion ratio of the convertible bond

We shall illustrate some of these concepts using the example of a recent issue of callable and puttable convertible bonds.

Callable Convertible Bond	*Example*
Issuer	Alaska Air Group Inc.
Issue Size	$75 Million of Convertible Subordinated Debentures
Issue Date	June 20, 1989
Maturity Date	June 15, 2014
Coupon	6.875%
Price	100
Call Feature	Callable after July 1, 1992 at 104.8, declining annually to 100 on June 15, 1999.
Put Feature	Puttable by the holder at par plus accrued interest, in the event of a change in control.
Sinking Fund Feature	Annual sinking fund, beginning in 1999, to retire at least 60% of the debentures before maturity.
Security	Unsecured
Rating	Ba3 (Moody's)

We shall ignore the call feature of the issue and focus on the convertibility feature alone. The price of a non-convertible bond with the same promised payments would be:

$$\frac{6.875/2}{[1 + y\% / 2]} + \frac{6.875/2}{[1 + y\%/2]^2} + \ldots + \frac{100 + 6.875/2}{[1 + y\%/2]^{50}}$$

If the market yield for such a bond was 12%, the price would be 59.61. Since the actual price is par or 100, the value of the convertibility feature *plus* the put feature *minus* the call feature is 40.39. Of course, in principle, the value of the convertibility and call features could have been computed directly, although the methods for doing so are quite complex.

The empirical evidence regarding the decision to call convertible bonds seems to indicate departures from the conceptual framework discussed above. We shall discuss two empirical studies of the call policies of firms that issued callable, convertible bonds. The earlier study by Ingersoll (1977) found that out of 179 such issues in the period 1968–1975, the call announcements on all but 9 were "delayed," i.e., well after the conversion value had exceeded the call price. The median company in the sample waited until the conversion value of its bonds exceeded the call price by as much as 43.9%.

In more recent research, Acharya and Handa (1988) found somewhat different call behavior. Out of a sample of 230 convertible bonds that were called between 1980 and 1984, 73 were called when the conversion value was *less* than the respective call price. Indeed, the median firm in the sub-sample of 73 firms called when the conversion value was significantly *less* (by 48.5%) than the call price.

Based on these studies, the empirical evidence on the call behavior of firms issuing callable, convertible bonds is somewhat mixed. As in the case of non-convertible bonds, convertible bonds appear to be called too "early" or too "late" in relation to the valuation framework discussed earlier. As mentioned in the case of non-convertible bonds, a possible explanation for such behavior may be a scenario where the managers of a firm issuing convertible bonds have superior information about the firm's prospects compared to the bondholders. For example, the firm may call a bond early, if the managers know about a potential increase in firm value, of which the bondholders are, as yet, unaware.[18]

9.7 WARRANTS

A warrant is a security that gives the owner the right to purchase an underlying asset at a prespecified price (exercise price) before an expiration date. Although warrants are sometimes issued on bonds, they are, in most cases, issued on common stocks. A warrant is, thus, similar to a call option on stocks. A warrant, however, differs from a call in two fundamental aspects.

First, a warrant is issued by a corporation rather than by an another investor. Warrants are issued on their own by firms to raise capital or, more often than not, with bonds to be included in a package of "bonds with warrants attached," as illustrated by the following example:

---

[18]For an analysis along these lines of asymmetric information between the managers of the firm and its bondholders, see Harris and Raviv (1985).

Bond with Warrants Attached	*Example*
Issuer	Texaco Capital NV (guaranteed by Texaco Inc.)
Issue Size	$200 Million with 200,000 warrants attached.
Issue Date	November 15, 1983.
Maturity Date	November 15, 1990.
Coupon	10 1/2%.
Price	98.
Call Feature	Callable on or after November 16, 1987 at par plus accrued interest.
Sinking Fund Feature	None.
Security	Unsecured.
Rating	Aaa (Moody's)
Exercise Price	$20
Exercise Period	4 years.

Warrants are sometimes also issued to corporate managers or investment bankers as part of their incentive compensation.

Second, unlike the case of a call option on equity, the exercise of warrants results in the dilution of the value of the underlying equity. This results from the fact that, upon the exercise of warrants, the firm issues new shares and receives the exercise price of the warrants, which is less than the prevailing market price of shares. Such a dilution effect makes the valuation of warrants more complex than that of call options.

A third issue, although not fundamental, is important in the valuation of warrants. The expiration dates of warrants are typically several years from the issue date, in contrast to those for most exchange-traded call options on stocks, which typically have expiration dates less than a year away. This difference has implications for the valuation of options including problems relating to uncertainty of the volatility parameter and uncertain interest rates. These issues are not analyzed in this chapter.

Due to the dilution effect, a warrant can be valued more easily when viewed as a call option on the *total* equity value of the firm (the value of the current equity plus the value of the new shares issued, when the warrants are exercised), rather than on just the *current* equity value of the firm. To see this, consider an all-equity firm with n shares of stock currently outstanding.

Suppose the firm now issues m European warrants at a price per warrant, W, and an exercise price, X. Each warrant entitles the holder to receive one share, upon exercise. The total value of the firm, after the warrants are issued, then becomes $V = nS + mW$, where S is the current stock price. On the expiration date of the warrants, their payoff will be:

$$W_T = \max [0, (V_T + mX) / (n + m) - X]$$
$$= \max [0, (V_T - nX) / (n + m)], \qquad (9.20)$$

where V_T denotes the value of the firm just before the exercise of the warrants on their expiration date. After the warrants are exercised, the value of the firm increases to $V_T + mX$ and the number of shares to $n + m$. Thus, $(V_T + mx)/(n + m)$ is the diluted share value after the exercise of the warrants. Equation (9.20) also shows that warrants will be exercised only if $V_T > nX$.

What is the relationship between warrants on stocks and call options on stocks (which are exercised only when $S_T > X$)? The answer to this question depends on the capital structure of the firm on whose stock the warrants and call options are written. We shall consider two different capital structures: one with equity and warrants, and the other with only equity.

Consider first a European call option on the stock of a firm with equity and European warrants outstanding. Assume that the call options and the warrants expire the same day and have the same exercise price, X. Given that a call option will be exercised only if the share price, S_T, on the expiration date satisfies the condition, $S_T > X$, the payoff to the call option on the expiration date is $\max [S_T - X, 0]$. If the warrants are exercised, then $S_T = (V_T + mX) / (n + m)$ since m more shares are issued for X each. In this case, $S_T > X$, only if $V_T > nX$. We know from equation (9.20) that the warrants will be exercised only if $V_T > nX$. Thus, the condition for, and the payoff from, the exercise decision are the same for both warrants and call options. Therefore, the value of a warrant should be the same as the value of a call option on the stock of the firm with both equity and warrants.

We cannot, however, use the Black-Scholes call option pricing model *directly* to value warrants if they are viewed as being written on the stock rather than on the total value of the firm. This is because a potential dilution of equity value resulting from the exercise of warrants will affect the current market price of stock and the process of its evolution. In particular, the distribution of equity return will not be stationary; the volatility of stock returns is not constant over time. In principle, to value warrants viewed as written on the *stock*, the impact of dilution on the stock price process should be simultaneously incorporated into pricing warrants. No closed form solution, however, exists in this more realistic and yet more complicated case.[19] Here, in order to value warrants in a manner similar to call options written on the stock, we consider an alternative approach where warrants are compared with call options written on the stock of an all-equity firm, rather than on the value of the firm as a whole.

Suppose there is an all-equity firm on which European call options are written. Now, consider an otherwise identical firm with warrants in the capital structure. In order to make the two firms identical except in terms of their capital structures, we need to assume that the (real) investment policies (i.e., the assets) of the two firms are the same. For this to be true, let us suppose that the proceeds from issue of warrants are paid out as dividends rather than being invested in the firm. Note that the value of an all-equity firm and the value of the firm with warrants outstanding, before the exercise of warrants, are the same: $V_T = nS_T$. The payoff to a warrant is then related to that of a call option in the following manner:

$$
\begin{aligned}
W_T &= \max \left[(nS_T + mX) / (n + m) - X, 0 \right] \\
&= \max \left[n(S_T - X) / (n + m), 0 \right] \\
&= \{ \max [S_T - X, 0] \} \, (1 - df) \\
&= C_T \, (1 - df)
\end{aligned}
\tag{9.21}
$$

where $df = m / (n + m)$ is a dilution factor (i.e., the number of warrants per share outstanding upon exercise of warrants) and C_T is the payoff to a call option on the expiration date. The dilution factor df is similar to a for convertible bonds.

Based on the expression above, we can make two inferences. First, a European warrant will be exercised whenever the undiluted share value, S_T, is sufficiently large to trigger the exercise of a call option on the stock of an identical firm without warrants. Second, the payoff to a warrant is proportionately smaller than that to a call option on the stock of an identical firm without warrants, where the proportionality factor is a function of a dilution factor, df. Thus, in order to preclude arbitrage, the values of a warrant and a call option should differ only by the dilution factor as in equation (9.21):

$$
W = C \, (1 - df)
\tag{9.22}
$$

In other words, the value of a warrant is equal to the value of a call option

---

[19]See Bensoussan, Crouhy, and Galai (1991), for details.

on the stock of an otherwise identical firm without warrants, at the same exercise price and maturity, but adjusted by the dilution factor.

There are two additional factors to keep in mind in valuing warrants relative to call options. First, if the proceeds from issuing warrants are invested in the firm's assets which have a positive present value rather than paid out as dividends, the value of a warrant will be larger than it would otherwise be as in equation (9.20). In this case, the firm's investment policy is being changed and the value of a warrant and the stochastic process generating the total value of the firm should be solved for simultaneously.

Second, for American warrants, it may not be optimal to exercise all warrants with identical terms at the same time. For American call options, however, as discussed in Chapter 4, it is *always* optimal to exercise all call options with identical terms at the same time, if an exercise of a call option pays at all. This difference in the optimal exercise policy between warrants and call options is a direct consequence of the dilution effect associated with an exercise of warrants. Thus, for example, if one individual holds all the warrants with identical terms, it may be beneficial to him to sequentially exercise the warrants. If, on the other hand, competing individuals constrained from making side-payments to each other or colluding in other ways hold the warrants, the payoff to an investor's warrants depends on how other investors exercise their warrants.[20]

Numerical Example 6: Consider an all-equity firm that has only one share on which no dividends are paid at time 1. Suppose that the value of this firm follows the binomial process shown in the lower panel of Figure 9–3. If a European call option is written on the stock of this firm with an exercise price equal to the current value of the firm, 150, the current value of the call option is 23.38, as shown in Figure 9–10.

Suppose the same firm issues one European warrant with an exercise price of 150 and pays the proceeds W to shareholders as dividends. If the firm value moves up in consecutive periods, the warrant will be exercised on the expiration date as shown in Figure 9–11. Only in this state, does the diluted share value exceed the exercise price. Note that the current value of the warrant, 11.69, is one-half of the value of a call option with a similar exercise price and maturity, since the dilution factor df is equal to one half (i.e., one warrant per share outstanding) in this case.

Finally, we value a warrant when the proceeds from issuing warrants

---

[20]In general, the value of a warrant then depends on the game-theoretic exercise strategies of all individuals holding the warrants. The valuation problem in such an interesting and complex situation is, however, yet to be resolved.

FIGURE 9–10
Possible values of a call option on an all-equity firm's stock over two periods

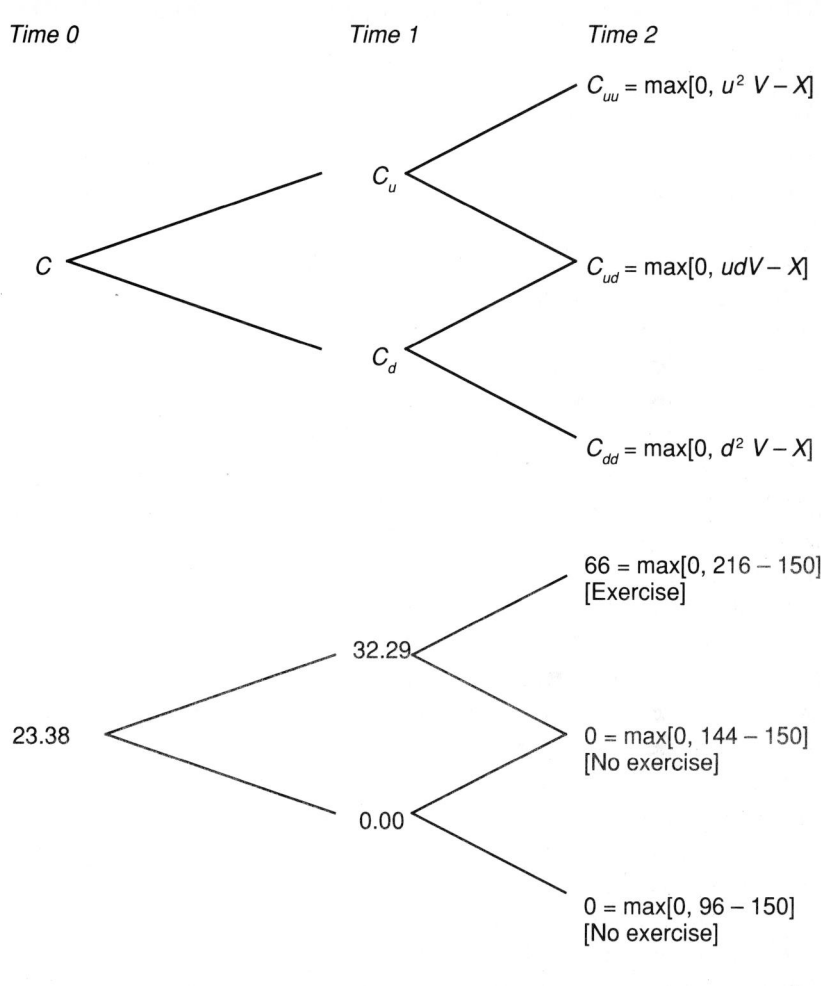

Time 0	Time 1	Time 2

$C_{uu} = \max[0,\ u^2\ V - X]$

C_u

C

$C_{ud} = \max[0,\ udV - X]$

C_d

$C_{dd} = \max[0,\ d^2\ V - X]$

$66 = \max[0,\ 216 - 150]$
[Exercise]

32.29

23.38

$0 = \max[0,\ 144 - 150]$
[No exercise]

0.00

$0 = \max[0,\ 96 - 150]$
[No exercise]

are invested in the firm's assets. When a warrant is issued, the total value of the firm is $V = 150 + W$. This current firm value will move up by $u - 1$ or move down by $d - 1$ in each of the two periods. Figure 9–12 shows the possible values of the firm and the warrant, respectively. As expected, the value of a warrant, 19.26, exceeds its value when the proceeds are paid out

FIGURE 9–11
Possible values of a warrant over two periods

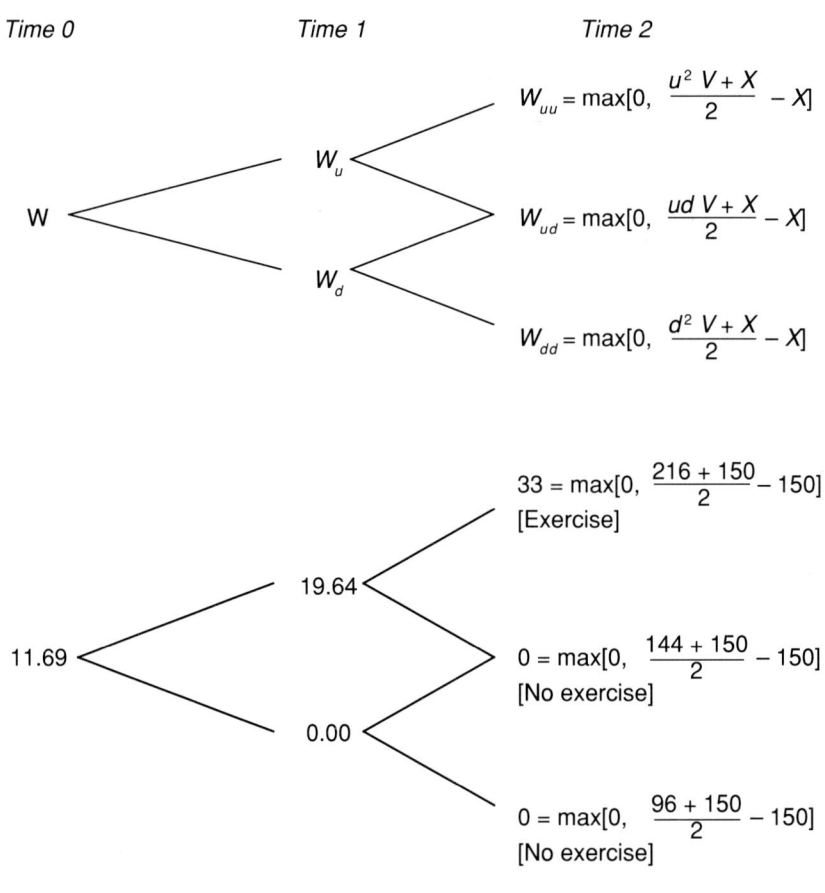

as dividends. As noted before, however, a warrant or a call option written on the *stock* cannot be valued directly using the Black-Scholes model because the distribution of returns on the the stock of a firm with warrants outstanding is not stationary. Readers may confirm from the current example (see Figure 9–13) that the value of the stock, $S = V - W$, in each period changes by different magnitudes of u and d in each period. Hence, the volatility of the stock returns is changing over time.[21]

---

[21]See Bensoussan, Crouhy, and Galai (1991) for a detailed analysis.

FIGURE 9–12
Possible values of the firm and the warrant when the warrant proceeds are invested in the firm's assets over two periods

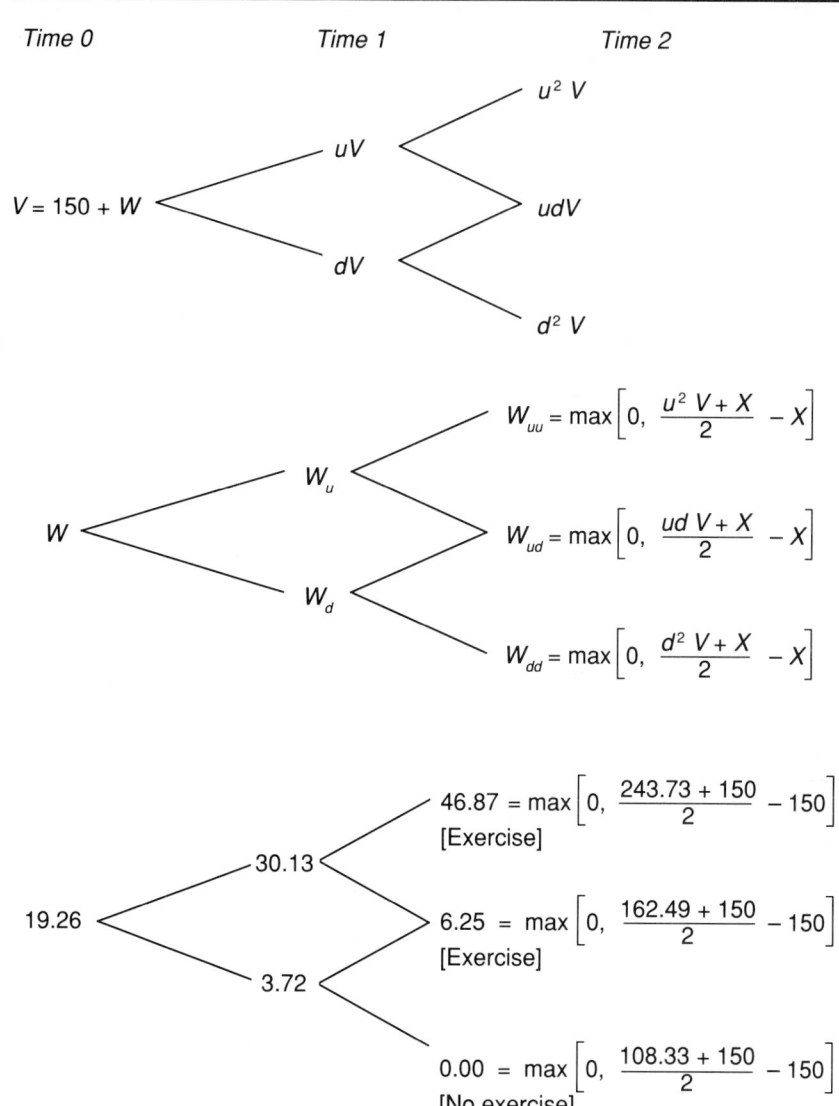

9.8 CONCLUSION

In this chapter, we have established the correspondence between options and corporate securities. We have also shown how a simple option pricing model can be applied to value corporate securities, ranging from such basic securities as stocks and (zero) coupon bonds without explicit option features to more complex securities with explicit option features such as callable and convertible bonds and warrants.

Besides the corporate securities we have analyzed in this chapter, there are a number of other corporate securities with option features, most of which are rather recent innovations. Examples of such securities include puttable bonds, retractable/extendible bonds, bonds with an interest rate cap or floor, foreign exchange-linked bonds, commodity-linked bonds, and bonds with interest payments convertible from fixed rate to floating rate basis, or vice-versa. In addition there are various types of hybrid securities, which have features of both debt and equity, such as preferred stock, exchangeable bonds and exchangeable warrants.

In practice, it is fairly difficult to value corporate securities with option

FIGURE 9–13
Possible values of the stock of the firm with warrants over two periods

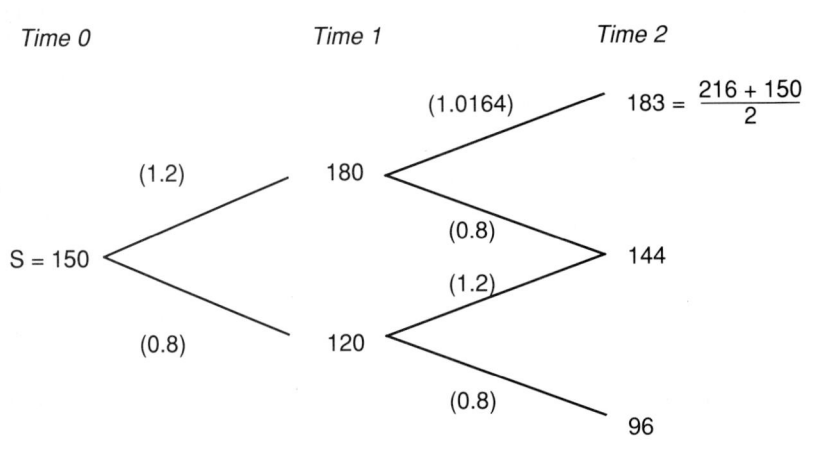

*The numbers in the parentheses represent u or d.

features using the Black-Scholes model or its variants. This difficulty arises from the following four facts. First, there are multiple sources of risk for most corporate securities. Although we have in this chapter considered only default risk that stems from firm value uncertainty, all corporate bonds are also subject to interest rate risk. Furthermore, if a corporate bond contains foreign exchange-related options, it is subject to foreign exchange risk as well. Many corporate securities thus have two or more sources of risk, among which there are interactions. Modelling the behavior of the underlying asset variables with the potential interactions among them properly taken into account is then a principal source of difficulty in valuing corporate securities. The analysis becomes even more complex if exercise decisions are triggered by this interaction.

Second, typical corporate bonds have much longer maturities than traded stock options. For long term options, we cannot assume, as the Black-Scholes model does, that the volatility per unit of time of the underlying asset value is constant over time. Also, the short-term interest rate is stochastic over the life of long term options. This problem, closely related to the first one, makes the valuation of corporate securities fairly involved.

Third, corporate bonds contain numerous indenture provisions that are designed to control conflicts of interests between stockholders and bondholders. Typical indenture provisions include safety covenants (e.g., debt that is secured by specific assets owned by the firm and hence has a prior claim on those assets in the event of default), subordination arrangements (e.g., restrictions on issue of additional debt by the firm that ranks *pari passu* or senior to the existing debt), and restrictions on the financing of interest and dividend payments (e.g., restrictions on how large the dividend payments can be in relation to present and past earnings). Each of these indenture provisions implies a boundary condition of firm value at which the firm is reorganized. Although some of the boundaries are given *exogenously* by the contract specifications, others may be determined *endogenously* as part of an optimal decision problem, such as the exercise of various options. If such bonds have American-style options such as call and/or conversion privileges, the optimal exercise policies also have to be incorporated as boundary conditions in the valuation problem. It would then be nearly an insurmountable task at this stage of theoretical and practical development to value these securities with reasonable accuracy and generality.

Finally, the analysis here has assumed that the total market value of the assets is independent of financing policies. This assumption may be questioned on several grounds. As noted earlier, the taxation of corporations and investors may influence the valuation of the firm. Default by the corporation on one of its securities may impose a "dead-weight" cost on the value of all claims issued by the firm. Perhaps most importantly, informational considerations may influence the valuation of the firm's assets. There is a vast and growing literature on the effect of asymmetric information between managers, stockholders and bondholders on their decisions and, in turn, the valuation of the firm's assets. Incorporation of these effects, especially the last one, into the valuation framework is a challenging task and is the focus of current research in corporate finance.

An important caveat regarding the application of option pricing concepts to the valuation of corporate securities is worth emphasizing. In the case of traded options such as options on stocks or foreign exchange, for example, the assumption that arbitrage between the price of the option and the price of the underlying asset is the basis for pricing of the option, is quite reasonable, since the option and the underlying asset are actively traded. In the case of corporate securities, the underlying asset, the sum total of the firm's assets, may not be tradeable at all. Further, several of the claims issued by the firm such as some of its short term debt, implicit claims to employees and customers etc., may not be traded either. This makes a literal application of the hedging and arbitrage concepts underlying option pricing difficult to justify. However, the broad conceptual foundations of option pricing still serve as a useful basis for analysis.

Notwithstanding these difficulties, the option pricing framework provides us with a very useful tool in analyzing the important features in corporate securities. As interest rate risk, foreign exchange risk, and default risk persist, we can anticipate that corporate securities with new types of option features will emerge. Indeed, hardly a week goes by without a new type of security or financing arrangement being introduced in world capital markets. A related development is the increasing attention being paid to the conflicts of interest between the claimants on a firm, especially in the context of leveraged buyouts and mergers and acquisitions. The strategies of investors and the financing strategies of firms will become more complex and less amenable to simple analysis. The insights from an option pricing model will then prove to be even more essential in designing tools for analyzing financial strategies.

APPENDIX TO CHAPTER 9

This appendix illustrates the valuation of corporate securities using a continuous-time model similar to that used by Black and Scholes (1973) in their well-known article. The development here is similar in spirit to that in the appendix to Chapter 3. We shall first list the important assumptions underlying the valuation model:

A.1   The capital market is perfect and competitive.

A.2   There are no taxes or transactions costs for trading in assets.

A.3   Trading in assets takes place continuously in time.

A.4   The term structure of interest rates is flat and non-stochastic. I.e., the price of a riskless pure discount bond which promises a payment of one dollar at time T years from today is e^{-rT}, where r is the instantaneous riskless rate of interest, which is the same for all maturities T.

A.5   The value of the firm, V, evolves through time according to the following stochastic process:

$$dV = (\mu V - c)dt + \sigma V dz$$

where
   dV represents the infinitesimal change in the value of the firm,
   μ is the instantaneous expected rate of return on the firm's assets per unit of time,
   c is the total dollar payout by the firm as coupon payments/dividends, per unit of time,
   σ is the instantaneous standard deviation of the rate of return on the firm's assets per unit of time,
   dt is a infinitesimally small interval of time,
   dz is an infinitesimal random variable with a mean and variance of the same order as dt.

Consider a corporate security, i.e., any claim issued by the firm, whose market value, Y, at any point in time can be written as a function of the underlying asset, the value of the firm, and time, $Y = Y(V, t)$. Formally, the value of this corporate security evolves through time according to the equation:

$$dY = (\mu_y Y - c_y)dt + \sigma_y Y dz \qquad (9A.1)$$

where μ_y and σ_y are the instantaneous mean and standard deviation, respectively, of the return on the corporate security, Y, and c_y is the dollar payout per unit of time to this security.

We now form a portfolio of the firm's assets and the particular corporate security, Y, and the riskless bond in such a way that (a) the net investment in the portfolio is zero, and (b) the portfolio is riskless. In order to preclude the possibility of arbitrage, i.e., riskless profit, the return on this portfolio with zero net investment must equal zero. This no-arbitrage condition translates into the following second-order partial differential equation to be satisfied by the corporate security, Y:

$$\frac{1}{2}\sigma^2 V^2 \frac{\partial^2 Y}{\partial V^2} + (rV - c)\ \frac{\partial Y}{\partial V} - rY + \frac{\partial Y}{\partial t} + c_y = 0 \qquad (9A.2)$$

A complete description of the partial differential equation requires, in addition to (9A.2) above, a specification of two boundary conditions and one end-point condition, very similar to the discussion in the appendix to Chapter 3. Here, it is important to note that what distinguishes one contingent claim, i.e., one corporate security, from another contingent claim issued by the firm is precisely the specification of these boundary conditions.

As a specific example, consider the risky discount bond issued by a firm that pays no dividends until the maturity date of the bond. This firm has no other claims outstanding, besides the debt and the equity. In this case, $c = c_y = 0$. Denoting by T the length of time until maturity, we can rewrite (9A.2) for the value of the discount bond, B, as:

$$\frac{1}{2}\sigma^2 V^2 \frac{\partial^2 B}{\partial V^2} + rV \frac{\partial B}{\partial V} - rB - \frac{\partial B}{\partial T} = 0 \qquad (9A.3)$$

For the discount bond, the boundary conditions and the end-point condition are:

$$B(V = 0, T) = 0 \qquad (9A.4a)$$

$$B(V, T) \le V \qquad (9A.4b)$$

$$B(V, T = 0) = \min [V, F] \qquad (9A.4c)$$

The condition (9A.4a) states that the bond is worthless when the value of the firm is zero. The condition (9A.4b) constrains the value of the bond not to exceed the value of the firm. Finally, the end-point condition (9A.4c) represents the contractual payoff function for the discount bond on the maturity date, as described in Section 9.2 in the chapter.

Solving the partial differential equation (9A.3) subject to the conditions (9A.4a), (9A.4b), and (9A.4c), yields the value of the bond at any point in time before the maturity date:

$$B = V N(h_1) + Fe^{-rT} N(h_2)$$

$$= Fe^{-rT} [N(h_2) + \frac{1}{\ell} N(h_1)]$$

(9A.5)

where $\ell \equiv Fe^{-rT}/V$ is the "quasi" debt-to-total value ratio where the debt is valued at the present value (assuming no default) of its face value,

$h_1 = -[\sigma^2 T/2 - \log(\ell)] / \sigma \sqrt{T}$,

$h_2 = -[\sigma^2 T/2 + \log(\ell)] / \sigma \sqrt{T}$, and

$N(\cdot)$ represents the cumulative normal density function.

The expression (9A.5) is a variant of the Black-Scholes model developed in Chapter 3. To derive (9A.5) from the Black- Scholes model, first note that the risky bond can be thought of as the value of the firm minus the equity. Since the equity can be written as a call option on the value of the firm, risky debt can be written as the value of the underlying asset minus the value of the call, (a "covered-write" position), where the latter is given by the Black-Scholes model.

Examination of equation (9A.5) shows that the value of the bond can be written as $B(V, F, \sigma, T, r)$. Differentiating B with respect to each determinant results in the following comparative statics: $\partial B / \partial V, \partial B / \partial F > 0$ and $\partial B / \partial \sigma, \partial B / \partial T, \partial B / \partial r < 0$. In other words, the value of the risky bond is, as expected, an increasing function of the current value of the firm and the face value of the bond, and a decreasing function of the business risk of the firm, the time to maturity and the riskless rate of interest.

Given the value of the bond in (9A.5), we can compute the yield to maturity, R, from the definition $e^{-RT} \equiv F/B$. We can then rewrite equation (9A.5) to obtain the function for the default risk premium, $H = R - r$, as,

$$H = -\frac{1}{T} \log \left[N(h_2) + \frac{1}{\ell} N(h_1) \right] \qquad (9A.6)$$

Inspection of equation (9A.6) shows that the default risk premium can be written as H (ℓ, σ,T): the default risk premium depends on the capital structure through the quasi debt-to-total value ratio, ℓ, the business risk represented by the volatility parameter, σ, and the time to maturity, T.

Differentiating H with respect to each variable results in the following comparative statics: $\partial H / \partial \ell$, $\partial H / \partial \sigma > 0$, and $\partial H / \partial T >$ or < 0. The first two inequalities show that the default risk premium, for a given maturity, always increases as the volatility parameter, σ, increases and as the debt-to-total value ratio, ℓ, increases. The third inequality, however, shows that the time to maturity has no such simple effect on the default risk premium. This is because there are two different effects of the time to maturity: one through the riskless interest rate (in determining the present value of the promised payment, F) and the other through the volatility parameter, σ, in relation to the quasi debt-to-total value ratio, ℓ. These two effects work in opposite directions in the same fashion as for a European put option as described in Chapter 3.

Further examination of the default premium function, $H(\cdot)$, shows that the default premium is related to the time to maturity as illustrated in Figure 9–14. This figure can be intuitively interpreted for different levels of the quasi debt-to-total value ratio. Specifically, when the time to maturity is very short, a firm with a debt ratio, ℓ, greater than one, is very likely to default at maturity, since there is not much time for the firm value to increase. On the other hand, a firm with a debt ratio, ℓ, smaller than one is very likely to stay solvent. As the time to maturity increases, however, the probability that a firm that is highly levered, ($\ell > 1$), will default decreases. For a firm that is currently solvent, ($\ell < 1$), on the other hand, the probability of default first increases with time to maturity and then declines for very large values of T.

Other corporate securities such as coupon debt, callable debt, convertible debt, warrants etc., can be analyzed in a very similar manner. The main differences in the analysis will be in the specifics of the boundary and end-point conditions. Also, in many practical cases, the early exercise feature may be important, since the options may be American-style. Closed form expressions for value may not exist for these cases and numerical methods outlined in Chapters 8 and 14 may be required to solve the valuation problem.

FIGURE 9–14
Default risk premium vs. maturity at different values of the "quasi-debt ratio," ℓ.

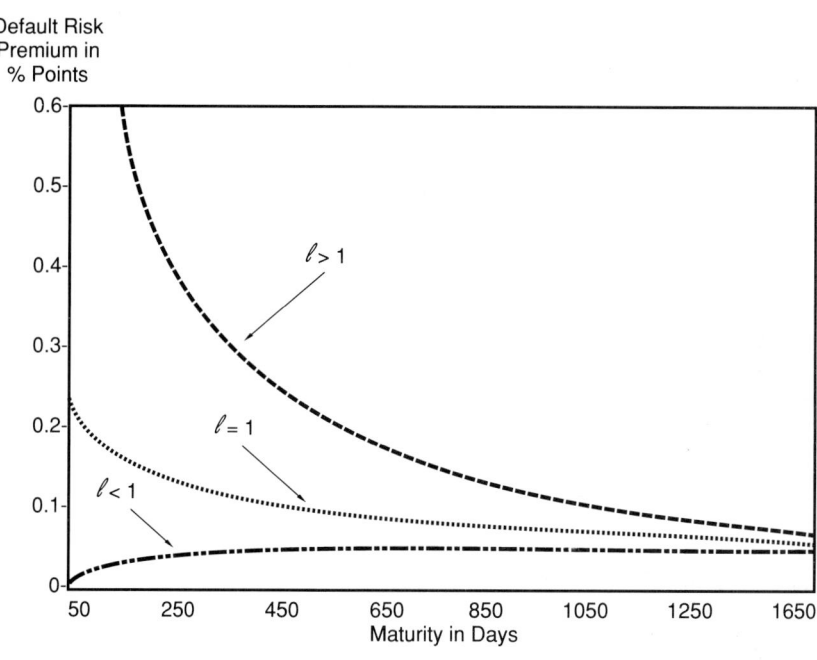

References

Acharya, S., and Handa, P. (June 1988). Early calls of convertible debt: New evidence and theory. New York University, Salomon Brothers Center for the Study of Financial Institutions working paper.

Bensoussan, A., Crouhy, M., and Galai, D. (December 1991). Black-Scholes approximation of warrant prices. Unpublished manuscript.

Black, F., and Cox, J. (May 1976). Valuing corporate securities: Some effects of bond indenture provisions. *Journal of Finance, 31,* 351–68.

Black, F., and Scholes, M. (May/June 1973). The pricing of options and corporate liabilities. *Journal of Political Economy, 81,* 637–59.

Brennan, M., and Schwartz, E. (November 1980). Analyzing convertible bonds. *Journal of Financial and Quantitative Analysis, 15,* 907–29.

Constantinides, G., and Grundy, B. (January 1987). Call and conversion of

Constantinides, G., and Rosenthal, R. (February 1984). Strategic analysis of the competitive exercise of certain financial options. *Journal of Economic Theory, 32,* 128–38.

Courtadon, G., and Merrick, J., Jr., (Fall 1983). The option pricing model and the valuation of corporate securities. *Midland Corporate Finance Journal, 1,* 43–57.

Crouhy, M., and Galai, D. (June 1988). Warrant valuation and equity volatility. Centre HEC working paper.

Emmanual, D., (August 1983). Warrant valuation and exercise strategy. *Journal of Financial Economics, 12,* 211–36.

Galai, D., and Masulis, R. (January/March 1976). The option pricing model and the risk factor of stock. *Journal of Financial Economics, 33,* 53–81.

Galai, D., and Schneller, M. (December 1978). Pricing warrants and the value of the firm. *Journal of Finance, 33,* 1333–42.

Geske, R., (November 1977). The valuation of corporate liabilities as compound options. *Journal of Financial Quantitative Analysis, 12,* 541–52.

Harris, M., and Raviv, A. (December 1985). A sequential signalling model of convertible debt call policy. *Journal of Finance, 40,* 1263–82.

Ingersoll, J., Jr., (May 1977). An examination of convertible call policies on convertible securities. *Journal of Finance, 32,* 463–78.

Ingersoll, J., Jr., (May 1977). A contingent-claims valuation of convertible securities. *Journal of Financial Economics, 4,* 289–322.

Mason, S., and Merton, R. (1983). The role of contingent claims analysis in corporate finance. In E. Altman and M. Subrahmanyam (eds.), *Recent advances in corporate finance.* Homewood, Illinois: Richard D. Irwin, Inc.,

Merton, R., (May 1974). On the pricing of corporate debt: The risk structure of interest rates. *Journal of Finance, 29,* 449–70.

Modigliani, F., and Miller, M. (June 1958). The cost of capital, corporation finance and the theory of investment. *American Economic Review, 48,* 261–97.

Smith, C., Jr., (January/March 1976). Option pricing: A review. *Journal of Financial Economics, 3,* 3–51.

Smith, C., Jr., (1979). Applications of option pricing analysis. In J. Bicksler (ed.), *Handbook of financial economics.* Amsterdam: North-Holland,.

Vu, J. (June 1986). An empirical investigation of calls of non-convertible bonds. *Journal of Financial Economics, 16,* 235–65.

CHAPTER 10

THE OPTION FEATURE IN MORTGAGES

Robert I. Gerber
Andrew S. Carron [*]

10.1 INTRODUCTION

Mortgages represent the largest single sector of the U.S. debt market, surpassing even the federal government. In mid-1988, mortgage debt outstanding (residential, farm, and commercial) totalled over $3 trillion— 35 percent of total credit market debt owed by domestic nonfinancial sectors. By comparison, federal government and agency debt amounted to just over $2 trillion.[1]

Because of the enormous volume of mortgages and the importance of housing in the U.S. economy, numerous mechanisms have developed to facilitate the provision of credit to this sector. The predominant method by which this has been accomplished is securitization, the bundling of individual mortgage loans into capital market instruments. More than $870 billion

---

[*]The authors are Vice President and Director, respectively, The First Boston Corporation.
[1]Federal Reserve Board, Flow of Funds Accounts.

in mortgage backed securities are now outstanding, an amount comparable to consumer credit, corporate bonds, or municipal securities.[2]

Mortgage-backed securities

A mortgage-backed security is a bond which is backed by a pool (group) of mortgage loans. Principal and interest payments received from the underlying loans are passed through to the bondholders. These securities contain at least one type of embedded option due to the right of the home buyer to prepay the mortgage loan before maturity. A wide variety of loan types and security structures has led to substantial product diversity. Option features concomitantly range from the simple to the exceedingly complex.

In 1970 the Government National Mortgage Association (GNMA) launched the mortgage-backed securities market. GNMA, a federal government agency, guarantees investors timely receipt of mortgage principal and interest. The strength of this agency guarantee virtually eliminates credit risk. A high market price reflects this credit quality, and ensures that the vast majority of eligible loans are securitized as GNMAs. The Federal National Mortgage Association (FNMA) and the Federal Home Loan Mortgage Corporation (FHLMC) also securitize loans and provide "near-government" agency guarantees: the federal government bears no direct responsibility for bond performance, but has an interest in the success of the FNMA/FHLMC programs. These securities—GNMA, FNMA, and FHLMC—comprise the agency-backed sector of the market. Private firms also create mortgage-backed securities. The "private-label," or "AA," sector of the market refers to nonagency issues.

Mortgage-backed securities were first packaged using the pass-through structure. The pass-through's essential characteristic is that investors receive a pro rata share of the cash flows that are generated by the pool of mortgages—interest, scheduled amortization, and principal prepayments. Exercise of mortgage prepayment options has pro rata effects on all investors; consequently, the analytical techniques used for individual mortgages can simply be applied to the pass-through security. Substantial complication, however, was introduced with the advent of multi-class structures, such as the collateralized mortgage obligation (CMO).

A CMO is a multi-class mortgage-backed security in which two or more series of bonds ("tranches") receive sequential, rather than pro rata,

---

[2]Ibid.

principal paydown. Interest payments are generally made on all tranches.
A two tranche CMO is a simple example. Assume that there is $100 in
mortgages backing two $50 tranches. Both tranches receive interest, like
a pass-through security, but principal payments are initially used to pay
down only the first, or "A" tranche. For example, if $1 in mortgage
amortization and prepayments is collected the first month, the balance of the
"A" tranche is reduced (paid down) by $1. No principal on the "B" tranche
is paid until the "A" tranche is fully retired. Then the remaining $50 in
mortgage principal pays down the $50 "B" tranche. In effect, the "A" or
"fast-pay" tranche has been assigned all of the early mortgage prepayments
and reaches its maturity sooner than would an ordinary pass-through
security. The "B" or "slow-pay" tranche has only the later mortgage
prepayments; it begins paying down much later than an ordinary pass-
through security.

CMO's are backed by whole mortgage loans and/or pass-through
securities. As originally intended, the basic CMO structure significantly
alters the option features of the underlying collateral. Prepayments do not
equally affect all bondholders. Sequential tranche paydown can be interpreted as meaning that prepayment options must be sequentially exercised.
In the previous example, the options to prepay the A tranche must be
exercised, or expire, before options on the B tranche can be exercised.[3]

Elaborate CMO structures, each with different option features, have
proliferated. "Floaters", "strips," and "PACs" are among the most common
new structures.[4] Floaters are floating rate tranches, usually with coupon
caps, and often collateralized by fixed rate mortgages. Strips (stripped
mortgage-backed securities) are securities in which one tranche receives all
or most principal payments (PO or principal only strip) and the other tranche
all or most interest payments (IO or interest only strip). PACs, planned amortization classes, are tranches in which principal paydowns are announced
and fixed at issue; these planned payments will be made, as long as bond
collateral prepayments fall within certain bands. Complex bond structures
lead to complicated option features.

---

[3]Most CMOs have a "clean-up call," which allows issuers to retire the bonds once the outstanding
principal falls belows a specified level (usually about 10%).

[4]The Tax Reform Act of 1986 created a new legal entity—the Real Estate Investment Conduit (REMIC).
The REMIC legislation makes economically viable some additional security structures (e.g., senior/
subordinated pass-through). As of 1990, REMIC selection will be mandatory for multi-class mortgage-
backed securities. Until then, a CMO selection is also possible.

Analyzing mortgages

Complexity in the mortgage-backed securities market can appear daunting. Nonetheless, securities can usually be analyzed as variations on the basic fixed-rate, mortgage pass-through. Examination of the prepayment option is central to understanding the entire class of securities. It is the building block for the majority of other options, and the analytical tools it engenders can be broadly applied to more complicated security structures.

The typical residential mortgage, the primary ingredient of these securities, is a level-payment amortizing loan. Homeowners ("mortgagors") have the right, but not the obligation, to prepay their loans at any time. This embedded prepayment option, an American-style call, is common to all residential mortgages.[5] However, loans vary by contractual provisions and mortgagor demographic characteristics. These differences often give rise to additional option features and disparities in the value and exercise strategy of the prepayment option.

Mortgage contracts specify loan "term" (maturity), coupon (interest or "contract" rate), and prepayment constraints. Original stated term, which can be 30, 25, or 15 years, determines the loan amortization schedule. Mortgage coupon rate, whether fixed or adjustable, provides the main impetus to refinance (that is, to pay off the existing mortgage by taking out a new loan at a lower rate). The greater the mortgage contract rate relative to the current mortgage market rate ("current coupon"), the greater the incentive to refinance. With an adjustable-rate mortgage (ARM) this relationship is very subtle. Coupon rate varies according to a formula, periodically resetting in accordance with an index of market interest rates.[6] Limits on the magnitudes of the resets (which are called caps) are often included in the formula. As was discussed in Chapter 6, caps can be interpreted as put or call options, which are automatically exercised when optimal.

Prepayment constraints and mortgagor "noneconomic" behavior lead to otherwise suboptimal prepayment (call exercise) strategies. Mortgagors vary in their financial sophistication and economic resources. Individuals lacking sufficient assets and access to credit may not be able to refinance

---

[5]In effect, mortgagors also have a default option. Homeowners, by discontinuing monthly payments, can "put" their house back to the mortgagee. The real estate value of the property is the option's exercise price. Default options, however, are secondary to the evaluation of most mortgage-backed securities. Consequently, an explicit discussion of their impact is not presented.

[6]Caps on monthly mortgage payments are also a common feature of ARMs.

their mortgages even when it is financially desirable. Moreover, the financial incentives to prepay existing mortgages are usually not the primary determinant of a homeowner's decision to relocate. Due-on-sale clauses in a mortgage contract, which require full payment of principal upon sale of the house, can thus precipitate noneconomic prepayments. Mortgages lacking due-on-sale clauses are called assumable,[7] because the new owner "assumes" the responsibility for making payments under the existing mortgage.

The mortgage securities markets

Because of the size and importance of the mortgage securities market, considerable effort is expended in attempting to value the options embedded in these instruments. Accurate prepayment forecasting is critical for proper valuation and hedging. Historically, prepayment rates on the more common mortgage securities have ranged from as low as 2 percent of the remaining balance per year to as high as 40 percent; rates of 0 percent and 100 percent on some more esoteric mortgage instruments are not unheard of.

Institutional investors—including insurance companies, pension funds, banks, savings and loans, and investment banks—typically try to match the duration of their assets to that of their liabilities. When mortgage prepayments change, the duration of mortgage security assets changes. It is as if an investor discovered that her 7-year bonds of the night before had mysteriously turned into 2-year (or 20-year!) bonds by morning.

In the spring of 1986, market interest rates were falling rapidly. Many investors had long positions in mortgage securities, which they had hedged with short positions in Treasury securities or matched against equivalent liabilities. As interest rates declined, the value of the mortgages rose. But prepayments increased also, as borrowers refinanced their mortgages, and mortgage duration was reduced. So mortgage securities prices barely rose above par even as Treasury prices soared higher and higher. The short Treasury positions created losses much larger than the corresponding gains on the mortgage positions. The hedging problem really required shorting 10-year Treasuries against a rise in interest rates while shorting 3-year

---

[7]Some mortgage contracts preclude or discourage prepayment through the use of financial charges (prepayment penalities). These features are most often present in multifamily and commercial mortgages.

Treasuries against a decline in interest rates. Using explicit options instead of short positions could have accomplished this goal, but at a cost that was felt to outweigh any yield advantage inherent in the mortgages.

The remainder of this chapter will expand upon the concepts we have just raised. Section 10.2 describes the basic fixed-rate mortgage loan and outlines an approach to mortgage valuation. Optimal prepayment strategies are presented for a frictionless world, the effects of market imperfections are examined, and empirically observed strategies are discussed. In Section 10.3 the generic fixed-rate, mortgage pass-through is evaluated. The analytical techniques developed in Section 10.3 are then briefly applied to more complicated securities in Section 10.4. The Appendix gives a glossary of mortgage-related terms.

10.2 THE BASIC FIXED-RATE MORTGAGE

A residential mortgage is a loan secured by a house and land. Historically, the market has been dominated by the fixed-rate, level-pay, fully amortizing loan. Moreover, examination of these loans provides insight into the analysis of most other mortgages and mortgage-backed securities.

Fixed-rate mortgages usually have two essential features. First, the loans fully amortize. Level monthly mortgage payments include interest and principal. The payments are calculated so that, over the life of a loan, the principal component of payments is scheduled to sum to the original loan balance. Second, mortgagors generally have the right to prepay their loan in full, or in part, at any time. In effect, the lender has purchased (long) a fully amortizing bond, and sold (short) an American call. The cash flow from a mortgage is therefore dependent on whether (and when) it is prepaid, and the prepayment decision is a function of interest rate levels (among other considerations).

As a loan with call features, there are three steps in the proper valuation of a mortgage. First, the process which governs future interest rate behavior must be specified. Second, a method to discount cash flows must be developed. Finally, the relationship between interest rates and cash flow patterns must be ascertained for interest, amortization, and prepayment. Each issue is addressed in turn.

Valuing a Simple Bond
In our example, a simple binomial interest model is selected for its intuitive

appeal, and its convenience of use.[8] The short-term interest rate, $r(t)$, is the only source of uncertainty. In each period it can move up or down by a specified amount. The process can be described as follows:

For $t = 0$, $r(0) = 0.10$

For $t > 0$, $r(t) = u\, r(t-1) = r_u$ (10.1)

         or

$r(t) = d\, r(t-1) = r_d$

where $u = 1.3$
       $d = 0.7$

A value of r_u denotes the up-state, while r_d refers to the down-state. A three period tree is constructed in Exhibit 10–1 to reflect this process. At each node in the tree, the price of a one period default-free bond is equal to par, discounted by the spot interest rate. Nodes in the tree, denoted by $N(t, n)$, are identified by time and the cumulative number of up-states. For example, $N(2, 2)$ is the node at time two, having witnessed two up-states; the interest rate associated with the node is 16.9%.

Simple arbitrage arguments (see Cox, Ross, and Rubinstein [1979]) can be used to value any interest sensitive security. The price of any default-free, option-free bond can be calculated using:

$$B(r(t), t) = [1/(1 + r(t))] \times$$
(10.2)
$$[p\, B(r_u, t+1) + (1-p)\, B(r_d, t+1) + pmt(t)],$$

where $B(r(t), t)$ = bond price in period t,
       $B(r_u, t+1)$ = bond price in an up-state in period $t+1$,
       $B(r_d, t+1)$ = bond price in a down-state in period $t+1$,
       $pmt(t)$ = bond cash flow in period t (e.g., coupon payments, amortization), and
       p = the "risk adjusted" (or "risk neutral") probability of an up-state.

---

[8]Conclusions based upon the binomial model are robust. The process has very desirable limiting properties. It can be used to approximate a variety of continuous diffusion processes [see Cox, Ross, and Rubinstein (1979)].

EXHIBIT 10–1
Binomial interest rate process

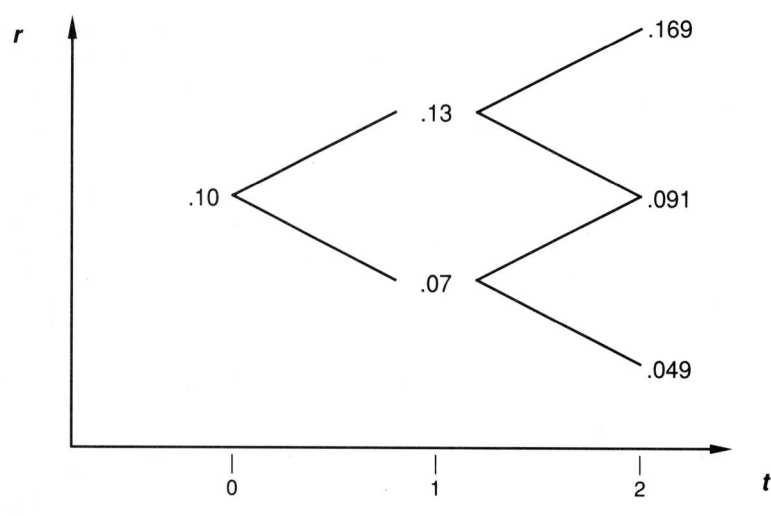

Because p will usually differ from the the true probability of an up-state, the second term in brackets in (10.2) will not usually equal the true expected value of the bond's future payoff. As we have seen in earlier chapters, equation (10.2) is the basic valuation equation for any security whose value depends on the interest rate. This includes mortgage instruments with prepayment options.

The value of p may vary over time and with interest rate levels. Arbitrage restrictions require, however that at a given node in the tree, the same value of p be used to evaluate all risky securities. Therefore, only one p need be computed at each node. It can be backed out of equation (10.2) if, for any risky asset, next-period prices are known in both the up- and down-state.

Using the price of a two-period zero coupon bond, p can easily be calculated. Next period the bond's price is equal to that of a one-period zero coupon bond. In each state the price of a one period zero is solely determined by the state's interest rate. Given the interest rate process and current yield curve information, the (time varying) values of p and the prices of all option free bonds can be calculated at each node in the probability tree.[9]

An example of arbitrage-free pricing is provided in Exhibit 10–2. The current zero coupon Treasury yield curve is displayed. With the current price of a two-period bond at 81.16, the initial value of p is calculated to be 0.843. The yield curve and interest rate process can be used to compute implied forward values of p. Assuming that p does not change over time in this example, bond prices are calculated. These will be used in all future examples.

The binomial method can also be used to price an amortizing bond, denoted $AB(t)$. In equation (10.1), $pmt(t)$ must include amortization plus interest. Periodic payments, $pmt(t)$, and the face value, $F(t)$, can be expressed, respectively, as follows[10]:

$$pm(t) = \$100 \times c \times \frac{(1+c)^T}{(1+c)^T - 1} \qquad (10.3)$$

$$F(t) = \$100 \times \frac{(1+c)^T - (1+c)^t}{(1+c)^T - 1} \qquad (10.4)$$

where T = original term (maturity) of the loan, and
   c = periodic interest rate on the loan.

From equations (10.3) and (10.4) it is clear that the loan produces a constant periodic stream of payments, and the principal balance is constrained at origination ($100) and maturity ($0). Cumulative amortization at any time can be expressed as the difference between the original and current face values. Exhibit 10–3 illustrates the relationship of principal and interest payments over time.

Amortizing bonds

The previous methods can easily be extended to the analysis of an amortizing bond. Two equivalent valuation methods can be used. First, equation (10.2) can be directly applied. Second, a portfolio of zero coupon Treasury

---

[9]The yield curve at a given moment in time does not provide enough information to determine unique values of p at all subsequent nodes. The practitioner is thus provided some modeling flexibility. One alternative is to calculate forward values of p, similar in spirit to implied forward interest rates.
[10]See Fabozzi (1988), pp. 294–304, for mortgage formulas.

EXHIBIT 10–2
Arbitrage-free pricing

Current Treasury Market

Maturity	Yield	Price
1-period	.100	90.91
2-period	.110	81.16
3-period	.121	70.97

Calculation of p from equation 10.2 with pmt = 0 (for zero-coupon bond)

$$p = \frac{(1 + r(t))\, B(r(t),\, t) - B(r_d,\, t + 1)}{B(r_u,\, t + 1) - B(r_d,\, t + 1)}$$

$$= \frac{(1 + .1)81.16 - 93.46}{88.50 - 93.46} = .843$$

Bond Prices

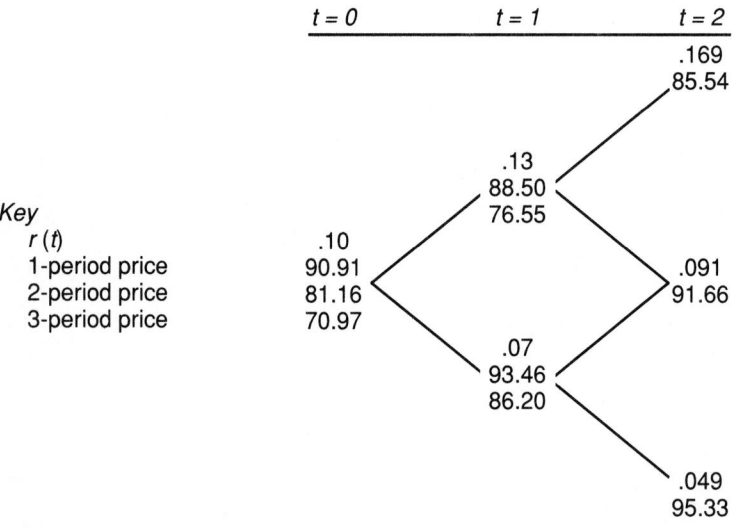

	t = 0	*t = 1*	*t = 2*
			.169
			85.54
		.13	
		88.50	
Key		76.55	
r (t)	.10		
1-period price	90.91		.091
2-period price	81.16		91.66
3-period price	70.97		
		.07	
		93.46	
		86.20	
			.049
			95.33

securities can be constructed which replicates the bond's cash flows. The lack of arbitrage opportunities implies that the amortizing bond and the replicating portfolio have the same price. Exhibit 10–4 presents an analysis of a simple amortizing bond.

EXHIBIT 10–3
Cash flows of a fully amortizing bond

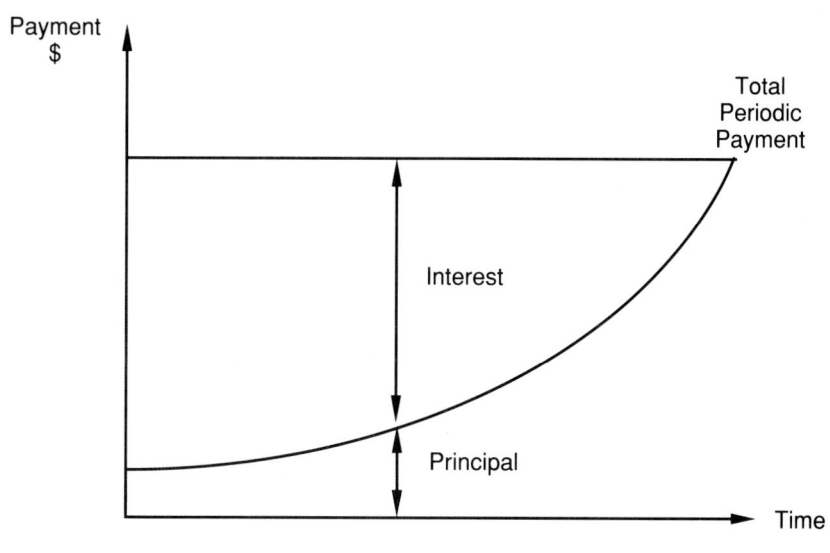

A $100 bond, with a 10% coupon, is examined in Exhibit 10–4. Amortization occurs over three periods. Periodic payments, equal to $40.21, are broken down into principal and interest. The interest component decreases, and the principal component increases, over the life of the loan. Cumulative principal payments are equal to $100. In order to evaluate the bond, assume it is liquid and default-free, and thus does not require a credit premium over the Treasury yield curve. Cash flows from the bond can be replicated by three zero-coupon Treasuries, with one-, two-, and three-period maturities. The current portfolio price is $97.72, which is consistent with equation (10.1).

Prepayments

Most residential mortgages can be prepaid at any time prior to maturity. Borrowers can make partial prepayments, which reduce the outstanding balance, and therefore shorten the remaining term to maturity or allow for a reduction in the monthly payment. In most cases of prepayment, the entire remaining balance is paid off; for analytical purposes, all prepayments are assumed to be of this type. The process is relatively simple: the borrower

EXHIBIT 10–4
Payments on a fully amortizing 3-period bond—10% coupon

Period[a]	Payment[b]	Interest	Principal	Price	Value = Price × Payment / 100
0	40.21	10.00	30.21	90.91	36.55
1	40.21	6.98	33.23	81.16	32.63
2	40.21	3.66	36.56	70.97	28.54
					97.72

[a]Period t begins at date t and ends at $t + 1$. The period t payment occurs at date $t + 1$ (see text).
[b]Interest plus principal may not sum to payment due to rounding.

presents a check to the lender for the remaining balance, and the lender returns the cancelled mortgage document to the borrower.

Some mortgages require the borrower to pay a penalty if the loan is prepaid in the early years; these fees are generally modest. Loans on apartment buildings and commercial structures often prohibit prepayment for some number of years, or require the borrower to compensate the lender for loss of interest income over the remaining life of the loan. For purposes of this discussion, we assume all mortgages are prepayable at par.

The prepayment option embedded in a mortgage can be viewed as an American-style call. Valuation is similar, but slightly more complicated, than for European-style calls. It is thus instructive to recall briefly the pricing of a European call. The option is valued according to equation (10.2) with the option value replacing the bond value in the equation and the minor modification that payment only occurs at exercise. Alternatively, option value can be established via a replication argument—a portfolio can be constructed which replicates the option's cash flows.

Using the binomial tree for interest rates shown in Exhibit 10–2, Exhibit 10–5 analyzes a European call on a one-period Treasury bond to illustrate option valuation in our example. Consider a call on a one-period Treasury, with strike price $90.00, set to expire in one period. In the event of an up-state in interest rates, the exercise price exceeds the price of a one-period bond, and the option expires worthless. However, if a down-state occurs, the call is worth $3.46 = $93.46 – $90.00. A replicating portfolio

EXHIBIT 10–5
Valuation of a European call

Method 1—Direct Valuation in a Binomial Framework

Strike Price = 90.00
$C(t)$ = call price at time t

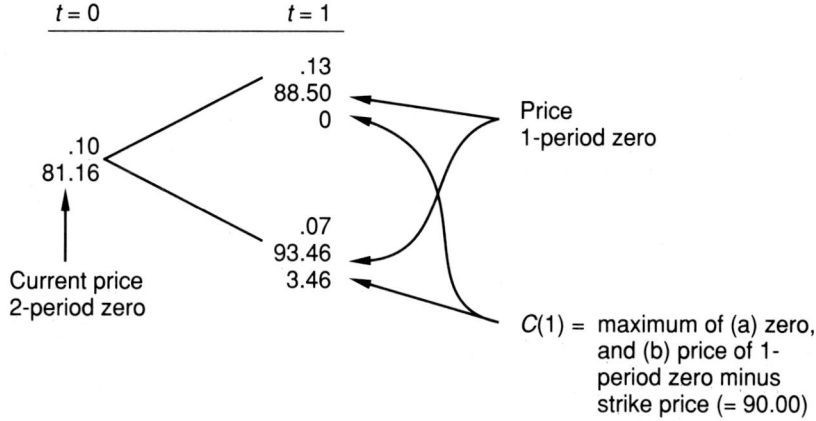

$$C(0) = \frac{1}{1 + r(0)} \; [C(r_u, t+1)\, p + C(r_d, t+1)\, (1-p)]$$

$$= \frac{1}{1.1} \; [0 \times .843 + 3.46 \times .157] = .49$$

Method 2—Valuing the Replicating Portfolio of Zero-Coupon Bonds

(a) Purchase .698 2-period zeros at 81.16
(b) Borrow 56.16 short-term at .10

Portfolio Value = $81.16 \times .698 - 56.16 = .49$

Payouts:

In up-state	$88.50 \times .698 - 56.16 \times 1.1 = 0$
In down state	$93.46 \times .698 - 56.16 \times 1.1 = 3.46$

can be constructed with a long position in two-period Treasuries, and a short position in one-period Treasuries such that in both up- and down-states the payoff is identical to the option . Therefore, the option price must be equal to $0.49, the cost of the portfolio.

An American style option can be exercised before expiration. More-over, periodic principal and interest payments of an amortizing bond can be interpreted as dividends and, as described in Chapter 4, often lead to early exercise of in-the-money options. As the loan ages, the amortization rate increases, as does the incentive for early exercise. To account for this change, equation (10.2) must be modified as follows:

$$C(r, t) \ = \ \max[C' \ (r, t), C_e], \qquad\qquad (10.5)$$

where $C(r, t)$ = call value,
   $C'(r, t)$ = call value if not exercised at time t (from equation (10.2)),
   C_e = $\max(AB(t) - X, 0)$ = call value if exercised at time t (the intrinsic value), and
   X = strike price of the option.

Equation (10.5), alone or in conjunction with a replication argument, can be used to calculate the value of $C(r, t)$. Possibility of early exercise complicates the calculation, but does not alter the essential characteristics of the analysis.

Strike price plays a major role in determining exercise strategy and option value. For most mortgages, face value is the stated exercise price of the prepayment option. Market "frictions," such as taxes, credit premiums, prepayment penalties, due-on-sale clauses, and transaction costs, increase the effective prepayment strike price. Nonetheless, the assumption of frictionless markets is a reasonable starting point for discussing optimal exercise strategy. The presence of frictions does not alter basic valuation techniques. Afterwards, the introduction of frictions can be used to explain much of the observed "suboptimal" prepayment behavior.

Most mortgages can be prepaid at face value. After inserting face value as the strike price, equation (10.5) can be used to value the call option. In order to apply the formula, next period's option price for both up- and down-states must be known. A backward induction argument can be employed to ascertain these values. The procedure works as follows. The call is first evaluated at each terminal node of the probability tree. Using this information, a value can be placed on the call in each of the next-to-last nodes. Continuing backwards, the value of the call at all nodes can be established. As an added twist, the possibility of immediate exercise must always be considered.

Exhibit 10–6 provides an example of the valuation of a call on the sample three-period amortizing bond. The strike price at each point is equal to the unpaid principal balance as of that date, so it declines from 100 to 69.79 in period 1 and finally to 36.56 in period 2. At each node in the tree, three steps are followed. First, the intrinsic value of the call, the greater of its value if immediately exercised and zero, is calculated. Second, the backward induction formula in equation (10.2) is used to derive the call

EXHIBIT 10–6
Valuation of a call on a fully amortizing 3-period bond

Strike Price = Outstanding Principal

Node	Outstanding Principal	Market Value of Cash Flows	Intrinsic[a] Value	Call[b] Value	Value[c] Alive
0,0	100.00	97.72	0.00	0.38	0.38
1,1	69.79	66.37	0.00	0.04	0.04
1,0	69.79	72.24	2.45	2.45	0.50
2,2	36.56	34.40	0.00	0.00	0.00[d]
2,1	36.56	36.86	0.30	0.30	0.00[d]
2,0	36.56	38.33	1.77	1.77	0.00[d]

$t = 0$ $t = 1$ $t = 2$

```
                                               .169
                                               0.00
                              .13
                              0.04
          .10                                  .091
          0.38                                 0.30
                              .07
                              2.45
                                               .049
                                               1.77
```

[a]Intrinsic Value = max(0, Market Value of Cash Flows − Strike Price).
[b]Maximum of Intrinsic Value and Value Alive
[c]Using equation (10.5) with $p = .843$.
[d]Call expires if not exercised.

value if alive (not exercised). Third, the call value is established as the greater of its intrinsic and alive values. For example, at the nodes $N(2,1)$ and $N(2,0)$ the option's intrinsic values are, respectively, \$0.30 (= \$36.86 − \$36.56) and \$1.77 (= 38.33 − \$36.56). These are also the call values because, if unexercised, the option expires worthless. Using these as up- and down-state option values, equation (10.2) can easily be applied to establish a \$0.50 alive call value at $N(1,0)$. However, the intrinsic value at $N(1,0)$ is \$2.45. Therefore, the option is worth \$2.45 and is immediately exercised at $N(1,0)$.

In general, the option is exercised (i.e., the mortgage is prepaid) if, and only if, the market value of the mortgage (long bond-short call) exceeds the face value of the loan.[11] If the mortgage price exceeds its face value, rational exercise of the call is indicated because calling the loan will increase the mortgagor's net worth. These conclusions, however, must be slightly modified when there are significant market frictions.

Exercise with market frictions

Rational prepayment strategies are altered by market frictions. Due-on-sale clauses often force prepayments on discount mortgages (price below face value). Furthermore, many premium mortgages (price above face value) are not prepaid. Mortgagors are often exposed to significant refinancing costs, such as loan points and legal fees, which decrease prepayment incentives. Moreover, homeowners with premium loans will usually put off refinancing if they plan to relocate in the near future. Complications along these lines are easily included in the basic model via suitable adjustments to contractual features of the mortgage.

Market frictions can be interpreted as driving a wedge between effective and stated loan characteristics. Suitable adjustments to the stated option strike price or loan amortization schedule can be used to better explain empirically observed prepayment patterns. For example, a mortgage due-on-sale clause will reduce the effective strike price to the home-owner who is compelled to relocate. Alternatively, if refinancing is costly, the effective strike price to the mortgagor will exceed the outstanding loan balance.

The existence of significant refinancing costs is perhaps the most significant financial barrier to prepayment. Moreover, this friction will often cause the mortgagor (borrower) and the mortgagee (lender) to place

---

[11]Merton (1974) discusses optimal exercise strategies for American-style options.

different values on the option. In the event of a refinancing, the benefits to the mortgagor are reduced by these costs, but there is no change in the financial loss to the lender. As an example, modify Exhibit 10–6 by supposing that refinancing costs increase the mortgagor's effective strike price by $2.00. At each node, intrinsic value to the mortgagor must decline. Before considering these costs, intrinsic value exceeds $2.00 only at $N(1,0)$; it is now the only node at which refinancing is an optimal decision. Including costs, intrinsic value declines to $0.45 = $2.45 – $2.00. However, at $N(0,1)$ the lender must still exchange a bond worth $72.24 for $69.79— a loss of $2.45.

Refinancing costs often interact with homeowner relocation plans to further reduce prepayment frequency. A homeowner intending to move within a short period has essentially exchanged a long-term, fully amortizing loan for a shorter maturity, partially amortizing loan with a large balloon payment. The mortgagor will not readily swap large refinancing costs for a small, temporary reduction in interest costs. Sufficient time to recoup up-front refinancing costs is necessary to inspire an optional prepayment. In our simple three-period example, suppose a relocation-induced prepayment will occur at date $t = 2$. In Exhibit 10–7 it is shown that when refinancing costs are $2.00, refinancing is no longer rational at node $N(1,0)$, because intrinsic value declines to 0 ($71.75 – $69.79 – $2.00 $= -.04$).

As illustrated above, rational mortgagors with identical loans will not always possess the same prepayment exercise strategy. Although the incentives to refinance premium loans appear compelling, refinancing costs and future relocation plans may alter prepayment decisions. Mortgage pools, which are composed of many similar mortgages, will reflect the distribution of mortgagor characteristics. Consequently, many empirical factors must be addressed in mortgage-backed securities analysis. Exhibit 10–8 compares the historical prepayment experience for GNMA pass-throughs to the rational exercise strategy in the absence of refinancing costs.

10.3 OPTION VALUATION FOR MORTGAGE PRICING

The essential features of the option valuation approach to mortgage pricing have been discussed. These results are now extended to the analysis of mortgage pass-through securities. Valuation methods in current use are described.

EXHIBIT 10–7
Call valuation with moving costs and premature relocation

Cash Flows with Prepayment at t = 2 Due to Relocation

Period	Payment	Interest	Principal	Price	Value = Price × Payment / 100
0	40.21	10.00	30.21	90.91	36.55
1	76.77	6.98	69.79	81.16	62.31

Option Valuation (Effective Strike Price = Outstanding Principal + $2.00)

Node	Outstanding Principal	Market Value of Cash Flows	Intrinsic Value
0,0	100.00	98.86	0.00
1,1	69.79	67.94	0.00
1,0	69.79	71.75	0.00 [a]

[a]Equals max(0, 71.75 – 69.79 – 2.00)

Accurate mortgage analysis has been shown to require careful consideration of both bond and option features. In application, however, entire securities are analyzed at one time. Components are not individually valued and summed. There are two interrelated reasons for this practice. First, separate option valuation is not necessary because an active market for prepayment options does not exist. Second, piecewise valuation does not offer a computational advantage. Actual prepayments do not reflect a purely optimal exercise strategy, and are thus best represented by an empirically derived (and complicated) mathematical function. Therefore, an explicit option valuation formula, which would greatly increase computation speed, is not forthcoming. Numerical techniques, which directly value the mortgage as a whole, must be used.

Current valuation techniques have four main parts—reminiscent of the simple analysis in Section 10.2. First, a yield curve process that creates multiple interest rate paths must be specified. Second, an empirical model of prepayment behavior must be constructed. Third, a cash flow generator

EXHIBIT 10–8
Observed prepayment rates on GNMA securities

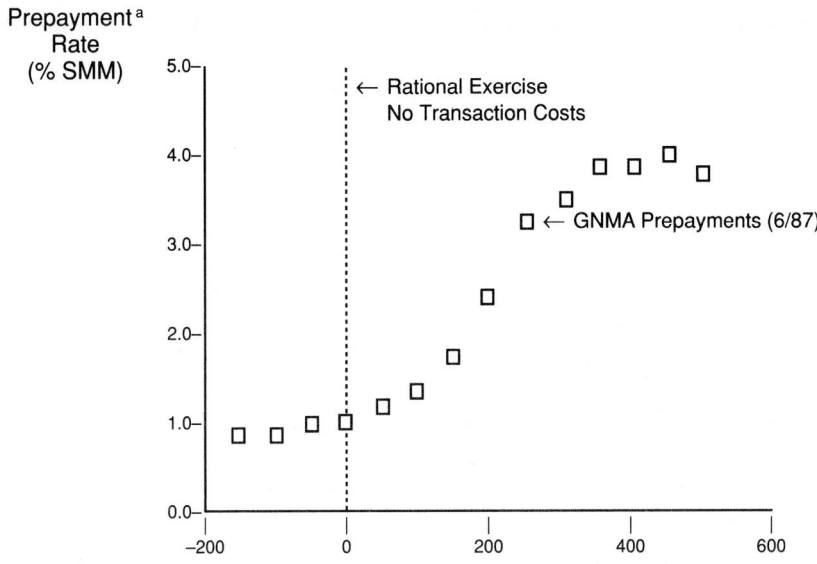

Prepayment[a]
Rate
(% SMM)

← Rational Exercise
No Transaction Costs

□ ← GNMA Prepayments (6/87)

Pass-through Rate minus Current Coupon Rate (basis points)

[a]Prepayment rate = percent of outstanding mortgages prepaid in current month.

is necessary to create periodic principal and interest flows that are consistent with each interest rate path and the prepayment model. Finally, results must be aggregated, weighted, and summarized.

At the heart of the procedure is the examination of the performance of a security under varying sets of assumptions. Each scenario is typically defined by a sequence of interest rates over time.

Interest rates

Most models begin with the Treasury yield curve as it exists on the evaluation date. It is then assumed that the fair non-call yield curve for mortgages is at a fixed spread over the zero coupon Treasury yield curve.

Mortgage securities are less liquid than Treasuries and are more difficult to monitor and evaluate. All other things equal, then, they should provide the investor with an incremental return over Treasury securities. For example, GNMA mortgage securities might be evaluated relative to a yield curve constructed 50 basis points above the zero coupon Treasury yield curve. This is referred to as an "option-adjusted spread" of 50 basis points.

An interest rate path is a random sequence of short-term discount rates consistent with this non-call yield curve. Arbitrage-free restrictions require that the average short rates reflect the forward rates implied by the yield curve. The use of forward rates builds in the assumption that the Treasury market is fairly priced.

These average short rates define the random way that discount rates move through time. Each scenario, or path, is a random sequence of these short-term discount rates. In order for these random paths to be relevant to a particular analysis, certain constraints are imposed on them, in the form of a probability distribution. A lognormal distribution, the standard assumption, implies that the proportional change in interest rates is a random variable that is normally distributed around a constant mean. It results in interest rates that are expected to move by a larger absolute amount at higher yield levels than at lower yield levels, and guarantees that rates will never be negative. Paths that are always near the average values are assigned a higher probability than those which deviate further. Paths that have jumps anywhere are assigned zero probability. Four paths illustrating a lognormal distribution are presented in Exhibit 10–9.

Volatility is defined as the standard deviation of the percentage change in interest rates. It is generally expressed on an annualized basis. An assumption of 25% volatility for a security whose present yield is 8% therefore implies a standard deviation of roughly 200 basis points (25% of 8%). Higher volatility means a greater probability of extreme interest rate moves.

Volatility itself is not a constant; it is therefore the most difficult parameter to estimate to run the model. There are three main ways of deriving a volatility assumption: historical, implied, and projected. The historical method calculates volatility based on actual yield movements over some recent period, from two weeks to two years. This is the most direct measurement possible, but to use it in an options model means to assume that the size of rate movements in the future will continue at the historical level. The implied volatility method uses market prices on bond options together with a theoretical option pricing model, solving for volatility. This is probably the best measure of the market's expectations, but it can be affected by technical factors in the options market. Implied

EXHIBIT 10–9
Possible discount rate scenarios yield curve as of January 3, 1988

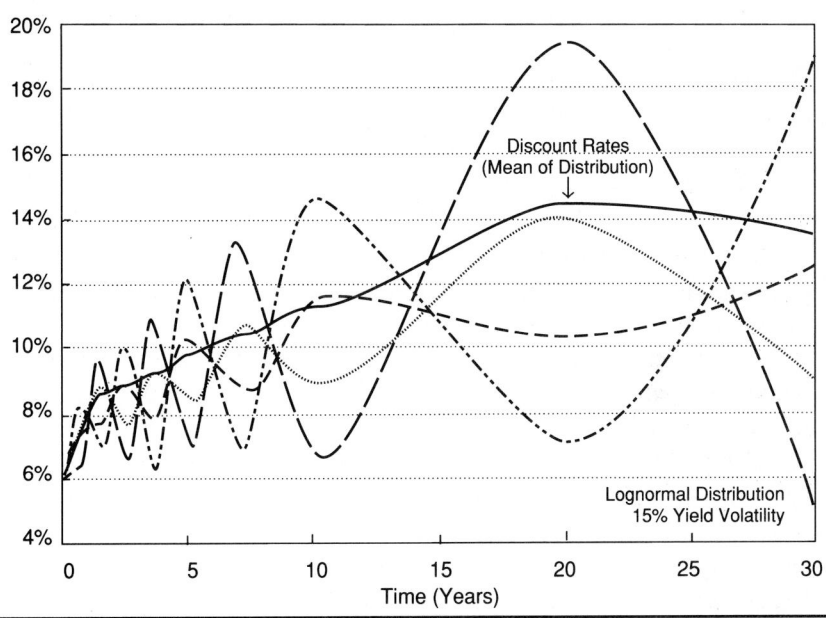

volatility in any case is a short-term measure, and may not be appropriate for evaluation of a very long-term security. Finally, a volatility assumption may be projected, based on an economic forecast or an investor's own views on the market.

Prepayment Model
The prepayment model is the single most important component of an option valuation methodology for mortgages. At the same time, it is the part of the model that varies the most from one analyst to another; no two use precisely the same methodology in creating a prepayment model. Hence most of the differences in the absolute option-adjusted spreads obtained from different analysts may be traced to the prepayment functions employed. The range of variation is shown in Exhibit 10–10, a compilation of thirteen investment banking firms' prepayment projections for various GNMA securities.

In Exhibit 10–10, prepayments are measured in terms of PSA; it is one of the three standards used to quote prepayment rates. "Single monthly

EXHIBIT 10–10
GNMA prepayment projections from various analysts as of November 20, 1987

PSA[a]

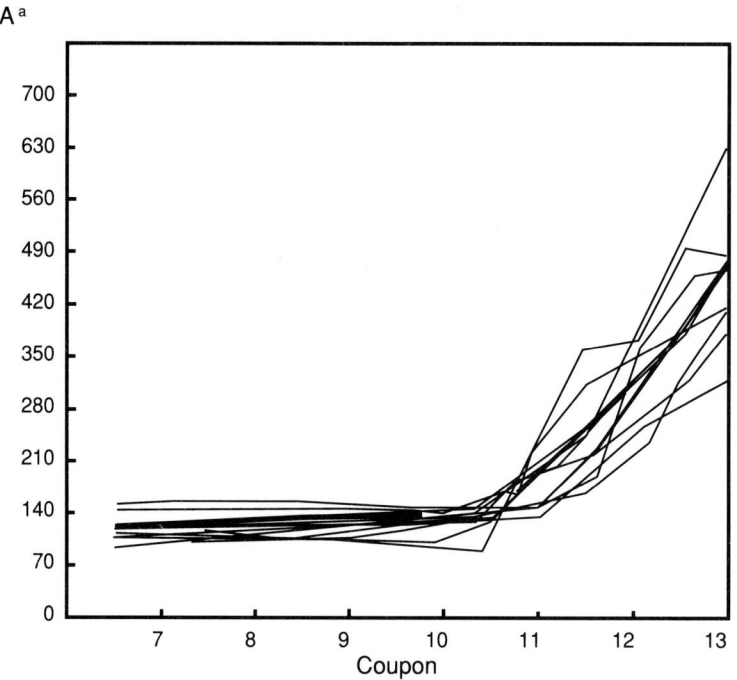

aPrepayment projections as a percent of the PSA Standard Prepayment Model (see text).

mortality" (SMM) is defined as the percentage of the outstanding balance that prepays per month. The "conditional prepayment rate" (CPR) is the annualized value of SMM. As a result of compounding, however, CPR is not a simple multiple of SMM. The Public Securities Association standard (PSA) measures prepayment relative to an assumed series of CPRs (roughly based on historical experience). For 100% PSA, prepayments are assumed to rise linearly from 0% CPR at origination to 6% CPR at month 30. From then on, prepayments remain at 6% CPR. For 200% PSA, simply double all CPRs in this series.

Prepayment models include many components. Age of the mortgage pool and relative coupon, however, are by far the most important. Relative coupon is usually defined as the coupon on the underlying mortgages less the current coupon rate for similar mortgages. Exhibit 10–11 shows that

EXHIBIT 10–11
Example of projected GNMA prepayment rates from a prepayment model

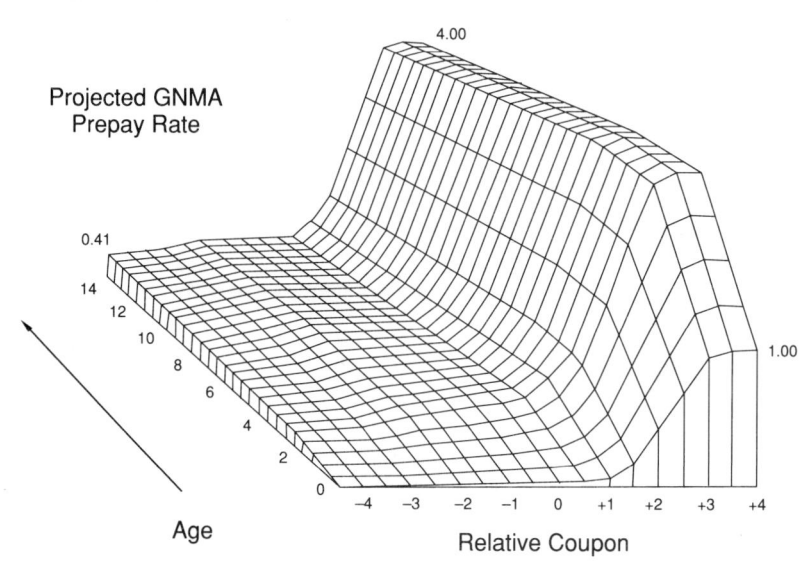

prepayments increase with both age and relative coupon, up to a point. For very seasoned mortgages (for example, over 5 years) and for very high premium securities (for example, more than 3 percentage points above the current coupon), further increases in age or relative coupon have little or no effect on the prepayment assumption. Each mortgage type (government-insured, conventional, and so forth) has a different set of parameters.

Cash Flow Generator

Each path is defined by a sequence of interest rates. We calculate a current coupon rate for every point of the path, and from it, a prepayment speed. For this given path and set of prepayment rates, all of the cash flows on a mortgage security can be determined. The initial balance, coupon, and maturity define the amortization schedule. Interest payments are simply the periodic coupon rate times the remaining balance. Total cash flow is coupon interest, scheduled principal, and prepaid principal.

An example of cash flow generation is presented in Exhibit 10–12. The falling interest rate path composed of nodes $N(0,0)$, $N(1,0)$ and $N(2,0)$

EXHIBIT 10–12
Cash flow generation along a path

Time	Node	Interest	Scheduled Amortization	Prepaid Principal	Total Cash Flow
$t = 1$	0,0	10.00	30.21	0.00	40.21
$t = 2$	1,0	6.98	33.23	36.56	76.77
$t = 3$	2,0	0.00	0.00	0.00	0.00

in our example is examined. Prepayments are assumed to reflect perfectly rational decisions based upon zero refinancing costs. As shown in Exhibit 10–6, the prepayment option will be exercised at $N(1,0)$. Therefore, cash flows are equal to scheduled amortization and interest at $t = 1$, scheduled payments plus full prepayment at $t = 2$, and zero at $t = 3$.

Valuation

The basic idea in valuation is to determine a value for the security for each path and then to aggregate the results across scenarios. Once the set of interest rate paths and cash flows is generated, a price has to be assigned to each path. The price associated with a path is the present value of its cash flows. The discount rates are used in a way that is consistent with their definition as forward rates. The cash flow in any period is discounted only one period by the discount rate for that period. The discount rate for the next (earlier) period is at the rate associated with that period. In this way, the cash flow in any period is discounted altogether by the compounded product of all prior rates. Hence the individual rates are short-term discount rates at various points in time, and are closely related to today's forward rates.

We call this method one of "discounting along paths." Since distant forward rates are higher than nearby rates when the yield curve is positively sloped, the cash flows in the early years are treated in a way that is compatible with our treatment of short-term debt, while cash flows in later years are discounted at rates appropriate for longer-term debt. The method gives this result without knowing in advance whether the security has a long or short duration, average life, or maturity.

Aggregation Procedure

We have described how the value associated with one scenario is calculated. The most common way to aggregate the values is to generate a number of paths randomly and simply average the resulting prices. This method is called sampling. If more paths are used, and if each path is a series of monthly rather than annual cash flows, one has better confidence that the results are accurate.

The number and periodicity of paths required to be generated depends on the information and precision desired. Fewer paths, each with less frequent observations, are needed for an accurate estimate of price than for an accurate estimate of duration and convexity.

As an alternative to sampling, the backward induction pricing method can be used. It works backward in time, computing all possible prices of a mortgage, across a variety of initial interest rate levels, for successively longer times from maturity. Eventually, the price at the settlement date for the actual initial interest rate is obtained.

For example, suppose we are trying to price a mortgage security with three time periods remaining until maturity. For simplicity we will assume that only three interest rate levels are possible between now and then, and that today's short-term interest rate is the middle level. Exhibit 10–13 represents the "state space" (the set of possible interest rate levels over time) and solid lines represent possible state transitions. Each transition has a probability of occurrence that depends on the yield curve and volatility. We begin our analysis by noting that the bond returns its par value at maturity for each interest rate. We then step one period back from maturity. For each possible interest rate, we know the transition probabilities for the rates next period, the prepayment rates according to the prepayment model, the coupon rate, and the short-term interest rates. We also know all possible future values, so we can compute the probability-weighted average present value for each interest rate. Once these prices are computed, we proceed to price the mortgage for each rate two periods from maturity, relying on the prices known for one period from maturity. Finally we proceed to price the mortgage at the beginning. The price corresponding to the middle interest rate is the fair price at today's interest rate. The simulation method would have required 27 scenarios to model the same process.

The method has two advantages over the simpler simulation method. The first advantage is that it is faster, enabling us to calculate more precise answers. This is particularly important for the calculation of durations, where less precise methods can lead to serious errors. The second advantage over simulation is that the method can value explicit American options on mortgage securities. Both methods can value the homeowner's prepayment option, and both are able to handle a string of European options, such

EXHIBIT 10–13
The backward induction approach for a 3-period model

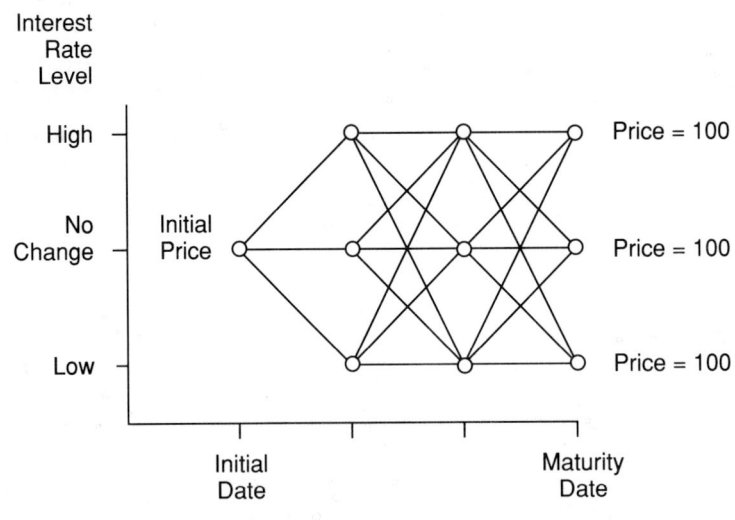

as coupon caps and floors. But only the backward induction method can value explicit American options, such as a CMO trustee's clean-up call or an over-the-counter option on a mortgage security.

Outputs from the Model

The spread over the non-call yield curve summarizes the relative attractiveness of the mortgage security. In the simplest case, this is analogous to the situation with non-callable corporate bonds. If a bond is initially priced at 50 basis points over the Treasury curve and is still priced at the same spread at the end of the holding period, it will have returned roughly 50 basis points over the Treasury security.

For securities with option components, the spread over the non-call yield curve is maintained for each interest rate path. This means the value of the mortgage instrument, including options, should earn the Treasury yield plus the "option-adjusted" spread (OAS) over its remaining term. These spreads have the same caveats as simple yield spreads. But the size of the spread gives a good indication of whether the security is relatively attractive over the short term, and also gives an indication of its long-term attractiveness over Treasury securities. We do not view these spreads, however, as something that can be locked in or guaranteed. Exhibit 10–14 describes the relationship between two scenario interest-rates, an OAS level, and period-by-period discount rates.

Depending on how the models are run, the option-adjusted spread is either an input or an output. On the one hand, we can assume a spread and calculate a price. The spread is both a prediction of the fair spread that the security will eventually be priced to return and also the fair return over Treasuries for the interim. On the other hand, we can specify today's market price and calculate the spread it implies.

This spread compensates the mortgage holder for the nuisance of receiving monthly cash flows and the credit risk of holding agency rather than Treasury debt with the accompanying partial guarantees. But in practice it also must compensate the holder for volatility risk (actual volatility differs from that assumed) and for non-systematic prepayment model risk (the difference between actual experienced prepayments and those our models would predict given the realized yield history outcome).

The results of an option pricing analysis are intended to expose the cost, likelihood, and timing of exercise of the homeowner's prepayment option. The value of a mortgage security that is arrived at through this methodology is generally less than what would be calculated for the same average discount rates under an assumption of a static yield curve. A prepayment function is generally assumed for the static analysis, as it is for the expected value analysis, so the difference in value between the two methods is not a result of the *level* of prepayments. Rather, it is a representation of the cost to the lender (and value to the borrower) of the *variation* in option exercise in response to unanticipated changes in economic conditions. Hence the expected value computed through this method of analysis is said to be "option based" or "option adjusted." The difference between option-adjusted and static value is the cost imposed by the short call option position of the security and the effect of discounting cash flows from different points in time at different rates.

Duration and Convexity

In order to hedge mortgage-backed securities against interest-rate risk, accurate measures of their price sensitivity must be obtained. For noncallable securities, participants in fixed-income markets have come to rely upon (modified) duration and convexity to quantify interest-rate sensitivity.

EXHIBIT 10–14
Discounting along paths (option adjusted spread)

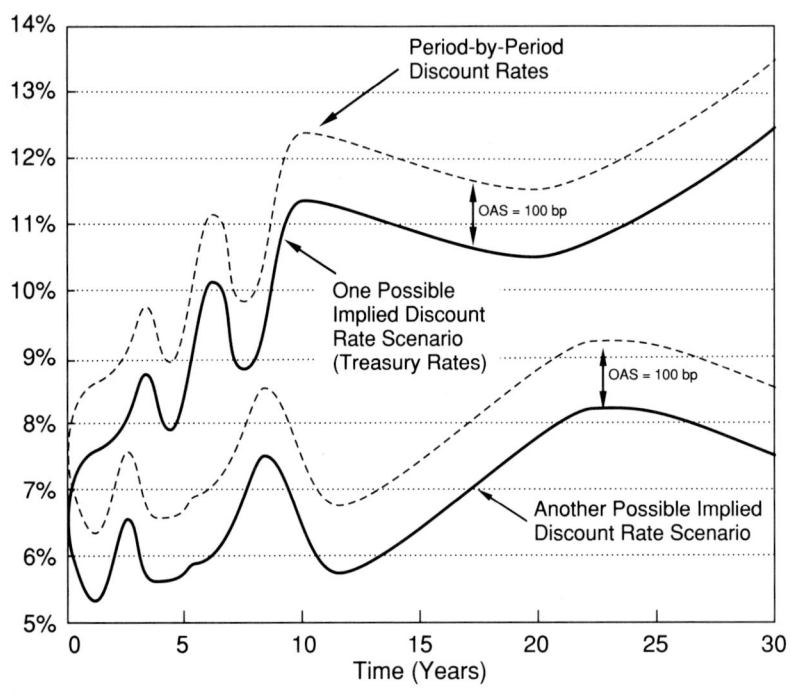

Duration is equal to the percentage change in price resulting from a small change in yield, and convexity is used to adjust duration for large yield movements.

Standard, static definitions of duration and convexity are not appropriate hedging tools for securities with embedded options. Consequently, "effective" measures of duration and convexity have been developed which take into account how the value of prepayment options responds to interest rate movements. Effective duration is computed by shifting the yield curve up and down slightly, holding option adjusted spread constant, and calculating the security's price. The average percentage price change is a measure of duration, and by measuring the difference in price change from upward and downward movements in yields, convexity can be calculated. This procedure is discussed in more detail in Chapter 8.

10.4 COMPLICATED MORTGAGE-BACKED SECURITIES

Mortgage-backed securities have become increasingly complicated. Nonetheless, the basics of mortgage valuation outlined in Section 10.2 remain intact. Mortgages are amortizing bonds with embedded prepayment options, and exercise strategies reflect refinancing costs and anticipated tenure decisions. Methods described in Section 10.3 must be employed to analyze mortgage-backed securities.

Securities have evolved in two directions since the advent of the GNMA pass-through. Each of these avenues can be viewed as a reaction to interest rate risk. First, risk-averse investors have sought to reallocate the embedded option feature of mortgages. Multi-class securities, collateralized mortgage obligations (CMOs) and mortgage strips, have been the response to this demand. A CMO is typically composed of several bonds (tranches) with different priorities over the cash flows from a mortgage pool. Second, mortgage lenders have often offered borrowers attractive rates on adjustable rate mortgages (ARMs) in order to achieve a better asset/liability match. Although some instruments combine multi-class and adjustable rate features, it is simpler to examine the two elements separately. For the sake of simplicity, all multi-class derivatives (CMOs) are assumed to have fixed coupons and fixed-rate mortgage collateral.

CMO derivative analysis is a straightforward extension of the fixed rate pass-through methodology. Interest rate paths, prepayment frequencies and amortization rates are generated as before. Only one modification is necessary. Redirection of collateral cash flows must be considered. At each node along an interest rate path, tranches receive different principal and interest amounts. Even though this modification is conceptually simple, the complexity and variety of paydown rules can create confusion. Moreover, the added computational burden of analyzing these securities is considerable.

CMO tranches receive sequential, rather than pro rata, principal paydown. Due to their sequential nature, tranche amortization and option features differ from those of the underlying collateral. Many tranches have an initial nonamortization period. After paydown begins, amortization speed is much quicker than that of the underlying collateral. Prepayments follow a similar pattern.

The simple two-tranche CMO of section 10.1 can be used to illustrate the sequential pay structure. The CMO is backed by $100 of mortgages with a 10% coupon and 10 periods to maturity. Exhibit 10–15 describes the periodic principal and interest payments going to each tranche under two scenarios: zero prepayments, and annual prepayments equal to 5% of outstanding collateral balance.

Adjustable-rate mortgages (ARMs) add another twist to the analysis of mortgage-backed securities. Ideally, the mortgage coupon is intended to fully reflect current market rates. The ideal ARM security will be priced close to par, and refinancings will rarely occur. However, ARM coupons imperfectly adjust to changes in market interest rates, which leads to substantial deviations from the ideal.

ARM coupon levels differ from market rates for four reasons. First, mortgage lenders usually offer an initial below market, "teaser" rate to attract borrowers. Second, floating coupons are often tied to an index of market rates (e.g., the 1-year Constant Maturity Treasury Index), which does not exactly correspond to current market rates. Third, coupons only adjust (reset) to index movements periodically. Finally, coupon adjustments are often constrained by periodic and lifetime ceilings (caps) and floors.

ARM performance can be viewed as being like a combination of the ideal floater and a fixed-rate security, as shown schematically in Exhibit 10–16. When interest rates change, the coupon on a pure floater changes as well, and the value remains at par. At the other extreme, the value of a fixed-rate instrument will show a sharp decline when interest rates rise. In the exhibit, percentage price changes are shown for a 1 percentage point increase in market interest rates. Most ARMs will fall between the floater and the fixed-rate security. Rigidities in coupon adjustments can produce price deviations from par, which can induce optimal exercise of the prepayment option. However, deviations from par are usually fairly small and temporary, and prepayment options are usually not in-the-money for long. An exception to the price reversion to par of an ARM occurs when the coupon level "caps out." For example, suppose an ARM has a maximum 2% coupon adjustment per year, its present coupon level is 8%, and the index of current market rates is 13%. The mortgage will be priced at a discount to par.

Coupon caps can be viewed as options which are always optimally exercised. From the standpoint of the mortgagor (borrower), a coupon ceiling can be interpreted as a long put and a floor as a short call. When an

EXHIBIT 10–15
Projected cash flows of a two tranche CMO

| | Zero Prepayment Case | | | | | | Prepayments at 5% SMM | | | | | |
| | Interest | | | Principal | | | Interest | | | Principal | | |
Period	A	B	Total[a]	A	B	Total	A	B	Total	A	B	Total
0	5.00	5.00	10.00	6.27	0.00	6.27	5.00	5.00	10.00	10.96	0.00	10.96
1	4.37	5.00	9.37	6.90	0.00	6.90	3.90	5.00	8.90	10.68	0.00	10.68
2	3.68	5.00	8.68	7.59	0.00	7.59	2.84	5.00	7.84	10.43	0.00	10.43
3	2.90	5.00	7.92	8.35	0.00	8.35	1.79	5.00	6.79	10.20	0.00	10.20
4	2.09	5.00	7.09	9.19	0.00	9.19	0.77	5.00	5.77	7.73	2.27	10.00
5	1.17	5.00	6.17	10.11	0.00	10.11	0.00	4.77	4.77	0.00	9.82	9.82
6	0.16	5.00	5.16	1.59	9.53	11.12	0.00	3.79	3.79	0.00	9.66	9.66
7	0.00	4.05	4.05	0.00	12.23	12.23	0.00	2.83	2.83	0.00	9.53	9.53
8	0.00	2.82	2.82	0.00	13.45	13.45	0.00	1.87	1.87	0.00	9.41	9.41
9	0.00	1.48	1.48	0.00	14.80	14.80	0.00	0.93	0.93	0.00	9.32	9.32
	50.00	50.00		50.00	50.00	100.00	50.00	50.00		50.00	50.00	100.00

[a]Columns may not sum due to rounding.

EXHIBIT 10–16
Change in value of a typical ARM when interest rates rise one percent

Coupon Reset Frequency	Maximum Reset Amount				
	0%	1%	2%	No Limit	
Instantaneous		−0.09	−0.08	0	Floater
Every year		−1.17	−0.93	−0.89	
Every 2 years		−1.94	−1.59	−1.47	
Every 3 years		−2.37	−2.02	−1.79	
Never	−3.17				
	(Fixed Rate)				

index rises above the ceiling, the mortgagor has effectively put a discount bond to the mortgagee (lender) at par. The discount bond has a coupon equal to the ceiling. When a floor is reached, the mortgagee has effectively called a premium bond from the mortgagor at par.

Complications, such as coupon adjustment caps, can be examined using the methods already discussed. For each interest rate path, however, coupon levels must be adjusted to correspond to the exact specification of the ARM under consideration. Moreover, the prepayment model must also be modified to accurately account for the rigidities in the coupon adjustment process and the demographic features of the borrowers. As before, demographic characteristics may alter the effective strike price of the prepayment option and the terms of the loan.

References

Carron, A., and Hogan, M. (June 1988). The option valuation approach to mortgage pricing. *Journal of Real Estate Finance and Economics, 1,* 131–49.

Cox, J., Ingersoll, J., and Ross, S. (1985). A theory of the term structure of interest rates. *Econometrica, 53,* 385–407.

Cox, J., Ross, S., and Rubinstein, M. (1979). Option pricing: A simplified approach. *Journal of Financial Economics, 7,* 229–63.

Dunn, K., and McConnell, J. (1981).   Valuation of GNMA mortgage-backed securities. *Journal of Finance, 36,* 599–616.

Fabozzi, F., ed. (1988). *The handbook of mortgage securities.* (Revised edition). Chicago: Probus Publishing Co.

Merton, R. (1973).   Theory of rational option pricing. *Bell Journal of Economics and Management Science, 4,* 141–83.

APPENDIX TO CHAPTER 10

GLOSSARY OF MORTGAGE-RELATED TERMS

Accrual Bond   Deferred coupon tranche of a CMO. An accrual bond receives payments of neither principal nor interest until all tranches preceding it are retired. In effect, an accrual bond is a deferred interest obligation, resembling a zero coupon bond prior to the time that the preceding tranches are retired, except that accrual bonds carry an explicit coupon rate. The accrual bond then receives cash payments representing interest and principal on the accrued amount outstanding.   Accrual bonds are purchased most frequently by investors who require the greatest degree of protection against reinvestment and call risk, or who seek the greater price leverage afforded by these classes. Also called Accretion Bond and Z Bond.

Adjustable Rate Mortgage (ARM)   A mortgage whose interest rate is periodically readjusted to reflect movements in market interest rates. ARMs are usually tied to a government index, with limitations on the rate change within a period and a rate cap for the life of the loan.

Amortization   The scheduled principal portion of a mortgage payment.

Assumable   A mortgage that a homebuyer is permitted to take over from the seller.

Cap   An upper limit on the interest rate that may be paid on a floating rate security.

Collateral   The mortgages underlying a mortgage-backed security.

Collateralized Mortgage Obligation (CMO)   A corporate bond backed by a pool of mortgages in which the principal cash flows of the pool are channeled, usually sequentially, into two or more series of bonds (tranches). Interest payments are made on all tranches except, in some CMOs, accrual bonds (Z) or principal-only (PO) bonds.

Conditional Prepayment Rate (CPR)   See Constant Prepayment Rate.

Constant Prepayment Rate (CPR)   A prepayment model in which the average monthly prepayment rate (SMM) in percent is annualized using the formula $(1 - CPR/100) = (1 - SMM / 100)^{12}$ *Note:* To transform an SMM to the corresponding CPR, use the following conversion:

$$CPR = 100 \times \left[1 - \left(1 - \frac{SMM}{100} \right)^{12} \right].$$

Coupon   With respect to mortgage securities, it is the mortgage rate less servicing, guarantee and/or securitization fees.

Conventional Loan   A mortgage loan usually granted by a bank or thrift institution.   The loan is based on real estate value as security, recourse to the homeowner and/or private mortgage insurance, rather than being insured or guaranteed by a government agency.

Convexity   A measure of the change in duration with respect to changes in interest rates.   Convexity is the second derivative of a bond's price with respect to yield.   The more convex a bond is, the more its duration will change given a change in interest rates.   Modified duration assumes that prices change linearly with interest rates; it therefore becomes increasingly imprecise in estimating price changes as yield changes increase.   If a bond is convex, its change in price given a specified change in yield will be of a different magnitude than that predicted by modified duration.   If the interest rates change and the ending bond price is greater than that predicted by modified duration, the bond has positive convexity.   Conversely, if the price is less than that predicted by modified duration, the bond has negative convexity.

Credit Risk   The risk that an issuer will default on its bonds.

Current Coupon   The interest rate on mortgage-backed pass-through securities currently trading at a price close to par.

Discount   The difference between par and the price of an issue for issues selling below par.

Due-on-sale   A mortgage clause requiring a mortgage to be prepaid upon transfer of ownership of the property.   A due on sale clause is not enforceable in some states.   It applies only to conventional mortgages; all government-backed loans are assumable.

Duration   A measure of a bond's price sensitivity, expressed in years.   As defined by Frederick Macaulay in 1938, it is a measure of the interest rate risk of a bond, taking into consideration that there may be cash flows before the maturity date and that the cash flows must be considered in terms of their present value.   Duration is similar to, but much more precise than, average life.   It is a measure of the number of years until the average dollar—in present value terms—is received from coupon and principal payments.   As such, it is one measure of systematic risk.   Average life, on the other hand, is a measure of the time to receive a dollar of principal only—it takes into consideration neither interest payments nor present value.   Duration is computed by multiplying the time to each principal and interest payment by its present value, summing these products, and dividing by the full price of the bond.

11th District Cost of Funds Index   An ARM index.   The 11th District Cost of Funds is the weighted average interest rate paid by the 11th Federal Home Loan Bank District member savings institutions on their sources of funds.

Face Value   The principal amount the bondholder receives upon maturity. Alternatively, the amount which, when multiplied by the percentage coupon rate, gives the amount of interest payable to the bondholder.

Federal Home Loan Mortgage Corporation (FHLMC)   A corporate instrumentality of the United States, created by an act of Congress on July 24, 1970 in order to increase the availability of mortgage credit for the financing of housing. FHLMC issues securities backed by pools of conventional mortgages: Participation Certificates (PCs), Guaranteed Mortgage Certificates (GMCs), Collateralized Mortgage Obligations (CMOs) or REMICs. Also called Freddie Mac.

Federal National Mortgage Association (FNMA)   A government-sponsored corporation owned entirely by private stockholders established in 1938 to provide additional liquidity to the mortgage market. In 1968, the original FNMA was broken into two corporations: the privately owned FNMA and the government owned GNMA. FNMA predominantly issues securities backed by conventional mortgages. Also called Fannie Mae.

Fixed Rate Interest   Interest on a security that is calculated as a constant specified percentage of the current principal amount and paid with respect to specified interest periods (annually, semiannually, quarterly, monthly, or biweekly) until maturity.

Fixed Rate Loan   A loan for which the interest rate is fixed for life.

Floater   Floating rate security.

Forward Rate   An interest rate for a holding period that begins in the future.

Fully Amortizing   Describes a loan whose payments are designed so that the principal balance will be completely paid over the term of the loan without requiring a large "balloon" payment at the end.

Government Insured   Describes a mortgage loan warranted against default by the Federal Housing Administration or the Veterans Administration.

Government National Mortgage Association (GNMA)   A wholly-owned U.S. Government corporation within the Department of Housing and Urban Development, established in 1968 as a spinoff from the Federal National Mortgage Association (FNMA). GNMA took over the assets and liabilities and operation of the special assistance functions and the management and liquidating functions of FNMA. GNMA issues securities backed by pools of mortgages (see Pass-Through). Primary functions of GNMA are the purchase and sale of certain FHA and VA mortgages pursuant to various programs to support the housing market, and the guaranteeing of mortgage-backed securities issued against pools of FHA and VA mortgages.

Index   A market interest level off of which ARM coupons are set, including Treasury bills, cost of funds, LIBOR, and Constant Maturity Treasury.

Interest   An amount of money charged to a borrower by a lender for the use of money.

Interest Only (IO)   Stripped mortgage-backed security in which the investor receives all of the interest and none of the principal of the underlying security.

Level Pay   Amortization schedule in which payments of principal plus interest are kept constant for the life of the loan.

Lifetime Cap   Maximum interest rate for the life of an adjustable rate mortgage loan.

Lifetime Floor   Minimum interest rate for the life of an adjustable rate mortgage loan.

Loan Points   Fee paid by a mortgagor at the initiation of a mortgage, not included in the interest rate, expressed as a percentage of the loan amount.

Maturity   The date on which the principal or stated value of a debt security becomes due and payable in full to the holder.

Mortgage   Conveyance of an interest in real property given as security for the payment of a debt.

Mortgage-Backed Security (MBS)   An ordinary bond backed by an undivided interest in a pool of mortgages or trust deeds. Income from the underlying mortgages or trust deeds is used to pay off the securities.

Mortgagee   A person or firm to whom the title to property is conveyed as security for a loan.

Mortgagor   One who borrows money, giving as security a mortgage or deed of trust on real property.

Negative Convexity   See Convexity.

Option-Adjusted Spread   Yield spread over the Treasury yield curve adjusted for the value of the option embedded in the security.

Pass-Through   A mortgage-backed security for which the payments on the underlying mortgages are passed from the mortgage holder through the servicing agency (who usually keeps a portion as a fee) to the security holder.

Paydown   Payment of principal on a loan.

Periodic Cap   Maximum amount (up or down) by which an adjustable rate mortgage loan rate may change per reset interval.

Planned Amortization Class (PAC)   A type of CMO tranche that has a planned amortization schedule. Principal payments are made on a priority basis to the PAC bonds before being made to the other tranches. The payment schedule causes the weighted average life of the PAC bond to remain relatively constant over a wide range of prepayment experience.

Premium   The difference between the price of an issue and par, for issues selling above par.

Prepayment   Any payment made before its originally scheduled payment date. In particular, the full or partial repayment of a mortgage loan before such payment is due.

Prepayment Model   Predictive model of prepayment rates. Models include Twelve-Year Life or Prepaid Life, FHA experience, Single Monthly Mortality (SMM), Conditional prepayment Rate (CPR), Constant Percent Prepayment (CPP), the PSA (Public Securities Association) Standard Prepayment Model, the Absolute Prepayment Model (ABS) for asset-backed securities and proprietary models.

Prepayment Penalty   A fee paid by a mortgagor to a mortgagee for exercising the option to prepay a loan. For single-family mortgages, prepayment penalties typically amount to a small percentage of the loan balance and apply only during the first few years. For commercial loans, the penalty may require the mortgagor to pay the present value of any forgone interest income (the difference between the remaining scheduled interest payments and then-current market rates for a similar loan).

Principal   The face amount or par value of a security; the amount exclusive of interest or premium due the holder at maturity. It is the sum used to compute interest. Also called Face or Nominal Amount.

Principal Only (PO)   Stripped mortgage-backed security in which the investor receives all of the principal payments and none of the interest on the underlying security. See Interest Only.

Private Label Pass-Through   A pass-through not issued by a government agency and therefore not containing a government or agency guarantee. Private pass-throughs are also referred to as AA pass-throughs, reflecting the typical credit rating of issuers, such as Citicorp and Bank of America.

PSA Standard Prepayment Model   FHA experience specifies standard prepayment percentages for each year of a mortgage's life. PSA, on the other hand, specifies a standard percentage for each month, and annualizes that percentage. 100% PSA calls for prepayment rates of 0.2% CPR in the first month, 0.4% CPR in the second month, 0.6% in the third month, and so on until, in months 30 and beyond, the mortgage (or mortgage pool) will prepay at an annual rate of 6% CPR. Also called Standard Prepayment Assumption.

Real Estate Mortgage Investment Conduit (REMIC)   A mortgage securities vehicle, authorized by the Tax Reform Act of 1986, that holds commercial or residential mortgages and issues securities representing interests in those mortgages. A REMIC can be formed as a corporation, partnership, or segregated pool of assets. The REMIC itself is generally exempt from federal income tax, but the income from the mortgages is reported by investors. For investment purposes, REMIC securities are nearly indistinguishable from CMOs.

Refinancing   The prepayment of a mortgage with funds borrowed at a lower interest rate.

Relative Coupon   The difference between the Coupon and the Current Coupon; used as a measure of the borrower's incentive to refinance.

Scheduled Amortization   See Amortization.

Seasoned   A mortgage on which payments have been made for a relatively long period, typically 2-3 years.

Single Monthly Mortality (SMM)   A prepayment model originally developed as an alternative to FHA experience. The SMM rate of a mortgage pool is the percentage of outstanding mortgages assumed to terminate each month. Unlike the FHA model, the SMM model assumes that a pool of mortgages will prepay at a fixed percentage rate, regardless of the age of the mortgages. Other prepayment models, such as CPR and CPP, are similar to SMM, but express prepayments on an annual basis. CPR and CPP differ from each other in the way they annualize the SMM figures.

Strip   A mortgage-backed security created by altering the distribution of interest and principal on a pass-through from a pro rata to an unequal yet concurrent allocation.

Tranche   A part of a security, typically a CMO, that shares documentation with other parts but has different terms (e.g., in a $200 million issue, one tranche of $100 million may have a maturity of five years and the second tranche of $100 million may have a maturity of ten years). Also called Class.

Volatility   The susceptibility of a quantity or entity to change. For securities, volatility is typically stated as the standard deviation of possible ending prices (or yields, or returns) over a one-year period.

Whole Loan   A mortgage that is not part of a mortgage-backed security.

Yield Curve   A graph showing the relationship between yield and maturity for a set of similar securities. Generally refers to the most recent issues of each maturity in the U.S. Treasury market if not otherwise specified.

Yield Spread   The difference between the yield of two securities.

Z Bond   See Accrual Bond.

CHAPTER 11

PORTFOLIO INSURANCE AND RELATED DYNAMIC TRADING STRATEGIES

Mark Kritzman[*]

11.1 INTRODUCTION

Portfolio insurance is an option-based dynamic trading strategy designed to protect a portfolio from market declines while preserving the opportunity to participate in market advances. In effect, it is equivalent to a protective put option strategy, but it does not require investment in options. Instead, portfolio insurance is implemented by shifting a portfolio between a risky asset and a riskless asset, thus replicating the payoff of a put option synthetically.

At its peak in popularity, prior to the 1987 worldwide stock market crash, approximately $90 billion of institutional assets were under the administration of portfolio insurance strategies.[1] Investor enthusiasm for portfolio insurance came to an abrupt end, however, with the stock market crash, as many investment experts attributed the magnitude of the crash, if not the event itself, to portfolio insurance. Perhaps neither the investor enthusiasm that propelled its ascent nor the post crash criticism that

[*]Mr. Kritzman is currently a Partner at Windham Capital Management in New York.
[1]*Report of the Presidential Task Force on Market Mechanisms,* N. Brady, Chairman, 1988.

precipitated its demise fairly reflects the merits and limitations of portfolio insurance. Certainly, its intent is worthwhile, as evidenced by the assets it attracted. Yet, the investment market conditions upon which its success depends are perhaps more restrictive than many practitioners originally estimated.

The purpose of this chapter is to review portfolio insurance and related dynamic trading strategies from an analytical perspective as well as from an historical perspective. The chapter is divided into five sections. In section 11.2, we discuss the motivation for portfolio insurance, its basic structure, and its historical development. In section 11.3, we describe several other dynamic trading strategies that have emerged as extensions of portfolio insurance. Next, in section 11.4, we review in detail the correspondence of portfolio insurance to option valuation within the framework of the binomial option pricing model. In section 11.5, we present two real world applications of dynamic trading strategies: a specific example of portfolio insurance and an example of a related strategy called surplus insurance. Finally, in section 11.6, we address two important procedural issues: estimating volatility and executing the strategy. We conclude the chapter with a brief summary.

11.2 THE MARKET FOR OPTION REPLICATION

Why Replicate Options?
As we mentioned at the beginning of the chapter, portfolio insurance is designed to provide the same outcome as a protective put option strategy. Such a strategy enables us to acquire an asset which we hope will appreciate in value and, at the same time, to limit the extent of our potential loss should the asset fall in value. Based on put-call parity (See Chapter 2), we know that we could achieve the same outcome by combining a riskless asset with a call option.

Suppose, however, we wish to protect a portfolio which includes several assets instead of a single asset. We could purchase a put option on each of the component assets as a means of protecting the overall portfolio. This approach, however, would be unnecessarily expensive if a fairly priced option on the total portfolio were available. Option prices are determined, in part, by the total risk of the underlying asset. A portfolio's total risk is typically lower than the average of the component assets' total risk because, to the extent the assets are not perfectly correlated with each other, some of their specific risk is diversified away in a portfolio. Consequently, an option on a portfolio is typically less expensive than a portfolio of options.

Consider, for example, two assets that are both priced at $50, have standard deviations of 30 percent, and are uncorrelated with each other. Suppose a put option with a strike price of $45 is available on each of these assets and that these options expire in three months. Further, suppose that we can purchase a Treasury bill that yields 8 percent annually. If we insert these values into the Black-Scholes formula, we find that each option is worth $.80. Thus, if we wished to protect a portfolio consisting of 500 shares of each asset from declining in value below $45,000, we would have to purchase 1,000 put options at a total cost of $800.

Now suppose we could purchase a single put option whose value is determined, not by the risk of each component asset, but instead by the risk of the overall portfolio. What is the fair value of such an option? The total value of the portfolio is $50,000, and the cumulative strike price equals $45,000. The standard deviation of this portfolio, however, is not 30 percent but 21.21 percent,[2] because the portfolio's risk is reduced by diversification. Again, using the Black-Scholes formula, we find that the fair value of this option position is $294, which is $506 less than it would cost to achieve the same level of protection by purchasing a put option on each of the component assets. This example demonstrates that as long as the component assets of a portfolio are not perfectly correlated with each other, it is less expensive to purchase an option on a portfolio than it is to purchase a portfolio of options on each of the component assets. See section 2.6 of Chapter 2 for a somewhat more general discussion of this notion.

If we were interested in protecting the S&P 500 index portfolio, for example, we could purchase a put option on this index so long as our investment horizon coincided with the term of an available option. We should certainly prefer this strategy to a strategy of purchasing individual

---

[2]This value is computed as:

$$\sqrt{\sigma_1^2 w_1 + \sigma_2^2 w_2 + 2\rho\,\sigma_1\, w_1\, \sigma_2\, w_2}$$

where,

σ_1 = Standard deviation of asset 1
σ_2 = Standard deviation of asset 2
w_1 = Percent invested in asset 1
w_2 = Percent invested in asset 2
ρ = Correlation between asset 1 and asset 2

put options on each of the 500 securities. In many instances, however, we might be interested in protecting a portfolio for which options are not available or for longer periods than the typical term of traded options. The desire to achieve portfolio protection in these and similar situations motivated the development of portfolio insurance and other dynamic trading strategies to generate option-like results.

Portfolio Insurance: The Basic Strategy

The name, portfolio insurance, is in one sense appropriate and in another sense inappropriate. It is appropriate because the terms of portfolio insurance relate easily to the terms of conventional insurance. However, in another sense the strategy is inappropriately named since it does not depend on the principle of pooling risk; rather, it depends on the concept of hedging. Thus, the features of portfolio insurance also correspond directly to familiar notions of option valuation.

In order to implement portfolio insurance, we start by specifying some minimum value we wish to prevent the portfolio from penetrating, or equivalently, a minimum return which we wish to be certain of achieving. This minimum value or minimum return is called the *floor*. It corresponds to the strike price in a protective put option strategy.

The protection, of course, pertains to a specific *investment horizon*. The investment horizon is analogous to the term of the insurance policy and, in the context of option valuation, it corresponds to the time remaining to expiration.

The difference between the initial portfolio value and the floor value is called the *deductible*. As with conventional insurance, the lower the deductible, the higher the expected cost of the strategy.

The expected cost of portfolio insurance can be thought of as the insurance premium or, in the context of option valuation, as the price of a protective put option.

A related notion to cost is *upside capture*, which refers to the percentage of the risky asset's terminal value that is "captured" by the insured portfolio's terminal value. Note that upside capture is defined in terms of total portfolio value, not returns. For example, if the risky asset increases from $100 to $120 while the portfolio increases from $100 to $115, upside capture equals 95.83 percent (115/120). At the inception of a portfolio insurance strategy, we would expect upside capture to equal the initial value of the portfolio, less the cost of the implicit put option that the strategy is designed to replicate, all divided by the portfolio's initial value. Thus, in the above example the cost of the implicit or shadow put option equals 4.17%.

Finally, the *hedge ratio* in a portfolio insurance strategy equals the percentage of the portfolio that is allocated to the risky asset. It corresponds to the delta of the overall portfolio in a protective put option strategy.

These terms are illustrated in Figure 11–1, which compares the payoff functions of a risky asset and a portfolio insurance strategy.

Although portfolio insurance is intended to produce the same outcome as a protective put option strategy, it does not require investment in options. Instead, we can achieve the same result by shifting a portfolio's assets to a risky component as its value rises and to a riskless component as the portfolio's value falls; hence, it is a dynamic trading strategy.

At first, it may seem counterintuitive to follow a strategy that requires us to buy high and sell low. When our intuition fails, it is sometimes best to resort to an explicit example. In Chapter 3, in the discussion of the binomial option pricing model, we learned how options can be replicated by

FIGURE 11–1
Payoffs on risky strategy and portfolio insurance

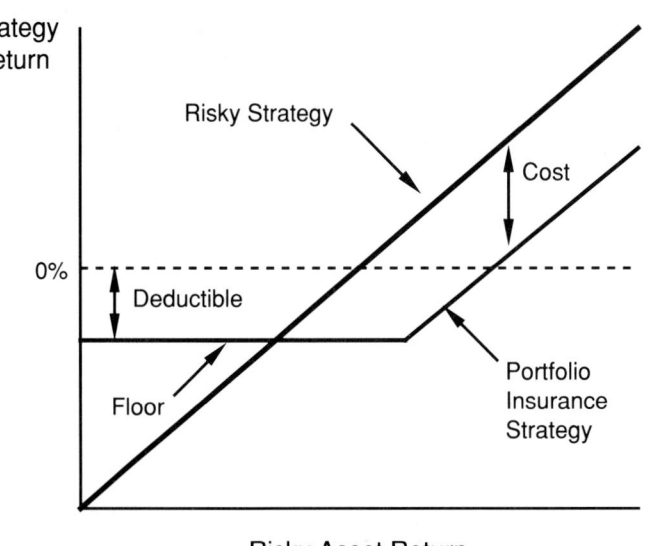

investing in a risky asset along with borrowing or lending. Specifically, we can replicate a put option by selling short some amount of the underlying risky asset and lending at the riskless rate of interest. For example, suppose we wish to replicate a one year put option on a $100 risky asset with a strike price of $95, and suppose that the risky asset can either increase 20 percent to $120 or decrease 10 percent to $90. Furthermore, suppose the riskless rate of interest equals 8 percent. If we follow the procedures described in Chapter 3, we find that the value of such an option equals $1.85 and that we could replicate the same outcome by selling short $16.67 of the risky asset and lending $18.52 at the riskless rate.

To see this equivalence consider the return of the put option and the replication strategy if the risky asset value falls to $90. The put option will return $5 which, after its cost of $1.85, leaves a net profit of $3.15. The short position in the risky asset will return $1.67 which, when added to the proceeds from lending $18.52 at 8 percent, also leaves a net profit of $3.15. Now consider what happens if the risky asset increases to $120. The option expires worthless for a net loss of $1.85 (its cost). The short position loses $3.33 which, when added to the proceeds of lending $18.52 at 8 percent, produces an identical loss of $1.85.

We have just shown that, assuming that the risky asset can take on only two alternative values, we can replicate a put option by selling short some quantity of the risky asset and lending at the riskless rate. In order to replicate a protective put option *strategy*, we simply need to add the underlying investment in our risky asset portfolio to these positions that replicate the put option, resulting in a net long position of $83.33 in the risky asset and $18.52 in the riskless asset.

If the risky asset value increased to $102, with u and d remaining at 1.2 and .9, repeating the above calculation would show that the corresponding investment in the risky and riskless assets needed to replicate a protective put option strategy with a $95 strike price would equal $91.33 and $11.85 respectively. If, on the other hand, the risky asset decreased to $98, we would replicate a protective put option strategy by investing $75.33 in the risky asset and $25.19 in the riskless asset.

It is not our intention with this example to describe in detail the correspondence between option valuation and dynamic hedging. We will expand upon this notion in section 11.4. At this point, however, we wish merely to introduce the concept that option-like results can be achieved by shifting a portfolio to a risky asset as the portfolio's value rises (buy high) and to a riskless asset as the portfolio's value falls (sell low).

The Rise and Fall of Portfolio Insurance

It is difficult to trace the theoretical origins of portfolio insurance, since several academic papers contain insights and views that can be construed, at the very least, as sympathetic if not actually descriptive of portfolio insurance.[3] Even the timing of the arrival of portfolio insurance as a practical investment strategy is open to debate, since we can cite examples of portfolio insurance products that date as far back as 1956.[4] Nonetheless, most investors agree that the dynamic trading strategy widely referred to today as portfolio insurance was introduced by Berkeley professors, Hayne Leland and Mark Rubinstein in 1976.[5]

At first, the investment community was reluctant to embrace portfolio insurance for a variety of reasons. For many investors, it was intuitively unacceptable to follow a strategy that caused them to buy high and sell low. However, as investors developed a better understanding of the product and, in particular, its correspondence to option strategies, this concern gradually subsided.

But investor enthusiasm was also restrained by a legitimate concern. The revision rules prescribed by the strategy implied a high level of trading, since the theoretically correct hedge ratio (i.e., the percent of the portfolio allocated to the risky asset) changed as the portfolio value changed and with the passage of time. Investors worried that transaction costs might be prohibitively expensive, especially for large institutional funds. The introduction of stock index futures in 1982 solved this problem. Instead of trading a portfolio's assets in the open market, an investor could buy or sell financial futures, with much lower transaction costs, to achieve the appropriate exposure to the risky and riskless assets. Moreover, with financial futures a portfolio insurance program could be executed by a third party so that it was completely "transparent" to the manager of the insured portfolio. For example, if an endowment fund had $50 million invested in an index fund, a portfolio insurance manager could buy and sell stock index futures without affecting the index fund manager in order to achieve the appropriate exposures for the insurance strategy.

---

[3]For example, see: R. Merton, "Optimum Consumption and Portfolio Rules in a Continuous-Time Model," *Journal of Economic Theory*, December 1971; and F. Black, "Individual Investment and Consumption Strategies Under Uncertainty," in *Portfolio Insurance: A Guide to Dynamic Hedging*, D. Luskin, (ed.), John Wiley & Sons, 1988.

[4]R. Litzenberger, "Other Approaches to Asset Allocation," *Asset Allocation for Institutional Portfolios*, The Institute of Chartered Financial Analysts, Dow Jones Irwin, 1987.

[5]H. Leland and M. Rubinstein, "The Evolution of Portfolio Insurance," in *Portfolio Insurance: A Guide to Dynamic Hedging*, D. Luskin (ed.), John Wiley & Sons, 1988.

Needless to say the emergence of financial futures accelerated the penetration of portfolio insurance into the institutional investment industry. The Brady Commission estimated that by the fall of 1987, between $60 and $90 billion of equity assets had been allocated to portfolio insurance programs.[6] Furthermore, the success of LOR, a firm started by Leland and Rubinstein and a third partner, John O'Brien, attracted a number of large players to the market, including LOR licensees Aetna Insurance Company and Wells Fargo Bank, as well as Bankers Trust Company and Morgan Bank, who chose to rely on their own technology.

Despite the popularity of portfolio insurance, it was not without critics. Some investors found it to be deficient because the changes in asset mix were partly dependent on the chosen investment horizon. For example, as the end of the horizon approached, if the portfolio value was significantly above the floor, the portfolio would be allocated almost entirely to the risky component. If the portfolio value was below the floor, the portfolio would be allocated almost entirely to the riskless component. In order to resume the strategy over a subsequent period the portfolio would have to be re-allocated to a new, substantially different asset mix. Investors were troubled that, although their willingness to accept risk had not changed from one day to the next, the risk exposure of their fund changed drastically and abruptly when they restarted the strategy at the beginning of a new investment horizon.

The popularity of portfolio insurance, together with the criticisms that were directed at it, generated interest in alternative dynamic trading strategies. At almost exactly the same time in the summer of 1986, Fischer Black and Robert Jones[7] of Goldman Sachs and André Perold[8] of Harvard circulated papers describing a strategy called "Constant Proportion Portfolio Insurance." Constant Proportion Portfolio Insurance also protected a portfolio from declining below a pre-specified value, but the term of the protection was not restricted to a finite investment horizon, and the revision rule was not based strictly on option replication.

As the investment community gained experience with portfolio insurance, other variations of the strategy were introduced including a strategy

---

[6]*Report of the Presidential Task Force on Market Mechanisms,* N. Brady, Chairman, 1988.
[7]F. Black and R. Jones, "Simplifying Portfolio Insurance," *Goldman Sachs Research Report,* August 1986.
[8]A. Perold, "Constant Proportion Portfolio Insurance," Harvard Business School working paper, August 1986.

for protecting the surplus value of a pension fund, that is, its assets minus projected liabilities. This strategy, in particular, attracted widespread attention from pension plan sponsors in the wake of Financial Accounting Standard Number 87, which required stricter valuation and disclosure requirements for pension assets and liabilities. Still, the most common application of portfolio insurance was to protect institutionally managed equity portfolios. Pension officers and other institutional investors found comfort in a strategy that set a floor below which their fund would not fall, yet allowed the fund to participate in the rising stock market. Moreover, implementing portfolio insurance did not require them to forecast the risky asset's return, since an arbitrage-based strategy does not depend on expected return (see Chapter 3). And finally, the strategy was typically executed by a third party who traded financial futures without any disruption to the manager of the underlying portfolio. Implementing portfolio insurance with financial futures also made it easier and cheaper than altering market exposure by buying and selling stocks and bonds.

As the bull market entered its fifth year in 1987, investors found a new rationale for portfolio insurance. Equity valuation levels were approaching historical extremes, with the price-earnings ratio of the S&P 500 above 20 and its dividend yield below 3 percent. At these valuation extremes, many investors, especially those who were "value oriented," would have normally retreated from the stock market and held cash (i.e., short term money market instruments), a process that by itself would have tended to temper the market's rise. Many of these investors, however, viewed portfolio insurance as a substitute for cash. They reasoned that they would be protected should the market fall, so why sacrifice upside potential? Partly as a consequence of this reasoning, the volume of assets administered under portfolio insurance programs increased fourfold in 1987 alone. However, both the suppliers and the consumers of portfolio insurance misjudged a crucial fact. They over-estimated the liquidity of the stock market.

On October 19, 1987, the stock market fell more than 20 percent, nearly double the largest previous single day decline. Moreover, the October 19th plunge followed a week of sharply falling prices. The market value of all outstanding U.S. stocks was reduced by $1 trillion, a decline of more than 30 percent.

As prices began to fall, portfolio insurers sold stock index futures to protect their portfolios. This activity in the futures market led to more selling in the cash market as program traders attempted to arbitrage the spreads between the cash market and the futures market.[9] Some portfolio insurers had been experimenting with rules designed to minimize transaction costs. Instead of trading immediately in response to a significant market decline, they waited, expecting a bounce back that would enable them to transact at more favorable prices. However, the opportunities for such trades were few and far between. As a result, by the close of the market on Friday, October 16, many insurers had not sold enough futures to achieve the appropriate reduced risk exposure, given the market's level.

Since the mechanics of the strategy were well known to the investment community, it was obvious that portfolio insurers would be substantial net sellers of equities the following Monday. But neither the cash market nor the futures market was sufficiently liquid to absorb the selling pressure on Monday, October 19th. Consequently, at the close of trading, the December S&P 500 stock index future sold at an incredible 20 point discount to the cash index (implying annualized arbitrage profits in excess of 60%). The Dow Jones Industrial Average closed at 1,738, but the S&P futures price implied a level closer to 1,400. This decoupling of the cash market and the futures market made it virtually impossible to calculate appropriate positions for portfolio insurance programs.

It is a widely held belief that portfolio insurance was responsible for the magnitude of the stock market crash. This belief, to some extent, can be traced to the Brady Commission which stated in its report to the President, "First, reactive selling by institutions, which followed portfolio insurance strategies and sought to liquidate large fractions of their stock holdings regardless of price, played a prominent role in the market break."[10] The news media contributed further to this belief with such comments as, "Analysts, traders and academics have long fretted about the price battering potential of portfolio insurers..." and "...their initial wave of selling soon expanded to an avalanche..."[11]

Did portfolio insurance really cause the Crash? Of course, we can only surmise the answer to this question. Nonetheless, some facts are pertinent.

---

[9]It is possible to trade a basket of stocks constructed to match a particular index. Traders can sometimes profit by purchasing an undervalued futures contract on an index and simultaneously selling the basket of stocks that matches that index, because at expiration the value of the index and the futures contract must match. If the futures contract were overvalued, traders could profit by reversing the above transaction.

[10]*Report of the Presidential Task Force on Market Mechanisms,* N. Brady, Chairman, 1988.

[11]S. McMurray, "Chicago's Shadow Markets Led Free Fall In a Plunge that Began Right at the Opening," *The Wall Street Journal,* October 20, 1987.

One full year after the Crash, the stock market was valued 20 percent below the pre-Crash peak reached in August 1987, despite the fact that earnings were 30 percent higher while long term interest rates were only moderately higher. Since portfolio insurance activity had declined by 90 percent as of October 1988, it might seem reasonable to assume that if portfolio insurance was responsible for the Crash, its absence would have allowed the market to rise to its pre-Crash level, especially in light of the improved fundamentals. One hypothesis is that portfolio insurance did not necessarily cause the market to crash, but that it contributed to the severity of the crash by allowing the market to rise above a level that could be justified by the underlying fundamentals prior to the Crash. And perhaps it accelerated the market's return to reasonable valuation levels. Although it would imply investor irrationality, this explanation is consistent with the relationship between market levels and portfolio insurance activity both before and after the Crash.

After the Fall

Burton Malkiel[12] compared portfolio insurers after the Crash to the cat in Mark Twain's aphorism. Twain observed that a cat that sits on a hot stove once will not do it a second time. Malkiel perceptively points out that the cat would not be inclined to sit on a cold stove either. It is true that portfolio insurance, as it was once practiced and loved (and then hated), is no longer a force in the market. But option replication strategies have not disappeared; Only the term "portfolio insurance" has disappeared. Since the Crash, investors have implemented a variety of option replication strategies, and since these strategies do indeed vary, they tend not to strain the market's capacity to absorb the requisite trading. Furthermore, no individual strategy has attracted the following that traditional portfolio insurance enjoyed at its pinnacle. Some of the more popular post-Crash option replication strategies are described in section 5.2, and in Chapter 5.

11.3 RELATED DYNAMIC TRADING STRATEGIES

In this section we will examine several trading strategies that are different from portfolio insurance, but are related to it because they involve option replication.

---

[12]B. Malkiel, "The Brady Commission Report: A Critique," *The Journal of Portfolio Management,* Summer, 1988.

Surplus Insurance

Surplus insurance is a strategy for protecting the net worth of a pension fund. This notion gained considerable credibility when the Financial Accounting Standards Board revised pension accounting rules by requiring corporate pension fund sponsors to disclose pension assets and liabilities on their balance sheets if the liabilities exceed the assets. Within this expanded pension investment context, it no longer makes much sense just to protect pension assets, since even in a favorable asset market environment pension liabilities could increase at a faster pace than pension assets, and lead to an underfunded situation.

To understand this notion, consider an example in which interest rates fall sharply. The pension fund assets that are invested in stocks and bonds would probably appreciate in value. But since pension liabilities are valued at market,[13] their value will also rise with declining interest rates. Moreover, pension liabilities equal the present value of benefit obligations that are due many years in the future. Thus they are typically more sensitive to changes in interest rates than are stocks or bonds. It is quite likely that with falling rates the pension liabilities would increase in value more than the pension assets, resulting in a reduction in the fund's surplus.

Surplus insurance differs from conventional portfolio insurance in that the "riskless" asset is now a portfolio that is chosen to track the value of the liabilities. In this context, Treasury bills are risky because they do not track liabilities. Over an accounting period, bonds are usually the least risky asset because they are highly correlated with pension liabilities. Over longer time periods equities may be less risky than bonds since both equities and liabilities grow with inflation and with productivity gains.[14]

Arbitraging Volatility

The price of an option depends on the price of the underlying asset, the strike price, the rate of interest, the time remaining to expiration, and the volatility of the underlying asset. All of these determinants are observable except

---

[13]Pension liabilities are computed as the present value of future benefit obligations. These benefit obligations are discounted to a present value based on prevailing levels of interest rates on fixed income instruments of similar duration; hence the value of these liabilities changes inversely with changes in interest rate levels.

[14]Over the short run, such as an accounting period, benefit obligations are relatively constant. However, over longer periods, inflation and increases in productivity will drive up wages, and since benefit obligations are typically indexed to wages, they too will grow with inflation and productivity gains. Thus equities, which also trend up over long time periods, can hedge long term liability growth better than bonds.

volatility. Therefore, when an option trades at a particular price, that price implies a particular level of volatility on the underlying asset. If we believe that the implied volatility on a stock index option, for example, is too high, we can exploit this belief by selling the stock index option and following a dynamic trading strategy to replicate it. If we are correct in our judgment, the premium we collect for selling the option will exceed the cost of replicating the option, and the difference will be our profit. This strategy would have been extremely successful immediately after the Crash, when implied volatilities were more than double the subsequent experienced volatility. Of course, we could pursue the inverse of this arbitrage strategy if we believed that option prices underestimated volatility.

Dynamic Strategies to Generate Convex or Concave Payoffs

Some investment strategies can be characterized by a payoff function which relates the terminal value of the underlying asset to the profits of a particular strategy. For example, the payoff function of a portfolio insurance strategy is the solid line shown in Figure 11–2. The dashed line represents the payoff function of a buy/hold strategy of dividing the portfolio equally between a risky asset and a riskless asset.

The portfolio insurance strategy provides a higher return than the buy/hold strategy if the risky asset does very well or very poorly. The buy/hold strategy produces a higher return than the portfolio insurance strategy if the risky asset's performance is unexceptional in either direction. The portfolio insurance payoff function is convex and, in general, convex payoff functions are desirable if we expect extreme outcomes, i.e., high volatility.

However, we do not necessarily have to replicate an option strategy to generate a convex payoff function. We can simply follow a "linear investment rule" that amplifies changes in asset mix that result from changes in the relative prices of the assets. For example, suppose that we divide $100 equally between a riskless and a risky asset so that our initial mix is 50 percent in each asset. Now suppose the risky asset's value increases 10 percent to $55 while the other asset remains the same. This relative performance changes our mix to 52.4 percent of the portfolio held in the risky asset (55/105 = .524), and 47.6 percent in the riskless asset.

If we do not rebalance our portfolio, its value as the risky asset price changes is just given by the straight line in Figure 11–2. However, we might rebalance the portfolio proportions as a function of the realized asset returns. For example, we might multiply the market driven changes in

FIGURE 11–2
Portfolio insurance vs. buy/hold strategy

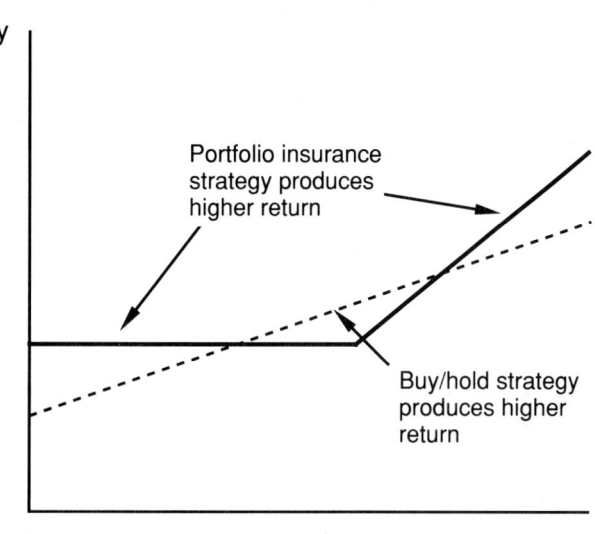

Strategy
Return

Portfolio insurance
strategy produces
higher return

Buy/hold strategy
produces higher
return

Risky Asset Return

portfolio weights, in the first case +2.4 percent, and in the second case –2.4 percent, by some factor greater than 1, say 5, and add these values (+12 percent and –12 percent) to the prior target allocations. Rebalancing the portfolio accordingly will lead to 62 percent and 38 percent in the risky and riskless assets, respectively. This strategy will generate a convex payoff function.

These types of strategies are used as substitutes for option replication strategies because they are simple to implement and simple to understand. Moreover, they are time invariant in the sense that they do not pertain to a particular investment horizon. They continue indefinitely. A linear investment rule that multiplied the price driven changes in asset mix by a number less than 1 would tend to reverse them and would produce a concave payoff function. For example, if we chose a factor of .3 instead of 5, the rule we described above would produce a concave payoff function. In general, if we anticipated that risky asset prices would follow a mean reversion process within a relatively narrow band (so that price moves in one direction would tend to lead to reversals back toward the mean), we would prefer a concave payoff function. On the other hand, if we believed that relative asset prices followed trends leading to divergent prices, we would prefer a convex payoff function. These relationships are illustrated impressionistically in Figure 11–3.

In the next section, we review the theoretical basis of option replication strategies and, in particular, their correspondence with option valuation.

FIGURE 11–3
Linear, concave, and convex payoff functions

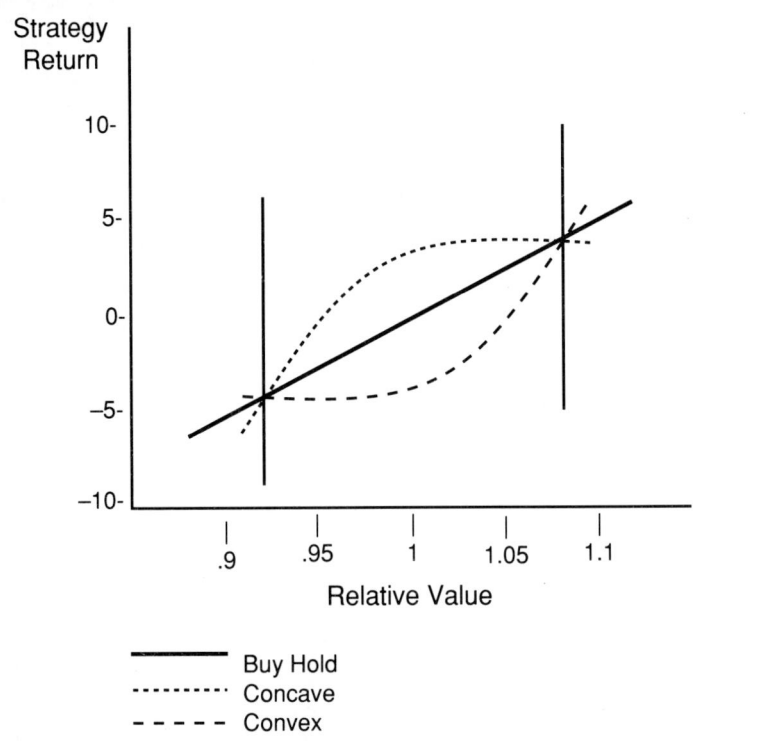

11.4 VALUATION

The Binomial Approach to Portfolio Insurance

In Chapter 3, we saw how a binomial tree could be used to derive the value of an option, and we presented an abbreviated example of this notion in Section 1 of this chapter. Now we will employ the same approach to derive in more detail the expected cost and the hedge ratio to be used in a portfolio insurance strategy.

Suppose we wish to invest $100.00 so that it will capture the return of a risky asset if it does well and at the same time lose no more than 5 percent should the risky asset produce poor performance. In effect, we wish to replicate the same outcome that we could achieve by investing in the risky asset along with a protective put option, or equivalently, investing in a riskless asset and buying a call option on the risky asset. Let us begin by deriving the value of a put option with a strike price of $95 on a risky asset that is valued at $100. As before, we will start by assuming that this asset can either increase 20 percent or decrease 10 percent. We will also assume that the riskless rate of interest is 8 percent. We can represent the possible changes in the risky asset's value as shown in Figure 11–4.

FIGURE 11–4

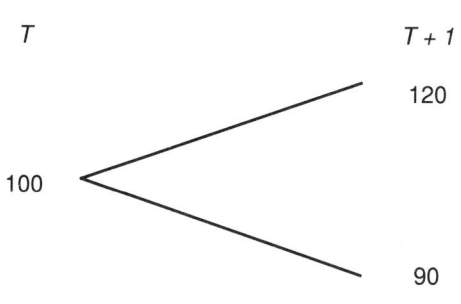

The possible values for the put option at expiration are obvious. They equal the maximum of zero or the strike price less the asset price. These values are shown in Figure 11–5.

FIGURE 11–5

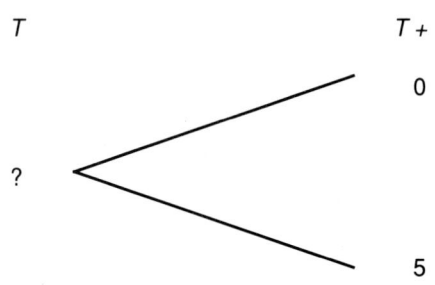

The value of the option at the beginning of the period is not obvious, however. So our next task is to determine this value. The payoff for a put option can be replicated by selling short some fraction of the risky asset position and lending some amount at the riskless rate of interest (as demonstrated in Section 1). We can determine the amount to sell short and to lend by solving the following equations simultaneously.

$$N \times 120.00 + 1.08 \times L = 0.00$$

$$N \times 90.00 + 1.08 \times L = 5.00$$

If we proceed as described in Chapter 3, we find that the fraction of the risky asset we should sell, N, equals 16.67 percent of the portfolio and the amount we should lend, L, equals $18.52.

Moreover, since we can replicate a put option by selling short $16.67 of the underlying asset and lending $18.52, its value at the beginning of the period must equal the sum of our short position and the amount we lend; that is, $1.85.

$$P = -16.67 + 18.52 = 1.85$$

Portfolio insurance, however, is not equivalent to being long a put option. Rather, it is intended to replicate investment in an underlying risky asset together with a put option. Thus to replicate a protective put option strategy, we must add the underlying risky asset position to our short position, in this case resulting in a net exposure of $83.33 in the risky asset.

In Order To Replicate	Amount to Invest In Risky Asset	Amount to Lend
Put Option	−16.67	18.52
Risky Asset	100.00	0.00
Protective Put Option Strategy	83.33	18.52

There is only one problem with this strategy. We cannot afford it. It will cost us $101.85. We started with $100.00 to invest and we determined how much it would cost to purchase a put option that would prevent us from losing more than 5 percent. However, in order to achieve this protection we must spend $1.85 for the put option. Thus our total outlay is $101.85. In order to be certain of not losing more than 5 percent on our $100.00 investment, we must scale back the amount of the risky asset that we purchase such that when we include the cost of the put option we will have spent exactly $100.00. The combination of investment in the risky asset and strike price on the put so that the total position has a floor of $95.00 and costs exactly $100.00 must be found by trial and error. We must repeat the process described above, substituting different values for the risky asset amount. If we continue in this fashion, we find that it would cost $2.78 to protect $97.22 of the risky asset using a protective put strategy (the sum of $97.22 plus $2.78 = $100). At these values, N equals −.2572 and L equals 27.79; thus we can replicate the put option part of the strategy by selling 25.72 percent of our $97.22 in the risky asset and lending $27.79 at 8 percent. This equivalence is shown below.

Risky Asset Return = 20%

Put Payoff:	0.00	Risky Asset Payoff:	−5.00
		($-.2572 \times 97.22 \times .20$)	
Put Cost:	2.78	Lending Payoff:	2.22
		($27.79 \times .08$)	
Profit:	−2.78		−2.78

Risky Asset Return = –10%

Put Payoff:	7.50	Risky Asset Payoff:	2.50
$(95 - .9 \times 97.22)$		$(-.2572 \times 97.22 \times -.10)$	
Put Cost:	2.78	Lending Payoff:	2.22
		$(27.79 \times .08)$	
Profit:	4.72	Profit:	4.72

As shown earlier, we start our option replication strategy by combining these positions with our underlying investment in the risky asset. Therefore, we invest $72.21 in the risky asset (that is, $(1.00 - .2572)$ times $97.22) and $27.79 in the riskless asset (which, of course, is tantamount to lending at the riskless rate). Then as the value of the portfolio changes and as we approach the end of the investment horizon, we repeat this valuation process regularly to determine the adjustments necessary to maintain this level of protection.

This example permits us to assign values to the insurance terms we defined earlier.

- The floor equals $95.00 which implies a minimum return of –5.00 percent on our initial investment of $100.00.
- The investment horizon equals one year.
- The deductible equals $5.00, which is computed as the difference between the initial portfolio value and the floor value.
- The cost of the insurance is $2.78, the value of the implicit put option.
- Upside capture is expected to equal 97.22 percent which is computed as the implicit value of the risky asset we can afford to protect, as a percentage of the total portfolio value. We can also compute upside capture as the total portfolio value less the implicit value of the put option, all divided by the total portfolio value.
- The initial hedge ratio equals 72.21 percent, which is computed as the amount invested in the risky asset as a percentage of the total portfolio value.

In this valuation example, we have assumed implicitly that the values we derived by using the binomial model with only one interval are correct. In fact, these values are only rough approximations that approach the true values as we increase the number of intervals in the binomial tree. In the next section, we will describe how to implement two option replication strategies using continuous-time models.

11.5 APPLICATIONS

A Specific Example of Portfolio Insurance

Suppose that we are retained by a corporate pension fund sponsor to insure a $100 million S&P 500 index fund managed by another manager. Furthermore, suppose that we are restricted to transacting in the futures market completely independently of the index fund manager. The customer will deposit the necessary funds to satisfy initial margin requirements, and the customer's trustee and our broker's bank will wire funds back and forth each day to cover variation margin. The customer wants to be reasonably certain that the total portfolio value will not fall below $95 million one year from now, and he wants to participate in the return of the index fund should it perform favorably. Currently, we can purchase a riskless asset maturing in one year to yield 8 percent. How should we proceed?

First of all, we need to determine the initial hedge ratio for the portfolio. Already we know that the strike price is $95 million, the riskless rate of interest is 8 percent, and the time remaining to expiration is one year. The only additional information we need is an estimate of volatility. Because we will be using stock index futures to implement the strategy, there are two sources of volatility: the standard deviation of the index fund and the tracking error between the index fund and the futures contract. We can infer the market's view of the standard deviation of the S&P 500 index by deriving the estimate that is consistent with the price of an index option that was traded recently. This estimate for the standard deviation is called the implied volatility. We can also estimate standard deviation by examining historical data from a period we believe is representative of the future. Tracking error, the other source of volatility, represents the variability of the price of the futures contract around its fair value. We can estimate this value from historical experience. Total volatility equals the square root of the sum of these two values squared. For example, suppose that we estimate the standard deviation of the S&P 500 index fund as 15 percent and the tracking error as 2.5 percent. Total volatility equals the square root of the sum of .15 squared plus .025 squared, which is 15.21 percent.

An important issue concerns the treatment of dividends and other cash distributions paid by the securities in the investment portfolio. It is an essential feature of the portfolio insurance strategy that the underlying asset is taken to be the portfolio as a whole. As long as dividends are simply reinvested within the portfolio, the fact that they are paid and then reinvested does not affect its total value. The option formulas that are used in the replication procedure are therefore not adjusted for dividends.

On the other hand, if the insured portfolio itself makes cash distributions (whether they are related to dividends received from the securities or not), they should be treated as dividends and the appropriate option model should be used to take account of them. In this example, we assume all dividends are reinvested when they are received.

We start by substituting the values shown below into the Black-Scholes formula for a put option.

Risky Asset Value (millions)	$S =$	100.00
Strike Price (millions)	$X =$	95.00
Risky Asset Standard Deviation	$\sigma =$	15.21%
Riskless Rate of Interest	$r =$	8.00%
Time to Expiration	$T =$	1.00

We find that the put option value equals $1.53 million, which presents us with the same problem we encountered in our binomial example. We cannot afford to purchase both a portfolio valued at $100 million and a put option valued at $1.53 million. Thus, we must start again with a lower value for the risky asset. Eventually we will discover that we can afford to purchase $98.11 million of the risky asset along with a 95 strike put option on it valued at $1.89 million, exactly exhausting our available funds. But our intention is to replicate this strategy, not to actually buy the option. We accomplish this by investing an amount equal to 1 minus the put's delta times the risky asset value in the risky asset and the balance in the riskless asset.

For a risky asset equal to $98.11 million, $(1 - N(D)) = .792$, which means that we should invest $77.70 million in the S&P 500 and $22.30 million in the riskless asset. Our customer, however, already has $100 million dollars invested in an S&P 500 index fund. Therefore, we can create the appropriate exposure by selling S&P 500 stock index futures contracts against this position. Suppose that the S&P 500 index is at 300. The value of a single contract equals the S&P index times $500 or $300 \times $500 = $150,000. Thus we should sell about 149 contracts short to create the equivalence of a $77.70 million allocation to the S&P 500 and a $22.30 million exposure to the riskless asset.

Suppose that after we implement this strategy, both the S&P index fund and the S&P futures contract decline in value. We must substitute the new value for the risky asset into the Black-Scholes formula along with the current time remaining to expiration in order to find the new hedge ratio. Then we rebalance the portfolio to accord with the new hedge ratio by trading the appropriate number of futures contracts.

In theory, we should buy and sell futures contracts continuously as time passes and as the value of the portfolio changes, but continuous trading would be prohibitively expensive (not to mention impossible). In practice, we impose a "transaction filter" to balance the cost of frequent trading against the imprecision that could result from infrequent trading. There are several approaches for filtering transactions. We can simply rebalance at specified time intervals, or we can rebalance when the portfolio value changes by a specified amount. We can also filter transactions by establishing a band around the theoretically correct hedge ratio. If the actual hedge ratio is within the band, we would not transact. If the actual ratio is above the band, we would bring it in line with the upper boundary. If it is below the band, we would bring it in line with the lower boundary. This rule assumes implicitly that the portfolio value vibrates within a narrow interval. Hence we should only trade when its value moves outside of this "noise" interval.

Suppose we continue with our strategy, buying and selling futures contracts as dictated by changes in the hedge ratio and tempered by our transaction filter. If, after one year, the index fund declines in value below $95 million, the value of the total portfolio, reflecting the value of the index fund, the futures position, and the investment in the riskless asset, should equal or exceed $95 million. If, on the other hand, the index fund increases significantly in value, the insurance strategy should capture 98.11 percent of the terminal value.

The actual value of the total portfolio, however, may differ from the expected value for a variety of reasons. The experienced volatility of the index fund could be different than the standard deviation that we anticipated. If it is higher than we anticipated, it will cost more to replicate the option, and upside capture will typically be lower than we estimated. If the experienced volatility is lower than we anticipated, upside capture will probably be higher than our estimate.

Also, tracking error between the index fund and the futures contract may be different than we expected, which would have a similar impact on upside capture as an incorrect volatility estimate. Even if tracking error is no different than we expected, if, on average, we sell futures when they are undervalued relative to their theoretical relationship with the cash index and buy them when they are overvalued, upside capture will be lower than we expected. If we are fortunate enough to transact at favorable futures prices, we could capture more of the portfolio's terminal value than we expected.

Upside capture may also differ from our expectations because we do not trade continuously. This problem is especially acute when there are market breaks such as the Crash on October 19, 1987, especially if the futures market and the cash market are decoupled as they were when the cash/futures arbitrage broke down on that date. If the break is severe enough and the index fund falls below the floor value, the total portfolio could violate the floor. Many insurance strategies experienced this problem in 1987.

The bottom line is that the upside capture and the level of protection of an actual portfolio insurance strategy may differ significantly from what is implied by the fair value of a theoretical put option. Thus sometimes portfolio insurers manage the strategy as if the floor were actually higher than specified by the customer or overestimate volatility intentionally when quoting the expected cost of the strategy.

Surplus Insurance

Suppose that a corporate pension fund sponsor wishes to ensure that the value of the pension fund, which currently equals 110 percent of the present value of the liabilities, will equal or exceed 100 percent of the pension liabilities one year from now. Keep in mind that the future value of the pension liabilities is uncertain; hence this outcome could not be assured by investment in a riskless asset such as Treasury bills. In fact, in this context, Treasury bills are risky because their returns are uncorrelated or possibly negatively correlated with the changes in the present value of the liabilities. Suppose, for example, that long term interest rates were to decrease sharply over the course of the year. If the portfolio were invested in Treasury bills, its value would only rise at approximately the riskless rate over that period. The liabilities, however, could increase substantially in value because the stream of benefit payments would be discounted by a lower rate of interest. Consequently, pension assets, if invested in Treasury bills, would rise only moderately, while liabilities would rise sharply, leading to a possible underfunded situation.

In this context, a riskless asset is not an asset whose return is relatively constant, but a portfolio whose value tracks the changes in the present value of the liabilities. We will call this portfolio a "liability mimicking" portfolio. Typically, a liability mimicking portfolio would include long duration bonds, since pension liabilities have long average durations. If our investment horizon is much longer than a year, however, the liability mimicking portfolio should probably include some equities to hedge the inflation and productivity driven growth in liabilities.

Suppose we construct a portfolio that is almost perfectly correlated with pension liabilities and that its standard deviation is 12 percent. And suppose that we choose an S&P 500 index fund as our risky asset, because we believe that it has the best chance of minimizing the long run costs of funding the benefit obligations. Suppose that the standard deviation of the index fund is 15 percent and that it is 50 percent correlated with the liability mimicking portfolio. Finally, suppose that we are proscribed from using financial futures, but that we can buy and sell units in both the index fund and the liability mimicking portfolio whenever we like. We can use a variant of the Black-Scholes model to determine the initial hedge ratio and the changes to the hedge ratio over time so as to ensure that the pension assets will equal or exceed the pension liabilities one year from now.

In effect, we wish to replicate an option to exchange the liability mimicking portfolio with the S&P index fund.[15] Alternatively, we can view this strategy as investment in the index fund with a protective put option whose strike price is indexed to the value of the liabilities. The relevant option pricing model differs from the Black-Scholes model in two important ways. First, return in this context is measured as the portfolio's return minus the change in the present value of the liabilities; hence the riskless "return" equals 0 percent (the return of the liability mimicking portfolio minus itself). Second, risk is also measured net of the risk of the liabilities.

Specifically, the value of an option to exchange an S&P index fund for a liability mimicking portfolio can be evaluated as:

$$C = I\,N(D_1) - L\,N(D_2)$$

$$D_1 = \frac{\ln(I\,/\,L) + 1/2\,\sigma_\rho^2\ T}{\sigma_\rho\,\sqrt{T}}$$

$$D_2 = D_1 - \sigma_\rho\,\sqrt{T}$$

---

[15] The valuation of this option was first described in W. Margrabe's "The Value of an Option to Exchange One Asset for Another," *The Journal of Finance,* March, 1978

where,

C   = option to exchange index fund for liability mimicking portfolio
I   = total value of the index fund
L   = total value of the liability mimicking portfolio
σ_I = volatility of the index fund
σ_L = volatility of the liability mimicking portfolio
ρ = correlation between returns on the index fund and the liability
       mimicking portfolio
σ_ρ = volatility of the overall position
       = $\sigma_I^2 + \sigma_L^2 - 2\rho\,\sigma_I\,\sigma_L$
T   = investment horizon
$N(\cdot)$ = cumulative normal distribution function

With the assumptions made above, we have σ_I = 15.0%, σ_L = 12.0%, ρ = .50, and T = 1 year.

    This expression (which the reader might recognize as equation (3.23), the value of an option to exchange one risky asset for another) is identical to the Black-Scholes model with the riskless rate equal to 0 and volatility measured as the volatility of the risky asset and the liability mimicking portfolio held in combination. In fact, we can use the Black-Scholes model for this calculation if we simply enter 0 as the riskless rate and net risk as the standard deviation of the risky asset. Net risk in this case will be

$$[(15.0)^2 + (12.0)^2 - 2\,(.5)(15.0)(12.0)]^{.5} = 13.7\%$$

    Now just as with conventional portfolio insurance, we are interested in replicating a strategy whereby we purchase as much of the index fund as possible along with a protective put option. Therefore, we must solve iteratively for the amount of the index fund we can afford to purchase so that when we add the cost of a protective put option on that portfolio, we will spend all of our available funds. Then, instead of purchasing the index fund and the put option (which, of course, does not exist), we allocate our portfolio to the index fund and the liability mimicking portfolio according to the hedge ratio that is consistent with the protective put strategy. If we proceed in this fashion, we find that in theory we can afford to purchase $107.22 million of the index fund along with a put option valued at $2.78 million, assuming our portfolio value equals $110 million. With this combination, we can be certain that the pension assets will equal or exceed the pension liabilities one year from now. We can replicate this strategy by investing $76.98 million in the index fund and $33.02 million in the liability mimicking portfolio at the start of the horizon and adjusting the exposure as dictated by the hedge ratio that results through time as we insert the new values for the portfolio, the liabilities, and the time remaining in the investment horizon. Also, just as with conventional portfolio insurance, the precision with which we replicate the option strategy will depend on: our ability to trade positions in the two portfolios as required, the accuracy of our estimates for standard deviation and correlation, and the closeness of the liability mimicking portfolio with the actual liabilities.

Because the index fund and the liability mimicking portfolio are positively correlated with each other, their returns are naturally hedged. Thus changes in the hedge ratio of this strategy are typically smaller than changes in the hedge ratio of conventional portfolio insurance (remember, it is changes in their *relative* values that cause the hedge ratio to change). Moreover, it is quite likely that a conventional portfolio insurer would be selling equities when a surplus insurer would be purchasing equities, so that the strategies provide liquidity to each other.

To see this last point, consider a scenario where interest rates rise. Equity values would probably fall, so that the conventional insurer would reduce the exposure to equities to protect the fund. But pension liabilities typically are more sensitive to changes in interest rates than equities. So, although the equity value would fall as interest rates rose, the present value of the liabilities would fall by a greater amount, resulting in an increase in the ratio of assets to liabilities. In such a case, the surplus insurer would increase the exposure to equities. The opposite would occur if interest rates fall.

11.6 PROCEDURAL ISSUES

Volatility Estimation
If we wish to replicate an option with a dynamic trading strategy, we can observe all of the required inputs except volatility. As we mentioned earlier, there are several elements of volatility to be estimated: the standard deviation of the underlying asset; the tracking error between the underlying asset and the futures contract if we use futures to implement the strategy; and the correlation coefficient between the risky assets if we wish to replicate an option to exchange risky assets.

If there are exchange traded options on the risky asset, we can infer the standard deviation from the prices at which these options are traded. Since all of the other required inputs of the Black-Scholes model are observable, we simply need to try different values for the standard deviation in the Black-Scholes formula until the price that we compute equals the price at which the option was traded. It is important that the observed values we use be contemporaneous or else our estimate of the implied volatility could be incorrect. A particularly efficient search procedure is the Newton Raphson Method (See Chapter 13). According to this procedure we start with some reasonable guess for standard deviation. We then change this guess by an amount that equals the option pricing function evaluated using our guess less the true price, all divided by the derivative of the function with respect to standard deviation evaluated at our guess. This procedure usually converges to a solution in two or three tries. A simpler search procedure called Bisection is also discussed in Chapter 13.

Of course, there are many risky assets for which traded options are unavailable. In these situations it is fairly standard to extrapolate historical experience. We are also limited to historical evidence in estimating tracking error and correlations. In doing so, we should take care to select a measurement period which we believe reflects the market conditions we can expect over our investment horizon. For example, the Federal Reserve changed its operating policy in October 1979, with the result that bond returns have been much more volatile since 1979 than they were previously. Consequently, the volatility of bond returns prior to 1979 should probably be weighted less than evidence since 1979. Regardless of which approach we use to estimate volatility, it is prudent to increase our estimates by some factor to account for the inevitable errors in our estimates.

Execution

As we suggested earlier, the success with which we replicate an option through a dynamic trading strategy depends importantly on execution. If fairly priced, liquid financial futures are available and there are no significant trading interruptions, we should be able to achieve reasonably precise results. In practice, although markets aren't quite perfect, we can still replicate options with varying degrees of success through such techniques as program trading and by blending exchange-traded options with a dynamic trading strategy.

If our option replication strategy involves a portfolio of reasonably liquid securities (relative to the amounts we need to invest), we can arrange to have this portfolio traded as a package. Such an arrangement is known as program trading. In fact, we can also arrange for a brokerage firm to guarantee the prices at which the trade will occur. Of course, the more risk that we transfer to the broker, the more he or she will charge us to execute the trade. Alternatively, we can assume the market risk and pay a lower commission for the execution. Since brokerage firms generally try to make sure they are compensated adequately for bearing risk, it is probably less expensive over the long run to conduct program trading on a "best efforts" basis as opposed to a "guaranteed price" basis.

We must also face the possibility of an interruption in trading. In such a situation, we may not be able to adjust the hedge ratio as expediently as necessary, with the result that we could violate the floor of the insurance strategy. To guard against this outcome, we can include some exchange-traded options in our portfolio as a safety net. Even if we are insuring a portfolio that is different from the underlying index of the exchange-traded option, we can at least hedge the portfolio against the systematic component of its total risk. By combining exchange-traded options in our portfolio, we can effectively minimize the sensitivity of the hedge ratio to changes in the portfolio's price.[16]

11.7 SUMMARY

Portfolio insurance is a dynamic strategy for trading between a risky asset and a riskless asset that is designed to generate the same outcome as a protective put option strategy. Portfolio insurance, however, does not require investment in options. Instead, we can protect a portfolio from declining below a prespecified level while preserving upside potential by shifting funds in the portfolio into riskless assets as its value falls and into risky assets as the portfolio's value rises.

Portfolio insurance was introduced in 1976 by Hayne Leland and Mark Rubinstein, but it was not until the emergence of financial futures in 1982 that it attracted widespread attention. At its peak in popularity prior to the 1987 stock market crash, the Brady Commission estimated that

---

[16]This strategy is described in S. Figlewski's "Insuring Portfolio Insurance," *First Boston Publication,* November 18, 1987.

between \$60 billion and \$90 billion was under the administration of portfolio insurance strategies. Many market experts attribute the magnitude of the stock market's crash to self-perpetuating selling pressure generated by portfolio insurance strategies.

Since the Crash, traditional portfolio insurance has become a smaller force in the market, although related dynamic trading strategies have emerged under different names. These include strategies to protect a pension fund's surplus value, strategies to arbitrage volatility, and simple linear investment rules to protect portfolios indefinitely rather than for a specific investment horizon as portfolio insurance does.

Computing the precise hedge ratio and expected cost of a portfolio insurance strategy is based on the arbitrage arguments that underlie the valuation of options. Given an option valuation model, we can produce the same conditional payoff as a put option by selling a fraction of the underlying asset short and lending some amount at the riskless rate of interest. Thus we can replicate a protective put option strategy by adding these positions to investment in the risky asset. This equivalence tells us how to protect a portfolio by varying its exposure to the risky asset and also how to estimate the cost of this protection.

To reduce transaction costs we would typically execute a portfolio insurance strategy by buying and selling financial futures rather than by transferring capital between a risky and riskless asset. For this reason, as well as other reasons, the actual results of a portfolio insurance strategy may differ from the results suggested by theoretical pricing relationships. For example, the actual cost of the protection would be higher than expected if, on balance, we bought overvalued futures contracts and sold undervalued contracts. We may also experience unexpected results if the asset that underlies the futures contract does not track the risky component of our portfolio precisely, or if we misestimate the risky asset's volatility, or finally, if we do not trade sufficiently often to capture changes in our portfolio's value.

Despite these practical restrictions, portfolio insurance remains a reasonably effective approach for risk control. The key innovation of portfolio insurance, though, is its application to institutional portfolio management of the principle that option strategy payoffs can be replicated without investment in options.

PART 3

IMPLEMENTATION

CHAPTER 12

MARKETMAKING IN OPTIONS: PRINCIPLES AND IMPLICATIONS

*William L. Silber**

12.1 INTRODUCTION

Focusing on a single price that balances supply and demand has been enormously helpful in identifying underlying forces of market equilibrium. In keeping with this tradition, the arbitrage models of the options pricing literature focus on an equilibrium price to isolate the underlying determinants of an option's fair value. For the most part, these discussions ignore the structure of markets, taking for granted that somehow the interested buyers and sellers find their way to the marketplace and transact at the equilibrium price.

Although this simplification is appropriate when trying to evaluate the fair value of an option, in practice it is not so easy to bring buyers and sellers together. To help solve this problem, at the center of most securities markets, including options markets, a marketmaker emerges who stands

*The author is Professor of Finance and Economics and Director, L. Glucksman Institute for Research in Securities Markets at the Stern School of Business, New York University. He wishes to thank Menachem Brenner, Stephen Brown and Stephen Figlewski for their comments.

ready to buy from the public at a bid price and to sell to the public at an offer price. By continuously quoting bids and offers, a marketmaker provides liquidity, and thereby facilitates the process of exchange. In particular, an investor wishing to sell an option immediately is always able to sell to the bid of a marketmaker and an investor wishing to buy immediately can always buy from the offer of a marketmaker. In the process of providing liquidity to market participants, marketmakers earn a profit based on the spread between the bid and offer prices and the volume of trading.

To those of us who have never actually engaged in marketmaking, the process by which a marketmaker arrives at a bid and offer quote, as well as the forces leading to revisions in quotations, have always been somewhat of a mystery. This is unfortunate because the marketmaker's bid-asked spread is a major component, along with commissions paid to a broker, of the cost of transacting. Since marketmakers play a major role in all types of options trading, our main objective is to understand the behavior of these marketmakers and to see exactly what determines the cost of transacting.

Section 12.2 describes the organizational structure of options markets, including an overview of the role of marketmakers in exchange traded options as well as in the more traditional over the counter (OTC) markets. Section 12.3 focuses on the optimizing behavior of marketmakers themselves, with special reference to the differences   between marketmaker behavior for derivative securities such as options, versus marketmaking more   generally. The remaining sections deal with guidelines used by options marketmakers to help quote bids and offers, including arbitrage and volatility relationships, and the practical problems confronting the marketmaker. The final section focuses on the investor's perspective: how should public traders respond to transactions costs?

12.2 MARKETMAKERS AND MARKET STRUCTURES

Before the Chicago Board Options Exchange (CBOE) came to life in 1973, all options were traded in the over the counter market. In this environment, various securities firms acted as marketmaking dealers, quoting bids and offers on puts and calls on individual stocks. An individual or institution wishing to buy or sell options would usually contact a brokerage firm to act as agent to buy from or sell to one of the option dealers. The cost of transacting included a commission paid to the broker and the expected bid-ask spread uncovered in the marketplace (which is a function, in part, of the cost of searching for the highest bid and lowest offer among competing market-makers).

Over the counter trading continues to flourish in a number of options markets, including most prominently, Treasury securities, foreign exchange, gold, silver, oil and other physical commodities. In most cases, the marketmaking dealers in these options are the very same firms that are established dealers in the underlying asset. Thus, many of the commercial banks and investment banks that are primary dealers in government securities also make markets in options on specific Treasury securities. Similarly, the banks that deal in foreign exchange are the largest market-makers in OTC foreign exchange options. And finally, the major bullion and oil trading firms are the primary marketmakers in options on these commodities.

Perhaps the single most important development in options markets was the establishment of exchange trading of options in 1973. The Chicago Board Options Exchange, an offshoot of the Chicago Board of Trade, applied the principles of standardized contract terms from futures markets to options. The CBOE introduced standardized strike prices and expiration dates for options on equities, where the underlying equities were listed for trading on the New York Stock Exchange or the American Stock Exchange. The CBOE's trading mechanism is a mixture of the specialist system adapted from the securities exchanges and a competitive marketmaker system adapted from futures markets. In particular, an employee of the CBOE coordinates an open auction and represents public limit orders much as would a specialist on the New York Stock Exchange. In addition, numerous "local traders" act as marketmakers by quoting bids and offers in the same trading pit, much as would traders on the futures exchanges.

Exchange trading of options accomplished a number of objectives. The centralized order flow reduced transactions costs by eliminating the search costs of uncovering the best bid and offer in over the counter trading. Standardized contract terms expanded the order flow to the marketplace, reducing the competitively determined bid-asked spread.[1] Finally, competing marketmakers emerged to offer continuously quoted bids and offers that facilitated immediate execution of public orders.

---

[1]See Demsetz [1968] for the first discussion of bid-asked spreads and why larger volume of trading reduces the spread.

The success of the CBOE's option trading induced other exchanges to sponsor trading in equity options, including the American Stock Exchange, the Pacific Stock Exchange, the Midwest Stock Exchange, the Philadelphia Stock Exchange and eventually even the New York Stock Exchange. Although most of these securities exchanges organized trading along lines of the specialist system, rather than following the CBOE's competitive marketmaker approach, the exchanges virtually eliminated over the counter trading in puts and calls on individual stocks. OTC trading in options was reserved for those equities that did not qualify for exchange listing, usually because the underlying stocks were too thinly capitalized. Thus, it seems that standardization of contract terms and centralized order flow are the key elements to the success of exchange options trading.[2]

Exchange trading of futures options was introduced in 1982.[3] Options on traditional futures contracts such as wheat, corn and soybeans as well as options on financial futures such as Treasury bonds, Eurodollars and stock indices now trade on the nation's futures exchanges. The trading mechanism for futures options is identical with the underlying futures contracts: an open outcry auction with competing marketmakers (sometimes called scalpers) freely quoting bids and offers.

Trading in futures options has been extremely successful, but it has not supplanted OTC options on the underlying commodities. As mentioned above, OTC options on Treasury bonds, gold, silver and crude oil trade actively alongside options on futures contracts. Although trading data do not exist for any OTC options, it is generally agreed that the volume of foreign exchange OTC options, for example, far exceeds the exchange-traded variety. There are a number of reasons for the success of OTC options on commodities. Hedgers in commodities frequently require customized strikes and expiration dates to reduce effectively their risk exposure. More importantly, marketmakers in OTC commodity options will frequently quote bids and offers that are good for much larger volume than the quotes of their exchange traded counterparts. Thus commercial hedgers who frequently must transact in large size, often prefer to execute trades in OTC

---

[2]It should not be surprising that the specialist system succeeded just about as well as the competing marketmaker system. The specialist is, after all, a marketmaker as well as auctioneer. The specialist quotes bids and offers that provide liquidity; potential competition from other exchange members keeps the specialist's quotes fair.

[3]Options on agricultural commodities were banned in the United States by the Commodity Exchange Act of 1936. The Commodity Futures Trading Commission, established by Congress in 1974 to replace the Commodity Exchange Authority, authorized a pilot program in options on futures contracts in 1982.

commodity options rather than in futures options listed on the various exchanges. The disadvantages of the OTC options are costly search for the highest bid and lowest offer as well as the non-negotiability of OTC options. Hedgers must balance these considerations in determining where to do their options business.

12.3 MARKETMAKER BEHAVIOR FOR
DERIVATIVE INSTRUMENTS

We have just seen that marketmakers play a central role in all types of options trading, including both the OTC and exchange-traded varieties. Since marketmaker quotations of bids and offers on options are a major determinant of transactions costs, it is useful to explore in somewhat greater detail marketmaker decision rules. An earlier study of marketmaker behavior in the competitive auction of futures exchanges (see Silber [1984]) provides a useful perspective on marketmaker activity. The overriding principle is that marketmakers provide the service of immediate execution of public orders by continuously quoting bids and offers. Thus a broker who enters the futures pit with a market order to buy can "lift the offer" of a marketmaker; a broker who has a market order to sell can "hit the bid" of a marketmaker. The marketmaker's objective is to sell at the offer what was bought at the bid and vice versa. More generally, the marketmaker's objective is to turn over inventory and earn the spread between bid and offer prices, rather than speculating on the direction of equilibrium price movements. In point of fact, the risk of change in the equilibrium price while the marketmaker temporarily has a nonzero inventory (because a bid has already been hit or an offer lifted) is one of the factors for which the marketmaker is compensated.

One of the skills required of a successful futures marketmaker is the ability to distinguish transient from permanent changes in order flow. In other words, the marketmaker must distinguish order flow which signals a change in the equilibrium price of the asset from order flow which will be reversed shortly, leaving the equilibrium price unchanged. In somewhat more practical terms, the marketmaker continuously assesses the probability of his or her bid being hit or offer lifted. The marketmaker revises the level of quotes whenever the flow of orders tends to be one-sided, i.e., whenever buyers or sellers predominate. Since marketmaking is more art than science, it is impossible to provide a simple rule prescribing when quotes should be revised up or down.

A marketmaker in options, whether it is options on futures, physicals, individual equities or index options has a similar set of objectives and requires a similar set of skills. One potential problem confronting an options marketmaker is the relatively sparse order flow usually experienced for any particular put or call. This makes it difficult for the marketmaker to estimate the equilibrium price. As a response, the marketmaker could quote a very wide bid-asked spread to compensate for the uncertainty and the price risk of the marketmaker's inventory. This is not only detrimental to the marketmaker because of the risk exposure, but it is also bad for the customer since wide bid-asked spreads imply large transactions costs.

In this context, the saving grace of options is that they are derivative securities so that their price movements are related directly to some underlying asset. Thus, an options marketmaker who buys call options because his or her bid was hit can offset the risk exposure of the unbalanced inventory position by selling short the underlying asset. Alternatively, if the marketmaker's bid for puts had been hit he or she can buy the underlying asset to offset risk. If the market for the underlying asset is liquid, so that the marketmaker can buy or sell sufficient quantities without inducing adverse price movements, the risk exposure could be hedged relatively cheaply, leading to a reduction in the bid-asked spread on the option. In section 12.5 below we will return to this discussion to show by specific example how the options marketmaker hedges in the underlying asset.

The options marketmaker can also offset risk exposure by buying or selling other options. For example, if the marketmaker's bid was hit for at-the-money calls on asset x expiring three months from now, a subsequent sale of at-the-money calls on asset x expiring four months from now would offset much of the marketmaker's inventory risk. Although order flow for any particular strike price and expiration date might very well be sparse, the order flow for all options on a particular underlying asset is much larger. Because options are derivative assets, all options on the same underlying asset are very close substitutes for each other. Marketmakers take advantage of this relationship to reduce their inventory risk. In the process, competition reduces the bid-ask spread quoted for each particular option.

It is interesting to note that the position of options marketmakers is a special case of marketmakers in thin securities whose returns are just highly correlated. A dealer in thin securities, such as CDs of small banks, can overcome the problem of sparse order flow in any particular issue by simultaneously making markets in many of these closely-related thin issues, e.g., by making markets in *all* small bank CDs. The dealer can then make a better informed estimate of the true equilibrium price of the generic security (small bank CDs), leading to a much narrower bid-asked spread than would be justified by the sparse order flow of each issue.[4] Options marketmakers, however, should be better off than these CD dealers because derivative securities such as options have closer price relationships with each other and the underlying asset than the substitute relationships among securities whose returns are highly correlated.

12.4 MARKETMAKER GUIDELINES: SIMPLE ARBITRAGE RELATIONSHIPS

To see how options marketmakers take advantage of the interrelationship among options in quoting bids and offers, we focus attention on some well-known arbitrage relationships. In particular, we will describe how market-makers use put-call parity and butterfly spreads to help in the marketmaking process. Although these are sometimes considered complicated relation-ships, they can be illustrated fairly simply. Along the way we will show that in the process of exploiting these arbitrage relationships, the marketmaker acts as the "options arbitrageur" of classical options theory. Thus, in addition to determining bids and offers we can also show how the market-maker influences the structure of options prices.

The best way to proceed is by way of specific examples. The simplest illustrations occur with options on futures contracts. This is so for two reasons: (a) options on futures trade alongside the underlying futures contract so that arbitrage is relatively inexpensive and easy for any member of the exchange; (b) since futures contracts require only margin deposits rather than a cash outlay, the examples can avoid the borrowing and lending component of the arbitrage relationships.

To provide a concrete framework for our examples, we assume that our marketmaker is a member of the New York Mercantile Exchange (NYMEX) and makes a market in crude oil options. The principles that emerge, however, are valid for all types of futures options. During the first half of 1988 the crude oil options market traded a daily average of about

---

[4]See Garbade [1982, p. 500] for more details of how a marketmaker in small bank CDs gains information by dealing in a number of such issues.

20,000 contracts. This was the most active nonfinancial futures option contract in the United States. On any particular day, approximately 50 members of NYMEX crowd into the crude oil options pit, which is located approximately 15 feet from the crude oil futures pit. Of these traders, about half are brokers who execute orders for off-floor hedgers and speculators, such as oil refiners, commercial users and brokerage houses; the other half are marketmakers trading for their own accounts or on behalf of larger marketmaker organizations.

Crude oil options are listed for trading in six consecutive expiration months. The specific strike prices listed vary with the historical price range of the futures contract; recently at least 8 different strikes have been the norm. Table 12–1 shows that on June 15, 1988, options were listed for expiration in August 1988 through January 1989 (futures contracts, by way of contrast were listed for June 1988 through July 1989). Strike prices (in the extreme lefthand column) ranged from $12 to $21 per barrel of oil. For each expiration month the table lists a column for puts and a column for calls, and for each type of option it lists a column for the settlement price ($P) and a column for the volume traded (vol). At the bottom of the table

TABLE 12–1
Crude oil options prices and trading volume for June 15, 1988

Strike Price	August 1988 Puts $P	Vol	Calls $P	Vol	September 1988 Puts $P	Vol	Calls $P	Vol	October 1988 Puts $P	Vol	Calls $P	Vol
$12	-	-	-	-	-	-	-	-	-	-	-	-
$13	-	-	-	-	-	-	-	-	-	-	-	-
$14	-	-	-	-	-	-	-	-	-	-	-	-
$15	.03	319	1.65	-	.10	172	1.75	-	.16	406	-	-
$16	.11	3,099	.74	380	.30	2,381	.95	-	.39	229	1.06	2
$17	.52	2,840	.14	2,196	.74	1,515	.39	607	.83	74	.50	17
$18	1.40	267	.03	2,580	1.50	250	.15	1,729	1.57	9	.24	237
$19	2.38	100	.01	806	2.39	-	.04	532	2.44	-	.11	32
$20	-	-			3.37	-	.02	410	-	-	.05	7
$21	-	-					.01	99	-	-	.02	-
Futures Price	$16.62				$16.65				$16.68			

there is a line for the settlement price of the futures contract for that particular month. Note that the total volume of options traded on June 15, 1988 was about 25,000 contracts, or just slightly more than the average daily trading volume for 1988.

The data listed in Table 12–1 are the settlement prices of the options at the close of business on June 15, 1988 and the number of contracts traded for each option on that day. For example, next to the 16 strike price under the August column, the price of the puts is listed as .11 and the price of the calls is listed as .74. Thus, the so-called August 16 puts cost 11 cents per barrel and the August 16 calls cost 74 cents per barrel. Since each contract is for 1,000 barrels of oil, that means the total cost of an August 16 put is $110.00 (.11 × 1,000) and the total cost of the August 16 call is $740.00. For our discussion purposes, we will always use the per barrel price since that is the way these options prices are quoted (this is similar to stock options whose prices are quoted per share even though the standard contract size is for 100 shares).

The first thing to notice about the table is that the volume of trading is concentrated in the "front months", i.e., August and September. In

TABLE 12–1, continued

Strike Price	November 1988 Puts $P	Vol	Calls $P	Vol	December 1988 Puts $P	Vol	Calls $P	Vol	January 1989 Puts $P	Vol	Calls $P	Vol
$12	-	-	-	-	-	-	-	-	-	-	-	-
$13	-	-	-	-	-	-	-	-	-	-	-	-
$14	-	-			.10	4			.15	25		
$15	..21	765			.27	160			.32	-	-	-
$16	.47	2,211			.54	20			-	-	-	-
$17	.93	300	.62	-	1.01	23	.71	1	1.08	-	-	-
$18	1.60	11	.29	10	1.67	2	.37	5	-	-	-	-
$19	-	-	.15	7	-	-	.21	20	-	-	-	-
$20	-	-	.08	702	-	-	.13	5	-	-	-	-
$21	-	-	.04	-	-	-	.07	-	-	-	-	-
Futures Price	$16.69				$16.70				$16.69			

particular, of the 25,582 contracts traded on June 15, 1988, 12,587 were in August puts and calls and 7,695 were in September puts and calls. More-over, of these 20,273 August and September options, almost all were concentrated in the 15 through 19 strike prices. Closer examination reveals that the most active puts and calls are the at-the-money or near out-of-the-money contracts. In particular, the August futures contract settled at $16.62 and September futures at 16.65. The most active puts were the 16 strike followed by the 17 strike and then the 15 strike. The most active calls were the 18 strike followed by the 17 and then the 19 strikes. These patterns of trading volume are typical of crude oil options generally as well as of all types of options.

Let us turn now to some basic pricing relationships. Settlement prices released by the exchange each day (recorded in Table 12–1 for June 15, 1988) are set to reflect the bid and offer represented in the pit at the close of trading. As described in section 12.3 above, a marketmaker quotes a bid and offer to keep a balanced inventory. This is a reasonable task for the actively traded puts and calls in August and September, since there is sufficient order flow to judge where the equilibrium price is. But for some of the options listed in Table 12–1 the volume of trading is relatively low (e.g., the August 19 puts traded only 100 contracts the entire day) or is nonexistent (e.g., the September 16 calls). This would seem to make the marketmaker's task difficult if not impossible, not just at the close of business, but throughout the trading day.

Applications of Put-Call Parity

One of the simplest concepts used by the marketmaker to quote bids and offers on infrequently traded options is put-call parity. Even without knowing the formal mathematical proofs, the marketmaker is aware that buying one put and buying one future is equivalent to buying one call at the strike of the put option. Similarly, the marketmaker is aware that buying one call and selling one future is equivalent to buying one put at the strike price of the call option. Thus, the marketmaker can use these so-called synthetic calls and puts to judge where the appropriate quotes should be.[5]

---

[5]The proof that long a call and short a future is a synthetic long put as well as the proof that long a put and long a future is a synthetic long call can be verified by constructing a payoff table for the synthetic position and the outright position on expiration. They will turn out to be the same. The next footnote has a specific example.

Here is a specific example. Suppose we are near the close of trading on June 15, 1988 and a broker enters the pit and asks for a market in September 16 calls. They have not traded all day so there is no clue about pricing from order flow in the calls. On the other hand, September 16 puts have traded over 2,000 contracts and are now quoted at .29 bid, offered at .31 (the midpoint, .30, is the settlement price on the September 16 calls). With September futures trading at 16.65, the marketmaker realizes that if he or she can buy one September 16 call at .94 and sell one September future at 16.65, the resulting position will be long a synthetic 16 put at .29. This follows from the payoff at expiration to the long call at .94 combined with a short future position at 16.65.[6] The only difference is the synthetic put requires an outlay of $940 per contract while buying the put outright would require an outlay of $290. Interest on the $650 difference until expiration of the September option (on August 12, 1988) at 7 percent amounts to approximately $7.50. Thus, the marketmaker is likely to bid .93 for the 16 call rather than .94 (to cover the interest expense). A similar line of reasoning suggests that if the marketmaker can sell the call at .96 and buy the future at 16.65, the resulting position will be short a synthetic 16 put at .31. This time interests works in the marketmaker's favor since he or she takes in .96 (rather than .31). Thus the call might be offered at .95.

The outcome of the story is that the broker asking for a quote on September 16 calls will hear .93 bid, offered at .95 or .94 bid, offered at .96 (if interest is ignored). In point of fact, uncertainty over where the market-maker will sell the futures contract (it could easily be 16.65, 16.64 or, less likely, 16.66) will widen the quote somewhat—.93 bid, offered at .96 is the most likely market for the September 16 calls.

Now let's see what the marketmaker does in response to a particular transaction. Suppose the broker sells one call to the marketmaker at .93 and the marketmaker sells a futures contract at 16.65, the marketmaker is long a synthetic put with a 16 strike price at a price of .28. The marketmaker could then try to offset completely the risk of the long synthetic put by

---

[6]Here is the numerical proof of this statement. If the future expires at $16.00, the call expires worthless—losing $.94. The short future at $16.65 gains $.65. Thus the position loses $.29. If the future expires anywhere above $16.00 the position still loses *exactly* .29 (e.g., at 16.20 the call is worth .20 so the loss on the call is only .94 - .20 or .74, but the profit on the short future is only 16.65 – 16.20, or .45; the total loss is .74 – .45 or .29). If the future expires anywhere below 16.00, the call expires worthless, losing .94 but the short future from 16.65 provides gains penny for penny with the decline in the futures. For example, at 15.71 the gain is 16.65 minus 15.71 or .94, so the net loss is zero. At 15.50 the short future is worth 16.65 minus 15.50 or 1.15 minus .94 for a net profit of .21. Notice that these last two cases have the same payoff as long a put with a 16 strike that costs .29, i.e., at 15.71 the long put position breaks even while at 15.50 it makes .50 – .29 or .21.

selling a put outright. We started off by noting that the market for September 16 puts was .29 bid offered at .31. Our marketmaker can sell a put simply by hitting a bid of .29, locking in a profit of .01 (the .29 sale of the put minus the .28 cost of the synthetic put), or $10 per contract. Alternatively, the marketmaker might choose to offer the put at .30 (bettering the existing offer of .31), hoping that some anxious buyer bidding .29 will step up and buy the put at .30; in this case the marketmaker locks in a profit of .02, or $20 per contract. Notice that once the marketmaker has bought one call, sold one future and sold one put, the position, known as a reverse conversion or reversal, is riskless. No matter what happens to the price of the futures contract, the marketmaker's $10 or $20 profit remains.[7]

Alternatively, suppose the broker had bought a call from the market-maker at .96. The marketmaker then buys a future at 16.65 and tries to buy a put at .30 (bettering other bids of .29). If the marketmaker is successful, the short call-long put-long futures position, known as a conversion, is riskless and locks in a profit of $10 (the difference between selling the synthetic put at .31 and buying the put outright at .30). No matter what happens to the price of the futures contract the $10 profit remains.[8]

It is clear that the principle of synthetic puts and calls allows the marketmaker to quote bid and offer prices for options that have little or no order flow. The consequence for pricing relationships among options is known as put-call parity. More specifically, unless synthetic puts are valued at the same price as outright puts and unless synthetic calls are valued at the same price as outright calls (all adjusted for interest costs), a riskless profitable transaction is available. Because of low transactions costs and expertise in executing trades, marketmakers respond quickly to such risk-less arbitrages. Thus, price quotations always reflect the principles of put-call parity. That is not to say such riskless transactions do not take place— they most certainly do. But they are reserved for marketmakers with low transactions costs who put in the time and effort to monitor continuously order flow in the options and futures pits.

---

[7]The only risk exposure facing the marketmaker is when the futures contract expires at or near the strike price. Under those circumstances, the marketmaker does not always know whether the short put (in this case) will be exercised. In particular, even if the option is slightly in the money, it may not be exercised. The option holder may not want the futures position that comes with exercising the option. This risk of not knowing a position can induce marketmakers to limit the number of such positions they put on.

[8]In both conversions and reversals the marketmaker must worry about financing variation margin payments on the short or long futures position. This can be accomplished by selling or buying e^{-rt} futures for each conversion or reversal rather than hedging with futures on a one to one basis.

The settlement prices in Table 12–1, in fact, reflect put-call parity within a .01 or .02 discrepancy.[9] The \$10 or \$20 profit opportunities are well within the usual bid-asked spread. Thus, they do not represent riskless profitable transactions for public customers. If settlement prices did indicate that larger profits were possible, it probably means an error was made in recording those prices.

Applications of Butterfly Spreads

A glance at Table 12–1 reveals an apparently serious problem for the marketmaker. Some strike prices—even for the active August and September expirations—have no volume of trading for either puts *or* calls. How, then do marketmakers quote bids and offers when confronted by a broker's request? One response is for the marketmaker to quote a very wide bid-asked spread, leaving plenty of room for error concerning the true equilibrium price. This is the usual response in any market. But with options, the marketmaker has a handy reference point, using so-called butterfly spreads, that can help sharpen the precision of the marketmaker's quotes. The best way to understand the process is by way of specific example.

Suppose a broker enters the options pit and asks for a market in October 21 calls. Table 12–1 shows that there was zero volume in October 21 puts and calls, so the marketmaker has no help from order flow or put-call parity. In point of fact, a marketmaker only needs to know where the October 19 call and October 20 call are quoted in order to quote a market in the 21 calls. Assume, as suggested by the settlement prices, that the 19 calls are .10 bid, offered at .12 and the 20 calls are .04 bid, offered at .06. The marketmaker would then be willing to quote the 21 calls as .01 bid, offered at .03, or to be on the safe side, .01 bid, offered at .04. The marketmaker is comfortable with such a quote, especially if the broker hits the .01 bid. In that case, if the marketmaker buys a 21 call at .01 he or she

---

[9]Put-call parity is often stated in the following way: the price of the synthetic long futures contract—long a call, short a put—must equal the price of the futures contract. In Table 12–1 you can verify these relationships by adding the price of the call to the exercise price of the option, subtracting the price of the put, and comparing that number with the settlement price of the futures contract. In formal terms, if C is the call price, P is the put price, F is the price of the underlying futures contract, X is the exercise price, r is the risk free interest rate and T is the time to option expiration, then put-call parity implies the following price relationship:

$$C - P = e^{-rT} (F-X).$$

would bid aggressively for a 19 call, perhaps bettering the existing .10 bid and buying from an anxious seller at .11. At the same time the marketmaker tries to sell two 20 calls at the .06 offering price. If the marketmaker is successful, the resulting position is long one 19 call, long one 21 call and short two 20 calls, with the total dollar outlay of zero (the .11 plus .01 cost of the 19's and 21's is offset by the sale of two 20's at .06).

This position is known as long a butterfly spread, where the 19 calls and 21 calls are called the wings. The payoff to a long butterfly has a minimum of zero (if the futures contract settles on expiration below 19 or above 21) and a maximum of $1.00 per butterfly spread (the payoff is 1.00 if the futures contract settles *exactly* at 20, so that everything is worthless except the 19 call which has a value of $1.00). Clearly, the marketmaker would eagerly incur a cost of zero to put on a position that has a zero chance of losing money but could wind up making a substantial profit. Thus the marketmaker is delighted to purchase the 21 calls at .01, especially if the order flow for the 20 calls suggests that sales at .06 are reasonable. The marketmaker is less happy about selling those 21 calls at the .03 offer since if he or she establishes a short butterfly position (short the wings and long the center) the payoff is a large loss if the option contract expires when the future is at the center strike. Nevertheless, if the option is far away from the current price of the underlying and there is not that much time to expiration left, a sale at .03 is reasonable. Just to be sure, however, we tacked on a .01 to the offer price which makes for a safer sale of the 21 calls at .04.

Butterfly spreads usually cannot be put on at zero cost. Only a marketmaker with low transactions costs who continuously monitors the market can hope to do it—and even then only if the center of the butterfly is relatively far away from the current price of the underlying futures contract, so that there is relatively little chance that the butterfly will produce a profit. This was the case in our example with the 19-20-21 butterfly (the futures contract was trading at 16.65). In all other cases, marketmaker competition for long butterfly spreads will lead to a positive cost of every butterfly combination.

The implications of this very last point are rather interesting as far as the structure of options pricing is concerned. The fact that butterfly spreads should, in general, cost something means that for any three options that have equally spaced strike prices, the value of the middle option is always less than a simple average of the other two. A quick review of Table 12–1 will reveal the accuracy of this statement—both for puts and for calls. A formal proof of this point and other "butterfly" price relationships is found in Chapter 2.

Before turning to how marketmakers use some of the sophisticated options technology developed in recent years, let's take one more step in the simple arbitrage process and examine the role of over the counter marketmakers. Our discussion in section 12.2 above suggested that for assets such as Treasury bonds, foreign exchange, gold, silver, oil and others, a thriving market exists for both exchange-traded and OTC options. OTC marketmakers have one major advantage over their exchange-based counterparts: OTC marketmakers see order flow in options that marketmakers on the exchange floor do not have access to. Thus, a so-called upstairs marketmaker can often buy or sell OTC options and then lay off some or all of the risk by selling or buying exchange-traded options with similar strikes and expiration dates. Thus OTC marketmakers can and do put on options positions that are almost, but not quite, riskless arbitrage positions. Since OTC customers are likely to search among OTC marketmakers for the best bid and offer, competition and arbitrage should bring the prices of OTC options into line with exchange-traded options. Unfortunately, there are no data available on OTC options to substantiate this proposition.

12.5 ADVANCED MARKETMAKER TECHNOLOGY: DELTAS AND MODELS

Although conversions, reversals and other arbitrage-type relationships provide important guidelines for options marketmakers, exclusive reliance on such techniques leaves the marketmaker at the mercy of order flow in options to offset inventory risk. This is less than desirable considering the sparse order flow problem in most options. As pointed out in section 12.3 above, however, the fact that options are derivative instruments leaves open the possibility of hedging in the underlying asset. Marketmakers who take advantage of this possibility will be able to distinguish themselves from other traders (see Silber [1984]) by quoting bids and offers continuously and over a wide range of options. As usual, we illustrate these principles first by way of specific example, and only then introduce formal option pricing models into the decisionmaking process. To set the stage for the model-based analysis, however, our example uses some of the formal terminology of the options pricing literature.

The first part of our discussion shows how hedging in the underlying asset is designed to protect the marketmaker's option position from small movements in the price of the underlying asset. The next step describes the risks that remain in these hedged positions. Finally, we describe how marketmakers use formal option pricing models to help implement the entire process.

Delta-Neutral Hedging

Suppose a broker enters the crude oil options pit on June 15, 1988 and asks for a market in the September 17 calls. Although approximately 1,500 of these calls and 600 September 17 puts traded on this day, order flow is often quite sparse at any particular point in time. The bulk of trading is usually done during the first and last hour of the day, rather than continuously. Thus, although marketmakers may know where the puts and calls have been trading, fifteen minutes can easily elapse before another order to buy or sell this particular option enters the pit. A marketmaker who relies only on conversions and reversals or butterflies will be reluctant to quote a market. In particular, if the marketmaker's bid is hit or offer is lifted he or she is long or short options, with the associated price risk should crude oil futures move up or down. However, a marketmaker who knows how the price movement in the 17 calls is related to the price movement in the futures contract, can buy or sell futures in the proper ratio in order to neutralize the inventory risk of the options position.

Based on experience, a good options marketmaker knows that the price of an at-the-money futures option moves about half as much as the price of the underlying asset. More specifically, the so-called *delta* of an at-the-money call is approximately plus .5, while the delta of an at-the-money put is approximately minus .5, i.e., the call moves half as much in the same direction as the future, while the put moves half as much in the opposite direction. Armed with this information, when the broker enters the options pit and asks for the market in September 17 calls, the marketmaker checks the September futures contract to see where it is trading. Since order flow in futures is much more dense than options, the most recent trade in futures is likely to be only a few seconds old. If the September futures contract is trading at 16.65, the marketmaker would probably quote the September 17 call at .38 bid offered at .40 (see Table 12–1 where .39 is listed as the value of the 17 call when September futures are trading 16.65). If the broker sells ten contracts to the marketmaker, the marketmaker immediately orders a sale of five futures contracts (since the delta is approximately .5), hoping the sale is completed at a price of 16.65. This sale would then offset the price risk of the marketmaker's long call position. For example, if the price of

September futures subsequently falls to 16.55 and the value of the September 17 calls falls to .34, the .05 loss on the ten calls in the marketmaker's position is offset by a gain of .10 on the five contract short position in futures. This is called *delta-neutral hedging* because the proper number of futures used to offset the risk exposure of the option position is based on the delta of the option.

The ultimate objective of the marketmaker is, of course, to sell at the offering price the calls that were just bought on the bid side of the market. Recall that the marketmaker always wants to buy at the bid and sell at the offer. The advantage of hedging in the underlying is that it allows the marketmaker to reduce inventory risk while bridging the gap between asynchronously arriving buy and sell orders for options. In a sense, the immediate sale of the five futures contracts is a surrogate for the immediate sale of the options contracts. Thus, if a broker subsequently enters the options pit and lifts the marketmaker's offer on the 17 calls, the marketmaker will buy back the futures contracts that were sold to protect the inventory.

It should be clear that as long as marketmakers are risk averse, a marketmaker who hedges inventory risk will be able to compete successfully against one who does not hedge, by quoting a narrower bid-asked spread. Recall from section 12.2 above that one of the major determinants of the bid asked spread is the risk exposure of the resulting inventory position. Hedging the options inventory in the more liquid futures market in a sense transfers the liquidity of the futures market to the options market. Thus, the customer is better off because the bid-asked spread is narrower, and so is the marketmaker because inventory risk has been minimized.

A similar hedging strategy can be followed with puts except this time the marketmaker buys futures when buying puts and sells futures when selling puts. The reason is straightforward: puts decrease in value when the market rises, therefore, a long futures position is needed to offset the loss on a long put position as futures prices rise.

Risk in Delta-Neutral Portfolios

Offsetting the price risk of options inventory by delta-based purchases and sales of the underlying, produces a delta-neutral portfolio for the marketmaker. In particular, the value of the marketmaker's portfolio is insulated from the effects of small price changes in the underlying asset in either direction. Although this situation is preferable to a naked options position, the marketmaker is still at risk in a number of dimensions. First, a delta-neutral position that is long options (as in our example) will lose money over time because options are wasting assets. As the expiration date of the option moves closer, the value of the option above its intrinsic value declines. The dollar value of the decline in the option each day is called *theta*. Thus, a long options position loses theta (times the number of options in the position) each day, while a short options position gains theta each day.

This last point suggests that marketmakers should prefer delta-neutral positions that are short options because they earn the erosion in the value of the option over time. The problem, as usual, is that there is no such thing as a free lunch. Delta-neutral options positions are hedged for small movements in the price of the underlying asset, as suggested above, but not for large price movements. The problem arises because the delta of the option changes as the price of the underlying moves up and down. The change in delta per unit change in the price of the underlying is called *gamma*. If the marketmaker's portfolio is short options (either puts or calls) and he or she wishes to remain delta-neutral at all times (thereby avoiding a view of market price direction), the marketmaker must rebalance the hedge by buying futures when the market goes up and selling when the market goes down.[10] Thus, volatility in the underlying asset in conjunction with the gamma of an option imply that a delta-neutral position that is short options will lose money when the price of the underlying is volatile. On the other hand, a delta-neutral position that is long options benefits from price volatility. In particular, rebalancing a long delta-neutral options position requires selling futures when the market rises and buying futures when the market falls.[11]

It is interesting to note that theta and gamma tend to compensate for

---

[10]An example of why rebalancing the hedge is necessary when the price of the underlying moves up and down, and why short options positions lose money in this case is as follows. Suppose the marketmaker is short ten at-the-money 17 calls and long five futures contracts at a price of 16.95. The position is delta-neutral because the delta of the 17 calls is .5 when the futures price is 16.95. As the price of the futures contract rises, say to 17.50, the calls become in-the-money and their delta rises, say to .6. The market-maker must now buy one futures contract at a price of 17.50 to remain in a delta-neutral position. If the futures price then declines to where it was before, the marketmaker must sell out one futures contract at a price of 16.95 to remain delta-neutral. The end result is that the marketmaker's position is exactly where it was (long ten 17 calls and short five futures), except in the interim he or she has bought a futures contract at 17.50 and sold it at 16.95 for a loss of .55 (or $550.00).

[11]To prove this, see the previous footnote and recreate the example except this time assume the marketmaker is long ten 17 calls and short five futures.

one another. In particular, a delta neutral position that is long options loses money because of theta each day, but makes money when the market moves up and down because of gamma. On the other hand, a delta neutral position that is short options makes money because of theta each day, but loses money when the market moves up and down because of gamma. Nevertheless, marketmakers are not usually indifferent between these two characteristics. Theta erosion in the value of an option occurs fairly smoothly over time, while loses from gamma rebalancing can be large and discontinuous. The latter occurs when there is a sharp price movement in the underlying that prevents the marketmaker from continuously rebalancing the portfolio. This often occurs when there is a sharp jump or drop in price between the close of trading on one day and the opening on the following.

The implication of all of this is that marketmakers prefer ultimately to balance their portfolios by buying some options and selling others rather than by being net buyers or sellers of options versus futures. This reinforces the notion that marketmakers view delta-hedging in the underlying asset as a temporary substitute for an option transaction. More specifically, continuing our previous example, once our marketmaker has bought the September 17 calls and sold futures to hedge price exposure, he or she is likely to be a more anxious seller of options the next time around. Thus, if a broker asks for a market in the September 18 calls, the marketmaker might bid .14 and offer at .15, hoping that the relatively low offer is lifted by the broker. If the broker buys twenty-five of the 18 calls, the marketmaker would have to buy enough futures to be delta-neutral again. It just so happens that the delta on the 18 calls is about .20, so the marketmaker would buy back the five futures contracts that were sold to offset the marketmakers purchase of the ten 17 calls. Thus the marketmaker's position is long ten September 17 calls and short twenty-five 18 calls. This position is delta-neutral as before, but the theta-based loss associated with being long ten September 17 calls is more or less offset by the short position in the September 18 calls. Thus, the marketmaker can plan to earn the bid-asked spread without worrying about the erosion in the value of the options portfolio.[12]

---

[12]The marketmaker cannot relax completely with this position since theta, as well as gamma, change with the price of the underlying asset. Thus, the thetas (and gammas) of the long ten 17 calls and short twenty-five 18 calls are roughly in balance when the price of the underlying asset is about $17.00. But if the price of the underlying jumps to $18.00, for example, the short position in the 18 calls dominates the long position in the 17 calls. The marketmaker will then make money from theta erosion but lose money when the market is volatile because of gamma.

Using a Valuation Model

Our somewhat complicated example suggests that marketmaking in options requires more than just reading the balance of order flow in the options market. A fair amount of technical information—deltas, gammas and thetas—can be brought to bear on the situation. Marketmakers may rely on experience to assess some of these factors, but modern options pricing models, from the simple binomial to complicated modifications of Black-Scholes, are frequently utilized to help manage the options position of an active marketmaker. This is especially important because the sparse order flow of each individual option usually forces a marketmaker to become short and long options with many different strike prices and expiration dates. A formal model can keep track of portfolio deltas, gammas, thetas and more, with greater efficiency than even the most experienced marketmaker.

In a somewhat related vein, marketmakers frequently use option pricing models to help gauge the fair values of an option. The example of marketmaking presented above assumed that the futures price was 16.65, so that the value of the 17 and 18 calls were .39 and .15, as indicated by the settlement prices recorded in Table 12–1. But when the futures price moves, so does the price of the option that is likely to balance the flow of buy and sell orders. Marketmakers use experience and trial and error to move their quotes when the price of the underlying asset moves, but they also rely upon fair values derived from option pricing models to help in the quotation process. Moving quoted bids and offers to the proper level helps to avoid unwanted shifts in inventory (as would occur when bids that are too high are hit or when low offers are lifted).

Although there are a variety of option pricing models to choose from, any one can demonstrate how they contribute to marketmaking. Since we have been dealing with options on crude oil futures, let us illustrate our discussion with Black [1976] which models a European option on futures and forward contracts.

The model developed in Black [1976] generates the fair value of an option, defined as the option price which does not offer any riskless arbitrage opportunities, as a function of the price of the underlying asset, the strike price of the option, the number of days to expiration, the short term interest rate (until expiration) and some measure of the price volatility of the underlying asset. In addition, the model provides the delta, gamma and theta of the option, as well as *kappa* (sometimes called *vega*), which measures the sensitivity of the option price to a change in volatility (to be discussed below). Obviously, when the marketmaker is asked by the broker to quote a bid and offer for the September 17 call, it would be useful to have the fair value and the delta of the option as estimated by the model in Black [1976]. The fair value helps the marketmaker center the quotes and the delta prescribes the number of futures contracts required to hedge the position

In practice, using the model is both trivially easy and extremely difficult. The five items listed above as determining the fair value of an option can be fed into the computer, along with the formula from Black [1976], producing the option's price, the delta and so on, within seconds. The process is straightforward with four of the five items influencing the option's value: the price of the futures contract, the expiration date of the option, the short term interest rate and the strike price of the option are known with certainty at the time the option must be priced. The price volatility of the underlying asset, on the other hand, is a problem. It is a problem because the option's value depends on the price volatility of the underlying asset (defined as the annualized standard deviation of the percentage price change), from now until the expiration date of the option. Thus, in the case of the September 17 calls, it depends on the price volatility of crude oil futures between June 15, 1988 (the date of the price quote) and August 12, 1988 (the date September crude oil options expire). Although we will be able to calculate precisely what that was after the option expires on August 12, 1988, the marketmaker can only offer an estimate of price volatility on June 15, 1988.

Marketmakers use a variety of techniques to estimate volatility. One approach is to calculate historical price volatility over some previous period—10 days, 20 days, 30 days and so on and enter that value into the formula. This is tantamount to assuming that the best estimate of the market's volatility in the future is past volatility. Variations on this approach include statistically generated weighted averages of past price volatility that have been superior predictors of future volatility.

A popular alternative to historical volatility that is used by many marketmakers is the implied volatility of the option. The option pricing formula can produce the fair value of an option if given all five inputs, including volatility. Alternatively, if the price of the option is entered into the formula along with everything but volatility, the model generates a volatility number that is consistent with the other variables. This number is called implied volatility because it is the volatility that is implied by the price of the option.

Marketmakers who use implied volatility to generate fair values calculate implied volatility from options and futures prices at some earlier point in time, usually the previous day's settlement prices. These implied volatilities are then fed into the formula to generate fair values, deltas and so on for the current day.[13] Table 12–2 shows a sample marketmaker fair value table for June 16, 1988 for September crude oil options, based on the implied volatilities from the options and futures settlement prices of June 15, 1988. It is useful to review this table in some detail.

There are eight columns of option strikes, labelled September 13 through September 20, at the top of Table 12–2. The extreme left-hand column lists various prices of the September crude oil futures contract, ranging from $16.00 at the top of the page down to $16.95 at the bottom. Associated with each price is the fair value of the call and the put as well as the delta for each option. For example, under the September 13 column there are two columns of numbers, the left column is the price of the option, the right column is the delta. The first pair of entries in the column are the fair value and delta of the September 13 call when the futures price is 16.00 and the second pair of entries is the fair value and delta for the September 13 put when the futures price is 16.00, and so on. Thus the September 13 call has a fair value of $3.01 and a delta of .94, while the September 13 put has a fair value of $.04 and a delta of minus .05, when the September futures price is $16.00 (the put has a negative delta because its price moves opposite the future's price).

The remaining entries of Table 12–2 record the fair values and deltas for alternative futures prices. For example, look at the fair values for the puts and calls when the September futures contract has a price of 16.65. We see that the 15 and 16 puts and the 17, 18 and 19 calls have the same fair values as the settlement prices recorded in Table 12–1. This is not terribly surprising. The fair values in Table 12-2 were, in fact, based on the settlement prices in Table 12–1, including the settlement price of 16.65 for the September future. The only difference is the passage of one day in the option's life. However, one day's theta erodes fair value by less than one cent (theta is listed at the top of each column, e.g., $T = .005$ in the column

---

[13]Over the counter marketmakers have access to real time computer programs that recalculate implied volatility with each transaction. Most marketmakers would not revise their estimates of volatility so frequently.

for the 17 strike). In general, the fair value of the option does not have much overnight theta erosion until it has less than one month to expiration

The fair value table can be very helpful to the marketmaker in a number of ways. Recall that in our earlier example, the marketmaker estimated the delta of the 17 calls at .5 since the calls were "just about at the money." Table 12–2 shows that when the September future is 16.65 a more precise estimate of the delta of the 17 call is .41. Thus the marketmaker should have sold only four futures, rather than five, when buying ten 17 calls from the broker in order to be properly hedged.

The fair value table is also extremely useful at the opening of trading if the futures price changes substantially overnight. For example, if September futures open down .35 cents at 16.30 on June 16, 1988, and a broker asks for a market in the 17 calls right at the opening, the marketmaker sees from the table that based on yesterday's implied volatility the fair value would be .26. He or she might then quote the market as .24 bid, offered at .28. Thus, the marketmaker can use the fair value table as a guideline for centering bid and offer quotes. Without such help the marketmaker would have quoted a much wider bid-asked spread to protect against ignorance over where the true market really is. Note that it is quite normal for marketmakers to quote wider spreads at the opening of trading because they are less certain of where the balance in order flow will be. Although fair value tables help, they are only as good as the volatility entered into the pricing formula. Yesterday's implied volatility reflects yesterday's market environment. It may be the best estimate available for today, but it is only an estimate. Thus our example suggested a bid-asked spread of .04 for the opening quote rather than the more usual .02 spread, even with the help of the fair value table.

12.6 PERSPECTIVES ON VOLATILITY

Since volatility is the crucial unknown component to estimating fair values of options, it makes sense to examine the numbers somewhat more carefully. At the top of each strike price column in Table 12–2, the implied volatility underlying the fair value calculation is listed. For example, under the September 17 strike price $I = 20.46$ means that the implied volatility for that strike is 20.46%. In the column for the September 16 strike price, the implied volatility used is 21.80. Recall that these numbers for implied

TABLE 12–2
Fair value table for crude oil options (June 16, 1988)

Commodity: CRUDE 16.650
Rate: 7.500
Current Date: JUN 16 88

	SEP	SEP	SEP	SEP	SEP	SEP	SEP	SEP
	X = 13.00	X = 14.00	X = 15.00	X = 16.00	X = 17.00	X = 18.00	X = 19.00	X = 20.00
	I = 32.16	I = 28.61	I = 23.48	I = 21.80	I = 20.46	I = 21.61	I = 21.29	I = 24.16
	V = 0.004	V = 0.008	V = 0.014	V = 0.024	V = 0.026	V = 0.019	V = 0.010	V = 0.006
	T = 0.001	T = 0.002	T = 0.003	T = 0.004	T = 0.005	T = 0.004	T = 0.002	T = 0.001
16.00	3.01 0.94	2.08 0.88	1.20 0.76	0.55 0.51	0.18 0.24	0.06 0.09	0.01 0.02	0.00 0.01
	0.04 −0.05	0.10 −0.11	0.21 −0.23	0.55 −0.48	1.16 −0.75	2.03 −0.90	2.98 −0.97	3.96 −0.98
16.05	3.05 0.95	2.12 0.89	1.24 0.77	0.57 0.53	0.19 0.25	0.06 0.10	0.01 0.03	0.00 0.01
	0.04 −0.05	0.10 −0.10	0.20 −0.22	0.52 −0.46	1.13 −0.74	1.99 −0.89	2.93 −0.96	3.91 −0.98
16.10	3.10 0.95	2.17 0.89	1.27 0.78	0.60 0.54	0.20 0.26	0.07 0.10	0.01 0.03	0.00 0.01
	0.04 −0.04	0.09 −0.10	0.19 −0.21	0.50 −0.45	1.09 −0.73	1.94 −0.88	2.88 −0.96	3.86 −0.97
16.15	3.15 0.95	2.21 0.89	1.31 0.79	0.63 0.55	0.21 0.28	0.07 0.11	0.02 0.03	0.00 0.01
	0.03 −0.04	0.09 −0.09	0.18 −0.20	0.48 −0.44	1.06 −0.71	1.90 −0.88	2.83 −0.96	3.81 −0.97
16.20	3.20 0.95	2.26 0.90	1.35 0.80	0.66 0.57	0.23 0.29	0.08 0.12	0.02 0.03	0.00 0.02
	0.03 −0.04	0.08 −0.09	0.17 −0.19	0.46 −0.42	1.02 −0.70	1.86 −0.87	2.79 −0.96	3.77 −0.97
16.25	3.24 0.95	2.30 0.90	1.39 0.81	0.68 0.58	0.24 0.30	0.08 0.12	0.02 0.04	0.00 0.02
	0.03 −0.04	0.08 −0.09	0.16 −0.18	0.44 −0.41	0.99 −0.69	1.81 −0.86	2.74 −0.95	3.72 −0.97
16.30	3.29 0.96	2.35 0.91	1.43 0.82	0.71 0.59	0.26 0.31	0.09 0.13	0.02 0.04	0.01 0.02
	0.03 −0.04	0.07 −0.08	0.15 −0.17	0.42 −0.39	0.95 −0.67	1.77 −0.86	2.69 −0.95	3.67 −0.97
16.35	3.34 0.96	2.39 0.91	1.47 0.82	0.74 0.61	0.28 0.33	0.10 0.14	0.02 0.04	0.01 0.02
	0.03 −0.03	0.07 −0.08	0.14 −0.16	0.40 −0.38	0.92 −0.66	1.73 −0.85	2.64 −0.95	3.62 −0.97
16.40	3.39 0.96	2.44 0.93	1.52 0.83	0.78 0.62	0.29 0.34	0.10 0.15	0.02 0.04	0.01 0.02
	0.03 −0.03	0.06 −0.07	0.13 −0.16	0.38 −0.37	0.88 −0.65	1.69 −0.84	2.60 −0.94	3.57 −0.97

TABLE 12–2—continued

	SEP	SEP	SEP	SEP	SEP	SEP	SEP	SEP
	X = 13.00	X = 14.00	X = 15.00	X = 16.00	X = 17.00	X = 18.00	X = 19.00	X = 20.00
	I = 32.16	I = 28.61	I = 23.48	I = 21.80	I = 20.46	I = 21.61	I = 21.29	I = 24.16
	V = 0.004	V = 0.008	V = 0.014	V = 0.024	V = 0.026	V = 0.019	V = 0.010	V = 0.006
	T = 0.001	T = 0.002	T = 0.003	T = 0.004	T = 0.005	T = 0.004	T = 0.002	T = 0.001
	0.96	0.92	0.84	0.63	0.35	0.16	0.05	0.02
	-0.03	-0.07	-0.15	-0.35	-0.63	-0.83	-0.94	-0.97
16.45	3.43	2.48	1.56	0.81	0.31	0.11	0.03	0.01
	0.02	0.06	0.12	0.36	0.85	1.64	2.55	3.52
16.50	3.48	2.53	1.60	0.84	0.33	0.12	0.03	0.01
	0.02	0.06	0.12	0.34	0.82	1.60	2.50	3.47
16.55	3.53	2.57	1.64	0.87	0.35	0.13	0.03	0.02
	0.02	0.05	0.11	0.33	0.79	1.56	2.45	3.43
16.60	3.58	2.62	1.69	0.90	0.37	0.14	0.04	0.02
	0.02	0.05	0.10	0.31	0.76	1.52	2.41	3.38
16.65	3.63	2.67	1.73	0.94	0.39	0.15	0.04	0.02
	0.02	0.05	0.10	0.30	0.73	1.48	2.36	3.33
16.70	3.68	2.71	1.77	0.97	0.41	0.16	0.04	0.02
	0.02	0.05	0.09	0.28	0.70	1.44	2.32	3.28
16.75	3.72	2.76	1.82	1.01	0.43	0.17	0.05	0.02
	0.02	0.04	0.09	0.27	0.68	1.40	2.27	3.24
16.80	3.77	2.81	1.86	1.04	0.45	0.18	0.05	0.02
	0.02	0.04	0.08	0.25	0.65	1.36	2.22	3.19
16.85	3.82	2.86	1.90	1.08	0.47	0.19	0.05	0.03
	0.01	0.04	0.08	0.24	0.62	1.33	2.18	3.14
16.90	3.87	2.90	1.95	1.12	0.50	0.20	0.06	0.03
	0.01	0.04	0.07	0.23	0.60	1.29	2.13	3.09
16.95	3.92	2.95	1.99	1.15	0.52	0.21	0.06	0.03
	0.01	0.03	0.07	0.21	0.57	1.25	2.09	3.05

volatility are based on the previous day's settlement prices for puts, calls and the future. More specifically, since out-of-the-money puts and out-of-the-money calls are most actively traded, the implied volatility numbers are derived from these options. Thus, the implied volatilities for the 16 strike and below are based on put prices, while for the 17 strike and above implied volatilities are based on call prices. Although put-call parity should make the volatilities the same for any particular strike, no matter whether the put or call price is used in the calculation, sometimes settlement prices do not reflect put-call parity. In those cases the procedure just described resolves the issue.

The most interesting characteristic of the implied volatilities in Table 12–2 is that the volatilities differ across strike prices. In particular, for the three strikes below the current futures price of 16.65, the implied volatilities rise from 21.80 (at the 16 strike) to 28.61 (at the 14 strike). On the other hand, the implied volatilities for the three strike prices above 16.65 are all about the same (21 percent). The observed pattern stems from the way we calculated implied volatility—a numerical solution of the Black [1976] option pricing formula based on the settlement price of each option. From the marketmaker's perspective, as long as the structure of implied volatilities across strike prices is stable from day to day, it makes sense to use that pattern as a guideline for quoting bids and offers. In point of fact, the skewed structure of volatilities across different strikes shown in Table 12–2 has been present with brief exceptions, since the inception of crude oil options trading in 1986. Thus, marketmakers can and do rely upon fair value numbers that reflect different volatilities for different strike prices in crude oil options (as well as for other kinds of options.)

From a conceptual perspective, we should try to understand what this observed pattern for implied volatilities really means. After all, there is only one actual volatility for the underlying asset. Moreover, using historical volatility as an input to the option pricing formula, described above as an alternative to the implied volatility approach, would obviously produce only a single number for volatility. What then does the structure of volatility across different strike price reflect? To some extent, the resolution of this question requires a theoretical discussion that goes beyond our scope. Nevertheless, a brief overview might prove helpful.

The volatility component of Black [1976], as well as the original Black-Scholes [1973] option pricing model, reflects the simplifying assumption that asset prices follow a smooth, continuous, evolution over time (called a *diffusion process*). In particular, no discontinuous price jumps (either up or down) are allowed for. Real world prices, however, do sometimes exhibit discontinuous price movements. Moreover, such sharp price jumps are especially beneficial to buyers of out-of-the-money options, and especially detrimental to sellers of out-of-the-money options. For example, the buyer of a September put with a 15 strike price would benefit considerably if there were an overnight $2.00 collapse in oil prices, so that the relatively cheap deep out-of-the-money puts suddenly became very valuable in-the-money puts. Sellers of such puts are especially vulnerable under such circumstances for two reasons: (1) there is no chance to rebalance the hedge between yesterday's close and today's opening; (2) the deltas on such out-of-the-money options change dramatically with precipitous price movements (in our example from about minus .1 to over minus .5).

The explanation for why deep out-of-the-money puts have relatively high implied volatilities is now fairly straightforward. Enthusiastic buyers and reluctant sellers push up the market clearing price for the option above the level suggested as the fair value based on a simple diffusion process for price movements in the underlying asset. When this price is fed into the Black [1976] options pricing formula along with the four other predetermined option characteristics (strike, futures price, expiration and interest rate), the model produces a high value for the residual unknown factor—labelled *implied volatility*.

Although this explanation seems reasonable, it leaves open the question of why the out-of-the-money call options in Table 12–2 do not reflect a similar pattern. In other commodity options, such as gold, both out-of-the-money puts and out-of-the-money calls have higher implied volatilities than the at-the-money options. The answer in the case of crude oil options rests with the market's assessment of the probability of price jumps. Since the Organization of Petroleum Exporting Countries (OPEC) is a major force in the oil market, and since the potential collapse of this cartel in recent years has been a greater threat than the likelihood of stricter control over oil supplies, the probability of a sharp collapse in oil prices is much greater than the probability of a sharp increase. Thus, out-of-the-money put prices are bid up while out-of-the-money call prices reflect the normal probabilities associated with a smooth evolution in the price of the underlying asset. This discussion indicates that, in practice, the implied volatility parameter for a given option reflects things other than just a trader's forecast of price volatility, including estimates of the size and direction of price jumps, risk aversion and so on.

Some marketmakers have taken advantage of option pricing models such as Merton [1976] that explicitly take account of potential jumps in the price of the underlying. By and large, these more sophisticated models require information, such as the frequency of potential jumps, that the marketmaker can only guess at. Since marketmakers utilize these models primarily as guidelines for centering quoted bids and offers (as well as for managing options positions), the added sophistication of an options pricing model with a jump process is probably not worth the effort.

The most vexing problem confronting options marketmakers is that volatility, however measured, has a large amount of uncertainty associated with it. Recall that volatility is supposed to measure the standard deviation of the percentage price change of the underlying asset during the life of the option. From this perspective, it is possible that either true volatility or expected volatility can change over time, implying a change in the fair value of the options. True volatility can change for fundamental reasons, such as in the case of crude oil options, the announcement of an OPEC meeting, or in the case of Treasury bond options, the announcement of a change in Federal Reserve operating techniques. Expected volatility moves up and down as market participants reassess their subjective view of the economic environment, and the prospects for price volatility in the asset underlying their particular option.

Marketmakers are affected in two ways by fluctuations in volatility over time and the associated change in the fair values of options. First, the marketmaker must change quoted bids and offers. Second, the value of the marketmaker's portfolio of options changes as well. As far as bid-ask quotes are concerned, marketmakers using implied volatility as input to the fair value calculation automatically revise their estimate of volatility every day. Other marketmakers will adjust their bids and offers to order flow in the marketplace. On the other hand, the impact of a change in volatility on an option's value (called kappa or vega), and the effect on the value of the marketmaker's portfolio, is a more serious problem. In fact, this "kappa risk," along with theta and gamma, is something that marketmakers take into account when deciding how to balance their options portfolio.

To provide an idea of the magnitudes involved, look at the top of each column in Table 12–2 where the value for V gives the impact of a one percentage point change in volatility on the value of the option (at yesterday's settlement price). In the September 17 column, $V = .026$, suggesting that the value of the 17 call (which was .39) would fall to .364 if volatility declined one percentage point (to 19.46) or would rise to .416 if volatility increased by one percentage point (to 21.46). A marketmaker who is long ten September 17 calls (and short futures to be delta-neutral) could gain or lose more than $200 simply because the market's estimate of volatility changed by one percentage point. Since such changes in volatility are quite frequent, marketmakers have still another reason to prefer a balance of long and short options in their portfolios. In this way the "kappa risk" of being long the 17 calls, for example, would be partially offset by being short the 18 calls.

The end of the story is that marketmakers would like to earn the bid-asked spread and manage their options positions to be delta, gamma, theta and kappa neutral. Since this is a difficult if not impossible task, market-making in options turns out to be a complicated business. Marketmakers apply intuition, order flow, fancy models and anything else that helps them to understand and manage options positions.

12.7 CONCLUSIONS FOR PUBLIC TRADERS

This overview has provided some insight into the decision rules and guidelines followed by options marketmakers quoting bids and offers in the marketplace. Unless one is thinking about becoming a marketmaker, much of the detail is probably of academic interest. There are some lessons, however, that can be drawn from our descriptions that might be useful for public traders who utilize the liquidity services of marketmaking dealers in options.

Perhaps the most important outcome of our overview is that the liquidity costs implied by bid and offer quotes are not written in stone. They are negotiating points from which a marketmaker will sometimes depart, depending upon his or her inventory position. Thus, public traders should always inquire about the bid and offer and then instruct the broker who will execute the order to improve on the marketmaker's bid when buying (by entering a higher bid) and improve on the marketmaker's offer when selling (by entering a lower offer). The trader's improved bid or offer might just uncover an anxious seller or buyer, allowing the trader to buy or sell at better prices than the quoted bid or offer. The broker should be instructed, however, to lift offers or hit bids in the event that the broker's market is not acted upon within a short time period. Thus, liquidity costs might be reduced, without necessarily sacrificing the liquidity services of the market-maker, if proper instructions are given to a broker.

A public trader should not waste time trying to uncover nearly riskless arbitrage trades. They exist, for relatively brief time periods (seconds in a futures option pit), and immediately find their way into a marketmaker's position. Public traders do not have the time, the low transactions costs, or the execution facilities to compete with marketmakers in this area.

A trader should avoid placing orders during the opening of trading. Marketmakers have relatively poor information about where the true equilibrium quote should be at that time. This translates into a wider bid-asked spread, hence larger transactions costs for the trader. Unless there are overriding considerations, avoid trading during the opening few minutes.

Public traders who deal with OTC marketmakers must be especially careful to search for the best bid or offer. Without centralized order flow there is no guarantee that the highest bid and lowest offer have been uncovered. Moreover, the larger the volume the trader wants to buy or sell, the more dealers he or she should contact. The dollar saving varies directly with the size of the transaction. It pays to incur search costs (a bid or offer may even "expire" in the process) if a large trade must be completed.

Finally, and perhaps most importantly, as a general rule, use the marketmakers' liquidity services by hitting bids and lifting offers. Do not attempt to play marketmaker by monitoring order flow and trying to beat a marketmaker to a bid or offer that is represented in the marketplace by some other public trader. Marketmakers will prevail in such contests nine times out of ten. The cost of chasing a market up and down as marketmakers' bids and offers are revised continuously will usually be substantially more expensive than the bid-asked spread. Public traders should surely try to execute at better prices, as pointed out above. But once a broker has exercised due diligence in that regard, the best advice is to hit bids and lift offers; paying the liquidity costs is usually the least expensive component of a speculative transaction.

References

Black, F. (January/March 1976). The pricing of commodity contracts. *Journal of Financial Economics.*

Black, F., and Scholes, M. (May/June 1973). The pricing of options and corporate liabilities. *Journal of Political Economy.*

Demsetz, H. (February 1968). The cost of transacting. *Quarterly Journal of Economics.*

Garbade, K. (1983). *Securities markets.* New York: McGraw-Hill.

Merton, R. (January/March 1976). Option pricing when the underlying stock returns are discontinuous. *Journal of Financial Economics.*

Silber, W. (September 1984). Marketmaker behavior in an auction market: An analysis of scalpers in futures markets. *Journal of Finance.*

CHAPTER 13

ESTIMATING VOLATILITY

Stephen J. Brown[*]

13.1 INTRODUCTION

Any application of option pricing theory to the pricing of derivative securities requires measures of volatility. One can observe in the market the price of the underlying asset and the interest rate. The option contract gives the strike price and time to expiration. However volatility cannot be observed directly and must be estimated. The need to obtain accurate estimates of volatility is crucial. As previous chapters have shown, the option price is very sensitive to volatility, this sensitivity being measured by *kappa* or κ. Thus, one must obtain accurate estimates of this quantity. In addition, as we shall discuss, the use of estimates in place of the parameters called for in the theory will in general lead to a biased measure of the option price, where the bias is a function of just how precisely we measure volatility.

Chapter 3 gives the simplest and most straightforward approach to estimating volatility. In the example given, the estimate of volatility based on closing values for the Standard and Poor's 500 index from February 1,

*Stephen J. Brown is Yamaichi Faculty Fellow and Professor of Finance, Leonard N. Stern School of Business, New York University.

1988 through February 29, 1988 was .159. This estimate was obtained by estimating the sample variance of the 19 day to day changes in the natural logarithms of closing values for each trading day in February. This calculation, illustrated in Table 3–2 yields .000098. We annualize this estimate of day to day variance by multiplying it by a factor of 260 (approximately the number of trading days in the year). This yields .0254 as the annual variance. The square root of this number, or .159, is then the estimate of volatility σ that appears in the option pricing formula.

As a general rule, statisticians prefer simple estimation procedures to more complex ones when the assumptions of the model may not hold exactly in the data. The assumption in this case is that the change in the logarithm of asset prices is distributed as Normal with constant variance. A suggestion that this assumption may not hold *exactly* can be found by examining Figure 13–1. This figure shows the results of the volatility calculation for the S&P 500 index for every month of 1986. While volatility measured using data for the entire year, .1499, is less than the estimate for February 1988, volatility measures seem to change greatly from month to month. Either the true measure of volatility changes through time, or the measure of volatility simply is not estimated very precisely. Unfortunately, without further analysis the results reported in Figure 13–1 may be consistent with either interpretation.

There are two general approaches to this problem. One approach is to augment the set of information to obtain more precise estimates of volatility. In the simple case, this might mean increasing the sample size from one month to one year of data. This approach will not help if volatility does in fact change over the course of the year. A variant of this approach is to keep the period of time fixed at one month, but to use information derived from trades within each day — the high, low and close or even trade by trade data, if such is available. The difficulty here is to ensure that the data are not contaminated by short term trading phenomena, such as the effects of the bid-ask spread. The second general approach is to account for changes in volatility by inferring this quantity from option values themselves. While generally most favored in practice, these so called *implied volatility* measures raise issues of interpretation and statistical inference. The remainder of this chapter shall review these approaches to the estimation of volatility.

In section 13.2 we examine the use of historical data to estimate volatility. We first discuss the straightforward approach suggested in Chap-

FIGURE 13–1
Volatility[a] estimates by month, 1986—S&P 500 Index

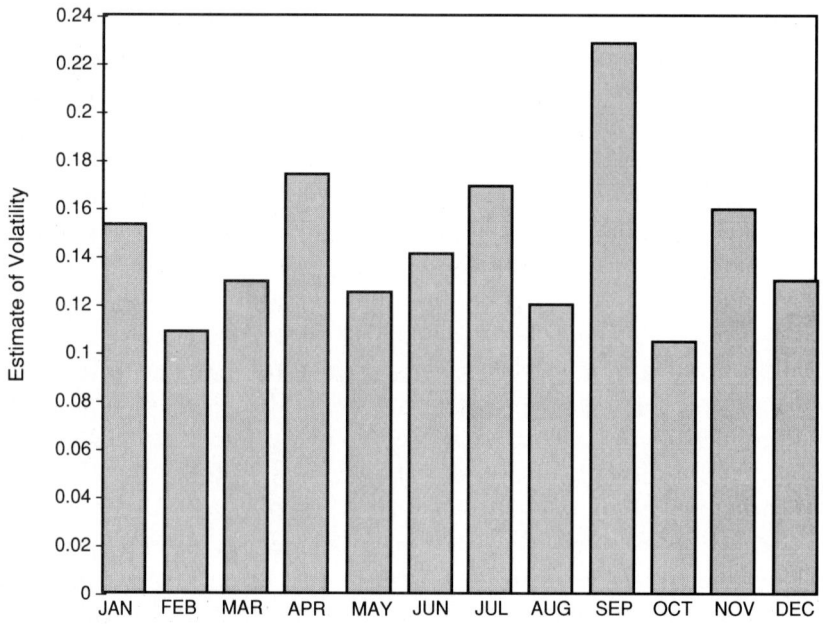

[a]Volatility estimated using annual data is .1499

ter 3, and the necessary adjustment for the fact that trading days are not the same as calendar days. This estimate of volatility will change from month to month. Then we show how to determine whether sampling variability is enough to explain these changes. If the data do indicate significant shifts in volatility, then further analysis is required. We discuss the use and significant limitations of transaction to transaction data and high-low information in this context.

The alternative approach discussed in section 13.3 is to infer the volatility from the option prices themselves. The implied volatility is introduced, and computational issues are addressed. We then discuss how to combine measures of implied volatility obtained from different options trading on the same underlying asset. Section 13.4 presents some concluding remarks.

13.2 THE USE OF TIME SERIES DATA TO ESTIMATE VOLATILITY

The simple approach

If the assumptions of the Black-Scholes model are correct, and changes in the logarithms of prices are indeed normally distributed with constant variance, most statisticians would agree that the simple approach outlined in Chapter 3 for the estimation of volatility is indeed reasonable. One assumption many find difficult to live with is the assumption that volatility is not affected by the time interval between successive closing price quotations. In the Chapter 3 example, it is assumed that the volatility for the period between Thursday and Friday, February 4 and 5, 1988 is the same as that for the period that includes the weekend, February 5 through 8, 1988. Some practitioners modify the simple approach by defining the squared deviation that appears in Table 3–2 as

$$\text{Squared Deviation} = (y_t - \text{diff}_t \times \bar{y})^2 / \text{diff}_t$$

where diff_t is the number of days between successive closes and the mean $\bar{y}$ is defined as the sum of changes in logarithms divided by the number of calendar days in the month, 29. In the February 5 through 8 case, the difference is three days. Hence, the squared difference recorded for February 8 on Table 3–2 should be .000076 instead of the value .000100 reported in that table. This leads to a smaller daily variance of .000072. However, variance is now annualized by multiplying by 365.25 (the number of *calendar* days in the year) instead of 260 (the number of *trading* days). Hence, the standard deviation measured on an annual basis is 0.162, not substantially different from the .159 number reported in the table.[1]

The sample estimate of variance is said to be unbiased in the sense that potential deviations from the true or underlying variance have an expected value of zero. It is also said to be a minimum variance estimator in that the variance of such deviations is minimized. However, it should be emphasized that the square root of this estimate measures the volatility parameter

---

[1]Recent work by French and Roll (1986) suggests that the process generating close to open differences in price may differ substantially from that governing price changes during the trading day. If this is so, the calendar day correction may be misleading.

of the option pricing formula with error.[2] Naive use of sample estimates in the option pricing formula can lead to significant pricing errors. The extent to which such estimates are useful depends on the precision of the volatility estimate.

Changes in volatility

The precision with which volatility is measured increases as more information is used to estimate it. With actively traded assets, the precision of the estimate of volatility should be arbitrarily high given the large amount of trade price information. However, volatility changes.[3] Volatility may indeed be considered stable over the remaining life of any given option, consistent with the standard option pricing formulae. However, events of the recent and not so recent past may provide a poor index of the market's anticipation of future volatility. As we use data extending further back in time, the estimate of volatility may become more precise. At the same time, it may prove less relevant.

Estimates of volatility can and do change from month to month. This is illustrated in Figure 13–1. One reasonable explanation for such a result is that the month by month estimates of volatility are simply not very precise. One month of close to close data may be too short a period of time to provide useful estimates of volatility. An alternative hypothesis is that these data reflect changes in underlying volatility. Standard statistical procedures can determine whether sampling variability is sufficient to explain observed changes in volatility from month to month. The simplest example of such a procedure is *Bartlett's test*.

---

[2]Many practitioners believe that the estimation of volatility is a mere statistical problem unrelated to the more central problem of valuing traded options. One simply obtains an estimate of volatility and plugs it into the valuation equation. Boyle and Ananthanarayanan (1977) observe that the estimation error can have valuation consequences. One can think of the estimate of volatility, σ, as being given by the true volatility σ, plus or minus some estimation error e. Using a Taylor series expansion, the value of a call given the estimate of volatility $C(s)$ is related to the true value of the call $C(s)$ by the approximate relation:

$$C(s) \approx C(\sigma) + \kappa \times e + .5 \times (dk \ / \ ds) \times e^2$$

Obviously, if the estimate of volatility differs from the true volatility, the option will be incorrectly valued to the extent that the option price depends on volatility, *kappa*, or k. This is captured by the second term of this expression. The third term captures an additional source of bias related to the efficiency with which the volatility is measured (given by the average value or expected value of e^2). This latter source of bias is negligible in the case of European call options, since *kappa* does not vary greatly with volatility ($d\kappa \ / \ d\sigma$ is small in magnitude). In cases where it may be large (such as in the case of certain compound options), Butler and Schachter (1986) discuss how to adjust for this source of bias.

[3]For evidence on the extent to which volatility varies through time for stocks, see Officer (1973) and Christie(1982).

The intuition behind this test is to consider whether variance estimated for subperiods of the data differs significantly from variance estimated using the entire period of data, allowing for the possibility that mean returns may differ from period to period. The steps that go into the calculation of the test statistic are reasonably straightforward. First, as with the volatility calculation, sums of squared deviations from the mean change in the logarithm of prices are computed for each month of the year. Each month's variance is estimated by dividing the sum of squares for that month by the number of trading days less one. The annual variance is computed by adding up all sums of squares and dividing by the number of trading days in the year less the number of months (since there are 12 estimates of the mean that go into the calculation of the month by month sums of squares). The results of these calculations are summarized on Table 13–1. Bartlett's test statistic is then given by the formula:

$$\text{Bartlett's test statistic} = \sum_{i=1}^{12} (n_i - 1) \ln (\hat{\sigma}^2 / \hat{\sigma}_i^2) = 24.92$$

where

$\hat{\sigma}_i^2$ is the variance estimated for month i

$\hat{\sigma}^2$ is the variance estimated for the entire year

n_i is the number of trading days in month i

This test statistic is simply the difference between the logarithm of annual variance $\hat{\sigma}^2$ and the average value of the logarithm of monthly variance $\hat{\sigma}_i^2$. It thus measures the extent to which monthly variances differ from annual variances. Given sampling variability from month to month, this difference will be distributed approximately as Chi-square with 11 degrees of freedom (12 months – 1). A value of 24.92 would be exceeded with probability .0093. Thus we reject the hypothesis that the measures of volatility are the same across months, at the one percent level.[4]

For this reason, in such circumstances past data is of limited relevance. To take an extreme example, the data prior to October 19, 1987 gave little

---

[4]This test statistic is known to be sensitive to departures of the data from a Normal distribution, so that rejection of the hypothesis that the variances are equal may simply tell us that the distribution of changes in the logarithm of prices is not Normal. This may not be so great a problem as it would appear, since many alternatives to the Normal distribution for stock returns, such as the Student t and Cauchy distributions can be characterized as Normal distributions for which the variance changes from period to period [see, e.g., Praetz (1972)]. If variance is hypothesized to vary in some predictable fashion, there exist robust nonparametric tests for changes in variance [see Giaccotto and Ali (1982)].

TABLE 13–1
Calculation of Bartlett's test statistic on the basis of data for 1986

Month	Mean	Sum of Squares	Variance	$(n_i-1)\ln(\hat{\sigma}_i^2/\hat{\sigma}^2)$	Number of Trading Days
Jan	0.00049	0.00187	0.00009	-1.97396	21
Feb	0.00363	0.00083	0.00005	10.89261	19
Mar	0.00257	0.00123	0.00006	5.10108	20
Apr	-0.00065	0.00245	0.00012	-6.79049	22
May	0.00233	0.00124	0.00006	6.14908	21
Jun	0.00067	0.00159	0.00008	1.19760	21
Jul	-0.00275	0.00230	0.00011	-5.39564	22
Aug	0.00327	0.00102	0.00005	10.11867	21
Sep	-0.00425	0.00396	0.00020	-17.03093	21
Oct	0.00232	0.00086	0.00004	16.96553	23
Nov	0.00112	0.00172	0.00010	-2.18783	19
Dec	-0.00130	0.00122	0.00006	7.87504	22
Year	0.00057	0.02029	0.00008	24.92074	252

indication of the increase in volatility that occurred subsequent to that date. One approach to this problem is to use data for only the very recent past. For example, if one were to have priced an index option in March 1988 with one month to expiration, it might be appropriate to use only data for February to estimate volatility.

A less extreme approach to this problem is to emphasize the most recent data in constructing an estimate of volatility. In the context of the Chapter 3 example, instead of finding a simple average of changes in the logarithm of stock prices and of the squared deviations from the average, one might take weighted averages, where the weights sum to one and decrease as one goes further back in time. This and related ad hoc procedures are discussed in Sharpe [1985] p. 503. The method of exponential smoothing is an example of this method. Assume the average of changes in the logarithm of prices is known, or for simplicity set equal to zero. Then, for each successive squared deviation, sd_t, the prior estimate of variance $\hat{\sigma}_{t-1}^2$ is updated by the formula:

$$\hat{\sigma}_t^2 = \alpha\, sd_t + (1-\alpha)\, \hat{\sigma}_{t-1}^2$$

where the weighting constant α is determined by experience to be a number between zero and one. This is in fact a weighted average scheme, where the weights α, $\alpha(1-\alpha)$, $\alpha(1-\alpha)^2$, .. sum to one and decrease as one goes further back in time.

To illustrate the method of exponential smoothing, suppose we set α equal to .05. In a Bayesian interpretation of the procedure, the prior estimate of variance $\hat{\sigma}^2_{t-1}$ is assumed to be equivalent to a data sample of size equal to the reciprocal of the weighting constant α. In this instance the equivalent sample size is 20 trading days. To refer back to the Table 13–1 example, the variance estimate for the month of January is .000093, implying an annualized standard deviation of .154. The S&P 500 index stood at 211.78 at the end of January and was 213.96 on February 3, 1986. The volatility estimate for February 3 is obtained as follows. The squared difference in logarithm of prices is .000105. This quantity times .05 plus the prior estimate of variance .000093 times .95 yields .000094, the new estimate of variance, which yields .156 as an annualized volatility measure. This procedure can be repeated for each day for which data is available. Using data just for the month of October 1986 to estimate volatility yields .10 which appears to be unreasonably low. The exponential smoothing procedure yields estimates of volatility that range from .19 at the beginning of the month to .14 by the end of the month.

Obviously, such measures of volatility depend crucially on an appropriate choice of weighting constants. Advanced statistical procedures have recently been developed to estimate appropriate values for these constants from the data.[5] However, these methods assume the variance evolves in a fashion inconsistent with the standard option pricing formulae, which assume the variance will be constant over the remaining life of the option.

Another approach is to increase the frequency with which the data is measured. If data prior to last month are considered of limited use in determining volatility, an obvious approach is to use trade to trade data if available.

---

[5]Such weighting schemes can be interpreted in an ARCH framework. ARCH is an acronym for Auto-Regressive Conditional Heteroscedasticity, and assumes that the true variance evolves in a fashion similar to the exponential smoothing equation given in the text. If this is so, then the parameter α can be estimated using the method of maximum likelihood. See Engle (1982).

The use of trade to trade and high-low data to estimate volatility

The technique for estimating volatility using trade to trade data is essentially the same as that described in Chapter 3 where, instead of closing prices, transaction prices are used.[6] However, the use of such data can lead to estimates of volatility that differ significantly from estimates derived from close to close data.

For example, on the basis of data for the S&P 500 Index Futures contract for October, 1986 the close to close estimate of volatility is .158. This number is higher than the previous number computed on the basis of the S&P 500 close data for October 1986. In part this is to be explained by the difference between the cash and derivative markets. The number is close to the standard deviation estimated on the basis of the annual S&P 500 close data. However, using the same period of data to estimate volatility on a transaction to transaction basis yields a much higher estimate.

There are 9,185 minute by minute transaction records for the month of October 1986. Utilizing the correction for unequal intervals between transactions given above,[7] the sum of squared deviations from the mean is .002423. The estimate of variance is then the average of this sum of squared deviations, or 2.6383×10^{-7}. This yields an estimate of volatility of .372 on an annualized basis. This volatility estimate is more than twice the magnitude of the close to close number. If instead of minute by minute transactions, we use transactions recorded every 15 minutes, we obtain a somewhat lower number of .369. Transactions recorded every hour yield an estimate of volatility of .324. If the assumptions of the model were indeed correct, these numbers should all be of a similar magnitude. In fact, the extent to which the estimate of volatility falls as the measurement interval increases has been proposed as a test of the assumptions of the model applied to this kind of data.[8]

The decrease in volatility as the differencing interval increases is

---

[6]In this context, it is considered necessary to control for the fact that the time between successive transaction prices can vary. The appropriate correction is described in section 13.2 of this chapter, where the time between prices is measured as a fraction of a calendar day. Such a correction assumes that the asset in question is traded continuously. If this is not the case, the time between transactions may itself represent the appropriate unit of time. See, for example, Harris (1986).

[7]Excluding all intervals between transactions of greater than one minute (close to open differences, for example) led to very similar results. The numbers we report here are thus not sensitive to use of the correction for different intervals between transactions.

[8]See, for example, the work of Lo and McKinley (1988).

consistent with negative serial covariance of successive differences in the logarithm of prices. Such negative serial covariances exist in this data and are statistically significant for the minute to minute and even hour to hour differences. Such negative serial covariances are consistent with trades that occur within the bid-ask spread; Roll [1984] suggests that this negative serial covariance may actually be used as a measure of the bid-ask spread. Others have suggested that the reduction in volatility over somewhat longer intervals is consistent with mean-reversion in asset markets — the tendency of asset prices once disturbed by trading behavior to revert to some index of long term value (Poterba and Summers [1989]).

A significant reduction in volatility as the measurement interval increases strongly suggests the existence of short term trading processes in the market that may not be particularly relevant for the pricing of options and other derivative securities. While it is possible to model these short term trading processes and estimate volatility using sophisticated maximum likelihood procedures of the type described by Garbade and Lieber [1977], as a general rule one should avoid use of transaction data to estimate volatility where such reductions in estimated volatility occur.[9]

Even if trade to trade data were appropriate, such trade data are not always readily available. But if the assumptions of the model are correct, knowledge of the highs and lows of trading on a day by day basis can yield an estimate of volatility superior to that obtained by looking only at successive close to close data. In fact, it is possible to show that using the high-low data for a given month will yield an estimate of volatility as precise as one estimated using five to six times the amount of close to close data.[10] Incorporating the open and close prices will lead to further improvements.

The estimate of volatility is given by the formula:

$$\hat{\sigma} = \sqrt{\frac{.361}{n} \sum_{i=1}^{n} [\ln (H_i) - \ln(L_i)]^2}$$

[9]This observation also calls into question the use of close-to-close data, to the extent that trading processes may unduly affect the price behavior around the close. This has been documented by Harris (1986) among others. Some use 3 p.m. to 3 p.m. data to avoid such problems [see, for example, McKinley and Ramaswamy (1988)]. Use of such data in the S&P 500 index futures example yields an estimate of volatility equal to .137, lower than the close-to-close number. In that month, minute-to-minute changes in the logarithm of price were negatively correlated, with a correlation coefficient of −.19 in the last fifteen minutes of trading.

[10]Both this result on relative precision and the estimator derived using high-low data are taken from Parkinson (1980).

where

> H_i is the trading high for day i
>
> L_i is the trading low for day i
>
> n is the number of trading days under consideration

In other words, simply take the average value of the squared difference in logarithms between the high and the low price for each trading day. We then multiply this quantity by the factor[11] .361 to obtain the estimate of variance. The square root of this estimate is then the desired measure of volatility.

To see how to apply this measure, consider the S&P 500 Index data. The high for Wednesday, October 1, 1986, was 235.64 and the low was 231.45. This yields a squared difference in logarithms multiplied by .361 of .000116. The average of these numbers for the month yields an estimate of daily variance equal to .000087. The annualized measure of daily standard deviation is .15. This estimate is quite close to that obtained using annual data, and as noted above, has a precision from five to six times that of the close to close number. Use of open and close data is said to lead to even greater precision.[12]

In many instances, measures of volatility based on historical data are unreliable where volatility changes through time. In many applications, only data for the very recent past is considered. This limitation implies that such measures of volatility will be imprecise. Use of intra-day trading data to increase the precision of the volatility estimate may lead to problems if intra-day trading phenomena obscure the measure of volatility, although use of high-low data can alleviate some of this problem. The difficult tradeoff between the appropriate specification of the volatility measure and the precision with which it is measured has led most practitioners to

---

[11]The expected value of the square of the range high-low (in natural logarithms) is four times the variance times the natural logarithm of two if the assumptions of the model are correct. Thus, an estimate of the variance is given by the average squared range multiplied by the reciprocal of four times the natural logarithm of two, or .361.

[12]See Garman and Klass (1980). However, we do not recommend this refinement. To the extent that opening and closing prices are unduly subject to short-term trading processes, the refined measures will yield unreliable estimates of the underlying volatility. The extremes of trading typically occur within a few minutes of the open and close. For example, the measure that accounts for opening and closing prices, and makes the appropriate volatility (σ_6 in the parlance of Garman and Klass) equal to .376 in the S&P 500 example, numerically indistinguishable from the .372 estimate obtained using trade-to-trade data.

consider another approach to the estimation of volatility. This approach uses as a measure of volatility that quantity implied by the price at which the option trades. Such a measure is called an *implied volatility.*

13.3 THE USE OF OPTION VALUES TO ESTIMATE VOLATILITY

Implied volatility

As noted in the introduction to this chapter, volatility is the only parameter of the option pricing formula that we cannot observe directly. However, we can observe option values in the market. Since such values are increasing functions of volatility it should be possible, at least in principle, to obtain a measure of volatility from the option price itself. Such measures are called *implied volatilities.*

To understand the concept of an implied volatility, it will be helpful to reconsider the example given in Chapter 3, section 4. In that example, the Black-Scholes model value of a three month at-the-money call option is $3.74 given the following set of parameter values:

Initial Asset Price: $S = \$100$
Exercise Price: $X = \$100$
Time to Expiration: $T = 91/365 = .2493$ (three months)
Interest Rate: $r = \ln(1.06) = .05827$ (6 percent annual)
Volatility: $\sigma = .15$

Of course, this example assumes that volatility is known to be equal to .15. What if this information were not available? Figure 13–2 plots the value of this call option as a function of the unknown volatility measure, assuming that the Black-Scholes model correctly values the option. If such an option actually trades at $3.74 we might infer from this figure that volatility is approximately .15. This value is obtained by finding where the horizontal line drawn at the call value of $3.74 intersects with the option value line in the figure. This graphical approach is intuitively appealing. However, to obtain useful volatility measures in this way requires many calculations (and a steady hand!).

While simpler and more accurate methods of calculating implied volatilities exist and will be covered in this section, there appears to be a

FIGURE 13–2
Option values and volatility

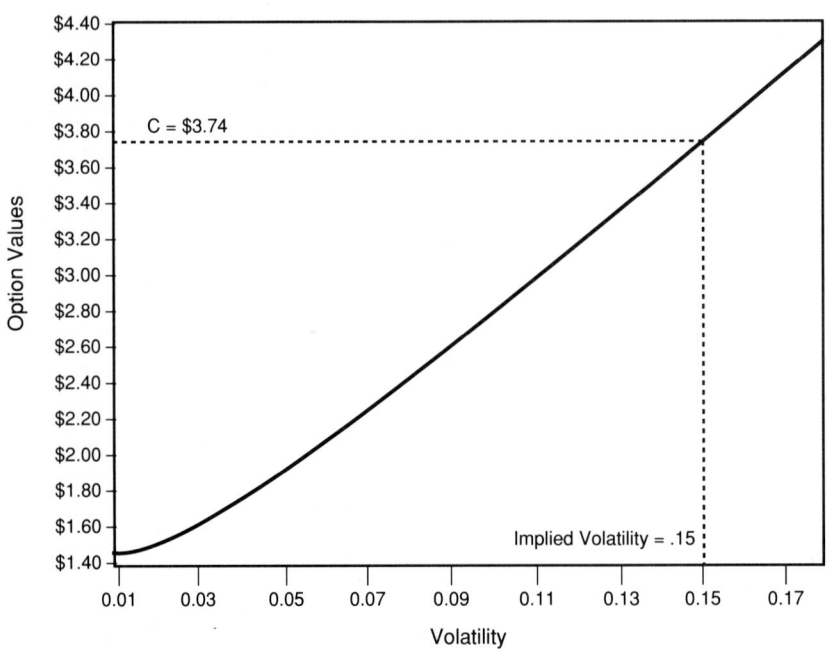

circularity in the reasoning behind this measure. If traded options are correctly valued, why bother calculating volatilities at all? The reason is that
more than one option may be written on a given asset. While any particular
option may trade at a price that deviates from the model price, the sense is
that a weighted average of implied volatilities will be an appropriate
measure of the volatility of the underlying asset on which the options are
written. This section will conclude with a discussion of some suggested
weighting schemes.

Methods of Calculating Implied Volatility

The most popular computational method for deriving measures of implied
volatility is the *Newton-Raphson algorithm*. This method is highly efficient
and accurate in the context of European call options. It does not work as well

for American options on dividend paying securities, and may not work at all for other kinds of derivative securities. Another algorithm, the *Method of Bisection* involves about the same number of computations, but is somewhat simpler to apply and is guaranteed to work for all classes of derivative securities. We will now examine how the two procedures work.

The computational problem is to find the volatility measure σ_o such that the value of the option (in this case, a European call) expressed as a function of volatility, $C(\sigma_o)$, is equal to the observed option price, C_o. The Newton-Raphson algorithm starts out with the presumption that the option value is to a first approximation given by a linear function of volatility:

$$[C_o - C(\sigma)] \approx \kappa \cdot (\sigma_o - \sigma)$$

where κ or *kappa,* is the derivative of the option value as a function of volatility. For any given value of σ, the implied volatility σ_o may be approximated by:

$$\hat{\sigma}_o \approx \sigma + [C_o - C(\sigma)] / \kappa$$

The method proceeds by first specifying a starting value for volatility, computing $C(\sigma)$ and κ for that value of σ, and approximating the implied volatility using the above formula. This approximation is not exact. How close it is can be judged by the extent to which the option value given that estimate, $C(\hat{\sigma}_o)$, comes close to the observed price C_o. A closer approximation can be found by substituting the approximate measure of volatility $\hat{\sigma}_o$ into the above formula again. The process continues for about three to four iterations, until the implied option price equals C_o and there is no further change in the successive estimates of volatility.[13]

The method can best be understood by means of the example used above. First, we need a good starting value (although nearly any starting value can be used—it may just take the procedure more iterations to converge). Note that the implied volatility is approximately proportional to the ratio between the call value and the value of the underlying asset for at-the-money calls:[14]

---

[13]The properties of this approach to estimating implied volatilities is discussed in Manaster and Koehler (1982).

[14]See Brenner and Subrahmanyam (1987).

$$\sigma_o \approx [\, C_o / S\,] / [.398 \sqrt{T}]$$
$$= [3.74 / 100] / [.398 \sqrt{.2493}\,] = .1882$$

This calculation provides a good starting value. For this value of volatility and other parameters given above, the calculation of implied volatility is outlined in Table 13–2:

TABLE 13–2
Calculation of implied volatility using the Newton-Raphson algorithm

	σ	D	$N(D)$	C	κ	$\hat{\sigma}_o$
Iteration 1:	0.188197	0.201580	0.579877	4.485896	19.51913	0.149984
Iteration 2:	0.149984	0.231428	0.591509	3.742112	19.39340	0.149875
Iteration 3:	0.149875	0.231542	0.591553	3.740000	19.39289	0.149875

For the initial estimate of volatility given as .1882, the theoretical call value would have been $4.49. Applying these numbers, along with *kappa,* into the formula above for the implied volatility yields a close estimate of .14998. Substituting this measure into the option formula yields 3.7421, a value slightly in excess of the trading price. A further approximation of implied volatility, .149875, gives us the option value exactly.

In certain applications, *kappa* may be difficult to compute. In some instances it may not even be well defined. While one could always define a numerical measure of *kappa* as the change in option value per (small) unit change in volatility, the Newton-Raphson procedure will not work well in such cases. There is a better way.

Where the standard Black-Scholes formula gives a close approximation to the value of other options to which, strictly speaking it does not apply (such as an at-the-money American option on a dividend paying security), this Newton-Raphson method is recommended. However, the method does not work very well where *kappa* varies greatly as a function of volatility. As noted above, for certain derivative securities, *kappa* may be difficult to compute and may not even exist. The Method of Bisection is an alternative approach which does not require any estimate of *kappa* and is not sensitive to choice of starting values. From a computational viewpoint, it is almost as efficient.

Figure 13–3 illustrates the method. The solid line in the figure represents the value of some hypothetical compound option. This option increases in value with volatility, but perhaps not in the perfectly smooth fashion assumed for the Newton-Raphson algorithm. In particular, *kappa* may not be defined at certain points where the value of the option may change abruptly with the level of volatility. Such a point is denoted by the kink in the solid line given in the figure.

To demonstrate how the Method of Bisection works, first choose a 'low' estimate of implied volatility σ_L, which would correspond to an option value of C_L, and a 'high' estimate σ_H, corresponding to C_H, so that C_o lies between C_L and C_H. The estimate of implied volatility is given as the linear interpolation between those two points:

$$\hat{\sigma}_o = \sigma_L + (C_o - C_L) \times (\sigma_H - \sigma_L) / (C_H - C_L)$$

If the value of the option given this estimate of implied volatility is equal to the traded option value, C_o, stop. Otherwise, if the value $C(\hat{\sigma}_o)$ is less than C_o, replace σ_L with this value and repeat the exercise. If it is greater, use it to replace σ_H. This alternative method should converge on the correct measure of implied volatility very quickly.[15]

Despite the fact that the Newton-Raphson algorithm is more familiar to practitioners and is, indeed, widely available as a computer software product, we recommend the method of bisection because it is more general, requiring only that the user specify the appropriate option valuation model. Furthermore, it is nearly as efficient as the alternative approach which requires estimates of *kappa* at each iteration.

Weighting Implied Volatilities

Implied volatilities estimated for different options trading on the same underlying security will typically differ. In Table 13–3 we report the implied volatilities computed for different Chicago board options on the

---

[15]This simple approach to finding the implied volatility is actually referred to as the *Secant Method* in the technical literature. Properties of this method, and improvements on it are described in Brent (1973, chapters 3 and 4). It is a useful exercise to verify that the method described will yield the same numerical quantity for the implied volatility as will the Newton-Raphson method with the same number of iterations.

FIGURE 13–3
Illustration of the method of bisection

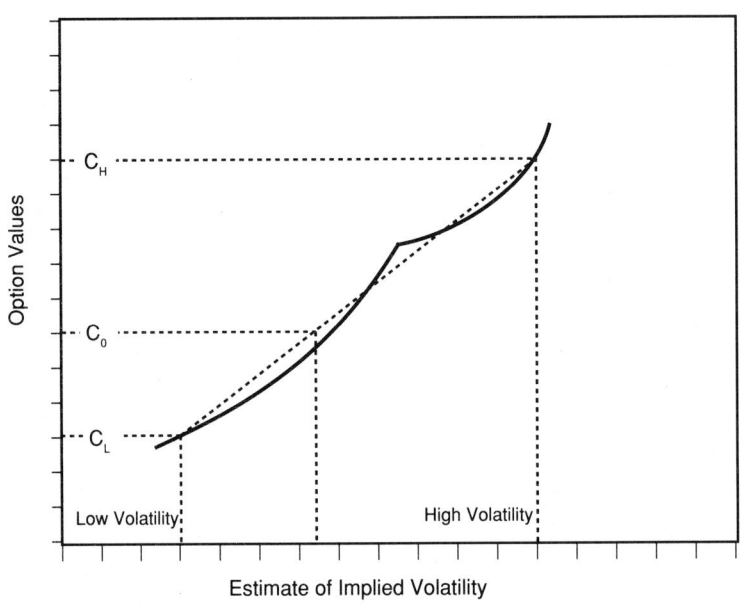

S&P 500 Index as of October 2, 1986. These volatilities were computed on the basis of a closing price of 233.92 using a risk-free rate assumption of 4.98 percent.[16]

As we see, implied volatility varies with each option, from .128 to .207, depending on which option is under study. In what sense do these different numbers reflect the market's anticipation of volatility of the underlying asset over the period to expiration? Practitioners believe that cross-sectional differences in implied volatility are due to errors in the data: prices of the option and the underlying security may not be quoted at exactly the same point in time, and price changes are only quoted in fractional

---

[16]These numbers were taken from *The Wall Street Journal* of October 3, 1986. Figures for the dividends to be paid on the index portfolio were provided by Shearson Lehman.

TABLE 13–3
Implied volatilities computed for the options on the S&P 500
futures contract, October 2, 1986.

		October			November				December			
Strike	C^a	σ_i	λ	κ	C	σ_i	λ	κ	C	σ_i	λ	κ
225	9-3/8	.128	23.5	.061								
230	5-7/8	.178	27.8	.166	8-1/2	.182	16.9	.329	9-7/8	.175	14.4	.412
235	3-3/8	.198	33.0	.189					7-5/8	.182	15.5	.428
240	1-3/8	.184	44.9	.157	4-1/8	.190	21.3	.328	5-3/4	.189	16.7	.410
245	7/16	.178	58.5	.093	3-1/8	.207	21.6	.197	3-3/4	.180	19.5	.384
250	3/16	.193	62.2	.052					2-9/16	.181	21.3	.335
255	1/16	.199	69.2	.024					1-11/16	.190	35.5	.182

[a]C is the closing price of the option on the S&P 500 index. $\hat{\sigma}_i$ is the implied volatility given by the Black-Scholes formula for a European call, correcting for dividends and other parameters in the text. λ is the elasticity of the option given by *delta* times the ratio of the index level to the option price, and κ is *kappa,* the sensitivity of the option price to volatility.

units.[17] Presumably, one might also allow for transitory pricing errors. Suppose the option value can be approximated by a linear function of volatility in a region of the true volatility. In that case a weighted average of implied volatility measures would provide a good estimate of the parameter to use in the option pricing formula.[18] The issue is to determine the appropriate set of weights.

The simplest approach is to use equal weights, or at least to weight the implied volatilities according to the value outstanding of the options in question. The simple average of volatility measures in the above example is .184. Since the values of certain options (such as call options at-the-money) are more sensitive to choice of the correct measure of volatility than others, it would make sense to weight those options more heavily than

---

[17]See Cox and Rubinstein (1985) for a discussion of this. Brenner and Galai (1986) discuss the effect of such errors in pricing (as well as the impact of bid-ask spread) on the measures of implicit volatility. For a somewhat different interpretation of volatility estimates from various options, see section 6 of Chapter 12 in this volume.

[18]One might argue that this proposition would be true even if the option pricing formula were misspecified (for example, by not accounting for changes in volatility), but that the option price were locally a linear function of a parameter we might call "volatility." I am indebted to Haim Reisman for this observation.

others (which may be deep in-the-money or out-of-the-money). This is especially true where we expect such options to be less sensitive to data errors of the type described above.[19] Thus one might compute kappa as the appropriate weighting factor for each option. The sum of *kappa* in the above example is 4.314. Adding up the measure of implied standard deviation times *kappa* for each option, divided by 4.314 yields .185 as the measure of implied volatility.[20]

There is an alternative procedure that implicitly weights according to *kappa*. Define the measure of implied volatility as that single measure of σ that minimizes the expression

$$\text{Sum of Squares} = \sum_{i=1}^{n} [\, C_{io} - C_i(\sigma) \,]^2$$

where

C_{io} is the trading price of option i

n is the total number of options used to estimate implied volatility

The motivation here is to allow for the possibility of quotation errors. The standard implied volatility measures assume an identity between the option value and observed option price. This approach instead seeks a single measure of volatility that brings the theoretical option value as close as possible to the observed data.

In the S&P 500 example, to compute such a number simply tabulate the theoretical option prices for volatility ranging in value from .128 to .207.[21] The value of volatility that minimizes the sum of squares is .1842. To see the relationship to *kappa* weighting, note that the sum of squares is minimized where

$$\sum_{i=1}^{n} [\, C_{io} - C_i(\sigma) \,]\, \kappa_i = 0$$

---

[19]Beckers (1981) suggests that use of the option most sensitive to changes in volatility *alone* will yield a measure of volatility as good as some of the less extreme weighting schemes discussed here.

[20]Cox and Rubinstein (1985) suggest using the elasticity of the option, defined as *delta* ($\Delta C / \Delta S$) times S / C, as the appropriate weighting factor. This elasticity is given as λ in Table 13–3. Weighting volatilities in this way yields .186 as the measure of volatility.

[21]This can be done in LOTUS 1-2-3, using the *Data Table 1* option.

All these weighting methods yield results that are not significantly different. This is not surprising, given that the range of implied volatilities is not great. As a practical matter, if the implied volatilities were very different, the practitioner would be advised to check carefully for errors in the data or misalignment of price quotations.

Black has suggested a relatively complicated weighting scheme that combines both historical estimates of volatility and implied volatility and seems to account for several empirical regularities in the equity option markets.[22] There seems to be a market factor in volatilities: volatilities of related securities tend to move together. Volatilities tend to be mean-reverting in that extreme volatilities, either low or high, tend to return to average values over time. Finally, volatility seems to fall as the price of a given security rises. It is yet to be seen whether the empirical formula that accounts for these different elements has applicability beyond the equity option markets. Until this formula is validated for these other markets, it is not possible to recommend its general application. However, it is a promising approach worthy of further study.

13.4 CONCLUSION

The simplest approach to estimating volatility for the option pricing model may not be appropriate where volatility changes through time. One resolution of this problem is to refine the estimation procedures to make use of trade-to-trade data to get as precise a measure of volatility as possible on the basis of a limited amount of historical data. An alternative approach is to use volatility estimated from the trading prices of the options themselves. In either case, one has to be careful interpreting the results of the analysis since such results depend crucially on the quality of the data used to estimate the measure of volatility.

---

[22]Black's formula is described in detail in Cox and Rubinstein (1985).

References

Amihud, Y., and Mendelson, H. (1987). Trading mechanisms and stock returns: An empirical investigation. *Journal of Finance,42*, 533–53.

Beckers, S. (1981). Standard deviations implied in option prices as predictors of future stock price variability. *Journal of Banking and Finance, 5*, 363–82.

Boyle, P. and Ananthanarayanan, A. (1977). The impact of variance estimation in option valuation models. *Journal of Financial Economics, 5*, 375–88.

Brenner, M. and Galai, D. (1986). Estimation of errors in the implied standard deviation. New York, NY: New York University unpublished working paper.

Brenner, M. and Subrahmanyam, M. (1987). A simple formula to compute the implied standard deviation. *Financial Analysts Journal,* forthcoming

Brent, R. (1973). *Algorithms for minimization without derivatives.* Englewood Cliffs, NJ: Prentice-Hall, Inc.

Butler, J.S. and Schachter, B. (1986). Unbiased estimation of the Black/Scholes formula. *Journal of Financial Economics, 15*, 341–57.

Christie, A. (1982). The stochastic behavior of common stock variances. *Journal of Financial Economics, 10*, 407–32.

Cox, J., and Rubinstein, M. (1985). *Options markets.* Englewood Cliffs, NJ: Prentice-Hall, Inc.

Engle, R. (1982). Autoregressive conditional heteroscedasticity with estimates of the variance of United Kingdom inflation. *Econometrica, 50*, 987–1007.

French, K., and Roll, R. (1986). Stock return variances: The arrival of information and the reaction of traders. *Journal of Financial Economics, 17*, 5–26.

Garbade, K and Lieber, Z. (1977). On the independence of transactions on the New York Stock Exchange. *Journal of Banking and Finance, 1*, 151–72.

Garman, M. and Klass, M. (1980). On the estimation of security price volatilities from historical data. *Journal of Business, 53*, 67–78.

Giaccotto, C. and Ali, M. (1982). Optimum distribution-free tests and further evidence of heteroscedasticity in the market model. *Journal of Finance, 38*, 1247–57.

Harris, L. (1986). Cross security tests of the mixture of distributions hypothesis. *Journal of Financial and Quantitative Analysis, 21*, 39–46.

Harris, L. (1986). A transaction data study of weekly and intradaily patterns in stock returns. *Journal of Financial Economics, 16*, 19–118.

Lo, A.W. and McKinley, A. C. (1988). Stock market prices do not follow random walks: Evidence from a simple specification test. *Review of Financial Studies, 1*, 41–66.

Manaster, S. and Koehler, G. (1982). The calculation of implied variances from the Black-Scholes formula. *Journal of Finance, 37*, 227–30.

Marsh, T., and Rosenfeld, E. (1986). Non-trading, market making, and estimates of stock price volatility. *Journal of Financial Economics, 15*, 359–72.

McKinley, C. and Ramaswamy, K. (1988). *Review of Financial Studies, 1*, 137–58.

Officer, R. (1973). The variability of the market factor of the New York Stock Exchange. *Journal of Business, 46*, 434–52.

Parkinson, M. (1980). The extreme value method for estimating the variance of the rate of return. *Journal of Business ,53*, 61–65.

Poterba, J., and Summers, L. (1988). Mean reversion in stock prices: Evidence and implications. *Journal of Financial Economics, 22*, 27–59.

Praetz, P. (1972). The distribution of share prices. *Journal of Business, 45*, 49–55.

Roll, R. (1984). A simple implicit measure of the bid ask spread in an efficient market. *Journal of Finance, 39*, 1127–1159.

Sharpe, W. (1985). *Investments.* (3rd edition). Englewood Cliffs, NJ: Prentice-Hall, Inc.

CHAPTER 14

AN INTRODUCTION TO NUMERICAL METHODS IN OPTION PRICING

*Georges Courtadon**

This chapter presents advanced material describing the various methods for deriving approximate solutions to option valuation problems. The reader should be familiar with the material presented in Chapter 3 and its appendices. Because of the technical complexity of the material, it has not been possible to follow the same notation as in the previous chapters. The reader should be alert for the differences.

14.1 INTRODUCTION

The last ten years have witnessed tremendous growth in the field of theoretical option pricing. During this time, the original approach proposed by Black and Scholes (1973) has been extended to the valuation of many other types of options. All of the different valuation models have one point in common: in each of them, option values can be obtained by solving a

*The author is a Vice President in the North American Investment Bank of Citicorp and head of Derviative Products Research.

partial differential equation of the parabolic type subject to a set of boundary conditions.

A few of these valuation problems lend themselves to closed form solutions, such as the Black-Scholes equation for a European option on a non-dividend paying stock. One of the common methods to obtain a closed form solution is to represent the value of the option by the value of an integral, and to solve this integral as a function of known mathematical functions. The appendices to Chapter 3 illustrate this approach for the Black-Scholes model. The option's expected value at expiration is obtained by integrating its payoff over the probability density for the stock price at that date. The expected payoff is then discounted back to the present to give the option value. Under some regularity conditions, this method can be shown to be general for all partial differential equations of the parabolic type [see Friedman (1976)].

This method was first specifically applied to option pricing by Cox and Ross (1976) who showed that option valuation will not directly depend on investors' risk preferences as long as a hedging argument is used to derive the valuation equation.[1] As discussed in earlier chapters, this means the value of the option can be determined by assuming that investors are risk neutral and expected rates of return on the option and on the underlying instrument are equal to a constant riskless rate of interest. The concept of risk neutral valuation was then generalized by Cox, Ingersoll and Ross (1985) to allow for stochastic interest rates.[2]

Though closed form solutions are desirable, most option valuation problems do not have closed form solutions and must be solved by using numerical methods, that is, methods that attempt only to compute an approximate solution for a specific set of parameters. Two main categories of numerical solutions have been used in the option pricing literature. The first category attempts to solve the integral equation representing the value of the option, while the second category directly solves the partial differential equation. One can include in the first category the Binomial approach of Sharpe (1978) and Cox, Ross and Rubinstein (1979), the Trinomial

---

[1]Investors' preferences will affect the valuation problem only to the extent that they determine the equilibrium process followed by the price of the instrument underlying the option.

[2]Under interest rate uncertainty, it is not possible as a general rule to separate the calculation of the expected value of the option payout at maturity from its discounting back to the present. The expected value of the option payout at maturity must be computed over the joint probability distribution of the discount rate and the price of the underlying instrument on the option maturity date.

approach of Parkinson (1977) and the Monte-Carlo simulation approach first proposed by Boyle (1977). The second category includes all of the finite difference approximation techniques which have been used in the finance literature, starting with the work of Brennan and Schwartz (1976).

In this chapter, we will introduce the reader to both types of numerical methods. The numerical methods presented are illustrated by the example of valuing an American put option on a stock paying a dividend. In the next section, we show how approaches like the Binomial or the Trinomial methods can be applied to solve this problem.

In the third section, we present the standard finite difference approximation techniques which can be used to solve the American put option valuation problem. We will first present the different tools which transform the partial differential equation describing the value of the option into a difference equation. We will then outline the two main approaches to approximating a partial differential equation by finite differences: the explicit and implicit difference methods. We will conclude the section by introducing a more accurate finite difference scheme which increases the degree of accuracy of the numerical approximation.

The fourth section of this chapter will present a numerical example that permits comparison among the different numerical methods described in the second and third sections. We will conclude in the fifth section. Finally, two appendices present advanced material. Appendix A contains a discussion of issues of convergence and stability of the finite difference approximation methods, and Appendix B describes Parkinson's Trinomial model for American options.

14.2 VALUATION BY SOLVING THE INTEGRAL EQUATION

In the next three sections of this chapter, we will use the case of an American put option on a stock that pays dividends to illustrate the different types of numerical methods. We will make the standard assumptions of the continuous time literature. These assumptions were discussed in Chapter 3, and can be summarized as follows:

(A1)   The markets are frictionless and trading is continuous. In particular, there are no restrictions on short sales.

(A2)   The annual risk free rate of interest is constant and equal to r. This rate is assumed to be continuously compounded.

(A3)   The stock price follows a geometric Wiener process of the form $dS = (\alpha - d)Sdt + \sigma Sdz$, where α and σ are, respectively, the annual mean and standard deviation of the continuously compounded rate of return on the stock. The stock is also assumed to pay a continuous and proportional annual dividend rate of d. Finally, dz is a standard Brownian motion with mean zero and variance dt.

Given these assumptions, it can be easily shown that the value at time t, $W(S, t)$, of a put option maturing at time T satisfies the following system of equations:[3]

$$\frac{1}{2} \sigma^2 S^2 \frac{\partial^2 W}{\partial S^2} + (r - d) S \frac{\partial W}{\partial S} - rW + \frac{\partial W}{\partial t} = 0 \qquad (14.1a)$$

subject to: $\qquad\qquad W(S, T) = \text{Max}[0, E - S] \qquad\qquad (14.1b)$

$$W(S, s) = \text{Max}[W^*(S, s), E - S] \text{ for } t < s < T \qquad (14.1c)$$

where E is the exercise price of the option and $W^*(S, s)$ represents the value of the option at time s if it is not exercised, i.e., it is left alive for the next instant of time. Boundary condition (14.1b) accounts for the fact that the payout of the put option at maturity will be zero if the stock price is greater than or equal to the exercise price, and equal to the difference between the exercise price and the stock price if the stock price is less than the exercise price. Boundary condition (14.1c) represents the decision that the holder of an American put option has to take at every point in time during the life of the option. The option holder can either keep the option alive, in which case the position will be worth $W^*(S, s)$, or exercise it if $E - S$ is greater than $W^*(S, s)$.

This valuation problem does not have a closed form solution and must

---

[3]See, for example, Brennan and Schwartz (1977) or Parkinson (1977). The difference between equation (14.1a) and (3A.16) is in the adjustment for the dividend on the stock, that is assumed to be paid out continuously at a constant rate (meaning the dollar amount varies with the stock price).

be solved numerically. To simplify the exposition of the different numerical methods, we will make the change of variable, $X = \log(S)$, in the valuation problem defined by the system of equations (14.1a) to (14.1c). We will now define the value of the put option by $U(X, t)$. The system of equations (14.1a) to (14.1c) becomes:

$$\frac{1}{2} \sigma^2 \frac{\partial^2 U}{\partial X^2} + (r - d - \frac{1}{2} \sigma^2) \frac{\partial U}{\partial X} - rU + \frac{\partial U}{\partial t} = 0 \qquad (14.2a)$$

subject to: $\qquad\qquad U(X, T) = \text{Max}[0, E - \exp(X)] \qquad\qquad (14.2b)$

$$U(X, s) = \text{Max}[U^*(X, s), E - \exp(X)] \qquad \text{for } t < s < T \quad (14.2c)$$

where $U^*(X, s)$ is equal to $W^*(S, s)$. Equation (14.2a) is obtained from equation (14.1a) by replacing the derivatives of $W(S, t)$ with respect to S and t by the derivatives of $U(X, t)$ with respect to X and t. We have:

$$\frac{\partial W}{\partial t} = \frac{\partial U}{\partial t}, \qquad\qquad \frac{\partial W}{\partial S} = \frac{1}{S} \frac{\partial U}{\partial X}$$

and $\qquad$
$$\frac{\partial^2 W}{\partial S^2} = \frac{1}{S^2} \frac{\partial^2 U}{\partial X^2} - \frac{1}{S^2} \frac{\partial U}{\partial X}$$

The reader can easily verify that equation (14.2a) follows from equation (14.1a) once this substitution is made. Finally, equations (14.2b) and (14.2c) are simple transformations of equations (14.1b) and (14.1c).

As already mentioned in the introduction, one of the approaches which can be used to solve the valuation problem corresponding to equations (14.2a) to (14.2c) is to solve the integral representation of the solution to this valuation problem. This method was first proposed by Cox and Ross (1976) for European options. Cox and Ross show that the value of the option is equal to the discounted expected value of the payout of the option at maturity. Recall that under risk neutrality the expected rates of return on the option and the underlying instrument are equal to the riskless rate of interest. The expected value of the price of the underlying instrument is taken with respect to a risk neutral density function such that it is expected to earn the riskless rate up to the maturity date of the option. The result is then discounted at the riskless rate.

Therefore, following the Cox and Ross analysis, the price of the otherwise equivalent European put option will be such that:

$$U(X_t, t) = EV_t\{U(X_T, T)\exp[-r(T - t)]\} \tag{14.3}$$

where EV_t is the expected value operator at time t with respect to the risk neutral density function. X_t and X_T are, respectively, the values of X at time t and at time T. X_T is assumed to be normally distributed with mean $X_t + (r - d - \frac{1}{2}\sigma^2)(T - t)$ and variance $\sigma^2(T - t)$. The valuation principle derived by Cox and Ross is also applicable to American option valuation since it will also hold between the value of the option at time s and the value of the option at time $s + k$ where k is a small interval of time and $t < s < T$. We have:

$$U(X_s, s) = EV_s\{U(X_{s+k}, s + k)\}\exp[-rk] \tag{14.4}$$

where EV_s is defined similarly to EV_t. Equation (14.4) defines a recursive relationship between the value of an American option at time $s + k$ and its value at time s. Consequently, given the value of the option on its maturity date, we can solve for the value of the option at time $T - k$ and proceed backwards by solving for the value of the option every period of time of length k back to time t.

The Binomial and Trinomial methods are simple numerical implementations of this recursive valuation method where the probability distribution of X_{s+k} given X_s is approximated by a binomial or a trinomial process.

The Binomial Approach

The Binomial model for option valuation was developed in Chapter 3 and applied throughout the book. The principle of risk neutral valuation means that the option value depends on the volatility of the stock return but not on its mean. As we have seen, this gives us considerable flexibility in setting up a stock price tree for the Binomial model. For example, at times it has been useful to pick up and down values so that the risk neutral probabilities were each .5.

But while the approach will "work" under many different combinations of u and d, the behavior of the model as a discrete approximation to a continuous process is not independent of these assumptions. One combination may provide more accurate answers for a given number of steps than another. This subsection and the next will present two different Binomial approaches. Section 14.4 will compare their performance in a numerical example.

In the first subsection, we construct the Binomial stock price tree explicitly to approximate the risk neutral diffusion process we have been discussing above. The risk neutral diffusion process followed by the logarithm of the stock price is:

$$dX = (r - d - \tfrac{1}{2}\sigma^2)dt + \sigma\,dz \tag{14.5}$$

The simplest way to make this process discrete is to assume that over a short period of time k, the change in logarithm of the stock price can only take two possible values, each with probability $\tfrac{1}{2}$. These two values are:

$$
\begin{array}{ccc}
 & \overset{\tfrac{1}{2}}{\nearrow} & X + (r - d - \tfrac{1}{2}\sigma^2)k + \sigma\sqrt{k} \\
X & & \\
 & \underset{\tfrac{1}{2}}{\searrow} & X + (r - d - \tfrac{1}{2}\sigma^2)k - \sigma\sqrt{k}
\end{array}
\tag{14.6}
$$

This discrete process correctly approximates the distribution of X_T given X_t. Equation (14.6) implies that the mean and variance of dX are, respectively, equal to $(r - d - \tfrac{1}{2}\sigma^2)k$ and $\sigma^2 k$. If k is taken to be a small interval of time, the number of time steps over the interval of time $T - t$ will be sufficiently large for the Law of Large Numbers to hold. Therefore, $X_T - X_t$ will be approximately normally distributed with mean $(r - d - \tfrac{1}{2}\sigma^2)(T - t)$ and variance $\sigma^2(T - t)$. From equation (14.6) we can see that the discrete stock price process over the time interval k is:

$$
\begin{array}{ccc}
 & \overset{\tfrac{1}{2}}{\nearrow} & S\exp[(r - d - \tfrac{1}{2}\sigma^2)k + \sigma\sqrt{k}] = Su \\
S & & \\
 & \underset{\tfrac{1}{2}}{\searrow} & S\exp[(r - d - \tfrac{1}{2}\sigma^2)k - \sigma\sqrt{k}] = Sv
\end{array}
\tag{14.7}
$$

where u and v denote the up and down price steps.

This process is called a geometric random walk and is path independent. The stock price is only affected by the number of up and down moves over a period of time and not by the sequence of the moves. Consequently, after M time steps of size k, the stock price can take one of $M + 1$ values.[4]

Let us suppose that we are at time t, valuing an option which matures at time $t + k$. Within our binomial approximation, this only represents one time step. We can represent the value of the option at time t as a function of its value at time $t + k$ in the following way:

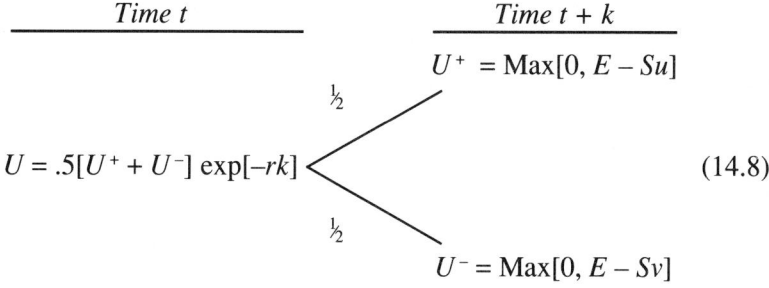

Time t	*Time t + k*

$$U^+ = \text{Max}[0, E - Su]$$

$$U = .5[U^+ + U^-]\exp[-rk] \qquad (14.8)$$

$$U^- = \text{Max}[0, E - Sv]$$

Here, the superscripts "$+$" and "$-$" refer to the option value after an up-move and a down-move in the stock, respectively. If the option is of the American type, the value of the option at time t if kept alive up to time $t + k$, which is given by equation (14.8), should be compared to its value exercised.

The method can easily be extended to more than one period. Suppose that we are pricing an option which matures two periods from time t. The stock prices at the different time periods will be given by the following tree:

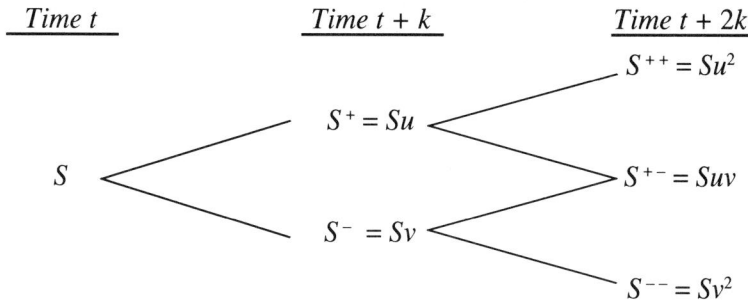

Time t	*Time t + k*	*Time t + 2k*

$$S^{++} = Su^2$$
$$S^+ = Su$$
$$S$$
$$S^{+-} = Suv$$
$$S^- = Sv$$
$$S^{--} = Sv^2$$

---

[4]This is one of the limitations of the Binomial model. Certain types of stock price processes are not path independent, so that the ending price is a function of both up and down moves and also the order in which they occur. In this case, the number of possible stock prices after M time steps is 2^M.

The corresponding option prices will be:

Time t	Time t + k	Time t + 2k

$$U^{++} = \text{Max}[0, E - S^{++}]$$

$$U^{+} = \text{Max}[.5(U^{++} + U^{+-})\exp(-rk), E - S^{+}]$$

$$U = \text{Max}[.5(U^{+} + U^{-})\exp(-rk), E - S]$$

$$U^{+-} = \text{Max}[0, E - S^{+-}]$$

$$U^{-} = \text{Max}[.5(U^{+-} + U^{--})\exp(-rk), E - S^{-}]$$

$$U^{--} = \text{Max}[0, E - S^{--}]$$

This method is generalized to more than two time steps in the normal way.

The Binomial method that we have presented is similar to the method proposed by Jarrow and Rudd (1983). It differs from the approach proposed by Cox, Ross and Rubinstein (1979) since we do not use their duplicating portfolio approach to derive risk neutral probabilities for the up and down moves, and we directly discretize the risk neutral density function. The methods are equivalent, however, since they both approximate the risk neutral density function for sufficiently small time steps. In the next subsection, we present a binomial model which follows the Cox, Ross and Rubinstein approach.

The Binomial Approach According to Cox, Ross and Rubinstein

In this approach, the discretization of the stock price process will be made to approximate the empirical probability density function of the stock price and not its risk neutral probability density function. The stock price process defined in assumption (A3) will be approximated by the following discrete process. Over a small interval of time k, the stock price will either go up to Su with probability q or go down to Sv with probability $(1 - q)$. We have:

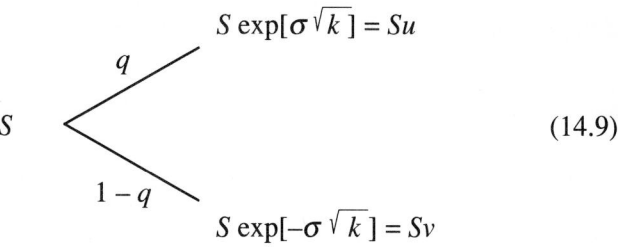

$$S \exp[\sigma \sqrt{k}] = Su$$

$$S \qquad\qquad (14.9)$$

$$S \exp[-\sigma \sqrt{k}] = Sv$$

The probability q must be defined so that the probability distribution of the difference between the logarithm of the stock price at time T and the logarithm of the stock price at time t is normal with mean $(\alpha - d - \frac{1}{2}\sigma^2)(T-t)$ and variance $\sigma^2(T-t)$. This means $q \log(Su \,/\, S) + (1-q) \log(Sv \,/\, S) = (\alpha - d - \frac{1}{2}\sigma^2)k$ and q must be equal to $.5 + .5[(\alpha - d - \frac{1}{2}\sigma^2)/\sigma]\sqrt{k}$.

With this discrete stock price process, we can now attempt to value the put option. Let us suppose that we have at time t a put option maturing at time $t + k$. Given the value of the stock price at time t, we know from equation (14.9) the two possible values of the stock at time $t + k$. Since the option matures at that time, we also know how to value the option at that time. We have:

Time t	*Time t + k*

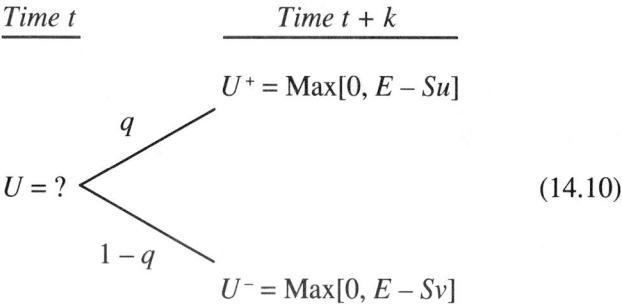

$$U^+ = \text{Max}[0, E - Su]$$

$$U = ? \qquad\qquad (14.10)$$

$$U^- = \text{Max}[0, E - Sv]$$

The first step in valuing the put option is to create a portfolio at time t which duplicates the payout of the put option at time $t + k$. If such a portfolio exists, the value of the option should be equal to the value of this portfolio. Let us conjecture that this portfolio is a combination of Δ shares of stock and a riskless lending position, B. This portfolio will duplicate the option if it pays the same as the option at time $t + k$. Consequently Δ and B should be such that:

$$\Delta \, Su\{\exp(dk)\} + B \exp(rk) = U^+$$

$$\Delta \, Sv\{\exp(dk)\} + B\exp(rk) = U^-$$

If we solve this system of two equations in two unknowns, we find that:

$$\Delta = \frac{U^+ - U^-}{S(u - v)\{\exp(dk)\}}$$

and,

$$B = \frac{U^+ v - U^- u}{(v - u)\{\exp(rk)\}}$$

The value of the option at time t is therefore equal to:

$$U = \Delta S + B = \exp(-rk)[pU^+ + (1 - p)U^-], \qquad (14.11)$$

with

$$p = \frac{\exp[(r - d)k] - v}{u - v}$$

Equation (14.11) is similar to equation (14.8) except that the probability of an up move is no longer 1/2 but is equal to p. Finally, it must be pointed out that the probability p implies that the density function of the difference between the logarithm of the stock price at time T and the logarithm of the stock price at time t is normal with mean $(r - d - \frac{1}{2}\sigma^2)(T - t)$ and variance $\sigma^2(T - t)$. In other words, it is the risk neutral density function. The remainder of the derivation of the Binomial method is similar to the one followed above except that equation (14.11) must be used in place of equation (14.8).

Other methods different from the Binomial approach can be used to approximate equation (14.4). We present a method in Appendix 14–B that can be characterized as a Trinomial method. At every time step, the logarithm of the stock price can go up by a fixed amount, go down by the same amount or stay the same. This procedure was first proposed by Parkinson (1977).

Furthermore, stock price processes which are not lognormal can be applied to option valuation in a binomial or trinomial framework. The interested reader can examine the method proposed by Cox and Ross (1976, footnote 1) which uses a trinomial approximation method to solve for the value of a stock option when the stock price follows a square root process. The square root process is similar to the lognormal process of assumption (A3) except that the instantaneous standard deviation of the stock price in the square root process is proportional to the square root of the stock price rather than the stock price itself.

14.3 VALUATION BY FINITE DIFFERENCE APPROXIMATION

Equation (14.4) can also be used to achieve a better understanding of finite difference approximations of the valuation problem (14.2a) to (14.2c). As demonstrated by equation (14.4), the valuation equation gives the value of the option at time s as a function of the value of the option at time $s + k$ where k is a small interval of time and $t \leq s < T$. Consequently, we can apply a solution technique similar to the one used in the case of the Binomial model. Given the boundary condition that the option value on the option maturity date, T, is its intrinsic value, we can use the partial differential equation to solve for the value of the option at time $T - k$. The procedure can then be followed every interval of time back to time t.

Let us therefore assume that the time dimension has M subintervals of length k such that $T - t = Mk$. The finite difference approximation will differ from a binomial method since, at every time step, the method will compute the option value for N values of the stock price. To do so, the method will assume that the option takes value on a bounded interval of logarithms of stock price $[X_{min}, X_{max}]$.[5]

The finite difference approximation technique therefore fits a grid of $N \times M$ points to the space over which the option takes value and computes the value of the option for each of these $N \times M$ combinations of time and stock price, as shown in Figure 14-1. Instead of valuing the option on all points in the space $[t, T] \times [X_{min}, X_{max}]$, the numerical method will only evaluate the option on the $N \times M$ points of the grid. As in the Binomial model, the method starts from the maturity date, T, and proceeds backwards along the time dimension by solving for the value of the option at time $T - k$, $T - 2k$, ..., back to time t (which is equal to $T - Mk$).

---

[5]X_{min} will be the value of the logarithm of the stock price which is sufficiently small for $\partial U / \partial X = -\exp[X_{min}]$ for $t \leq s < T$. X_{max} will be the value of the logarithm of the stock price which is sufficiently large for $U(X_{max}, s) = 0$ for $t \leq s < T$.

FIGURE 14–1
Lattice of price and time points for finite difference approximation

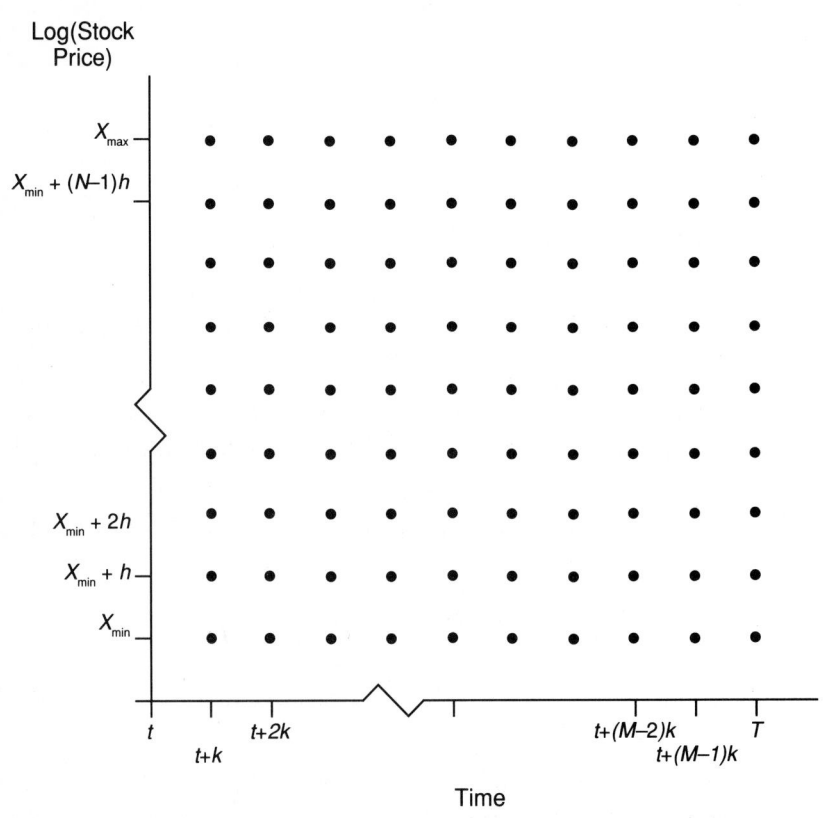

The Basic Tools

The principal tool in the derivation of difference approximations is Taylor's expansion. Taylor's expansion says that the value of the option at the point (X, s) satisfies the following equations:[6]

$$U(X + h, s) = U(X, s)$$

$$+ h \ \frac{\partial U}{\partial X} + \frac{1}{2} h^2 \ \frac{\partial^2 U}{\partial X^2} + \frac{1}{6} \ h^3 \frac{\partial^3 U}{\partial X^3} + O(h^4) \quad (14.12)$$

$$U(X - h, s) = U(X, s)$$

$$- h \ \frac{\partial U}{\partial X} + \frac{1}{2} h^2 \ \frac{\partial^2 U}{\partial X^2} - \frac{1}{6} \ h^3 \frac{\partial^3 U}{\partial X^3} + O(h^4) \quad (14.13)$$

Consequently, by adding equation (14.12) to equation (14.13), we can obtain a finite difference approximation of the second derivative, $\partial^2 U / \partial X^2$:

$$\frac{\partial^2 U}{\partial X^2} = \frac{U(X + h, s) - 2U(X, s) + U(X - h, s)}{h^2} + O(h^2) \quad (14.14)$$

In finite difference form, this can be approximated by:

$$\left. \frac{\partial^2 U}{\partial X^2} \right|_{ij} = \frac{U_{i+1,j} - 2U_{ij} + U_{i-1,j}}{h^2} \quad (14.15)$$

where the expression on the left is the second derivative of $U(X, s)$ with respect to X and U_{ij} is the finite difference approximation of $U(X, s)$ at the point $X = X_{min} + ih$ and $s = t + jk$.

Similarly, subtracting equation (14.13) from equation (14.12) will give us the following finite difference approximation of the first derivative with respect to X:

$$\frac{\partial U}{\partial X} = \frac{U(X + h, s) - U(X - h, s)}{2h} + O(h^2) \quad (14.16)$$

---

[6]$O(h^4)$ means that the error is "of the order of h^4." There exists a positive constant K such that $|O(h^4)| < K(h^4)$ as h tends to zero. In equation (14.12), for example, as h, the size of the interval between log stock prices in our grid goes to zero, the error we make by just using the first four terms on the right hand side as an approximation to $U(X + h, s)$ also goes to zero, and at a fast enough rate that it is less than $K(h^4)$ for any h. In general the higher the order of h in our approximation, the more accurate it is.

or in finite difference terms:

$$\frac{\partial U}{\partial X}\bigg|_{ij} = \frac{U_{i+1,j} - U_{i-1,j}}{2h} \tag{14.17}$$

Finally, the finite difference approximation of the time derivative can be obtained by expanding the value of the option as a function of time:

$$U(X, s + k) = U(X, s) + k\frac{\partial U}{\partial t} + O(k^2) \tag{14.18}$$

$$U(X, s - k) = U(X, s) - k\frac{\partial U}{\partial t} + O(k^2) \tag{14.19}$$

Equations (14.18) and (14.19) imply two different approximations of the time derivative. Equation (14.18) implies that:

$$\frac{\partial U}{\partial t} = \frac{U(X, s + k) - U(X, s)}{k} + O(|k|) \tag{14.20}$$

which corresponds to the following approximation:

$$\frac{\partial U}{\partial t}\bigg|_{ij} = \frac{U_{i,j+1} - U_{ij}}{k} \tag{14.21}$$

This approximation of the time derivative will produce a finite difference approximation of the partial differential equation known as the "implicit" scheme, illustrated in Figure 14-2.

Equation (14.19), on the other hand, implies that:

$$\frac{\partial U}{\partial t} = \frac{U(X, s) - U(X, s - k)}{k} + O(|k|) \tag{14.22}$$

or a finite difference approximation of:

$$\frac{\partial U}{\partial t}\bigg|_{ij} = \frac{U_{i,j} - U_{ij-1}}{k} \tag{14.23}$$

This approximation, shown in Figure 14-3, will give rise to what is known as the "explicit" scheme.

FIGURE 14–2
Typical lattice element in "implicit" finite difference approximation

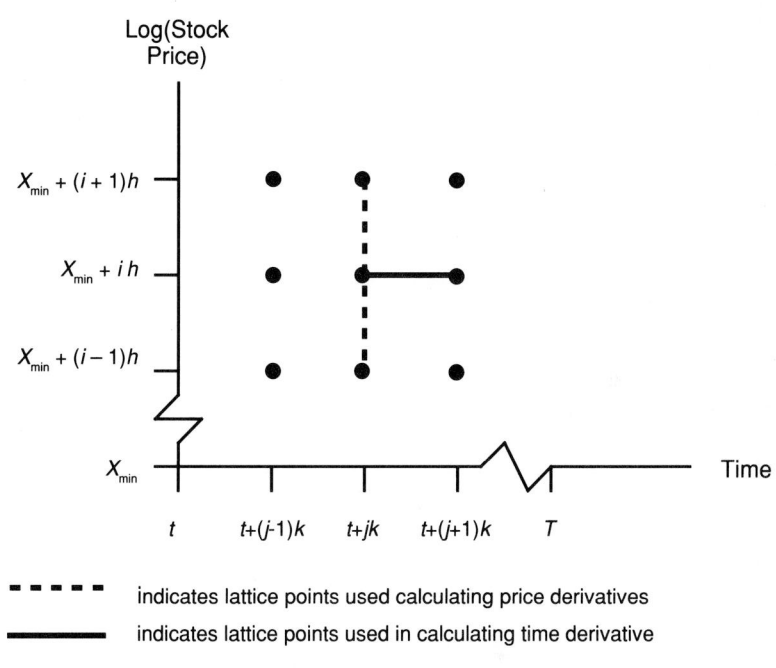

indicates lattice points used calculating price derivatives

indicates lattice points used in calculating time derivative

We will see below that more accurate finite difference schemes can be derived by keeping the term of order k^2 in the Taylor expansion of the value of the option as a function of time.

The Explicit Scheme

In the previous subsection, we derived finite difference approximations for the derivatives of the option price with respect to the logarithm of the stock price and time. We can now substitute these approximations in the original valuation equation. Let us first substitute equations (14.15), (14.17) and (14.23) for the second and first derivatives with respect to the stock price and for the first derivative with respect to time. The partial differential equation is now replaced at every time step by a system of $N-1$ difference equations:

FIGURE 14–3
Typical lattice element in "explicit" finite difference approximation

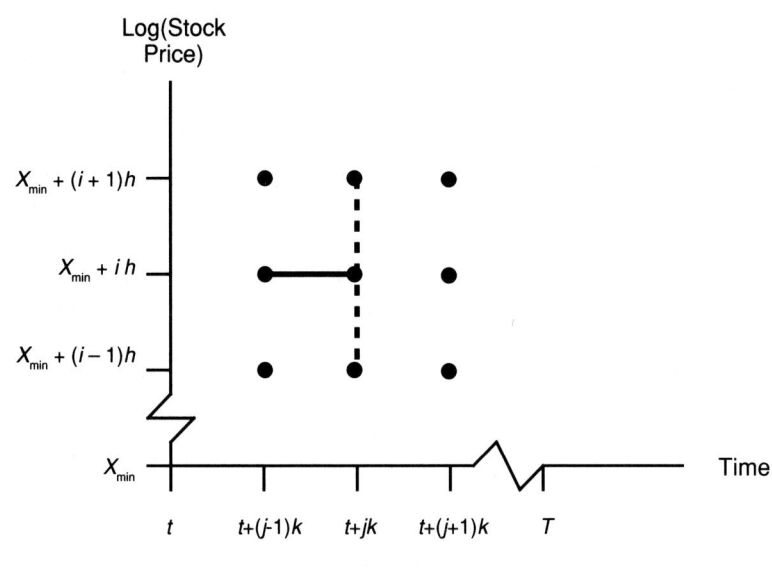

$\blacksquare\;\blacksquare\;\blacksquare\;\blacksquare\;\blacksquare$ indicates lattice points used calculating price derivatives

$\rule{2cm}{1.2mm}$ indicates lattice points used in calculating time derivative

$$\frac{1}{2}\,\sigma^2\,\frac{U_{i+1,j} - 2U_{ij} + U_{i-1,j}}{h^2} + (r - d - \tfrac{1}{2}\,\sigma^2)\frac{U_{i+1,j} - U_{i-1,j}}{2h} - rU_{ij}$$

$$+\;\frac{U_{ij} - U_{i,j-1}}{k} = 0 \qquad \text{for } 1 \le i \le N-1$$

If we regroup the terms which are functions of $U_{i,j-1}$, $U_{i-1,j}$, U_{ij}, and $U_{i+1,j}$ in these equations, we obtain the following system of equations at every time step:

$$U_{i,j-1} = aU_{i-1,j} + bU_{ij} + cU_{i+1,j} \qquad (14.24)$$
$$1 \le i \le N-1$$

with

$$a = k[\tfrac{1}{2}\,(\sigma/h)^2 - \tfrac{1}{2}(r-d-\tfrac{1}{2}\sigma^2)/h]$$
$$b = (1 - rk - (\sigma/h)^2\,k)$$
$$c = k[\tfrac{1}{2}\,(\sigma/h)^2 + \tfrac{1}{2}(r-d-\tfrac{1}{2}\sigma^2)/h]$$

This system of $N-1$ equations gives the value of the option at time $j-1$ directly as a function of the value of the option at time j.

Since our grid does not extend from minus infinity to infinity at each time step, we must add boundary conditions appropriate for the option we are valuing, an American put in this case, to specify what happens to the function U at the lower and upper limits. First, we assume that at every time step j, the first derivative at the grid point $(0, j)$, i.e., X_{min} is equal to $-\exp[X_{min}]$. This implies that $U_{0j} = U_{1j} + h\{\exp[X_{min}]\}$. Secondly, we set $U_{Nj} = 0$.

We can now express this system of equations in matrix terms in the following way:[7]

$$
\begin{bmatrix}
U_{1j-1} - K \\
U_{2j-1} \\
U_{3j-1} \\
\cdot \\
\cdot \\
\cdot \\
U_{N-2j-1} \\
U_{N-1j-1}
\end{bmatrix}
\begin{bmatrix}
b^* & c & & & & & \\
a & b & c & & & & \\
& a & b & c & & & \\
& & & \cdots & & & \\
& & & & \cdots & & \\
& & & & & \cdots & \\
& & & & a & b & c \\
& & & & & a & b
\end{bmatrix}
\begin{bmatrix}
U_{1j} \\
U_{2j} \\
U_{3j} \\
\cdot \\
\cdot \\
\cdot \\
U_{N-2j} \\
U_{N-1j}
\end{bmatrix}
$$

If we denote this tridiagonal matrix of coefficients by A, the column vector of values $U_{1j-1}, U_{2j-1}, \ldots, U_{N-1j-1}$ by $\bar{U}_{j-1}$ and the column vector of values $U_{1j}, U_{2j}, \ldots, U_{N-1j}$ by $\bar{U}_j$, we can rewrite the previous expression in the following way:

$$\bar{U}_{j-1} = A\bar{U}_j \qquad (14.25)$$

---

[7] b^* is equal to $a + b$ and the constant K is equal to $ah\{\exp[X_{min}]\}$. K and b^* are obtained by incorporating the two additional boundary conditions in the system of equations (14.24).

The value of the American put option at time $j - 1$ is therefore an explicit function of the value of the American put option at time j. The value of the option at time t will be obtained by consecutively solving for the value of the option at time $T - k, T - 2k, \ldots, T - Mk$ and comparing, at each grid point and at every time step, the value obtained from equation (14.25) to the value of the option if exercised. At each grid point, the greater of these two values should be entered as U_{ij} to account for the early exercise privilege of the American put option.

The Implicit Scheme

A slightly different finite difference scheme can be obtained by using equation (14.21) rather than equation (14.23) to approximate the derivative of the option value with respect to time. The partial differential equation given by equation (14.2a) is now replaced at every time step by the following system of $N - 1$ difference equations:

$$\frac{1}{2}\,\sigma^2\,\frac{U_{i+1,j} - 2U_{ij} + U_{i-1,j}}{h^2} + (r - d - \tfrac{1}{2}\,\sigma^2)\frac{U_{i+1,j} - U_{i-1,j}}{2h} - rU_{ij}$$

$$+ \frac{U_{i,j+1} - U_{ij}}{k} = 0 \qquad \text{for } 1 \leq i \leq N - 1$$

If we regroup the terms which are functions of $U_{i,j+1}$, $U_{i-1,j}$, U_{ij}, and $U_{i+1,j}$ in these equations, we obtain the following system of equations at every time step:

$$aU_{i-1,j} + bU_{ij} + cU_{i+1,j} = U_{i,j+1} \qquad\qquad (14.26)$$
$$1 \leq i \leq N - 1$$

with

$$
\begin{aligned}
a &= k[-\tfrac{1}{2}\,(\sigma/h)^2 + \tfrac{1}{2}(r - d - \tfrac{1}{2}\sigma^2)/h] \\
b &= (1 + rk + (\sigma/h)^2\,k) \\
c &= -k[\tfrac{1}{2}(\sigma/h)^2 + \tfrac{1}{2}(r - d - \tfrac{1}{2}\sigma^2)/h]
\end{aligned}
$$

This system of equations is different from the one in equation (14.24), since the value of the U_{ij}'s cannot be solved for explicitly as a function of the $U_{i,j+1}$'s. The system of equations corresponding to equation (14.26) can also be written in matrix form. We have:[8]

---

[8]As done previously, we assume that the first derivative at X_{min} is equal to $-\exp[X_{min}]$ and that $U_{Nj} = 0$. This implies that $U_{0j} = U_{1j} + h\{\exp[X_{min}]\}$. Consequently $b^* = a + b$ and K is equal to $ah\{\exp[X_{min}]\}$.

$$
\begin{bmatrix}
b^* & c & & & & & \\
a & b & c & & & & \\
 & a & b & c & & & \\
 & & & \ldots & & & \\
 & & & & \ldots & & \\
 & & & & & \ldots & \\
 & & & & a & b & c \\
 & & & & & a & b
\end{bmatrix}
\begin{bmatrix}
U_{1j} \\
U_{2j} \\
U_{3j} \\
\cdot \\
\cdot \\
\cdot \\
U_{N-2j} \\
U_{N-1j}
\end{bmatrix}
=
\begin{bmatrix}
U_{1j+1} - K \\
U_{2j+1} \\
U_{3j+1} \\
\cdot \\
\cdot \\
\cdot \\
U_{N-2j+1} \\
U_{N-1j+1}
\end{bmatrix}
$$

Similarly, if we denote the tridiagonal matrix of coefficients by B, the column vector of values $U_{1j},\ U_{2j},\ \ldots,\ U_{N-1j}$ by $\bar{U}_j$, and the column vector of values $U_{1j+1},\ U_{2j+1},\ \ldots, U_{N-1j+1}$ by $\bar{U}_{j+1}$, we can write:

$$B\bar{U}_j = \bar{U}_{j+1} \tag{14.27}$$

Consequently, the vector $\bar{U}_j$ of U_{ij}'s for $1 \leq i \leq N - 1$ can only be obtained by inverting the tridiagonal matrix of coefficients, B.

Several methods can be used to invert this matrix. One of the most common is the Gauss elimination method.[9] Inverting the matrix, we have:

$$\bar{U}_j = B^{-1} \bar{U}_{j+1} \tag{14.28}$$

The value of the option at time t is then obtained as in the explicit case by successively solving for $\bar{U}_M, \ \bar{U}_{M-1}, \ \ldots$ up to $\bar{U}_0$. However, at every time step, before going to the next time step the value of the option alive obtained from equation (14.28) should be compared to the value of the option exercised and the larger of the two values should be kept for the next time step.

More Accurate Finite Difference Approximations

As mentioned above, it is possible to increase the level of accuracy that can be obtained from a given grid by using different approximations for the time

---

[9]For a description of this method, see Smith (1978).

derivative. The following technique was first presented in Courtadon (1982).

To simplify the exposition, we will separate the computation of the expected value of the option as of time t from the discounting of the expected value. This can be done by solving the valuation problem for $V(X, t) = U(X, t)\exp[r(T - t)]$. The valuation problem (14.2a) to (14.2c) becomes:

$$\frac{1}{2} \sigma^2 \frac{\partial^2 V}{\partial X^2} + (r - d - \tfrac{1}{2} \sigma^2) \frac{\partial V}{\partial X} + \frac{\partial V}{\partial t} = 0 \qquad (14.29a)$$

subject to: $\qquad\qquad V(X, T) = \text{Max}[0, E - \exp(X)] \qquad\qquad (14.29b)$

$$V(X, s) = \text{Max}[V^*(X, s), (E - \exp(X))\exp(r(T - s))] \qquad (14.29c)$$

where $V^*(X, s)$ is defined similarly to $U^*(X, s)$.

The only difference between this new finite difference approximation and the approximations presented above comes from the fact that we will approximate the partial differential equation at the points $X = X_{min} + ih$ and $s = t + (j + 1/2)k$ for $0 < i < N$ and $0 < j < M$, rather than at the points $X = X_{min} + ih$ and $s = t + jk$. This can be done even though we do not explicitly solve for the value of the option at time $t + (j + 1/2)k$, given that the approximations derived for the derivatives only depend on the knowledge of the option value at time $t + jk$ and at time $t + (j + 1)k$. Figure 14-4 indicates schematically how the system works.

The following approximations can then be derived for the derivatives with respect to X and the derivative with respect to t:

$$\left.\frac{\partial^2 V}{\partial X^2}\right|_{i,j+1/2} = \frac{V_{i+1,j} - 2V_{ij} + V_{i-1,j} + V_{i+1,j+1} - 2V_{i,j+1} + V_{i-1,j+1}}{2h^2} \qquad (14.30)$$

$$\left.\frac{\partial V}{\partial X}\right|_{i,j+1/2} = \frac{V_{i+1,j} - V_{i-1,j} + V_{i+1,j+1} - V_{i-1,j+1}}{4h} \qquad (14.31)$$

$$\left.\frac{\partial V}{\partial t}\right|_{i,j+1/2} = \frac{V_{i,j+1} - V_{i,j}}{k} \qquad (14.32)$$

FIGURE 14–4
Typical lattice element in "more accurate" finite difference approximation

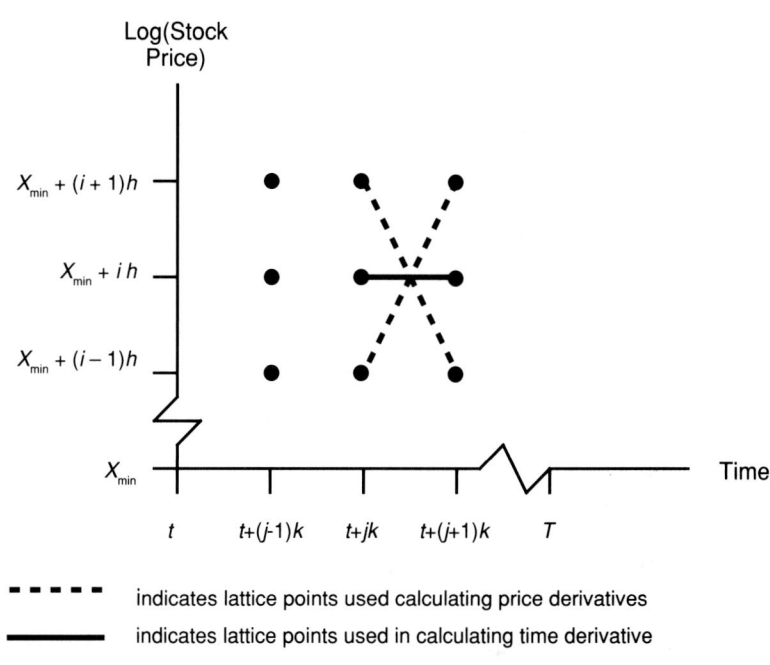

indicates lattice points used calculating price derivatives

indicates lattice points used in calculating time derivative

where V_{ij} is the finite difference approximation of $V(X, s)$ at the point $X = X_{min} + ih$ and $s = t + jk$. The level of accuracy of these approximations is of the order $O(h^2) + O(k^2)$. By substituting equations (14.30), (14.31) and (14.32) in equation (14.29a), we obtain the following approximation of the partial differential equation:

$$aV_{i-1,j} + bV_{ij} + cV_{i+1,j} = d_{ij} \qquad (14.33)$$

$$\text{for } 1 \leq i \leq N - 1$$

with: $a = k[-\tfrac{1}{4}(\sigma/h)^2 + \tfrac{1}{4}(r - d - \tfrac{1}{2}\sigma^2)/h]$
     $b = (1 + \tfrac{1}{2}(\sigma/h)^2 k)$
     $c = -k[\tfrac{1}{4}(\sigma/h)^2 + \tfrac{1}{4}(r - d - \tfrac{1}{2}\sigma^2)/h]$
     $d_{ij} = -aV_{i-1,j+1} + (1 - \tfrac{1}{2}(\sigma/h)^2 k) V_{i,j+1} - cV_{i+1,j+1}$

If we call C the $(N-1) \times (N-1)$ tridiagonal matrix of coefficients a, b, and c, we can rewrite the system of equations corresponding to equation (14.34) in matrix form. We have:

$$C\overline{V}_j = [2I - C]\ \overline{V}_{j+1} \qquad (14.34)$$

or, equivalently:

$$\overline{V}_j = C^{-1}\ [2I - C]\ \overline{V}_{j+1} = [2C^{-1} - I]\overline{V}_{j+1} \qquad (14.35)$$

where I is an $(N-1) \times (N-1)$ identity matrix and where $\overline{V}_j$ and $\overline{V}_{j+1}$ are, respectively, the vectors of $N-1$ option values for $0 < i < N$ at time $t + jk$ and at time $t + (j+1)k$.

14.4 NUMERICAL EXAMPLES

This section will present numerical implementations of the different methods described in the previous two sections. In doing so, we will address issues of convergence and computational speed. Given that the American put option valuation model does not have a closed form solution, in order to study the convergence of the different numerical methods to the true option value, we apply these methods to the valuation of a European put option for which an exact closed form solution exits. The closed form solution is:

$$W(S, t) = E \exp[-r(T-t)]N(-X_2) - S\exp[-d(T-t)]N(-X_1) \ (14.36)$$

where

$$X_1 = \frac{\ln(S/E) + (r - d + \sigma^2/2)(T-t)}{\sigma\sqrt{T-t}}$$

$$X_2 = X_1 - \sigma\sqrt{T-t}$$

The parameters and variables are defined as in section 14.2.

The following tables present the results of such an investigation when we assume that the interest rate r is 10%, dividend payout d is 5%, volatility

σ is 20% and the strike price E is 1. The results are given for a time to maturity of 1 year and different values of S, .95, .975, 1., 1.025 and 1.05, in other words, from 5 percent in the money to 5 percent out of the money.

TABLE 14–1
Modified Black-Scholes Model Put Values

	Stock Price				
	.95	.975	1.0	1.025	1.05
Put Value	.0726	.0622	.0530	.0449	.0379

TABLE 14–2
Binomial Model Put Values

Time	CPU	S				
Steps	Time	.95	.975	1.0	1.025	1.05
30	.03	.0730	.0619	.0536	.0452	.0376
60	.08	.0729	.0621	.0533	.0448	.0381
90	.15	.0728	.0622	.0531	.0450	.0378
120	.26	.0728	.0622	.0530	.0451	.0379

TABLE 14–3
Cox-Ross-Rubinstein Binomial Model Put Values

Time	CPU	S				
Steps	Time	.95	.975	1.0	1.025	1.05
30	.03	.0729	.0627	.0524	.0453	.0383
60	.09	.0723	.0625	.0527	.0452	.0377
90	.16	.0727	.0624	.0528	.0451	.0379
120	.26	.0727	.0623	.0529	.0450	.0380

TABLE 14–4
Explicit Model Put Values

N	M	CPU Time	S				
			.95	.975	1.0	1.025	1.05
50	100	.02	.0725	.0628	.0538	.0461	.0392
50	400	.09	.0725	.0625	.0532	.0453	.0382
50	600	.12	.0725	.0624	.0531	.0452	.0381
50	1000	.21	.0725	.0624	.0531	.0451	.0380

TABLE 14–5
Implicit Model Put Values

N	M	CPU Time	S				
			.95	.975	1.0	1.025	1.05
50	15	.01	.0720	.0618	.0523	.0444	.0372
50	30	.02	.0722	.0621	.0527	.0447	.0376
50	60	.03	.0723	.0622	.0528	.0449	.0377
50	90	.04	.0724	.0623	.0529	.0449	.0378

TABLE 14–6
More Accurate Implicit Model Put Values

N	M	CPU Time	S				
			.95	.975	1.0	1.025	1.05
50	15	.01	.0725	.0624	.0530	.0450	.0379
50	30	.02	.0725	.0624	.0530	.0450	.0379
50	60	.04	.0725	.0624	.0530	.0450	.0379
50	90	.05	.0725	.0624	.0530	.0450	.0379

The CPU time is given in seconds for a Vax 8700 computer. The time displayed on each line of Tables 14–2 and 14–3 is the time necessary to compute the corresponding five option prices while the time displayed on each line of Tables 14–4, 14–5 and 14–6 represents the time required to compute the entire grid of option prices for the given number of steps in the time and stock price dimensions.

The results show that similar levels of accuracy can be achieved by the five different methods, but at different costs in terms of CPU time. It is important to note that binomial methods do not have a significant edge over implicit finite difference methods in terms of CPU time. This is even more apparent if accuracy is taken into account. Indeed, this can be shown directly by comparing Table 14–2 with Table 14–6. The CPU time required in Table 2 to compute the five option prices with 60 time steps is equal to .08 seconds while the computation of 50 option prices in Table 14–6 takes .01 seconds for 15 time steps and .02 seconds for 30 time steps. The model in Table 14–6 converges rapidly enough that there is no change even in the 4th decimal place by making the grid finer in the time dimension.

In addition, the level of accuracy achieved by the implicit finite difference approximation method is better than the one achieved by the binomial approximation. Model accuracy can be examined by comparing root mean squared errors. For each model, we take the approximation errors for the five stock price values, square them, take the square root of the average. The root mean squared error of the Binomial method in Table 14–2 is .00022 while the same statistic in Table 14–6 is .00011. Further investigation of the different methods indicates that implicit finite difference approximations are preferable to binomial approximations for deriving the different option risk parameters like deltas and gammas.[10] The deltas and gammas derived from an implicit finite difference methodology are more stable than those derived from binomial models.

The results also show that the cost of the explicit finite difference method in terms of CPU time becomes prohibitive very quickly. In Appendix A of this chapter we will show that the size of the step in the time dimension must remain small relative to the size of the step in the stock price dimension for the explicit approximation method to converge. Consequently, the number of time steps will have to increase when the maturity of the option increases and the rate of convergence of the explicit approximation to the true option value will be sensitive to the ratio of the step size in the stock price dimension to the step size in the time dimension.

Before concluding this section, it is interesting to illustrate the differences between the different methods in pricing American options. We will use the same example as above except that we will now apply the methods to the pricing of the corresponding American option. We only

---

[10]The delta is the first derivative of the option price with respect to the price of the underlying while the gamma is the second derivative of the option price with respect to the price of the underlying.

report the values of the American option for the two Binomial models and the more accurate implicit finite difference scheme.

TABLE 14–7
Binomial Model Put Values

Time Steps	CPU Time	S				
		.95	.975	1.0	1.025	1.05
30	.03	.0829	.0699	.0596	.0501	.0415
60	.09	.0828	.0701	.0595	.0497	.0419
90	.16	.0828	.0701	.0594	.0499	.0418
120	.33	.0827	.0701	.0593	.0500	.0417

TABLE 14–8
Cox-Ross-Rubinstein Binomial Model Put Values

Time Steps	CPU Time	S				
		.95	.975	1.0	1.025	1.05
30	.03	.0828	.0705	.0590	.0501	.0421
60	.11	.0825	.0704	.0591	.0501	.0417
90	.21	.0827	.0703	.0592	.0500	.0417
120	.36	.0827	.0702	.0592	.0500	.0418

TABLE 14–9
More Accurate Implicit Model Put Values

N	M	CPU Time	S				
			.95	.975	1.0	1.025	1.05
50	15	.04	.0818	.0699	.0588	.0496	.0414
50	30	.06	.0821	.0701	.0590	.0498	.0416
50	60	.13	.0822	.0702	.0591	.0499	.0416
50	90	.18	.0823	.0702	.0591	.0499	.0417
100	30	.12	.0824	.0700	.0591	.0497	.0417
100	60	.22	.0825	.0701	.0592	.0498	.0417
100	90	.33	.0825	.0701	.0593	.0498	.0417
100	120	.48	.0826	.0701	.0593	.0499	.0417
150	90	.58	.0826	.0701	.0593	.0498	.0417
150	120	.71	.0826	.0701	.0593	.0498	.0417

Most of the previously derived results still hold. In the remainder of this section, we will assume that the true option prices are given by the implicit finite difference approximation of Table 14–9 with N equal to 150 and M equal to 120. Given these values, the root mean squared error (RMSE) of the Binomial method of Table 14–7 is .00012 for 90 time steps and .0001 for 120 time steps. These two computations respectively represent .16 and .33 second of CPU time. A similar level of accuracy can be obtained with the finite difference approximation of Table 14–9 in the same amount of CPU time. In Table 14–9, for the case where N equals 100 and M equals 30 the RMSE is equal to .00014 and the CPU time is equal to .12 second, while for N equal to 100 and M equal to 60 the RMSE is equal to .00006 and the CPU time is equal to .22 second. In addition, as in the case of the European option, the estimates of the risk parameters like delta and gamma derived from the finite difference approximation of Table 14–9 are more stable than those derived from the binomial approximations. Note that delta, gamma, and theta for a finite difference method can be obtained directly because they are computed in the approximation algorithm. To compute kappa (vega) one must calculate a numerical derivative by changing the volatility parameter by a small amount and rerunning the valuation procedure.

14.6 CONCLUSION

Numerical methods have an increasingly important role to play in option pricing. Indeed, as we mentioned in the introduction, except for European options it is nearly impossible to find closed form solutions to most option valuation problems. Even in the case of European option valuation, simple modifications of the assumptions, like making the volatility a function of the level of the price of the underlying instrument, will prevent a closed form solution.

In this chapter, we have presented the two main categories of numerical methods which have been used in the option pricing literature. The first category is the family of methods similar to the Binomial or Trinomial approach, sometimes referred to as lattice methods. The second category is the family of finite difference approximation methods. The first category attempts to solve numerically the martingale representation of the solution of the partial differential equation, while the second category directly approximates the partial differential equation without using the martingale representation of the solution. Therefore, the first category will tend to have a more intuitive economic flavor, involving the concept of risk neutral valuation, while the second category will tend to be more mechanical in nature. It should be said, however, that the second category of methods is more general than the first. Indeed, solving the martingale representation of the solution is only feasible computationally if the joint probability density function of the underlying sources of risk is known. This is not the case for the finite difference approximation methods. Given a partial differential equation, finite difference approximation methods can always be used.

Finally, it should be mentioned that the material contained in this chapter is only an introduction to the large amount of work which has been done in the numerical analysis and option pricing literature. A more complete survey should include the work which extends these methods to more than one source of risk. The interested reader can achieve some understanding of these extensions by examining the work of McKee and Mitchell (1970) and Brennan and Schwartz (1980), and (1982) for finite difference approximation methods, as well as Boyle (1987) and Heath, Jarrow and Morton (1988) for lattice methods.

APPENDIX A TO CHAPTER 14

Stability and Convergence of the Finite Difference Schemes

This topic has been extensively studied in the finite difference approximation literature. This Appendix will only give a brief introduction to the problems of stability and convergence of finite difference approximation methods. A more complete exposition of the problem can be found in Smith (1978) or Mitchell and Griffiths (1980). Before going further, it is important to understand what is meant by convergence and stability. Let us call the difference between the exact solution, U_{ij}^e, of the partial differential equation and its numerical approximation, U_{ij}, the discretization error. The finite difference approximation method is said to be convergent if the discretization error tends to zero as the grid sizes tend to zero. Stability, on the other hand, looks at the problem of propagation of errors as the numerical method unwinds through time for given grid sizes in the time and stock price dimensions.

Smith (1978) indicates that convergence may be difficult to prove directly since the discretization error is usually expressed in terms of unknown derivatives for which no bounds can be estimated. However, in the case of linear and parabolic partial differential equations, stability will imply convergence if and only if the difference equation approximating the partial differential equation can be shown to be "consistent." Let:

$$F(U_{ij}) = a \, U_{i-1,j} + b \, U_{ij} + c \, U_{i+1,j} - U_{i,j-1} \qquad (14A.1)$$

represent the difference approximation of the partial differential equation at the grid point i, j for the case of the explicit finite difference approximation. The finite difference approximation is said to be consistent with the partial differential equation if $F(U_{ij}^e)$, otherwise called the local truncation error, tends to zero as the grid sizes tend to zero. The same approach could be followed to prove the convergence of the implicit finite difference approximation. In the remainder of this section, we will present the conditions under which the explicit and implicit finite difference approximations are consistent and stable.

The Explicit Case

We will first address the issue of the convergence of the explicit scheme. To prove this convergence, we will assume that we have already proven that the approximation method is stable. Consequently, it is necessary and sufficient to prove that the difference approximation is consistent. To do so, we have to derive the local truncation error of the explicit scheme. This can be done by expressing $F(U_{ij}^e)$ in terms of the partial derivatives of the exact option price with respect to the stock price and time. We have:

$$F(U_{ij}^e) = \left[-\frac{1}{2} \, k \, \frac{\partial^2 U}{\partial t^2} + \frac{1}{6} \, (r - d - \frac{1}{2} \, \sigma^2) h^2 \, \frac{\partial^3 U}{\partial X^3} + \frac{1}{24} \, \sigma^2 h^2 \frac{\partial^4 U}{\partial X^4} \right]$$

$$= O(k) + O(h^2)$$

Therefore $F(U_{ij}^e)$ tends to zero as the grid sizes, k and h, tend to zero.[11]

---

[11] We assume that the derivatives in equation (14.2a) are bounded.

As explained previously, the stability of the solution is established if one can prove that the effect of an error at some time step is not amplified by the finite difference scheme, and actually diminishes as the number of time steps increases. The stability of the solution is usually studied by examining the eigenvalues of matrix A corresponding to equation (14.25). A sufficient condition for the method to be stable is that all the eigenvalues of the matrix have a modulus which is less than 1. A detailed derivation of this result can be found in Smith [1978, pp. 81–85].[12]

A more intuitive proof of stability is provided by Brennan and Schwartz (1978). They look at the coefficients a, b, and c of equation (14.24) as probabilities which relate the values of the option at time j to the value of the option at time $j-1$. Their analysis is directly applicable to the analysis of the stability of our explicit finite difference approximation even though our approximation is slightly different from theirs.[13] Given that the sum of the coefficients, a, b, and c in equation (14.24) is equal to $1-rk$, the numerical approximation will be stable if these coefficients are all positive. In this way, all the coefficients will be less than 1 and any error will dissipate when the numerical approximation unfolds. Given equation (14.24), we can show that this will be the case if:

$$h < \frac{\sigma^2}{|r-d-.5\,\sigma^2|} \quad \text{and} \quad k < \frac{h^2}{r\,h^2+\sigma^2}$$

This result is equivalent to the one derived by Brennan and Schwartz if we set $d=0$ and to the one derived by Geske and Shastri ($k/h^2 < \tfrac{1}{2}$) if we set $r=d=0$ and $\sigma=\sqrt{2}$.

The Implicit Case

Similar methods can be followed to show the convergence and the stability of the implicit scheme. As in the case of the explicit finite difference approximation, the local truncation error can be shown to tend to zero as the grid sizes tend to zero and the implicit scheme can be shown to be stable. The stability of the finite difference scheme can be analyzed in a manner

---

[12]Geske and Shastri (1985) outline Smith's proof.
[13]Brennan and Schwartz use a different approximation for the term rU in the partial differential equation. They approximate the term at time $j-1$ rather than at time j. In this way, the coefficients a, b and c in equation (8) of their paper sum to 1 and can be interpreted as probabilities. In our case, the coefficients sum to $1-rk$ and could be interpreted as discounted probabilities.

similar to that used for the explicit scheme. However, given that we now have to invert matrix B in equation (14.27) to get a relationship similar to equation (14.25), the derivation of the probabilities which relate the value of the option at time j to the value of the option at time $j - 1$ is not as straightforward as in the explicit case. This derivation was done by Brennan and Schwartz (1978). An easier way to prove the stability of the implicit scheme is to use the eigenvalue approach. To show stability, we have to show that all the eigenvalues of the matrix B^{-1} have a modulus less than 1.

To do so, we must use two general results on eigenvalues. In the first place the eigenvalues of the inverse of any square matrix are equal to the inverse of the eigenvalues of this matrix. Secondly, the eigenvalues of a common tridiagonal matrix such as B are equal to:[14]

$$\lambda_i = b + 2c(a \, / \, c)^5 \cos(i \, \pi/N) \quad \text{for } 1 \leq i \leq N-1 \qquad (14A.3)$$

Given this result, we can show that:[15]

$$\lambda_i = 1 + rk + (\sigma \, / \, h)^2 \, k \; - k \sqrt{(\sigma/h)^4 - (r-d-.5\,\sigma^2)^2 \, / \, h^2} \; \cos(i\pi/N)$$

$$> 1 + rk + (\sigma^2 \, / \, h)^2 \, k - k(\sigma \, / \, h)^2 \cos(i\pi \, / \, N)$$

$$= 1 + rk + 2k(\sigma \, / \, h)^2 \sin^2(i\pi \, / \, 2N) > 1$$

All the eigenvalues of B have a modulus greater than 1. Consequently, the eigenvalues of B^{-1} which are equal to the inverse of the eigenvalues of B all have a modulus less than 1. This proves that the implicit finite difference approximation method is stable.

Convergence and Stability of the More Accurate Finite Difference Approximation

This method can be shown to be stable and convergent. We will prove stability and leave to the reader the proof of convergence. The stability of the method can be proven by using the eigenvalue method. In this case, we need to compute the eigenvalues of the matrix $[2C^{-1} - I]$. It is relatively easy

---

[14]In this proof, we ignore the boundary condition at X_{min}. Therefore b^* is equal to b in equation (14.25).
[15]This result is derived under the assumption that $(\sigma \, /h)^4$ is greater than $(r-d-.5\sigma^2)^2 \, / \, h^2$. This implies that we have the following constraint on h: $h^2 < \sigma \, ^4/(r-d-.5\sigma^2)^2$. This condition is the same as the one derived by Brennan and Schwartz (1978).

to show that if λ is an eigenvalue of matrix C, $[2C^{-1} - I]$ will have a corresponding eigenvalue equal to $(2/\lambda - 1)$. Therefore, we will show stability of the numerical approximation if we can prove that the modulus of λ is always greater than 1. To derive the eigenvalues of C, we can apply equation (14A.3). We have:[16]

$$\lambda_i = 1 + .5(\sigma/h)^2\, k - .5k\sqrt{(\sigma/h)^4 - (r-d-.5\,\sigma^2)^2/h^2}\, \cos(i\pi/N)$$

$$> 1 + .5(\sigma/h)^2\, k - .5k(\sigma/h)^2\cos(i\pi/N)$$

$$= 1 + k(\sigma/h)^2\sin^2(i\pi/2N) > 1$$

Therefore the numerical method corresponding to equation (14.34) is stable. Courtadon (1982) extends the probabilistic approach of Brennan and Schwartz to this more accurate finite difference scheme to show the stability of the finite difference approximation corresponding to equation (14.34).

APPENDIX B TO CHAPTER 14

The Parkinson American Option Valuation Approach

In this Appendix, we show how the Parkinson approach can be used to solve for the value of the American put option. As previously, we solve for $U(X, t) = W(S, t)$ where $X = \ln(S/E)$.

The valuation equation for $U(X, t)$ simplifies to:

$$\frac{1}{2}\sigma^2\frac{\partial^2 U}{\partial X^2} + (r - d - .5\sigma^2)\frac{\partial U}{\partial X} - rU + \frac{\partial U}{\partial t} = 0 \qquad (14B.1)$$

subject to:

$$U(X, T) = \text{Max}[O, E - \exp(X)] \qquad (14B.2)$$

---

[16] As in the case of the implicit difference approximation, this result is derived under the assumption that $(\sigma/h)^4$ is greater than $(r-d-.5\sigma^2)^2/h^2$. This implies that we have the following constraint on h: $h^2 < \sigma^4/(r-d-.5\sigma^2)^2$.

$$U(X, s) = \text{Max}[U^*(X, s), E - \exp(X)] \qquad (14\text{B}.3)$$

where U^* is the option value at time s if not exercised at this point. To solve this problem we will assume that the option can be exercised every k units of time. For k small enough, the solution that we will obtain will be a good approximation of the American option value. Given this assumption, the American option valuation problem can be approximated by the following dynamic programming model:

$$U(X, t) = \exp(-rk)\text{Max}[EV_t\{U(X, t + k)\}, E - \exp(X)]$$

$$U(X, t + k) = \exp(-rk)\text{Max}[EV_{t+k}\{U(X, t + 2k)\}, E - \exp(X)]$$

$$\vdots \qquad \vdots$$

$$U(X, t+(M - 1)k) = \exp(-rk)\text{Max}[EV_{t+(M-1)k}\{U(X, t + Mk)\}, E - \exp(X)]$$

$$U(X, t + Mk) = \text{Max}[O, E - \exp(X)]$$

M is such that $Mk = (T - t)$ and $EV_{t+jk}\{\ \}$ is the expected value operator at time $t + jk$. If we define the value of X at time $t + jk$ by X_j and the value of X at time $t + (j + 1)k$ by X_{j+1}, we know from equation (14B.1) that X_{j+1} is distributed normally with mean $X_j + (r - d - .5\sigma^2)k$ and variance $\sigma^2 k$. As in Parkinson, we will approximate the normal distribution by a trinomial. X_{j+1} will take three possible values: $X_j + h$ with probability p^+, X_j with probability p, and $X_j - h$ with probability p^-. Given the mean and variance of X_{j+1}, p^+, p, and p^- are such that:

$$p^+ = .5\sigma^2\, kh^{-2} + .5\,(r - d - .5\sigma^2)kh^{-1} + .5(r - d - .5\sigma^2)^2\, k^2\, h^{-2}$$

$$p = 1 - \sigma^2\, kh^{-2} - (r - d - .5\sigma^2)^2\, k^2\, h^{-2}$$

$$p^- = .5\sigma^2\, kh^{-2} - .5(r - d - .5\sigma^2)\, kh^{-1} + .5(r - d - .5\sigma^2)^2\, k^2\, h^{-2}$$

The previous dynamic programming problem becomes:

$$U(X, t) = \text{Max}[p^+U(X + h, t + k)+pU(X, t + k)$$
$$+ p^-U(X - h, t + k), E - \exp(X)]\exp(-rk)$$

where: (allowing the dummy variable Y to denote the price variable for the node of the tree in question).

$$U(Y, t + k) = \text{Max}[p^+U(Y + h, t + 2k) + pU(Y, t + 2k)$$
$$+ p^-U(Y - h, t + 2k), E - \exp(Y)]\exp(-rk)$$

$$\vdots$$

$$U(Y, t + (M - 1)k) = \text{Max}[p^+U(Y + h, t + Mk) + pU(Y, t + Mk)$$
$$+ p^-U(Y - h, t + Mk), E - \exp(Y)]\exp(-rk)$$

$$U(Y, t + Mk) = \text{Max}[O, E - \exp(Y)]$$

The value of the American put option, $W(S, t)$, is simply equal to $U(X, t)$.

References

Black, F. and Scholes, M. (1973). The pricing of options and corporate liabilities. *Journal of Political Economy, 81,* 637–59.

Boyle, P.P. (May 1977). Options: A Monte Carlo approach. *Journal of Financial Economics, 4,* 323–38.

Boyle, P.P. (February 1987,). A lattice framework for option pricing with two state variables. University of Waterloo, Ontario, working paper.

Brennan, M.J., and Schwartz, E. (June 1976). The pricing of equity-linked life insurance policy with an asset value guarantee. *Journal of Financial Economics, 3,* 195–214.

Brennan, M.J., and Schwartz, E. (May 1977). The valuation of American put options. *Journal of Finance, 32,* 449–62.

Brennan, M.J., and Schwartz, E. (September 1978). Finite difference methods and jump processes arising in the pricing of contingent claims: A synthesis. *Journal of Financial and Quantitative Analysis, 13,* 461–74.

Brennan, M.J., and Schwartz, E. (November 1980). Analyzing convertible bonds. *Journal of Financial and Quantitative Analysis, 15,* No. 4.

Brennan, M.J., and Schwartz, E. (September 1982). An equilibrium model of bond pricing and a test of market efficiency,. *Journal of Financial and Quantitative Analysis, 17,* No. 3, 301–29.

Courtadon, G., (December 1982). A more accurate finite difference approximation for the valuation of options. *Journal of Financial and Quantitative Analysis, 17,* 677–704.

Cox, J., Ingersoll, J., and Ross, S. (March 1985). A theory of the term structure of interest rates. *Econometrica, 53,* No. 2, 385–407.

Cox, J., and Ross, S. (January/March 1976). The valuation of options for alternative stochastic processes. *Journal of Financial Economics, 3,* 145–66.

Cox, J., Ross, S., and Rubinstein, M. (September 1979). Option pricing: A simplified approach. *Journal of Financial Economics, 7,* No. 3.

Friedman, A. (1976). *Stochastic differential equations and applications.* (vol. 1). New York: Academic Press.

Geske, R., and Shastri, K. (March 1985). Valuation by approximation: A comparison of alternative valuation techniques. *Journal of Financial and Quantitative Analysis, 20,* 45–71.

Heath D., Jarrow, R., and Morton, A. (August 1988). Bond pricing and the term structure of interest rates: A discrete time approximation. Cornell University working paper.

Jarrow, R., and Rudd, A. (1983). *Option pricing.* Homewood, Illinois: Richard D. Irwin.

McKee, S., and Mitchell, A. (February 1970). Alternate direction methods for parabolic equations in two space dimensions with mixed derivatives. *Computer Journal.*

Mitchell, A. R., and Griffiths, D. F. (1980). *The finite difference method in partial differential equations.* New York: Wiley.

Parkinson, M. (January 1977). Option pricing: The American put. *Journal of Business, 50.*

Sharpe, W. F. (1978). *Investments.* Englewood Cliffs, New Jersey: Prentice-Hall.

Smith, G. (1978). *Numerical solutions of partial differential equations: Finite difference methods.* Oxford: Clarendon Press.

INDEX